Read, Reason, Write

AN ARGUMENT TEXT AND READER

THIRTEENTH EDITION

Dorothy U. Seyler
Allen Brizee

READ, REASON, WRITE

Published by McGraw Hill LLC, 1325 Avenue of the Americas, New York, NY 10019. Copyright ©2024 by McGraw Hill LLC. All rights reserved. Printed in the United States of America. No part of this publication may be reproduced or distributed in any form or by any means, or stored in a database or retrieval system, without the prior written consent of McGraw Hill LLC, including, but not limited to, in any network or other electronic storage or transmission, or broadcast for distance learning.

Some ancillaries, including electronic and print components, may not be available to customers outside the United States.

This book is printed on acid-free paper.

1 2 3 4 5 6 7 8 9 LCR 28 27 26 25 24 23

ISBN 978-1-266-22201-6
MHID 1-266-22201-4

Cover Image: *JUPITERIMAGES/Thinkstock/Alamy Images*

All credits appearing on page or at the end of the book are considered to be an extension of the copyright page.

The Internet addresses listed in the text were accurate at the time of publication. The inclusion of a website does not indicate an endorsement by the authors or McGraw Hill LLC, and McGraw Hill LLC does not guarantee the accuracy of the information presented at these sites.

mheducation.com/highered

About the Authors

DOROTHY SEYLER is professor emerita of English at Northern Virginia Community College. A Phi Beta Kappa graduate of the College of William & Mary, Dr. Seyler holds advanced degrees from Columbia University and the State University of New York at Albany. She taught at Ohio State University, the University of Kentucky, and Nassau Community College before moving with her family to Northern Virginia.

In addition to articles published in both scholarly journals and popular magazines, Dr. Seyler is the author of ten college textbooks, including *Introduction to Literature, Doing Research, Steps to College Reading,* and *Patterns of Reflection. Read, Reason, Write* was first published in 1984. In 2007, she was elected to membership in the Cosmos Club in Washington, D.C., for "excellence in education."

Professor Seyler is also the author of *The Obelisk and the Englishman: The Pioneering Discoveries of Egyptologist William Bankes* (2015), a "fascinating story," according to *Kirkus Reviews,* "of a figure who deserves to be much better known." She enjoys tennis, golf, and travel—and writing about both sports and travel.

ALLEN BRIZEE is associate professor of English and Director of Writing Across the Curriculum at Saint Louis University. Professor Brizee teaches graduate and undergraduate courses in writing, rhetoric, writing center theory and practice, as well as writing across the curriculum.

Professor Brizee began his professional journey as a student of Dorothy's at Northern Virginia Community College (NVCC). After graduating, he transferred to Virginia Tech, where he earned a BA in English (Phi Beta Kappa) and MA in English. Professor Brizee taught at NVCC, The George Washington University, and the University of Maryland while working as a technical writer. He then completed his PhD in rhetoric and composition at Purdue University, and while there he worked on the widely used Purdue Online Writing Lab (OWL).

Professor Brizee's research interests include rhetorical theory, writing pedagogy, technology, and public/digital humanities. He has published articles in a variety of academic journals. He also coauthored *Partners in Literacy: A Writing Center Model for Civic Engagement* and coedited *Commitment to Justice in Jesuit Higher Education,* third edition. Professor Brizee is currently working on his next book *Via Media: The Rhetoric of the Middle Way in Isocrates, Queen Elizabeth I, and the Anglican Church.* He enjoys collaborating with community groups on work like The Baltimore Project: Learning and Living Racial Justice and gaming in all its forms. He lives in St. Louis, Missouri, with his wife, Stephanie, and his son, Harry.

Brief Contents

Contents

Preface

Read, Reason, Write teaches critical thinking, reading, and composing through a step-by-step approach to inquiry, analysis, and writing. Guided by decades of classroom experience and by research and theory in composition and rhetoric, this text introduces students to various genres and guides them in analyzing style, rhetorical construction, and effectiveness. To support this, *Read, Reason, Write* offers the following features.

Three Books in One

When using *Read, Reason, Write* with Connect, students receive access to:

- *Read, Reason, Write* eBook
- The *Connect Composition Essentials Handbook*
- The *McGraw Hill Composition Reader* with 100+ readings

Clear and Exemplified Writing Instruction

Read, Reason, Write provides instruction for beginning, drafting, completing, and then revising summaries, analyses, and arguments. Guided by convention expectations, the text provides instruction in overall organization, paragraph structure, and sentence-level issues such as tone, mechanics, and attribution tailored to various genres. Writing instruction is supported by:

- A genre approach to argument is informed by the writer's response to the rhetorical situation. Students move through material on the rhetorical situation to help them determine which argumentative genre fits their call to write. Instruction for analyzing and using visuals is designed to support students in thinking critically about—and also producing–visually enhanced communication. Coverage includes analysis of new visual media like memes but also traditional images like graphs, charts, and tables.
- Guidelines features, found in relevant chapters, provide concrete guidelines for drafting, revising, and finalizing writing assignments. Following best practices in writing pedagogy, the text helps students understand and practice the recursive process of composition based in rhetorical theory.
- Thorough and easy-to-reference coverage of both MLA and APA documentation requirements.
- Model student essays that illustrate the kinds of writing students will be asked to prepare in the course–summaries, analyses, arguments, and formally documented papers. In many cases, the student essays are accompanied by prework to illustrate different stages of the writing process and project management tools to help them plan and follow through on writing assignments.

- *Writing Assignment* allowing students to draft assignments while also benefiting from just-in-time learning resources. The built-in grammar checker and originality detection alert students to issues before they submit their work and offer resources that direct them on how to correct errors within the context of their own writing, empowering them to achieve their writing goals. Frequently used comments are automatically saved so instructors do not have to type the same feedback over and over. A peer review functionality allows students to review and comment on each other's work directly in the tool. Students can both receive feedback from peers and comment on peer submissions. Instructors can review all peer commenting and provide an overall peer review grade.
- The *Connect Composition Essentials Handbook*, featuring coverage of style, grammar, and mechanics, as well as up-to-date guidance on MLA and APA documentation. In Connect, teachers can assign a range of assessments, including quizzes, that are tied to the handbook.

Readings Focused on Current Issues Relevant to Students

Read, Reason, Write shares a rich collection of professional readings. To engage students, readings are both timely and classic, providing examples of the varied uses of language and strategies for argument. Current issues like the climate crisis are addressed in essays like "Air Pollution Kills" and "3 Indigenous Women Talk COP26 and What Real Climate Solutions Look Like." These two pieces use a problem-solution approach to argue for practical answers to our environmental challenges. Enduring topics like democracy and patriotism are addressed in pieces like the "Declaration of Independence" and the "Gettysburg Address." Students learn about the rhetorical concepts of induction, deduction, and the enthymeme used by the Founders in the "Declaration," as well as Lincoln's use of tone, word choice, and repetition in his historic Civil War speech.

- *Read, Reason, Write* includes 74 professional readings. New to this edition are 40 readings.
- An additional 100 readings are available in Connect. These can be assigned with scaffolding through Power of Process or on their own.
- In keeping with McGraw Hill's commitment to equity, diversity, and inclusion, 50% of the readings in both the text and in Power of Process are written by Black, Indigenous, and people of color (BIPOC) authors. This edition of *Read, Reason, Write* also includes readings by authors who self-identify as LGBTQIA+.

Support of Analysis and Critical Thinking

Read, Reason, Write supports students' ability to analyze and think critically in addition to writing effectively. Informed by the authors' decades of classroom experience, composition research, writing program administration, and writing assessment, this edition helps students achieve learning outcomes required by a variety of colleges and universities. Learning outcomes include analyzing and synthesizing information from a variety of credible sources; attributing and integrating these sources into ethical, persuasive arguments; and engaging in processes of invention and revision.

- Chapters begin with a Read/Reason/Write feature that prompts students to analyze the chapter-opening visual or concept introduced by the visual. This prepares students for thinking critically about upcoming chapter topics.

- Exercises, in relevant chapters, provide opportunities for students to practice what they are learning about to confirm understanding.
- Professional readings are followed by Questions for Reading; Questions for Reasoning and Analysis; and Questions for Reflection and Writing that move the reader from confirming their understanding of key concepts discussed in the reading to thinking critically about the example to planning for their own writing.
- Suggestions for Discussion and Writing provide options for classroom discussion and writing assignments that prompt student critical thinking and analysis.
- *Power of Process*, in Connect, provides strategies that guide students in learning how to critically read a piece of writing or consider a text as a possible source for incorporation in their own work. After they progress through the strategies, responding to prompts by annotating and highlighting, students are encouraged to reflect on their processes and interaction with the text. In this way, *Power of Process* guides students to engage with the text closely and critically so that they develop awareness of their process decisions. Instructors can choose from 100 readings in *Power of Process*, or upload selections from *Read, Reason, Write*. Additionally, they can choose to upload any personal selections, or have students submit their own writing.

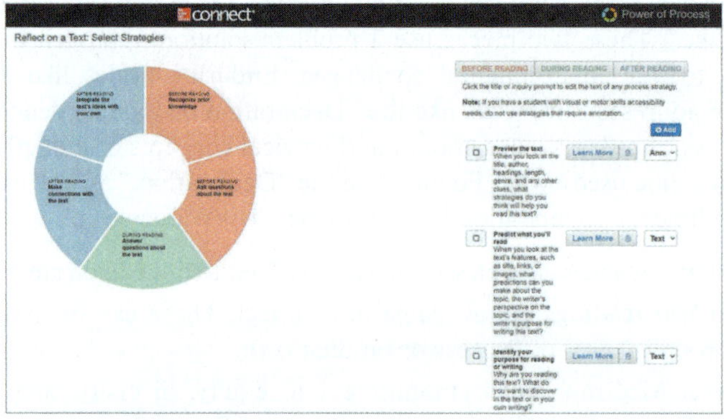

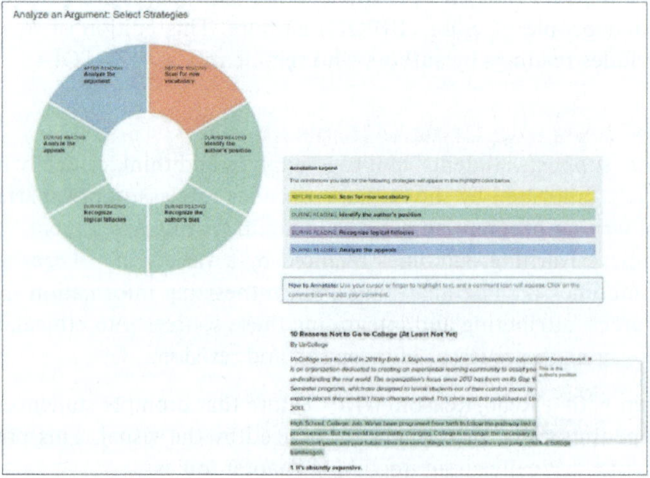

INSTRUCTION IN CLASSICAL AND CONTEMPORARY RHETORICAL THEORY

Read, Reason, Write provides instruction in both classical and contemporary rhetorical theory. Rhetorical concepts like *kairos, ethos, pathos,* and *logos* are covered in depth, as are induction, deduction, and the logical fallacies. These classical theories are paired with contemporary theories from Toulmin, visual rhetoric, and transfer theory. The text presents these rhetorical theories in an accessible way to help instructors teach and students learn these concepts. But, *Read, Reason, Write* also presents argument as contextual: written (or spoken) to a specific audience with the expectation of counterarguments. New to this edition are *stasis* theory as a model for inquiry and analysis and basic concepts from Kenneth Burke, as well as an expansion of visual rhetoric that covers memes and other online images.

Introduction to Analyzing Literature

Read, Reason, Write offers a brief but comprehensive introduction to reading and analyzing literature. Found in the appendix, this section also contains selections from the traditional literary canon, a student essay of literary analysis, and contemporary work from critically acclaimed authors. New to this edition are works from poets J Mase III and Crisosto Apache, as well as an award-winning short play by Alex Rubi, an undergraduate student majoring in English.

Opportunities for Confirmation of Key Concepts and Practice of Key Skills

- SmartBook 2.0, found online in Connect, uses adaptive assessments to create a personalized reading experience customized to individual student needs. By studying using SmartBook, students come prepared with the foundational knowledge needed to engage in analysis and critical thinking in class.
- Reading, writing, and research skills are further supported by Adaptive Learning Assignment. Found in Connect, *Adaptive Learning Assignment* provides each student with a personalized path to learning concepts instructors assign in their courses. The assignments continually adapt to the individual, identifying knowledge gaps and focusing on areas where remediation is needed. All adaptive content–including questions and integrated concept resources–is specifically targeted to, and directly aligned with, the individual learning objectives assessed in the course.

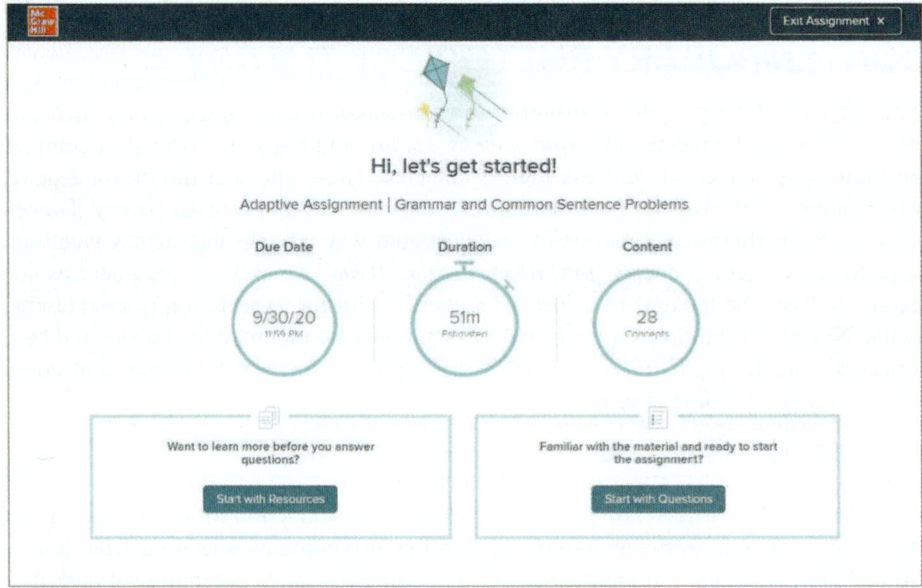

- The Connect Question bank includes practice quizzes as a formative assessment option.

Accessible eBook and Online Resources

This thirteenth edition of *Read, Reason, Write* offers an improved reading experience for all learners. Enhancements include improved eBook functionality for viewing and interacting with annotated readings. At McGraw Hill Higher Education, our mission is to accelerate learning through intuitive, engaging, efficient, and effective experiences, grounded in research. We are committed to creating universally accessible products that unlock the full potential of each learner, including individuals with disabilities.

New to the Thirteenth Edition

In the thirteenth edition, we have given greater attention to diversity, equity, and inclusion in text and illustrations, and when choosing the authors and subject matter of readings to better reflect the lives of our diverse students. Half of the professional readings in the text are written by Black or Indigenous writers or people of color.

All content has been updated to match current MLA and APA guidelines. Additionally, Learning Outcomes have been added to the start of each chapter to focus students and provide clarity for writing assessment.

Specific changes in each chapter follow.

Chapter 1: Writers and Their Sources

- New student analysis example
- Expanded Analytic Response "How Is It Written? How Does It Compare with Another Work?"
- Expanded Research Response "How Does It Help Me to Understand Other Works, Ideas, Events?"
- New student summary of "Toward Disability Justice: Don't Forget the Plastic that Gives Me Freedom"
- New student reading: "Toward Disability Justice: Don't Forget the Plastic that Gives Me Freedom"
- Updated grammar and style examples
- New reading: "Howard University's Removal of Classics Is a Spiritual Catastrophe"

Chapter 2: Responding Critically to Sources

- Added questions to "Traits of the Critical Reader/Thinker"
- Expanded bullets in "Who Is the Author?"
- Added content to "What Are the Author's Sources of Information?"
- Added bullets to "What Are the Author's Sources of Information?" to support accessibility
- New coverage of the "Level of Diction" to expand on the concept of style
- New reading: "The Seven Deadly Sins of Politi-Speak"
- Expanded coverage of "Writing about Style"
- Updated "Drafting the Style Analysis"
- New reading: " 'Us vs. Them' Thinking Is Tearing America Apart. But Here's Why I'm Still Hopeful About the Future"
- New student essay: "Albright Style Analysis with annotations"

Chapter 3: Understanding the Basics of Argument

- Updated coverage of "Arguments Should Be Ethical"
- "World of Argument" content updated
- Introductory examples updated
- New reading: "Lynching, Our National Crime"
- New reading: "Bans on Critical Race Theory Could Have a Chilling Effect on How Educators Teach about Racism"

Chapter 4: Writing Effective Arguments

- New student sample Audience Analysis table
- New reference chart: "A Continuum of Argumentative Language" with discussion questions
- "Guidelines for Drafting" expanded
- Updated "Revise Your Draft"
- Updated example of student revision
- Updated Revision checklist
- Added content to revision advice to cover collaborative tools Google Drive and Dropbox
- Added sample student essay with annotations

Chapter 5: Reading, Analyzing, and Using Visuals and Statistics in Argument

- Updated "Responding to Visual Arguments" to include more current means of visual communication
- Added discussion questions to "Responding to Visual Arguments"
- Updated "Reading Graphics" to include new examples
- Updated graphics for "Reading Graphics" practice exercises
- Updated "Reading Graphics" exercise questions
- Updated "The Uses of Authority and Statistics"
- Updated "Evaluating Statistics" to include most recent census
- Updated content for "Preparing Graphics for Your Essay" to include information about more current tools and best practices.
- Updated "Suggestions for Discussion and Writing" to contain current information and types of media (i.e., streaming services)

Chapter 6: Learning More about Argument: Induction, Deduction, Analogy, and Logical Fallacies

- Updated examples of fallacies statements

Chapter 7: Definition Arguments

- Revised introduction to include more contemporary examples of defining terms in an argument
- Revised "When Defining *Is* the Argument"
- Revised examples of "Developing a Definition"
- Updated "Evaluating Definition Arguments"
- New reading: "Opening Statement from Congresswoman Eleanor Holmes Norton for the Hearing on 'H.R. 51 Making D.C. the 51st State,' March 22, 2021."

Chapter 8: Evaluation Arguments

- Updated examples in introduction
- Updated example in "Preparing an Evaluation Argument"
- New reading: "One Way to Fix Plummeting Birthrates: Stop Bashing America"

Chapter 9: The Position Paper: Claims of Values

- New reading: "A People's Vaccine Against a Mutating Virus"
- New reading: "It's Wrong to Target Asian-American Scientists for Espionage Prosecution"
- New reading: "With Afghanistan's Fall, the U.S. Confronts a Moral Necessity It Faced Before"

Chapter 10: Arguments about Cause

- Revised "Suggestions for Discussion and Writing"

Chapter 11: Presenting Proposals: The Problem/Solution Argument

- New reading: "Air Pollution Kills. Making That Official Can Help Us Tackle It."
- Revised text in "Preparing a Problem/Solution Argument"
- New reading: "Doctors Can't Treat COVID-19 Effectively Without Recognizing the Social Justice Aspects of Health"
- New reading: "3 Indigenous Women Talk COP26 and What Real Climate Solutions Look Like"

Chapter 12: Locating, Evaluating, and Preparing to Use Sources

- Expanded coverage of using search engines and researching on the web

Chapter 13: Writing the Researched Essay

- Revised introductory text to expand on advice for writing an essay
- Updated Guidelines
- Updated examples in "Organizing the Paper"
- Expanded text in "Organizing the Paper"
- Updated phrasing regarding writing introductions to be more specific and to include terminology more appropriate for academic discourse
- Revised text to expand on pyramid paragraph style
- Updated examples in "Choose an Effective Title"
- New student sample paper: "Solutions to Combat High Maternal Mortality Rates for Black Women"

Chapter 14: Formal Documentation: MLA Style, APA Style

- Updated citation examples to reflect readings that are included in the current edition
- New sample paper: "Rhetorical Strategies and Genre in Obama's Remarks"

Chapter 15: The Media: Image and Reality

- New reading: "'I'm Prejudiced,' He Said. Then We Kept Talking"
- New reading: "Misinformation, Disinformation, and Hoaxes: What's the Difference?"
- New reading: "7 Ways to Avoid Becoming a Misinformation Superspreader"

Chapter 16: Misinformation, Disinformation, and the Role of Social Media

- New reading: "We Are All Propagandists Now"
- New reading: "Disinformation is Evolving to Move Under the Radar"
- "How to Combat Disinformation Targeting Black Communities"

Chapter 17: Race in America

- New reading: "What 'Shang–Chi and the Legend of Ten Rings' Gets Right about Chinese Food"
- New reading: "Texas Republicans to Investigate School Districts' Books that Mention Race and Sexuality"

Chapter 18: Gender and Gender Identity

- New reading: "Feminism's Legacy Sees College Women Embracing More Diverse Sexuality"
- New reading: "The Trans History You Weren't Taught in Schools"

Chapter 19: Laws and Rights: Issues of Gun Safety and Policing

- New reading: "Three Million More Guns"
- New reading: "The Sentencing of Derek Chauvin is Punishment—Not Justice"
- "End Police Violence Against Black Americans"
- "Gun Violence Research Matters. Here's Why"

Chapter 20: The Environment: How Do We Address the Climate Crisis?

- New reading: "How to Sabotage Climate Legislation? An Exxon Lobbyist Explains"
- New reading: "The Key to Beating Fossil Fuel Corps? Global Collaboration"
- New reading: "Missing from the COP26: Lifestyle Choices of Middle–Class and Rich Consumers"
- New reading: "An Ambitious Strategy to Preserve Biodiversity

Appendix: Understanding Literature

- New reading: "The Story of an Hour"
- New reading: "Josephine"
- New reading: "12. Carrizo"
- New reading: "The View from Mount Fuji"

Support for Instructors

Instructor's Manual

The Instructor's Manual is written with the diverse needs of composition instructors in mind. Faculty new to teaching reading will appreciate the brief presentations of theory that accompany the reading pedagogy in the textbook, as well as the suggestions for how to teach some of the more difficult argument writing skills. Faculty new to teaching writing will find help with ways to organize chapters into teachable sections and suggestions for selecting among the easier and more challenging readings.

Access to Readings for Use in Power of Process

All readings included in *Read, Reason, Write* are available for download through the Connect Online Learning Center. Instructors can choose to distribute copies of these readings or upload them into the *Power of Process* platform for critical and analytical reading.

Flexible Content for Your Argument Course: Customize *Read, Reason, Write* with Create™

As an alternative to the traditional text, instructors may use McGraw Hill Create™ to arrange chapters to align with their syllabus, eliminate those they do not wish to assign, and add any of the *Read, Reason, Write* content available only in Create™ to build one or multiple print or eBook texts, including Connect access codes. McGraw Hill Create™ is a self-service website that allows instructors and departments to create customized course materials using McGraw Hill's comprehensive, cross-disciplinary content and digital products. Through Create™, instructors may also add their own material, such as a course syllabus, a course rubric, course standards, and any specific instruction for students.

LMS and Gradebook Synching

McGraw Hill offers deep integration for a range of LMS products. Deep integration includes functionality such as single sign-on, automatic grade sync, assignment level linking and calendar integration.

Acknowledgments

It continues to be true that no book of value is written alone. Over its more than thirty years of life, a chorus of voices have enriched this text, too many now to list them all. Two editors should be given a special thanks, though: Steve Pensinger, who led the team through four early editions, and Lisa Moore, who brought new ideas to the sixth and seventh editions. Other portfolio managers, product developers, and content project managers have enriched the text through twelve editions and aided in the preparation of this thirteenth edition.

A special thanks to the instructors who use *Read, Reason, Write* and teach this course for their feedback and guidance throughout the revision process:

Larry Beason, University of South Alabama
Carl Becker, Delaware Technical Community College
Cecilia Bonner, Houston Community College, Northwest
Carol Bledsoe, Florida Gulf Coast College
Emily Cosper, Delgado Community College
Howard Cox, Angelina College
Courtney Danforth, College of Southern Nevada
Marie Eckstrom, Rio Hondo College
Renee Field, Moberly Area Community College
Chad Hammett, Texas State University
Mindy Hodge, Beckfield College
Steven Keeton, Baton Rouge Community College
Elizabeth Kelleher, Delaware Technical Community College
Marianne Layer, Grayson College
Edward Luter, Dallas College
Vickie Melograno, Atlantic Cape Community College
Kelly Paul, West Kentucky Community & Technical College
Michele Poulos, ECPI University
Carlos Rodriguez, Dominican University of California
Kimberly Russell, West Kentucky Community and Technical College
Melanie Salome, University of Houston
Ana Schnellmann, Lindenwood University
Naomi Seedberg, College for Creative Studies
Angela Spires, College of Southern Nevada
Brian Underwood, Pensacola State College
Jennifer Wingard, University of Houston
Syndee Wood, Palomar College

CHAPTER 1

Writers and Their Sources

LEARNING OUTCOMES

After reading Chapter 1, you will be able to:

- Recall the purpose of this textbook.
- Recount why this textbook is organized following the read, reason, write model.
- Describe the basic elements of critical reading.
- Identify the basic elements of critical analysis.
- Describe how to write a summary.
- Summarize how to attribute ideas that are not your own.

Prostock-studio/Shutterstock

READ: What is the situation in the photo? Who are the figures, where are they, and how do they differ?

REASON: What ideas are suggested by the photo?

WRITE: Why might this visual have been chosen for Chapter 1?

"Are you happy with your new car?" Sam asks.

"Oh, yes, I love my new car," Alex responds.

"Why?" queries Sam.

"Oh, it's just great—and Dad paid for most of it," Alex exclaims.

"So you like it because it was cheap," Sam says. "But wasn't your father going to pay for whatever car you chose?"

"Well, yes—within reason."

"Then why did you choose the Corolla? Why is it so great?"

Alex ponders a moment and then replies: "It's small enough for me to feel comfortable driving it, but not so small that I would be frightened by trucks. It gets good mileage, and Toyotas have a good reputation."

"Hmm. Maybe I should think about a Corolla. Then again, I wouldn't part with my Miata!" Sam proclaims.

A simple conversation, right? In fact, this dialogue represents an *argument.* You may not recognize it as a "typical" argument. After all, there is no real dispute between Sam and Alex—no yelling, no hurt feelings. But in its most basic form, an argument is a *claim* (Alex's car is great) supported by *reasons* (the car's size, mileage, and brand). Similar arguments could be made in favor of this car in other contexts. For instance, Alex might have seen (and been persuaded by) a television or online Toyota advertisement or might have read an article making similar claims in a magazine such as *Consumer Reports.* In turn, Alex might decide to develop that argument into an essay or speech for one of their courses.

READING, WRITING, AND THE CONTEXTS OF ARGUMENT

Arguments, it seems, are everywhere. Well, what about this textbook, you counter. Its purpose is to inform, not to present an argument. True—to a degree. But textbook authors also make choices about what is important to include and how students should learn the material. Even writing primarily designed to inform says to readers: Do it my way! Well, what about novels, you "argue." Surely they are not arguments. A good point—to a degree. The ideas about human life and experience we find in novels are more subtle, more indirect, than the points we meet head-on in many arguments. Still, expressive writing presents ideas, ways of seeing the world. It seems that arguments can be simple or profound, clearly stated or implied. And we can find them in many—if not most—of our uses of language.

You can accept this larger scope of argument and still expect that in your course on writing, argument, and critical thinking you probably will not be asked to write a textbook or a novel. You might, though, be asked to write a summary or a style analysis, so you should think about how those tasks might connect to the world of argument. Count on this: You will be asked to write! Why work on your writing skills? Here are good answers to this question:

- Effective communication is the single most important skill sought by employers.
- The better writer you become, the better reader you will be.
- The more confident a writer you become, the more efficiently you will handle written assignments in all your courses.
- The more you write, the more you learn about who you are and what really matters to you.

You are about to face a variety of writing assignments. Always think about what role each assignment asks of you. Are you a student demonstrating knowledge? An activist arguing for greater access to voting in response to voter restriction laws? A scholar presenting the results of research? A friend having a conversation about a new car? Any writer—including you—will take on different roles, writing for different audiences, using different strategies to reach each audience. There are many kinds of argument and many ways to be successful—or unsuccessful—in preparing them. Your writing course will be challenging. This text will help you meet that challenge.

RESPONDING TO SOURCES

If this is a text about *writing* arguments, why does it contain so many readings? (You noticed!) There are good reasons for the readings you find here:

- College and the workplace demand that you learn complex information through reading. This text will give you a lot of practice.
- You need to read to develop your critical thinking skills.
- Your reading will often serve as a basis for writing. In a course on argument, the focus of attention shifts from you to your subject, a subject others have debated before you. You will need to understand the issue, think carefully about the views of others, and only then join in the conversation.

THE GETTYSBURG ADDRESS

ABRAHAM LINCOLN

Fourscore and seven years ago our fathers brought forth on this continent a new nation, conceived in liberty and dedicated to the proposition that all men are created equal. Now we are engaged in a great civil war, testing whether that nation, or any nation so conceived and so dedicated, can long endure. We are met on a great battlefield of that war. We have come to dedicate a portion of that field as a final resting place for those who here gave their lives that that nation might live. It is altogether fitting and proper that we should do this. But, in a larger sense, we cannot dedicate—we cannot consecrate—we cannot hallow—this ground. The brave men, living and dead, who struggled here have consecrated it far above our poor power to add or to detract. The world will little note nor long remember what we say here, but it can never forget what they did here. It is for us, the living, rather to be dedicated here to the unfinished work which they who fought here have thus far so nobly advanced. It is rather for us to be here dedicated to the great task remaining before us—that from these honored dead we take increased devotion to that cause for which they gave the last full measure of devotion; that we here highly resolve that these dead shall not have died in vain; that this nation, under God, shall have a new birth of freedom; and that government of the people, by the people, for the people shall not perish from the earth.

Abraham Lincoln, "The Gettysburg Address," (1863).

To understand how critical thinkers may respond to sources, let's examine "The Gettysburg Address," Abraham Lincoln's famous speech dedicating the Gettysburg Civil War battlefield. We can use this document to see the various ways writers respond—in writing—to the writing of others.

What Does It Say? THE RESPONSE TO CONTENT

Instructors often ask students to *summarize* their reading of a complex chapter, a supplementary text, or a series of journal articles on library reserve. Frequently, book report assignments specify that summary and evaluation be combined. Your purpose in writing a summary is to show your understanding of the work's main ideas and of the relationships among those ideas. If you can put what you have read into your own words and focus on the text's chief points, then you have command of that material. Here is a sample restatement of Lincoln's "Address":

> Our nation was initially built on a belief in liberty and equality, but its future is now being tested by civil war. It is appropriate for us to dedicate this battlefield, but those who fought here have dedicated it better than we. We should dedicate ourselves to continue the fight to maintain this nation and its principles of government.

Sometimes it is easier to recite or quote famous or difficult works than to state, more simply and in your own words, what has been written. The ability to summarize reflects strong writing skills. For more coverage of writing summaries, see pp. 9–11. (For coverage of paraphrasing, a task similar to summary, see pp. 16–17.)

How Is It Written? How Does It Compare with Another Work? THE ANALYTIC RESPONSE

Summary requirements are often combined with analysis or evaluation, as in a book report. Most of the time you will be expected to *do something* with what you have read, and to summarize will be insufficient. Frequently you will be asked to analyze a work—that is, to explain the writer's choice of style or rhetorical strategies. This means examining sentence patterns, organization, metaphors, use of reasoning, and other techniques selected by the writer to influence and perhaps even persuade readers. Developing your skills in analysis will make you both a better reader and a better writer.

Many writers have examined Lincoln's word choice, sentence structure, and choice of metaphors to make clear the sources of power in this speech.* Analyzing Lincoln's style, you might examine, among other elements, his effective use of *tricolon:* the threefold repetition of a grammatical structure, with the three points placed in ascending order of significance.

---

* See, for example, Gilbert Highet's essay, "The Gettysburg Address," in *The Clerk of Oxenford: Essays on Literature and Life* (New York: Oxford UP, 1954), to which we are indebted in the following analysis.

> Lincoln uses two effective tricolons in his brief address. The first focuses on the occasion for his speech, the dedication of the battlefield: "we cannot dedicate—we cannot consecrate—we cannot hallow. . . ." The best that the living can do is formally dedicate; only those who died there for the principle of liberty are capable of making the battlefield "hallow." The second tricolon presents Lincoln's concept of democratic government, a government "of the people, by the people, for the people." The purpose of government—"for the people"—resides in the position of greatest significance.

A second type of analysis, a comparison of styles of two writers, is a frequent variation of the analytic assignment. By focusing on similarities and differences in writing styles, you can observe more clearly the role of choice in writing and may also examine the issue of the degree to which differences in purpose affect style. One student, for example, produced a thoughtful and interesting study of Lincoln's style in contrast to that of Martin Luther King, Jr.:

> Although Lincoln's sentence structure is tighter than King's, and King likes the rhythms created by repetition, both men reflect their familiarity with the King James Bible in their use of its cadences and expressions. Instead of saying eighty-seven years ago, Lincoln, seeking solemnity, selects the biblical expression "Fourscore and seven years ago." Similarly, King borrows from the Bible and echoes Lincoln when he writes "Five score years ago."

Lastly, you may have to analyze the rhetorical strategies a writer uses to inform and persuade readers. This is known as a rhetorical analysis. When completing a rhetorical analysis, you will study how an author develops their credibility, uses reasoning, and uses emotions to appeal to their audience.

For instance, in "The Gettysburg Address," Lincoln refers back to "The Declaration of Independence" to ground his argument in American history, thereby establishing his credibility as a leader connected to the nation's founding. He uses sound reasoning by building on the syllogism (deductive reasoning) established in "The Declaration of Independence" that asserts all people are created equal. And Lincoln appeals to the emotions of his audience by reminding them of the sacrifices made by living and dead Union soldiers.

Next, you might be asked to evaluate the effectiveness of these appeals.

Is It Logical? Is It Adequately Developed? Does It Achieve Its Purpose?

THE EVALUATION RESPONSE

Even when the stated purpose of an essay is "pure" analysis, the analysis implies a judgment. We analyze Lincoln's style and rhetorical strategies because we recognize that "The Gettysburg Address" is a great piece of writing and we want to see how it achieves its power. On other occasions, evaluation is the stated purpose for close reading and analysis. The columnist who challenges a previously published editorial has analyzed the editorial and found it flawed. The columnist may fault the editor's logic or lack of adequate or relevant support for the editorial's main idea. In each case the columnist makes a negative evaluation of the editorial, but that judgment is an informed one based on the columnist's knowledge of language and the principles of good argument.

Part of the ability to judge wisely lies in recognizing each writer's (or speaker's) purpose, audience, and occasion. It would be inappropriate to assert that Lincoln's address is weakened by its lack of facts about the battle. The historian's purpose is to record the number killed or to analyze the generals' military tactics. Lincoln's purpose was different.

> As Lincoln reflected upon this young country's being torn apart by civil strife, he saw the dedication of the Gettysburg battlefield as an opportunity to challenge the country to fight for its survival and the principles upon which it was founded. The result was a brief but moving speech that appropriately examines the connection between the life and death of soldiers and the birth and survival of a nation.

These sentences begin an analysis of Lincoln's train of thought and use of metaphors. The writer shows an understanding of Lincoln's purpose and the context in which he spoke.

How Does It Help Me to Understand Other Works, Ideas, Events?

THE RESEARCH RESPONSE

Frequently you will read not to analyze or evaluate but rather to use the source as part of learning about a particular subject. Lincoln's address is significant for the Civil War historian both as an event of that war and as an influence on our thinking about that war. "The Gettysburg Address" is also vital to the biographer's study of Lincoln's life or to the literary critic's study either of famous speeches or of the Bible's influence on English writing styles. Thus Lincoln's brief speech is a valuable source for students in a variety of disciplines. It becomes part of their research process. Able researchers study it carefully, analyze it thoroughly, place it in its proper historical, literary, and personal contexts, and use it to develop their own arguments.

Other work in this book will help you learn more about current events and how they affect you and the society in which you live. As you read these articles and essays, think about how you can use them in the research you may be doing for your class.

To practice reading and responding to sources, study the following article by Deborah Tannen. The exercises that follow will check your reading skills and your understanding of the various responses to reading just discussed. Use the prereading questions to become engaged with Tannen's essay.

Jonathan Timmes/ Courtesy of Deborah Tannen

WHO DOES THE TALKING HERE?

DEBORAH TANNEN

Professor of linguistics at Georgetown University, Deborah Tannen writes popular books on the uses of language by "ordinary" people. Among her many books are *Talking from 9 to 5* (1994) and *I Only Say This Because I Love You* (2004). Here she responds to the debate over who talks more, men or women.

PREREADING QUESTIONS What is the occasion for Tannen's article—what is she responding to? Who does most of the talking in your family—and are you okay with the answer?

It's no surprise that a one-page article published this month in the journal *Science* inspired innumerable newspaper columns and articles. The study, by Matthias Mehl and four colleagues, claims to lay to rest, once and for all, the stereotype that women talk more than men, by proving—scientifically—that women and men talk equally. 1

The notion that women talk more was reinforced last year when Louann Brizendine's "The Female Brain" cited the finding that women utter, on average, 20,000 words a day, men 7,000. (Brizendine later disavowed the statistic, as there was no study to back it up.) Mehl and his colleagues outfitted 396 college students with devices that recorded their speech. The female subjects spoke an average of 16,215 words a day, the men 15,669. The difference is insignificant. Case closed. 2

Or is it? Can we learn who talks more by counting words? No, according to a forthcoming article surveying 70 studies of gender differences in talkativeness. (Imagine—70 studies published in scientific journals, and we're still asking the question.) In their survey, Campbell Leaper and Melanie Ayres found that counting words yielded no consistent differences, though number of words per speaking turn did. (Men, on average, used more.) 3

This doesn't surprise me. In my own research on gender and language, I quickly surmised that to understand who talks more, you have to ask: What's the situation? What are the speakers using words for? 4

The following experience conveys the importance of situation. I was addressing a small group in a suburban Virginia living room. One man stood out because he talked a lot, while his wife, who was sitting beside him, said nothing at all. I described to the group a complaint common among women about men they live with: At the end of a day she tells him what happened, what she thought and how she felt about it. Then she asks, "How was your day?"—and is disappointed when he replies, "Fine," "Nothing much" or "Same old rat race." 5

The loquacious man spoke up. "You're right," he said. Pointing to his wife, he added, "She's the talker in our family." Everyone laughed. But he explained, "It's true. When we come home, she does all the talking. If she didn't, we'd spend the evening in silence." 6

The "how was your day?" conversation typifies the kind of talk women tend to do more of: spoken to intimates and focusing on personal experience, your own or others'. I call this "rapport-talk." It contrasts with "report-talk"—giving or exchanging information about impersonal topics, which men tend to do more. 7

Studies that find men talking more are usually carried out in formal experiments or public contexts such as meetings. For example, Marjorie Swacker observed an academic conference where women presented 40 percent of the papers and were 42 percent of the audience but asked only 27 percent of the questions; their questions were, on average, also shorter by half than the men's questions. And David and Myra Sadker showed that boys talk more in mixed-sex classrooms—a context common among college students, a factor skewing the results of Mehl's new study. 8

9 Many men's comfort with "public talking" explains why a man who tells his wife he has nothing to report about his day might later find a funny story to tell at dinner with two other couples (leaving his wife wondering, "Why didn't he tell me first?").

10 In addition to situation, you have to consider what speakers are doing with words. Campbell and Ayres note that many studies find women doing more "affiliative speech" such as showing support, agreeing or acknowledging others' comments. Drawing on studies of children at play as well as my own research of adults talking, I often put it this way: For women and girls, talk is the glue that holds a relationship together. Their best friend is the one they tell everything to. Spending an evening at home with a spouse is when this kind of talk comes into its own. Since this situation is uncommon among college students, it's another factor skewing the new study's results.

11 Women's rapport-talk probably explains why many people think women talk more. A man wants to read the paper, his wife wants to talk; his girlfriend or sister spends hours on the phone with her friend or her mother. He concludes: Women talk more.

12 Yet Leaper and Ayres observed an overall pattern of men speaking more. That's a conclusion women often come to when men hold forth at meetings, in social groups or when delivering one-on-one lectures. All of us—women and men—tend to notice others talking more in situations where we talk less.

13 Counting may be a start—or a stop along the way—to understanding gender differences. But it's understanding when we tend to talk and what we're doing with words that yields insights we can count on.

Deborah Tannen, "Who Does the Talking Here?" *Washington Post*, 15 Jul. 2007. Copyright ©2007 Deborah Tannen. Reprinted by permission.

QUESTIONS FOR READING AND REASONING

1. What was the conclusion of the researchers who presented their study in *Science?*
2. Why are their results not telling the whole story, according to Tannen? Instead of counting words, what should we study?
3. What two kinds of talk does Tannen label? Which gender does the most of each type of talking?
4. What is Tannen's main idea or thesis?

QUESTIONS FOR REFLECTION AND WRITING

5. How do the details–and the style–in the opening and concluding paragraphs contribute to the author's point? Write a paragraph answer to this question. Then consider: Which one of the different responses to reading does your paragraph illustrate?
6. Do you agree with Tannen that understanding how words are used must be part of any study of men and women talking? If so, why? If not, how would you respond to her argument?
7. "The Gettysburg Address" is a valuable document for several kinds of research projects. For what kinds of research would Tannen's essay be useful? List several possibilities and be prepared to discuss your list with classmates.

WRITING SUMMARIES

While in college and after you graduate, you will have to summarize material and present your summary to others. *A summary briefly restates, in your own words, the main points of a work in a way that does not misrepresent or distort the original.* A good summary shows your grasp of main ideas and your ability to express them clearly. You need to condense the original while giving all key ideas appropriate attention. As a student you may be assigned a summary to

- show that you have read and understood assigned works;
- complete a test question;
- have a record of what you have read for future study or to prepare for class discussion; or
- explain the main ideas in a work that you will also examine in some other way, such as in a book review.

When assigned a summary, pay careful attention to word choice. Avoid judgment words, such as "Brown then proceeds to develop the *silly* idea that. . . ." Follow these guidelines for writing good summaries.

GUIDELINES for Writing Summaries

1. **Write in a direct, objective style, using your own words.** Use few, if any, direct quotations, probably none in a one-paragraph summary.
2. **Begin with a reference to the writer (full name) and the title of the work, and then state the writer's thesis.** (You may also want to include where and when the work was published.)
3. **Complete the summary by providing other key ideas.** Show the reader how the main ideas connect and relate to one another.
4. **For short summaries, do not include specific examples, illustrations, or background sections. For longer summaries of a complex work, use specific examples sparingly.** Instead, paraphrase information from the original piece (see pp. 16–18 for more information on paraphrasing).
5. **Combine main ideas into fewer sentences than were used in the original.**
6. **Keep the parts of your summary in the same balance as you find in the original.** If the author devotes about 30 percent of the essay to one idea, that idea should get about 30 percent of the space in your summary.
7. **Select precise, accurate verbs to show the author's relationship to ideas.** Write Jones *argues*, Jones *asserts*, Jones *believes*. Do not use vague verbs that provide only a list of disconnected ideas. Do *not* write Jones *talks about*, Jones *goes on to say*.
8. **Do not make any judgments about the writer's style or ideas.** Do *not* include your personal reaction to the work.

EXERCISE: Summary

With these guidelines in mind, read the following two summaries of Deborah Tannen's "Who Does the Talking Here?" (see pp. 6–8). Then answer the question: What is flawed or weak about each summary? To aid your analysis, (1) underline or highlight all words or phrases that are inappropriate in each summary, and (2) put the number of the guideline next to any passage that does not adhere to that guideline.

SUMMARY 1

> I really thought that Deborah Tannen's essay contained some interesting ideas about how men and women talk. Tannen mentioned a study in which men and women used almost the same number of words. She goes on to talk about a man who talked a lot at a meeting in Virginia. Tannen also says that women talk more to make others feel good. I'm a man, and I don't like to make small talk.

SUMMARY 2

> In Deborah Tannen's "Who Does the Talking Here?" (published July 15, 2007), she talks about studies to test who talks more—men or women. Some people think the case is closed—they both talk about the same number of words. Tannen goes on to say that she thinks people use words differently. Men talk a lot at events; they use "report-talk." Women use "rapport-talk" to strengthen relationships; their language is a glue to maintain relationships. So just counting words does not work. You have to know why someone is speaking.

Although we can agree that the writers of these summaries have read Tannen's essay, we can also find weaknesses in each summary. Certainly the second summary is more helpful than the first, but it can be strengthened by eliminating some details, combining some ideas, and putting more focus on Tannen's main idea. Here is a much-improved version:

REVISED SUMMARY

> In Deborah Tannen's essay "Who Does the Talking Here?" (published July 15, 2007), Tannen asserts that recent studies to determine if men or women do the most talking are not helpful in answering that question. These studies focus on just counting the words that men and women use. Tannen argues that the only useful study of this issue is one that examines how each gender uses words and in which situations each gender does the most talking. She explains that men tend to use "report-talk" whereas women tend to use "rapport-talk." That is, men will do much of the talking in meetings when they have something to report. Women, on the other hand, will do more of the talking when they are seeking to connect in a relationship, to make people feel good. So, if we want to really understand the differences, we need to stop counting words and listen to what each gender is actually doing with the words that are spoken.

At times you may need to write a summary of a page or two rather than one paragraph. Frequently, long reports are preceded by a one-page summary. A longer summary may become part of an article-length review of an important book. Or instructors may want a longer summary of a lengthy or complicated article or text chapter. The following is an example of a summary of a lengthy article on plastic bans and their effects on people who use plastic to help live with chronic illnesses.

SAMPLE LONGER SUMMARY

In her article "Toward Disability Justice: Don't Forget the Plastic that Gives Me Freedom," Luticha Andre Doucette (*Yes! Magazine,* May 10, 2021) discusses the ableism that often excludes people with disabilities from important decisions, such as the plastic straw bans implemented in the past five years. The decision-making process that led to the bans, she argues, is an example of how "disabled people are relegated to having a nondisabled person determine what we need." Ultimately, Doucette asserts that "We all have to reimagine what a green world with disability justice at the center looks like, then create such a world."

Doucette begins by discussing another case of ableism, the criticism of supermarket chain Whole Foods selling "individually wrapped peeled oranges." She then provides an example of this criticism from social media: "Who is so lazy that they cannot peel their own orange?" Doucette points out that individually wrapped produce makes fruit available to "people who cannot peel oranges." She also argues that selling prepared food is safer for blind and low-vision people for whom "cooking on the stove top can be potentially dangerous."

Doucette then offers a personal example of how plastics help people with disabilities with everyday, life-saving tasks. She explains that silicon catheters are medical devices that provide a safer, less painful option to "catherization, the technique where a thin tube is inserted into the urethra so that you can relieve your bladder." She admits that she searched for a green alternative to her single-use catheter but couldn't find any. The only other choice is made from latex, to which she is allergic. Doucette concludes her article by asserting that environmentalists and disability justice activists can find compromise on these challenges and issues, but until they do, people with disabilities will continue using plastic.

Observe the differences between the longer summary of Luticha Andre Doucette's article and the paragraph summary of Deborah Tannen's essay:

- Some key ideas or terms may be presented in direct quotation.
- Examples may be described in some detail.
- Appropriate transitional and connecting words are used to show how the parts of the summary connect.
- The author's name is often repeated to keep the reader's attention on the article summarized, not on the author of the summary.

A Reminder on Writing Process

As you may remember from previous composition courses, writing is a recursive process that rarely follows a linear approach. For example, you may plan your essay, draft your outline, and write your introduction paragraph, only to find after reading your draft that your introduction works better as your first body paragraph. Likewise, after finishing your first body paragraph, it might make more sense to you to skip to your fourth body paragraph because you are distracted by an idea that you want to include in paragraph four and just cannot concentrate on paragraph three.

As you delve deeper into your own process of self-discovery in your writing, you may find that outlining helps you plan and draft. Alternatively, you may find that drafting your introduction helps you plan the rest of your paper, which then leads to your outline. What is most important to remember is that everyone writes differently. The concepts provided in this book are guidelines meant to help you become a better writer. You must find your own process–one that works for you. To give you a sense of what that process could be, review Figure 1.1:

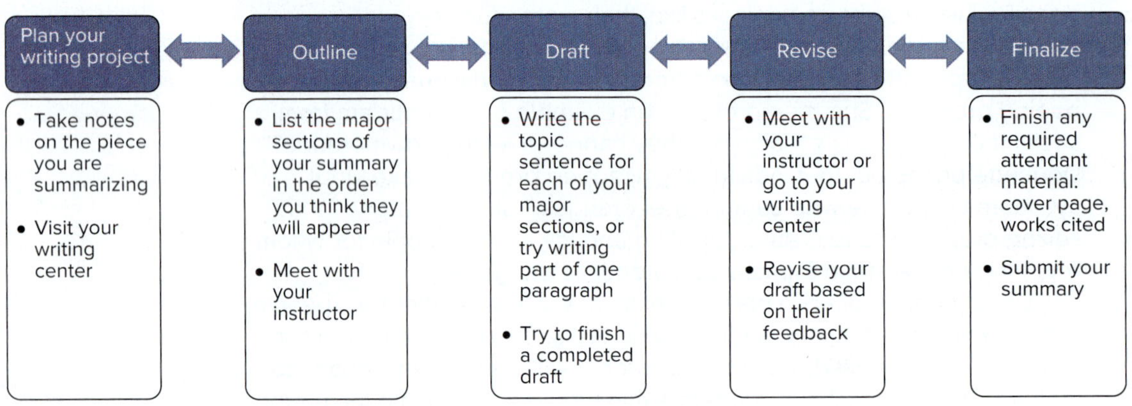

FIGURE 1.1 A Recursive Writing Process

1. Plan: Take notes on the piece you are summarizing; visit your writing center.
2. Outline: List the major sections of your summary in the order they will appear in your paper; meet with your instructor.
3. Draft: Write the topic sentences for each of your major sections, or try writing a part of one paragraph; try to finish a completed draft.
4. Revise: Meet with your instructor or go to your writing center; revise based on their feedback.
5. Finalize: Finish any required attendant material: cover page, works cited; submit your summary.

ACTIVE READING: USE YOUR MIND!

Reading is not about looking at marks on a page—or turning the pages as quickly as we can. Reading means constructing meaning, getting a message. This concept is often underscored by the term *active reading.* To help you always achieve active reading, not passive page turning, follow these guidelines.

GUIDELINES for Active Reading

1. **Understand your purpose in reading.** Do not just start turning pages to complete an assignment. Think first about your purpose. Are you reading for knowledge on which you will be tested? Focus on your purpose as you read, asking yourself, "What do I need to learn from this work?"
2. **Reflect on the title before reading further.** Titles are the first words writers give us. Take time to look for clues in a title that may reveal the work's subject and perhaps the writer's approach or attitude as well.
3. **Become part of the writer's audience.** Not all writers have you and me in mind when they write. As an active reader, you need to "join" a writer's audience by learning about the writer, about the time in which the piece was written, and about the writer's expected audience. For readings in this text you are aided by introductory notes; study them.
4. **Predict what is coming.** Look for a writer's main idea or purpose statement. Study the work's organization. Then use this information to anticipate what is coming. When you read "There are three good reasons for requiring a dress code in schools," you know the writer will list *three* reasons.
5. **Concentrate.** Slow down and give your full attention to reading. Turn off your messaging apps and social media when you're reading. Watch for transition and connecting words that show you how the parts of a text connect. Read an entire article or chapter at one time—or you will need to start over to make sense of the piece.
6. **Annotate as you read.** The more senses you use, the more active your involvement. That means marking the text as you read (or taking notes if the material is not yours). Underline key sentences, such as the writer's thesis. Then, in the margin, indicate that it is the thesis. With a series of examples (or reasons), label them and number them. When you look up a word's definition, write the definition in the margin next to the word. Draw diagrams to illustrate concepts; draw arrows to connect example to idea. Studies have shown that students who annotate their texts get higher grades.
7. **Keep a reading journal.** In addition to annotating what you read, you may want to develop the habit of writing regularly in a journal. A reading journal gives you a place to note impressions and reflections on your reading, your initial reactions to assignments, and ideas you may use in your next writing.

EXERCISE: Active Reading

Read the following essay, studying the annotations that are started for you. As you read, add your own notes. Then test your active reading by responding to the questions that follow the essay.

ACTUALLY, LET'S NOT BE IN THE MOMENT

RUTH WHIPPMAN

Courtesy of Ruth Whippman

Formerly a producer and director of BBC documentaries, Ruth Whippman now lives in California with her family and devotes her professional life to writing. She is the author of *The Pursuit of Happiness* and *America the Anxious* as well as essays that appear frequently in newspapers and magazines. The following article, drawn from her second book, was published November 27, 2016.

1 I'm at the kitchen sink, after a long day of work and kids and chores and the emotional exhaustion of a toxic election season, attempting to mindfully focus on congealed SpaghettiOs. My brain flits to the Netflix queue. I manhandle my thoughts back to the leaky orange glob in front of me. My brain flits to the president-elect.

Topic?

2 I'm making a failed attempt at "mindful dishwashing," the subject of a how-to article an acquaintance recently shared on Facebook. According to the practice's thought leaders, in order to maximize our happiness, we should refuse to succumb to domestic autopilot and instead be fully "in" the present moment, engaging completely with every clump of oatmeal and decomposing particle of scrambled egg. Mindfulness is supposed to be a defense against the pressures of modern life, but it's starting to feel suspiciously like it's actually adding to them. It's a special circle of self-improvement hell, striving not just for a Pinterest-worthy home, but a Pinterest-worthy mind.

"Not dishwashing —Idea of mindfulness,"

3 Perhaps the single philosophical consensus of our time is that the key to contentment lies in living fully mentally in the present. The idea that we should be constantly policing our thoughts away from the past, the future, the imagination or the abstract and back to whatever is happening *right now* has gained traction with spiritual leaders and investment bankers, armchair philosophers and government bureaucrats and human resources departments. Corporate America offers its employees mindfulness training to "streamline their productivity," and the United States military offers it to the Marine Corps. Americans now spend an estimated $4 billion each year on "mindfulness products." "Living in the Moment" has monetized its folksy charm into a multibillion-dollar spiritual industrial complex.

So does the moment really deserve its many accolades? It is a philosophy likely to be more rewarding for those whose lives contain more privileged moments than grinding, humiliating or exhausting ones. Those for whom a given moment is more likely to be "sun-dappled yoga pose" than "hour 11 manning the deep-fat fryer." 4

On the face of it, our lives are often much more fulfilling lived outside the present than in it. As anyone who has ever maintained that they will one day lose 10 pounds or learn Spanish or find the matching lids for the Tupperware will know, we often anticipate our futures with more blind optimism than the reality is likely to warrant. 5

Surely one of the most magnificent feats of the human brain is its ability to hold past, present, future and their imagined alternatives in constant parallel, to offset the tedium of washing dishes with the chance to be simultaneously mentally in Bangkok, or in Don Draper's bed, or finally telling your elderly relative that despite her belief that "no one born in the 1970s died," using a car seat isn't spoiling your child. It's hard to see why greater happiness would be achieved by reining in that magical sense of scope and possibility to outstare a SpaghettiO. 6

What differentiates humans from animals is exactly this ability to step mentally outside of whatever is happening to us right now, and to assign it context and significance. Our happiness does not come so much from our experiences themselves, but from the stories we tell ourselves that make them matter. 7

But still, the advice to be more mindful often contains a hefty scoop of moralizing smugness, a kind of "moment-shaming" for the distractible, like a stern teacher scolding us for failing to concentrate in class. The implication is that by neglecting to live in the moment we are ungrateful and unspontaneous, we are wasting our lives, and therefore if we are unhappy, we really have only ourselves to blame. 8

This judgmental tone is part of a long history of self-help-based cultural thought policing. At its worst, the positive-thinking movement deftly rebranded actual problems as "problematic thoughts." Now mindfulness has taken its place as the focus of our appetite for inner self-improvement. Where once problems ranging from bad marriages and work stress to poverty and race discrimination were routinely dismissed as a failure to "think positive," now our preferred solution to life's complex and entrenched problems is to instruct the distressed to be more mindful. 9

This is a kind of neo-liberalism of the emotions, in which happiness is seen not as a response to our circumstances but as a result of our own individual mental effort, a reward for the deserving. The problem is not your sky-high rent or meager paycheck, your cheating spouse or unfair boss or teetering pile of dirty dishes. The problem is you. 10

It is, of course, easier and cheaper to blame the individual for thinking the wrong thoughts than it is to tackle the thorny causes of his unhappiness. 11

So we give inner-city schoolchildren mindfulness classes rather than engage with education inequality, and instruct exhausted office workers in mindful breathing rather than giving them paid vacation or better health care benefits.

12 In reality, despite many grand claims, the scientific evidence in favor of the Moment's being the key to contentment is surprisingly weak. When the United States Agency for Healthcare Research and Quality conducted an enormous meta-analysis of over 18,000 separate studies on meditation and mindfulness techniques, the results were underwhelming at best.

13 Although some of the studies did show that mindfulness meditation or other similar exercises might bring some small benefits to people in comparison with doing nothing, when they are compared with pretty much any general relaxation technique at all, including exercise, muscle relaxation, "listening to spiritual audiotapes" or indeed any control condition that gives equal time and attention to the person, they perform no better, and in many cases, worse.

14 So perhaps, rather than expending our energy struggling to stay in the Moment, we should simply be grateful that our brains allow us to be elsewhere.

Ruth Whippman, "Actually, Let's Not Be in the Moment," *New York Times*, 27 Nov. 2016. Copyright ©2016 by Ruth Whippman. Used with permission of the author.

QUESTIONS FOR READING AND REASONING

1. What is the meaning of *mindfulness?* How do we practice it?
2. What are the presumed advantages of the practice of mindfulness?
3. What is the author's view of this new concept? State her view as a thesis–the claim of her essay.
4. How does Whippman support her claim? List specific details of her support.

QUESTIONS FOR REFLECTION AND WRITING

5. In paragraph 3, Whippman demonstrates the current popularity of mindfulness; what is clever about her discussion in this paragraph?
6. What is the most interesting piece of information or concept, for you, in Whippman's essay? Why? Write a journal entry–four or five sentences at least–in response to this question.

USING PARAPHRASE

Paraphrasing's goal is the same as summary's: an accurate presentation of the information and ideas of someone else. Unlike summary, we paraphrase an entire short work. This can be a poem (see pp. 477–478 for a paraphrase of a poem) or a complex section of prose that needs a simpler (but often longer than the original) restatement so that we are clear about its meaning. We paraphrase short but complex pieces; we summarize an entire essay or chapter or book.

Writers also use paraphrasing to restate *some* of the information or ideas from a source as part of developing their own work. They do this extensively in a researched essay, but they may also paraphrase parts of a source to add support to their discussion—or to be clear about another writer's ideas that they will evaluate or challenge in some way.

Now, to illustrate paraphrase, suppose you don't want to summarize Lincoln's entire speech, but you do want to use his opening point as a lead-in to commenting on our own times. You might write:

> Lincoln's famous speech at the dedication of the Gettysburg battlefield begins with the observation that our nation was initially built on a belief in liberty and equality, but the country's future had come to a point of being tested. We are not actually facing a civil war today, but we are facing a culture war, a war of opposing values and beliefs, that seems to be tearing our country apart.

Paraphrasing—putting Lincoln's idea into your own words—is a much more effective opening than quoting Lincoln's first two sentences. It's his idea that you want to use, not his language.

NOTE: Observe three key points:

1. The idea is Lincoln's but the word choice is entirely different. Resist the urge to borrow any of Lincoln's phrases—that would be quoting and would require quotation marks—and that does not serve your purpose.
2. You still give credit to Lincoln for the idea.
3. Summary, paraphrasing, and quoting all share this one characteristic: You let readers know that you are using someone else's information or ideas.

EXERCISE: Paraphrase

1. Find several examples of paraphrasing in Whippman's essay.
2. Assume that you are writing an essay on the disadvantages of mindfulness. Paraphrase the ideas in Whippman's paragraphs 9 and 10 to use in your assumed essay.
3. For an essay on the problems with the concept of mindfulness, evaluate the following two paragraphs that use some material from Whippman's essay.

PARAPHRASE 1

> The currently popular concept of mindfulness actually comes with problems. This concept seems to suggest that it's our fault if we are unhappy; we have failed to live each moment with positive thoughts. Mindfulness also shifts the focus from trying to address real problems in education and the workplace to teaching students and workers deep breathing exercises, as Ruth Whippman observes.

PARAPHRASE 2

> The currently popular concept of mindfulness actually comes with problems. In her essay "Actually, Let's Not Be in the Moment," Ruth Whippman worries that mindfulness seems to blame unhappy people for failing to live each moment with positive thoughts. As Whippman observes, mindfulness also shifts the focus from trying to address real problems in education and the workplace to teaching student and workers deep breathing exercises.

ACKNOWLEDGING SOURCES INFORMALLY

As you have seen in the summaries and paraphrases above, even when you are not writing a formally documented paper, you must identify each source by author. What follows are some of the conventions of writing to use when writing about sources.

Referring to People and Sources

Readers in academic, professional, and business contexts expect writers to follow specific conventions of style when referring to authors and to various kinds of sources. Study the following guidelines and examples, and then mark the next few pages for easy reference–perhaps by turning down a corner of the first and last pages.

References to People

- In a first reference, give the person's full name (both the given name and the surname): *Luticha Andre Doucette, Robert J. Samuelson.* In second and subsequent references, use only the last name (surname): *Doucette, Samuelson.*
- Do not use Mr., Mrs., or Ms. Special titles such as President, Chief Justice, or Doctor may be used in the first reference with the person's full name.
- Never refer to an author by her or his first name. Write *Tannen,* not *Deborah; Lincoln,* not *Abraham.*

References to Titles of Works

Titles of works must *always* be written as titles. Titles are indicated by capitalization and by either quotation marks or italics. The examples provided below show when to use quotation marks and when to use italics.

Guidelines for Capitalizing Titles

- The first and last words are capitalized.
- The first word of a subtitle is capitalized.

- All other words in titles are capitalized except
  - Articles (*a, an, the*).
  - Coordinating conjunctions (*and, or, but, for, nor, yet, so*).
  - Prepositions (*in, for, about*).

Titles Requiring Quotation Marks

Titles of works published within other works—within a book, magazine, or newspaper—are indicated by quotation marks.

ESSAYS	"Who Does the Talking Here?"
SHORT STORIES	"The Story of an Hour"
POEMS	"To Daffodils"
ARTICLES	"Toward Disability Justice: Don't Forget the Plastic That Gives Me Freedom"
CHAPTERS	"Writers and Their Sources"
LECTURES	"Crazy Mixed-Up Families"
TV EPISODES	"Winter Is Coming" (the first episode from *Game of Thrones,* a fantasy drama series from HBO)

Titles Requiring Italics

Titles of works that are separate publications and, by extension, titles of items such as works of art and websites are in italics.

PLAYS	*A Raisin in the Sun*
NOVELS	*The Prophets*
NONFICTION BOOKS	*Read, Reason, Write: An Argument Text and Reader*
BOOK-LENGTH POEMS	*The Odyssey*
MAGAZINES AND JOURNALS	*Wired*
NEWSPAPERS	*Washington Post*
FILMS	*Black Panther*
PAINTINGS	*New York in Transit*
TELEVISION PROGRAMS	*Reservation Dogs*
WEBSITES	*www.worldwildlife.org*
DATABASES	*ProQuest*

Read the following article and respond by answering the questions that follow. Observe, as you read, how the author refers to the various sources he uses to develop his article and how he presents material from those sources. We will use this article as a guide to handling quotations.

TOWARD DISABILITY JUSTICE: DON'T FORGET THE PLASTIC THAT GIVES ME FREEDOM

LUTICHA ANDRE DOUCETTE

Luticha Andre Doucette is the owner of Catalyst Consulting Associates, an organization that helps nonprofits, government institutions, and businesses integrate disability justice into their management and operations. She is also a community development activist who has worked with the city of Rochester, New York, on antipoverty initiatives as well as issues related to disabilities discrimination and related civil rights as protected under the 1990 Americans with Disabilities Act (ADA). Doucette earned her degree in Bioinformatics from Rochester Institute of Technology (RIT). As a Research Fellow at RIT, she also participated in genomics research working with new treatments for diseases. This article was published on May 10, 2021, in *Yes! Magazine,* an online publication dedicated to journalism focusing on solutions.

PREREADING QUESTIONS What do you think ableism is? What's your position on banning plastic disposable straws? Why do you feel this way?

1 It might seem surprising to many that plastics have provided a measure of freedom for many disabled individuals. During the "great plastic straw debate" in the late 2010s, many disabled activists took to social media to raise awareness about how straws were essential to us being able to live independently.

2 The straw provides the ability to drink freely, especially for those with limited movement. To many in disabled communities, the straw bans represented another instance that left us asking that our basic human dignity be honored. They also provided a microcosm of how movements do not include the disabled perspective. Drinking with straws was posed as an evil to the environment to be avoided lest people try to shame you. But shame shouldn't be an issue for a tool that can be the difference between being able or unable to drink at all. Often, disabled people are relegated to having a nondisabled person determine what we need.

3 Even before plastic straw bans, there have been instances in which the debate around personal use of plastics has been detrimental to disabled individuals. Several years ago, people on social media mocked Whole Foods when it began selling individually wrapped peeled oranges, adding captions like, "Who is so lazy that they cannot peel their own oranges?" Of course, because of ableism, none of them considered the fact that there are disabled people who cannot peel an orange, and that pre-peeled food provided access they'd never had before. Additionally, for those who are blind or have low vision, where cooking on the stove top can be potentially dangerous, prepped snacks or meals and yes, even, microwaved meals, can be the only means of access to good food, albeit prepackaged in plastic.

4 Furthermore, for many disabled people, plastics can touch the most intimate parts of our lives; they can be the difference between nutrition and malnutrition, safety and danger.

5 Many disabled people want to live plastic-free. However, doing so can be an insurmountable task for them. It's not just plastic straws that provide freedom,

but plastics in general have made life easier in other ways. As someone with a spinal cord injury, I use a lot of plastic for my everyday care. I was curious if ecofriendly options were available, so I began researching green products for such simple things as catheterization, the technique where a thin tube is inserted into the urethra so that you can relieve your bladder. The results were depressing at best. Latex is a common green alternative, however many disabled people, such as myself, are allergic. Not finding any good solutions, I began asking those who became paralyzed prior to the 1970s what they used; they said they used a metal tube to catheterize themselves. Ouch! Not having access to these plastic supplies is limiting at best and harmful at worst: using nothing, or reusing single-use supplies, putting oneself at an increased risk of infections and bed sores.

Overall, shaming and putting the onus of recycling and reducing the usage of plastics on the individual, especially for those who cannot avoid using plastics, puts an unfair burden on disabled individuals. Using single-use silicone catheters (which are made with plastic material) reduces my chances of getting a deadly urinary tract infection. Yes, throwing that plastic away hurts the environment, but in order to protect my body and health, I don't really have a choice. Recycling and manufacturing "green" medical supplies seems not to be an issue for environmentalists. 6

But it should be. 7

The best way environmentalists and plastic-free activists can help is to advocate for nondiscriminatory policies and the manufacturing of environmentally-friendly products that are disability-friendly. This intersectional approach can address the systemic equities and inequality, including health care coverage, which determines the quality of health disabled (and nondisabled) people can receive; it's not just a matter of who is impacted by policies around plastics, but what other systems need to change that also impact choice. We all have to reimagine what a green world with disability justice at the center looks like, then create such a world. 8

At the end of the day, disabled people want the same kind of access as anybody else without having to constantly fight to have our humanity and needs recognized. That is true freedom. 9

In the meantime, we have our plastics. 10

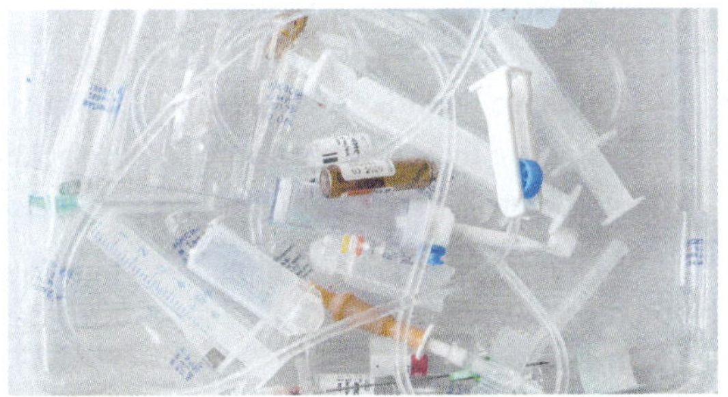

EleniyaChe/Shutterstock

Doucette, Luticha Andre. "Toward Disability Justice. Don't Forget the Plastic That Gives Me Freedom." Yes! Magazine, May 10, 2021. Used with permission.

QUESTIONS FOR READING AND REASONING

1. What is Doucette's subject? Where does she place her main argument?
2. What change is Doucette advocating to address the ableism that harms people with disabilities?
3. Summarize the evidence Doucette provides to support her argument.

4. If using plastic is necessary for some medical devices, how do you think we should responsibly dispose of them? Keep in mind that many medical devices cannot be recycled because they are considered hazardous material.
5. If we want to support Doucette's position, what should we do?
6. Doucette mentions shame in her article. What sort of shame is she discussing, and who was doing the shaming? Why do you think these people were shaming others?
7. Compromise is usually considered a positive thing, but it doesn't seem like Doucette is willing to compromise on some things. Why do you think this is? Do you agree? Why or why not?
8. How does Doucette identify her sources? She uses a primary source to find out more about nonplastic medical devices in the past. What did she do, and how did she attribute that information to others?

PRESENTING DIRECT QUOTATIONS: A GUIDE TO FORM AND STYLE

Although most of your papers will be written in your own words and style, you will sometimes use direct quotations. Just as there is a correct form for references to people and to works, there is a correct form for presenting borrowed material in direct quotations. Study the guidelines and examples and then mark these pages, as you did the others, for easy reference.

Reasons for Using Quotation Marks

We use quotation marks in four ways:

- To indicate dialogue in works of fiction and drama
- To indicate the titles of some kinds of works
- To indicate the words that others have spoken or written
- To separate ourselves from or call into question particular uses of words

The following guidelines apply to all four uses of quotation marks, but the focus will be on the third use.

A Brief Guide to Quoting

1. ***Quote accurately.*** Do not misrepresent what someone else has written. Take time to compare what you have written with the original.
2. ***Put all words taken from a source within quotation marks.*** (To take words from a source without using quotation marks is to plagiarize, a form of stealing punished in academic and professional communities.)
3. ***Never change any of the words within your quotation marks.*** Indicate any deleted words with ellipses [spaced periods (. . .)]. If you need to add words to make the meaning clear, place the added words in [square brackets], not (parentheses).

4. ***Always make the source of the quoted words clear.*** If you do not provide the author of the quoted material, readers will have to assume that you are calling those words into question–the fourth reason for quoting. Observe in the longer summary of Doucette's article that the author's full name is used in the beginning, and then her last name and pronouns (*her* and *she*) are interspersed throughout the rest of the summary. Be aware that many people are now communicating their preferred pronouns as "she/her/hers" or "they/them/theirs." Pay attention to people's preferences and write accordingly. If no preference is given, consider using the author's last name.
5. ***When quoting an author who is quoted by the author of the source you are using, you must make clear that you are getting that author's words from your source, not directly from that author.***

   For example:

   ORIGINAL: "Who is so lazy that they cannot peel their own oranges?"

   INCORRECT: Doucette seems to contradict herself, however, when she responds to Whole Foods selling individually wrapped produce: "Who is so lazy that they cannot peel their own oranges?"

   CORRECT: To make her point about the ableism that dominates our society, Doucette quotes a critical (and ableist) viewpoint from "people on social media": "Who is so lazy that they cannot peel their own oranges?"
6. ***Place commas and periods inside the closing quotation mark–even when only one word is quoted:*** Doucette argues that selling prepared food is safer for blind and low-vision people for whom "cooking on the stove top can be potentially dangerous."
7. ***Place colons and semicolons outside the closing quotation mark:*** To underscore how ableism dominates our society, Doucette includes the following critical (and ableist) observation from social media in her article "Toward Disability Justice": "Several years ago, people on social media mocked Whole Foods when it began selling individually wrapped peeled oranges, adding captions like, 'Who is so lazy that they cannot peel their own oranges?'"
8. ***Do not quote unnecessary punctuation.*** When you place quoted material at the end of a sentence you have written, use only the punctuation needed to complete your sentence.

   ORIGINAL: This intersectional approach can address the systemic equities and inequality, including health care coverage, which determines the quality of health disabled (and nondisabled) people can receive; it's not just a matter of who is impacted by policies around plastics, but what other systems need to change that also impact choice.

   INCORRECT: Doucette explains that "This intersectional approach can address the systemic equities and inequality ... disabled (and nondisabled) people can receive;."

   CORRECT: Doucette explains that "This intersectional approach can address the systemic equities and inequality ... disabled (and nondisabled) people can receive."

9. ***When the words you quote are only a part of your sentence, do not capitalize the first quoted word, even if it was capitalized in the source.*** **Exception:** You introduce the quoted material with a colon.

INCORRECT:	Doucette observes that "Often disabled people are relegated to having a nondisabled person determine what we need."
CORRECT:	Doucette observes that "often disabled people are relegated to having a nondisabled person determine what we need."
ALSO CORRECT:	Doucette provides helpful insight on ableism: "Often disabled people are relegated to having a nondisabled person determine what we need."

10. ***Use single quotation marks (the apostrophe key on your keyboard) to identify quoted material within quoted material:*** Doucette states that "during the 'great plastic straw debate' in the late 2010s, many disabled activists took to social media to raise awareness about how straws were essential to us being able to live independently."

11. ***Depending on the structure of your sentence, use a colon, a comma, or no punctuation before a quoted passage.*** A colon provides a formal introduction to a quoted passage. (See the example in item 9.) Use a comma only when your sentence requires it. Quoted words presented in a "that" clause are not preceded by a comma.

ORIGINAL:	"To many in disabled communities, the straw bans represented another instance that left us asking that our basic human dignity be honored."
CORRECT:	"To many in disabled communities," Doucette notes, "the straw bans represented another instance that left us asking that our basic human dignity be honored."
ALSO CORRECT:	Doucette observes that ableism influences many policy decisions and that "the straw bans represented another instance that left us asking that our basic human dignity be honored."

12. ***To keep quotations brief, omit irrelevant portions. Indicate missing words with ellipses.*** For example: Doucette explains that "to many in disabled communities, the straw bans . . . left us asking that our basic human dignity be honored." Some instructors want the ellipses placed in square brackets–[. . .]–to show that you have added them to the original. Modern Language Association (MLA) style does not require the square brackets unless you are quoting a passage that already has ellipses as part of that passage; in those cases, using square brackets distinguishes your added ellipses from the author's.

13. ***Consider the poor reader.***
    - Always give enough context to make the quoted material clear.
    - Do not put so many bits and pieces of quoted passages into one sentence that your reader struggles to follow the ideas.
    - Make sure that your sentences are complete and correctly constructed. Quoting is never an excuse for a sentence fragment or distorted construction.

NOTE: All examples of quoting given above are in the present tense. We write that "Doucette notes," "Doucette explains," "Doucette argues." Even though her article was written in the past, we use the present tense to describe her ongoing ideas. (APA style differs somewhat; if you are going to document in APA style, check guidelines for using present or past tense when writing about the ideas of others.)

FOR READING AND ANALYSIS

As you read the following article, practice active reading, including annotating the essay. Concentrate first on what the author has to say, but also observe the organization of the essay and the author's use of quotations and references to other authors and works.

HOWARD UNIVERSITY'S REMOVAL OF CLASSICS IS A SPIRITUAL CATASTROPHE

CORNEL WEST AND JEREMY TATE

Win McNamee/Getty Images

Cornel West has taught at some of the most distinguished universities in the world, including Yale, Princeton, the University of Paris, and Union Theological Seminary. Currently, West is Professor of the Practice of Public Philosophy at Harvard. He has published and edited over thirty books and is a prominent public intellectual who has appeared on TV and in movies while also producing spoken word albums. Jeremy Tate is the chief executive officer of the Classic Learning Test, a standardized exam alternative to the ACT and SAT.

PREREADING QUESTIONS: What type of institution is Howard University? Why do you think that it is meaningful for African American public scholar Cornel West to have cowritten this op-ed?

Upon learning to read while enslaved, Frederick Douglass began his great journey of emancipation, as such journeys always begin, in the mind. Defying unjust laws, he read in secret, empowered by the wisdom of contemporaries and classics alike to think as a free man. Douglass risked mockery, abuse, beating and even death to study the likes of Socrates, Cato and Cicero. 1

Long after Douglass's encounters with these ancient thinkers, the Rev. Martin Luther King Jr. would be similarly galvanized by his reading in the classics as a young seminarian—he mentions Socrates three times in his 1963 "Letter From Birmingham Jail." 2

Yet today, one of America's greatest Black institutions, Howard University, is diminishing the light of wisdom and truth that inspired Douglass, King and countless other freedom fighters. Amid a move for educational "prioritization," Howard University is dissolving its classics department. Tenured faculty will be dispersed to other departments, where their courses can still be taught. But the university has sent a disturbing message by abolishing the department. 3

Academia's continual campaign to disregard or neglect the classics is a sign of spiritual decay, moral decline and a deep intellectual narrowness running 4 amok in American culture. Those who commit this terrible act treat Western civilization as either irrelevant and not worthy of prioritization or as harmful and worthy only of condemnation.

5 Sadly, in our culture's conception, the crimes of the West have become so central that it's hard to keep track of the best of the West. We must be vigilant and draw the distinction between Western civilization and philosophy on the one hand, and Western crimes on the other. The crimes spring from certain philosophies and certain aspects of the civilization, not all of them.

6 The Western canon is, more than anything, a conversation among great thinkers over generations that grows richer the more we add our own voices and the excellence of voices from Africa, Asia, Latin America and everywhere else in the world. We should never cancel voices in this conversation, whether that voice is Homer or students at Howard University. For this is no ordinary discussion.

7 The Western canon is an extended dialogue among the créme de la créme of our civilization about the most fundamental questions. It is about asking "What kind of creatures are we?" no matter what context we find ourselves in. It is about living more intensely, more critically, more compassionately. It is about learning to attend to the things that matter and turning our attention away from what is superficial.

8 Howard University is not removing its classics department in isolation. This is the result of a massive failure across the nation in "schooling," which is now nothing more than the acquisition of skills, the acquisition of labels and the acquisition of jargon. Schooling is not education. Education draws out the uniqueness of people to be all that they can be in the light of their irreducible singularity. It is the maturation and cultivation of spiritually intact and morally equipped human beings.

9 The removal of the classics is a sign that we, as a culture, have embraced from the youngest age utilitarian schooling at the expense of soul-forming education. To end this spiritual catastrophe, we must restore true education, mobilizing all of the intellectual and moral resources we can to create human beings of courage, vision and civic virtue.

10 Students must be challenged: Can they face texts from the greatest thinkers that force them to radically call into question their presuppositions? Can they come to terms with the antecedent conditions and circumstances they live in but didn't create? Can they confront the fact that human existence is not easily divided into good and evil, but filled with complexity, nuance and ambiguity?

11 This classical approach is united to the Black experience. It recognizes that the end and aim of education is really the anthem of Black people, which is to lift every voice. That means to find your voice, not an echo or an imitation of others. But you can't find your voice without being grounded in tradition, grounded in legacies, grounded in heritages.

12 As German philosopher Hans-Georg Gadamer emphasized in the past century, traditions are inescapable and unavoidable. It is a question not of whether you are going to work in a tradition, but which one. Even the choice of no

tradition leaves people ignorantly beholden within a language they didn't create and frameworks they don't understand.

Engaging with the classics and with our civilizational heritage is the means to finding our true voice. It is how we become our full selves, spiritually free and morally great. 13

West, Cornel, and Jeremy Tate. "Howard University's Removal of Classics Is a Spiritual Catastrophe." the Washington Post, April 20, 2021. Used with permission.

QUESTIONS FOR READING

1. What are West and Tate discussing?
2. What event has occurred that called the authors to write this article?
3. Why do the authors believe that Howard University's actions are wrong?
4. What connections do the authors perceive between the events at Howard University and problems in our society?

QUESTIONS FOR REASONING AND ANALYSIS

5. West and Tate organize their opinion piece following the argumentative genre of problem-solution, also called a proposal. How do they explain the problem? How do they present their solution?
6. West and Tate are strongly committed to the classics, also called the "Great Works," of the Western tradition. Yet they do acknowledge some of the shortcomings and limitations of this canon. How do the authors balance the pros and cons of the classics?
7. The authors argue that schooling is not education. What do they say about this? What do they say has caused the breakdown between school and education?

QUESTIONS FOR REFLECTION AND WRITING

8. West and Tate argue for inclusion of the classics in higher education, and they mention a few examples: Socrates, Cato, Cicero. If you haven't already read these authors, has this article sparked your interest in finding out more about them and reading their work? Why or why not?
9. The authors argue that more education in the classics is needed now, not less. Do you agree? Why or why not?
10. The humanities (English, philosophy, history, classics, drama and music, languages, and theology) have fewer majors than they once did. Yet many successful people studied the humanities: Desmond Tutu, the late Anglican Bishop who helped topple apartheid in South Africa, studied theology. Billionaire George Soros studied philosophy. And *Harry Potter* author J. K. Rowling studied French and the classics. Why do you think people aren't majoring in the humanities? Are you considering a major or minor in the humanities? Why or why not?

SUGGESTIONS FOR DISCUSSION AND WRITING

1. Write a one-paragraph summary of the article by Cornel West and Jeremy Tate. Be sure that your summary clearly states the authors' main idea, the claim of their argument. Take your time and polish your word choice.

2. Western civilization has produced many positive achievements, but as the West and Tate note, it has also produced deeply troubling movements like the chattel slavery in America and white nationalism. Write a short essay on how you think colleges and universities balance the study of the positive attributes of Western civilization with its negative attributes.

3. Do some research on the courses at your college or university that include classical thinkers like Socrates, Cato, and Cicero. Write up a course plan that includes the classes you would like to take for your major during your time in college and then consider where one or two courses that include the classics might fit. Lastly, consider where you might include some courses on cultures outside of the Western tradition - courses that include information on the African diaspora, indigenous peoples, and the histories of Asia and Latin America.

CHAPTER 2

Responding Critically to Sources

LEARNING OUTCOMES

After reading Chapter 2, you will be able to:

- Recall the traits of a critical thinker.
- Describe the rhetorical context of sources.
- Outline how to analyze the style of a source.
- Describe how to write about style.
- Summarize how to write about and synthesize two or more sources when writing about style.

Spencer Platt/Getty Images

READ: What are the marchers protesting?

REASON: What information in the picture helps you determine the purpose of the protest march?

WRITE: What is the significance of the word "Nasty" in this protest sign?

In some contexts, the word *critical* carries the idea of harsh judgment: "The manager was critical of the assistant's long phone conversations." In other contexts, the term means to evaluate carefully. When we speak of the critical reader or critical thinker, we have in mind someone who reads actively, who thinks about issues, and who makes informed judgments. Here is a profile of the critical reader or thinker:

TRAITS OF THE CRITICAL READER/THINKER

- **Focused on the facts.**
  Give me the facts and show me that they are relevant to the issue.
- **Analytic.**
  What strategies has the writer/speaker used to develop the argument?
- **Open-minded.**
  Prepared to listen to different points of view, to learn from others.
- **Questioning/skeptical.**
  Who is the author, and what motivations and biases might they have?
  What other conclusions could be supported by the evidence presented?
  How thorough has the writer/speaker been?
  What persuasive strategies are used?
  What information has been omitted?
  Whose voices have been left out?
- **Creative.**
  What are some entirely different ways of looking at the issue or problem?
- **Intellectually active, not passive.**
  Willing to analyze logic and evidence.
  Willing to consider many possibilities.
  Willing, after careful evaluation, to reach a judgment, to take a stand on issues.

EXAMINING THE RHETORICAL CONTEXT OF A SOURCE

Reading critically requires preparation. Instead of "jumping into reading," begin by asking questions about the work's rhetorical context. Rhetoric is about using words, visuals, audio, and other symbolic mediums to communicate with others. Someone has chosen to shape a text in a particular way at this time for an imagined audience to accomplish a specific goal. The better you understand all of the decisions shaping a particular text, the better you will understand that work. And, then, the better you will be able to judge the significance of that work. So, try to answer the following five questions before reading. Then complete your answers while you read—or by doing research and thinking critically after you finish reading.

Who Is the Author?

Key questions to answer include:

- *Does the author have a reputation for honesty, thoroughness, and fairness?* Read the biographical note, if there is one. Ask your instructor about the author, or learn about the author in a biographical dictionary or online. Try *Book Review Digest* (available online, in your library, or through your library's database) for reviews of the author's books. When researching an author's reputation, think critically about who has written positively about them. Do people from one particular group or institution heap praise on the author? Or is the author well respected by people from across the political spectrum?
- *Is the author writing within an area of expertise?* People can voice opinions on any subject, but they cannot transfer expertise from one subject area to another. A football player endorsing a political candidate is a citizen with an opinion, not an expert on politics. This is especially important in areas like law, science, medicine, and politics. Some good questions to ask are as follows: Does the author write for broadly respected publications, such as newspapers of record (the *Washington Post,* the *New York Times,* the *Los Angeles Times, The Wall Street Journal*)? Does the author publish in scholarly journals? Or does the author just publish ideas on a personal website or on social media?
- *Is the author identified or affiliated with a particular group or set of beliefs? Does the biography place the writer or speaker in a particular institution or organization?* For example, a member of a Republican administration may be expected to favor a Republican president's policies. A Roman Catholic priest may be expected to take a stand against abortion. These kinds of details provide hints, but you should not decide, absolutely, what a writer's position is until you have read the work with care. Be alert to reasonable expectations but avoid stereotyping.

What Type—or Genre—of Source Is It?

Are you reading a researched and documented essay by a specialist–or the text of a speech delivered the previous week to a specific audience? Is the work an editorial–or a letter to the editor? Does the columnist (such as Adam Grant, who appears later in this chapter) write business columns? Is the cartoon a comic strip or a political cartoon from the editorial page of a newspaper? Know what kind of text you are reading before you start. That's the only way to give yourself the context you need to be a good critical reader.

What Kind of Audience Does the Author Anticipate?

Understanding the intended audience helps you answer questions about the depth and sophistication of the work and a possible bias or slant.

- *Does the author expect a popular audience, a general but educated audience, or a specialist audience of shared expertise? Does the author anticipate an audience that shares cultural, political, or religious values?* Often you can judge the expected audience by noting the kind of publication in which the article appears, the publisher of the book, or the venue for the speech. For example, *Reader's Digest* is written for a mass audience, and *Psychology Today* for a general but more knowledgeable reader. By contrast, articles in the *Journal of the American Medical Association* (*JAMA*) are written by physicians and research scientists for a specialized reader. (It would be inappropriate, then, for a general reader to complain that an article in *JAMA* is not well written because it is too difficult.)

- *Does the author expect a friendly audience? Or one with a "wait and see" attitude? Or even a hostile audience?* Some newspapers and television news organizations are consistently liberal, whereas others are noticeably conservative. (Do you know who owns your local paper and TV station? Do you know the political leanings of your local paper? Of the TV news that you watch? Of the blogs or websites you choose? Of the influencers you follow on Facebook, Twitter, Instagram, TikTok?) Remember: All arguments are "slanted" or "biased"–that is, they take a stand. That's as it should be. Just be sure to read or listen with an awareness of the author's particular background, interests, and possible stands on issues.

What Is the Author's Primary Purpose?

Is the work primarily informative or persuasive in intent? Designed to entertain or be inspiring? Think about the title. Read a book's preface to learn of the author's goals. Pay attention to tone as you read.

What Are the Author's Sources of Information?

Much of our judgment of an author and a work is based on the quality of the author's choice of sources. So always ask yourself: Where was the information obtained? Are sources clearly identified? Be suspicious of those who want us to believe that their unnamed "sources" are "reliable." Pay close attention to dates. A biography of King George III published in 1940 may still be the best source. An article urging more development based on county population statistics from the early 2000s is no longer reliable.

Due to the large amount of misinformation and disinformation available online and through social media, it is especially important that you think critically about your sources. What was once an exercise in "triangulating" your research by reading perhaps three sources to confirm information has now become a process of checking five, six, and even seven sources. And the sources you use must be vetted as well.

Figure 2.1 displays some of the steps that may help you respond critically to a source. Key questions about the source include:

- **Who is the author?** What is their reputation? Expertise? Affiliation?
- **What is the genre?** Is the piece an analysis? Op-ed? Informational?
- **Who is the audience?** Is the piece directed to those with undecided opinions? Those in agreement? Those in opposition?
- **What is the purpose?** Is the goal to inform? Persuade? Understand?
- **What sources are used?** Are any sources cited credible? Well-researched? Award-winning?

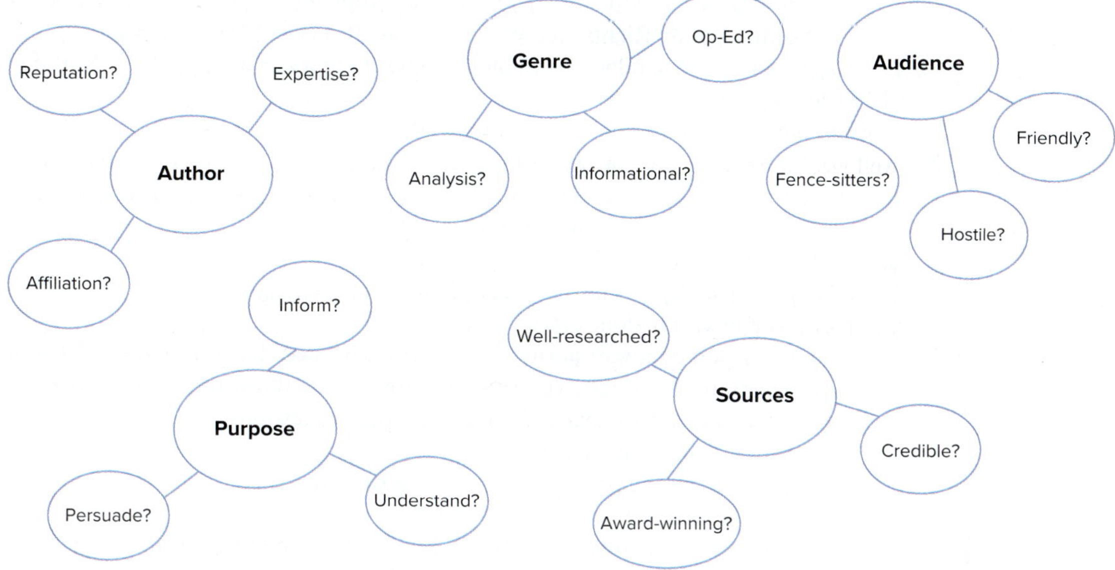

FIGURE 2.1 Examining Content Figure

NOTE: None of the readings in this textbook were written for publication in this textbook. They have all come from some other context. To read them with understanding you must identify the original context and think about how that should guide your reading.

EXERCISES: Examining the Context

1. For each of the following works, comment on what you might expect to find. Consider author, occasion, audience, and reliability.
   a. An article on the Republican administration, written by a former campaign worker for a Democratic presidential candidate.
   b. A discussion, published in the *Boston Globe,* of the New England Patriots' hope for the next Super Bowl.
   c. A letter to the editor about conservation, written by a member of the Sierra Club. (What is the Sierra Club? Check out its website.)
   d. A column in *The Wall Street Journal* on economics. (Look at the business and finance section of this newspaper. Your library has it or has access to it through a database.)
   e. A 2018 article in *Nutrition Today* on the best diets.
   f. A biography of Benjamin Franklin published by Oxford University Press.
   g. An article in *The Root* about a special vegetarian diet written by a physician. (Who is the audience for this magazine? Who publishes it?)

h. An editorial in the *New York Times* written after the Supreme Court's striking down of the Voting Rights Act of 1965 in the 2013 case *Shelby v. Holder.*
i. A speech on new handgun technology delivered at a convention of the National Rifle Association.
j. An editorial in your local newspaper titled "Stop Restricting Access to Voting."

2. Analyze an issue of your favorite publication. Look first at the editorial pages and the articles written by staff, then at articles contributed by other writers. Answer these questions for both staff writers and contributors:
   a. Who is the audience?
   b. What is the purpose of the articles and of the entire magazine?
   c. What type of article dominates the issue?
3. Select one environmental website and study what is offered. The EnviroLink Network (www.envirolink.org) will lead you to many sites. Write down the name of the site you chose and its address (URL). Then answer these questions:
   a. Who is the intended audience?
   b. What seems to be the primary purpose or goal of the site?
   c. What type of material dominates the site?
   d. For what kinds of writing assignments might you use material from the site?

ANALYZING THE STYLE OF A SOURCE

Critical readers read for implication and are alert to tone or nuance. When you read, think not only about *what* is said but also about *how* it is said. Consider the following passage:

> The fact that there are forty college football "bowl" games is a joke and shows that the NCAA and participating schools have sold their souls to corporate sponsors and just want to make a quick buck at the expense of student athletes.

This passage observes that the number of bowl games is large, that big money in college sports, especially football, can have negative repercussions, while student athletes are often exploited for their labor and sacrifices. But it actually says more than that, doesn't it? Note the writer's attitude toward the NCAA and colleges who belong to that organization, as well as the corporate partners who sponsor these games.

How can we rewrite this passage to make it more favorable? Here is one version produced by students in a group exercise:

> The large number of college football bowl games, now forty, may indicate that the NCAA and participating schools have lost focus on the purpose of athletics in American higher education by developing cozy relationships with corporate partners and their lucrative sponsorship deals.

The writers have not changed their critical view of the large number of college football bowl games and the risks of nonprofit educational institutions making a lot of money with big companies. But in this version the number of bowl games, the NCAA, and the colleges are not ridiculed. What are the differences in the two passages? The only differences are the word choice and the order in which those words appear in the sentence.

Denotative and Connotative Word Choice

The students' ability to rewrite the passage on college football bowl games to give it a positive attitude tells us that although some words may have similar meanings, they cannot always be substituted for one another without changing the message. Words with similar meanings have similar *denotations.* Often, though, words with similar denotations do not have the same connotations. A word's *connotation* is what the word suggests, what we associate the word with. The words *house* and *home,* for example, both refer to a building in which people live, but the word *home* suggests ideas—and feelings—of family and security. Thus the word *home* has a strong positive connotation. *House* by contrast brings to mind a picture of a physical structure only because the word doesn't carry any "emotional baggage."

> **NOTE:** Writers make choices; their choices reflect and convey their attitudes. *Studying the context in which a writer uses emotionally charged words is the only way to be sure that we understand the writer's attitude.*

EXERCISES: Connotation

1. For each of the following words or phrases, list at least two synonyms that have a more negative connotation than the given word.
   a. child
   b. persistent
   c. thin
   d. a large group
   e. scholarly
   f. trusting
   g. underachiever
   h. quiet
2. For each of the following words, list at least two synonyms that have a more positive connotation than the given word.
   a. notorious
   b. fat
   c. politician
   d. old (people)
   e. fanatic
   f. reckless
   g. drunkard
   h. cheap
3. Read the following paragraph and decide how the writer feels about the activity described. Note the choice of details and the connotative language that make you aware of the writer's attitude.

   Needing to complete a missed assignment for my physical education class, I dragged myself down to the tennis courts on a gloomy afternoon. My task was to serve five balls in a row into the service box. Although I thought I had learned the correct service movements, I couldn't seem to translate that knowledge into a decent serve. I tossed up the first ball, jerked back my racket, swung up on the ball—clunk—I hit the ball on the frame. I threw up the second ball, brought back my racket, swung up on the ball—ping—I made contact with the strings, but the ball dribbled down on my side of the net. I trudged around the court, collecting my tennis balls; I had only two of them.

4. Write a paragraph describing an activity that you liked or disliked without saying how you felt. From your choice of details and use of connotative language, convey your attitude toward the activity. (The paragraph in exercise 3 is your model.)
5. Select one of the words listed below and explain, in a paragraph, what the word connotes to you personally. Be precise; illustrate your thoughts with details and examples.
   a. nature
   b. mother
   c. romantic
   d. geek
   e. playboy
   f. artist

COLLABORATIVE EXERCISES: On Connotation

1. List all of the words you know for *human.* Then classify them by connotation (positive, negative, neutral) and by level of usage (formal, informal, slang). Is there any connection between type of connotation and level of usage? Why are some words more appropriate in some social contexts than in others? Can you easily list more negative words used for one category than for the other? Why?
2. Some words can be given a different connotation in different contexts. First, for each of the following words, label its connotation as positive, negative, or neutral. Then for each word with a positive connotation, write a sentence in which the word would convey a more negative connotation. For each word with a negative connotation, write a sentence in which the word would suggest a more positive connotation.
   a. natural
   b. old
   c. committed
   d. free
   e. chemical
   f. lazy
3. Each of the following groups of words might appear together in a thesaurus, but the words actually vary in connotation. After looking up any words whose connotation you are unsure of, write a sentence in which each word is used correctly. Briefly explain why one of the other words in the group should not be substituted.
   a. brittle, hard, fragile
   b. quiet, withdrawn, glum
   c. shrewd, clever, cunning
   d. strange, remarkable, bizarre
   e. thrifty, miserly, economical

Tone

We can describe a writer's attitude toward the subject as positive, negative, or (rarely) neutral. Attitude is the writer's position on, or feelings about, the subject. The way that attitude is expressed—the voice we hear and the feelings conveyed through that voice—is the writer's *tone.* Writers can choose to express attitude through a wide variety of tones. We may reinforce a negative attitude through an angry, somber, sad, mocking, peevish, sarcastic, or scornful tone. A positive attitude may be revealed through an enthusiastic, serious, sympathetic, jovial, light, or admiring tone. We cannot be sure that just because a writer selects a light tone, for example, the attitude must be positive. Humor columnists often choose a light tone to examine serious social and political issues. Given their subjects, we recognize that the light and amusing tone actually conveys a negative attitude toward the topic.

COLLABORATIVE EXERCISES: On Tone

With your class partner or in small groups, examine the following three paragraphs, which are different responses to the same event. First, decide on each writer's attitude. Then describe, as precisely as possible, the tone of each paragraph.

1. It is tragically inexcusable that this young athlete was not examined fully before he was allowed to join the varsity team. The physical examinations given were unbelievably sloppy. What were the coach and trainer thinking of not to insist that each youngster be examined while undergoing physical stress? Apparently they were not thinking about our boys at all. We can no longer trust our children to this inhumane system so bent on victory that it ignores their health—and indeed their very lives.
2. It was learned last night, following the death of varsity fullback Jim Bresnick, that none of the players was given a stress test as part of the physical examination. The oversight was attributed to laxness by the coach and trainer, who are described today as being "distraught." It is the judgment of many that the entire physical education program must be reexamined with an eye to the safety and health of all students.
3. How can I express the loss I feel over the death of my son? I want to blame someone, but who is to blame? The coaches, for not administering more rigorous physical checkups? Why should they have done more than other coaches have done before or than other coaches are doing at other schools? My son, for not telling me that he felt funny after practice? His teammates, for not telling the coaches that my son said he did not feel well? Myself, for not knowing that something was wrong with my only child? Who is to blame? All of us and none of us. But placing blame will not return my son to me; I can only pray that other parents will not have to suffer so. Jimmy, we loved you.

Level of Diction

In addition to responding to a writer's choice of connotative language, observe the *level of diction* used. An ancient Roman rhetorician, Cicero, divided style into three levels: the grand style, the middle style, and the plain style. Cicero asserted that writers and orators should use the grand style to move people to act. He argued that authors should use the middle style to please audiences and the plain style to teach. While writers might mix these styles in one piece for different reasons, thinking about these three levels may help you analyze the level of diction as you read.

Are the writer's words primarily typical of conversational language or of a more formal style? Does the writer use slang words or technical words? Is the word choice concrete and vivid or abstract and intellectual? These differences help to shape tone and affect our response to what we read. Lincoln's word choice in "The Gettysburg Address" (see p. 3) is formal and abstract. Lincoln writes "on this continent" rather than "in this land," "we take increased devotion" rather than "we become more committed." Another style, the technical, will be found in some articles in this text. The social scientist may write that "the child . . . is subjected to extremely punitive discipline," whereas a non-specialist, more informally, might write that "the child is controlled by beatings or other forms of punishment."

One way to create an informal style is to choose simple words: *land* instead of *continent.* To create greater informality, a writer can use contractions: *we'll* for *we will.* There are no contractions in "The Gettysburg Address."

> **NOTE:** In your academic and professional writing, you should aim for a style informal enough to be inviting to readers but one that, in most cases, avoids contractions or slang words.

Sentence Structure (Syntax)

Attitude is conveyed and tone created primarily through word choice, but sentence structure, also called syntax, and other rhetorical strategies are also important. Studying a writer's sentence patterns will reveal how they affect style and tone. When analyzing these features, consider the following questions:

1. *Are the sentences generally long or short, or varied in length?*

Are the structures primarily:

- *Simple* (one independent clause)

  In 1900, empires dotted the world.
- *Compound* (two or more independent clauses)

  A recent Gallup poll revealed that 20 percent of their Gen Z respondents identified as LGBTQIA+, but only 9.1 percent of characters on television between 2020 and 2021 identified as LGBTQIA+.
- *Complex* (at least one independent and one dependent clause)

  As nations grew wealthier, traditional freedom wasn't enough.

Sentences that are both long and complex create a more formal style. Compound sentences joined by *and* do not increase formality much because such sentences are really only two or more short, simple patterns hooked together. On the other hand, a long "simple" sentence with many modifiers will create a more formal style. The following example, from the article on the communication tendencies of men and women by Deborah Tannen, is more complicated than the sample compound sentence above: "One man stood out because he talked a lot, while his wife, who was sitting beside him, said nothing at all."

In "The Gettysburg Address" three sentences range from 10 to 16 words, six sentences from 21 to 29 words, and the final sentence is an incredible 82 words. All but two of Lincoln's sentences are either complex or compound-complex sentences. By contrast, in "Who Does the Talking Here?" Deborah Tannen includes a paragraph with five sentences. These sentences are composed of 14, 22, 35, 28, and 16 words each. All five are simple sentences.

2. *Does the writer use sentence fragments (incomplete sentences)?*

Although many instructors struggle to rid student writing of fragments, professional writers know that the occasional fragment can be used effectively for emphasis. Science fiction writer Bruce Sterling, thinking about the "melancholic beauty" of a gadget no longer serving any purpose, writes:

- Like Duchamp's bottle-rack, it becomes a found objet d'art. A metallic fossil of some lost human desire. A kind of involuntary poem.

The second and third sentences are, technically, fragments, but because they build on the structure of the first sentence, readers can add the missing words *It becomes* to complete each sentence. The brevity, repetition of structure, and involvement of the reader to "complete" the fragments all contribute to a strong conclusion to Sterling's paragraph.

3. *Does the writer seem to be using an overly simplistic style? If so, why?*

Overly simplistic sentence patterns, just like an overly simplistic choice of words, can be used to show that the writer thinks the subject is silly or childish or insulting. In one of her columns, Ellen Goodman objects to society's oversimplifying of addictions and its need to believe in quick and lasting cures. She makes her point with reference to two well-known examples—but notice her technique:

- Hi, my name is Jane and I was once bulimic but now I am an exercise guru. . . .
- Hi, my name is Oprah and I was a food addict but now I am a size 10.

4. *Does the writer use parallelism (coordination) or antithesis (contrast)?*

When two phrases or clauses are parallel in structure, the message is that they are equally important. Look back at an example from Deborah Tannen's essay. Tannen writes, "Women's rapport-talk probably explains why many people think women talk more. A man wants to read the paper, his wife wants to talk; his girlfriend or sister spends hours on the phone with her friend or her mother. He concludes: Women talk more." In this paragraph, Tannen coordinates two phrases, asserting the following:

- His wife wants to talk.
- His girlfriend or sister spends hours on the phone with her friend or mother.

Metaphors

When Whippman writes that advice about mindfulness is "like a stern teacher scolding us for failing to concentrate in class," she is using a *simile.* When Lincoln writes that the world will not remember, he is using a *metaphor*—actually *personification.* Metaphors, whatever their form, all make a comparison between two items that are not really alike. The writer is making a *figurative comparison,* not a literal one. The writer wants us to think about some ways in which the items are similar. Metaphors state directly or imply the comparison; similes express the comparison using a connecting word; personification always compares a nonhuman item to humans. The exact label for a metaphor is not as important as

- recognizing the use of a figure of speech,
- identifying the two items being compared,
- understanding the point of the comparison, and
- grasping the emotional impact of the figurative comparison.

REMEMBER: Pay attention to each writer's choice of metaphors. Metaphors reveal much about feelings and perceptions of life. And, like connotative words, they affect us emotionally even if we are not aware of their use. Become aware. Be able to "open up"—explain—metaphors you find in your reading.

EXERCISE: Opening Up Metaphors

During World War II, E. B. White, the essayist and writer of children's books, defined the word *democracy* in one of his *New Yorker* columns. His definition contains a series of metaphors. One is: Democracy "is the hole in the stuffed shirt through which the sawdust slowly trickles." We can open up or explain the metaphor this way:

> Just as one can punch a hole in a scarecrow's shirt and discover that there is only sawdust inside, nothing to be impressed by, so the idea of equality in a democracy "punches" a hole in the notion of an aristocratic ruling class and reveals that aristocrats, underneath, are ordinary people, just like you and me.[1]

Here are two more of White's metaphors on democracy. Open up each one in a few sentences.

> Democracy is "the dent in the high hat."
> Democracy is "the score at the beginning of the ninth."

Organization and Examples

Two other elements of writing, organization and choice of examples, also reveal attitude and help to shape the reader's response. When you study a work's organization, ask yourself questions about both placement and volume. Where are these ideas placed? At the beginning or end–the places of greatest emphasis–or in the middle, suggesting that they are less important? With regard to volume, ask yourself, "What parts of the discussion are developed at length? What points are treated only briefly?" *Note:* Sometimes simply counting the number of paragraphs devoted to the different parts of the writer's subject will give you a good understanding of the writer's main idea and purpose in writing.

Repetition

Well-written, unified essays will contain some repetition of key words and phrases. Some writers go beyond this basic strategy and use repetition to produce an effective cadence, like a drum beating in the background, keeping time to the speaker's fist pounding the lectern. In his repetition of the now-famous phrase "I have a dream," Martin Luther King Jr. gives emphasis to his vision of an ideal America. In the following paragraph, a student tried using repetition to give emphasis to a definition of liberty:

> Liberty is having the right to vote and not having other laws which restrict that right; it is having the right to apply to the university of your choice without being rejected because of race. Liberty exists when a gay man has the right to a teaching position and is not released from the position when the news of his orientation is disclosed. Liberty exists when a woman who has been offered a job does not have to decline for lack of access to day care for her children, or when a 16-year-old boy from the inner city can get an education and is not instead compelled to go to work to support his family.

These examples suggest that repetition generally gives weight and seriousness to writing and thus is appropriate when serious issues are being discussed in a forceful style.

Hyperbole, Understatement, and Irony

These three strategies create some form of tension to gain emphasis. Hyperbole overstates:

- "I will love you through all eternity!"

Understatement says less than is meant:

- Coming in soaking wet, you say, "It's a bit damp outside."

Irony creates tension by stating the opposite of what is meant:

- To a teen dressed in torn jeans and a baggy sweatshirt, the parent says, "Dressed for dinner, I see."

Quotation Marks, Italics, and Capital Letters

Several visual techniques can also be used to give special attention to certain words. A writer can place a word or phrase within quotation marks to question its validity or meaning in that context. Ellen Goodman writes, for example:

- I wonder about this when I hear the word "family" added to some politician's speech.[2]

Goodman does not agree with the politician's meaning of the word *family*. The expression *so-called* has the same effect:

- There have been restrictions on the Tibetans' so-called liberty.

Italicizing a key word or phrase or using all caps also gives additional emphasis. Dave Barry, in an essay satirizing "smart" technology, uses all caps for emphasis:

- Do you want appliances that are smarter than you? Of course not. Your appliances should be DUMBER than you, just like your furniture, your pets and your representatives in Congress.[3]

Capitalizing words not normally capitalized has the same effect of giving emphasis. As with exclamation points, writers need to use these strategies sparingly, or the emphasis sought will be lost.

EXERCISES: Recognizing Elements of Style

1. Name the technique or techniques used in each of the following passages. Then briefly explain the idea of each passage.
   a. We are becoming the tools of our tools. (Henry David Thoreau)[4]
   b. The bias and therefore the business of television is to *move* information, not collect it. (Neil Postman)[5]
   c. If guns are outlawed, only the government will have guns. Only the police, the secret police, the military. The hired servants of our rulers. Only the government—and a few outlaws. (Edward Abbey)[6]
   d. Having read all the advice on how to live 900 years, what I think is that eating a tasty meal once again will surely doom me long before I reach 900 while not eating that same meal could very well kill me. It's enough to make you reach for a cigarette! (Russell Baker)[7]
   e. If you are desperate for a quick fix, either legalize drugs or repress the user. If you want a civilized approach, mount a propaganda campaign against drugs. (Charles Krauthammer)[8]
   f. Oddly enough, the greatest scoffers at the traditions of American etiquette, who scorn the rituals of their own society as stupid and stultifying, voice respect for the customs and folklore of Native Americans, less industrialized people, and other societies they find more "authentic" than their own. (Judith Martin)[9]
   g. Text is story. Text is event, performance, special effect. Subtext is ideas. It's motive, suggestions, visual implications, subtle comparisons. (Stephen Hunter)[10]
   h. This flashy vehicle [the school bus] was as punctual as death: seeing us waiting at the cold curb, it would sweep to a halt, open its mouth, suck the boy in, and spring away with an angry growl. (E. B. White)[11]
2. Read the following essay by Erica Etelson. Use the questions that precede and follow the essay to help you determine Etelson's attitude toward her subject and to characterize her style.

THE SEVEN DEADLY SINS OF POLITI-SPEAK

ERICA ETELSON

Erica Etelson's work has appeared in *Salon,* the *Los Angeles Times, Medium,* the *San Francisco Chronicle,* and *The Nation.* Her first book, *Beyond Contempt: How Liberals Can Communicate Across the Great Divide,* was published in 2019, and the article included here was published in *Yes! Magazine* on June 28, 2021. In addition to working as a journalist, Etelson serves as a community activist dedicated to politics and the environment.

PREREADING QUESTIONS: What do you think "politi-speak" is, and why might it not be an effective way to connect with people who may not agree with you?

If you'd asked me six years ago to write a call to action to inspire people to participate in my social justice group, it would have gone something like this: 1

"The United States of Amerikkka has always been and will always be an ecocidal White supremacist settler-colonialist police state. Join our never-ending intersectional struggle to dismantle the hegemonic forces of racial capitalism, imperialism and cis-hetero-patriarchy." 2

I'm exaggerating, but only a little. (I would have used only one "k" in Amerika). Will you join my group? Wonderful, now we are a coalition of two. Two recent life changes landed me outside the left-activist bubble I'd inhabited for the past 30 years. In doing research for a book on how to communicate across lines of difference, I started talking with conservatives about issues we vehemently disagree on. From immigration to climate change to police violence, I gave—and received—an earful. 3

I also moved to a rural area, a place where most people, including many progressives, aren't tuned in to the latest Twitter dustup and aren't up to date on social justice jargon. By and large, folx are still folks, Latinx are still Latinos, and intersectionality is a street corner, not a way of understanding oppression. 4

Here's what I've learned: Academic and activist jargon and concepts obscure more than they clarify, and alienate more than they attract people to the cause. Likewise, overbearingly negative broadsides that paint our nation as hopelessly doomed make people pull the covers up over their heads. Once I got a little distance from what I'll call "politi-speak," I realized that it leaves me cold and demoralized, and that I remain involved in the struggle, not in the thrall of politi-speak, but despite it. 5

There are seven types of politi-speak that I believe repel more supporters than they attract. 6

1. BIG WORDS AND CONCEPTS

Terms that derive from the academic, legal, or policy world make people outside these circles feel confused, stupid or ashamed. To cope with these unpleasant feelings, they either withdraw or develop a feeling of anti-elitist resentment. This dynamic alienates people without advanced degrees and makes them more favorably inclined toward right-wing populist appeals. 7

Jargon can also generate distrust. If your meaning isn't clear, someone not already on your side might suspect that you're concealing your true intentions behind fancy words. Or that you're a showoff or a phony who doesn't even know what you're talking about. The lexicon of social justice is always changing, with many of the changes originating inside the academy. For those on the outside, all of a sudden, people are saying "BIPOC" as if by decree. And they're talking about toxic masculinity and White fragility. How many 8 ordinary Americans can even define these terms? One could be forgiven for thinking, "I don't know what they're talking about, but it sounds like they're dissing me."

9 If a new term is necessary, introduce and explain what important truth it illuminates. If it's hard to articulate its real-world value, it probably doesn't have much; in which case, save it for the classroom.

10 People with advanced degrees may worry about "dumbing down" the discourse or insulting the intelligence of their audience. But being plain-spoken says nothing about the intelligence of the speaker or the audience. The bigger risk runs in the other direction—insulting people by speaking in a highbrow manner that excludes people who don't know the lingo.

2. OTHERING LANGUAGE

11 Social justice advocates paint a multiracial future but sometimes use language that belittles or even demonizes certain groups of people, typically those who are White, male and/or straight. There is, among progressives, gleeful anticipation of the day when all the old White dinosaurs die off and leave us in peace, and this sentiment has not escaped the old White dinosaurs' notice.

12 Lifting up marginalized groups doesn't require putting down others. If people perceive themselves to be cast aside as second-class citizens, they are going to be extremely wary if not outright hostile to the goals of those who are doing the othering.

13 Dr. Martin Luther King's "beloved community" stands as a model for the kind of radical inclusivity that can dispel the White minority's fear of losing ground. Punching down at "white trash" does the opposite. It kills solidarity. At a time when many on the political right cast themselves as the persecuted victims of woke cancel culture, we win by throwing our arms open wide and inviting everyone into a future that is altruistic, inclusive, and gracious, not competitive, vindictive, or petty.

14 When considering whether to amplify a derogatory meme or label, I ask myself whether it adds anything that can help explain or solve a problem. And if it passes the first test, I ask who the audience is and whether anyone who doesn't already "get it" is more likely to be enlightened or antagonized. For example, if I want White women to wear masks in stores, [a negative] "Karen" meme fails on both counts.

15 If any mask resister was swayed by [a negative Karen] meme, I'll eat my mask for lunch.

3. LECTURES

16 This is a hard one. There's so much wrong in the world and, in a modern, complex society, the problems tend to be multilayered and interconnected. The temptation to fully explain and contextualize is ever present, but doing so often takes the form of abstraction and, worse, browbeating the audience for not "getting it."

A good organizer or messenger knows how to convey the nub of the problem in ways just about everyone can understand. And they do it without making anyone feel stupid for not having already seen the light. 17

Let's say you're organizing to shut down a local industrial polluter. Which call to action is going to be more motivating? 18

"Once again, the forces of extractive capitalism are externalizing their losses on the frontline poor and BIPOC people of this community. We demand the decolonization of structures of oppression that exploit our bodies and natural resources." 19

OR 20

"I'm mad at the company that's dumping waste in our drinking water and is too cheap to clean it up—who else is mad and wants to do something about it?" 21

Every minute spent lecturing is a minute of not listening. People will remember how you made them feel (heard or unheard, appreciated or belittled, inspired or hopeless) more than they will remember what you said. It's the compassion, humor, and positive vibes, not the pedagogy, that will keep them coming back for more. 22

4. RANTS

A rant is a lecture delivered with anger and without compassion, and it tends to backfire pretty spectacularly. Unless the audience already completely agrees with you, a rant will make them recoil or lash back with a counter-rant. 23

The rant puts the ranter at the center at the cost of getting to understand and connect more deeply with the other person. The legendary organizer George Goehl, director of People's Action, believes that helping people make meaning of their lives—and the root causes of their suffering—is the essential task of organizing, and that this happens when the organizer gives people the space to open up. Rants suck all the oxygen out of the room. 24

5. DOOMSAYING

Nobody's a bigger Debbie Doomsday than I am. I understand the compulsion to broadcast everything I think I know about how utterly fucked we are. I also know that there's nothing more demobilizing than telling people there's no hope. Reagan promised "morning in America." Trump predicted "so much winning." If you're a pessimist, you may see optimists as suckers for con artists like Trump. But if you take away people's hope, they will look to someone who will restore it. 25

"You have to give the people hope," said Harvey Milk, California's first openly gay elected official. Meanwhile, progressive activists keep reminding us that "justice is a constant struggle," a statement as demoralizing as it is true. 26

6. DEHUMANIZING CATEGORIES

When I first started hearing the terms "BIPOC" and "Latinx," I had a negative reaction but didn't know why. What I've come to realize is that, in my mind, these 27 terms dehumanize the people they are meant to lift up. For me, "people of color" conjures up just that. . . *people* of color. The acronym BIPOC strikes me as clinical and degrading. References to "Black bodies" instead of "Black people" also trigger some alarm bells in my mind—do they want me to see African Americans as whole people or merely as "bodies"? If we want people to join a human rights campaign, it's crucial that the humans whose rights are at stake be full human beings, not political props.

7. SELF-RIGHTEOUSNESS

28 You can be pissed off and you can be depressed and you can be in pain, but as soon as you start calling people out for not being as oppressed, as compassionate, or as well-informed as you, your hurt moves into the background, and all the other person sees is your negative judgment of them. Disdain, no matter how justified you believe it to be, alienates all but the already converted. If you're on your high horse, someone will try to knock you off it.

29 One of the holy grails of organizing and communicating is to meet people where they're at, not where you wish they were at. If I'm a personal trainer with a client who hasn't exercised in 10 years, the first thing I'd do is have them walk (if they're able) for 10 minutes on the treadmill, not kill themselves in an hourlong kickboxing class. I'm not going to lecture them about their sedentary lifestyle. I'm going to give them workouts they're willing and able to do and, bit by bit, move them toward running the half-marathon.

30 The same goes for engaging people politically. If people aren't likely to know what a word means, or are apt to react negatively to it, then the question that must be asked is whether the tradeoff is worth it. Is it so mission-critical to introduce a word or concept that it's worth the risk of turning off the not-yet-converted? Is a sarcastic tweet, however clever, going to galvanize new supporters or paint your cause in a negative light?

31 A few years ago, I participated in a direct action against a bank that finances fossil fuel development. We sat in a circle in a downtown intersection chanting protest movement classics such as, "The people united will never be defeated." Someone suggested a song. What song? We brainstormed. How about "This Land is Your Land?" a 60-something White woman offered. A youngish White woman who had been leading the chants snorted in disgust. "No, we're *not* going to sing that." The older woman, looking confused, asked why not. After some eye rolling, the younger woman said, "If you don't know. . .I'm not going to get into it right now." The older woman looked downward and got very quiet while the rest of the group exchanged smug, knowing glances. We had all collaborated in the humiliation of a fellow activist who was so committed she was willing to spend a day in jail but who hadn't received the memo about how an old folk tune negates Indigenous land claims. Instead of meeting her where she was at, we acted superior and risked repelling her from the movement.

Listen to where people are at and to how they talk about their problems, the 32
words they use and those they do not. What keeps them up at night or stoned all day? Who's messing with them and who else is suffering the same injuries? What good things do they want in their lives and who else wants those good things? For those of us in the hope-and-change business, our job is to listen to people's problems, connect them with kindred souls and work together to create a roadmap to the promised land. If the signposts on the map are incomprehensible—or obscured by a fog of snark—we are all lost.

Etelson, Erica. "The Seven Deadly Sins of Politi-Speak." *Yes! Magazine*, June 28, 2021. Used with permission.

QUESTIONS FOR READING AND REASONING

1. What is Etelson's primary claim?
2. Humor can be very effective for disarming hostile audiences, but it can also backfire spectacularly. What does Etelson say about using the humor of memes as a persuasive strategy for improving public health and building bridges with people who disagree with you?
3. Where does the phrase "seven deadly sins" come from, and why do you think Etelson uses this term in her title?
4. Why do you think Etelson focuses so much on language, tone, and style in her article?
5. Reread Etelson's list. What alternatives does she provide to help people avoid the seven deadly sins she discusses?

QUESTIONS FOR REFLECTION AND WRITING

6. How does Etelson use the communication strategies she is advocating?
7. Which of the seven deadly sins do you find the most egregious? Why?

WRITING ABOUT STYLE

Why is style important? As noted above, the Roman rhetorician Cicero divided style into three categories (grand, middle, and plain) because he understood the importance of tailoring style in response to rhetorical situations (purpose, audience, genre, etc.). By determining the style that a writer is using, you can begin to understand their purpose and audience.

Contemporary writers and orators sometimes mix styles depending on their rhetorical situation. You can determine which level of style–or mixture of styles–a writer is using by doing a style analysis.

What does it mean to "do a style analysis"? A style analysis answers the question "How is it written?" Let's think through the steps in preparing a study of a writer's choice and arrangement of language.

Understanding Purpose and Audience

A style analysis is not the place for challenging the ideas of the writer. A style analysis requires the discipline to see how a work has been put together *even if you disagree with the writer's views.* You do not have to agree with writers to appreciate their skill in writing.

If you think about audience in the context of your purpose, you should conclude that a summary of content does not belong in a style analysis. Why? Because we write style analyses for people who have already read the work. Remember, though, that your reader may not know the work in detail, so give examples to illustrate the points of your analysis.

Planning the Essay

As noted in Chapter 1, writing is a recursive process that rarely follows a linear approach. What follows, then, is just one way of working through the iterative writing process that is, at times, messy and full of starts and stops.

First, organize your analysis according to elements of style, not according to the organization of the work. Scrap any thoughts of "hacking" your way through the essay, commenting on the work paragraph by paragraph. This approach invites summary and means that you have not selected an organization that supports your purpose in writing. Think of an essay as like the pie in Figure 2.2. We could divide the pie according to key ideas–if we were summarizing. But we can also carve the pie according to elements of style, the techniques we have discussed in this chapter. This is the general plan you want to follow for your essay.

Choose those techniques you think are most important in creating the writer's attitude, and discuss them one at a time. Do not try to include the entire pie; instead, select three or four elements to examine in detail. If you were asked to write an analysis of the Erica Etelson article, for example, you might select her use of sentence structure, hyperbole, and irony. These are three techniques that stand out in Etelson's writing.

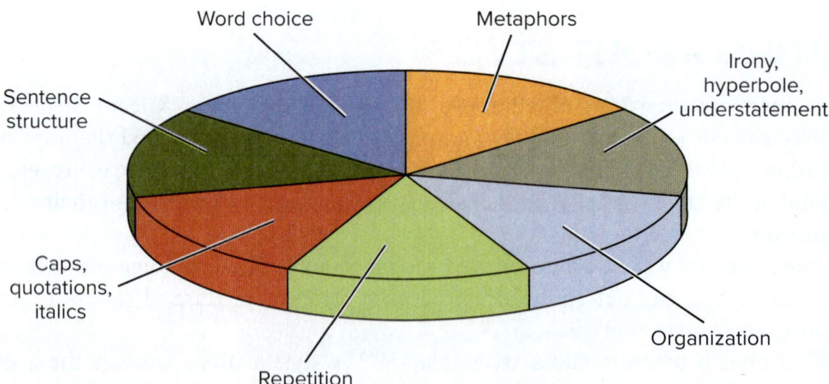

FIGURE 2.2 Analyzing Style

Drafting the Style Analysis

If you were to select three elements of style, as in the Erica Etelson example above, your essay might look something like this:

Paragraph 1: Introduction	1. Attention-getter 2. Author, title, publication information of article/book 3. Brief explanation of author's subject 4. Your thesis–that you will be analyzing style
Paragraph 2: First body paragraph	Analysis of sentence structure. (See below for more details on body paragraphs.)
Paragraph 3: Second body paragraph	1. Topic sentence that introduces of organization as the second element of style to be analyzed 2. Three or more examples of how the author uses organization 3. Explanation of how each example connects to the author's thesis–that is, how the example of organization conveys style. That is your analysis.
Paragraph 4: Third body paragraph	Analysis of word choice–with the same three parts listed above.
Paragraph 5: Conclusion	Restate your thesis: We can understand Etelson's point through a study of these three elements of her style.

A CHECKLIST FOR REVISION

When revising and polishing your draft, use these questions to complete your essay.

- ☐ Have I handled all titles correctly?
- ☐ Have I correctly referred to the author?
- ☐ Have I used quotation marks correctly when presenting examples of style? (Use the guidelines in Chapter 1 for these first three questions.)
- ☐ Do I have an accurate, clear presentation of the author's subject and thesis?
- ☐ Do I have enough examples of each element of style to show my readers that these elements are important?
- ☐ Have I connected examples to the author's thesis? That is, have I shown my readers how these techniques work to develop the author's attitude?

To reinforce your understanding of style analysis, read the following essay by Madeleine Albright, answer the questions that follow, and then study the student essay that analyzes Albright's style.

"US VS. THEM" THINKING IS TEARING AMERICA APART. BUT HERE'S WHY I'M STILL HOPEFUL ABOUT THE FUTURE

Marc Bryan-Brown/ WireImage/Getty Images

MADELEINE ALBRIGHT

Madeleine Albright (1937–2022) received her PhD from Columbia University in 1975. From 1997 to 2001, she served as the first female U.S. Secretary of State under President Bill Clinton. After leaving government, Albright worked as a distinguished professor in Georgetown University's School of Foreign Service and served on the board of directors for the Council of Foreign Relations. In 2012, President Barack Obama awarded her the Presidential Medal of Freedom for her work in foreign policy and diplomacy. She was the author of seven books, including *Hell and Other Destinations: A 21-Century Memoir* published in 2020. This article was published January 12, 2021, by *Time* magazine.

PREREADING QUESTIONS: Who is "us"? Who is "them"?

1 At this moment of shock, sadness, and hope, it might be wise to reflect on the two most dangerous words in the human vocabulary: "us" and "them." Last week, we received a dramatic reminder of this peril when our nation's political divisions erupted into a spectacle of lawlessness on Capitol Hill.

2 The impulse to choose sides is inherent in our species. Psychologists point to our desire to be safe by joining groups with which we have an affinity, our fear of the unknown, and our vanity; we want to think of ourselves as better or smarter than the other. These traits are ingrained. For better or worse, we are clannish beings, and this has done much to shape our history.

3 As a child of Europe, my own life was knocked off course early on by Hitler's race-based conception of "us vs. them," and later by Stalin's more ideological one. While in government, my daily preoccupations were with blood-drenched rivalries in the Balkans, Caucasus, Africa, and Middle East. In those years, the United States worked hard to help countries in faraway places to cool clashes related to ethnicity, religion, race, and political philosophy. In so doing, we pointed to our nation as a model; often citing the motto *E Pluribus Unum,* out of many, one.

4 Now, even as we prepare for the inauguration of a new president, we do not see ourselves as much of a model. Immensely destructive forces have been unleashed in our country. The trend has been evident for at least a quarter century, but has, in the past four years, assumed the strength of a hurricane. By now,

our nerve endings have been rubbed raw. Political rallies have devolved into exhibitions of hate. Public figures are threatened and harassed, their homes vandalized. Debates have been supplanted by shouting matches. At the very highest level, democratic institutions have been undermined and mocked. Surveys indicate that a growing number of Americans view partisan opponents not only as misguided but also as agents of evil. Each day, our biases are reinforced by the broadcast news and social media sources we select and by the likeminded people with whom we associate.

Many among us would apparently prefer to live in a country where the rest of us, i.e. "them," have no place. This attitude led directly to the debacle we witnessed on January 6, when a mob broke into the U.S. Capitol in support of a Republican president's effort to reverse the lawful result of a national election. One imagines that Abraham Lincoln, the party's founder, wept. 5

In today's not-so-United States, we must acknowledge that our divisions extend far beyond matters of political affiliation to include religion, race, gender, education, ethnicity, sexual orientation, and urban vs. rural. Confronted by this reality, many citizens are tempted either to retreat more deeply into their respective group identities or to insist piously that such categories are irrelevant and should not matter. Neither approach works. Exacerbating our differences is one road to disaster; denying them is another. Instead of fantasizing about a harmony that is out of reach, we should focus on ensuring that our inevitable disagreements lead whenever possible to constructive outcomes. Democracy was designed to aid such a process, based on the premise–severely tested in recent years–that voters will ultimately prefer builders to bullies and healers to heels. 6

As I approach the midpoint of my ninth decade, I see glimmers of light amid the darkness. Voter turnout this year was at a record high. President-elect Biden has been setting exactly the right tone and judges and officials in key swing states deserve medals for valor. The recent pandemic relief bill was a gift, albeit an imperfect one, from moderates in both parties. Senator McConnell and some other Republican leaders, after waiting far too long, ultimately chose loyalty to the Constitution over obeisance to a demented commander-in-chief. We should be conscious, too, that America has shown resilience in the past when dealing with sharp divisions, up to and including a civil war. As a country, we have a habit of veering in one direction or another before recovering our sense of balance. In my time as an adult, our electorate has switched control of the White House from one party to another nine times. 7

It should be clear given both our national experience (and world history) that no group has a monopoly on truth or virtue. However we conceive of "us," we have ample grounds for humility. I can speak only for myself, but I have been wrong many times. My attitudes and opinions are always changing as I learn more and perhaps forget a few things here and there. There is no question that we all have a right to quarrel with one another; that's the democratic way. But we also have a responsibility to talk frankly and to listen carefully, to recognize 8 our own faults, and to refrain from pinning dehumanizing labels on those with whom we disagree. It would be helpful, too, if the professional political class would stop describing America as split between red states and blue. The habit is lazy and unhelpful, and the picture it creates is at odds with the shared needs, aspirations, and values of most citizens. Notwithstanding the recent tumult, we remain one country, not two.

9 There is immense folly in thinking that, just because we have important differences, Americans have nothing equally or more important in common. Lacking that conviction, we would have neither the ability nor the credibility to lead internationally. At home, only by acting on that conviction can we avoid paralysis. Going forward, let us advocate vigorously on behalf of causes that concern us as individuals or groups; but let us also never forget that we belong in addition to a larger circle. No matter how we define "us"; no matter how we define "them"; "We the People," is an inclusive phrase.

Albright, Madeleine. "'Us vs. Them' Thinking Is Tearing America Apart. But Here's Why I'm Still Hopeful About the Future." *Time*, February 8, 2021. Used with permission.

QUESTIONS FOR READING AND REASONING

1. How does the title of Albright's article serve as a lead-in to her subject?
2. What is Albright's main idea or thesis?
3. What examples illustrate the problem Albright discusses in her article? What evidence does she present to support her main idea or thesis?
4. What solutions does Albright suggest?

QUESTIONS FOR REFLECTION AND WRITING

5. How does Albright organize her article?
6. What sort of sentence structure (syntax) does Albright use to convey her ideas?
7. How does the author's word choice affect the tone of the article?
8. Does Albright's writing style contribute to or detract from the persuasiveness of the article?
9. Do you think that the divisions in our society are a problem? Why or why not? What are the causes of these divisions?
10. Do you agree with Albright's solutions? Why or why not? How would you go about addressing the "us vs. them" division in America?

STUDENT ESSAY

STYLE ANALYSIS OF MADELEINE ALBRIGHT'S "'US VS. THEM' THINKING"

Student begins style analysis with a concise title that explains the topic and purpose of the essay.

I understand and will uphold the ideals of academic honesty as stated in the Honor Code.

Not every instructor will require an honor code statement, but you should be prepared to write one.

Hannah Peek

ENGL 1900-07

Prof. Brizee

29 September 2021

In a world of uncertainty and unprecedented times, Madeleine Albright calls us all to action in her article, "'Us vs. Them' Thinking Is Tearing America Apart. But Here's Why I'm Still Hopeful About the Future." This *Time* article was written on January 15, 2021, in response to the January 6, 2021, insurrection at the Capitol building in Washington, DC. Albright uses her many years of experience working in the government, some of which were spent as the Secretary of State, to persuade her audience to come together for the common good. She attempts to appeal to both sides of the political spectrum in her article by using stylistic word choice and organization. This analysis will focus on the unique and approachable choice of words and phrases throughout Albright's article as well as how she organizes her ideas to persuade us to come together for a common cause.

Introduction provides information about the article, when it was written, where it was published, and its author.

The introduction concludes with a purpose and thesis statement.

One main way in which Albright persuades us to take action in our divided nation is with her word choice. She uses phrases such as "us vs. them won't work" and "we the people" to convince people that our current political divisions are not going to work anymore. Albright believes that we must come together if we are ever going to solve the problems we face as a country. She tells us that we may need to compromise on our beliefs to find a middle ground. She also uses some emotional and potentially polarizing strategies like calling the president "demented," calling politicians "lazy and unhelpful," and

Student provides a clear topic sentence.

the phrase "not-so-United States" (Albright). Albright took a chance on these words as she may have alienated fervent Trump supporters or politicians. However, these words stir up emotions in the average reader, even the more moderate Republican. Using these types of words could have convinced someone on the political fence to hop over to her side. Albright also strayed away from too many technical terms in her article. By sounding less academic, her article became much more approachable for the average reader. Albright chose words for this article that furthered her goal; she worked to call her readers to action (Albright).

Clear transition sentence leading to a clear topic sentence.

Another method that Albright uses to persuade her readers is the way she organizes her article. Looking at the very beginning and very end of her article gives us a great idea of what she planned to accomplish in her writing. The beginning and end of an article are important because these are the parts that people remember the most. The introduction must also grab readers' attention to ensure that the audience will continue reading. Albright does this by using many 'us' and 'we' statements in the beginning and end of her article. This underscores her main idea in the article of coming together as a nation to address our problems. Albright peppers her experiences as a veteran politician throughout the middle of the article to avoid making the article about her; this also reminds the reader of her expertise so that they can trust the subject of her writing more.

Student uses paraphrasing rather than direct quotes in this short analysis to ensure that it is her voice that drives the essay rather than stringing together a series of direct quotes.

Another way Albright organizes her article is by providing examples of division in the country and explaining how these have wreaked havoc in our society. She speaks of rallies becoming hateful and disagreements often resulting in violence. To ensure that readers do not lose hope while reading these sections, Albright also includes a paragraph that details some of the areas that have been going right in the political world. She speaks of the COVID relief bill and the compromises made by the Republican politicians. By having these contrasting events near one another in the article, Albright is able to prove her point that when people come together and embrace their differences, they can solve issues. Also, by placing the more optimistic examples toward the end of the article, she leaves the reader with a bit of hope about the future (Albright).

Albright wrote and organized "'Us vs. Them' Thinking" in a way that persuades readers to take action in a world of chaos and divisiveness. The words she chose to use further emphasizes her point and stirs up emotion even in the most apolitical reader. Albright uses her expertise as a politician to demonstrate to her reader that to solve any issues currently facing our country, we must collaborate as a nation; she wants us to join together with our differences and use them to find solutions.

The conclusion restates all the main ideas from the analysis.

WORK CITED

Even though only one source was used for the style analysis, the student still includes a Work Cited page to meet the requirements of the assignment.

Albright, Madeleine. "'Us vs. Them' Thinking Is Tearing America Apart. But Here's Why I'm Still Hopeful About the Future." *Time,* 15 Jan. 2021, time.com/5929843/madeleine-albright-us-vs-them-thinking/.

Courtesy of Hannah Peek.

ANALYZING TWO OR MORE SOURCES

Scientists examining the same set of facts do not always draw the same conclusions; neither do historians and biographers agree on the significance of the same documents. How do we recognize and cope with these disparities? As critical readers we analyze what we read, pose questions, and refuse to believe everything we find in print or online. To develop these skills in recognizing differences, instructors frequently ask students to contrast the views of two or more writers. In psychology class, for example, you may be asked to contrast the views of Sigmund Freud and John B. Watson on child development. In a communications course, you may be asked to contrast the moderator styles of two talk-show hosts. We can examine differences in content or presentation, or both. Here are guidelines for preparing a contrast of sources.

GUIDELINES for Preparing a Contrast Essay

- **Work with sources that have something in common.** Think about the context for each, that is, each source's subject and purpose. (There is little sense in contrasting a textbook chapter, for example, with a TV talk show because their contexts are so different.)
- **Read actively to understand the content of the two sources.** Stream films, TV shows, or podcasts so that you can watch or listen to them several times, just as you would read a written source more than once.
- **Analyze for differences, focusing on your purpose in contrasting.** If you are contrasting the ideas of two writers, for example, then your analysis will focus on ideas, not on writing style. To explore differences in two news accounts, you may want to consider all of the following: the impact of placement in the newspaper/magazine, accompanying photographs or graphics, length of each article, what is covered in each article, and writing styles. Prepare a list of specific differences.
- **Organize your contrast.** It is usually best to organize by points of difference. If you write first about one source and then about the other, the ways that the sources differ may not be clear for readers. Take the time to plan an organization that clearly reveals your contrast purpose in writing. To illustrate, a paper contrasting the writing styles of two authors can be organized according to the following pattern:

  Introduction: Introduce your topic and establish your purpose to contrast styles of writer A and writer B.

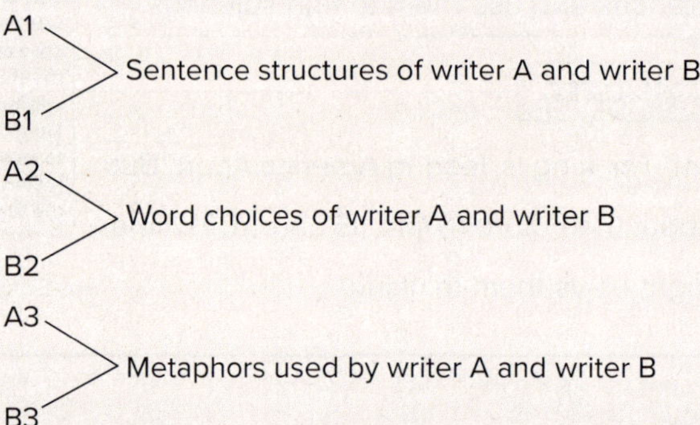

  Conclusion: Explain the effect of the differences in style of the writers.

- **Illustrate and discuss each of the points of difference for each of the sources.** Provide examples and explain the impact of the differences.
- **Always write for an audience who may be familiar with your general topic but not with the specific sources you are discussing.** Be sure to provide adequate context (names, titles of works, etc.).

SYNTHESIZING TWO OR MORE SOURCES

Sometimes we have the writing goal of synthesizing sources rather than contrasting them because the goal is to show the sources basically agree. You can still use the contrast structure even though your purpose is to demonstrate similarities rather than differences. If the sources contain some differences, you might want to begin by noting those, but then proceed to organize by points of similarity.

Remember that summarizing first one source and then the other does not produce a synthesis. Instead, you are actually leaving your reader with the task of finding the similarities. But when you group points of similarity, you are then doing the analysis for the reader, fulfilling your purpose in writing.

EXERCISE: Analyzing Two Sources

In Chapter 1, Ruth Whippman has written to question the popular current view that we need to develop "mindfulness." You will find that many have written about the topic of mindfulness. Locate a second article on this subject, and read to see if the author agrees with Whippman or supports the concept of mindfulness. If there is agreement, prepare a synthesis of the two articles. If there is disagreement, prepare a contrast of the two articles. You may be asked to prepare just an outline, rather than completing an essay. You may be asked to prepare the outline on your own or with a classmate who has the same second article as you do.

WHY I TAUGHT MYSELF TO PROCRASTINATE

ADAM GRANT

Courtesy of Adam Grant

Adam Grant, a Phi Beta Kappa graduate from Harvard with a PhD in organizational psychology from the University of Michigan, is The Wharton School's top-rated professor. He is the author of two books, *Originals* (how individuals champion new ideas) and *Give and Take,* named one of the best books of 2013. He has been widely recognized for his work in business innovation as well as for his guidelines in developing both creative and moral children.

PREREADING QUESTIONS Why would anyone recommend procrastinating? What might be Grant's twist on this topic?

Normally, I would have finished this column weeks ago. But I kept putting it off because my New Year's resolution is to procrastinate more. 1

I guess I owe you an explanation. Sooner or later. 2

We think of procrastination as a curse. Over 80 percent of college students are plagued by procrastination, requiring epic all-nighters to finish papers and prepare for tests. Roughly 20 percent of adults report being chronic procrastinators. We can only guess how much higher the estimate would be if more of them got around to filling out the survey. 3

But while procrastination is a vice for productivity, I've learned—against my natural inclinations—that it's a virtue for creativity. 4

For years, I believed that anything worth doing was worth doing early. 5
In graduate school I submitted my dissertation two years in advance. In college, I wrote my papers weeks early and finished my thesis four months before the due date. My roommates joked that I had a productive form of obsessive-compulsive disorder. Psychologists have coined a term for my condition: pre-crastination.

6 Pre-crastination is the urge to start a task immediately and finish it as soon as possible. If you're a serious pre-crastinator, progress is like oxygen and postponement is agony. When a flurry of emails land in your inbox and you don't answer them instantly, you feel as if your life is spinning out of control. When you have a speech to give next month, each day you don't work on it brings a creeping sense of emptiness, like a dementor is sucking the joy from the air around you (look it up—now!).

7 In college, my idea of a productive day was to start writing at 7 a.m. and not leave my chair until dinnertime. I was chasing "flow," the mental state described by the psychologist Mihaly Csikszentmihalyi in which you are so completely absorbed in a task that you lose a sense of time and place. I fell so deeply into that zone of concentration that my roommates once gave a party while I was writing and I didn't even notice.

8 But procrastinators, as the writer Tim Urban describes it on the blog *Wait But Why*, are at the mercy of an Instant Gratification Monkey who inhabits their brains, constantly asking questions like "Why would we ever use a computer for work when the Internet is sitting right there waiting to be played with?"

9 If you're a procrastinator, overcoming that monkey can require herculean amounts of willpower. But a pre-crastinator may need equal willpower to *not* work.

10 A few years ago, though, one of my most creative students, Jihae Shin, questioned my expeditious habits. She told me her most original ideas came to her after she procrastinated. I challenged her to prove it. She got access to a couple of companies, surveyed people on how often they procrastinated, and asked their supervisors to rate their creativity. Procrastinators earned significantly higher creativity scores than pre-crastinators like me.

11 I wasn't convinced. So Jihae, now a professor at the University of Wisconsin, designed some experiments. She asked people to come up with new business ideas. Some were randomly assigned to start right away. Others were given five minutes to first play Minesweeper or Solitaire. Everyone submitted their ideas, and independent raters rated how original they were. The procrastinators' ideas were 28 percent more creative.

12 Minesweeper is awesome, but it wasn't the driver of the effect. When people played games before being told about the task, there was no increase in creativity. It was only when they first learned about the task and then put it off that

they considered more novel ideas. It turned out that procrastination encouraged divergent thinking.

Our first ideas, after all, are usually our most conventional. My senior thesis in college ended up replicating a bunch of existing ideas instead of introducing new ones. When you procrastinate, you're more likely to let your mind wander. That gives you a better chance of stumbling onto the unusual and spotting unexpected patterns. Nearly a century ago, the psychologist Bluma Zeigarnik found that people had a better memory for incomplete tasks than for complete ones. When we finish a project, we file it away. But when it's in limbo, it stays active in our minds. 13

Begrudgingly, I acknowledged that procrastination might help with everyday creativity. But monumental achievements are a different story, right? 14

Wrong. Steve Jobs procrastinated constantly, several of his collaborators have told me. Bill Clinton has been described as a "chronic procrastinator" who waits until the last minute to revise his speeches. Frank Lloyd Wright spent almost a year procrastinating on a commission, to the point that his patron drove out and insisted that he produce a drawing on the spot. It became Fallingwater, his masterpiece. Aaron Sorkin, the screenwriter behind *Steve Jobs* and *The West Wing,* is known to put off writing until the last minute. When Katie Couric asked him about it, he replied, "You call it procrastination, I call it thinking." 15

So what if creativity happens not in spite of procrastination, but because of it? I decided to give it a try. The good news is that I am no stranger to self-discipline. So I woke up one morning and wrote a to-do list for procrastinating more. Then I set out to achieve the goal of not making progress toward my goals. It didn't go excellently. 16

My first step was to delay creative tasks, starting with this article. I resisted the temptation to sit down and start typing, and instead waited. While procrastinating (i.e., thinking), I remembered an article I had read months earlier on pre-crastination. It dawned on me that I could use my own experiences as a pre-crastinator to set the stage for readers. 17

Next, I drew some inspiration from George Costanza on *Seinfeld,* who made it a habit to quit on a high note. When I started writing a sentence that felt good, I stopped in the middle of it and walked away. When I returned to writing later that day, I was able to pick up where I had left the trail of thought. Mitch Albom, author of *Tuesdays With Morrie,* uses the same trick. "If you quit in the middle of a sentence, that's just great," he told me. "You can't wait to get back to it the next morning." 18

Once I did finish a draft, I put it away for three weeks. When I came back to it, I had enough distance to wonder, "What kind of idiot wrote this garbage?" and rewrote most of it. To my surprise, I had some fresh material at my disposal: During those three weeks, for example, a colleague had mentioned the fact that Mr. Sorkin was an avid procrastinator. 19

20 What I discovered was that in every creative project, there are moments that require thinking more laterally and, yes, more slowly. My natural need to finish early was a way of shutting down complicating thoughts that sent me whirling in new directions. I was avoiding the pain of divergent thinking—but I was also missing out on its rewards.

21 Of course, procrastination can go too far. Jihae randomly assigned a third group of people to wait until the last minute to begin their project. They weren't as creative either. They had to rush to implement the easiest idea instead of working out a novel one.

22 To curb that kind of destructive procrastination, science offers some useful guidance. First, imagine yourself failing spectacularly, and the ensuing frenzy of anxiety may jump-start your engine. Second, lower your standards for what counts as progress, and you will be less paralyzed by perfectionism. Carving out small windows of time can help, too: The psychologist Robert Boice helped graduate students overcome writer's block by teaching them to write for 15 minutes a day. My favorite step is pre-commitment: If you're passionate about gun control, go to the app *stickK* and fork over some cash in advance. If you don't meet your deadline, your money will be donated to the National Rifle Association. The fear of supporting a cause you despise can be a powerful motivator.

23 But if you're a procrastinator, next time you're wallowing in the dark playground of guilt and self-hatred over your failure to start a task, remember that the right kind of procrastination might make you more creative. And if you're a pre-crastinator like me, it may be worth mastering the discipline of forcing yourself to procrastinate. You can't be afraid of leaving your work un

Adam Grant, "Why I Taught Myself to Procrastinate," *New York Times*, 16 Jan. 2016. Copyright ©2016 by Adam Grant. Used with permission of the author.

QUESTIONS FOR READING

1. What does a good procrastinator allow for?
2. What does *pre-crastination* mean? Which term best describes the author?
3. Who are some of the most famous procrastinators? What happened when Grant chose to procrastinate while writing this essay?

QUESTIONS FOR READING AND ANALYSIS

4. What is Grant's thesis–the claim of his argument? Try to state it with precision.
5. Although the author can be said to have a serious topic, how does he avoid preaching? Find several examples of style elements that add a light touch to his essay.

QUESTIONS FOR REFLECTION AND WRITING

6. Have you experienced an "in the flow" level of concentration that would have let you work in the midst of a party? If so, how did you do it? If not, why not?
7. Are you a pro- or a pre-crastinator? A good or a bad procrastinator? Are you likely to try Grant's advice for becoming a good procrastinator? Why or why not?

SUGGESTIONS FOR DISCUSSION AND WRITING

1. Analyze the style of one of the essays from section 5 of this text. Do not comment on every element of style; select several elements that seem to characterize the writer's style and examine them in detail. Remember that style analyses are written for an audience familiar with the work, so summary is not necessary.

2. Many of the authors included in this text have written other articles that you will find in your library or online. Select one that interests you, read it, and prepare a review of it that synthesizes summary, analysis, and evaluation. Prepare a review of about 150 words; assume that the book has just been published.

3. Choose two newspaper and/or magazine articles that differ in their discussion of the same person, event, or product. You may select two different articles on a person in the news, two different accounts of a news event, an advertisement and a *Consumer Reports* analysis of the same product, or two reviews of a book or movie. Analyze differences in both content and presentation, and then consider why the two accounts differ. Organize by points of difference, and write to an audience not necessarily familiar with the articles.

4. Choose a recently scheduled public event (the Super Bowl, the Olympics, a presidential election, the Academy Award presentations, the premiere of a new television series), and find several articles written before and several after the event. First compare articles written after the event to see if they agree factually. If not, decide which article appears to be more accurate and why. Then examine the earlier material and decide which was the most and which the least accurate. Write an essay in which you explain the differences in speculation before the event and why you think these differences exist. Your audience will be aware of the event, but not necessarily aware of the articles you are studying.

CREDITS

1. E. B. White. "The Meaning of Democracy." *New Yorker,* 3 July 1943.
2. Ellen Goodman. "Family Ties Pulled Tight at Holiday Dinners." *Washington Post,* 24 Nov. 1989.
3. Dave Barry. "Remote Control." *Washington Post,* 5 Mar. 2000.
4. Henry David Thoreau. *Walden* (1854).
5. Neil Postman. *The Disappearance of Childhood.* Vintage Books, 1994, p. 82.
6. Edward Abbey. *Abbey's Road.* Dutton, 1979.
7. Russell Baker. "Sunday Observer: Eat What You Are." *New York Times Magazine,* 10 Oct. 1982.
8. Charles Krauthammer. "Legalize? No. Deglamorize." *Washington Post,* 20 May 1988.
9. Judith Martin. "The Roles of Manners." *The Responsive Community,* Spring 1996.
10. Stephen Hunter. "Look Out Below: At the Movies, Subtext Plays a Summer Role." *Washington Post,* 18 Aug. 2002, p. G01.
11. E. B. White. "Education" in *One Man's Meat.* Harper & Row, 1944.

CHAPTER 3

Understanding the Basics of Argument

LEARNING OUTCOMES

After reading Chapter 3, you will be able to:

- Describe the characteristics of argument.
- Summarize the shape of argument as envisioned by Aristotle.
- Identify the language of argument.
- Summarize the shape of argument as envisioned by Toulmin.

stockbroker/123RF

READ: What is the situation? Why is it useful to be able to argue effectively in these types of situations?

REASON: Most of the seated people are smiling, but two people are not. Why might these people not be smiling? What do you think the people are thinking?

WRITE: Compose a dialogue of what happens next. What do the two people who are not smiling say? How does the speaker respond? Does the discussion get heated? What's the outcome?

In this section we will explore the processes of thinking logically and analyzing issues to reach informed judgments. Remember: Mature people do not need to agree on all issues to respect one another's good sense, but they do have little patience with uninformed or illogical statements masquerading as argument.

CHARACTERISTICS OF ARGUMENT

Argument Is Conversation with a Goal

When you enter into an argument (as speaker, writer, or reader), you become a participant in an ongoing debate about an issue. Because you are probably not the first to address the issue, you need to be aware of the ways that the issue has been debated by others and then seek to advance the conversation. Kenneth Burke, a contemporary rhetorician, developed a metaphor to describe this process: a parlor. Burke writes, "Imagine that you enter a parlor. You come late. When you arrive, others have long preceded you, and they are engaged in a heated discussion, a discussion too heated for them to pause and tell you exactly what it is about."[1] As you listen to the ongoing conversation, Burke argues, you learn enough about the topic to engage in the discussion. Someone might agree with you and support your points, but others might disagree. Eventually, you have to leave the parlor, and the discussion continues as you exit.

Your ability to persuade others in the parlor depends on your argument remaining focused and reasoned. If you were to merely repeat what others were saying, you would not add much to the conversation, and your ability to support your points would not be as successful. This is why you need to make useful additions to your readers' understanding of a topic and compose reasoned arguments. In this way, argument becomes a meaning-making process developed through discourse.

Argument Takes a Stand on an Arguable Issue

A meaningful argument focuses on a debatable issue. We usually do not argue about facts. "Professor Nuri's postcolonial literature class meets at 10:00 on Mondays" is not arguable. It is either true or false. We can check the schedule of classes to find out. (Sometimes the facts change; new facts replace old ones.) We also do not debate personal preferences for the simple reason that they are just that–personal. If the debate is about the appropriateness of boxing as a sport, for you to declare that you would rather play soccer is to fail to advance the conversation. You have expressed a personal preference, interesting perhaps, but not relevant to the debate.

Argument Uses Reasons and Evidence

Some arguments merely "look right." That is, conclusions are drawn from facts, but the facts are not those that actually support the assertion, or the conclusion is not the only or the best explanation of those facts. To shape convincing arguments, we need more than an array of facts. We need to think critically, analyze the issue, see relationships, weigh evidence. We need to avoid the temptation to "argue" from emotion only, or to believe that just stating our opinion is the same thing as building a sound argument.

Argument Incorporates Values

Arguments are based not just on reason and evidence but also on the beliefs and values we hold and think that our audience may hold as well. In a reasoned debate, you want to make clear the values that you consider relevant to the argument. In an editorial defending the sport of boxing, one editor wrote that boxing "is a sport because the world has not yet become a place in which the qualities that go into excellence in boxing [endurance, agility, courage] have no value" (*Washington Post,* February 5, 1983). But James J. Kilpatrick also appeals to values when he argues, in an editorial critical of boxing, that we should not want to live in a society "in which deliberate brutality is legally authorized and publicly applauded" (*Washington Post,* December 7, 1982). Observe, however, the high level of seriousness in the appeal to values. Neither writer settles for a simplistic personal preference: "Boxing is exciting" or "Boxing is too violent."

Arguments Should be Ethical

One criticism of Aristotle, the ancient Greek rhetorician, is that he did not combine ethics with his theories of rhetoric. While he did leave us with an entire work on ethics, *Nicomachean Ethics,* his definition of rhetoric omits any mention of ethics. In his work *On Rhetoric,* he defines rhetoric as follows: "Let rhetoric be [defined as] an ability, in each [particular] case, to see the available means of persuasion."[2] Today, his definition has been simplified to "Finding the available means of persuasion in any given situation."

Divorcing rhetoric from ethics is dangerous because rhetoric and argument are powerful ways of creating meaning and persuading others. Rhetoric and argument can be used for good or ill. History has taught us that charismatic leaders can use rhetoric and argument to bring about positive change (e.g., Abraham Lincoln) or very negative change (e.g., Adolf Hitler). So perhaps a better way of defining rhetoric and argument would be in this way: "Finding the *ethical* means of persuasion for any given situation."

Argument Recognizes the Topic's Complexity

Much false reasoning (the logical fallacies discussed in Chapter 6) results from a writer's oversimplifying an issue. A sound argument begins with an understanding that most issues are complicated. The wise person approaches such ethical concerns as abortion or euthanasia or such public policy issues as tax cuts with the understanding that there are many philosophical, moral, and political issues that complicate discussions of these topics. Recognizing an argument's complexity may also lead us to an understanding that there can be more than one "right" position. The thoughtful arguer respects the views of others, seeks common ground when possible, and often chooses a conciliatory approach.

THE SHAPE OF ARGUMENT: WHAT WE CAN LEARN FROM ARISTOTLE

While Aristotle doesn't integrate ethics with rhetoric, he does provide us with effective ways of analyzing argument. Still one of the best ways to understand the basics of argument is to reflect on what Aristotle describes as the three "players" in any argument:

the *writer* (or *speaker*), the *argument itself,* and the *reader* (or *audience*). Aristotle also reminds us that a writer's credibility (*ethos*) and appeals to the reader's logic (*logos*) and emotions (*pathos*) are important in understanding and evaluating an argument. Moreover, he notes that the occasion or "situation" (*kairos*) should be considered. Let's examine each part of this model of argument.

Ethos (about the Writer/Speaker)

It seems logical to begin with *ethos* because without this player we have no argument. We could, though, end with the writer because Aristotle asserts that this player in any argument is the most important.

For Aristotle, how a rhetor presents an argument builds credibility. For Isocrates, the influential Greek philosopher who opened the first school of rhetoric in Athens, the rhetor's experience and life history determined their credibility. You can learn from both approaches to ethos by incorporating them into your model of analysis and by keeping them in mind when you write your own arguments. How you construct your arguments will be as important as your reputation, so reason well and be careful about what you post online!

No argument, no matter how logical, no matter how appealing to one's audience, can succeed if the audience rejects the arguer's credibility, his or her *ethical* qualities.

Think how often in political contests those running attack their opponent's character rather than the candidate's programs. Remember the smear campaign against Obama—he is (or was) a Muslim and therefore unfit to be president, the first point an error of fact, the second point an emotional appeal to voters' fears. Candidates try these smear tactics, even without evidence, because they understand that every voter they can convince of an opponent's failure of *ethos* is a citizen who will vote for them.

Logos (about the Logic of the Argument)

Logos refers to the argument itself—to the assertion and the support for it. Aristotle maintains that part of an arguer's appeal to an audience lies in the logic of the argument and the quality of the support provided. Even the most credible of writers will not move thoughtful audiences with inadequate evidence or sloppy reasoning. Yes, "arguments" that appeal to emotions, to our needs and fantasies, will work for some audiences—look at the success of advertising, for example. But if you want to present a serious claim to critical readers, then you must pay attention to your argument. Paying attention means not only having good reasons but also organizing them clearly. Your audience needs to see *how* your evidence supports your point. Consider the following argument in opposition to the war on Iraq.

> War can be justified only as a form of self-defense. To initiate a war, we need to be able to show that our first strike was necessary as a form of self-defense. The Bush administration argued that Iraq had weapons of mass destruction and intended to use them against us. Responding to someone's "intent" to do harm is always a difficult judgment call. But in this case, there were no weapons of mass destruction, so there could not have been any intent to harm the United States, or at least none that was obvious and immediate. Thus we must conclude that this war was not the right course of action for the United States.

You may disagree (many will) with this argument's assertion, but you can respect the writer's logic, the clear connecting of one reason to the next. One good way to strengthen your credibility is to get respect for clear reasoning.

Pathos (about Appeals to the Audience)

Argument implies an audience, those whose views we want to influence in some way. Aristotle labels this player *pathos,* the Greek word for both passion and suffering (hence *pathology,* the study of disease). Arguers need to be aware of their audience's feelings on the issue, the attitudes and values that will affect their response to the argument. There are really two questions arguers must answer: "How can I engage my audience's interest?" and "How can I engage their sympathy for my position?"

Some educators and health experts believe that childhood obesity is a major problem in the United States. Other Americans are much more focused on the economy—or their own careers. Al Gore is passionately concerned about the harmful effects of global warming; others, though increasingly fewer, think he lacks sufficient evidence of environmental degradation. How does a physician raise reader interest in childhood obesity? How does Gore convince doubters that we need to reduce carbon emissions? To prepare an effective argument, we need always to plan our approach with a clear vision of how best to connect to a specific audience—one that may or may not agree with our interests or our position.

Kairos (about the Occasion or Situation)

While *ethos, logos,* and *pathos* create the traditional three-part communication model, Aristotle adds another term to enhance our understanding of any argument "moment." The term *kairos* refers to the occasion for the argument, the situation that we are in. What does this moment call for from us? Is the lunch table the appropriate time and place for an argument with your coworker over the failure to meet a deadline that is part of a joint project? You have just received a 65 on your history test; is this the best time to e-mail your professor to protest the grade? Would the professor's office be the better place for your discussion than an e-mail sent just a few minutes after you have left class?

The concept of *kairos* asks us to consider what is most appropriate for the occasion, to think through the best time, place, and genre (type of argument) to make a successful argument and choose the ethical course of action. This concept has special meaning for students in a writing class who sometimes have difficulty thinking about audience at all. When practicing writing for the academic community, you may need to modify the language or tone that you use in other situations.

We argue in a specific context of three interrelated parts, as illustrated in Figure 3.1.

We present support for an assertion to a specific audience whose expectations and character we have given thought to when shaping our argument. And we present ourselves as informed, competent, and reliable so that our audience will give us their attention.

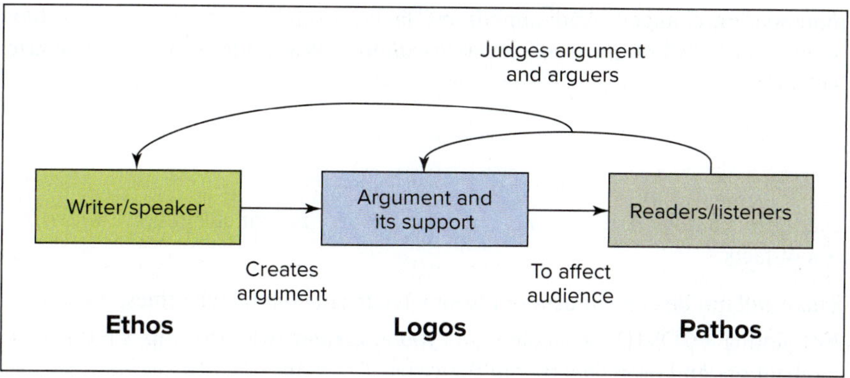

FIGURE 3.1 Aristotelian Structure of Argument

THE LANGUAGE OF ARGUMENT

We could title this section the *languages* of argument because arguments come in visual language as well as in words. But visual arguments–images, cartoons, photos, ads, memes, infographics, videos–are almost always accompanied by some words: figures speaking in bubbles, a caption, a slogan (Nike's "Just Do It!"). So we need to think about the kinds of statements that make up arguments, whether those arguments are legal briefs or cartoons, casual conversations or scholarly essays. To build an argument we need some statements that support other statements that present the main idea or claim of the argument.

- Claims: usually either inferences or judgments, for these are debatable assertions.
- Support: facts, opinions based on facts (inferences), or opinions based on values, beliefs, or ideas (judgments) or some combination of the three.

Let's consider what kinds of statements each of these terms describes.

Facts

Facts are statements that are verifiable. Factual statements refer to what can be counted or measured or confirmed by reasonable observers or trusted experts.

> There are twenty-six desks in Room 110.
>
> In the United States, more people have died of COVID-19 than died during the influenza pandemic of 1918.

These are factual statements. We can verify the first by observation–by counting. The second fact comes from medical records. We rely on trusted record-keeping sources and medical experts for verification. By definition, we do not argue about the facts. Usually. Sometimes "facts" change, as we learn more about our world. For example, when the COVID-19 epidemic first appeared in the United States, medical experts did not recommend wearing masks, but as public health officials learned more about the virus, that recommendation changed. And sometimes "facts" are false facts. These are statements that sound like facts but are incorrect. For example: Windmills and turbines cause cancer. Not so.

Inferences

Inferences are opinions based on facts. Inferences are the conclusions we draw from an analysis of facts.

> There will not be enough desks in Room 110 for upcoming fall-semester classes.
>
> Not getting a COVID-19 vaccine puts you at greater risk of serious illness, hospitalization, and even death from the virus.

Predictions of an increase in student enrollment for the coming fall semester lead to the inference that most English classes scheduled in Room 110 will run with several more students per class than last year. The dean should order new desks. Similarly, we infer from the number of deaths that COVID-19 is a health problem; statistics show more people dying from COVID-19 than from flu during the 1918 pandemic.

Inferences vary in their closeness to the facts supporting them. That the sun will "rise" tomorrow is an inference, but we count on its happening, acting as if it is a fact. However, the first inference stated above is based not just on the fact of twenty-six desks but on another inference–a projected increase in student enrollment–and two assumptions. The argument looks like this:

FACT:	There are twenty-six desks in Room 110.
INFERENCE:	There will be more first-year students next year.
ASSUMPTIONS:	1. English will remain a required course.
	2. No additional classrooms are available for English classes.
CLAIM:	There will not be enough desks in Room 110 for upcoming fall-semester classes.

This inference could be challenged by a different analysis of the facts supporting enrollment projections. Or, if additional rooms can be found, the dean will not need to order new desks. Inferences can be part of the support of an argument, or they can be the claim of an argument.

Judgments

Judgments are opinions based on values, beliefs, or philosophical concepts. (Judgments also include opinions based on personal preferences, but we have already excluded these from argument.) Judgments concern right and wrong, good and bad, better or worse, should and should not:

> No more than nineteen students should be enrolled in English composition classes.
>
> Non tenure track instructors and graduate teaching assistants who teach composition courses should be paid more and receive benefits.

NOTE: Placing such qualifiers as "I believe," "I think," or "I feel" in an assertion does not free you from the need to support that claim. The statement "I believe that President Obama was a great president" calls for an argument based on evidence and reasons.

To support the first judgment, we need to explain what constitutes overcrowding, or what constitutes the best class size for effective teaching of writing. If we can support our views on effective teaching, we may be able to convince the college dean that ordering more desks for Room 110 is not the best solution to an increasing enrollment in English composition classes. The second judgment also offers a solution to a problem, in this case a labor problem. To increase the well-being—and in turn increase the quality of teaching—of non tenure track instructors and graduate students teaching composition, colleges and universities should pay them a living wage and provide benefits. The underlying assumption: People who are fairly compensated for their labor will be happier and teach more effectively.

EXERCISE: Facts, Inferences, and Judgments

Compile a list of three statements of fact, three inferences, and three judgments. Try to organize them into three related sets, as illustrated here:

- Smoking is prohibited in some restaurants.
- Secondhand smoke is a health hazard.
- Smoking should be prohibited in all restaurants.

We can classify judgments to see better what kind of assertion we are making and, therefore, what kind of support we need to argue effectively.

FUNCTIONAL JUDGMENTS (guidelines for judging how something or someone works or could work)

Babe Ruth was the best player during the Golden Age of baseball.

Antismoking advertising will reduce the number of smokers.

AESTHETIC JUDGMENTS (guidelines for judging art, literature, music, or natural scenes)

The sunrise was beautiful.

A Raisin in the Sun's structure, characters, and symbols are perfectly wedded to create the play's vision of racism in South Chicago in the 1950s and 1960s.

ETHICAL JUDGMENTS (guidelines for group or social behavior)

Lawyers should not advertise.

It is discourteous to talk during a film or lecture.

MORAL JUDGMENTS (guidelines of right and wrong for judging individuals and for establishing legal principles)

Taking another person's life is wrong.

Equal rights under the law should not be denied on the basis of race or gender identification.

Functional and aesthetic judgments generally require defining key terms and establishing criteria for the judging or ranking made by the assertion. How, for example, do we compare DJs? On the amount of money they earn? The number of tournaments won? Or the consistency of winning throughout one's career? What about the DJ's quality and range of style? Ethical and moral judgments may be more difficult to support because they depend not just on how terms are defined and criteria established but on values and beliefs as well. If taking another person's life is wrong, why isn't it wrong in war? Or is it? These are difficult questions that require thoughtful debate.

EXERCISES: Understanding Assumptions, Facts, False Facts, Inferences, and Judgments

1. Categorize the judgments you wrote for the previous exercise (p. 69) as aesthetic, moral, ethical, or functional. Alternatively, compile a list of three judgments that you then categorize.
2. For each judgment listed for exercise 1, generate one statement of support, either a fact or an inference or another judgment. Then state any underlying assumptions that are part of each argument.
3. Read the following article and then complete the exercise that follows. This exercise tests both careful reading and your understanding of the differences among facts, inferences, and judgments.

YOUR BRAIN LIES TO YOU

SAM WANG and SANDRA AAMODT

Dr. Samuel S. H. Wang is a professor of molecular biology and neuroscience at Princeton, where he manages a research lab. Dr. Sandra Aamodt, former editor of *Nature Neuroscience,* is a freelance science writer. Drs. Wang and Aamodt are the authors of *Welcome to Your Brain: Why You Lose Your Car Keys but Never Forget How to Drive and Other Puzzles of Everyday Life* (2008). They also manage a blog—*Welcome to Your Brain.*

False beliefs are everywhere. Eighteen percent of Americans think the sun revolves around the earth, one poll has found. Thus it seems slightly less egregious that, according to another poll, 10 percent of us think that Senator Barack Obama, a Christian, is instead a Muslim. The Obama campaign has created a Web site to dispel misinformation. But this effort may be more difficult than it seems, thanks to the quirky way in which our brains store memories—and mislead us along the way. 1

The brain does not simply gather and stockpile information as a computer's hard drive does. Current research suggests that facts may be stored first in the hippocampus, a structure deep in the brain about the size and shape of a fat man's curled pinkie finger. But the information does not rest there. Every time we recall it, our brain writes it down again, and during this re-storage, it is also reprocessed. In time, the fact is gradually transferred to the cerebral cortex and is separated from the context in which it was originally learned. For example, you know that the capital of California is Sacramento, but you probably don't remember how you learned it. 2

This phenomenon, known as source amnesia, can also lead people to forget whether a statement is true. Even when a lie is presented with a disclaimer, people often later remember it as true. 3

With time, this misremembering only gets worse. A false statement from a non-credible source that is at first not believed can gain credibility during the months it takes to reprocess memories from short-term hippocampal storage to longer-term cortical storage. As the source is forgotten, the message and its implications gain strength. This could explain why, during the 2004 presidential campaign, it took some weeks for the Swift Boat Veterans for Truth campaign against Senator John Kerry to have an effect on his standing in the polls. 4

Even if they do not understand the neuroscience behind source amnesia, campaign strategists can exploit it to spread misinformation. They know that if their message is initially memorable, its impression will persist long after it is debunked. In repeating a falsehood, someone may back it up with an opening line like "I think I read somewhere" or even with a reference to a specific source. 5

In one study, a group of Stanford students was exposed repeatedly to an unsubstantiated claim taken from a Web site that Coca-Cola is an effective paint thinner. Students who read the statement five times were nearly one-third more likely than those who read it only twice to attribute it to *Consumer Reports* (rather than *The National Enquirer,* their other choice), giving it a gloss of credibility. 6

7 Adding to this innate tendency to mold information we recall is the way our brains fit facts into established mental frameworks. We tend to remember news that accords with our worldview, and discount statements that contradict it.

8 In another Stanford study, 48 students, half of whom said they favored capital punishment and half of whom said they opposed it, were presented with two pieces of evidence, one supporting and one contradicting the claim that capital punishment deters crime. Both groups were more convinced by the evidence that supported their initial position.

9 Psychologists have suggested that legends propagate by striking an emotional chord. In the same way, ideas can spread by emotional selection, rather than by their factual merits, encouraging the persistence of falsehoods about Coke—or about a presidential candidate.

10 Journalists and campaign workers may think they are acting to counter misinformation by pointing out that it is not true. But by repeating a false rumor, they may inadvertently make it stronger. In its concerted effort to "stop the smears," the Obama campaign may want to keep this in mind. Rather than emphasize that Mr. Obama is not a Muslim, for instance, it may be more effective to stress that he embraced Christianity as a young man.

11 Consumers of news, for their part, are prone to selectively accept and remember statements that reinforce beliefs they already hold. In a replication of the study of students' impressions of evidence about the death penalty, researchers found that even when subjects were given a specific instruction to be objective, they were still inclined to reject evidence that disagreed with their beliefs.

12 In the same study, however, when subjects were asked to imagine their reaction if the evidence had pointed to the opposite conclusion, they were more open-minded to information that contradicted their beliefs. Apparently, it pays for consumers of controversial news to take a moment and consider that the opposite interpretation may be true.

13 In 1919, Justice Oliver Wendell Holmes of the Supreme Court wrote that "the best test of truth is the power of the thought to get itself accepted in the competition of the market." Holmes erroneously assumed that ideas are more likely to spread if they are honest. Our brains do not naturally obey this admirable dictum, but by better understanding the mechanisms of memory perhaps we can move closer to Holmes's ideal.

Wang, Sam, and Sandra Aamodt. "Your Brain Lies to You." *New York Times,* 27 June 2008. Reprinted by permission of the authors.

Label each of the following sentences as F (fact), FF (false fact), I (inference), or J (judgment).

______ 1. Campaigns have trouble getting rid of misinformation about their candidate.

______ 2. When we reprocess information we may get the information wrong, but we always remember the source.

______ 3. The Obama campaign should have stressed that he became a Christian as a young man.

_____ 4. Most of us remember information that matches our view of the world.

_____ 5. When students were told to be objective in evaluating evidence, they continued to reject evidence they disagreed with.

_____ 6. Coca-Cola is an effective paint thinner.

_____ 7. True statements should be accepted and false statements rejected.

_____ 8. Justice Holmes was wrong about the power of truth to spread more widely than falsehood.

_____ 9. The more we understand about the way the world works, the better our chances of separating truth from falsehood.

_____ 10. Americans do not seem to understand basic science.

THE SHAPE OF ARGUMENT: WHAT WE CAN LEARN FROM TOULMIN

British philosopher Stephen Toulmin adds to what we have learned from Aristotle by focusing our attention on the basics of the argument itself. First, consider this definition of argument: *An argument consists of evidence and/or reasons presented in support of an assertion or claim that is either stated or implied.* For example:

CLAIM:	We should not go skiing today
GROUNDS:	because it is too cold.
GROUNDS:	Because some laws are unjust,
CLAIM:	civil disobedience is sometimes justified.
GROUNDS:	It's only fair and right for academic institutions to
CLAIM:	accept students only on academic merit.

The parts of an argument, Toulmin asserts, are actually a bit more complex than these examples suggest. Each argument has a third part that is not stated in the preceding examples. This third part is the "glue" that connects the support–the evidence and reasons–to the argument's claim and thus fulfills the logic of the argument. Toulmin calls this glue an argument's *warrants.* These are the principles or assumptions that allow us to assert that our evidence or reasons–what Toulmin calls the *grounds*–do indeed support our claim. Figure 3.2 illustrates these basics of the Toulmin model of argument.

CLAIM:	Academic institutions should accept students only on academic merit.
GROUNDS:	It is only fair and right.
WARRANT:	(1) Fair and right are important values. (2) Academic institutions are only about academics.

FIGURE 3.2 The Toulmin Structure of Argument

Look again at the sample arguments to see what warrants must be accepted to make each argument work:

CLAIM: We should not go skiing today.

GROUNDS: It is too cold.

WARRANTS: When it is too cold, skiing is not fun; the activity is not sufficient to keep one from becoming uncomfortable. AND: Too cold is what is too cold for me.

CLAIM: Civil disobedience is sometimes justified.

EVIDENCE: Some laws are unjust.

WARRANTS: To get unjust laws changed, people need to be made aware of the injustice. Acts of civil disobedience will get people's attention and make them aware that the laws need changing.

Warrants play an important role in any argument, so we need to be sure to understand what they are. Note, for instance, the second warrant operating in the first argument: The temperature considered uncomfortable for the speaker will also be uncomfortable for companions—an uncertain assumption. In the second argument, the warrant is less debatable, for acts of civil disobedience usually get media coverage and thus dramatize the issue. The underlying assumptions in the third example stress the need to know one's warrants. Both warrants will need to be defended in the debate over selection by academic merit only.

COLLABORATIVE EXERCISE: Building Arguments

With your class partner or in small groups, examine each of the following claims. Select two, think of one statement that could serve as evidence for each claim, and then think of the underlying assumption(s) that complete each of the arguments.

1. Professor X is not a good instructor.
2. Americans need to reduce the fat in their diets.
3. Armin van Burren is a great DJ.
4. Military women should be equally represented in the command ranks.
5. College newspapers should be free of supervision by faculty or administrators.

Toulmin was particularly interested in the great range or strength or probability of various arguments. Some kinds of arguments are stronger than others because of the language or logic they use. Other arguments must, necessarily, be heavily qualified for the claim to be supportable. Toulmin developed his language to provide a strategy for analyzing the degree of probability in a given argument and to remind us of the need to qualify some kinds of claims. You have already seen how the idea of warrants, or assumptions, helps us think about the "glue" that presumably makes a given argument work. Taken together, Toulmin terms and concepts help us analyze the arguments of others and prepare more convincing arguments of our own.

Here are all of the elements of the Toulmin model of argument, which are explained in detail below:

CLAIM (fact value, or policy):	The argument
GROUNDS (data or evidence):	Reasons supporting the claim
WARRANT:	Why readers should believe that the grounds support the claim
BACKING:	Information showing that the evidence is credible
QUALIFIER:	Information indicating that the claim may not be absolute
REBUTTAL:	Information recognizing that counter arguments to the claim likely exist and that address those counter arguments

Keep in mind that arguments using the Toulmin model do not always progress from Claim to Grounds to Warrant to Backing, etc., in a linear fashion. Also, the Toulmin model does not always have to contain all of the elements outlined above. Sophisticated writers will often intersperse Toulmin's elements if and when they seem most effective to support their argument.

Claims

A claim is what the argument asserts or seeks to prove. It answers the question "What is your point?" In an argumentative speech or essay, the claim is the speaker's or writer's main idea or thesis. Although an argument's claim "follows" from reasons and evidence, we often present an argument–whether written or spoken–with the claim stated near the beginning of the presentation. We can better understand an argument's claim by recognizing that we can have claims of fact, claims of value, and claims of policy.

Claims of Fact

Although facts usually support claims, we do argue over some facts. Historians and biographers may argue over what happened in the past, although they are more likely to argue over the significance of what happened. Scientists also argue over the facts, over how to classify an unearthed fossil, or whether the fossil indicates that the animal had feathers. For example:

CLAIM: The small, predatory dinosaur *Deinonychus* hunted its prey in packs.

This claim is supported by the discovery of several fossils of *Deinonychus* close together and with the fossil bones of a much larger dinosaur. Their teeth have also been found in or near the bones of dinosaurs that have died in a struggle.

Assertions about what will happen are sometimes classified as claims of fact, but they can also be labeled as inferences supported by facts. Predictions about a future event may be classified as claims of fact:

CLAIM: The United States will win the most gold medals at the 2024 Olympics.

CLAIM: I will get an A on tomorrow's psychology test.

What evidence would you use to support each of these claims? (And, did the first one turn out to be correct?)

Claims of Value

These include moral, ethical, and aesthetic judgments. Assertions that use such words as *good* or *bad, better* or *worse,* and *right* or *wrong* will be claims of value. The following are all claims of value:

CLAIM: Lionel Messi is a better soccer player than Cristiano Ronaldo.

CLAIM: *A Raisin in the Sun* is one of the most significant American plays.

CLAIM: Cheating hurts others and the cheater too.

CLAIM: Abortion is wrong.

Arguments in support of judgments demand relevant evidence, careful reasoning, and an awareness of the assumptions one is making. Support for claims of value often include other value statements. For example, to support the claim that censorship is bad, arguers often assert that the free exchange of ideas is good and necessary in a democracy. The support is itself a value statement.

Claims of Policy

Finally, claims of policy are assertions about what should or should not happen, what the government ought or ought not to do, how to best solve social problems. Claims of policy debate, for example, college rules, state gun laws, or federal aid to racial and ethnic communities that suffered disproportionately from the COVID-19 pandemic. The following are claims of policy:

CLAIM: College newspapers should not be controlled in any way by college authorities.

CLAIM: States should not have laws allowing people to carry concealed weapons.

CLAIM: The federal government must provide more aid to communities that suffered disproportionately from COVID-19.

Claims of policy are often closely tied to judgments of morality or political philosophy, but they also need to be grounded in feasibility. That is, your claim needs to be doable, to be based on a thoughtful consideration of the real world and the complexities of public policy issues.

Grounds (or Data or Evidence)

The term *grounds* refers to the reasons and evidence provided in support of a claim. Although the words *data* and *evidence* can also be used, note that *grounds* is the most general term because it includes reasons or logic as well as examples or statistics. We determine the grounds of an argument by asking the question "Why do you think that?"

or "How do you know that?" When writing your own arguments, you can ask yourself these questions and answer by using a *because* clause:

CLAIM:	Smoking should be banned in restaurants because
GROUNDS:	secondhand smoke is a serious health hazard.
CLAIM:	Lionel Messi is a better soccer player than Cristiano Ronaldo because
GROUNDS:	1. he is the highest scorer in La Liga's history;
	2. he has the most assists in La Liga's history; and
	3. he has a higher season goal average.

Warrants

Why should we believe that your grounds do indeed support your claim? Your argument's warrants answer this question. They explain why your evidence really is evidence. Sometimes warrants reside in language itself, in the meanings of the words we are using. If I am *younger* than my brother, then my brother must be *older* than I am. In a court case attempting to prove that Jones murdered Smith, the relation of evidence to claim is less assured. If the police investigation has been properly managed and the physical evidence is substantial, then Smith may be Jones's murderer. The prosecution has–presumably beyond a reasonable doubt–established motive, means, and opportunity for Smith to commit the murder. In many arguments based on statistical data, the argument's warrant rests on complex analyses of the statistics–and on the conviction that the statistics have been developed without error.

Still, without taking courses in statistics and logic, you can develop an alertness to the "good sense" of some arguments and the "dubious sense" of others. You know, for example, that good SAT scores are a predictor of success in college. Can you argue that you will do well in college because you have good SATs? No. We can determine only a statistical probability. We cannot turn probabilities about a group of people into a warrant about one person in the group. (In addition, SAT scores are only one predictor. Another key variable is motivation.)

What is the warrant for the Messi claim?

CLAIM:	Messi is a better soccer player than Ronaldo.
GROUNDS:	The three facts above.
WARRANT:	It is appropriate to judge and rank soccer players on these kinds of facts. That is, the better player is the one who has the highest number of goals in a top-level league, has the most assists in that league's history, and has a higher season goal average.

Backing

Standing behind an argument's warrant may be additional *backing.* Backing answers the question "How do we know that your evidence is good evidence?" You may answer this question by providing authoritative sources for the data used (for example, the Census Bureau or Goal.com). Or, you may explain in detail the methodology of the experiments performed or the surveys taken. When scientists and social scientists present the results of their research, they anticipate the question of backing and automatically provide a detailed explanation of the process by which they acquired their evidence. In criminal trials, defense attorneys challenge the backing of the prosecution's argument. They question the handling of blood samples sent to labs for DNA testing, for instance. The defense attorneys want jury members to doubt the *quality* of the evidence.

This discussion of backing returns us to the point that one part of any argument is the audience. To create an effective argument, ask yourself: Will my warrants and backing be accepted? Is my audience likely to share my values, religious beliefs, or scientific approach? If you are speaking to a group at your church, then backing based on the religious beliefs of that church may be effective. If you are preparing an argument for a general audience, then using specific religious assertions as warrants or backing probably will not result in an effective argument.

Qualifiers

Some arguments are absolute; they can be stated without qualification. *If I am younger than my brother, then he must be older than I am.* Most arguments need some qualification; many need precise limitations. If, when playing bridge, I am dealt eight spades, then my opponents and partner together must have five spade cards—because there are thirteen cards of each suit in a deck. My partner *probably* has one spade but *could* be void of spades. My partner *possibly* has two or more spades, but I would be foolish to count on it. When bidding my hand, I must be controlled by the laws of probability. Look again at the smoking-ban claim. Observe the absolute nature of both the claim and its support. If second-hand smoke is indeed a health hazard, it will be that in *all* restaurants, not just in some. With each argument ask what qualification is needed for a successful argument.

Sweeping generalizations often come to us in the heat of a debate or when we first start to think about an issue. For example: *Gun control is wrong because it restricts individual rights.* But on reflection surely you would not want to argue against all forms of gun control. (Remember: An unqualified assertion is understood by your audience to be absolute.) Would you sell guns to felons in jail or to children on the way to school? Obviously not. So, let's try the claim again, this time with two important qualifiers:

QUALIFIED CLAIM: Adults without a criminal record should not be restricted in the purchase of guns.

Others may want this claim further qualified to eliminate particular types of guns or to control the number purchased or the process for purchasing. The gun-control debate is not about absolutes; it is all about which qualified claim is best.

Rebuttals

Arguments can be challenged. Smart debaters assume that there are people who will disagree with them. They anticipate the ways that opponents can challenge their arguments. When you are planning an argument, you need to think about how you can counter or rebut the challenges you anticipate. Think of yourself as an attorney in a court case preparing your argument *and* a defense of the other attorney's challenges to your argument. If you ignore the important role of rebuttals, you may not win the jury to your side.

USING TOULMIN'S TERMS TO ANALYZE ARGUMENTS

Terms are never an end in themselves; we learn them when we recognize that they help us to organize our thinking about a subject. Toulmin's terms can aid your reading of the arguments of others. You can "see what's going on" in an argument if you analyze it, applying Toulmin's language to its parts. Not all terms will be useful for every analysis because, for example, some arguments will not have qualifiers or rebuttals. But to recognize that an argument is *without qualifiers* is to learn something important about that argument.

First, here is a simple argument broken down into its parts using Toulmin's terms:

GROUNDS: Because Dr. Bradshaw has an attendance policy,

CLAIM: students who miss more than seven classes will

QUALIFIER: most likely (last year, Dr. Bradshaw did allow one student, in unusual circumstances, to continue in the class) be dropped from the course.

WARRANT: Dr. Bradshaw's syllabus explains her attendance policy, a

BACKING: policy consistent with the concept of a discussion class that depends on student participation and consistent with the attendance policies of most of her colleagues.

REBUTTAL: Although some students complain about an attendance policy of any kind, Dr. Bradshaw does explain her policy and her reasons for it the first day of class. She then reminds students that the syllabus is a contract between them; if they choose to stay, they agree to abide by the guidelines explained on the syllabus.

This argument is brief and fairly simple. Let's see how Toulmin's terms can help us analyze a longer, more complex argument. Read actively and annotate the following essay while noting the existing annotations using Toulmin's terms. Then answer the questions that follow the article.

THE UNCHECKED POWER OF POLICE UNIONS

ROBERT REICH

Steve Russell/Toronto Star/Getty Images

Robert Reich has spent his career working, teaching, and publishing on civil rights and public policy. He served in four administrations under Presidents Gerald Ford, Jimmy Carter, Bill Clinton, and Barack Obama. Reich is a Rhodes Scholar and holds a J.D. from Yale. He has taught at Brandeis University and Harvard, and he now works as the Chancellor's Professor of Public Policy at the University of California Berkeley. He has been widely published by the *Wall Street Journal,* the *New York Times,* and the *Harvard Business Review* and has written over eighteen books. He appears regularly on TV. This article was published by *Salon* on July 7, 2021.

PREREADING QUESTIONS:

Police officers can be a positive force in communities, ensuring public safety. Similarly, unions can be a positive force in the workplace ensuring workers' safety and collective bargaining. Why do you think Reich is concerned about police unions in this article?

Introduction

Primary claim (policy)

1 Police unions abuse collective bargaining to shield their members from accountability for the killings of unarmed Black people and other heinous misconduct. No progress can be made without reining in the unchecked power of police unions.

Warrant

First additional claim (fact)

2 Look, I was Secretary of Labor. I'm in favor of unions. But police unionizing can have deadly consequences.

Grounds supporting first additional claim

3 One study found that extending collective bargaining rights to Florida sheriffs' offices led to an estimated 40 percent increase in violent police misconduct.

More grounds supporting first additional claim

4 Another study found that the protections built into the police union contracts in America's 100 largest cities were significantly correlated with the killing of unarmed civilians.

5 Another study suggests that the increase in police unionization from the 1950s through the 1980s resulted in "about 60 to 70" additional civilians killed by police each year—the majority of whom were people of color.

Second additional claim (value)

6 Experts believe the protections in police union contracts give too many officers the sense they can abuse their power.

Grounds supporting the second additional claim

7 Police contracts often have provisions allowing departments to erase disciplinary records within a few years, enabling officers with histories of misconduct to clear their records.

More grounds supporting second additional claim

8 Others allow accused officers to access their investigative files before being questioned, letting them manipulate their story. Others set strict time limits for citizens to file complaints about officers; some prevent anonymous complaints from being investigated at all.

All these provisions allow officers with histories of misconduct to stay on the force. 9

Third additional claim (facts)

Derek Chauvin, for instance, had at least 17 complaints lodged against him, 10
and never faced any discipline beyond two letters of reprimand. Needless to say, other public sector employees are not afforded these extraordinary protections.

Grounds supporting third additional claim

Even if an officer is fired, there's an extensive appeals process that usually 11
works out in their favor.

In Philadelphia, 62 percent of officers fired from 2006 to 2017 were rein- 12
stated. In San Antonio, 70 percent were. When New York police officer Daniel Pantaleo was finally fired, five years after choking Eric Garner to death, the NYPD's largest union responded by threatening a work slowdown.

More grounds supporting third additional claim

Police unions fight cities that enact even mild reforms, like establishing civilian 13
review boards. The result? Review boards are notoriously ineffective by design.

Fourth additional claim (value)

Some police union contracts with cities forbid them even creating a review 14
board. In the tragic case of Breonna Taylor, Louisville's review board could not start an investigation, take complaints from citizens, or recommend discipline for the officers. All it could do was make recommendations for policy or training changes.

It's the same in other cities: oversight boards have no investigative power, no subpoena power, and no discipline power.

Grounds supporting fourth additional claim

Police unions also wield enormous political clout. A Guardian investigation 15
found police unions spent about $87 million influencing state and local legislation over the past two decades, and at least $47.3 million on campaign contributions and lobbying at the federal level. In 2017, police unions spent $2 million to influence legislation in California alone.

Fifth additional claim (fact)

Grounds supporting fifth additional claim

Now, don't get me wrong. Stopping the abuses of police unions must not 16
become a stalking horse for attacking public sector unions generally. But the unchecked powers of police unions urgently need to be addressed.

Anticipated challenge and qualifier

Rebuttal

To start, lawmakers must change state labor laws to restrict the subjects 17
police unions can bargain over.

Primary claim (policy) restated through different terms

They should limit negotiations to pay and benefits, not how police do their 18
jobs, how and when they use force, and how and when they are disciplined.

Explanation of primary claim

For decades, police unions have shielded officers from accountability, bul- 19
lied cities into doing their bidding, and attacked lawmakers who took them on. It's past time to ensure they can no longer block accountability under the guise of collective bargaining.

Additional claims restated

Primary claim (policy) restated through different terms

Reich, Robert. "The Unchecked Power of Police Unions." *Salon.com*, July 7, 2021. Used with permission.

QUESTIONS FOR READING

1. What events is Reich responding to in this article?
2. According to Reich, what happened when the police unionized?
3. What do some police contracts allow police officers and departments to do that might discourage disciplinary action for officers who don't follow department regulations or who receive complaints?
4. How much money did police unions spend in one year in one state influencing legislation according to Reich?

QUESTIONS FOR REASONING AND ANALYSIS

5. Why is Reich a credible source to write this article?
6. What is Reich's argument?
7. How does the author organize this article, and what sort of information does he use to support his argument?

QUESTIONS FOR REFLECTION AND WRITING

8. Are you persuaded by Reich's argument? Why or why not?
9. Review the section in this book that discusses Toulmin's approach to argument. What elements of Toulmin's strategy can you identify in Reich's article?
10. Working in law enforcement is one of the most challenging professions anyone can choose. Do you know someone in law enforcement, and if you do, ask them what they think about Reich's idea. How did they respond? If you don't know someone in law enforcement, do some initial research to see how police unions respond to people who suggest limiting their influence to negotiating pay and benefits. What did you find? What's your position on this issue? Why do you feel this way?

Toulmin's terms can help you to see what writers are actually "doing" in their arguments. Just remember that writers do not usually follow the terms in precise order. Indeed, you can find both grounds and backing in the same sentence, or claim and qualifiers in the same paragraph, and so on. Still, the terms can help you to sort out your thinking about a claim you want to support. Now use your knowledge of argument as you read and analyze the following arguments.

FOR ANALYSIS AND DEBATE

Pictorial Press Ltd/ Alamy Stock Photo

LYNCHING, OUR NATIONAL CRIME

IDA B. WELLS

Ida B. Wells (1862–1931) was an early civil rights leader and investigative journalist who wrote extensively about racism and lynching in the United States from the late 1800s to the time of her death in 1931. She was born into an enslaved family in Mississippi but was freed by the Emancipation Proclamation in 1862. Wells worked as a teacher before joining the *Memphis Free Speech and Headlight,* an African American–owned newspaper in 1889. In 1909, she cofounded the National Association for the Advancement of Colored People along with W. E. B. Du Bois and other civil rights leaders. In this speech, given in New York City in 1909, Wells uses strongly held beliefs, judgments, facts, and inferences to argue for national action against lynching.

PREREADING QUESTIONS: Why do you think it is important to learn about the history of systemic racism and violence against people of color in America?

The lynching record for a quarter of a century merits the thoughtful study of the American people. It presents three salient facts: First, lynching is color-line murder. Second, crimes against women is the excuse, not the cause. Third, it is a national crime and requires a national remedy. Proof that lynching follows the color line is to be found in the statistics which have been kept for the past twenty-five years. During the few years preceding this period and while frontier law existed, the executions showed a majority of white victims. Later, however, as law courts and authorized judiciary extended into the far West, lynch law rapidly abated, and its white victims became few and far between. Just as the lynch-law regime came to a close in the West, a new mob movement started in the South. 1

This was wholly political, its purpose being to suppress the colored vote by intimidation and murder. Thousands of assassins banded together under the name of Ku Klux Klans, "Midnight Raiders," "Knights of the Golden Circle," et cetera, et cetera, spread a reign of terror, by beating, shooting and killing colored in a few years, the purpose was accomplished, and the black vote was suppressed. But mob murder continued. From 1882, in which year fifty-two were lynched, down to the present, lynching has been along the color line. Mob murder increased yearly until in 1892 more than two hundred victims were lynched and statistics show that 3,284 men, women and children have been put to death in this quarter of a century. During the last ten years from 1899 to 1908 inclusive the number lynched was 959. Of this number 102 were white, while the colored victims numbered 857. No other nation, civilized or savage, burns its criminals; only under that Stars and Stripes is the human holocaust possible. Twenty-eight human beings burned at the stake, one of them a woman and two of them children, is the awful indictment against American civilization—the gruesome tribute which the nation pays to the color line. 2

Why is mob murder permitted by a Christian nation? What is the cause of this awful slaughter? This question is answered almost daily—always the same shameless falsehood that "Negroes are lynched to protect womanhood." Standing before a Chautauqua assemblage, John Temple Graves, at once champion of lynching and apologist for lynchers, said: "The mob stands today as the most potential bulwark between the women of the South and such a carnival of crime as would infuriate the world and precipitate the annihilation of the Negro race." This is the never-varying answer of lynchers and their apologists. All know that it is untrue. The cowardly lyncher revels in murder, then seeks to shield himself from public execration by claiming devotion to woman. But truth is mighty and the lynching record discloses the hypocrisy of the lyncher as well as his crime. 3

The Springfield, Illinois, mob rioted for two days, the militia of the entire state was called out, two men were lynched, hundreds of people driven from their 4 homes, all because a white woman said a Negro assaulted her. A mad mob went to the jail, tried to lynch the victim of her charge and, not being able to find him, proceeded to pillage and burn the town and to lynch two innocent men. Later, after the police had found that the woman's charge was false, she published a retraction, the indictment was dismissed and the intended victim discharged. But the lynched victims were dead. Hundreds were homeless and Illinois was disgraced.

5 As a final and complete refutation of the charge that lynching is occasioned by crimes against women, a partial record of lynchings is cited; 285 persons were lynched for causes as follows: Unknown cause, 92; no cause, 10; race prejudice, 49; miscegenation, 7; informing, 12; making threats, 11; keeping saloon, 3; practicing fraud, 5; practicing voodooism, 1; refusing evidence, 2; political causes, 5; disputing, 1; disobeying quarantine regulations, 2; slapping a child, 1; turning state's evidence, 3; protecting a Negro, 1; to prevent giving evidence, 1; knowledge of larceny, 1; writing letter to white woman, 1; asking white woman to marry, 1; jilting girl, 1; having smallpox, 1; concealing criminal, 2; threatening political exposure, 1; self-defense, 6; cruelty, 1; insulting language to woman, 5; quarreling with white man, 2; colonizing Negroes, 1; throwing stones, 1; quarreling, 1; gambling, 1.

6 Is there a remedy, or will the nation confess that it cannot protect its protectors at home as well as abroad? Various remedies have been suggested to abolish the lynching infamy, but year after year, the butchery of men, women and children continues in spite of plea and protest. Education is suggested as a preventive, but it is as grave a crime to murder an ignorant man as it is a scholar. True, few educated men have been lynched, but the hue and cry once started stops at no bounds, as was clearly shown by the lynchings in Atlanta, and in Springfield, Illinois.

7 Agitation, though helpful, will not alone stop the crime. Year after year statistics are published, meetings are held, resolutions are adopted and yet lynchings go on. Public sentiment does measurably decrease the sway of mob law, but the irresponsible bloodthirsty criminals who swept through the streets of Springfield, beating an inoffensive law-abiding citizen to death in one part of the town, and in another torturing and shooting to death a man who for threescore years had made a reputation for honesty, integrity and sobriety; had raised a family and had accumulated property; were not deterred from their heinous crimes by either education or agitation.

8 The only certain remedy is an appeal to law. Lawbreakers must be made to know that human life is sacred and that every citizen of this country is first a citizen of the United States and secondly a citizen of the state in which he belongs. This nation must assert itself and protect its federal citizenship at home as well as abroad. The strong arm of the government must reach across state lines whenever unbridled lawlessness defies state laws and must give to the individual under the Stars and Stripes the same measure of protection it gives to him when he travels in foreign lands.

9 Federal protection of American citizenship is the remedy for lynching. Foreigners are rarely lynched in America. If, by mistake, one is lynched, the

national government quickly pays the damages. The recent agitation in California against the Japanese compelled this nation to recognize that federal power must yet assert itself to protect the nation from the treason of sovereign states. Thousands of American citizens have been put to death and no President has yet raised his hand in effective protest, but a simple insult to a native of Japan was quite sufficient to stir the government at Washington to prevent the threatened wrong. If the government has power to protect a foreigner from insult, certainly it has power to save a citizen's life.

The practical remedy has been more than once suggested in Congress. 10
Senator Gallinger, of New Hampshire, in a resolution introduced in Congress called for an investigation "with the view of ascertaining whether there is a remedy for lynching which Congress may apply." The Senate Committee has under consideration a bill drawn by A. E. Pillsbury, formerly Attorney General of Massachusetts, providing for federal prosecution of lynchers in cases where the state fails to protect citizens or foreigners. Both of these resolutions indicate that the attention of the nation has been called to this phase of the lynching question.

As a final word, it would be a beginning in the right direction if this con- 11
ference can see its way clear to establish a bureau for the investigation and publication of the details of every lynching, so that the public could know that an influential body of citizens has made it a duty to give the widest publicity to the facts in each case; that it will make an effort to secure expressions of opinion all over the country against lynching for the sake of the country's fair name; and lastly, but by no means least, to try to influence the daily papers of the country to refuse to become accessory to mobs either before or after the fact.

Several of the greatest riots and most brutal burnt offerings of the mobs have 12
been suggested and incited by the daily papers of the offending community. If the newspaper which suggests lynching in its accounts of an alleged crime, could be held legally as well as morally responsible for reporting that "threats of lynching were heard"; or, "it is feared that if the guilty one is caught, he will be lynched"; or, "there were cries of 'lynch him,' and the only reason the threat was not carried out was because no leader appeared," a long step toward a remedy will have been taken.

In a multitude of counsel there is wisdom. Upon the grave question pre- 13
sented by the slaughter of innocent men, women and children there should be an honest, courageous conference of patriotic, law-abiding citizens anxious to punish crime promptly, impartially and by due process of law, also to make life, liberty and property secure against mob rule.

Time was when lynching appeared to be sectional, but now it is national—a 14
blight upon our nation, mocking our laws and disgracing our Christianity. "With malice toward none but with charity for all" let us undertake the work of making the "law of the land" effective and supreme upon every foot of American soil—a shield to the innocent; and to the guilty, punishment swift and sure.

Wells, Ida B. Lynching Our National Crime. Address at the National Negro Conference. New York. June 1, 1909.

Label each of the following as F (fact), FF (false fact), I (inference), SHB (strongly held belief), or J (judgment).

_____ 1. More Black people have been lynched than white people.

_____ 2. At least 959 Black people were lynched between 1899 and 1908.

_____ 3. Black people represented a higher number of people lynched because they commited more crimes.

_____ 4. Black people were lynched to protect white women.

_____ 5. Lynchers were bloodthirsty cowards.

_____ 6. Holding lynchers accountable under the rule of law will reduce lynching.

_____ 7. Federal protection of Americans will also help reduce lynching.

_____ 8. Investigating and publicizing lynching will divide our nation and make race issues worse.

_____ 9. States should handle racial violence because the federal government is inefficient.

_____ 10. States can be trusted to handle racial violence because their track record is successful.

Some contemporary racial justice activists have said that police violence against people of color is a form of lynching. Reread Wells's speech considering this perspective and then do some research on the increased reporting of police violence against minorities through the use of cell phone videos.

BANS ON CRITICAL RACE THEORY COULD HAVE A CHILLING EFFECT ON HOW EDUCATORS TEACH ABOUT RACISM

NICHOLAS ENSLEY MITCHELL

Nicholas Ensley Mitchell received his PhD from Louisiana State University in 2016 and is currently an Assistant Professor of Curriculum Studies at the University of Kansas, where he teaches graduate and undergraduate courses in pedagogy and curriculum development. His research focuses on critical race studies, public policy analysis, and multicultural education. He has published in scholarly journals and media outlets, such as the *Journal of the American Association for the Advancement of Curriculum Studies* and the Jesuit Social Research Institute's *Just South Quarterly.* This article was published on July 13, 2021, in *The Conversation.*

PREREADING QUESTIONS: Critical race theory has received a lot of attention in recent years, but most definitions of this analytical approach are either misinformed or incorrect. What do you know about critical race theory, and where did you learn about it?

Perhaps no topic has dominated education news in 2021 like the debate over whether or not critical race theory should be taught—or whether it is even being taught—in America's schools.

Critical race theory is an academic framework that holds that racism is embedded in American society and its institutions.

The debate about whether K-12 students should be exposed to this theory has prompted some Republican-controlled state legislatures to pass laws to make sure that never happens. As of early July 2021, six states have passed laws that seek to ban instruction on critical race theory in K-12 schools, although the laws rarely mention critical race theory by name.

The new laws in Idaho, Texas, Oklahoma, Iowa, New Hampshire and Tennessee all prohibit teaching that any race is superior. The laws also prohibit teaching that anyone should be subjected to discrimination or treated badly because of their race or sex. In short, it appears that these laws protect all students against racism and sexism in the classroom.

But the problem emerges when the laws seek to control what teachers can say about whether a state or the nation itself was racist from inception, or whether the U.S. or any states sought to promote white supremacy through their laws.

A TEACHER'S DILEMMA

Will these newly adopted laws require educators to paint a rosy picture of America's past? Or do they still permit legitimate discussions about the role that racism played in legally sanctioned racist practices, such as slavery and racial segregation?

As a curriculum theorist who studies how school curricula portray different events in history, I am concerned that the laws will lead teachers to avoid topics that they worry could get them into trouble, even though it's unclear what kind of trouble that could be.

But first, let's take a look at what some of these laws actually say.

In Iowa and Tennessee, the laws say teachers cannot teach that the United States is "fundamentally racist."

How can a teacher in Iowa or Tennessee explain that the United States was not "fundamentally racist," yet at the time of its founding, race-based slavery was legal and stayed that way until after the Civil War?

The Texas law requires teaching that slavery and racism were strictly "deviations from, betrayals of, or failures to live up to, the authentic founding principles of the United States, which include liberty and equality."

Does that mean a Texas teacher now has to say that Founding Fathers George Washington, Thomas Jefferson and James Madison betrayed the "authentic founding principles" of liberty and equality because they owned slaves?

These are not philosophical questions.

WHAT IS DISTORTION?

Not all of the measures against critical race theory come in the form of law.

In Florida, for instance, the Department of Education adopted a new policy that states teachers "must be factual and objective." It also says they cannot "suppress or distort significant historical events, such as the Holocaust, slavery, the Civil War and Reconstruction."

But the policy also states that distortion includes teaching critical race theory. The policy makes clear that it is referring to "the theory that racism is not merely the product of prejudice, but that racism is embedded in American society and its legal systems in order to uphold the supremacy of white persons."

The policy further prohibits the use of material from the 1619 Project. That was a series of articles in the *New York Times* that connect the founding of America to a slave ship that arrived in Virginia in 1619.

The Florida policy also says teachers "may not define American history as something other than the creation of a new nation based largely on universal principles stated in the Declaration of Independence." Instruction also must include the U.S. Constitution, the Bill of Rights and subsequent amendments, the policy states.

POTENTIAL CONFLICTS

These restrictions create quite a few concerns for, say, a Florida social studies teacher. Now, such a teacher must figure out how to tell students what the Founding Fathers really meant when they wrote "We the people" in the U.S. Constitution, without saying the Founding Fathers were racist for excluding Black people from the meaning of that phrase.

Teachers may be torn between whether they should follow these new laws and policies or follow their professional code of ethics, which says teachers "shall not deliberately suppress or distort subject matter relevant to the student's progress."

How do teachers explain the motivation behind the Florida law that forbade unmarried interracial couples from spending the night together until the U.S. Supreme Court struck it down in 1964? How do teachers explain why Japanese Americans were kept in internment camps during the Second World War?

These are questions that lawmakers have essentially forced teachers to confront before they set out to teach American history. But there are no satisfactory answers for teachers, who will be forced to "distort" history one way or another.

Either they will "distort" history in the eyes of lawmakers who say it's wrong to teach that America was racist from the start. Or they will distort history by ignoring the fact that–as the U.S. Supreme Court once noted itself in 1857–Black people were "not intended" to be regarded as "citizens" under the U.S. Constitution and therefore had no constitutional rights.

Mitchell, Nicholas Ensley. "Bans on Critical Race Theory Could Have a Chilling Effect on How Educators Teach about Racism." *The Conversation*, July 13, 2021. Used with permission.

QUESTIONS FOR READING

1. What problem does Mitchell discuss in his article?
2. What examples does Mitchell provide to explain the problem?
3. What is critical race theory according to Mitchell?
4. According to Mitchell, how do some people incorrectly define critical race theory?

QUESTIONS FOR REASONING AND ANALYSIS

5. What is the author's claim?
6. What support does Mitchell provide to support his claim?
7. How does this support divide into facts, inferences, assumptions, and judgments?
8. Reread the article and see if you can find any functional judgments, aesthetic judgments, ethical judgments, and/or moral judgments?

QUESTIONS FOR REFLECTION AND WRITING

9. Reflect on the author's position regarding critical race theory and the threat of banning the teaching of racial injustice in America. Do you believe Mitchell's claim? Do you agree with his conclusion?
10. Do some research on the teaching of racial history in your state. What are teachers allowed to teach, and what are they not allowed to teach? Do you think that people who are not experts in teaching and history should decide what children should or should not learn? Who should decide what is taught in public schools in America? What are your thoughts on teaching about race in America?

SUGGESTIONS FOR DISCUSSION AND WRITING

1. Compare the style and tone of Wells's and Mitchell's essays. Has each one written in a way that works for the author's approach to this issue? Be prepared to explain your views or develop them into a comparative analysis of style.

2. Reread and study the essay "Your Brain Lies to You" (pp. 70-73) and then analyze the argument's parts, using Toulmin's terms.

3. Student drinking–including binge and underage drinking–remains an issue on college campuses. Should colleges actively seek to control binge and underage drinking on campus? Draw on your own experience as well as what statistics and discussions of this problem that you may find online to develop a claim that you can support.

CREDITS

1. Kenneth Burke. *The Philosophy of Literary Form*. Berkeley: University of California Press, 1941.
2. George A. Kennedy. *Classical Rhetoric and Its Christian and Secular Tradition*. Chapel Hill, U of North Carolina Press.

CHAPTER 4

Writing Effective Arguments

LEARNING OUTCOMES

After reading Chapter 4, you will be able to:

- Detail how to analyze your audience.
- Describe how to determine your writing purpose.
- Explain how to move from topic to claim to possible support.
- Describe how to draft your argument.
- Explain how to revise your draft.

John Parrot/Stocktrek Images/Getty Images

READ: Who are the figures in the painting? What are they doing?

REASON: What details in the painting help to date the scene?

WRITE: What is significant about the moment captured in this painting?

The basics of good writing remain much the same for works as seemingly different as the personal essay, the argument, and the researched essay. Good writing is focused, organized, and clear. Effective essays are written in a style and tone that are suited to both the audience and the writer's purpose. These are sound principles, all well known to you. But how, exactly, do you achieve them when writing argument? This chapter will help you answer that question.

KNOW YOUR AUDIENCE

Too often, students plunge into writing without thinking much about audience, for, after all, their "audience" is only the instructor who has given the assignment, and their purpose is to complete the assignment and get a grade. These views of audience and purpose are likely to lead to badly written arguments. First, if you are not thinking about readers who may disagree with you, you may not develop the best defense of your claim. Second, you may ignore your essay's needed introductory material on the assumption that the instructor, knowing the assignment, has a context for understanding your writing. To avoid these pitfalls, use the following questions to sharpen your understanding of audience.

Who Is My Audience?

If you are writing an essay for the student newspaper, your audience consists—primarily—of students, but do not forget that faculty and administrators also read the student newspaper. If you are preparing a letter-to-the-editor refutation of a recent column in your town's newspaper, your audience will be the readers of that newspaper—that is, adults in your town. Some instructors give assignments that create an audience such as those just described so that you will practice writing with a specific audience in mind.

If you are not assigned a specific audience, imagine your classmates, as well as your instructor, as part of your audience. In other words, you are writing to readers in the academic community. These readers are intelligent and thoughtful, expecting sound reasoning and convincing evidence. From diverse cultures and experiences, these readers also represent varied values and beliefs. Do not confuse the shared expectations of writing conventions with shared beliefs.

Completing an audience analysis table like the one shown in Table 4.1 will help you develop a better idea of what your readers will be expecting when you write and enable you to determine your rhetorical approach and your tone. The following audience analysis table was prepared by first-year writing student Zaryn Kamara for "Solutions to Combat High Maternal Mortality Rates for Black Women," the student essay that appears on pp. 310–318 in Chapter 13. The purpose of this assignment was to conduct research on a problem facing a local community, in this case St. Louis, Missouri, and propose some ways to address this problem.

What Will My Audience Know about My Topic?

What can you expect a diverse group of readers to know? Whether you are writing on a current issue or a centuries-old debate, you must expect most readers to have some

TABLE 4.1 Student Sample: Audience Analysis

READER	NEEDS	BELIEFS	VIEWPOINT
Gatekeeper - The board of directors of hospitals who create policies.	Create better policies regarding the health of mothers, and work with physicians to create assessments that might lower these numbers.	Cost-effective and efficient plans of treatment for their hospital regardless of issues.	May be defensive and not compliant.
Primary - Physicians, specifically OB/GYNs.	To better understand racial disparities and create a diverse workforce.	Caring for patients to the best of their ability.	Some physicians may believe that no change is needed to combat maternal mortality.
Secondary - Organizations who strive to reduce maternal mortality and the disparities within it.	Find investors who are willing to fund research and tools to combat maternal mortality.	Reducing maternal mortality and all of its stipulations.	Determined to create change.
Shadow - Those who want to change the racial disparities in hospitals and reduce maternal mortality. - Those affected by maternal mortality.	Spread more information about the topic of maternal mortality and all of its stipulations.	Relating to the issue and hoping to stop anyone else from experiencing their own difficulties.	Remain hopeful that change will be implemented.

knowledge of the issues. Their knowledge does not free you from the responsibility of developing your support fully, though. In fact, their knowledge creates further demands. For example, most readers know the main arguments on both sides of the abortion issue. For you to write as if they do not—and thus to ignore the arguments of the opposition—is to produce an argument that probably adds little to the debate on the subject.

On the other hand, what some readers "know" may be little more than an overview of the issues from TV news—or the emotional outbursts of a family member. Some readers may be misinformed or prejudiced, but they embrace their views enthusiastically nonetheless. So, as you think about the ways to develop and support your argument, you will have to assess your readers' knowledge and sophistication. This assessment will help you decide how much background information to provide or what false facts need to be revealed and dismissed.

Where Does My Audience Stand on the Issue?

Expect readers to hold a range of views, even if you are writing to students on your campus or to an organization of which you are a member. It is not true, for instance, that all students want coed dorms or pass/fail grading. And if everyone already agrees with

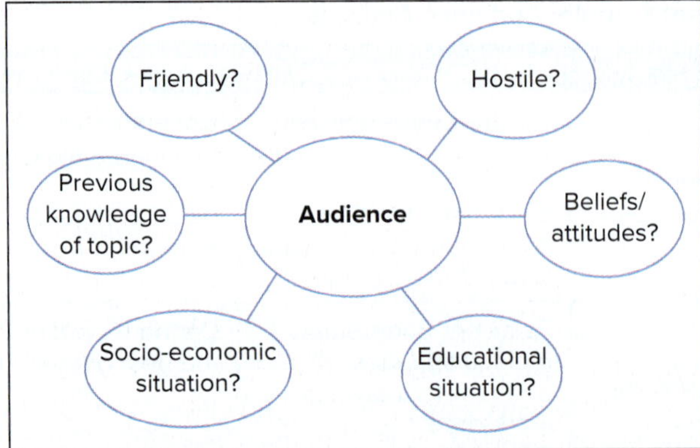

FIGURE 4.1 Questions to Ask about Your Audience

you, you have no reason to write. An argument needs to be about a topic that is open to debate. So:

- Assume that some of your audience will probably never agree with you but may offer you grudging respect if you compose an effective argument.
- Assume that some readers do not hold strong views on your topic and may be open to convincing if you present a good case.
- Assume that those who share your views will still be looking for a strong argument in support of their position.
- Assume that if you hold an unpopular position your best strategy will be a conciliatory approach. (See pp. 96–97 for a discussion of the conciliatory argument.)

Figure 4.1 presents the types of questions you should ask about your audience. Is your audience friendly? Is your audience hostile?

What are your audience's beliefs?

What is your audience's educational situation?

What is your audience's socio-economic situation?

What previous knowledge of the topic does your audience have?

How Should I Speak to My Audience?

Your audience will form an opinion of you based on how you write and how you reason. The image of argument—and the arguer—that we have been creating in this text's discussion is of thoughtful claims defended with logic and evidence. However, the heated debate at yesterday's lunch does not resemble this image of argument. Sometimes the word *persuasion* is used to separate the emotionally charged debate from the calm, intellectual tone of the academic argument. Unfortunately, this neat division between argument and persuasion does not describe the real world of debate. The thoughtful arguer also wants to be persuasive, and highly emotional presentations can contain relevant facts in support of a sound idea. Instead of thinking of two separate categories—argument and persuasion—think instead of a continuum from the most rigorous logic to extreme flights of fantasy. Figure 4.2 suggests this continuum with some kinds of arguments placed along it.

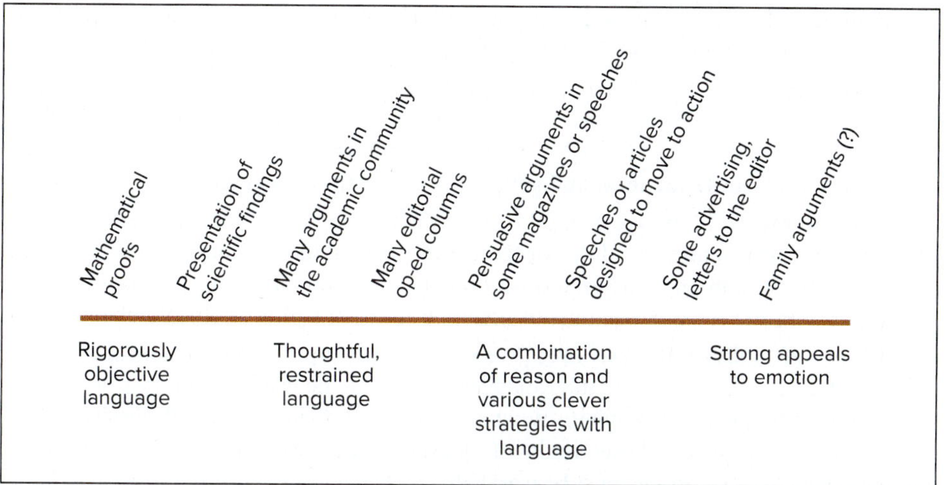

FIGURE 4.2 A Continuum of Argumentative Language

Where should you place yourself along this continuum of language? You will have to answer this question with each specific writing context. Much of the time you will choose "thoughtful, restrained language," as expected by the academic community, but there may be times that you will use various persuasive strategies. Probably you will not select "strong appeals to emotion" for your college or workplace writing. Remember that you have different roles in your life, and you use different *voices* as appropriate to each role. Most of the time, you will want to use the serious voice you normally select for serious conversations with other adults. This is the voice that will help you establish your credibility, your *ethos.*

UNDERSTAND YOUR WRITING PURPOSE

There are many types or genres of argument and different reasons for writing—beyond wanting to write convincingly in defense of your views. Different types of arguments require different approaches, or different kinds of evidence. It helps to be able to recognize the kind of argument you are contemplating.

What Type (Genre) of Argument Am I Preparing?

Here are some useful ways to classify arguments and think about their support.

- **Investigative paper similar to those in the social sciences.** If you are asked to collect evidence in an organized way to support a claim about advertising strategies or violence in children's TV programming, then you will be writing an investigative essay. You will present evidence that you have gathered and analyzed to support your claim.
- **Evaluation.** If your assignment is to explain why others should read a particular book or take a particular professor's class, then you will be preparing an evaluation

argument. Be sure to think about your criteria: What makes a book or a professor good? Why do you dislike Lady Gaga? Is it her music–or her lifestyle?

- **Definition.** If you are asked to explain the meaning of a general or controversial term, you will be writing a definition argument. What do we mean by *wisdom?* What are the characteristics of *cool?* A definition argument usually requires both specific details to illustrate the term and general ideas to express its meaning.
- **Claim of values.** If you are given the assignment to argue for your position on euthanasia, trying juveniles as adults, or the use of national identification cards, recognize that your assignment calls for a position paper, a claim based heavily on values. Pay close attention to your warrants or assumptions in any philosophical debate.
- **Claim of policy.** If you are given a broad topic: "What should we do about ______________?" and you have to fill in the blank, your task is to offer solutions to a current problem. What should we do about childhood obesity? About home foreclosures? These kinds of questions are less philosophical and more practical. Your solutions must be workable.
- **Refutation or rebuttal.** If you are given the assignment to find a letter to the editor, a newspaper editorial, or an essay in this text with which you disagree, your job is to write a refutation essay, a specific challenge to a specific argument. You know, then, that you will refer repeatedly to the work you are rebutting, so you will need to know it thoroughly.

What Is My Goal?

It is also helpful to consider your goal in writing. Does your topic call for a strong statement of views (i.e., "These are the steps we must take to reduce childhood obesity")? Or is your goal an exploratory one, a thinking through of possible answers to a more philosophical question ("Why is it often difficult to separate performance from personality when we evaluate a star?")? Thinking about your goal as well as the argument's genre will help to decide on the kinds of evidence needed and on the approach to take and tone to select.

Will the Rogerian or Conciliatory Approach Work for Me?

Psychologist Carl Rogers asserts that the most successful arguments take a conciliatory approach. The characteristics of this approach include

- showing respect for the opposition in the language and tone of the argument,
- seeking common ground by indicating specific facts and values that both sides share, and
- qualifying the claim to bring opposing sides more closely together.

In their essay "Euthanasia–A Critique," authors Peter A. Singer and Mark Siegler provide a good example of a conciliatory approach. They begin their essay by explaining and then rebutting the two main arguments in favor of euthanasia. After stating the two arguments in clear and neutral language, they write this in response to the first argument:

> We agree that the relief of pain and suffering is a crucial goal of medicine. We question, however, whether the care of dying patients cannot be improved without resorting

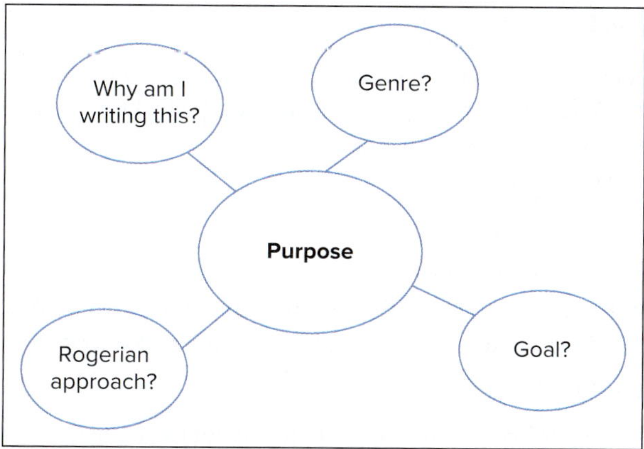

FIGURE 4.3 **Questions to Ask about Your Audience**

to the drastic measure of euthanasia. Most physical pain can be relieved with the appropriate use of analgesic agents. Unfortunately, despite widespread agreement that dying patients must be provided with necessary analgesia, physicians continue to underuse analgesia in the care of dying patients because of the concern about depressing respiratory drive or creating addiction. Such situations demand better management of pain, not euthanasia.[1]

In this paragraph the authors accept the value of pain management for dying patients. They go even further and offer a solution to the problem of suffering among the terminally ill—better pain management by doctors. They remain thoughtful in their approach and tone throughout, while sticking to their position that legalizing euthanasia is not the solution.

Consider how you can use the conciliatory approach to write more effective arguments. It will help you avoid "overheated" language and maintain your focus on what is doable in a world of differing points of view. There is the expression that "you can catch more flies with honey than with vinegar." Using "honey" instead of "vinegar" might also make you feel better about yourself.

Figure 4.3 presents the questions you should ask about your purpose.

Why am I writing this? What is the genre? What is the goal? Is this a Rogerian approach?

MOVE FROM TOPIC TO CLAIM TO POSSIBLE SUPPORT

When you write a letter to the editor of a newspaper, you have chosen to respond to someone else's argument that has bothered you. In this writing context, you already know your topic and, probably, your claim as well. You also know that your purpose will be to refute the article you have read. In composition classes, the context is not always so clearly established, but you will usually be given some guidelines with which to get started.

Selecting a Topic

Suppose that you are asked to write an argument that is in some way connected to First Amendment rights. Your instructor has limited and focused your topic choice and purpose. Start thinking about possible topics that relate to freedom of speech and censorship issues. To aid your topic search and selection, use one or more invention strategies:

- Brainstorm (make a list).
- Freewrite (write without stopping for ten minutes).
- Map or cluster (connect ideas to the general topic in various spokes, a kind of visual brainstorming). See Chapter 12 for an example of an idea map.
- Read through this text for ideas.

Your invention strategies lead, let us suppose, to the following list of possible topics:

Administrative restrictions on the college newspaper
Hate speech restrictions or codes
Deleting certain books from high school reading lists
Controls and limits on alcohol and cigarette advertising
Restrictions on violent TV programming
Dress codes/uniforms

Looking over your list, you realize that the last item, dress codes/uniforms, may be about freedom but not freedom of speech, so you drop it from consideration. All of the other topics have promise. Which one do you select? Two considerations should guide you: interest and knowledge. First, your argument is likely to be more thoughtful and lively if you choose an issue that matters to you. But unless you have time for study, you are wise to choose a topic about which you already have some information and ideas. Suppose that you decide to write about television violence because you are concerned about violence in American society and have given this issue some thought. It is time to phrase your topic as a tentative thesis or claim.

Drafting a Claim

Good claim statements will keep you focused in your writing–in addition to establishing your main idea for readers. Give thought both to your position on the issue and to the wording of your claim. *Claim statements to avoid:*

- Claims using vague words such as *good* or *bad.*

VAGUE: TV violence is bad for us.
BETTER: We need more restrictions on violent TV programming.

- Claims in loosely worded "two-part" sentences.

UNFOCUSED: Campus sexual assault is a serious problem, and we need to do something about it.
BETTER: College administrators and students need to work together to reduce both the number of campus sexual assaults and the fear of sexual assault.

- Claims that are not appropriately qualified.

OVERSTATED: Violence on television is making us a violent society.

BETTER: TV violence is contributing to viewers' increased fear of violence and insensitivity to violence.

- Claims that do not help you focus on your purpose in writing.

UNCLEAR: PURPOSE Not everyone agrees on what is meant by violent TV programming.

(Perhaps this is true, but more important, this claim suggests that you will define violent programming. Such an approach would not keep you focused on a First Amendment issue.)

BETTER: Restrictions on violent TV programs can be justified.

(Now your claim directs you to the debate over restrictions of content.)

Listing Possible Grounds

As you learned in Chapter 3, you can generate grounds to support a claim by adding a "because" clause after a claim statement. We can start a list of grounds for the topic on violent TV programming in this way:

We need more restrictions on violent television programming *because*

- Many people, including children and teens, watch many hours of TV (get stats).
- People are affected by the dominant activities/experiences in their lives.
- There is a connection between violent programming and desensitizing and fear of violence and possibly more aggressive behavior in heavy viewers (get detail of studies).
- Society needs to protect young people.

You have four good points to work on, a combination of reasons and inferences drawn from evidence.

Listing Grounds for the Other Side or Another Perspective

Remember that arguments generate counterarguments. Continue your exploration of this topic by considering possible rebuttals to your proposed grounds. How might someone who does not want to see restrictions placed on television programming respond to each of your points? Let's think about them one at a time:

We need more restrictions on violent television programming because

1. *Many people, including children and teens, watch many hours of TV.*

Your opposition cannot really challenge your first point on the facts, only its relevance to restricting programming. The opposition might argue that if parents think their children are watching too much TV, they should turn it off. The restriction needs to be a family decision.

2. *People are affected by the dominant activities/experiences in their lives.*

It seems common sense to expect people to be influenced by dominant forces in their lives. Your opposition might argue, though, that many people have the TV on for many hours but often are not watching it intently for all of that time. The more dominant forces in our lives are parents and teachers and peers, not the TV. The opposition might also argue that people seem to be influenced to such different degrees by television that it is not fair or logical to restrict everyone when perhaps only a few are truly influenced by their TV viewing to a harmful degree.

3. *There is a connection between violent programming and desensitizing and fear of violence and possibly more aggressive behavior in heavy viewers.*

Some people are entirely convinced by studies showing these negative effects of violent TV programming, but others point to the less convincing studies or make the argument that if violence on TV were really so powerful an influence, most people would be violent or fearful or desensitized.

4. *Society needs to protect young people.*

Your opposition might choose to agree with you in theory on this point–and then turn again to the argument that parents should be doing the protecting. Government controls on programming restrict adults as well as children, whereas it may only be some children who should watch fewer hours of TV and not watch adult "cop" shows at all.

Working through this process of considering opposing views can help you see

- where you may want to do some research for facts to provide backing for your grounds,
- how you can best develop your reasons to take account of typical counterarguments, and
- if you should qualify your claim in some ways.

Planning Your Approach

Now that you have thought about arguments on the other side, you decide that you want to argue for a qualified claim that is also more precise:

> To protect young viewers, we need restrictions on violence in children's programs and ratings for prime-time adult shows that clearly establish the degree of violence in those shows.

This qualified claim responds to two points of the rebuttals. Our student hasn't given in to the other side but has chosen to narrow the argument to emphasize the protection of children, an area of common ground.

Next, it's time to check some of the articles in this text or go online to get some data to develop points 1 and 3. You need to know that 99 percent of homes have at least one TV; you need to know that by the time young people graduate from high school, they have spent more time in front of the TV than in the classroom. Also, you can find the average number of violent acts by hour of TV in children's programs.

Then, too, there are the various studies of fearfulness and aggressive behavior that will give you some statistics to use to develop the third point. Be sure to select reliable sources and then cite the sources you use. *Citing sources is not only required and right; it is also part of the process of establishing your credibility and thus strengthening your argument.*

Finally, how are you going to answer the point about parents controlling their children? You might counter that in theory this is the way it should be–but in fact not all parents are at home watching what their children are watching, and not all parents care enough to pay attention. However, all of us suffer from the consequences of those children who are influenced by their TV watching to become more aggressive or fearful or desensitized. These children grow up to become the adults the rest of us have to interact with, so the problem becomes one for the society as a whole to solve. If you had not disciplined yourself to go through the process of listing possible rebuttals, you may not have thought through this part of the debate.

DRAFT YOUR ARGUMENT

Many of us can benefit from a step-by-step process of invention–such as we have been exploring in the last few pages. In addition, the more notes you have from working through the Toulmin structure, the easier it will be to get started on your draft. Students report that they can control their writing anxiety when they generate detailed notes. A page of notes that also suggests an organizational strategy can remove that awful feeling of staring at a blank computer screen. See Chapter 12 for more information on the recursive writing process.

In the following chapters on argument, you will find specific suggestions for organizing the various kinds of arguments. But you can always rely on one of these two basic organizations, regardless of the specific genre:

PLAN 1: ORGANIZING AN ARGUMENT
Attention-getting opening (why the issue is important, or current, etc.)
Claim statement
Reasons and evidence in order from least important to most important
Challenge to potential rebuttals or counterarguments
Conclusion that reemphasizes claim

PLAN 2: ORGANIZING AN ARGUMENT
Attention-getting opening
Claim statement (or possibly leave to the conclusion)
Order by arguments of opposing position, with your challenge to each
Conclusion that reemphasizes (or states for the first time) your claim

GUIDELINES for Drafting

- **Try to get a complete draft in one sitting so that you can read the whole piece.** At the very least, try to write the topic sentences of each of your paragraphs so you know the information that you will place in those sections.
- **If you can't think of a clever opening, state your claim and move on to the body of your essay.** After you draft your reasons and evidence, a good opening may occur to you.
- **If you find that you need something more in some parts of your essay, leave space there as a reminder that you will need to return to that paragraph later.**
- **Try to avoid using either a dictionary or thesaurus while drafting.** Your goal is to get the ideas down. You will polish later.
- **Learn to draft at your computer.** Revising is so much easier that you will be more willing to make significant changes if you work at your PC. If you are handwriting your draft, leave plenty of margin space for additions or for directions to shift parts around.

REVISE YOUR DRAFT

If you have drafted at the computer, begin revising by printing a copy of your draft. Most of us cannot do an adequate job of revision by looking at a computer screen. Then remind yourself that revision is a three-step process: rewriting, editing, and proofreading.

Rewriting

You are not ready to polish the writing until you are satisfied with the argument. Look first at the total piece. Do you have all the necessary parts: a claim, support, some response to possible counterarguments? Examine the order of your reasons and evidence. Do some of your points belong, logically, in a different place? Does the order make the most powerful defense of your claim? Be willing to move whole paragraphs around to test the best organization. Also reflect on the argument itself. Have you avoided logical fallacies? Have you qualified statements when appropriate? Do you have enough support? The best support?

Consider development: Is your essay long enough to meet assignment requirements? Are points fully developed to satisfy the demands of readers? One key to development is the length of your paragraphs. If most of your paragraphs are only two or three sentences, you have not developed the point of each paragraph satisfactorily. It is possible that some paragraphs need to be combined because they are really on the same topic. More typically, short paragraphs need further explanation of ideas or examples to illustrate ideas. Compare the following paragraphs for effectiveness:

First Draft of a Paragraph from an Essay on Gun Control

One popular argument used against the regulation of gun ownership is the need of citizens, especially in urban areas where the crime rate is higher, to possess a handgun for personal protection, either carried or kept in the home.

Some citizens may not be aware of the dangers to themselves or their families when they purchase a gun. Others, more aware, may embrace the myth that "bad things only happen to other people."

Revised Version of the Paragraph with Statistics Added

One popular argument used against the regulation of gun ownership is the need of citizens, especially in urban areas where the crime rate is higher, to possess a handgun for personal protection, whether it is carried or kept in the home. Although some citizens may not be aware of the dangers to themselves or their families when they purchase a gun, they should be. According to the Brady Center to Prevent Gun Violence, from their web page "Key Statistics," "access to a gun in the home increases the risk of death by suicide by 300%." The Center also reports that "every 16 hours a woman is shot dead by her current or former partner" and "every day eight children and teens are shot unintentionally by family fire."

A quick online search has provided this student with some facts to support his argument. Observe how he has referred informally but fully to the source of his information. (If your instructor requires formal MLA documentation in all essays, then you will need to add a Works Cited page and give a full reference to the website. See Chapter 14.)

Editing

Make your changes, print another copy, and begin the second phase of revision: editing. As you read through this time, pay close attention to unity and coherence, sentence patterns, and word choice. Read each paragraph as a separate unit to be certain that everything is on the same subtopic. Then look at your use of transition and connecting words, both within and between paragraphs. Ask yourself: Have you guided the reader through the argument using appropriate connectors such as *therefore, in addition, as a consequence, also,* and so forth?

Read again, focusing on each sentence, checking to see that you have varied sentence patterns and length. Read sentences aloud to let your ear help you find awkward constructions or unfinished thoughts. Strive as well for word choice that is concrete and specific, avoiding wordiness, clichés, trite expressions, or incorrect use of specialized terms. Observe how Sam edited one paragraph in her essay "Balancing Work and Family:"

Some specific words you may want to eliminate include prepositions (*to, in, for, of*) and forms of the verb "to-be" (*is, was, are, were*). Once you have eliminated those, replace the to-be verbs with active verbs and revise your sentence so that the subject is in the action spot. Here is an example:

Original

To begin the process of revision, the editing was completed on the paper.

Revision

The student began revising their paper by editing.

This revision is clearer, and it contains fewer words.

Draft Version of Paragraph

Vague reference. Wordy.

Short sentences.

Vague reference.

Women have come a long way in equalizing themselves, but inequality within marriages do exist. One reason for this can be found in the media. Just last week America turned on thier televisions to watch a grotesque dramatization of skewed priorities. On *Who Wants to Marry a Millionaire,* a panel of women vied for the affections of a millionaire who would choose one of them to be his wife. This show said that women can be purchased. Also that men must provide and that money is worth the sacrifice of one's individuality. The show also suggests that physical attraction is more important than the building of a complete relationship. Finally, the show says that women's true value lies in thier appearance. This is a dangerous message to send to both men women viewers.

Edited Version of Paragraph

Although women have come a long way toward equality in the workplace, inequality within marriages can still be found. The media may be partly to blame for this continued inequality. Just last week Americans watched a grotesque dramatization of skewed priorities. On *Who Wants to Marry a Millionaire,* a panel of women vied for the affections of a millionaire who would choose one of them to be his wife. Such displays teach us that women can be purchased, that men must be the providers, that the desire for money is worth the sacrifice of one's individuality, that physical attraction is more important than a complete relationship, and that women's true value lies in their appearance. These messages discourage marriages based on equality and mutual support.

Sam's editing has eliminated wordiness and vague references and has combined ideas into one forceful sentence. Support your good argument by taking the time to polish your writing.

A Few Words about Word Choice and Tone

You have just been advised to check your word choice to eliminate wordiness, vagueness, clichés, and so on. Here is a checklist of problems often found in student papers with some ways to fix the problems:

- *Eliminate clichés.* Do not write about "the fast-paced world we live in today" or the "rat race." First, do you know for sure that the pace of life for someone who has a demanding job is any faster than it was in the past? Using time effectively has always mattered. Also, clichés suggest that you are too lazy to find your own words.
- *Avoid jargon.* In the negative sense of this word, *jargon* refers to nonspecialists who fill their writing with "heavy-sounding terms" to give the appearance of significance.

Watch for any overuse of "scientific" terms such as *factor* or *aspect,* or other vague, awkward language.

- *Avoid language that is too informal for most of your writing contexts.* What do you mean when you write: "*Kids* today watch too much TV"? Alternatives include *children, teens, adolescents.* These words are less slangy and more precise.
- *Avoid nasty attacks on the opposition.* Change "those jerks who are foolish enough to believe that TV violence has no impact on children" to language that explains your counterargument without attacking those who may disagree with you. After all, you want to change the thinking of your audience, not make them resent you for name-calling.
- *Avoid all discriminatory language and use inclusive language instead.* In the academic community and the adult workplace, most people are bothered by language that belittles any one group. This includes language that is racist or sexist or reflects negatively on older or differently abled persons or those who do not share your sexual orientation or religious beliefs. Just don't do it!

Proofreading

You also do not want to lose the respect of readers because you submit a paper filled with "little" errors—errors in punctuation, mechanics, and incorrect word choice. Most readers will forgive one or two little errors but will become annoyed if they begin to pile up. So, after you are finished rewriting and editing, print a copy of your paper and read it slowly, looking specifically at punctuation, at the handling of quotations and references to writers and to titles, and at those pesky words that come in two or more "versions": *to, too,* and *two; here* and *hear; their, there,* and *they're;* and so forth. If instructors have found any of these kinds of errors in your papers over the years, then focus your attention on the kinds of errors you have been known to make.

Refer to Chapter 1 for handling references to authors and titles and for handling direct quotations. Use a glossary of usage for homonyms (words that sound alike but have different meanings), and check a handbook for punctuation rules. Take pride in your work and present a paper that will be treated with respect. What follows is a checklist of the key points for writing good arguments that we have just examined.

Collaborative Writing

Lastly, as you revise, edit, and proofread, consider using a collaborative writing platform like GoogleDrive or Dropbox. These tools allow you to share your work with your classmates, so that in-class workshop collaboration is easier. You might also consider continuing your workshop collaboration outside of class. With the increase of online coursework, students are using these types of tools more often. However, be sure to let your instructor know if you are workshopping your work with other students.

A CHECKLIST FOR REVISION

- ☐ Have I selected an issue and purpose consistent with assignment guidelines?
- ☐ Have I stated a claim that is focused, appropriately qualified, and precise?
- ☐ Have I developed sound reasons and evidence in support of my claim?
- ☐ Have I used Toulmin's terms to help me study the parts of my argument, including rebuttals to counterarguments?
- ☐ Have I taken advantage of a conciliatory approach and emphasized common ground with opponents?
- ☐ Have I found a clear and effective organization for presenting my argument?
- ☐ Have I edited my draft thoughtfully, concentrating on producing unified and coherent paragraphs and polished sentences?
- ☐ Have I eliminated wordiness, clichés, jargon?
- ☐ Have I selected an appropriate tone for my purpose and audience?
- ☐ Have I used my word processor's spell-check and proofread a printed copy with great care?
- ☐ Have I eliminated discriminatory language and used inclusive language instead?

FOR ANALYSIS AND DEBATE

FIVE MYTHS ABOUT TORTURE AND TRUTH

DARIUS REJALI

Courtesy of Darius Rejali

A professor of political science at Reed College, Iranian-born Darius Rejali is a recognized expert on the causes and meaning of violence, especially on torture, in our world. His books *Torture and Democracy* (2007) and *Spirituality and the Ethics of Torture* (2009) have won acclaim and resulted in frequent interviews for Rejali. The following essay appeared on December 16, 2007, in the *Washington Post*.

PREREADING QUESTIONS Can you think of five myths about torture? What do you expect Rejali to cover in this essay?

1 *So the CIA did indeed torture Abu Zubaida, the first al-Qaeda terrorist suspect to have been waterboarded. So says John Kiriakou, the first former CIA employee directly involved in the questioning of "high-value" al-Qaeda detainees to speak out publicly. He minced no words last week in calling the CIA's "enhanced interrogation techniques" what they are.*

2 *But did they work? Torture's defenders, including the wannabe tough guys who write Fox's "24," insist that the rough stuff gets results. "It was like flipping a switch," said Kiriakou about Abu Zubaida's response to being waterboarded. But the al-Qaeda operative's confessions—descriptions of fantastic plots from a man who intelligence analysts were convinced was mentally ill—probably didn't give the CIA any actionable intelligence. Of course, we may never know the whole truth, since the CIA destroyed the videotapes of Abu Zubaida's interrogation. But here are some other myths that are bound to come up as the debate over torture rages on.*

1. Torture worked for the Gestapo. Actually, no. Even Hitler's notorious 3
secret police got most of their information from public tips, informers and inter-agency cooperation. That was still more than enough to let the Gestapo decimate anti-Nazi resistance in Austria, Czechoslovakia, Poland, Denmark, Norway, France, Russia and the concentration camps.

Yes, the Gestapo did torture people for intelligence, especially in later years. 4
But this reflected not torture's efficacy but the loss of many seasoned professionals to World War II, increasingly desperate competition for intelligence among Gestapo units and an influx of less disciplined younger members. (Why do serious, tedious police work when you have a uniform and a whip?) It's surprising how unsuccessful the Gestapo's brutal efforts were. They failed to break senior leaders of the French, Danish, Polish and German resistance. I've spent more than a decade collecting all the cases of Gestapo torture "successes" in multiple languages; the number is small and the results pathetic, especially compared with the devastating effects of public cooperation and informers.

2. Everyone talks sooner or later under torture. Truth is, it's surprisingly 5
hard to get anything under torture, true or false. For example, between 1500 and 1750, French prosecutors tried to torture confessions out of 785 individuals. Torture was legal back then, and the records document such practices as the bone-crushing use of splints, pumping stomachs with water until they swelled and pouring boiling oil on the feet. But the number of prisoners who said anything was low, from 3 percent in Paris to 14 percent in Toulouse (an exceptional high). Most of the time, the torturers were unable to get any statement whatsoever.

And such examples could be multiplied. The Japanese fascists, no strangers 6
to torture, said it best in their field manual, which was found in Burma during World War II: They described torture as the clumsiest possible method of gathering intelligence. Like most sensible torturers, they preferred to use torture for intimidation, not information.

3. People will say anything under torture. Well, no, although this is a favor- 7
ite chestnut of torture's foes. Think about it: Sure, someone would lie under torture, but wouldn't they also lie if they were being interrogated without coercion?

In fact, the problem of torture does not stem from the prisoner who *has* infor- 8
mation; it stems from the prisoner who doesn't. Such a person is also likely to lie, to say anything, often convincingly. The torture of the informed may generate no more lies than normal interrogation, but the torture of the ignorant and innocent overwhelms investigators with misleading information. In these cases, nothing is indeed preferable to anything. Anything needs to be verified, and the CIA's own 1963 interrogation manual explains that "a time-consuming delay results"—hardly useful when every moment matters.

Intelligence gathering is especially vulnerable to this problem. When police 9
officers torture, they know what the crime is, and all they want is the confession. When intelligence officers torture, they must gather information about what they don't know.

4. Most people can tell when someone is lying under torture. Not so—and 10
we know quite a bit about this. For about 40 years, psychologists have been

testing police officers as well as normal people to see whether they can spot lies, and the results aren't encouraging. Ordinary folk have an accuracy rate of about 57 percent, which is pretty poor considering that 50 percent is the flip of a coin. Likewise, the cops' accuracy rates fall between 45 percent and 65 percent—that is, sometimes less accurate than a coin toss.

11 Why does this matter? Because even if torturers break a person, they have to recognize it, and most of the time they can't. Torturers assume too much and reject what doesn't fit their assumptions. For instance, Sheila Cassidy, a British physician, cracked under electric-shock torture by the Chilean secret service in the 1970s and identified priests who had helped the country's socialist opposition. But her devout interrogators couldn't believe that priests would ever help the socialists, so they tortured her for another week until they finally became convinced. By that time, she was so damaged that she couldn't remember the location of the safe house.

12 In fact, most torturers are nowhere near as well trained for interrogation as police are. Torturers are usually chosen because they've endured hardship and pain, fought with courage, kept secrets, held the right beliefs and earned a reputation as trustworthy and loyal. They often rely on folklore about what lying behavior looks like—shifty eyes, sweaty palms and so on. And, not surprisingly, they make a lot of mistakes.

13 **5. You can train people to resist torture.** Supposedly, this is why we can't know what the CIA's "enhanced interrogation techniques" are: If Washington admits that it waterboards suspected terrorists, al-Qaeda will set up "waterboarding-resistance camps" across the world. Be that as it may, the truth is that no training will help the bad guys.

14 Simply put, nothing predicts the outcome of one's resistance to pain better than one's own personality. Against some personalities, nothing works; against others, practically anything does. Studies of hundreds of detainees who broke under Soviet and Chinese torture, including Army-funded studies of U.S. prisoners of war, conclude that during, before and after torture, each prisoner displayed strengths and weaknesses dependent on his or her own character. The CIA's own "Human Resources Exploitation Manual" from 1983 and its so-called Kubark manual from 1963 agree. In all matters relating to pain, says Kubark, the "individual remains the determinant."

15 The thing that's most clear from torture-victim studies is that you can't train for the ordeal. There is no secret knowledge out there about how to resist torture. Yes, there are manuals, such as the IRA's "Green Book," the anti-Soviet "Manual for Psychiatry for Dissidents" and "Torture and the Interrogation Experience," an Iranian guerrilla manual from the 1970s. But none of these volumes contains specific techniques of resistance, just general encouragement to hang tough. Even al-Qaeda's vaunted terrorist-training manual offers no tips on how to resist torture, and al-Qaeda was no stranger to the brutal methods of the Saudi police.

16 And yet these myths persist. "The larger problem here, I think," one active CIA officer observed in 2005, "is that this kind of stuff just makes people feel better, even if it doesn't work."

Rejali, Darius. "Five Myths About Torture and Truth." *Washington Post*, 17 Dec. 2007. Reprinted by permission of the author.

QUESTIONS FOR READING

1. What context for his discussion does the author provide in the opening two paragraphs?
2. What worked better than torture for the Gestapo? What led to an increase in torture in the Gestapo?
3. What do the data show about getting people to speak by torturing them?
4. Who are the people most likely to lie under torture?
5. Why are interrogators not very good at recognizing when the tortured are lying?

QUESTIONS FOR REASONING AND ANALYSIS

6. What structure does the author use? What kind of argument is this?
7. What is Rejali's position on torture, the claim of his argument?
8. What grounds does he present in support of his claim?
9. Describe Rejali's style; how does his style of writing help his argument?

QUESTIONS FOR REFLECTION AND WRITING

10. Which of the five discussions has surprised you the most? Why?
11. Has the author convinced you that all five myths lack substance? Why or why not? If you disagree, how would you refute Rejali?
12. Why do intelligence and military personnel continue to use harsh interrogation strategies even though the evidence suggests that what, if anything, they learn will not be useful? Ponder this question.

HOW THE FUTURE WILL JUDGE US

KWAME ANTHONY APPIAH

Courtesy of Kwame Anthony Appiah

The son of a Ghanian lawyer and politician and British novelist, Appiah was educated in both Ghana and England. He holds a PhD in philosophy from Cambridge University, and, since 2002, he has held appointments in both the philosophy department at Princeton University and is now at New York University. Appiah is the author of many books, including *The Ethics of Identity* (2003) and *The Honor Code: How Moral Revolutions Happen* (2010). He is recognized as one of the world's most significant contemporary thinkers.

PREREADING QUESTIONS Given Appiah's areas of study and interest, what kinds of current problems do you think he will select for future judgment? What have we repudiated from our country's past?

1 Once, pretty much everywhere, beating your wife and children was regarded as a father's duty, homosexuality was a hanging offense, and water-boarding was approved—in fact, invented—by the Catholic Church. Through the middle of the 19th century, the United States and other nations in the Americas condoned plantation slavery. Many of our grandparents were born in states where women were forbidden to vote. And well into the 20th century, lynch mobs in this country stripped, tortured, hanged and burned human beings at picnics.

2 Looking back at such horrors, it is easy to ask: What were people thinking?

3 Yet, the chances are that our own descendants will ask the same question, with the same incomprehension, about some of our practices today.

4 Is there a way to guess which ones? After all, not every disputed institution or practice is destined to be discredited. And it can be hard to distinguish in real time between movements, such as abolition, that will come to represent moral common sense and those, such as prohibition, that will come to seem quaint or misguided. Recall the book-burners of Boston's old Watch and Ward Society or the organizations for the suppression of vice, with their crusades against claret, contraceptives and sexually candid novels.

5 Still, a look at the past suggests three signs that a particular practice is destined for future condemnation.

6 First, people have already heard the arguments against the practice. The case against slavery didn't emerge in a blinding moment of moral clarity, for instance; it had been around for centuries.

7 Second, defenders of the custom tend not to offer moral counterarguments but instead invoke tradition, human nature or necessity. (As in, "We've always had slaves, and how could we grow cotton without them?")

8 And third, supporters engage in what one might call strategic ignorance, avoiding truths that might force them to face the evils in which they're complicit. Those who ate the sugar or wore the cotton that the slaves grew simply didn't think about what made those goods possible. That's why abolitionists sought to direct attention toward the conditions of the Middle Passage, through detailed illustrations of slave ships and horrifying stories of the suffering below decks.

9 With these signs in mind, here are four contenders for future moral condemnation.

OUR PRISON SYSTEM

10 We already know that the massive waste of life in our prisons is morally troubling; those who defend the conditions of incarceration usually do so in non-moral terms (citing costs or the administrative difficulty of reforms); and we're inclined to avert our eyes from the details. Check, check and check.

11 Roughly 1 percent of adults in this country are incarcerated. We have 4 percent of the world's population but 25 percent of its prisoners. No other

nation has as large a proportion of its population in prison; even China's rate is less than half of ours. What's more, the majority of our prisoners are nonviolent offenders, many of them detained on drug charges. (Whether a country that was truly free would criminalize recreational drug use is a related question worth pondering.)

And the full extent of the punishment prisoners face isn't detailed in any judge's sentence. More than 100,000 inmates suffer sexual abuse, including rape, each year; some contract HIV as a result. Our country holds at least 25,000 prisoners in isolation in so-called supermax facilities, under conditions that many psychologists say amount to torture. 12

INDUSTRIAL MEAT PRODUCTION

The arguments against the cruelty of factory farming have certainly been around a long time; it was Jeremy Bentham, in the 18th century, who observed that, when it comes to the treatment of animals, the key question is not whether animals can reason but whether they can suffer. People who eat factory-farmed bacon or chicken rarely offer a moral justification for what they're doing. Instead, they try not to think about it too much, shying away from stomach-turning stories about what goes on in our industrial abattoirs. 13

Of the more than 90 million cattle in our country, at least 10 million at any time are packed into feedlots, saved from the inevitable diseases of overcrowding only by regular doses of antibiotics, surrounded by piles of their own feces, their nostrils filled with the smell of their own urine. Picture it—and then imagine your grandchildren seeing that picture. In the European Union, many of the most inhumane conditions we allow are already illegal or—like the sow stalls into which pregnant pigs are often crammed in the United States—will be illegal soon. 14

THE INSTITUTIONALIZED AND ISOLATED ELDERLY

Nearly 2 million of America's elderly are warehoused in nursing homes, out of sight and, to some extent, out of mind. Some 10,000 for-profit facilities have arisen across the country in recent decades to hold them. Other elderly Americans may live independently, but often they are isolated and cut off from their families. (The United States is not alone among advanced democracies in this. Consider the heat wave that hit France in 2003: While many families were enjoying their summer vacations, some 14,000 elderly parents and grandparents were left to perish in the stifling temperatures.) Is this what Western modernity amounts to—societies that feel no filial obligations to their inconvenient elders? 15

Sometimes we can learn from societies much poorer than ours. My English mother spent the last 50 years of her life in Ghana, where I grew up. In her final years, it was her good fortune not only to have the resources to stay at 16 home, but also to live in a country where doing so was customary. She had family next door who visited her every day, and she was cared for by doctors and nurses who were willing to come to her when she was too ill to come to them. In short, she had the advantages of a society in which older people are treated with respect and concern.

17 Keeping aging parents and their children closer is a challenge, particularly in a society where almost everybody has a job outside the home (if not across the country). Yet the three signs apply here as well: When we see old people who, despite many living relatives, suffer growing isolation, we know something is wrong. We scarcely try to defend the situation; when we can, we put it out of our minds. Self-interest, if nothing else, should make us hope that our descendants will have worked out a better way.

THE ENVIRONMENT

18 Of course, most transgenerational obligations run the other way—from parents to children—and of these the most obvious candidate for opprobrium is our wasteful attitude toward the planet's natural resources and ecology. Look at a satellite picture of Russia, and you'll see a vast expanse of parched wasteland where decades earlier was a lush and verdant landscape. That's the Republic of Kalmykia, home to what was recognized in the 1990s as Europe's first man-made desert. Desertification, which is primarily the result of destructive land-management practices, threatens a third of the Earth's surface; tens of thousands of Chinese villages have been overrun by sand drifts in the past few decades.

19 It's not as though we're unaware of what we're doing to the planet: We know the harm done by deforestation, wetland destruction, pollution, overfishing, greenhouse gas emissions—the whole litany. Our descendants, who will inherit this devastated Earth, are unlikely to have the luxury of such recklessness. Chances are, they won't be able to avert their eyes, even if they want to.

20 Let's not stop there, though. We will all have our own suspicions about which practices will someday prompt people to ask, in dismay: What were they thinking?

21 Even when we don't have a good answer, we'll be better off for anticipating the question.

Appiah, Kwame Anthony. "How the Future Will Judge Us." *Washington Post,* 26 Sept. 2010. Reprinted by permission of the author.

QUESTIONS FOR READING

1. On what basis are current practices likely to be repudiated by future Americans? What three signs mark a practice for future condemnation?
2. How do the three signs suggest that our prison system is likely to be condemned?
3. What are the problems with our industrial meat production?
4. What in our work situations contributes to the isolation of the elderly? What happened to many older people in France in 2003?
5. How will the next generation have to react to the environment?

QUESTIONS FOR REASONING AND ANALYSIS

6. What is Appiah's claim? (You will need a complex statement that combines both a general idea and specific practices.)
7. How do Appiah's four practices illustrate his idea of the three warning signs?
8. What else does the author provide to defend his choice of the specific four practices?
9. Appiah is making some devastating judgments of people past and present. How would you describe his tone? How does his tone help him keep readers from feeling attacked or judged?

QUESTIONS FOR REFLECTION AND WRITING

10. Has Appiah convinced you that the future will judge the four practices he discusses? Why or why not?
11. Did any of the four practices chosen by the author surprise you? If so, which one(s)? Why?
12. If you had been asked to select four current practices for condemnation, would you have included any of Appiah's? Why or why not? What other(s) would have been on your list? Why?

This op-ed was written by Hayley Knapik (she/her/they/them), a first-year undergraduate student at Saint Louis University where they are majoring in Psychology and pursuing a Bachelor of Science. This paper contains many of the rhetorical strategies discussed in this chapter. Can you identify some of them?

STUDENT ESSAY: OP ED

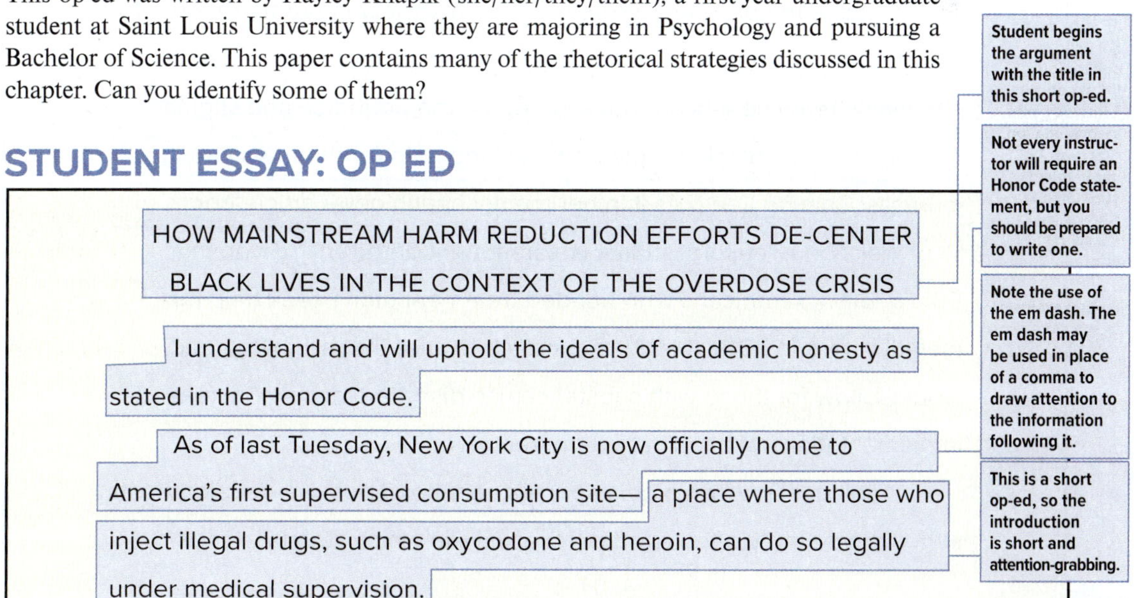
HOW MAINSTREAM HARM REDUCTION EFFORTS DE-CENTER BLACK LIVES IN THE CONTEXT OF THE OVERDOSE CRISIS

I understand and will uphold the ideals of academic honesty as stated in the Honor Code.

As of last Tuesday, New York City is now officially home to America's first supervised consumption site—a place where those who inject illegal drugs, such as oxycodone and heroin, can do so legally under medical supervision.

Op-eds generally follow AP (Associated Press) style, so contractions are permissible.

Colons are usually used to introduce a list. However, they may also be used to introduce an independent clause that is closely related to the subject of the independent clause preceding it.

For those who aren't familiar with the concept of harm reduction (or who still cling to the outdated moral model of addiction), this may come as a shock. It certainly did before the movement gained traction at the height of the HIV/AIDS epidemic, when the use of shared, unsterilized needles among people who injected drugs was one of the most prevalent and underrepresented causes for the spread of the virus. Now, finally, we're seeing a paradigm shift in our social perspective of drug use: this perspective prioritizes saving the lives of people who use drugs over allowing them to die as punishment for their failure to stop using.

Because this is a short op-ed, the student quickly arrives at the opinions presented in the article.

Student provides examples and uses sound reasoning to support the op-ed's claims.

One might glance at the astronomical increase in overdose deaths among Black Americans in recent years and take no issue with commemorating this achievement. However, what the media often fails to address is that, historically, institutionalized healthcare resources have been disproportionately accessible to members of different racial groups, with Black communities receiving the least of the benefits despite needing them the most. The media underrepresents the disparity in access to harm reduction resources between racial groups by prioritizing its development over its accessibility.

AP style does not italicize publication titles, nor does it include parenthetical citation. However, AP does require attribution of sources, which the student provides.

Further examples to support claims.

Despite the progress we've made as a society in our treatment of people with substance use disorders, the transition of harm reduction into mainstream healthcare doesn't negate the prejudice and stigma that often deters Black people from seeking help for them. As health journalist Shanon Lee puts it in her mental health news article from Very Well Mind, "cultural stigma is a treatment deterrent." Given that 50% of Black Americans who needed treatment didn't seek help for mental illness in 2018, it isn't a far stretch to infer that a similar trend would follow for those with substance use disorders despite increased implementations of harm reduction treatment.

Additionally, when media sources commend positive developments in healthcare, they often overlook the ways in which structural racism limits marginalized groups from taking advantage of them in terms of practical and financial deficits. Historically, drugs such as buprenorphine have been used by a greater percentage of white people since their inception, according to the National Institute on Drug Abuse. This is primarily due to the financial inaccessibility of such treatments, given that they are paid for out of pocket or through private insurance. Because insurance is determined by one's employer, the latter option is less accessible to people of color, given that they receive both fewer job opportunities and harsher collateral consequences for drug-related arrests.

Reporting progress in the field of addiction resources without acknowledging how marginalized groups have historically been denied access to similar resources is another way in which an inherently racist social institution—the media—centers white lives over Black lives. By commemorating the introduction of publicly funded and accessible addiction clinics without acknowledging the disproportionate influence that stigma will inevitably have on the attendance of Black and Brown people, the media is centering strategies that will better serve white people as a solution to an issue that is now disproportionately affecting Black populations at an increased rate.

The op-ed concludes by restating main argument.

Courtesy of Hayley Knapik

SUGGESTIONS FOR DISCUSSION AND WRITING

1. Read Rejali and Appiah again and then write an analysis of their differences in style and tone.
2. Appiah lists the prison system, industrial meat production, treatment of the elderly, and the environment as the areas people of the future will most harshly judge. Can you think of any more? Write a one-page essay on them and why they should be added to Appiah's list.
3. Reflect on what you have learned about torture from Rejali and then consider: What may be the greatest "unknown" part of the equation in the use of interrogation as a strategy for finding people who have broken the law? Or, put another way, what do you see as the biggest problem to ensuring success from questioning people under pressure to get intelligence from them?
4. The debate over the use of enhanced interrogation techniques and of hidden sites continues. Bloche mentions several studies in his discussion. Go online and see what more you can learn about this debate. Ponder this question: Why do some continue these strategies when studies fail to confirm that they work?
5. Should the debate over enhanced interrogation procedures be about effectiveness or ethics? And if it should be about effectiveness, then how much evidence is needed to defend torture on the grounds that it works? Ponder these questions.

CREDIT

1. Peter A. Singer and Mark Siegler. "Euthanasia–A Critique." *New England Journal of Medicine,* 28 June 1990, vol. 322, pp. 1881–1888.

CHAPTER 5

Reading, Analyzing, and Using Visuals and Statistics in Argument

LEARNING OUTCOMES

After reading Chapter 5, you will be able to:

- Describe how to respond to visual arguments.
- Illustrate how to read graphics.
- Explain how to determine the uses of authority and statistics.
- Describe how to write an investigative argument.

George Tames/The New York Times/Redux

READ: This is a photo of President John F. Kennedy; where was it taken?

REASON: What is your initial reaction to the photo? How does it make you feel? What does it make you think about?

WRITE: There are many images of President Kennedy; why would we select this one for your consideration? What comment does it make that extends beyond one particular president?

We live in a visual age. Many of us go to movies to appreciate and judge the film's visual effects. The web is awash in pictures, colorful icons, animated GIFs, and videos. Perhaps the best print symbol of our visual age in print is *USA Today,* a paper filled with color photos and many tables and other graphics as a primary way of presenting information. *USA Today* has forced the more traditional papers to add color to compete. We also live in a numerical age. We refer to the events of September 11, 2001, as 9/11—without any disrespect. This chapter brings together these markers of our times as they are used in argument—and as argument. Finding statistics and visuals used as part of argument, we also need to remember that cartoons and advertisements are arguments in and of themselves.

RESPONDING TO VISUAL ARGUMENTS

Many arguments bombard us today in visual forms. These include photos, political cartoons, and advertising. Most major newspapers include work from political cartoonists whose drawings appear regularly on the editorial page. Some comic strips are also political in nature, at least some of the time. These cartoons are designed to make a political point in a visually clever and amusing way. (That is why they are both "cartoons" and "political" at the same time.) Their uses of irony and caricatures of known politicians make them among the most emotionally powerful, indeed stinging, of arguments.

Photographs accompany many newspaper and magazine articles, and they often tell a story. Indeed, some photographers are famous for their ability to capture a personality or a newsworthy moment. So accustomed to these visuals today, we sometimes forget to study photographs. Be sure to examine each photo, remembering that authors and editors have selected each one for a reason.

Lastly, images, memes, and videos on social media like Facebook, Twitter, Instagram, and TikTok flood our senses with visual and even auditory messages. These mediums of communication are incredibly powerful, so we must use our critical thinking to analyze and discern their messages. Thinking critically about these messages is especially important given the large amount of mis/disinformation clogging these platforms.

Advertisements are among the most creative and powerful forms of argument today. Remember that ads are designed to take your time (for shopping) and your money. Their messages need to be powerful to motivate you to action. With some products (what most of us consider necessities), ads are designed to influence product choice, to get us to buy brand A instead of brand B. With other products, ones we really do not need or that may actually be harmful to us, ads need to be especially clever. Some ads do provide information (car X gets better gas mileage than car Y). Other ads (perfume ads, for example) take us into a fantasy land so that we will spend $50 on a small but pretty bottle. Another type of ad is the "image advertisement," an ad that assures us that a particular company is top-notch. If we admire the company, we will buy its goods or services. Understanding a few basic design principles, outlined below, will help you read, analyze, and even create these types of visual arguments.

Visual Rhetoric and Visual Literacy

Because visual argument, also known as visual rhetoric, is such a common and powerful form of communication, you will be expected to read, analyze, and even create communication that mixes text with images—this is known as visual literacy. More than merely making something "pretty," visual literacy is based in cognitive psychology, as well as cultural and rhetorical theory. The basic concepts below—Gestalt principles, reading patterns, focal points, and colors—provide an introduction to visual rhetoric and visual literacy.

Gestalt Principles and the C.A.R.P. Design Model

The Gestalt principles of design evolved from Gestalt theory, a psychological approach to analyzing human perceptions and human behavior first theorized by the Berlin School of Experimental Psychology. When applied to visuals, Gestalt principles hold that certain designs and graphic forms have a greater impact on people when used in specific combinations with one another. For example, the first element of the C.A.R.P. model, contrast, refers to the visual and cognitive impact something like black text can have when placed on a white background. When the contrast decreases, for example if gray text is used on a white background, the visual and cognitive impact decreases: Decrease contrast and you decrease impact. Take a look at the design of this book; notice that the text, text boxes, and images contrast with their backgrounds to ensure impact and readability. The elements of the C.A.R.P. model are explained below:

The C.A.R.P. Design Model

- **Contrast:** Design elements, such as text, have more impact and are more readable when placed over backgrounds that are a different color or shade. For example, the guidelines boxes below create contrast with the text within them but also with the white page behind them.
- **Alignment:** Design elements are carefully placed in some way to create a notable pattern and establish a connection with one another. Note the guidelines boxes again: Even though the boxes are separate, the red line on the left continues in each box, creating alignment between them.
- **Repetition:** Design elements, such as logos, icons, or colors, help readers understand that they are still within the larger piece of work. For example, the pages of the MLA section of *Read, Reason, Write* are edged in blue to help you find them within the text and to help you understand that you are still in the MLA section.
- **Proximity:** Design elements are placed near one another if they share similar concepts or ideas. For example, navigation links on a website are not randomly placed around a page. Rather, navigation links are placed near one another, usually in navigation bars at the top or on the edges of a webpage. Because navigation links share the similar purpose of helping users move around the website, they are placed in proximity to one another.

Reading Patterns

In cultures that read from left to right, readers looking at a print document usually begin in the top left corner, move right and then down the page in a Z pattern. Similarly, online readers usually move down a webpage in an F pattern, which is influenced by the location of navigation bars and headings. Of course, reading patterns also depend on the location of design elements, such as focal points and colors, so remember that the design of the work will have an impact on the reading pattern of the audience.

Focal Points

Focal points are design elements that immediately catch readers' attention and draw their eyes to them. For example, human faces or the faces of animals, especially cute ones like puppies and kittens, are strong focal points. Circles and spheres, whether complete or just partially visible, are also strong focal points. But a document's focal point does not have to be a face or a sphere; white space may also form a focal point, especially if it is placed near a dense collection of text.

Colors

Colors are some of the most powerful design features used in visual rhetoric. They can form focal points (see the text in red below), influence reading patterns, and serve as essential elements of the C.A.R.P. design principles. But colors are also culturally dependent; that is, the meaning of colors sometimes depends on the cultural context. For example, in Western cultures, red means **ALARM,** but in some Asian cultures, red means good luck and good fortune. In Western cultures, white means purity, but in some Asian cultures, it means death. So, why do you think wedding dresses in China are red, while wedding dresses in America are white? Because in China, it is customary to wish the couple good luck in their marriage. Americans have inherited traditional expectations of purity on wedding days. Note that when creating images using colors, you also need to remember that some segment of your audience, especially males, may have some sort of color vision deficiency. The most common color vision deficiency is red-green color blindness.

New Line Cinema

Memes

Memes are images, GIFs, or short videos posted online that mimic, parody, or alter an original idea, resulting in a clever or humorous visual. Memes usually present information through images and text, though this is not always the case. Two aspects of memes set them apart from other types of images. First, memes rarely remain unaltered in some way by online users. Second, memes' success can be measured by their journey through

New Line Cinema

virtual platforms (blogs, websites), social media (Facebook, Twitter, Instagram, TikTok), and by the variations they inspire.

For example, the meme depicting the character Boromir (Sean Bean) from the movie *The Fellowship of the Ring* based on the book by J. R. R. Tokien first showed Boromir saying, "One does not simply walk into Mordor."

But soon, people were replacing the original line from the movie with all sorts of humorous variations. One example is "One does not simply eat one tic tac."

The meme was so successful that it spread through multiple virtual platforms and spawned hundreds of variations. The meme even left the virtual world when entrepreneurial designers included variations on infant onesies and T-shirts.

Due to their humor and visual design, memes can be very influential, which is why it's so important to use critical thinking to analyze them. Sometimes memes are simply funny. Other times, memes can carry subtle political messages you may not be aware of. By "liking," retweeting, or sharing harmful memes, you might inadvertently imply that you agree with a political message you do not support.

New Line Cinema

Also, since authorship can be difficult to determine, you have no way of checking the credibility of the person who designed the meme. In fact, the meme may not have a human designer at all. The latest in meme design uses artificial intelligence algorithms to create memes! These AI-generated memes may make sense, or they may make no sense at all, though the results are often clever and funny.

Below are general guidelines for reading visuals and guidelines for reading arguments presented in photographs, political cartoons, and advertisements. You can practice these steps with the exercises that follow.

GUIDELINES for Reading Visuals

- **What is the context and purpose of the visual and who is the audience?**
- **Does the visual follow the C.A.R.P. model?** If not, why not?
- **How is the visual designed?** Does the visual follow the Z reading pattern or the F reading pattern?
- **What is the focal point?**
- **Are colors used, or is the image grayscale or black and white?**
- **What is the rhetorical situation?**
- **What is the intended message?**
- **What are the connotative and denotative meanings in the visual?**
- **Has the designer used any tropes (irony, sarcasm, understatement, metaphor, etc.)?**
- **What topics, genres, or political, or cultural ideas has the designer integrated into the visual?**

GUIDELINES for Reading Photographs

- **Is a scene or situation depicted?** If so, study the details to identify the situation.
- **Identify each figure in the photo.**
- **What details of scene or person(s) carry significance?**
- **How does the photograph make you feel?**

GUIDELINES for Reading Political Cartoons

- **What scene is depicted?** Identify the situation.
- **Identify each of the figures in the cartoon.** Are they current politicians, figures from history or literature, the "person in the street," or symbolic representations?
- **Who speaks the lines in the cartoon?**
- **What is the cartoon's general subject?** What is the point of the cartoon, the claim of the cartoonist?

GUIDELINES for Reading Advertisements

- **What product or service is being advertised?**
- **Who seems to be the targeted audience?**
- **What is the ad's primary strategy?** To provide information? To reinforce the product's or company's image? To appeal to particular needs or desires? For example, if an ad shows a group of young people having fun and drinking a particular beer, to what needs/desires is the ad appealing?
- **Does the ad use specific rhetorical strategies such as humor, understatement, or irony?**
- **What is the relation between the visual part of the ad (photo, drawing, typeface, etc.) and the print part (the text, or copy)?** Does the ad use a slogan or catchy phrase? Is there a company logo? Is the slogan or logo clever? Is it well known as a marker of the company? What may be the effect of these strategies on readers?
- **What is the ad's overall visual impression?** Consider both images and colors used.

EXERCISES: Analyzing Photos, Cartoons, and Ads

1. Analyze the photo on p. 117, using the guidelines previously listed.
2. Review the photos that open Chapters 1, 4, 5, 8, 19, and 21. Select the one you find most effective. Analyze it in detail to show why you think it is the best.
3. Identify a cartoon in a recently published newspaper or magazine (print or online). Analyze the cartoon, explaining why it is effective, or how it could be improved.
4. Analyze the ads on pp. 123–125, again using the guidelines listed above. After answering the guideline questions, consider these as well: Will each ad appeal effectively to its intended audience? If so, why? If not, why not?

U.S. Food and Drug Administration

Education for All? We're All In.

Every student deserves the chance to succeed. In college and beyond.

We offer a range of affordable, engaging learning solutions wrapped in dedicated support services to aid effective teaching and learning. Faculty and students enjoy the freedom to choose, based on their needs and course goals.

mheducation.com

McGraw Hill; Graduation Photo: PeopleImages/Getty Images

Positive Futures Network; Photo: Jasmin Merdan/Getty Images

READING GRAPHICS

Graphics—photographs, diagrams, tables, charts, and graphs—present a good bit of information in a condensed but also visually engaging format. Graphics are everywhere: in newspapers, the web, and social media. It's a rare training session or board meeting that is conducted without the use of graphics to display information. So, you want to be able to read graphics and create them, when appropriate, in your own writing. First, study the chart on page 126 that illustrates the different uses of various visuals. General guidelines for reading graphics follow. The guidelines will use Figure 5.1 to illustrate points. Study the figure repeatedly as you read through the guidelines.

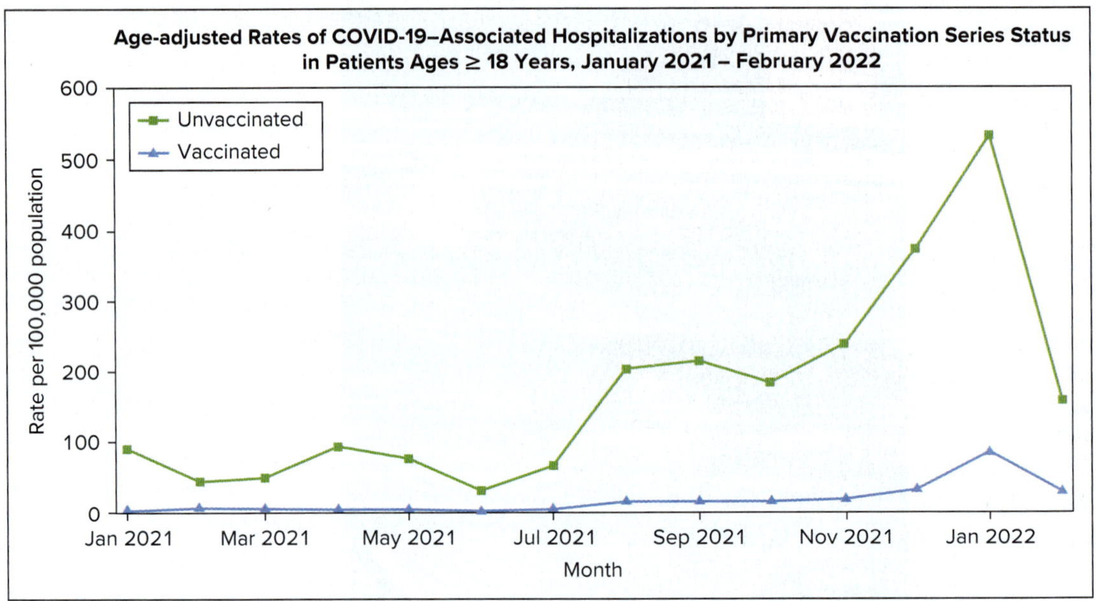

FIGURE 5.1 Age-Adjusted Rates of COVID-19–Associated Hospitalizations by Vaccine Status in Adults Ages > 18 Years, January–August 2021

Data from https://covid.cdc.gov/covid-data-tracker/#covidnet-hospitalizations-vaccination

Understanding How Graphics Differ

Each type of visual serves specific purposes (Figure 5.2). You can't use a pie chart, for example, to explain a process; you need a diagram or a flowchart. So, when reading graphics, understand what each type can show you. When preparing your own visuals, select the graphic that will most clearly and effectively present the particular information you want to display.

TYPE	PURPOSE	EXAMPLE
Diagram	show details, demonstrate process	drawing of knee tendons, photosynthesis
Table	list numerical information	income of U.S. households
Bar chart	comparative amounts of related numbers	differences in suicide rates by age and race
Pie chart	relative portions of a whole	percentages of Americans by educational level
Flowchart	steps in a process	purification of water
Graph	relationship of two items	income increases over time
Map	information relative to a geographical area	locations of world's rain forests
Infographic	show steps in a process, research findings, complex ideas, combination of graphics (diagrams, tables, charts)	NIH infographic showing how to improve your chances of remaining safe and healthy during the COVID-19 pandemic by wearing masks, washing hands, and getting vaccinated

FIGURE 5.2 Types of Graphics
Centers for Disease Control and Prevention

GUIDELINES for Reading Graphics

1. **Locate the particular graphic referred to in the text and study it at that point in your reading.** Graphics may not always be placed on the same page as the text reference. Stop your reading to find and study the graphic; that's what the writer wants you to do. Find Figure 5.1.
2. **Read the title or heading of the graphic.** Every graphic is given a title. What is the subject of the graphic? What kind of information is provided? Figure 5.1 shows age-adjusted rates of COVID-19–associated hospitalizations by vaccine status in adults ages 18 and over, January–February 2022.
3. **Read any notes, description, and the source information at the bottom of the graphic.** Figure 5.1 came from the Centers for Disease Control on March 30, 2022. Critical questions: What is this figure showing me? Is the information coming from a reliable source? Is it current enough to still be meaningful?
4. **Study the labels—and other words—that appear as part of the graphic.** You cannot draw useful conclusions unless you understand exactly what is being shown. Observe in Figure 5.1 that the line graph shows the hospitalization rates of vaccinated and unvaccinated adults ages 18 years and over from January 30, 2021, to February 2022.
5. **Study the information, making certain that you understand what the numbers represent.** Data were collected from January 30, 2021, to February 26, 2022, and are displayed in units of 10 per 100,000. So to know exactly how many unvaccinated people were hospitalized for COVID-19–associated illness, we need to know how many people were hospitalized for COVID-19–related illness in the U.S. population. The line graphic does not give us this information. It give us comparative rates per 100,000 people in both categories and tells us that almost by September, about 205 in every 100,000 people hospitalized were not vaccinated. In January 2022, when the Omicron variant of COVID-19 hit the United States, over 500 in every 100,000 people hospitalized were not vaccinated.
6. **Draw conclusions.** Think about the information in different ways. Critical questions: What does the author want to accomplish by including these figures? How are they significant? What conclusions can you draw from Figure 5.1? Answer these questions to guide your thinking:
   a. Which group of people were at most risk of being hospitalized for COVID-19–related illness? Would you have guessed this group? Why or why not? What might be some of the causes for the greater risk to this group?
   b. By June 2021, COVID-19–related hospitalizations were down. But then the Delta variant began spreading across the United States. Why do you think that the rate of COVID-19–related hospitalizations increased among the unvaccinated at this point? Do you think there is a causal relationship? Why or why not?
   c. The rate of COVID-19–related hospitalizations remained consistently low among people who were vaccinated. Why do you think this occurred? Why do you think there was a small uptick in COVID-19–related hospitalizations in January 2022 among vaccinated people?

Graphics provide information, raise questions, explain processes, engage us emotionally, make us think. Study the various graphics in the exercises that follow to become more expert in reading and responding critically to visuals.

EXERCISES: Reading and Analyzing Graphics

1. Study the pie charts in Figure 5.3 and then answer the following questions.

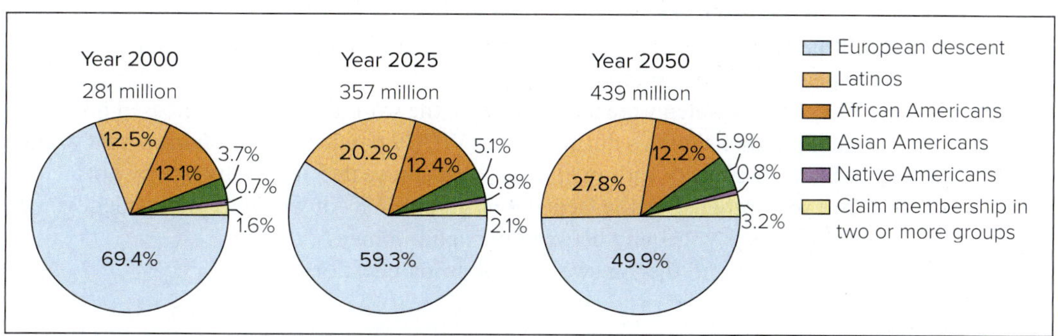

FIGURE 5.3 The Shifting of U.S. Racial-Ethnic Mix

Data from https://www.census.gov/library/stories/2021/08/improved-race-ethnicity-measures-reveal-united-states-population-much-more-multiracial.html.

   a. What is the subject of the charts?
   b. In addition to the information within the pie charts, what other information is provided?
   c. Which group increases by the greatest relative amount? How would you account for that increase?
   d. Which figure surprises you the most? Why?

2. Study the line graphs in Figure 5.4 and then answer the following questions.

FIGURE 5.4 Gender Pay Gap in the United States

The gender pay gap has remained stable in recent years but is narrower among young workers.

Data from https://www.pewresearch.org/fact-tank/2021/05/25/gender-pay-gap-facts/

a. What two subjects are treated by the graphs?
b. In 2015, what percentage of men's median income did women in both age categories earn?
c. During which five-year period did women's income in both age categories increase the most?
d. If the current trends continue, by what year should women between ages 25 and 34 earn the same amount as men?
e. Given that women were forced to leave the workforce due to increased home and family responsibilities during the COVID-19 pandemic, do you think that women will achieve parity with men in the next five years? Ten? Why or why not?
f. Are you bothered by the facts in this graph? Why or why not? What might you do to address pay inequity between men and women?

3. Study Table 5.1 and then answer the following questions.

TABLE 5.1 Earnings Summary Measures by Selected Characteristics: 2018 and 2019

CHARACTERISTIC	2018			2019			PERCENT CHANGE (2019 LESS 2018)*	
		MEDIAN EARNINGS (DOLLARS)			MEDIAN EARNINGS (DOLLARS)			
	NUMBER (THOUSANDS)	ESTIMATE	MARGIN OF ERROR[1] (±)	NUMBER (THOUSANDS)	ESTIMATE	MARGIN OF ERROR[1] (±)	ESTIMATE	MARGIN OF ERROR[1] (±)
PEOPLE WITH EARNINGS								
All Workers	**167,555**	**40,976**	**206**	**169,802**	**41,537**	**188**	***1.4**	**0.63**
Men	88,115	47,588	414	89,023	48,769	822	*2.5	1.79
Women	79,440	33,246	703	80,779	35,826	266	*7.8	2.32
Full-Time, Year-Round Workers	**118,000**	**51,570**	**206**	**119,158**	**52,000**	**212**	***0.8**	**0.49**
Men	67,205	56,293	483	67,123	57,456	865	*2.1	1.59
Women	50,795	45,914	495	52,035	47,299	367	*3.0	1.26
Female-to-male earnings ratio	X	0.816	0.0100	X	0.823	0.0126	0.9	1.79

(Earnings in 2019 dollars, adjusted using the CPI-U-RS. People 15 years and older as of March of the following year with earnings. For information on confidentiality protection, sampling error, nonsampling error, and definitions, see <https://www2.census.gov/programs-surveys/cps/techdocs/cpsmar20.pdf>)

*An asterisk preceding an estimate indicates change is statistically different from zero at the 90 percent confidence level.

X Not applicable.

[1] A margin of error (MOE) is a measure of an estimate's variability. The larger the MOE in relation to the size of the estimate, the less reliable the estimate. This number, when added to and subtracted from the estimate, forms the 90 percent confidence interval. MOEs shown in this table are based on standard errors calculated using replicate weights. For more information, see "Standard Errors and Their Use" at <https://www2.census.gov/library/publications/2020/demo/p60-270sa.pdf>.

Note: Inflation-adjusted estimates may differ slightly from other published data due to rounding.

Source: U.S. Census Bureau, Current Population Survey, 2019 and 2020 Annual Social and Economic Supplements (CPS ASEC).

Source: https://nces.ed.gov/programs/raceindicators/indicator_ree.asp#info

a. What is being presented and compared in this table?
b. What, exactly, do the numerals in the Full-time, Year-Round Workers, Men line represent? What, exactly, do the numerals in the Full-Time, Year-Round Workers, Women line represent? (Be sure that you understand what these numbers mean.)
c. Based on the information provided in the Full-Time, Year-Round Workers, Female-to-male earnings ratio line, about how many more years should it take for women to achieve parity with men's pay?
d. Which figure surprises you the most? Why?

4. Maps can be used to show all kinds of information, not just the locations of cities, rivers, or mountains. Study the map in Figure 5.5, and then answer the questions that follow.

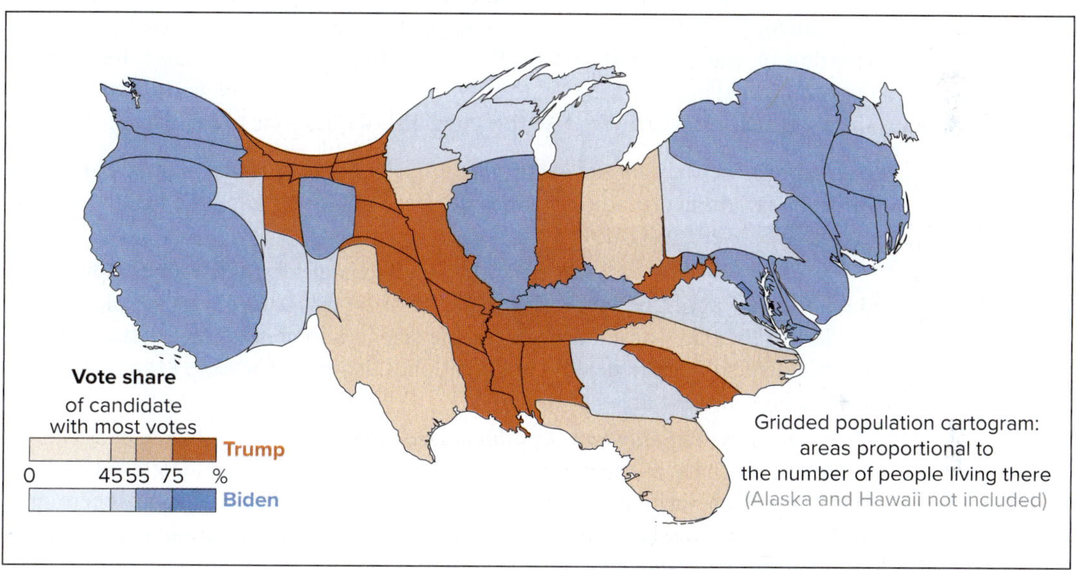

FIGURE 5.5 2020 Election Results A gridded population cartogram showing areas proportional to the number of people living there (Alaska and Hawaii not included).

a. What, exactly, does the map show? Why does the map look strange?
b. Which states have the largest population, and how does the presentation of the voting data in this map encourage a different perspective on the electoral college?
c. Do some research on the electoral college. How are electoral votes distributed by state, and how was this distribution developed?
d. What do you think about using the electoral college to select presidents of the United States? If you are not sure, do some more research and then see if you can answer the question.

THE USES OF AUTHORITY AND STATISTICS

Most of the visuals you have just studied provide a way of presenting statistics—data that many today consider essential to defending a claim. One reason you check the source information accompanying graphics is that you need to know—and evaluate—the authority of that source. When a graphic's numbers have come from the Census Bureau, you know you have a reliable source. When an author writes that "studies have shown . . . ," you should be suspicious of the authority of the data. All elements of the arguments we read—and write—affect a writer's credibility.

Judging Authorities

We know that movie stars and sports figures are not authorities on soft drinks and watches. But what about *real* authorities? When writers present the opinions or research findings of authorities as support for a claim, they are saying to readers that the authority is trustworthy and the opinions valuable. But what they are asserting is actually an assumption or warrant, part of the glue connecting evidence to claim. Remember: Warrants can be challenged. If the "authority" can be shown to lack authority, then the logic of the argument is destroyed. Use this checklist of questions to evaluate authorities:

- ☐ *Is the authority actually an authority on the topic under discussion?* A medical doctor who specializes in neuroradiology does not have authority in public health or infectious diseases like COVID-19.
- ☐ *Is the work of the authority still current?* Times change; expertise does not always endure. Galileo would be lost in the universe of today's astrophysicists. Be particularly alert to the dates of information in the sciences in general, in genetics and the entire biomedical field, in health and nutrition. It is very difficult to keep up with the latest findings in these areas of research.
- ☐ *Does the authority actually have legitimate credentials?* Are the person's publications in respected journals? Is the person respected by others in the same field? Have their publications been verified by newer research, or have their conclusions been questioned or even dismissed by the latest scholarship? *Just because it's in print or online does not mean it's a reliable source!*
- ☐ *Do experts in the field generally agree on the issue?* If there is widespread disagreement, then referring to one authority does not do much to support a claim. This is why you need to understand the many sides of a controversial topic before you write on it, and you need to bring knowledge of controversies and critical thinking skills to your reading of argument. This is also why writers often provide a source's credentials, not just a name, unless the authority is quite famous.
- ☐ *Are the author's research methods sound and appropriately applied to answer the research question?* If an author claims that "Americans support the freedom to choose whether to wear a mask during a deadly pandemic," but has only surveyed 100 people in the Florida Panhandle, then you should question those findings.
- ☐ *Is the authority's evidence reliable, so far as you can judge, but the interpretation of that evidence seems odd, or seems to be used to support strongly held beliefs?* Does the evidence actually connect to the claim? A respected authority's work can be stretched or manipulated in an attempt to defend a claim that the authority's work simply does not support.

EXERCISES: Judging Authorities

1. Jane Goodall has received worldwide fame for her studies of chimpanzees in Gombe and for her books on those field studies. Goodall is a vegetarian. Should she be used as an authority in support of a claim for a vegetarian diet? Why or why not? Consider:
   a. Why might Goodall have chosen to become a vegetarian?
   b. For what arguments might Goodall be used as an authority?
   c. For what arguments might she be used effectively for emotional appeal?
2. Suppose a respected zoologist prepares a five-year study of U.S. zoos, compiling a complete list of all animals at each zoo. He then updates the list for each of the five years, adding births and deaths. When he examines his data, he finds that deaths are one and one-half times the number of births. He considers this loss alarming and writes a paper arguing for the abolishing of zoos on the grounds that too many animals are dying. Because of his reputation, his article is published in a popular science magazine. How would you evaluate his authority and his study?
   a. Should you trust the data? Why or why not?
   b. Should you accept his conclusions? Why or why not?
   c. Consider: What might be possible explanations for the birth/death ratio?

Understanding and Evaluating Statistics

There are two useful clichés to keep in mind: "Statistics don't lie, but people lie with statistics" and "There are lies, damned lies, and statistics." The second cliché is perhaps a bit cynical. We don't want to be naïve in our faith in numbers, but neither do we want to become so cynical that we refuse to believe any statistical evidence. What we do need to keep in mind is that when statistics are presented in an argument, they are being used by someone interested in winning that argument.

Some writers use numbers without being aware that the numbers are incomplete or not representative. Some present only part of the relevant information. Some may not mean to distort, but they do choose to present the information in language that helps their cause. There are many ways, some more innocent than others, to distort reality with statistics. Use the following guidelines to evaluate the presentation of statistical information.

GUIDELINES for Evaluating Statistics

- **Is the information current and therefore still relevant?** Crime rates in your city based on 2015 census data probably are no longer relevant, certainly not current enough to support an argument for increased (or decreased) police department spending.
- **If a sample was used, was it randomly selected and large enough to be significant?** Sometimes in medical research, the results of a small study are publicized to guide researchers to important

new areas of study. When these results are reported in the press or on TV, however, the small size of the study is not always made clear. Thus one week we learn that coffee is bad for us, the next week that it is okay.

- **What information, exactly, has been provided?** When you read "Two out of three chose the Ford Focus for its dependability," you must ask yourself, "Two-thirds of how many altogether?"
- **How have the numbers been presented?** And what is the effect of that presentation? Numbers can be presented as fractions, whole numbers, or percentages. Writers who want to emphasize budget increases will use whole numbers—billions of dollars. Writers who want to de-emphasize those increases select percentages. Writers who want their readers to respond to the numbers in a specific way add words to direct their thinking: "a *mere* 3 percent increase" or "the *enormous* $5 billion increase."

WRITING THE INVESTIGATIVE ARGUMENT

The first step in writing an investigative argument is to select a topic to study. Composition students can write successful investigative essays on the media, on campus issues, and on various local concerns. Although you begin with a topic–not a claim–since you have to gather evidence before you can see what it means, you should select a topic that holds your interest and that you may have given some thought to before choosing to write. For example, you may have noticed some clever ads for jeans or beer, or perhaps you are bothered by plans for another shopping area along a major street near your home. Either one of these topics can lead to an effective investigative, or inductive, argument.

Gathering and Analyzing Evidence

Let's reflect on strategies for gathering evidence for a study of magazine ads for a particular kind of product (the topic of the sample student paper that follows).

- Select a time frame and a number of representative magazines.
- Have enough magazines to render at least twenty-five ads on the product you are studying.
- Once you decide on the magazines and issues to be used, pull *all* ads for your product. Your task is to draw useful conclusions based on adequate data objectively collected. You can't leave some ads out and have a valid study.
- Study the ads, reflecting on the inferences they allow you to draw. The inferences become the claim of your argument. You may want to take the approach of classifying the ads, that is, grouping them into categories by the various appeals used to sell the product.

More briefly, consider your hunch that your area does not need another shopping mall. What evidence can you gather to support a claim to that effect? You could locate all existing strip or enclosed malls within a ten-mile radius of the proposed new mall site, visit each one, and count the number and types of stores already available. You may discover that there are plenty of malls but that the area really needs a grocery store. No one really goes to big bookstores anymore. Only small, coffee-shop-type bookstores are surviving Amazon. So instead of reading to find evidence to support a claim, you are creating the statistics and doing the analysis to guide you to a claim. Just remember to devise objective procedures for collecting evidence so that you do not bias your results.

Planning and Drafting the Essay

You've done your research and studied the data you've collected; how do you put this kind of argument together? Here are some guidelines to help you draft your essay.

Analyzing Evidence: The Key to an Effective Argument

This is the thinking part of the process. Anyone can count stores or collect ads. What is your point? How does the evidence you have collected actually support your claim? You must guide readers through the evidence. Consider this example:

GUIDELINES for Writing an Investigative Argument

- **Begin with an opening paragraph that introduces your topic in an interesting way.** Possibilities include beginning with a startling statistic or explaining what impact the essay's facts will have on readers.
- **Devote space early in your paper to explaining your methods or procedures, probably in your second or third paragraph.** For example, if you have obtained information through questionnaires or interviews, recount the process: the questions asked, the number of people involved, the basis for selecting the people, and so on.
- **Classify the evidence that you present.** Finding a meaningful organization is part of the originality of your study and will make your argument more forceful. It is the way you see the topic and want readers to see it. If you are studying existing malls, you might begin by listing all of the malls and their locations. But then do not go store by store through each mall. Rather, group the stores by type and provide totals.
- **Consider presenting evidence in several ways, including in charts and tables as well as within paragraphs.** Readers are used to visuals, especially in essays containing statistics.
- **Analyze evidence to build your argument.** Do not ask your reader to do the thinking. No data dumps! Explain how your evidence *is* evidence by discussing the connection between facts and the inferences they support.

In a study of selling techniques used in computer ads in business magazines, a student, Brian, found four major selling techniques, one of which he classifies as "corporate emphasis." Brian begins his paragraph on corporate emphasis thus:

> In the technique of corporate emphasis, the advertiser discusses the whole range of products and services that the corporation offers, instead of specific elements. This method relies on the public's positive perception of the company, the company's accomplishments, and its reputation.

Brian then provides several examples of ads in this category, including an IBM ad:

> In one of its eight ads in the study, IBM points to the scientists on its staff who have recently won the Nobel Prize in physics.

But Brian does not stop there. He explains the point of this ad, connecting it to the assertion that this technique emphasizes the company's accomplishments:

> The inference we are to draw is that IBM scientists are hard at work right now in their laboratories developing tomorrow's technology to make the world a better place in which to live.

Preparing Graphics for Your Essay

Tables, bar charts, and pie charts are particularly helpful ways to present statistical evidence you have collected for an inductive argument. One possibility is to create a pie chart showing your classification of ads (or stores or questions on a questionnaire) and the relative amount of each item. For example, suppose you find four selling strategies. You can show in a pie chart the percentage of ads using each of the four strategies.

Computers help even the technically unsophisticated prepare simple charts. You can also do a simple table. When preparing graphics, keep these points in mind:

- Every graphic must be introduced and referred to in the text at the appropriate place–where you are discussing the information in the visual. Graphics are not disconnected attachments to an argument. They give a complete set of data in an easy-to-digest form, but some of that data must be discussed in the essay.
- Every graphic (except photographs) needs a label. Use Figure 1, Figure 2, and so forth. Then, in the text refer to each graphic by its label.
- Every graphic needs a title. Always place a title after Figure 1 (and so forth), on the same line, at the top or bottom of your visual.
- Use applications preloaded on your computer or available through your college to design your visuals. MS Excel is a good tool to use if you need to input numbers and convert them to pie charts, bar graphs, line charts, or other visuals. Adobe Illustrator and Photoshop are good applications to use for manipulating or creating graphics or pictures, though they are complicated programs to learn and use. You might consider MS Publisher or MS PowerPoint to develop simple graphics.

A CHECKLIST FOR REVISION

- ☐ Have I stated a claim that is precise and appropriate to the data I have collected?
- ☐ Have I fully explained the methodology I used in collecting my data?
- ☐ Have I selected a clear and useful organization?
- ☐ Have I presented and discussed enough specifics to show readers how my data support my conclusions?
- ☐ Have I used graphics to present the data in an effective visual display?
- ☐ Have I revised, edited, and proofread my paper?

STUDENT ESSAY

BUYING TIME

Garrett Berger

Chances are you own at least one wristwatch. Watches allow us immediate access to the correct time. They are indispensable items in our modern world, where, as the saying is, time is money. Today the primary function of a wristwatch does not necessarily guide its design; like clothes, houses, and cars, watches have become fashion statements and a way to flaunt one's wealth.

Introduction connects to reader.

To learn how watches are being sold, I surveyed all of the full-page ads from the November issues of four magazines. The first two, *GQ* and *Vogue,* are well-known fashion magazines. *The Robb Report* is a rather new magazine that caters to the overclass. *Forbes* is of course a well-known financial magazine. I was rather surprised at the number of advertisements I found. After surveying 86 ads, marketing 59 brands, I have concluded that today watches are being sold through five main strategies: DESIGN/BRAND appeal, CRAFTSMANSHIP, ASSOCIATION, FASHION appeal, and EMOTIONAL appeal. The percentage of ads using each of these strategies is shown in Figure 1.

Student explains his methodology of collecting ads. Paragraph concludes with his claim.

In most DESIGN/BRAND appeal ads, only a picture and the brand name are used. A subset of this category uses the same basic strategy with a slogan or phrases to emphasize something about the brand or product.

Discussion of first category.

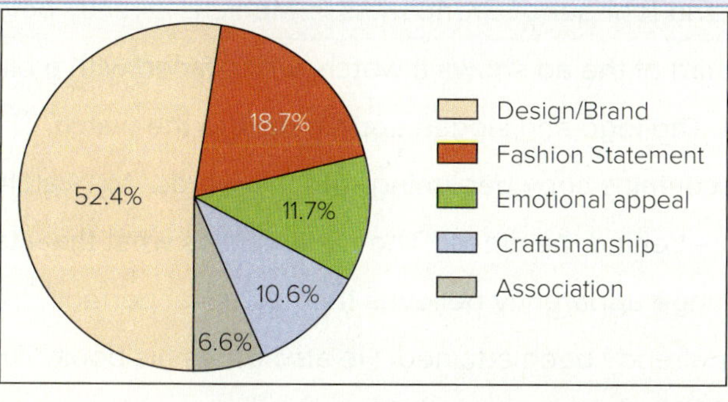

FIGURE 1 Percentage of Total Ads Using Each Strategy

A Mont Blanc ad shows a watch profile with a contorted metal link band, asking the question "Is that you?" The reputation of the name and the appeal of the design sell the watch. Rolex, perhaps the best-known name in high-end watches, advertises, in *Vogue,* its "Oyster Perpetual Lady-Datejust Pearlmaster." A close-up of the watch face showcases the white, mother-of-pearl dial, sapphire bezel, and diamond-set band. A smaller, more complete picture crouches underneath, showing the watch on its side. The model name is displayed along a gray band that runs near the bottom. The Rolex crest anchors the bottom of the page. Forty-five ads marketing 29 brands use the DESIGN/BRAND strategy. A large picture of the product centered on a solid background is the norm.

Discussion of second category.

CRAFTSMANSHIP, the second strategy, focuses on the maker, the horologer, and the technical sides of form and function. Brand heritage and a unique, hand-crafted design are major selling points. All of these ads are targeted at men, appearing in every magazine except *Vogue*. Collector pieces and limited editions were commonly sold using this strategy. The focus is on accuracy and technical excellence. Pictures of the inner works and cutaways, technical information, and explanations of movements and features are popular. Quality and exclusivity are all-important.

Detailed examples to illustrate second category.

A Cronoswiss ad from *The Robb Report* is a good example. The top third pictures a horologer, identified as "Gerd-R Lange, master watchmaker and founder of Cronoswiss in Munich," directly below. The middle third of the ad shows a watch, white-faced with a black leather band. The logo and slogan appear next to the watch. The bottom third contains copy beginning with the words "My watches are a hundred years behind the times." The rest explains what that statement means. Mr. Lange apparently believes that technical perfection in horology has already been attained. He also offers his book, *The Fascination of Mechanics,* free of charge along with the "sole distributor for North America" at the bottom. A "Daniel Roth" ad from the same magazine displays the name across the top of a white page; toward the top, left-hand corner a gold buckle and black band lead your eye to the center, where a gold watch with a transparent face displays its inner works exquisitely. Above and to the right, copy explains the exclusive and unique design accomplished by inverting the movement, allowing it to be viewed from above.

The third strategy is to sell the watch by establishing an ASSOCIATION with an object, experience, or person, implying that its value and quality are beyond question. In the six ads I found using this approach, watches are associated with violins, pilots, astronauts, hot air balloons, and a hero of the free world. This is similar to the first strategy, but relies on a reputation other than that of the maker. The watch is presented as being desirable for the connections created in the ad.

Discussion of third category.

Parmigiani ran an ad in *The Robb Report* featuring a gold watch with a black face and band illuminated by some unseen source. A blue-tinted violin rises in the background; the rest of the page is black. The brief copy reads: "For those who think a Stradivarius is only a violin. The Parmigiani Toric Chronograph is only a wristwatch." "The Moon Watch" proclaims an Omega ad from *GQ*. Inset on a white background is a picture of an astronaut on the moon saluting the American flag. The silver watch with a black face lies across the lower part of the page. Omega's logo appears at the top (Figure 2).

The fourth strategy is to present the watch simply as a FASHION statement. In this line of attack, the ads appeal to our need to be current, accepted, to fit in and be like everyone else, or to make a statement, setting us apart from others as hip and cool. The product is presented as a necessary part of our wardrobes. The watch is fashionable and will send the "right" message. Design and style are the foremost concerns; "the look" sells the watch.

Discussion of fourth category.

FIGURE 2 Example of Association Advertising
Omega

Techno Marine has an ad in *GQ* which shows a large close-up of a watch running down the entire length of the left side of the page. Two alternate color schemes are pictured on the right, separating small bits of copy. At the bottom on the right are the name and logo. The first words at the top read: "Keeping time—you keep your closet up to the minute, why not your wrist? The latest addition to your watch wardrobe should be the AlphaSport." Longines uses a similar strategy in *Vogue*. Its ad is divided in half lengthwise. On the left is a black-and-white picture of Audrey Hepburn. The right side is white with the Longines' logo at the top and two ladies' watches in the center. Near the bottom is the phrase "Elegance is an Attitude." Retailers appear at the bottom. The same ad ran in *GQ*, but with a man's watch and a picture of Humphrey Bogart. A kind of association is made, but quality and value aren't the overriding concerns. The point is to have an elegant attitude like these fashionable stars did, one that these watches can provide and enhance.

Discussion of fifth category.

The fifth and final strategy is that of EMOTIONAL appeal. The ads using this approach strive to influence our emotional responses and allege to influence the emotions of others towards us. Their power and appeal are exerted through the feelings they evoke in us. Nine out of ten ads rely on a picture as the main device to trigger an emotional link between the product and the viewer. Copy is scant; words are used mainly to guide the viewer to the advertiser's desired conclusions.

A Frederique Constant ad pictures a man, wearing a watch, mulling over a chess game. Above his head are the words "Inner Passion." The man's gaze is odd; he is looking at something on the right side of the page, but a large picture of a watch superimposed over the picture hides whatever it is that he is looking at. So we are led to the watch. The bottom third is white and contains the maker's logo and the slogan "Live your Passion." An ad in *GQ* shows a man holding a woman. He leans against a rock; she reclines in his arms. Their eyes are closed, and both have peaceful, smiling expressions. He is wearing a Tommy Hilfiger watch. The ad spans two pages; a close-up of the watch is presented on the right half of the second page. The only words are the ones in the logo. This is perhaps one of those pictures that are worth a thousand words. The message is he got the girl because he's got the watch.

Even more than selling a particular watch, all of these ads focus on building the brand's image. I found many of the ads extremely effective at conveying their messages. Many of the better-known brands favor the comparatively simple DESIGN/BRAND appeal strategy, to reach a broader audience. Lesser-known, high-end makers contribute many of the more specialized strategies. We all count and mark the passing hours and minutes. And society places great importance on time, valuing punctuality. But these ads strive to convince us that having "the right time" means so much more than "the time."

Strong conclusion; the effect of watch ads.

Courtesy of Garrett Berger

FOR READING AND ANALYSIS

EVERY BODY'S TALKING

Courtesy of Joe Navarro.

JOE NAVARRO

Joe Navarro spent more than twenty-five years in the FBI, specializing in counterintelligence and profiling. He is recognized as an authority on nonverbal messages, especially given off by those who are lying, and he continues to consult to government and industry. He has also turned his expertise to poker and has published, with Marvin Karlines, *Read, Em and Reap* (2006) and, on his own, *What Every Body Is Saying* (2008). The following essay appeared in the *Washington Post* on June 24, 2008.

PREREADING QUESTIONS What does the term "counterintelligence" mean? How much attention do you give to body language messages from others?

1 Picture this: I was sailing the Caribbean for three days with a group of friends and their spouses, and everything seemed perfect. The weather was beautiful, the ocean diaphanous blue, the food exquisite; our evenings together were full of laughter and good conversation.

2 Things were going so well that one friend said to the group, "Let's do this again next year." I happened to be across from him and his wife as he spoke those words. In the cacophony of resounding replies of "Yes!" and "Absolutely!" I noticed that my friend's wife made a fist under her chin as she grasped her necklace. This behavior stood out to me as powerfully as if someone had shouted, "Danger!"

3 I watched the words and gestures of the other couples at the table, and everyone seemed ecstatic—everyone but one, that is. She continued to smile, but her smile was tense.

4 Her husband has treated me as a brother for more than 15 years, and I consider him the dearest of friends. At that moment I knew that things between him and his wife were turning for the worse. I did not pat myself on the back for making these observations. I was saddened.

5 For 25 years I worked as a paid observer. I was a special agent for the FBI specializing in counterintelligence—specifically, catching spies. For me, observing human behavior is like having software running in the background, doing its job—no conscious effort needed. And so on that wonderful cruise, I made a "thin-slice assessment" (that's what we call it) based on just a few significant behaviors. Unfortunately, it turned out to be right: Within six months of our return, my friend's wife filed for divorce, and her husband discovered painfully that she had been seeing someone else for quite a while.

6 When I am asked what is the most reliable means of determining the health of a relationship, I always say that words don't matter. It's all in the language of the body. The nonverbal behaviors we all transmit tell others, in real time, what we think, what we feel, what we yearn for or what we intend.

Now I am embarking on another cruise, wondering what insights I will have about my travel companions and their relationships. No matter what, this promises to be a fascinating trip, a journey for the mind and the soul. I am with a handful of dear friends and 3,800 strangers, all headed for Alaska; for an observer it does not get any better than this. 7

While lining up to board on our first day, I notice just ahead of me a couple who appear to be in their early 30s. They are obviously Americans (voice, weight and demeanor). 8

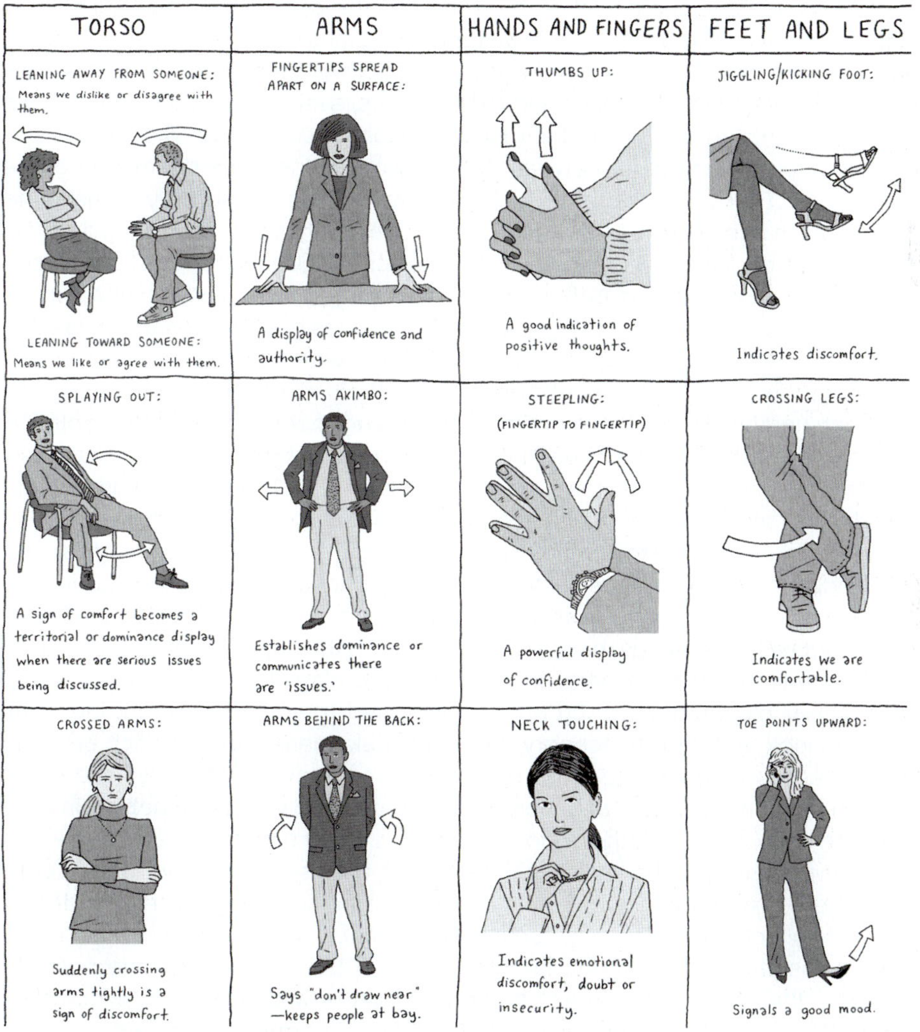

Illustrations in Joe Navarro, "Every Body's Talking," *Washington Post*, June 24, 2008. Illustrations by Peter Arkle. Reprinted by permission.

9 Not so obvious is their dysfunctional relationship. He is standing stoically, shoulders wide, looking straight ahead. She keeps whispering loudly to him, but she is not facing forward. She violates his space as she leans into him. Her face is tense and her lips are narrow slivers each time she engages him with what clearly appears to be a diatribe. He occasionally nods his head but avoids contact with her. He won't let his hips near her as they start to walk side by side. He reminds me of Bill and Hillary Clinton walking toward the Marine One helicopter immediately after the Monica Lewinsky affair: looking straight ahead, as much distance between them as possible.

10 I think everyone can decipher this one from afar because we have all seen situations like this. What most people will miss is something I have seen this young man do twice now, which portends poorly for both of them. Every time she looks away, he "disses" her. He smirks and rolls his eyes, even as she stands beside him. He performs his duties, pulling their luggage along; I suspect he likes to have her luggage nearby as a barrier between them. I won't witness the dissolution of their marriage, but I know it will happen, for the research behind this is fairly robust. When two people in a relationship have contempt for each other, the marriage will not last.

11 When it comes to relationships and courtship behaviors, the list of useful cues is long. Most of these behaviors we learned early when interacting with our mothers. When we look at loving eyes, our own eyes get larger, our pupils dilate, our facial muscles relax, our lips become full and warm, our skin becomes more pliable, our heads tilt. These behaviors stay with us all of our lives.

12 I watched two lovers this morning in the dining room. Two young people, perhaps in their late 20s, mirror each other, staring intently into each other's eyes, chin on hand, head slightly tilted, nose flaring with each breath. They are trying to absorb each other visually and tactilely as they hold hands across the table.

13 Over time, those who remain truly in love will show even more indicators of mirroring. They may dress the same or even begin to look alike as they adopt each other's nonverbal expressions as a sign of synchrony and empathy. They will touch each other with kind hands that touch fully, not with the fingertips of the less caring.

14 They will mirror each other in ways that are almost imperceptible; they will have similar blink rates and breathing rates, and they will sit almost identically. They will look at the same scenery and not speak, merely look at each other and take a deep breath to reset their breathing synchrony. They don't have to talk. They are in harmony physically, mentally and emotionally, just as a baby is in exquisite synchrony with its mother who is tracing his every expression and smile.

15 As I walk through the ship on the first night, I can see the nonverbals of courtship. There is a beautiful woman, tall, slender, smoking a cigarette outside. Two men are talking to her, both muscular, handsome, interested. She has crossed her legs as she talks to them, an expression of her comfort. As she holds her cigarette, the inside of her wrist turns toward her newfound friends. Her interest and comfort with them resounds, but she is favoring one of them. As he speaks to her, she preens herself by playing with her hair. I am not sure he is getting the message that she prefers him; in the end, I am sure it will all get sorted out.

16 At the upscale lounge, a man is sitting at the bar talking animatedly to the woman next to him and looking at everyone who walks by. The woman has begun

the process of ignoring him, but he does not get it. After he speaks to her a few times, she gathers her purse and places it on her lap. She has turned slightly away from him and now avoids eye contact. He has no clue; he thinks he is cool by commenting on the women who pass by. She is verbally and non-verbally indifferent.

The next night it is more of the same. This time, I see two people who just met talking gingerly. Gradually they lean more and more into each other. She is now dangling her sandal from her toes. I am not sure he knows it. Perhaps he sees it all in her face, because she is smiling, laughing and relaxed. Communication is fluid, and neither wants the conversation to end. She is extremely interested. 17

All of these individuals are carrying on a dialogue in nonverbals. The socially adept will learn to read and interpret the signs accurately. Others will make false steps or pay a high price for not being observant. They may end up like my friend on the Caribbean cruise, who missed the clues of deceit and indifference. 18

This brings me back to my friend and his new wife, who are on this wonderful voyage. They have been on board for four days, and they are a delight individually and together. He lovingly looks at her; she stares at him with love and admiration. When she holds his hand at dinner, she massages it ever so gently. Theirs is a strong marriage. They don't have to tell me. I can sense it and observe it. I am happy for them and for myself. I can see cues of happiness, and they are unmistakable. You can't ask for more. 19

Navarro, Joe. "Every Body's Talking." *Washington Post,* 24 June 2008. Used with permission of the author.

QUESTIONS FOR READING

1. What is Navarro's subject? (Do not answer "taking cruises"!)
2. What clues are offered to support the conclusion that the two cruise couples' relationships are about to dissolve?
3. What are the nonverbal messages that reveal loving relationships?
4. What nonverbal messages should the man in the lounge be observing?

QUESTIONS FOR REASONING AND ANALYSIS

5. What is Navarro's claim?
6. What kind of evidence does he provide?
7. How do the illustrations contribute to the argument? What is effective about the author's opening?

QUESTIONS FOR REFLECTION AND WRITING

8. Has the author convinced you that nonverbal language reveals our thoughts and feelings? Why or why not?
9. Can you "read" the nonverbal language of your instructors? Take some time to analyze each of your instructors. What have you learned? (You might also reflect on what messages you may be sending in class.)

SUGGESTIONS FOR DISCUSSION AND WRITING

For all investigative essays—inductive arguments—follow the guidelines in this chapter and use the student essay as your model. Remember that you will need to explain your methods for collecting data, to classify evidence and present it in several formats, and also to explain its significance for readers. Just collecting data does not create an argument. Here are some possible topics to explore:

1. Study print or online ads for one type of product (e.g., cars, cosmetics, cigarettes) to draw inferences about the dominant techniques used to sell that product. Remember that the more ads you study, the more support you have for your inferences. You should study at least twenty-five ads.

2. Study print or online ads for one type of product as advertised in different types of magazines or on different types of websites clearly directed to different audiences to see how (or if) selling techniques change with a change in audience. (Remember: To demonstrate no change in techniques can be just as interesting a conclusion as finding changes.) Study at least twenty-five ads, in a balanced number from the different magazines or websites.

3. Select a major figure currently in the news and conduct a study of bias in one of the newsmagazines (e.g., *Time* or *U.S. News & World Report*) or a newspaper. Use at least eight issues of the magazine or newspaper from the last six months and study all articles on your figure in each of those issues. To determine bias, look at the amount of coverage, the location (front pages or back pages), the use of photos (flattering or unflattering), and the language of the articles.

4. Conduct a study of amounts of violence in video games by analyzing the top ten bestselling video games of last year. Devise some classification system for types of violence based on your prior gaming experience before beginning your study, but be prepared to alter or add to your categories based on your viewing/playing/researching of each game. Note the types of violence occurring in the game, the explicitness, how often it occurs, how central to the game the violence is, and the context of the violence. Is it cartoon-type violence, or is it graphic, bloody violence? Is violence a central theme and a main part of winning or playing the game? Or is it only part of the game? You may also want to consider the game rating: M for mature players means that young children should not be playing that game, though they often find a way. If you're not a gamer, use the same process described above to analyze the ten most popular streaming shows.

5. As an alternative to topic 4, study the number and types of violent acts in children's programs streaming online. (This and topic 4 are best handled if you can play/watch several times.)

6. Conduct a survey and analyze the results on some campus issue or current public policy issue. Prepare questions that are without bias and include questions to get information about the participants so that you can correlate answers with the demographics of your participants (e.g., age, gender, race, religion, proposed major in college, political affiliation, or whatever else you think is important to the topic studied). Decide whether you want to survey students only or both students and faculty. Plan how you are going to reach each group.

CHAPTER 6

Learning More about Argument: Induction, Deduction, Analogy, and Logical Fallacies

LEARNING OUTCOMES

After reading Chapter 6, you will be able to:

- Describe induction.
- Explain deduction.
- Describe analogy.
- Identify logical fallacies.

MShieldsPhotos/Alamy Stock Photo

READ: "The School of Athens" was painted by the artist Raphael during the Italian Renaissance. Who are the two central figures in the painting?

REASON: Why do you think Raphael painted the central figure on our left pointing toward the heavens while the central person on our right gestures toward us?

WRITE: What makes this painting so compelling? Is it the subject matter? The colors? The depth and perspective? Or all of these elements together? Explain.

You can build on your knowledge of the basics of argument, examined in Chapter 3, by understanding some traditional forms of argument: induction, deduction, analogy, and logical fallacies. It is also important to recognize arguments that do not meet the standards of good logic.

INDUCTION

Induction is the process by which we reach inferences–opinions based on facts, or on a combination of facts and less debatable inferences. The inductive process moves from particular to general, from support to assertion. We base our inferences on the facts we have gathered and studied. In general, the more evidence, the more convincing the argument. No one wants to debate tomorrow's sunrise; the evidence for counting on it is too convincing. Most inferences, though, are drawn from less evidence, so we need to examine these arguments closely to judge their reasonableness.

The pattern of induction looks like this:

EVIDENCE: There is the dead body of Smith. Smith was shot in his bedroom between the hours of 11:00 a.m. and 2:00 a.m., according to the coroner. Smith was shot by a .32-caliber pistol. The pistol left in the bedroom contains Jones's fingerprints. Jones was seen, by a neighbor, entering the Smith home at around 11:00 the night of Smith's death. A coworker heard Smith and Jones arguing in Smith's office the morning of the day Smith died.

CLAIM: Jones killed Smith.

The facts are presented. The jury infers that Jones is a murderer. Unless there is a confession or a trustworthy eyewitness, the conclusion is an inference, not a fact. This is the most logical explanation. The conclusion meets the standards of simplicity and frequency while accounting for all of the known evidence.

The following paragraph illustrates the process of induction. In their book *Discovering Dinosaurs,* authors Mark Norell, Eugene Gaffney, and Lowell Dingus answer the question "Did dinosaurs really rule the world?"

> For almost 170 million years, from the Late Triassic to the end of the Cretaceous, there existed dinosaurs of almost every body form imaginable: small carnivores, such as *Compsognathus* and *Ornitholestes,* ecologically equivalent to today's foxes and coyotes; medium-sized carnivores, such as *Velociraptor* and the troödontids, analogous to lions and tigers; and the monstrous carnivores with no living analogs, such as *Tyrannosaurus* and *Allosaurus.* Included among the ornithischians and the elephantine sauropods are terrestrial herbivores of diverse body form. By the end of the Jurassic, dinosaurs had even taken to the skies. The only habitats that dinosaurs did not dominate during the Mesozoic were aquatic. Yet, there were marine representatives, such as the primitive toothed bird *Hesperornis.* Like penguins, these birds were flightless, specialized for diving, and probably had to return to land to reproduce. In light of this broad morphologic diversity [number of body forms], dinosaurs did "rule the planet" as

the dominant life form on Earth during most of the Mesozoic [era that includes the Triassic, Jurassic, and Cretaceous periods, 248 to 65 million years ago].[1]

Observe that the writers organize evidence by type of dinosaur to demonstrate the range and diversity of these animals. A good inductive argument is based on a sufficient volume of *relevant* evidence. The basic shape of this inductive argument is illustrated in Figure 6.1.

CLAIM:	Dinosaurs were the dominant life form during the Mesozoic era.
GROUNDS:	The facts presented in the paragraph.
ASSUMPTION: (WARRANT)	The facts are representative, revealing dinosaur diversity.

FIGURE 6.1 The Shape of an Inductive Argument

COLLABORATIVE EXERCISE: Induction

With your class partner or in small groups, make a list of facts that could be used to support each of the following inferences:

1. Fido must have escaped under the fence during the night.
2. Sue must be planning to go away for the weekend.
3. Students who do not hand in all essay assignments fail Dr. Bradshaw's English class.
4. The price of Florida oranges will go up in grocery stores next year.
5. Yogurt is a better breakfast food than bread.

DEDUCTION

Although induction can be described as an argument that moves from particular to general, from facts to inference, deduction cannot accurately be described as the reverse. Deductive arguments are more complex. *Deduction is the reasoning process that draws a conclusion from the logical relationship of two assertions, usually one broad judgment or definition and one more specific assertion, often an inference.* Suppose, on the way out of American history class, you say, "Abraham Lincoln certainly was a great leader." Someone responds with the expected question: "Why do you think so?" You explain: "He was great because he performed with courage and a clear purpose in a time of crisis." Your explanation contains a conclusion and an assertion about Lincoln (an inference) in support. But behind your explanation rests an idea about leadership, in the terms of deduction, *a premise.* The argument's basic shape is illustrated in Figure 6.2.

CLAIM:	Lincoln was a great leader.
GROUNDS:	1. People who perform with courage and clear purpose in a crisis are great leaders. 2. Lincoln was a person who performed with courage and a clear purpose in a crisis.
ASSUMPTION (WARRANT):	The relationship of the two reasons leads, logically, to the conclusion.

FIGURE 6.2 The Shape of a Deductive Argument

Traditionally, the deductive argument is arranged somewhat differently from these sentences about Lincoln. The two reasons are called *premises;* the broader one, called the *major premise,* is written first and the more specific one, the *minor premise,* comes next. The premises and conclusion are expressed to make clear that assertions are being made about categories or classes. When all three steps are used, the structure is called a *syllogism. Syllogisms* may also include more than one *minor premise,* but for now, we will just focus on the three-step deductive process. To illustrate:

MAJOR PREMISE: All people who perform with courage and a clear purpose in a crisis are great leaders.

MINOR PREMISE: Lincoln was a person who performed with courage and a clear purpose in a crisis.

CONCLUSION: Lincoln was a great leader.

If these two premises are correctly, that is, logically, constructed, then the conclusion follows logically, and the deductive argument is *valid.* This does not mean that the conclusion is necessarily *true.* It does mean that if you accept the truth of the premises, then you must accept the truth of the conclusion, because in a valid argument the conclusion follows logically, necessarily. How do we know that the conclusion must follow if the argument is logically constructed? Let's think about what each premise is saying and then diagram each one to represent each assertion visually. The first premise says that all people who act a particular way are people who fit into the category called "great leaders":

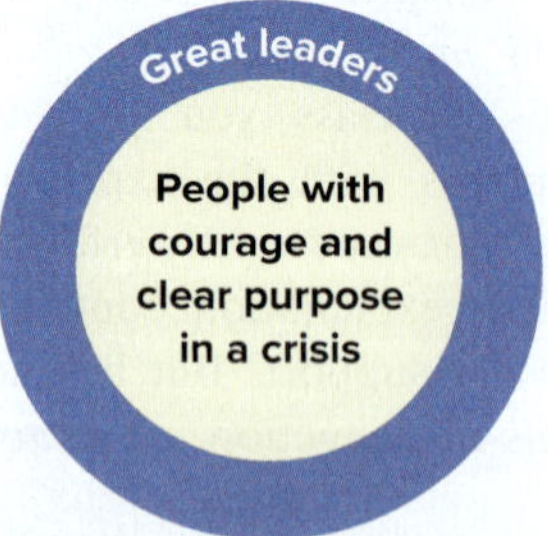

The second premise says that Lincoln, a category of one, belongs in the category of people who act in the same particular way that the first premise describes:

If we put the two diagrams together, we have the following set of circles, demonstrating that the conclusion follows from the premises:

We can also make negative and qualified assertions in a deductive argument. For example:

PREMISE:	No cowards can be great leaders.
PREMISE:	Falstaff was a coward.
CONCLUSION:	Falstaff was not a great leader.

Or, to reword the conclusion to make the deductive pattern clearer: No Falstaff (no member of this class) is a great leader. Diagramming to test for validity, we find that the first premise says no A's are B's:

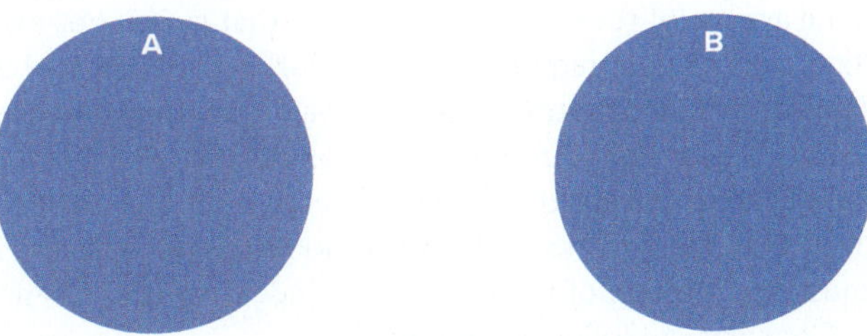

The second premise asserts all C's are A's:

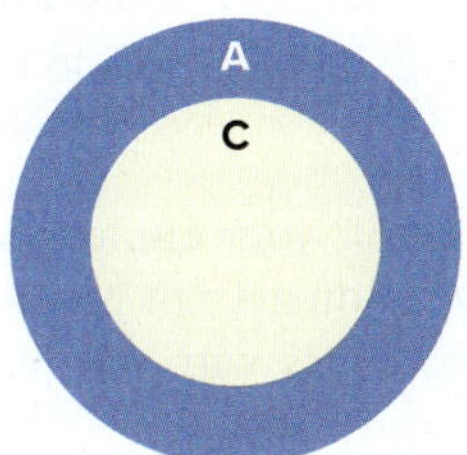

Put together, we see that the conclusion follows necessarily from the premises: No C's can possibly be members of class B.

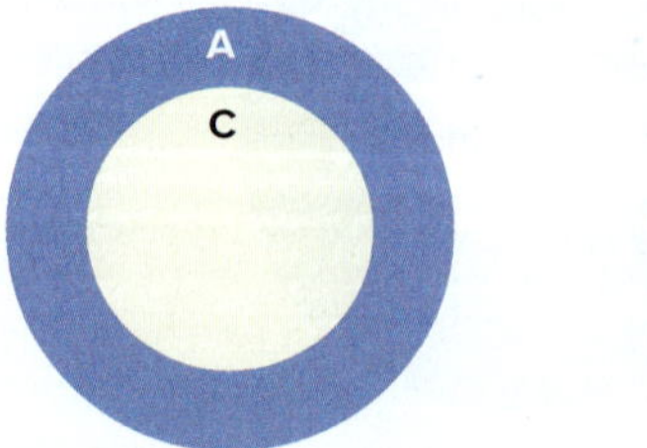

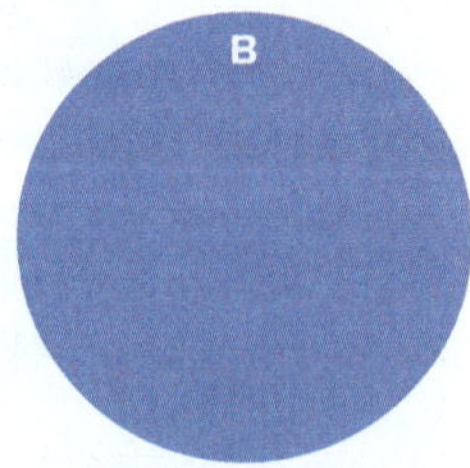

Some deductive arguments merely look right, but the two premises do not lead logically to the conclusion that is asserted. We must read each argument carefully or diagram each one to make certain that the conclusion follows from the premises. Consider the following argument: *Unions must be communistic because they want to control wages.* The sentence contains a conclusion and one reason, or premise. From these two parts of a deductive argument we can also determine the unstated premise, just as we could with the Lincoln argument: *Communists want to control wages.* If we use circles to represent the three categories of people in the argument and diagram the argument, we see a different result from the previous diagrams:

Diagramming the argument reveals that it is invalid; that is, it is not logically constructed because the statements do not require that the union circle be placed inside the communist circle. We cannot draw the conclusion we want from any two premises, only from those that provide a logical basis from which a conclusion can be reached.

We must first make certain that deductive arguments are properly constructed or valid. But suppose the logic works and yet you do not agree with the claim? Your complaint, then, must be with one of the premises, a judgment or inference that you do not accept as true. Consider the following argument:

MAJOR PREMISE:	(All) dogs make good pets.
MINOR PREMISE:	Fido is a dog.
CONCLUSION:	Fido will make a good pet.

This argument is valid. (Diagram it; your circles will fit into one another just as with the Lincoln argument.) However, you are not prepared to agree, necessarily, that Fido will make a good pet. The problem is with the major premise. For the argument to work, the assertion must be about *all* dogs, but we know that not all dogs will be good pets.

When composing a deductive argument, your task will be to defend the truth of your premises. Then, if your argument is valid (logically constructed), readers will have no alternative but to agree with your conclusion. If you disagree with someone else's logically constructed argument, then you must show why one of the premises is not true. Your counterargument will seek to discredit one (or both) of the premises. The Fido argument can be discredited by your producing examples of dogs that have not made good pets.

Sometimes, a deductive argument, or *syllogism,* does not include a premise. When a premise is missing from the deductive process, the syllogism becomes an *enthymeme.* Enthymemes are syllogisms that are missing a premise. A missing premise does not necessarily make a syllogism invalid or incorrect. In fact, omitting or skipping a *premise* is fairly common in everyday discourse. For instance, the syllogism above involving dogs makes sense–if you agree with the existing premises–even if one of the premises is omitted:

MINOR PREMISE:	Fido is a dog.
CONCLUSION:	Fido will make a good pet.
MISSING PREMISE (MAJOR PREMISE):	(All) dogs make good pets.

Or

MAJOR PREMISE:	(All) dogs make good pets.
CONCLUSION:	Fido will make a good pet.
MISSING PREMISE (MINOR PREMISE):	Fido is a dog.

As we have seen, this argument, with or without all three parts, fails on its logic. But upon first reading or hearing the enthymeme above, someone who is not paying attention might be misled.

Enthymemes are one of the most common ways people argue in conversations, and especially online, so it is important that you pay attention to information that may be missing. This process is known as critical thinking. If you do not use critical thinking, you may be manipulated into agreeing with an argument that you do not really support.

A deductive argument can serve as the core of an essay, an essay that supports the argument's claim by developing support for each of the premises. Since the major premise is either a broad judgment or a definition, it will need to be defended on the basis of an appeal to values or beliefs that the writer expects readers to share. The minor premise, usually an inference about a particular situation (or person), would be supported by relevant evidence, as with any inductive argument. You can see this process at work in the Declaration of Independence. Questions follow the Declaration to guide your analysis of this famous example of the deductive process.

THE DECLARATION OF INDEPENDENCE

In Congress, July 4, 1776
The unanimous declaration of the thirteen
United States of America

1 When in the course of human events, it becomes necessary for one people to dissolve the political bands which have connected them with another, and to assume among the powers of the earth, the separate and equal station to which the Laws of Nature and of Nature's God entitle them, a decent respect to the opinions of mankind requires that they should declare the causes which impel them to the separation.

2 We hold these truths to be self-evident, that all men are created equal, that they are endowed by their Creator with certain unalienable rights, that among these are life, liberty and the pursuit of happiness. That to secure these rights, governments are instituted among men, deriving their just powers from the consent of the governed. That whenever any form of government becomes destructive of these ends, it is the right of the people to alter or to abolish it, and to institute new government, laying its foundation on such principles and organizing its powers in such form, as to them shall seem most likely to effect their safety and happiness. Prudence, indeed, will dictate that governments long established should not be changed for light and transient causes; and accordingly all experience hath shown, that mankind are more disposed to suffer, while evils are sufferable, than to right themselves by abolishing the forms to which they are accustomed. But when a long train of abuses and usurpations, pursuing invariably the same object evinces a design to reduce them under absolute despotism, it is their right, it is their duty, to throw off such government, and to provide new guards for their future security. Such has been the patient sufferance of these Colonies; and such is now the necessity which constrains them to alter their former systems of government. The history of the present King of Great Britain is a history of repeated injuries and usurpations, all having in direct object the establishment of an absolute tyranny over these States. To prove this, let facts be submitted to a candid world.

3 He has refused his assent to laws, the most wholesome and necessary for the public good.

4 He has forbidden his Governors to pass laws of immediate and pressing importance, unless suspended in their operation till his assent should be obtained; and when so suspended, he has utterly neglected to attend to them.

5 He has refused to pass other laws for the accommodation of large districts of people, unless those people would relinquish the right of representation in the Legislature, a right inestimable to them and formidable to tyrants only.

6 He has called together legislative bodies at places unusual, uncomfortable, and distant from the depository of their public records, for the sole purpose of fatiguing them into compliance with his measures.

7 He has dissolved representative houses repeatedly, for opposing with manly firmness his invasions on the rights of the people.

He has refused for a long time, after such dissolutions, to cause others to be 8
elected; whereby the legislative powers, incapable of annihilation, have returned to the people at large for their exercise; the State remaining in the meantime exposed to all the dangers of invasion from without and convulsions within.

He has endeavoured to prevent the population of these States; for that purpose 9
obstructing the laws of naturalization of foreigners; refusing to pass others to encourage their migration hither, and raising the conditions of new appropriations of lands.

He has obstructed the administration of justice, by refusing his assent to 10
laws for establishing judiciary powers.

He has made judges dependent on his will alone, for the tenure of their 11
offices, and the amount and payment of their salaries.

He has erected a multitude of new offices, and sent hither swarms of officers 12
to harass our people, and eat out their substance.

He has kept among us, in times of peace, standing armies without the con- 13
sent of our legislatures.

He has affected to render the military independent of and superior to the 14
civil power.

He has combined with others to subject us to a jurisdiction foreign to our 15
constitution, and unacknowledged by our laws; giving his assent to their acts of pretended legislation:

For quartering large bodies of armed troops among us: 16

For protecting them, by a mock trial, from punishment for any murders which 17
they should commit on the inhabitants of these States:

For cutting off our trade with all parts of the world: 18

For imposing taxes on us without our consent: 19

For depriving us, in many cases, of the benefits of trial by jury: 20

For transporting us beyond seas to be tried for pretended offences: 21

For abolishing the free system of English laws in a neighbouring Province, 22
establishing therein an arbitrary government, and enlarging its boundaries so as to render it at once an example and fit instrument for introducing the same absolute rule into these Colonies:

For taking away our Charters, abolishing our most valuable laws, and alter- 23
ing fundamentally the forms of our governments:

For suspending our own Legislatures, and declaring themselves invested 24
with power to legislate for us in all cases whatsoever.

He has abdicated government here, by declaring us out of his protection 25
and waging war against us.

He has plundered our seas, ravaged our coasts, burnt our towns, and 26
destroyed the lives of our people.

He is at this time transporting large armies of foreign mercenaries to com- 27
plete the works of death, desolation and tyranny, already begun with circumstances of cruelty and perfidy scarcely paralleled in the most barbarous ages, and totally unworthy the head of a civilized nation.

He has constrained our fellow citizens taken captive on the high seas to 28
bear arms against their country, to become the executioners of their friends and brethren, or to fall themselves by their hands.

29 He has excited domestic insurrections amongst us, and has endeavoured to bring on the inhabitants of our frontiers, the merciless Indian savages, whose known rule of warfare, is an undistinguished destruction of all ages, sexes, and conditions.

30 In every stage of these oppressions we have petitioned for redress in the most humble terms; our repeated petitions have been answered only by repeated injury. A prince whose character is thus marked by every act which may define a tyrant is unfit to be the ruler of a free people.

31 Nor have we been wanting in attention to our British brethren. We have warned them from time to time of attempts by their legislature to extend an unwarrantable jurisdiction over us. We have reminded them of the circumstances of our emigration and settlement here. We have appealed to their native justice and magnanimity, and we have conjured them by the ties of our common kindred to disavow these usurpations, which would inevitably interrupt our connections and correspondence. They too have been deaf to the voice of justice and of consanguinity. We must, therefore, acquiesce in the necessity, which denounces our separation, and hold them, as we hold the rest of mankind, enemies in war, in peace friends.

32 We, therefore, the Representatives of the United States of America, in General Congress assembled, appealing to the Supreme Judge of the world for the rectitude of our intentions, do, in the name, and by the authority of the good people of these Colonies, solemnly publish and declare, That these United Colonies are, and of right ought to be Free and Independent States; that they are absolved from all allegiance to the British Crown, and that all political connection between them and the State of Great Britain, is and ought to be totally dissolved; and that as Free and Independent States, they have full power to levy war, conclude peace, contract alliances, establish commerce, and to do all other acts and things which Independent States may of right do. And for the support of this declaration, with a firm reliance on the protection of Divine Providence, we mutually pledge to each other our lives, our fortunes, and our sacred honor.

QUESTIONS FOR ANALYSIS

1. What is the Declaration's central deductive argument? State the argument in the shape illustrated above: major premise, minor premise, conclusion. Construct a valid argument. If necessary, draw circles representing each of the three terms in the argument to check for validity. (*Hint:* Start with the claim "George III's government should be overthrown.")
2. Which paragraphs are devoted to supporting the major premise? What kind of support has been given?
3. Which paragraphs are devoted to supporting the minor premise? What kind of support has been given?
4. Why has more support been given for one premise than the other?

EXERCISES: Completing and Evaluating Deductive Arguments

Turn each of the following statements into valid deductive arguments. (You have the conclusion and one premise, so you will have to determine the missing premise that would complete the argument. Draw circles if necessary to test for validity.) Then decide which arguments have premises that could be supported. Note the kind of support that might be provided. Explain why you think some arguments have insupportable premises. Here is an example:

PREMISE:	All Jesuits are priests.
PREMISE:	No women are priests.
CONCLUSION:	No women are Jesuits.

Since the circle for women must be placed outside the circle for priests, it must also be outside the circle for Jesuits. Hence the argument is valid. The first premise is true by definition; the term *Jesuit* refers to an order of Roman Catholic priests. The second premise is true for the Roman Catholic Church, so if the term *priest* is used only to refer to ordained people in the Roman Catholic Church, then the second premise is also true by definition.

1. Ms. Ferguson is a good teacher because she can explain the subject matter clearly.
2. Segregated schools are unconstitutional because they are unequal.
3. Michael must be a good driver because he drives fast.
4. The media clearly have a liberal bias because they make fun of religious fundamentalists.

ANALOGY

The argument from analogy is an argument based on comparison. Analogies assert that since A and B are alike in several ways, they must be alike in another way as well. The argument from analogy concludes with an inference, an assertion of a significant similarity in the two items being compared. The other similarities serve as evidence in support of the inference. The shape of an argument by analogy is illustrated in Figure 6.3.

GROUNDS:	A has characteristics 1, 2, 3, and 4. B has characteristics 1, 2, and 3.
CLAIM:	B has characteristic 4 (as well).
ASSUMPTION (WARRANT):	If B has three characteristics in common with A, it must have the key fourth characteristic as well.

FIGURE 6.3 The Shape of an Argument by Analogy

Although analogy is sometimes an effective approach to an issue because clever and imaginative comparisons are often moving, analogy is not as rigorously logical as either induction or deduction. Frequently, an analogy is based on only two or three points of comparison, whereas a sound inductive argument presents many examples to support its conclusion. Further, to be convincing, the points of comparison must be fundamental to the two items being compared. An argument for a county leash law for cats developed by analogy with dogs may cite the following similarities:

- Cats are pets, just like dogs.
- Cats live in residential communities, just like dogs.
- Cats can mess up other people's yards, just like dogs.
- Cats, if allowed to run free, can disturb the peace (fighting, making noise at night), just like dogs.

Does it follow that cats should be required to walk on a leash, just like dogs? If such a county ordinance were passed, would it be enforceable? Have you ever tried to walk a cat on a leash? In spite of legitimate similarities brought out by the analogy, the conclusion does not logically follow because the arguer is overlooking a fundamental difference in the two animals' personalities. Dogs can be trained to a leash; most cats (Siamese are one exception) cannot be so trained. Such thinking will produce sulking cats and scratched owners. But the analogy, delivered passionately to the right audience, could lead community activists to lobby for a new law.

Observe that the problem with the cat-leash-law analogy is not in the similarities asserted about the items being compared but rather in the underlying assumption that the similarities logically support the argument's conclusion. A good analogy asserts many points of comparison and finds likenesses that are essential parts of the nature or purpose of the two items being compared. The best way to challenge another's analogy is to point out a fundamental difference in the nature or purpose of the compared items. For all of their similarities, when it comes to walking on a leash, cats are *not* like dogs.

EXERCISES: Analogy

Analyze the following analogies. List the stated and/or implied points of comparison and the conclusion in the pattern illustrated in Figure 6.3. Then judge each argument's logic and effectiveness as a persuasive technique. If the argument is not logical, state the fundamental difference in the two compared items. If the argument could be persuasive, describe the kind of audience that might be moved by it.

1. College newspapers should not be under the supervision or control of a faculty sponsor. Fortunately, no governmental sponsor controls the *New York Times,* or we would no longer have a free press in this country. We need a free college press, too, one that can criticize college policies when they are wrong.
2. Let's recognize that college athletes are really professional and start paying all of them (since some NCAA programs are beginning to pay some top players). College athletes get a free education and spending money from boosters. They are required to attend practices and games, and–if they play football or basketball–they bring in huge revenues for their "organization." College coaches are also paid enormous

salaries, just like professional coaches, and often college coaches are tapped to coach professional teams. The only difference: Most of the college athletes who come from a lower socio-economic background don't get those big salaries and huge signing bonuses.

3. Just like any business, the federal government must be made to balance its budget. No company could continue to operate in the red as the government does and expect to be successful. A constitutional amendment requiring a balanced federal budget is long overdue.

LOGICAL FALLACIES

A thorough study of argument needs to include a study of logical fallacies because so many "arguments" fail to meet standards of sound logic and good sense. Why do people offer arguments that aren't sensible?

Causes of Illogic

Ignorance

One frequent cause for illogical debate is a lack of knowledge of the subject. Some people have more information than others. The younger you are, the less you can be expected to know about complex issues. On the other hand, if you want to debate a complex or technical issue, then you cannot use ignorance as an excuse. Instead, read as much as you can, listen carefully to discussions, ask questions, and select topics about which you have knowledge or will research before writing.

Egos

Ego problems are another cause of weak arguments. Those with low self-esteem often have difficulty in debates because they attach themselves to their ideas and then feel personally attacked when someone disagrees with them. Remember: Self-esteem is enhanced when others applaud our knowledge and thoughtfulness, not our irrationality.

Prejudices

The prejudices and biases that we carry around, having absorbed them "ages ago" from family and community, are also sources of irrationality. Prejudices range from the worst ethnic, religious, or sexist stereotypes to political views we have adopted uncritically (Democrats are all bleeding hearts; Republicans are all rich snobs) to perhaps less serious but equally insupportable notions (if it's in print, it must be right). People who see the world through distorted lenses cannot possibly assess facts intelligently and reason logically from them.

A Need for Answers

Finally, many bad arguments stem from a human need for answers–any answers–to the questions that deeply concern us. We want to control our world because that makes us feel secure, and having answers makes us feel in control. This need can lead to illogic from oversimplifying issues.

Based on these causes of illogic, we can usefully divide fallacies into (1) oversimplifying the issue and (2) ignoring the issue by substituting emotion for reason.

Fallacies That Result from Oversimplifying

Errors in Generalizing

Errors in generalizing include overstatement and hasty or faulty generalization. All have in common an error in the inductive pattern of argument. The inference drawn from the evidence is unwarranted, either because too broad a generalization is made or because the generalization is drawn from incomplete or incorrect evidence.

Overstatement occurs when the argument's assertion is unqualified–referring to all members of a category. Overstatements often result from stereotyping, giving the same traits to everyone in a group. Overstatements are frequently signaled by words such as *all, every, always, never,* and *none.* But remember that assertions such as "children love clowns" are understood to refer to "all children," even though the word *all* does not appear in the sentence. It is the writer's task to qualify statements appropriately, using words such as *some, many,* or *frequently,* as appropriate.

Overstatements are discredited by finding only one exception to disprove the assertion. One frightened child who starts to cry when the clown approaches will destroy the argument. Here is another example:

- Lawyers are only interested in making money.

  (What about lawyers who work to protect consumers, or public defenders who represent those unable to pay for a lawyer?)

Hasty or faulty generalizations may be qualified assertions, but they still oversimplify by arguing from insufficient evidence or by ignoring some relevant evidence. For example:

- Political life must lead many to excessive drinking. In the last six months the paper has written about five members of Congress who either have confessed to alcoholism or have been arrested on DUI charges.

  (Five is not a large enough sample from which to generalize about *many* politicians. Also, the five in the newspaper are not a representative sample; they have made the news because of their drinking.)

Forced Hypothesis

The *forced hypothesis* is also an error in inductive reasoning. The explanation (hypothesis) offered is "forced," or illogical, because either (1) sufficient evidence does not exist to draw any conclusion or (2) the evidence can be explained more simply or more sensibly by a different hypothesis. This fallacy often results from not considering other possible explanations. You discredit a forced hypothesis by providing alternative conclusions that are more sensible than or just as sensible as the one offered. Consider this example:

- Professor Redding's students received either As or Bs last semester. Professor Redding must be an excellent teacher.

  (The grades alone cannot support this conclusion. Professor Redding could be an excellent teacher, could have started with excellent students, or could be an easy grader.)

Non Sequitur

The term *non sequitur,* meaning literally "it does not follow," could apply to all illogical arguments, but the term is usually reserved for those in which the conclusions are not logically connected to the reasons. In a hasty generalization, for example, there is a connection between support (five politicians in the news) and conclusion (many politicians with drinking problems), just not a convincing connection. With the *non sequitur* there is no recognizable connection, either because (1) whatever connection the arguer sees is not made clear to others or because (2) the evidence or reasons offered are irrelevant to the conclusion. For example:

- The students will surely get good grades in physics; they earned As in biology class.

  (Doing well in one course, even one science course, does not support the conclusion that students will get a good grade in another course.)

Slippery Slope

The *slippery slope* argument asserts that we should not proceed with or permit A because if we do, the terrible consequences X, Y, and Z will occur. This type of argument oversimplifies by assuming, without evidence and usually by ignoring historical examples, existing laws, or any reasonableness in people that X, Y, and Z will follow inevitably from A. This kind of argument rests on the belief that most people will not want the final, awful Z to occur. The belief, however accurate, does not provide a sufficiently good reason for avoiding A. One of the best-known examples of slippery slope reasoning can be found in the gun-control debate:

- If we allow the government to register handguns, next it will register hunting rifles; then it will prohibit all citizen ownership of guns, thereby creating a police state or a world in which only outlaws have guns.

  (Surely no one wants the final dire consequences predicted in this argument. However, handgun registration does not mean that these consequences will follow. The United States has never been a police state, and its system of free elections guards against such a future. Also, citizens have registered cars, boats, and planes for years without any threat of their confiscation.)

False Dilemma

The *false dilemma* oversimplifies by asserting only two alternatives when there are more than two. The either–or thinking of this kind of argument can be an effective tactic if undetected. If the arguer gives us only two choices and one of those is clearly unacceptable, then the arguer can push us toward the preferred choice. For example:

- The Federal Reserve System must lower interest rates, or we will never pull out of the recession.

  (Clearly, staying in a recession is not much of a choice, but the alternative may not be the only or the best course to achieve a healthy economy. If interest rates go too low, inflation can result. Other options include the government's creating new jobs and patiently letting market forces play themselves out.)

False Analogy

When examining the shape of analogy, we also considered the problems with this type of argument. (See pp. 160–161.) Remember that you challenge a false analogy by noting many differences in the two items being compared or by noting a significant difference that has been ignored.

Post Hoc Fallacy

The term *post hoc,* from the Latin *post hoc, ergo propter hoc* (literally, "after this, therefore because of it"), refers to a common error in arguments about cause. One oversimplifies by confusing a time relationship with cause. Reveal the illogic of *post hoc* arguments by pointing to other possible causes:

- We should throw out the entire city council. Since the members were elected, the city has gone into deficit spending.

  (Assuming that deficit spending in this situation is bad, was it caused by the current city council? Or did the current council inherit debts? Or is the entire region suffering from a recession?)

EXERCISES: Fallacies That Result from Oversimplifying

1. Here is a list of the fallacies we have examined so far. Make up or collect from your reading at least one example of each fallacy.
   a. Overstatement
   b. Stereotyping
   c. Hasty generalization
   d. Forced hypothesis
   e. *Non sequitur*
   f. Slippery slope
   g. False dilemma
   h. False analogy
   i. *Post hoc* fallacy
2. Explain what is illogical about each of the following arguments. Then name the fallacy represented. (Sometimes an argument will fit into more than one category. In that case name all appropriate terms.)
   a. Everybody agrees that we need stronger drunk-driving laws.
   b. The upsurge in crime on Sundays is the result of the reduced rate of church attendance in recent years.
   c. The government must create new jobs. A factory in Illinois has laid off half its workers.
   d. Steve has joined the country club. Golf must be one of his favorite sports.
   e. Blondes have more fun.
   f. You'll enjoy your Tesla. Electric cars never break down.
   g. Gary loves jokes. He would make a great comedian.
   h. The economy is in bad shape because of the Federal Reserve Board. Ever since it expanded the money supply, the stock market has been declining.
   i. Either we improve the city's street lighting, or we will fail to reduce crime.
   j. DNA research today is just like the study of nuclear fission. It seems important, but it's just another bomb that will one day explode on us. When will we learn that government must control research?

k. To prohibit prayer in public schools is to limit religious practice solely to internal belief. The result is that Americans are religiously "free" only in their own minds.

l. Professor Johnson teaches in the political science department. I'll bet she's another socialist.

m. Coming to the aid of any country engaged in civil war is a bad idea. Next we'll be sending American troops, and soon we'll be involved in another Vietnam.

n. We must reject affirmative action in hiring or we'll have to settle for incompetent employees.

Fallacies That Result from Avoiding the Real Issue

There are many ways to divert attention from the issue under debate. Of the six discussed here, the first three try to divert attention by introducing a separate issue or "sliding by" the actual issue. The following three divert by appealing to the audience's emotions or prejudices. In the first three the arguer tries to give the impression of good logic. In the last three the arguer charges forward on emotional manipulation alone.

Begging the Question

To assume that part of your argument is true without supporting it is to *beg the question.* Arguments seeking to pass off as proof statements that must themselves be supported are often introduced with such phrases as "the fact is" (to introduce opinion), "obviously," and "as we can see." For example:

- Clearly, lowering grading standards would be bad for students, so a pass/fail system should not be adopted.

  (Does a pass/fail system lower standards? No evidence has been given. If so, is that necessarily bad for students?)

Red Herring

The *red herring* is a foul-smelling argument indeed. The debater introduces a side issue, some point that is not relevant to the debate:

- The senator is an honest woman; she loves her children and gives to charities.

  (The children and charities are side issues; they do not demonstrate honesty.)

Straw Man

The *straw man* argument attributes to opponents incorrect and usually ridiculous views that they do not hold so that their position can be easily attacked. We can challenge this illogic by demonstrating that the arguer's opponents do not hold those views or by demanding that the arguer provide some evidence that they do:

- Those who favor gun control just want to take all guns away from responsible citizens and put them in the hands of criminals.

  (The position attributed to proponents of gun control is not only inaccurate but actually the opposite of what is sought by gun-control proponents.)

Ad Hominem

One of the most frequent of all appeals to emotion masquerading as argument is the *ad hominem* argument (literally, argument "to the man"). When someone says that "those crazy liberals at the ACLU just want all criminals to go free," or a pro-choice demonstrator screams at those "self-righteous fascists" on the other side, the best retort may be silence, or the calm assertion that such statements do not contribute to meaningful debate.

Common Practice or Bandwagon

To argue that an action should be taken or a position accepted because "everyone is doing it" is illogical. The majority is not always right. Frequently, when someone is defending an action as ethical on the ground that everyone does it, the action isn't ethical and the defender knows it isn't. For example:

- There's nothing wrong with fudging a bit on your income taxes. After all, the super-rich don't pay any taxes, and the government expects everyone to cheat a little.

  (First, not everyone cheats on taxes; many pay to have their taxes done correctly. And if it is wrong, it is wrong regardless of the number who do it.)

Ad Populum

Another technique for arousing an audience's emotions and ignoring the issue is to appeal *ad populum,* "to the people," to the audience's presumed shared values and beliefs. Every Fourth of July, politicians employ this tactic, appealing to God, mother, apple pie, and "traditional family values." Simply reject the argument as illogical.

- Good, law-abiding Americans must be sick of the violent crimes occurring in our once godly society. But we won't tolerate it anymore; put the criminals in jail and throw away the key.

  (This does not contribute to a thoughtful debate on criminal justice issues.)

EXERCISES: Fallacies That Result from Ignoring the Issue

1. Here is a list of fallacies that result from ignoring the issue. Make up or collect from your reading at least one example of each fallacy.
   a. Begging the question
   b. Red herring
   c. Straw man
   d. *Ad hominem*
   e. Common practice or bandwagon
   f. *Ad populum*
2. Explain what is illogical about each of the following arguments. Then name the fallacy represented.
   a. Gold's book doesn't deserve a Pulitzer Prize. She had been married four times.
   b. I wouldn't vote for him; many of his programs are basically socialist.

c. Eight out of ten headache sufferers use Bayer asperin to relieve headache pain. It will work for you, too.
d. We shouldn't listen to Colman McCarthy's argument against liquor ads in college newspapers because he obviously thinks young people are ignorant and need guidance in everything.
e. My roommate Joe does the craziest things; he must be neurotic.
f. Since so many people obviously cheat the welfare system, it should be abolished.
g. She isn't pretty enough to win the contest, and besides she had her nose "fixed" two years ago.
h. Professors should chill out; everybody cheats on exams from time to time.
i. The fact is that bilingual education is a mistake because it encourages students to use only their native language and that gives them an advantage over other students.
j. Don't join those crazy liberals in support of the American Civil Liberties Union. They want all criminals to go free.
k. Real Americans understand that free-trade agreements are evil. Let your representatives know that we want American goods protected.

EXERCISE: Analyzing Arguments

Option 1: The Online Post. Posting online poses one of the most serious challenges to our communication and to our logic today. Yet, much of the information we use comes from online sources. It is vital, therefore, that you think critically about what you post and what you read online. Examine the following online post from a popular social media application. If you find logical fallacies, identify and explain them.

To My Online Friends

1 To my online friends: Over the past few weeks, I've been reading your posts about the benefits of the "environmental" regulations the EPA passed a few years ago. YOU PEOPLE ARE IDIOTS AND YOU DON'T KNOW WHAT YOU'RE TALKING ABOUT! Because of these regulations, I no longer have a job. Due to some over-educated scientists coming in here and finding some leaks from our plant into the river, the power-hungry bureaucrats at the EPA in Washington, D.C., fined us. Because of these fines, I was furloughed. Well, I got word today that this "furlough" is now permanent. I've been laid off. So now, Midville Steel is probably going to reduce production, hundreds of people are going to lose their

jobs, and the town itself is going to crumble. It's all the EPA's fault, and you liberals out there don't even know it!

2 I've tried to be patient with all of your posts, but now I have to explain the truth. Midville Steel has been a wonderful employer. They have refurbished *every* park in town, and they built our new baseball and softball fields. Every year, they sponsor our Fall Festival, and they contributed to our downtown revitalization project. The company and its employees don't deserve the punishment that the EPA is forcing on us. But most importantly, Midville Steel employs 2,700 people, and hundreds of them are going to lose their jobs because of unfair EPA regulations. The EPA just wants to impose strict regulations on American industry to help companies in other countries.

3 So I hope that all of you EPA-loving tree huggers out there are happy. And if you don't agree with my opinions, then just unfriend me now. Because if you don't like my opinion, then you don't like *me*. Good Americans recognize government overreach when they see it, and really, we only have two options here: shut down the EPA or shut down American industry.

Option 2: The Online Conversation. Online conversations can be a wonderful way to keep in touch with friends and family and to share information with people around the world. But as you probably already know, text messages, email, and other forms of digital media are imperfect mediums of communication. Conversations can quickly spiral out of control, and all involved can find themselves using insults and faulty logic to "win" an argument, especially about contentious issues. Examine the following social media conversation. If you find logical fallacies, identify and explain them.

Online Conversation

1 **Kim:** I just saw #algore's movie An Inconvenient Truth for the first time in my composition class. I'm shocked. I really had no idea things were so bad. If we don't do something about pollution now, the air we breathe is going to give us cancer, the seas are going to rise and flood the

coastlines, and our storms are just going to get worse. Maria, have you seen the movie?

2 **Maria:** OMG that movie is so old. I can't believe you think that stuff is true. My cousin works for the power company, and he says that the coal they burn isn't that bad. It's clean burning coal. Please don't turn into a tree hugging #hippie. They smell like #patchouli, get arrested protesting my cousin's plant, and are losers.

3 **Kim:** Wow. Chill out. Just because your cousin works at the plant doesn't mean he's an expert on #climatechange. That's probably why he drives that huge old #gasguzzler. And just because I care about the environment doesn't mean I'm a tree hugging hippie. How about you actually check your facts before getting so judgmental? We need to reduce pollution, or we're all going to get cancer. Don't you care about that?

4 **Maria:** Are you insulting my cousin? I'm unfriending you. #liberalloser!

5 **Kim:** Wtvs. Seeya. #planethater

6 **Maria:** #stinkyhippie

FOR READING AND ANALYSIS

DECLARATION OF SENTIMENTS

ELIZABETH CADY STANTON

Library of Congress, Prints & Photographs Division [LC-USZ62-48965]

Elizabeth Cady Stanton (1815–1902) was one of the most important leaders of the women's rights movement. Educated at the Emma Willard Seminary in Troy, New York, Stanton studied law with her father before her marriage. At the Seneca Falls Convention in 1848 (the first women's rights convention), Stanton gave the opening speech and read her "Declaration of Sentiments." She founded and became president of the National Women's Suffrage Association in 1869.

PREREADING QUESTION As you read, think about the similarities and differences between this document and the Declaration of Independence. What significant differences in wording and content do you find?

1 When, in the course of human events, it becomes necessary for one portion of the family of man to assume among the people of the earth a position different from that which they have hitherto occupied, but one to which the laws of nature and of nature's God entitle them, a decent respect to the opinions of mankind requires that they should declare the causes that impel them to such a course.

2 We hold these truths to be self-evident: that all men and women are created equal; that they are endowed by their Creator with certain inalienable rights; that among these are life, liberty, and the pursuit of happiness; that to secure these rights governments are instituted, deriving their just powers from the consent of the governed. Whenever any form of government becomes destructive of these ends, it is the right of those who suffer from it to refuse allegiance to it, and to insist upon the institution of a new government, laying its foundation on such principles, and organizing its powers in such form, as to them shall seem most likely to effect their safety and happiness. Prudence, indeed, will dictate that governments long established should not be changed for light and transient causes; and accordingly all experience hath shown that mankind are more disposed to suffer, while evils are sufferable, than to right themselves by abolishing the forms to which they were accustomed. But when a long train of abuses and usurpations, pursuing invariably the same object evinces a design to reduce them under absolute despotism, it is their duty to throw off such government, and to provide new guards for their future security. Such has been the patient sufferance of the women under this government, and such is now the necessity which constrains them to demand the equal station to which they are entitled.

3 The history of mankind is a history of repeated injuries and usurpations on the part of man toward woman, having in direct object the establishment of an absolute tyranny over her. To prove this, let facts be submitted to a candid world.

4 He has never permitted her to exercise her inalienable right to the elective franchise.

5 He has compelled her to submit to laws, in the formation of which she had no voice.

6 He has withheld from her rights which are given to the most ignorant and degraded men—both natives and foreigners.

7 Having deprived her of this first right of a citizen, the elective franchise, thereby leaving her without representation in the halls of legislation, he has oppressed her on all sides.

8 He has made her, if married, in the eye of the law, civilly dead.

9 He has taken from her all right in property, even to the wages she earns.

10 He has made her, morally, an irresponsible being, as she can commit many crimes with impunity, provided they be done in the presence of her husband. In the covenant of marriage, she is compelled to promise obedience to her

husband, he becoming, to all intents and purposes, her master—the law giving him power to deprive her of her liberty, and to administer chastisement.

He has so framed the laws of divorce, as to what shall be the proper causes, 11
and in case of separation, to whom the guardianship of the children shall be given, as to be wholly regardless of the happiness of women—the law, in all cases, going upon a false supposition of the supremacy of man, and giving all power into his hands.

After depriving her of all rights as a married woman, if single, and the owner 12
of property, he has taxed her to support a government which recognizes her only when her property can be made profitable to it.

He has monopolized nearly all the profitable employments, and from those 13
she is permitted to follow, she receives but a scanty remuneration. He closes against her all the avenues to wealth and distinction which he considers most honorable to himself. As a teacher of theology, medicine, or law, she is not known.

He has denied her the facilities for obtaining a thorough education, all col- 14
leges being closed against her.

He allows her in Church, as well as State, but a subordinate position, claim- 15
ing Apostolic authority for her exclusion from the ministry, and, with some exceptions, from any public participation in the affairs of the Church.

He has created a false public sentiment by giving to the world a differ- 16
ent code of morals for men and women, by which moral delinquencies which exclude women from society, are not only tolerated, but deemed of little account in man.

He has usurped the prerogative of Jehovah himself, claiming it as his right 17
to assign for her a sphere of action, when that belongs to her conscience and to her God.

He has endeavored, in every way that he could, to destroy her confidence 18
in her own powers, to lessen her self-respect, and to make her willing to lead a dependent and abject life.

Now in view of this entire disfranchisement of one-half the people of this 19
country, their social and religious degradation—in view of the unjust laws above mentioned, and because women do feel themselves aggrieved, oppressed, and fraudulently deprived of their most sacred rights, we insist that they have immediate admission to all the rights and privileges which belong to them as citizens of the United States.

In entering upon the great work before us, we anticipate no small amount 20
of misconception, misrepresentation, and ridicule; but we shall use every instrumentality within our power to effect our object. We shall employ agents, circulate tracts, petition the State and National legislatures, and endeavor to enlist the pulpit and the press in our behalf. We hope this Convention will be followed by a series of Conventions embracing every part of the country.

QUESTIONS FOR READING

1. Summarize the ideas of paragraphs 1 and 2. Be sure to use your own words.
2. What are the first three facts given by Stanton? Why are they presented first?
3. How have women been restricted by law if married or owning property? How have they been restricted in education and work? How have they been restricted psychologically?
4. What, according to Stanton, do women demand? How will they seek their goals?

QUESTIONS FOR REASONING AND ANALYSIS

5. What is Stanton's claim? With what does she charge men?
6. Most—but not all—of Stanton's charges have been redressed, however slowly. Which continue to be legitimate complaints, in whole or in part?

QUESTIONS FOR REFLECTION AND WRITING

7. Do we need a new declaration of sentiments for women? If so, what specific charges would you list? If not, why not?
8. Do we need a declaration of sentiments for other groups—children, underrepresented ethnic groups, the elderly, animals? If so, what specific charges should be listed? Select one group (that concerns you) and prepare a declaration of sentiments for that group. If you do not think any group needs a declaration, explain why.

IN DEFENSE OF POLITICS, NOW MORE THAN EVER BEFORE

PETER WEHNER

A senior fellow at the Ethics and Public Policy Center, Peter Wehner has served in the last three Republican administrations. Wehner is the author, with Michael Gerson, of *City of Man: Religion and Politics in a New Era* (2010). His articles have been published in many newspapers and magazines, and he appears frequently on radio and TV talk shows. This article first appeared in the *New York Times* in 2016.

PREREADING QUESTIONS Do you think it's possible to defend politics? If your answer is "Not at all," do you recognize a fallacy in your thinking?

1 One of John F. Kennedy's favorite books was John Buchan's 1940 memoir, *Pilgrim's Way*. Buchan, who served as a member of Parliament for the combined Scottish universities, wrote, "Public life is regarded as the crown of a career, and to young men it is the worthiest ambition." Politics, he added, "is still the greatest and most honorable adventure."

These days it would be hard to find a handful of people in America who agree with Buchan's sentiment. According to a 2015 Pew Research Center survey, trust in government is at one of the lowest levels in a half-century. Almost three-quarters of Americans believe elected officials put their own interests ahead of the country's interest. Much of the public has utter contempt for the political class. 2

Some of this is justified. Politicians aren't putting forward solutions to the problems facing many Americans. There's also their hypocrisy and corruption, as well as the triviality and rhetorical wasteland that characterizes much of public discourse. But that is hardly the whole of it. There are very good people who are quietly doing their jobs well and with integrity. I would hasten to point out, too, that voters are complicit in this problem, because they choose the people who represent them. The people who plant the flowers have some responsibility for the condition of the garden. 3

Repairing our politics begins with understanding the nature of the enterprise. Alleviating the public's bitter mistrust of politics requires coming to terms with its mundane realities and limits. 4

If the 20th-century American theologian Reinhold Niebuhr were to comment on the current state of affairs, he would warn us against cynicism and idealism, writes Wilfred M. McClay, a historian at the University of Oklahoma. Our disappointments arise from our excessive expectations. "We assume we are better people than we seem to be," according to Professor McClay, "and we assume that our politics should therefore be an endlessly uplifting pursuit, full of joy and inspiration and self-actualization rather than endless wrangling, head-butting, and petty self-interest." 5

Politics is less than perfect because we are less than perfect. We therefore need to approach it with some modesty. Politics is not like mathematics, where clear premises and deductive reasoning can lead to exact answers. We would all do better if we took to heart the words of the political scientist Harry Clor, author of "On Moderation." "There are truths to be discovered," he wrote, but they are "complex and many-sided; the best way to get to them is by engaging contrary ideas in a manner approximating dialogue." 6

In the throes of partisan disagreements, it can be tempting to think of American politics as a Manichaean struggle of good versus evil. As someone who has been involved in his share of intense political debates, and has been a senior White House aide, I'm keenly aware of how easy it is to adopt this parochial mind-set, to feel that one is part of a tribal community. 7

Instead, we need the self-confidence to admit that at best we possess only a partial understanding of the truth, which can be enlarged by refining our views in light of new arguments, new circumstances and new insights. But this requires us to listen to others, to weigh their arguments with care, and maybe even to learn from them. 8

"You used to not be able to talk about politics at a polite dinner party because you would probably have a fight," Lilliana Mason, who teaches political 9 science at the University of Maryland, recently told the *Washington Post,* in a revealing article about how most Trump voters in Virginia, where I live, don't know any Clinton voters and vice versa. "Increasingly, you can talk about politics at a dinner party because most of the people at the dinner party probably agree with you."

10 In creating a world that continually reinforces what we believe, it gets harder to comprehend the attitudes animating others. The more distant our opponents are, the more likely we are to dismiss and dehumanize them. There's no common ground, no acknowledgment that those who hold different views from us might have a legitimate point, an understandable grievance, a reasonable concern. This is when politics becomes blood sport.

11 We are living through an especially partisan time now, but factionalism has always been a problem, under every type of political system. One possible answer comes from Montaigne, who pretty much invented the essay as we know it: "I embark upon discussion and argument with great ease and liberty," he writes in "On the Art of Conversation." "Since opinions do not find in me a ready soil to thrust and spread their roots into, no premise shocks me, no belief hurts me, no matter how opposite to my own they may be."

12 "Whenever we meet opposition, we do not look to see if it is just, but how we can get out of it, rightly or wrongly," he wrote a little later in the same essay. "Instead of welcoming arms we stretch out our claws." Calmly, as always, he proposes a solution: "When I am contradicted it arouses my attention, not my wrath. I move toward the man who contradicts me: he is instructing me. The cause of truth ought to be common to both of us."

13 Our low regard for politics is leading us to undervalue the craft of governing, to lose sight of the idea that there is anything at all that "ought to be common to both of us," never mind truth. We are attracted to political novices and so-called outsiders, which leaves open the possibility of the rise of demagogic figures. Such a person might say, as the Republican nominee for president has: "I'll give you everything. I will give you what you've been looking for for 50 years. I'm the only one."

14 Our democratic belief that anyone can be a political leader paradoxically feeds into the anti-democratic belief that we should look to one person to quickly and easily save us. No one, alone, can fix it, and in our system of government, this authoritarian approach is a prescription for catastrophe. Our confusion about and contempt for politics is also blinding us to the possibility that it can advance the human good. There are those moments in American history when great issues of justice have been at stake, from ending slavery and segregation to opposing Communism and fascism to protecting the physically disabled and the unborn.

15 More often, though, politics is about making institutions work somewhat better, helping people's lives at the margins, giving men and women the room to make the most of their talents and skills. It's about making our schools better and our communities safer. The people who give up on politics and who reflexively denigrate those who are practitioners of it are doing a disservice to our country. Skepticism is fine; caustic cynicism is not.

16 "Political activity is a type of moral activity," the British political theorist Bernard Crick wrote in "In Defense of Politics." "It does not claim to settle every problem or to make every sad heart glad," he added, "but it can help some way

in nearly everything and, where it is strong, it can prevent the vast cruelties and deceits of ideological rule."

Thinking about politics as a moral activity may seem unimaginable during this malicious and degrading political year. But doing so, in a realistic and sober way, is the first step toward repairing America's shattered political culture and restoring politics to the pride of place it deserves in our national life. 17

Wehner, Peter. "In Defense of Politics, Now More than Ever." *New York Times,* 29 Oct. 2016. Used with permission of the author.

QUESTIONS FOR READING

1. What is the widely held view of politicians in America today? What are some legitimate reasons for this view? Who besides the politicians are also responsible for this problem?
2. What is a key reason that our politics often fail to meet expectations?
3. How do we need to change our thinking about who owns the "truth"? What was Montaigne's attitude toward those who contradicted him?
4. What can politics accomplish?
5. What are the dangers in believing that one leader can fix everything?

QUESTIONS FOR REASONING AND ANALYSIS

6. What set of views does the author seek to refute? How does he view political activity? What, then, is his central point, the claim of his argument?
7. What does Wehner accomplish in his three-paragraph opening?
8. How does the author develop and support his claim?

QUESTIONS FOR REFLECTION AND WRITING

9. Has anyone ever suggested to you that participation in public life should be viewed as "the crown of a career"? Why do you think our times have lost awareness of this concept?
10. What elected officials, serving currently or having recently served, do you admire? (Take time to reflect on this question; there are good people deeply involved in public service.) What do you admire about those on your list?
11. Do you agree with Wehner that truth is complex and many political problems lack easy solutions? If so, why? If not, how would you refute him?
12. How close do you come to meeting Montaigne's standard of openness to others with opposing views? What are the challenges to engaging in meaningful debate with others? Should we make the effort? Reflect on these issues that Wehner has raised.

CREDIT

1. Mark Norell, Eugene Gaffney, and Lowell Dingus. *Discovering Dinosaurs: In the American Museum of Natural History.* Alfred A. Knopf, 1995.

CHAPTER 7

Definition Arguments

LEARNING OUTCOMES

After reading Chapter 7, you will be able to:

- Describe definition as part of an argument.
- Explain when defining *is* the argument.
- Describe strategies for developing an extended definition.
- Summarize how to prepare a definition argument.

Drazen Zigic/Shutterstock

READ: What do these demonstrators seem to be protesting?

REASON: What are some events from the last five years that you can think of that might have sparked a protest like this one?

WRITE: From the events you recall, what are some key words from those events that are important to define?

"Define your terms!" someone yells in the middle of a heated debate. Although yelling may not be the best strategy, the advice is sound for writers of argument. People do disagree over the meaning of words. Although we cannot let words mean whatever we want and still communicate, we do recognize that many words have more than one meaning. In addition, some words carry strong connotations, the emotional associations we attach to them. For this reason, realtors never sell *houses;* they always sell *homes.* They want you to believe that the house they are showing will become the home in which you will feel happy and secure.

Many important arguments turn on the definition of key terms. If you can convince others that you have the correct definition, then you are well on your way to winning your argument. The civil rights movement, for example, really turned on a definition of terms. Leaders argued that some laws are unjust, that because it is the law does not necessarily mean it is right. Laws requiring separate schools and separate drinking fountains and seats at the back of the bus for Black people were, in the view of civil rights activists, unjust laws, unjust because they are immoral and as such diminish us as humans. If obeying unjust laws is immoral, then it follows that we should not obey such laws. And when we recognize that obeying such laws hurts us, we have an obligation to act to remove unjust laws. Civil disobedience–illegal behavior to some–becomes, by definition, the best moral behavior.

Here is an example of such logic: In 2018, the late civil rights leader and congressional representative from Georgia John Lewis (D) tweeted "Do not get lost in a sea of despair. Be hopeful, be optimistic. Our struggle is not the struggle of a day, a week, a month, or a year, it is the struggle of a lifetime. Never, ever be afraid to make some noise and get in good trouble, necessary trouble."

Recently, the definition of critical race theory has divided Americans and led to damaging mis/disinformation campaigns. To address this problem, Kimberlé Crenshaw, a legal scholar who helped develop critical race theory, argued in a 2021 CNN interview that "critical race theory is an approach based on the idea that the history of white supremacy still has a very real and lasting impact on our society and institutions today" (May 22, 2021).

DEFINING AS PART OF AN ARGUMENT

There are two occasions for defining words as a part of your argument:

- You need to define any technical terms that may not be familiar to readers–or that readers may not understand as fully as they think they do. David Norman, early in his book on dinosaurs, writes:

  > Nearly everyone knows what some dinosaurs look like, such as *Tyrannosaurus, Triceratops,* and *Stegosaurus.* But they may be much more vague about the lesser known ones, and may have difficulty in distinguishing between dinosaurs and other types of prehistoric creatures. It is not at all unusual to overhear an adult, taking a group of children around a museum display, being reprimanded sharply by the youngsters for failing to realize that a woolly mammoth was not a dinosaur, or–more forgivably–that a giant flying reptile such as *Pteranodon,* which lived at the time of the dinosaurs, was not a dinosaur either.[1]

  So what exactly is a dinosaur? And how do paleontologists decide on the groups they belong to?

Norman answers his questions by explaining the four characteristics that all dinosaurs have. He provides what is often referred to as a *formal definition.* He places the dinosaur in a class, established by four criteria, and then distinguishes this animal from other animals that lived a long time ago. His definition is not open to debate. He is presenting the definition and classification system that paleontologists, the specialists, have established.

- You need to define any word you are using in a special way. If you were to write: "We need to teach discrimination at an early age," you should add: "by *discrimination* I do not mean prejudice. I mean discernment, the ability to see differences." (*Sesame Street* has been teaching children this good kind of discrimination for many years.) The word *discrimination* used to have only a positive connotation; it referred to an important critical thinking skill. Today, however, the word has been linked to prejudice; to discriminate is to act on one's prejudice against some group. Writing today, you need to clarify when you are using the word in its original, positive meaning.

WHEN DEFINING *IS* THE ARGUMENT

Ibram X. Kendi begins each chapter of his book *How to Be an Anti-Racist* with definitions. In chapter 1, he writes, "Racist: One who is supporting a racist policy through their actions or inactions. Antiracist: One who is supporting an antiracist policy through their actions or expressing an antiracist idea" (13). He then goes on to define racism as "a marriage of racist policies and racist ideas that produces and normalizes racial inequity" (17–18). He explains that antiracism "is a powerful collection of antiracist policies that lead to racial equity" (20). Kendi follows by arguing that "Once we have a solid definition of racism and antiracism, we can start to make sense of the racialized world around us, before us" (21). In discussions such as Kendi's the purpose shifts. Instead of using definition as one step in an argument, definition becomes the central purpose of the argument. In his first chapter, Kendi points out how important it is to clearly define terms, and he argues that we cannot really address racism until we have a clear definition of that word and what it means to be antiracist.

STRATEGIES FOR DEVELOPING AN EXTENDED DEFINITION

Arguing for your meaning of a word provides your purpose in writing. But it may not immediately suggest ways to develop such an argument. Let's think in terms of what definitions essentially do: They establish criteria for a class or category and then exclude other items from that category. (A pen is a writing instrument that uses ink.) Do you see your definition as drawing a line or as setting up two entirely separate categories? For example:

When does interrogation become || torture?

One might argue that some strategies for making the person questioned uncomfortable are appropriate to interrogation (reduced sleep or comforts, loud noise). But at some point (stretching on a rack or waterboarding) one crosses a line to torture. To define torture, you have to explain where that line is—and how the actions on one side of the line are different from those on the other side.

What are the characteristics of wisdom as opposed to knowledge?

Do we cross a line from knowledge to become wise? Many would argue that wisdom requires traits or skills that are not found simply by increasing one's knowledge. The categories are separate. Others might argue that, while the categories are distinct, one does need knowledge to also be wise.

Envisioning these two approaches supports the abstract thinking that defining requires. Then what? Use some of the basic strategies of good writing:

- *Descriptive details.* Illustrate with specifics. List the traits of a leader or a courageous person. Explain the behaviors that we find in a wise person, or the behaviors that should be called torture. Describe the situations in which liberty can flourish, or the situations that result from unjust laws. Remember to use negative traits as well as positive ones. That is, show what is *not* covered by the word you are defining.
- *Examples.* Develop your definition with actual or hypothetical examples. Rev. Dr. Martin Luther King, Jr., Lincoln, and Franklin Delano Roosevelt can all be used as examples of leaders. The biblical Solomon is generally acknowledged as a good example of a wise person. You can also create a hypothetical wise or courteous person, or a person whose behavior you would consider virtuous.
- *Comparison and/or contrast.* Clarify and limit your definition by contrasting it with words of similar—but not exactly the same—meanings. For example, what are the differences between knowledge and wisdom or interrogation and torture? The goal of your essay is to establish subtle but important differences so that your readers understand precisely what you want a given word to mean. In an essay at the end of this chapter, Nicholas Haslam provides examples of horrible experiences people have endured to argue for a narrower definition of *trauma.*
- *History of usage or word origin.* The word's original meanings can be instructive. If the word has changed meaning over time, explore these changes as clues to how the word can (or should) be used. If you want readers to reclaim *discrimination* as a positive trait, then show them how that was part of the word's original meaning before the word became tied to prejudice. Word origin—etymology—can also give us insight into a word's meaning. Many words in English come from another language, or they are a combination of two words. The words *liberty* and *freedom* can usefully

be discussed by examining etymology. Most dictionaries provide some word origin information, but the best source is—always—the *Oxford English Dictionary.*

- *Use or function.* A frequent strategy for defining is explaining an item's use or function: A pencil is a writing instrument. A similar approach can give insight into more general or abstract words as well. For example, what do we have—or gain—by emphasizing virtues instead of values? Or, what does a wise person *do* that a non-wise person does not do?
- *Metaphors.* Consider using figurative comparisons. When fresh, not clichés, they add vividness to your writing while offering insight into your understanding of the word.

In an essay titled "Why I Blog," Andrew Sullivan, an early blogger, uses many of these strategies for developing a definition of the term *blog:*

- *Word origin.* "The word *blog* is a conflation of two words: *web* and *log.* . . . In the monosyllabic vernacular of the Internet, *web log* soon became the word *blog."*
- *One-sentence definition.* "It contains in its four letters a concise and accurate self-description: it is a log of thoughts and writing posted publicly on the World Wide Web."
- *Descriptive details.* "This form of instant and global self-publishing . . . allows for no retroactive editing. . . . [I]ts truth [is] inherently transitory."
- *Contrast.* "The wise panic that can paralyze a writer . . . is not available to a blogger. You can't have blogger's block."
- *Metaphors.* "A blog . . . bobs on the surface of the ocean but has its anchorage in waters deeper than those print media is technologically able to exploit."[2]

These snippets from Sullivan's lengthy essay give us a good look at defining strategies in action.

GUIDELINES for Evaluating Definition Arguments

When reading definition arguments, what should you look for? The basics of good argument apply to all arguments: a clear statement of claim, qualified if appropriate, a clear explanation of reasons and evidence, and enough relevant evidence to support the claim. How do we recognize these qualities in a definition argument? Use the following points as guides to evaluating:

- **Why is the word being defined?** Has the writer convinced you of the need to understand the word's meaning or change the way the word is commonly used?
- **How is the word defined?** Has the writer established the definition, clearly distinguishing it from what the writer perceives to be objectionable definitions? It is hard to judge the usefulness of the writer's position if the differences in meaning remain fuzzy. If Ibram Kendi is going to argue for antiracism, he needs to be sure that his readers know the difference between racism and antiracism.
- **What strategies are used to develop the definition?** Can you recognize the different types of evidence presented and see what the writer is doing in the argument? This kind of analysis can aid your evaluation of a definition argument.

- **What are the implications of accepting the author's definition?** Why does Ibram Kendi want readers to be antiracist rather than "not racist" or "race neutral" or even "color-blind"? Kendi's argument is not just about subtle points of language. His argument is also about attitudes that affect public policy issues. Part of any evaluation of a definition argument must include our assessment of the author's definition.
- **Is the definition argument convincing?** Do the reasons and evidence lead you to agree with the author, to accept the idea of the definition and its implications as well?

PREPARING A DEFINITION ARGUMENT

In addition to the guidelines for writing arguments presented in Chapter 4, you can use the following advice specific to writing definition arguments.

Planning

1. *Think:* Why do you want to define your term? To add to our understanding of a complex term? To challenge the use of the word by others? If you don't have a good reason to write, find a different word to examine.
2. *Think:* How are you defining the word? What are the elements/parts/steps in your definition? Some brainstorming notes are probably helpful to keep your definition concrete and focused.
3. *Think:* What strategies will you use to develop and support your definition? Consider using several of these possible strategies for development:
   - *Word origin or history of usage*
   - *Descriptive details*
   - *Comparison and/or contrast*
   - *Examples*
   - *Function or use*
   - *Metaphors*

Drafting

1. Begin with an opening paragraph or two that introduces your subject in an interesting way. Possibilities include the occasion that has led to your writing–explain, for instance, a misunderstanding about your term's meaning that you want to correct.
2. Do *not* begin by quoting or paraphrasing a dictionary definition of the term. "According to Webster . . ." is a tired approach lacking reader interest. If the dictionary definition were sufficient, you would have no reason to write an entire essay to define the term.
3. State your claim–your definition of the term–early in your essay, if you can do so in a sentence or two. If you do not state a brief claim, then establish your purpose in writing early in your essay. (You may find that there are too many parts to your definition to combine into one or two sentences.)

4. Use several specific strategies for developing your definition. Select strategies from the list above and organize your approach around these strategies. That is, you can develop one paragraph of descriptive details, another of examples, another of contrast with words that are not exactly the same in meaning.
5. Consider specifically refuting the error in word use that led to your decision to write your own definition. If you are motivated to write based on what you have read, then make a rebuttal part of your definition argument.
6. Consider discussing the implications of your definition. You can give weight and value to your argument by explaining the larger significance of your definition.

A CHECKLIST FOR REVISION

- ☐ Do I have a good understanding of my purpose? Have I made this clear to readers?
- ☐ Have I clearly stated my definition? Or clearly established the various parts of the definition that I discuss in separate paragraphs?
- ☐ Have I organized my argument, building the parts of my definition into a logical, coherent structure?
- ☐ Have I used specifics to clarify and support my definition?
- ☐ Have I used the basic checklist for revision in Chapter 4 (see p. 106)?

STUDENT ESSAY

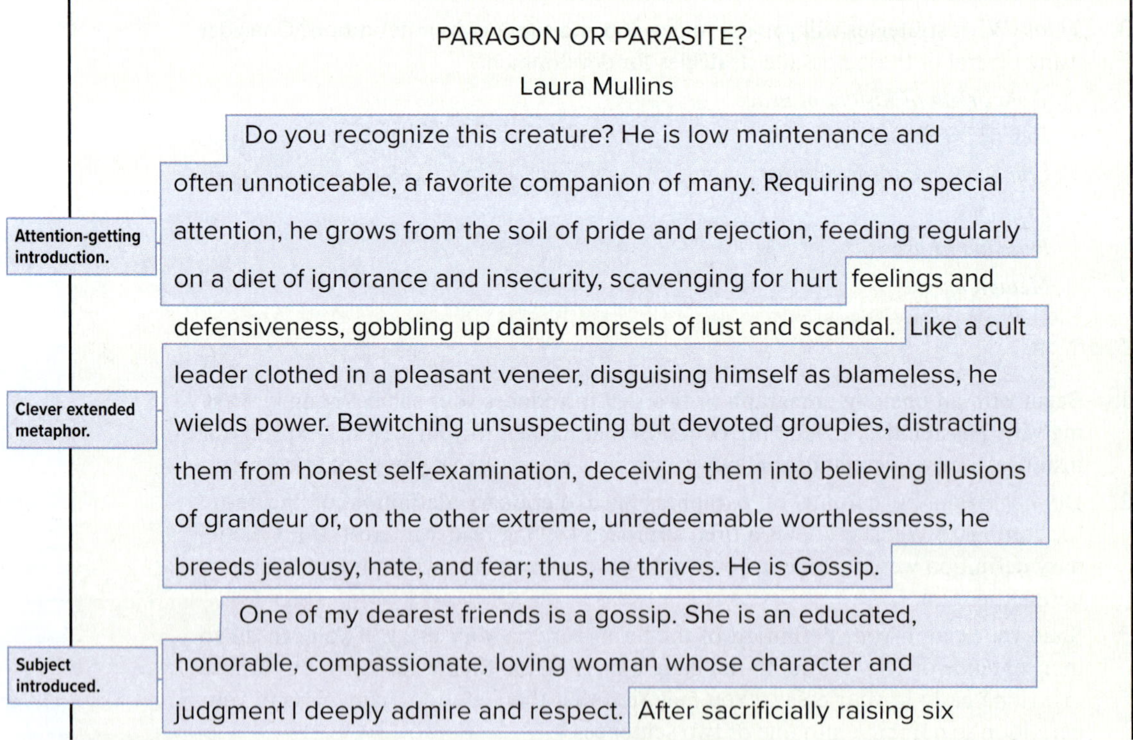
PARAGON OR PARASITE?

Laura Mullins

Do you recognize this creature? He is low maintenance and often unnoticeable, a favorite companion of many. Requiring no special attention, he grows from the soil of pride and rejection, feeding regularly on a diet of ignorance and insecurity, scavenging for hurt feelings and defensiveness, gobbling up dainty morsels of lust and scandal. Like a cult leader clothed in a pleasant veneer, disguising himself as blameless, he wields power. Bewitching unsuspecting but devoted groupies, distracting them from honest self-examination, deceiving them into believing illusions of grandeur or, on the other extreme, unredeemable worthlessness, he breeds jealousy, hate, and fear; thus, he thrives. He is Gossip.

Attention-getting introduction.

Clever extended metaphor.

One of my dearest friends is a gossip. She is an educated, honorable, compassionate, loving woman whose character and judgment I deeply admire and respect. After sacrificially raising six

Subject introduced.

children, she went on to study medicine and become a doctor who graciously volunteers her expertise. How, you may be wondering, could a gossip deserve such praise? Then you do not understand the word. My friend is my daughter's godmother; she is my gossip, or *godsib,* meaning sister-in-god. Derived from Middle English words *god,* meaning spiritual, and *sip/sib/syp,* meaning kinsman, this term was used to refer to a familiar acquaintance, close family friend, or intimate relation, according to the *Oxford English Dictionary.* As a male, he would have joined in fellowship and celebration with the father of the newly born; if a female, she would have been a trusted friend, a birth-attendant or midwife to the mother of the baby. The term grew to include references to the type of easy, unrestrained conversation shared by these folks.

Etymology of gossip and early meanings.

As is often the case with words, the term's meaning has certainly evolved, maybe eroded from its original idea. Is it harmless, idle chat, innocuous sharing of others' personal news, or back-biting, rumor-spreading, and manipulation? Is it a beneficial activity worthy of pursuit, or a deplorable danger to be avoided?

Current meanings.

In her article "Evolution, Alienation, and Gossip" (for the Social Issues Research Centre in Oxford, England), Kate Fox writes that "gossip is not a trivial pastime; it is essential to human social, psychological, and even physical well-being." Many echo her view that gossip is a worthy activity, claiming that engaging in gossip produces endorphins, reduces stress, and aids in building intimate relationships. Gossip, seen at worst as a harmless outlet, is encouraged in the workplace. Since much of its content is not inherently critical or malicious, it is viewed as a positive activity. However, this view does nothing to encourage those speaking or listening to evaluate or examine motive or purpose; instead, it seems to reflect the "anything goes" thinking so prevalent today.

Good use of sources to develop definition.

Conversely, writer and high school English and geography teacher Lennox V. Farrell of Toronto, Canada, in his essay titled "Gossip: An

Urban Form of Sorcery," presents gossip as a kind of "witchcraft . . . based on using unsubstantiated accusations by those who make them, and on uncritically accepting these by those enticed into listening." Farrell uses gossip in its more widely understood definition, encompassing the breaking of confidences, inappropriate sharing of indiscretions, destructive tale-bearing, and malicious slander.

Good use of metaphor to depict gossip as negative.

What, then, is gossip? We no longer use the term to refer to our children's godparents. Its current definition usually comes with derogatory implications. Imagine a backyard garden: You see a variety of greenery, recognizing at a glance that you are looking at different kinds of plants. Taking a closer look, you will find the gossip vine; inconspicuously blending in, it doesn't appear threatening, but ultimately it destroys. If left in the garden it will choke and then suck out life from its host. Zoom in on the garden scene and follow the creeping vine up trees and along a fence where two neighbors visit. You can overhear one woman saying to the other, "I know I should be the last to tell you, but your husband is being unfaithful to me." (Caption from a cartoon by Alan De la Nougerede.)

Conclusion states view that gossip is to be avoided—the writer's thesis.

The current popular movement to legitimize gossip seems an excuse to condone the human tendency to puff-up oneself. Compared in legal terms, gossip is to conversation as hearsay is to eyewitness testimony; it's not credible. Various religious doctrines abhor the idea and practice of gossip. An old Turkish proverb says, "He who gossips to you will gossip of you." From the Babylonian Talmud, which calls gossip the three-pronged tongue, destroying the one talking, the one listening, and the one being spoken of, to the Upanishads, to the Bible, we can conclude that no good fruit is born from gossip. Let's tend our gardens and check our motives when we have the urge to gossip. Surely we can find more noble pursuits than the self-aggrandizement we have come to know as gossip.

Courtesy of Laura Mullins.

FOR ANALYSIS AND DEBATE

NORTON OPENING STATEMENT AT HEARING ON D.C. STATEHOOD BILL

MAR 22, 2021 | PRESS RELEASE

Marvin Joseph/ The Washington Post/Getty Images

Born in Washington, D.C., Eleanor Holmes Norton graduated from Yale Law School in 1964 and was deeply involved with the civil rights movement. She then clerked for Federal District Court Judge A. Leon Higginbotham, Jr., and successfully argued a First Amendment case before the Supreme Court in 1969: *Brandenburg v. Ohio.* In 1982, she joined the Georgetown University Law Center, and she was elected to the House of Representatives as the nonvoting delegate for Washington, D.C., in 1990. Holmes Norton has been arguing for D.C. statehood ever since.

PREREADING QUESTIONS: Can you think of reasons why D.C. shouldn't become the fifty-first state? If so, are those reasons good enough to continue disenfranchising the 712,000 citizens of D.C.?

WASHINGTON, D.C.–Congresswoman Eleanor Holmes Norton (D-DC) released her opening statement, as prepared for delivery, from today's Committee on Oversight and Reform hearing on her District of Columbia statehood bill. 1

Opening Statement of Congresswoman Eleanor Holmes Norton House Committee on Oversight and Reform Hearing on "H.R. 51: Making D.C. the 51st State" March 22, 2021 2

Chairwoman Maloney, along with the residents of the District of Columbia, I greatly appreciate and thank you for this hearing today. This has been a historic year for D.C. statehood. I introduced H.R. 51 with a record 202 original cosponsors. Today, the bill has 215 cosponsors, which virtually guarantees passage in the House, even with cosponsors alone. The Senate version, S. 51, was introduced with a record 38 original cosponsors and now has 41 cosponsors. We are particularly grateful to our Senate sponsor, Senator Tom Carper, who gathered the largest number of original cosponsors ever. When the House passed the D.C. statehood bill last Congress, it was the first time in history a chamber of Congress had passed the bill. With Democrats controlling the House, the Senate and the White House, we have never been closer to statehood. 3

Under H.R. 51, the State of Washington, D.C. would consist of 66 of the 68 square miles of the present-day federal district. The reduced federal district, over which Congress would retain plenary authority, would be two square miles and consist of the Washington that Members of Congress and visitors associate with the nation's capital, including the U.S. Capitol complex, the White House, the Supreme Court, the principal federal monuments and the National Mall. It would be called the Capital. 4

H.R. 51 has both the facts and the Constitution on its side. The Constitution does not establish any prerequisites for new states, but Congress generally has 5 considered a prospective state's population and resources, support for statehood and commitment to democracy.

6 D.C.'s population of 712,000 is larger than that of two states and the State of Washington, D.C. would be one of seven states with a population under one million. D.C. pays more federal taxes per capita than any state and pays more federal taxes than 21 states. D.C.'s budget is larger than those of 12 states. Eighty-six percent of D.C. residents voted for statehood in 2016. In fact, D.C. residents have been petitioning for voting rights in Congress and local autonomy for 220 years.

7 The Constitution's Admissions Clause gives Congress the authority to admit new states, and all 37 new states have been admitted by an act of Congress. The Constitution's District Clause, which gives Congress plenary authority over the federal district, sets a maximum, not a minimum, size of the federal district. Congress previously has reduced the size of the federal district by 30 percent. The 23rd Amendment to the Constitution does not establish a minimum geographic or population size of the federal district. Conservative legal scholar and practitioner Viet Dinh, who served as an Assistant Attorney General in the George W. Bush Administration, has opined that the State of Washington, D.C. can be admitted by an act of Congress.

8 D.C. residents have fought in every American war, including the war that led to the creation of the nation, the Revolutionary War. The servicemembers from our nation's capital have helped get voting rights for people throughout the world, but continue to come home without those same rights or even the same rights of those with whom they served.

9 My own family has lived through almost 200 years of change in D.C. since my great-grandfather Richard Holmes, as a slave, walked away from a plantation in Virginia and made his way to D.C. Today, it is my great honor to serve in the city where my family has lived without equal representation for almost two centuries.

10 Congress can no longer allow D.C. residents to be sidelined in the democratic process, watching as Congress votes on matters that affect the nation with no say of their own, or watching as Congress votes to overturn the laws of the duly elected D.C. Council with no say of their own. Full democracy requires much more. D.C. residents deserve full voting representation in the Senate and the House and complete control over their local affairs. They deserve statehood.

11 Congress has two choices. It can continue to exercise undemocratic, autocratic authority over the American citizens who reside in our nation's capital, treating them, in the words of Frederick Douglass, as "aliens, not citizens, but subjects." Or it can live up to this nation's promise and ideals, end taxation without representation and pass H.R. 51.

12 Madam Chairwoman, thank you again for your leadership on D.C. equality.

Norton, Eleanor Holmes. "Opening Statement from Congresswoman Eleanor Holmes Norton for the Hearing on 'H.R. 51: Making D.C. the 51st State,'" 22 Mar. 2021.

QUESTIONS FOR READING

1. Why is Holmes Norton arguing that Washington, D.C. be defined as a state?
2. How do you think the tax-paying citizens of D.C., most of whom are Black, feel about not being able to vote for congressional representation?
3. What traits make up a U.S. state?
4. Explain the differences between an existing U.S. state and D.C. Explain the similarities.

QUESTIONS FOR REASONING AND ANALYSIS

5. How does Holmes Norton establish the exigency (*kairos*) of her argument?
6. How does Holmes Norton develop her argument, and what examples does she use?
7. According to Holmes Norton, what will be included in the State of Washington, D.C.? What will be excluded? Why do you think it's important to point this out?

QUESTIONS FOR REFLECTION AND WRITING

8. Holmes Norton asserts that "Congress generally has considered a prospective state's population and resources [as]. . . support for statehood and commitment to democracy." Why do you think the author establishes these attributes as criteria for statehood? Do you think these are accurate and realistic attributes? Why or why not?
9. Are there other attributes you would add to the criteria for statehood? If so, explain them.
10. Do you think Holmes Norton argues effectively for D.C. statehood? Why or why not?
11. Why do you think it's important for D.C. to be defined (or not defined) as a U.S. state?

CROSSING THE AEGEAN IS "TRAUMATIC." YOUR BAD HAIR DAY ISN'T.

NICHOLAS HASLAM

Professor and head of the School of Psychological Sciences at the University of Melbourne, Nick Haslam received his PhD in clinical and social psychology from the University of Pennsylvania and taught in the United States for several years before returning to Australia. Haslam has written in his academic areas of interest, but also frequently contributes to newspapers in several countries. His essay on trauma is one of those op-ed articles.

PREREADING QUESTIONS How do you use the word *trauma*? Based on his expertise and the title above, do you think Haslam is likely to agree with your use of the word?

1 These days, "trauma" seems epidemic.

2 A group of Columbia Law School students felt the "traumatic effects" of the Michael Brown grand jury decision so keenly, they argued, that they needed their finals postponed. A handful of Emory University students were "traumatized" by finding "Trump 2016" chalked on campus sidewalks. A young professor chronicled his traumatizing graduate training, which included discrimination and job anxiety. And in an interview, a "trauma-sensitive yoga" instructor talked through her "hair trauma": "I grew up with really curly, frizzy hair in Miami, Florida. When you're 13, a bad hair day is overwhelming," she said. "Even though I would never compare that to someone who was abused, it's an experience that shaped my identity and, at the time, was intolerable."

3 These aren't isolated incidents. Trauma is being used to describe an increasingly wide array of events. By today's standards, it can be caused by a microaggression, reading something offensive without a trigger warning or even watching upsetting news unfold on television. As one blogger wrote, "Trauma now seems to be pretty much anything that bothers anyone, in any way, ever."

4 This is not a mere terminological fad. It reflects a steady expansion of the word's meaning by psychiatrists and the culture at large. And its promiscuous use has worrying implications. When we describe misfortune, sadness or even pain as trauma, we redefine our experience. Using the word "trauma" turns every event into a catastrophe, leaving us helpless, broken and unable to move on.

5 Like democracy, alarm clocks and the Olympics, we owe "trauma" to the ancient Greeks. For them, trauma was severe physical injury; the word shares its linguistic root with terms for breaking apart and bruising. Of course, doctors still use "trauma" to describe physical harm. But more and more, we understand the term in a second way—as an emotional injury rather than a physical wound.

6 This shift started in the late 19th century, when neurologists such as Jean-Martin Charcot and Sigmund Freud posited that some neuroses were caused by deeply distressing experiences. The idea was revolutionary—a dawning recognition that shattered minds could be explained psychologically as well as biologically.

7 Ideas about psychological trauma continued to take shape in the 20th century, but the physical sense still dominated. In 1952, the first edition of *The Diagnostic and Statistical Manual of Mental Disorders,* which catalogues psychological illnesses, mentioned the term only in relation to brain injuries caused by force or electric shock.

8 By 1980, that had changed. The DSM's third edition recognized post-traumatic stress disorder for the first time, though the definition of a "traumatic event" was relatively focused—it had to be "outside the range of usual human experience" and severe enough to "evoke significant symptoms of distress in almost everyone." The DSM-III's authors argued that common experiences such as chronic illness, marital conflict and bereavement did not meet the definition.

Later editions of psychiatry's "bible"—really more like a field guide to the species of human misery—loosened the definition further, expanding it to incorporate indirect experiences such as violent assaults of family members and friends, along with "developmentally inappropriate sexual experiences" and occasions when people witness serious injury or death. One study found that 19 events qualified as traumatic in the DSM-IV; just 14 would have qualified in the revised edition of the DSM-III. 9

This broadening of the definition was justified in part by the finding that people who were indirectly exposed to stressful events could develop PTSD symptoms. Even so, researchers became concerned that elastic concepts of trauma "risk trivializing the suffering of those exposed to catastrophic life events." As psychologist Stephen Joseph explained in a 2011 interview, "The DSM over-medicalizes human experience. Things which are relatively common, relatively normal, are turned into psychiatric disorders." 10

An Army National Guard medic argued in *Scientific American* that "clinicians aren't separating the few who really have PTSD from those who are experiencing things like depression or anxiety or social and reintegration problems, or who are just taking some time getting over it." This, he worried, would lead to people being "pulled into a treatment and disability regime that will mire them in a self-fulfilling vision of a brain rewired, a psyche permanently haunted." 11

That hasn't stopped definition expansion. The federal Substance Abuse and Mental Health Services Administration, for example, now says trauma can involve ongoing circumstances rather than a distinct event—no serious threat to life or limb necessary. Trauma, by the agency's definition, doesn't even have to be outside normal experience. No wonder clinicians increasingly identify such common experiences as uncomplicated childbirth, marital infidelity, wisdom-tooth extraction and hearing offensive jokes as possible causes of PTSD. 12

This thinking has seeped into our culture as well. The word "trauma" itself has exploded in popularity in recent decades. A search of the 500 billion words that make up the Google Books database reveals that "trauma" appeared at four times the rate in 2005 as in 1965. According to Google Trends, interest in the word has grown by a third in the past five years. 13

How to explain this change? For one thing, the broadening of "trauma" coincides with other psychological shifts, such as a sense that our life outcomes are out of our control. According to one study, young people increasingly believe that their destinies are determined by luck, fate or powerful people besides themselves. People who hold these beliefs are more likely to feel helpless and unable to manage stress. Trauma is a way to explain life's problems as someone else's fault. 14

A second explanation can be found in my work on "concept creep." In recent decades, several psychological concepts have undergone semantic inflation. The definitions of abuse, addiction, bullying, mental disorder and prejudice have all expanded to include a broad range of phenomena. This reflects a growing sensitivity to harm in Western societies. By broadening the reach of these concepts—recognizing emotional manipulation as abuse, the spreading of rumors as bullying and increasingly mild conditions as psychiatric problems—we identify 15 more people as victims of harm. We express a well-intentioned unwillingness to accept things that were previously tolerated, but we also risk over-sensitivity: defining relatively innocuous phenomena as serious problems that require outside intervention. The expansion of the concept of trauma runs the same risk.

16 All of this is problematic. The way we interpret an experience affects how we respond to it. Interpreting adversity as trauma makes it seem calamitous and likely to have lasting effects. When an affliction is seen as traumatic, it becomes something overwhelming—something that breaks us, that is likely to produce post-traumatic symptoms and that requires professional intervention. Research shows that people who tend to interpret negative events as catastrophic and long-lasting are more susceptible to post-traumatic reactions. Perceiving challenging life experiences as traumas may therefore increase our vulnerability to them.

17 Our choice of language matters. A famous study by cognitive psychologist Elizabeth Loftus illustrates why. Loftus showed people films of traffic accidents and asked them to judge the speed of the cars involved, using subtly varying instructions. Different study participants were asked how fast the cars were going when they "smashed," "collided," "bumped," "hit" or "contacted" each other. Despite watching the very same collisions, people judged the cars to be traveling 28 percent faster when they were described as "smashing" rather than "contacting."

18 To define all adversities as traumas is akin to seeing all collisions as smashes. People collide with misfortune all the time: Sometimes it smashes them, but often they merely make contact.

19 Another fine invention of the ancient Greeks was stoicism. Contrary to popular opinion, the stoics did not think we should simply endure or brush off adversity. Rather, they believed that we should confront suffering with composure and rational judgment. We should all cultivate stoic wisdom to judge the difference between traumas that can break us apart and normal adversities that we can overcome.

Haslam, Nick. "Crossing the Aegean is 'Traumatic.' Your Bad Hair Day Isn't." *Washington Post*, 14 Aug. 2016. Used with permission of the author.

QUESTIONS FOR READING

1. What was the original meaning of the word *trauma?* What second meaning developed over time? When was trauma officially accepted as a psychological disorder?
2. How has the term expanded subsequent to the fourth edition of the DSM?
3. What kinds of human experience are now described as traumatic by the Substance Abuse and Mental Health Services Administration?
4. What causes does Haslam offer to account for the expanding meaning of trauma–and other concepts–in our culture?
5. Why does the author find these changing views distressing? What can happen when we see adversities as traumas?

QUESTIONS FOR REASONING AND ANALYSIS

6. What point does the author want to make about the changing definition of trauma? That is, what is Haslam's claim?
7. What specific strategies for defining are used by Haslam?
8. What does the author seek to accomplish in paragraph 15? How does this discussion of language advance his argument?
9. What is clever about Haslam's discussion of the Greek philosophy of Stoicism in the final paragraph?

QUESTIONS FOR REFLECTION AND WRITING

10. Which defining strategies are most effectively used by Haslam? Defend your selection.
11. Do you agree with Haslam that not only has the meaning of trauma been greatly expanded but also that this is a problem? If you disagree, how would you refute his argument? (*Note:* There is good evidence that our choice of language matters.)
12. Does your experience confirm Haslam's analysis that we tend today, as a culture, to label many kinds of unpleasant experiences as cause for trauma? If so, what examples can you add to this discussion?

SUGGESTIONS FOR DISCUSSION AND WRITING

1. In the student essay, Laura Mullins defines the term *gossip.* Select one of the following words to define and prepare your own extended definition argument, using at least three of the strategies for defining described in this chapter. For each word in the list, you see a companion word in parentheses. Use that companion word as a word that you contrast with the word you are defining. (For example, how does gossip differ from conversation?) The idea of an extended definition argument is to make fine distinctions among words similar in meaning.

   courtesy (manners)
   wisdom (knowledge)
   patriotism (chauvinism)
   hero (star)
   community (subdivision)
   freedom (liberty)

2. Select a word you believe is currently misused. It can be misused because it has taken on a negative (or positive) connotation that it did not originally have, or because it has changed meaning and lost something in the process. A few suggestions include *awful, awesome, fabulous, exceptional* (in education), *propaganda.*

3. Define a term that is currently used to label people with particular traits or values. Possibilities include *nerd, yuppie, freak, jock, redneck, bimbo, wimp.* Reflect, before selecting this topic, on why you want to explain the meaning of the word you have chosen. One purpose might be to explain the word to someone from another culture. Another might be to defend people who are labeled negatively by a term; that is, you want to show why the term should not have a negative connotation.

CREDITS

1. David Norman. *Dinosaur!* John Wiley & Sons, 1991.
2. Andrew Sullivan. "Why I Blog." *The Atlantic,* Nov. 2008.
3. Ibram X. Kendi. *How to Be an Antiracist.* One World, 2019.

Evaluation Arguments

LEARNING OUTCOMES

After reading Chapter 8, you will be able to:

- Describe characteristics of evaluation arguments.
- Identify types of evaluation arguments.
- Explain how to prepare an evaluation argument.
- Describe how to evaluate an argument through the rebuttal or refutation essay.

gorodenkoff/Getty Images

READ: What is the situation? Where are we?

REASON: Look at the faces; what do you infer to be the attitude of the participants?

WRITE: What is the photo's message?

"I really love Spencer's Camaro; it's so much more fun to go out with him than to go with Emery in his Volvo wagon," you confide to a friend. "On the other hand, Spencer always wants to see the latest horror movie–and 'wow' are they horrid! I'd much rather watch one of our teams play–whatever the season; sports events are so much more fun than horror movies!"

"Well, at least you and Spencer agree not to listen to Billie Eilish music. Her life is so messed up; why would anyone admire her music?" your friend responds.

CHARACTERISTICS OF EVALUATION ARGUMENTS

Evaluations. How easy they are to make. We do it all the time. So, surely an evaluation argument should be easy to prepare. Not so fast. Remember at the beginning of the discussion of argument in Chapter 3, we observed that we do not argue about personal preferences because there is no basis for building an argument. If you don't like horror movies, then don't go to them–even with Spencer! However, once you assert that sporting events are more fun than horror movies, you have shifted from personal preference to the world of argument, the world in which others will judge the effectiveness of your logic and evidence. On what basis can you argue that one activity is more fun than the other? And, always more fun? And, more fun for everyone? You probably need to qualify this claim and then you will need to establish the criteria by which you have made your evaluation. Although you might find it easier to defend your preference for a car for dates, you, at least in theory, can build a convincing argument for a qualified claim in support of sporting events. Your friend, though, will have great difficulty justifying her evaluation of Eilish based on Eilish's lifestyle. An evaluation of her music needs to be defended based on criteria about music–unless she wants to argue that any music made by people with unconventional lifestyles will be bad music, a tough claim to defend.

In a column for *Time* magazine, Charles Krauthammer argues that Tiger Woods is the greatest golfer ever to play the game. He writes:

> How do we know? You could try Method 1: Compare him directly with the former greatest golfer, Jack Nicklaus. . . . But that is not the right way to compare. You cannot compare greatness directly across the ages. There are so many intervening variables: changes in technology, training, terrain, equipment, often rules and customs.
>
> How then do we determine who is greatest? Method 2: The Gap. Situate each among his contemporaries. Who towers? . . . Nicklaus was great, but he ran with peers: Palmer, Player, Watson. Tiger has none.[1]

Krauthammer continues with statistics to demonstrate that there is no one playing now with Tiger who comes close in number of tournaments won, number of majors won, and number of strokes better in these events than the next player. He then applies the Gap Method to Babe Ruth in baseball, Wayne Gretzky in hockey, and Bobby Fischer in chess to demonstrate that it works to reveal true greatness in competition among the world's best.

Krauthammer clearly explains his Gap Method, his basic criterion for judging greatness. Then he provides the data to support his conclusions about who are or were the greatest in various fields. His is a convincing evaluation argument.

These examples suggest some key points about evaluation arguments:

- **Evaluation arguments are arguments, not statements of personal preferences.** As such, they need a precise, qualified claim and reasons and evidence for support, just like any argument.
- **Evaluation arguments are about "good" and "bad," "best" and "worst."** These arguments are not about what we should or should not do or why a situation is the way it is. The debate is not whether one should select a partner based on the kind of car they drive or why horror movies have so much appeal for many viewers. The argument is that sports events are great entertainment, or better entertainment than horror movies.
- **Evaluation arguments need to be developed based on a clear statement of the criteria for evaluating.** Eilish won Grammys for her music–why? By what standards of excellence do we judge a singer? A voice with great musicality and nuance? The selection of songs with meaningful lyrics? The ability to engage listeners–the way the singer can "sell" a song? The number of recordings sold and awards won? All of these criteria? Something else?
- **Evaluation arguments, to be successful, may need to defend the criteria, not just to list them and show that the subject of the argument meets those criteria.** Suppose you want to argue that sporting events are great entertainment because it is exciting to cheer with others, you get to see thrilling action, and it is good, clean fun. Are sports always "good, clean fun"? Some of the fighting in hockey matches is quite vicious. Some football players get away with dirty hits. Krauthammer argues that his Gap Method provides the better criterion for judging greatness and then shows why it is the better method. Do not underestimate the challenge of writing an effective evaluation argument.

TYPES OF EVALUATION ARGUMENTS

The examples we have examined above are about people or items or experiences in our lives. Tiger Woods is the greatest golfer ever, based on the Gap Method strategy. Sports events are more fun to attend than horror movies. We can (and do!) evaluate just about everything we know or do or buy. This is one type of evaluation argument. In this category we would place the review–of a book, movie, concert, or something similar.

A second type of evaluation is a response to another person's argument. We are not explaining why the car or college, sitcom or singer, is good or great or the best. Instead, we are responding to one specific argument we have read (or listened to) that we think is flawed–flawed in many ways or in one significant way that essentially destroys the argument. This type of evaluation argument is called a rebuttal or refutation argument.

Sometimes our response to what we consider a really bad argument is to go beyond the rebuttal and write a counterargument. Rather than writing about the limitations and flaws in our friend's evaluation of Eilish as a singer not to be listened to, we decide to write our own argument evaluating Eilish's strengths as a contemporary singer. This counterargument is best described as an evaluation argument, not a refutation. Similarly, we can disagree with someone's argument defending restrictions placed by colleges on student file sharing. But if we decide to write a counterargument defending students' rights to share music files, we have moved from rebuttal to our own position paper, our own argument based on values. Counterarguments are best seen as belonging to one of the other genres of argument discussed in this section of the text.

GUIDELINES for Analyzing an Evaluation Argument

The basics of good argument apply to all arguments: a clear statement of claim, qualified as appropriate, a clear explanation of reasons and evidence, and enough relevant evidence to support the claim. When reading evaluation arguments, use the following points as additional guides:

- **What is the writer's claim?** Is it clear, qualified if necessary, and focused on the task of evaluating?
- **Has the writer considered audience as a basis for both claim and criteria?** Your college may be a good choice for you, given your criteria for choosing, but is it a good choice for others? Qualifications need to be based on audience: College A is a great school for young people in need of B and with X amount of funds. Or: *The Da Vinci Code* is an entertaining read for those with some understanding of art history and knowledge of the Roman Catholic Church.
- **What criteria are presented as the basis for evaluation?** Are they clearly stated? Do they seem reasonable for the topic of evaluation? Are they defended if necessary?
- **What evidence and/or reasons are presented to show that the item under evaluation meets the criteria?** Specifics are important in any evaluation argument.
- **What are the implications of the claim?** If we accept the Gap Method for determining greatness, does that mean that we can never compare stars from different generations? If we agree with the rebuttal argument, does that mean that there are no good arguments for the claim in the essay being refuted?
- **Is the argument convincing?** Does the evidence lead you to agree with the author? Do you want to buy that car, listen to that music, read that book, see that film as a result of reading the argument?

PREPARING AN EVALUATION ARGUMENT

In addition to the guidelines for writing arguments presented in Chapter 4, you can use the following advice specific to writing evaluation arguments.

Planning

1. **Think:** Why do you want to write this evaluation? Does it matter, or are you just sharing your personal preferences? Select a topic that requires you to think deeply about how we judge that item (college, book, album, etc.).
2. **Think about audience:** Try to imagine writing your evaluation for your classmates, not just your instructor. Instead of thinking about an assignment to be graded, think about why we turn to reviews, for example. What do readers want to learn? They want to know if they should see that film. Your job is to help them make that decision.
3. **Think:** What are my criteria for evaluation? And, how will I measure my topic against them to show that my evaluation is justified? You really must know how you

would determine a great singer or a great tennis player before you write, or you risk writing only about personal preferences.

4. **Establish a general plan:** If you are writing a review, be sure to study the work carefully. Can you write a complete and accurate summary? (It is easier to review an album than a live concert because you can replay the album to get all the details straight.) You will need to balance summary, analysis, and evaluation in a review–and be sure that you do not mostly write summary or reveal the ending of a novel or film! If you are evaluating a college or a car, think about how to order your criteria. Do you want to list all criteria first and then show how your item connects to them, point by point? Or, do you want the criteria to unfold as you make specific points about your item?

   To analyze a film, consider the plot, the characters, the actors who play the lead characters, any special effects used, and the author's (and director's) "take" on the story. If the "idea" of the film is insignificant, then it is hard to argue that it is a great film. Analysis of style in a book needs to be connected to that book's intended audience. Style and presentation will vary depending on the knowledge and sophistication of the intended reader. If, for example, you have difficulty understanding a book aimed at a general audience, then it is fair to say that the author has not successfully reached that audience. But if you are reviewing a book intended for specialists, then your difficulties in reading are not relevant to a fair evaluation of that book. You can point out, though, that the book is tough going for a nonspecialist–just as you could point out that a movie sequel is hard to follow for those who did not see the original film.

Drafting

1. Begin with an opening paragraph or two that engages your reader while introducing your subject and purpose in writing. Is there a specific occasion that has led to your writing? And what, exactly, are you evaluating?
2. Either introduce your criteria next and then show how your item for evaluation meets the criteria, point by point, through the rest of the essay; or, decide on an order for introducing your criteria and use that order as your structure. Put the most important criterion either first or last. It can be effective to put the most controversial point last.
3. If you are writing a review, then the basic criteria are already established. You will need some combination of summary, analysis, and evaluation. Begin with an attention-getter that includes a broad statement of the work's subject or subject category: This is a *biography* of Benjamin Franklin; this is an *action film.* An evaluation in general terms can complete the opening paragraph. For example:

   > Kathleen Hall Jamieson's *Cyber-War: How Russian Hackers and Trolls Helped Elect a President* is destined to become a classic in journalism, communication studies, and political science.

4. The rest of the review will then combine summary details, analysis of presentation, and a final assessment of the work in the concluding paragraph. From the same review, after learning specifics of content, we read:

   > The target audience for this book includes students and professionals in journalism and political science. Additionally, anyone interested in social media and the 2020 elections will love this book.

5. Consider discussing the implications of your evaluation. Why is this important? Obviously for a book or film or art show, for example, we want to know if this is a "must read" or "must see." For other evaluation arguments, let us know why we should care about your subject and your perspective. Charles Krauthammer does not just argue that Tiger Woods is the greatest golfer ever; he also argues that his Gap Method is the best strategy for evaluation. That's why he shows that it works not just to put Woods ahead of Nicklaus but also to put other greats in their exalted place in other sports.

A CHECKLIST FOR REVISION

- ☐ Do I have a good understanding of my purpose? Have I made my evaluation purpose clear to readers?
- ☐ Have I clearly stated my claim?
- ☐ Have I clearly stated my criteria for evaluation—or selected the appropriate elements of content, style, presentation, and theme for a review?
- ☐ Have I organized my argument into a coherent structure by some pattern that readers can recognize and follow?
- ☐ Have I provided good evidence and logic to support my evaluation?
- ☐ Have I used the basic checklist for revision in Chapter 4? (See p. 106.)

STUDENT REVIEW

WINCHESTER'S ALCHEMY: TWO MEN AND A BOOK

Ian Habel

One can hardly imagine a tale promising less excitement for a general audience than that of the making of the *Oxford English Dictionary* (*OED*). The sensationalism of murder and insanity would have to labor intensely against the burden of lexicography in crafting a genuine page-turner on the subject. Much to my surprise, Simon Winchester, in writing *The Professor and the Madman: A Tale of Murder, Insanity, and the Making of the Oxford English Dictionary,* has succeeded in producing so compelling a story that I was forced to devour it completely in a single afternoon, an unprecedented personal feat.

The Professor and the Madman is the story of the lives of two apparently very different men and the work that brought them together.

Winchester begins by recounting the circumstances that led to the incarceration of Dr. W. C. Minor, a well-born, well-educated, and quite insane American ex-Army surgeon. Minor, in a fit of delusion, had murdered a man whom he believed to have crept into his Lambeth hotel room to torment him in his sleep. The doctor is tried and whisked off to the Asylum for the Criminally Insane, Broadmoor.

The author then introduces readers to the other two main characters: the *OED* itself and its editor James Murray, a lowborn, self-educated Scottish philologist. The shift in narrative focus is used to dramatic effect. The natural assumption on the part of the reader that these two seemingly unrelated plots must eventually meet urges us to read on in anticipation of that connection. As each chapter switches focus from one man to the other, it is introduced by a citation from the *OED,* reminding us that the story is ultimately about the dictionary. The citations also serve to foreshadow and provide a theme for the chapter. For example, the *OED* definition of *murder* heads the first chapter, relating to the details of Minor's crime.

Winchester acquaints us with the shortcomings of seventeenth- and eighteenth-century attempts at compiling a comprehensive dictionary of the English language. He takes us inside the meetings of the Philological Society, whose members proposed the compilation of the dictionary to end all dictionaries. The *OED* was to include examples of usage illustrating every shade of meaning for every word in the English language. Such a mammoth feat would require enlisting thousands of volunteer readers to comb the corpus of English literature in search of illustrative quotations to be submitted on myriad slips of paper. These slips of paper on each word would in turn be studied by a small army of editors preparing the definitions.

It is not surprising that our Dr. Minor, comfortably tucked away at Broadmoor, possessing both a large library and seemingly infinite free time, should become one of those volunteer readers. After all, we are still rightfully assuming some connection of the book's two plot lines. Yet what sets Dr. Minor apart from his fellow volunteers (aside from the details of his incarceration) is the remarkable efficiency with which he approached his task. Not content merely to fill out slips of paper for submission, Minor methodically indexed every possibly useful mention of any word appearing in his personal library. He then asked to be kept informed of the progress of the work, submitting quotations that would be immediately useful to editors. In this way he managed to "escape" his cell and plunge himself into the work of contemporaries, to become a part of a major event of his time.

Minor's work proved invaluable to the *OED*'s staff of editors, led by James Murray. With the two plot lines now intertwined, readers face such questions as "Will they find out that Minor is insane?" "Will Minor and Murray ever meet?" and "How long will they take to complete the dictionary?" The author builds suspense regarding a meeting of Minor and Murray by providing a false account of their first encounter, as reported by the American press, only to shatter us with the fact that this romantic version did not happen. I'll let Winchester give you the answers to these questions, while working his magic on you, drawing you into this fascinating tale of the making of the world's most famous dictionary.

Courtesy of Ian Habel.

EVALUATING AN ARGUMENT: THE REBUTTAL OR REFUTATION ESSAY

When your primary purpose in writing is to challenge someone's argument rather than to present your own argument, you are writing a *rebuttal* or *refutation.* A good refutation demonstrates, in an orderly and logical way, the weaknesses of logic or evidence in the argument. Study the following guidelines to prepare a good refutation essay and then study the sample refutation that follows. It has been annotated to show you how the author has structured his rebuttal.

GUIDELINES for Preparing a Refutation or Rebuttal Argument

1. **Read accurately.** Make certain that you have understood your opponent's argument. If you assume views not expressed by the writer and accuse the writer of holding those illogical views, you are guilty of the straw man fallacy, of attributing and then attacking a position that the person does not hold. Look up terms and references you do not know and examine the logic and evidence thoroughly.
2. **Pinpoint the weaknesses in the original argument.** Analyze the argument to determine, specifically, what flaws the argument contains. If the argument contains logical fallacies, make a list of the ones you plan to discredit. Examine the evidence presented. Is it insufficient, unreliable, or irrelevant? Decide, before drafting your refutation, exactly what elements of the argument you intend to challenge.
3. **Write your claim.** After analyzing the argument and deciding on the weaknesses to be challenged, write a claim that establishes that your disagreement is with the writer's logic, assumptions, or evidence, or a combination of these.
4. **Draft your essay, using the following three-part organization:**
   a. *The opponent's argument.* Usually you should not assume that your reader has read or remembered the argument you are refuting. Thus at the beginning of your essay, you need to state, accurately and fairly, the main points of the argument to be refuted.
   b. *Your claim.* Next make clear the nature of your disagreement with the argument you are rebutting.
   c. *Your refutation.* The specifics of your rebuttal will depend on the nature of your disagreement. If you are challenging the writer's evidence, then you must present the evidence that will show why the evidence used is unreliable or misleading. If you are challenging assumptions, then you must explain why they do not hold up. If your claim is that the piece is filled with logical fallacies, then you must present and explain each fallacy.

GLOBALIZATION SHOULDN'T BE A DIRTY WORD

DOUGLAS HOLTZ-EAKIN

Recognized as a scholar of applied economic policy, Douglas Holtz-Eakin served, between 2001 and 2008, in a number of government positions, including director of the Congressional Budget Office. He is currently president of the American Action Forum. His essay on globalization appeared in 2016.

Tom Williams/ CQ-Roll Call, Inc/ Getty Images

PREREADING QUESTIONS: Given the article's title and opening paragraph, what purpose do you expect the author to have? What does the term *globalization* mean to you?

1 "Globalization"—broadly defined as market-driven, cross-national flows of goods, services and investments—has become a dirty word. It is derided by U.S. presidential candidates, feared and rejected by the public, and evidently headed to the dustbin of policy ideals. This, despite its contributions in the past two

Attention-getting opening.

decades to dramatically reducing poverty in developing countries and improving productivity and standards of living in the developed world. What can get globalization back on track?

1st point of refutation: Globalization has been mischaracterized.

2 First, tell the truth about the successes and failures of globalization. The North American Free Trade Agreement was a success, both economically and strategically. In purely economic terms, it benefited Canada, Mexico and (modestly) the United States. It also solidified a democratic neighbor on the southern border. It was a success and should not be mischaracterized for cheap political gain.

3 The entry of China and India into the world trading system was also an enormously successful global anti-poverty program. But it is also true that its effect on global wage scales was far greater than anticipated, and Western policy responses were inadequate to deal with the fallout. Globalization is neither a resounding success nor an unmitigated disaster; the truth lies in between.

2nd point: Isolationism will hurt the U.S. economically.

4 Second, stop further deterioration. The toughest moment for globalization—the entrance of China and India—is in the rear-view mirror and won't be repeated. The greatest danger of *this* moment is not that additional steps on the path to globalization—the TPP or the Transatlantic Trade and Investment Partnership—will not go forward. Rather, the greatest danger is self-inflicted wounds—actively protectionist tariffs; retaliation and trade wars; and resulting global economic downdrafts. Preventing these will be the biggest test of near-term political leadership.

3rd point: Clearly state the steps needed to make globalization a success.

5 Third, improve the macro environment in which any future globalization discussion takes place. Everyday Americans recognize the post-World War II gains that accrued from aggregate growth north of 3 percent. They will similarly be acutely aware of the slow pace of economic advance that comes with our current 2 percent economic growth. Any notion that this "new normal" is somehow acceptable should be immediately discarded. Structural reforms to entitlements, the tax code, the regulatory state and education systems are necessary complements to trade agreements and globalization. Trade economics is *not* a zero-sum game, but the faster the economic growth, the more the general public will believe this.

4th point: Be honest about the effects of globalization.

6 Fourth, we must address the aftereffects. Shifts in the patterns of trade are accompanied by shifts in the pattern of employment, which may require more robust transition assistance in the form of income support or training. But this is just as true of shifts in domestic trade as it is international trade. Broadly supporting workers through job transitions will ease the fears of globalization.

5th point: Stress the relationship between trade agreements and U.S. strategic goals.

7 Finally, we must broaden the discussion. Any discussion of future trade agreements should openly feature their strategic importance. Just as the General Agreement on Tariffs and Trade knitted together the Western alliance and NAFTA strengthened North American democracy, agreements such as the TPP are just as important in terms of the U.S.-China strategic rivalry as they are for dollars and cents.

Holtz-Eakin, Douglas. "'Globalization' Shouldn't Be a Dirty Word." *Washington Post*, 20 Oct. 2016. Used with permission of the author.

QUESTIONS FOR READING

1. What does *globalization* mean?
2. What successes has this economic activity produced in the last two decades? What problem has it caused?
3. What can be done to stop further problems from globalization in the United States?
4. What will improve the macroeconomic environment? What do shifts in trade policies produce?
5. In what larger context should global trade agreements be discussed?

QUESTIONS FOR REASONING AND ANALYSIS

6. What is the author's claim? (Don't repeat the title; it is clever but not precise.)
7. Economic issues can be complex; how does Holtz-Eakin help readers follow his analysis?
8. What does the author mean when he writes that trade economics is "*not* a zero-sum game"?

QUESTIONS FOR REFLECTION AND WRITING

9. The author connects negative attitudes toward globalization with a lackluster economy. If we saw an increase in gross domestic production to 3 percent, would that help Americans see the advantages of globalization? Could you now explain to friends with this negative attitude why 3 percent growth should make them change their views?
10. Have you objected to globalization as producing nothing but trouble? If so, has Holtz-Eakin changed your thinking? If so, why? If not, why not?

FOR ANALYSIS AND DEBATE

ONE WAY TO FIX PLUMMETING BIRTHRATES: STOP BASHING AMERICA

JOSH HAMMER

Josh Hammer graduated from Duke University and holds a law degree from the University of Chicago Law School. He is the opinion editor for *Newsweek* and has published in numerous outlets, such as the *Los Angeles Times, National Review, The Times of Israel,* and *National Affairs.* He often speaks on college campuses, and he hosts *Newsweek*'s *The Josh Hammer Show* podcast. This article was published by *Newsweek* on May 6, 2021.

PREREADING QUESTIONS: Can you think of reasons that birthrates in the United States might be dropping other than people expressing their criticism of America's history of racism and current economic inequities? Consider the guidelines on refutation on page 199. How might you rebut the claims Hammer makes in this article?

1 The National Center for Health Statistics, a Centers for Disease Control and Prevention subagency, reported this week that America's fertility rate dropped for the sixth consecutive year. Total births declined by 4 percent in 2020, down to 1,637.5 children per 1,000 women. The statistical replacement rate for the U.S. population, by contrast, is roughly 2,100 births per 1,000 women. Overall, the 3,605,201 births last year in the U.S. represented the lowest number since the Jimmy Carter presidency.

2 It is perhaps too early to tell whether yet another annual incremental birthrate decline is anomalous, due to the COVID-19 pandemic, or flows naturally from existing demographic trendlines. Sociologists and demographers will pore over the data, but it is difficult to ignore the broader trend and place the blame squarely—or even predominantly—on the virus and the myriad draconian lifestyle restrictions the virus engendered. On the contrary, many had speculated before this week's report that the extended COVID lockdowns might lead to a one-time annual *increase* in the birthrate as couples sheltered in place together for months on end.

3 This bleak demographic reality is inconsonant with Americans' stated childrearing preferences. According to polling data revealed by American Compass in February, 45 to 50 percent of Americans who do not report that their families are still growing say they have fewer children than they would ideally desire, whereas 0 to 10 percent of Americans without growing families say they have more children than they ideally would have had. Put simply, Americans want more babies, but for various, complicated reasons, they are not having them. A drastic incongruence between stated preferences and lived reality is the definitional case for good public policy, and there has been a resurgence of interest of late on the Realignment Right to rediscover the tools of economic statecraft as it pertains to family policy.

4 Sen. Mitt Romney (R-UT) recently released his Family Security Act plan to provide direct monthly cash benefits for young and school-aged children. Sens. Marco Rubio (R-FL) and Mike Lee (R-UT) came out in support of a further increase in the Child Tax Credit for young children.

5 Sen. Josh Hawley (R-MO) unveiled a new "Parent Tax Credit" that the American Principles Project's Jon Schweppe has labeled the "most pro-family, pro-marriage, pro-life, pro-adoption, pro-work, pro-everything-that-conservatives-love economic proposal offered . . . in recent memory," and American Compass itself devised a rival "Family Income Supplemental Credit" policy. There are other competing ideas, too, such as University of Dallas professor Gladden Pappin's 2019 proposal for a generous direct support system called "FamilyPay."

6 This economic policy fermentation is deeply healthy. Elected Republicans in Washington, D.C., ought to eventually coalesce around one proposal, but for now, the intellectual vitality of the present policy discussion is intrinsically

beneficial. There are also innumerable avenues for *noneconomic* policy—the realms of sociology, technology, religion and so forth—to help lay the foundations for a possible new baby boom. Here is one exceedingly straightforward idea to add into the mix: Stop incessantly bashing America and telling young parents and children to hate America.

As a matter of public discourse and increasingly as a matter of education policy, impressionable young would-be parents and their even more impressionable children are indoctrinated in rank America-hatred. The most sordid forms of this indoctrination come packaged in woke-speak such as "critical race theory" and "anti-racism," which dovetail with the *New York Times'* insidious "1619 Project" in making an affirmative case for America's purported "systemic racism." This is no longer a fringe theory relegated to the cesspool that is the modern American academy; in the aftermath of Minneapolis police officer Derek Chauvin's recent guilty conviction, no less a figure than President Joe Biden himself seized the moment to decry the "systemic racism that is a stain on our nation's soul." Indeed, in the year 2021, condemning the United States' incorrigible "systemic racism" is perhaps the Democratic Party's foremost call to arms. 7

Holding aside the fact that this is a noxious lie—America has not been "systemically racist," with the possible exception of the anti-Asian racism of affirmative action education policies, since Jim Crow—there are tangible effects of this rhetoric for the body politic. Put simply, inculcating America-hatred logically ought to disincentivize young, healthy couples from procreating. After all, who would rationally want to bring forth new life into a country that is irredeemably "systemically racist" to its core? 8

Demographers often associate falling birthrates with falling confidence in a nation's future. The U.S. in the year 2021 is no exception. Fortunately, some of our plummeting confidence is baseless—and self-inflicted. The most straightforward way to help accelerate birthrates again could be as simple as ceasing the collective self-flagellation of leftist America-hatred. 9

Josh Hammer is Newsweek *opinion editor, a syndicated columnist and a research fellow with the Edmund Burke Foundation. Twitter: @josh_hammer.* 10

The views expressed in this article are the writer's own. 11

COPYRIGHT 2021 CREATORS.COM 12

Hammer, Josh. "One Way to Fix Plummeting Birthrates: Stop Bashing America." *Newsweek*, 6 May 2021. Used with permission.

QUESTIONS FOR READING

1. Who, in Hammer's view, is partially to blame for America's declining birthrate?
2. According to Hammer, what ideas are partially to blame for fewer births?
3. What does the *New York Times*' 1619 Project assert, and why do you think Hammer calls it "insidious"? What does Hammer call the "modern American academy," i.e., American higher education? Do you think that this is a fair assessment of colleges and universities in America? Why or why not?

QUESTIONS FOR REASONING AND ANALYSIS

4. Hammer writes about education policy, systemic racism, and affirmative action; how do these topics connect to give Hammer his general subject?
5. What, then, is the author's claim? Do you see a general theme that unites the many issues Hammer includes?
6. How does the author develop and support his claim? He includes statistics, and he highlights policies from politicians he supports. But do you notice any logical fallacies? If so, how would you challenge them?
7. Examine Hammer's style and tone. How would you characterize his tone? Is his approach likely to be effective for his primary audience? Do you think he is appealing to a friendly audience or a hostile audience? What about fence-sitters–those who haven't made up their minds on this subject?

QUESTIONS FOR REFLECTION AND WRITING

8. Beyond using statistical data that shows American birthrates dropping, does Hammer provide evidence that *directly* supports his claim, such as interview, focus group, or survey data? How do you think that the evidence he does use affects his argument? Are his positions inferences or judgments (review Chapter 3 to answer this question)?
9. Has Hammer supported his general claim and specific generalizations to your satisfaction? Why or why not?
10. Hammer argues that "America-hatred logically ought to disincentivize young, healthy couples from procreating." Is teaching about America's history of racist policies and its current racial injustice America-hating? If so, why? If not, why not? And what do you think Hammer would say about older couples with disabilities having or adopting children?
11. Given his educational background and law degree, what do you think about the state of Hammer's argument in this article?

SUGGESTIONS FOR DISCUSSION AND WRITING

1. Think about sports stars you know. Write an argument defending one player as the best in a particular sport. Think about whether you want to use Krauthammer's "Method 1" or "Method 2" or your own method for your criteria. (Remember that you can qualify your argument; you could write about the best college football player this year, for example.)
2. If you like music, think about what you might evaluate from this field. Who is the best rock band? Hip-hop artist? Country-western singer? And so forth. Be sure to make your criteria for evaluation clear.
3. You have had many instructors–and much instruction–in the last twelve-plus years. Is there one teacher who is/was the best? If so, why? Is there a teaching method that stands out in your memory for the excellence of its approach? Find an evaluation topic from your educational experiences.
4. Select an editorial, op-ed column, letter to the editor, or one of the essays in this text as an argument with which you disagree. Prepare a refutation of the work's logic or evidence or both. Follow the guidelines for writing a refutation or rebuttal in this chapter.
5. What is your favorite book? Movie? Television show? Why is it your favorite? Does it warrant an argument that it is really good, maybe even the best, in some way or in some category (sitcoms, for example)? Write a review, following the guidelines for this type of evaluation argument given in this chapter.

CREDIT

1. Charles Krauthammer, "The Greatness Gap," *Time*, 1 July 2002.

CHAPTER 9

The Position Paper: Claims of Values

LEARNING OUTCOMES

After reading Chapter 9, you will be able to:

- Describe the characteristics of the position paper.
- Explain how to prepare a position paper.

Congress of the United States
begun and held at the City of New York, on
Wednesday the Fourth of March, one thousand seven hundred and eighty nine

THE

RESOLVED

ARTICLES

Article the first.

Article the second.

Article the third.

Article the fourth.

Article the fifth.

Article the sixth.

Article the seventh.

Article the eighth.

Article the ninth.

Article the tenth.

Article the eleventh.

Article the twelfth.

ATTEST,

Frederick Augustus Muhlenberg, Speaker of the House of Representatives.

John Adams, Vice President of the United States, and President of the Senate

EXPLANATORY NOTES: *On September 25, 1789, the Congress proposed twelve articles of amendment to the Constitution of the United States. Except for the first two, they were ratified by the required number of States by December 15, 1791, and these became the first ten amendments. They have since been known as the Bill of Rights. The original is not legible in several places and this copy has been retouched for legibility.*

The articles in brief are: ARTICLE I—Regulating the number of Representatives according to the population of the State. ARTICLE II—Senators and Representatives cannot increase their salaries during their present term of office. ARTICLE III—Freedom of religion; Freedom of speech; Freedom of the press; Freedom of assembly; Right to petition the government for redress of grievances. ARTICLE IV—Right to keep and bear arms, since a well regulated militia is necessary for the security of a free State. ARTICLE V—No soldier to be quartered in any house in time of peace unless with the consent of the owner. ARTICLE VI—Freedom from unreasonable search and seizure. ARTICLE VII—Provisions concerning prosecution, trial and punishment; Just compensation for property taken for public use. ARTICLE VIII—Right to speedy and public trial, and provisions for its procedure. ARTICLE IX—Right of trial by jury. ARTICLE X—Excessive bail or fines and cruel punishment prohibited. ARTICLE XI—All rights to be retained by the people except those regulated in the Constitution. ARTICLE XII—The powers reserved to the States or to the people.

SuperStock/Getty Images

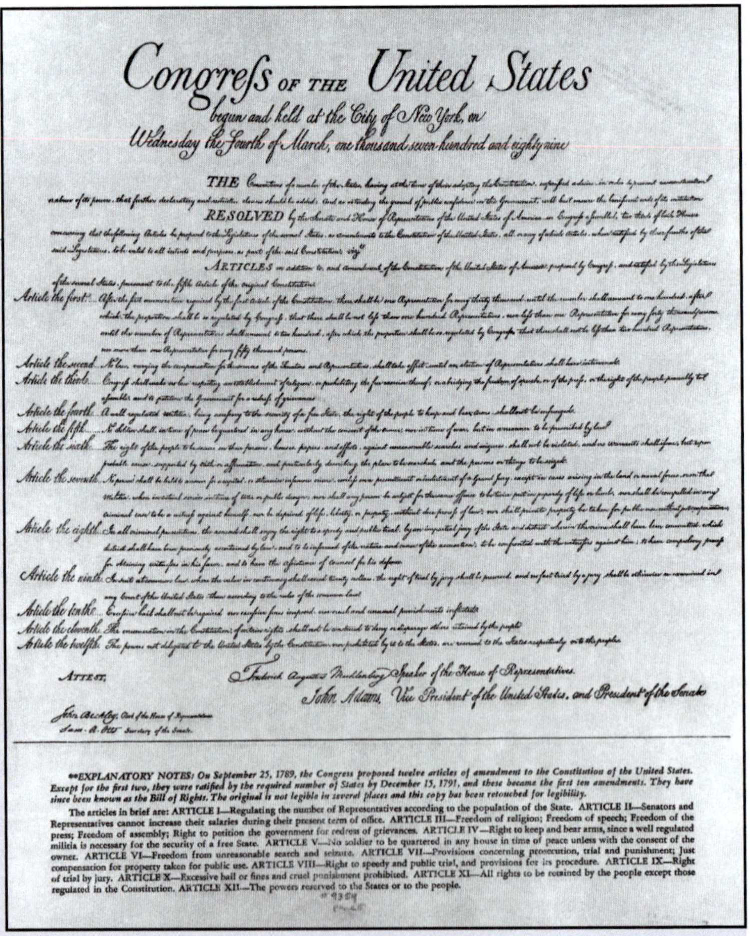

READ: The Bill of Rights, pictured here, was written to amend a very important document in U.S. history. What document does the Bill of Rights amend? Why was the Bill of Rights written?

REASON: What does the Bill of Rights establish for U.S. citizens? Why do you think the Bill of Rights is included as the picture representing this chapter?

WRITE: The original fourteen copies of the Bill of Rights were handwritten for distribution. What are the advantages of distributing a document like the Bill of Rights through today's mass media technology? What are the disadvantages?

As we established in Chapter 4, all arguments involve values. Evaluation arguments require judgment—thoughtful judgment, one hopes, based on criteria—but judgment nonetheless. If you believe that no one should spend more than $25,000 for a car, then you will not appreciate the qualities that attract some people to Mercedes. When one argues that government tax rates should go up as income goes up, it is because one believes that it is *right* for government to redistribute income to some degree: Rich people pay more in taxes, poor people get more in services. When countries ban the importing of ivory, they do so because they believe it is *wrong* to destroy the magnificent elephant just so humans can use their ivory tusks for decorative items. (Observe that the word *magnificent* expresses a value.)

Some arguments, though, are less about judging what is good or best, or less about how to solve specific problems, than they are about stating a position on an issue. An argument that defends a general position (segregated schools are wrong) may imply action that should result (schools should be integrated), but the focus of the argument is first to state and defend the position. It is helpful to view these arguments, based heavily on values and a logical sequencing of ideas with less emphasis on specifics, as a separate type—genre—of argument. These claims of values are often called position papers.

CHARACTERISTICS OF THE POSITION PAPER

The position paper, or claim of values, may be the most difficult of arguments simply because it is often perceived to be the easiest. Let's think about this kind of argument:

- A claim based on values and argued more with logic than specifics is usually more general or abstract or philosophical than other types of argument. Greenpeace objects to commercial fishing that uses large nets that ensnare dolphins along with commercial fish such as tuna. Why? Because we ought not to destroy such beautiful and highly developed animals. Because we ought not to destroy more than we need, to waste part of nature because we are careless or in a hurry. For Greenpeace, the issue is about values—though it may be about money for the commercial fishermen.
- The position paper makes a claim about what is right or wrong, good or bad, for us as individuals or as a society. Topics can range from capital punishment to pornography to reducing the amount of trash we toss.
- Although a claim based on values is often developed in large part by a logical sequencing of reasons, support of principles also depends on relevant facts. Remember the long list of specific abuses listed in the Declaration of Independence (see pp. 154–156). If Greenpeace can show that commercial fisheries can be successful using a different kind of net or staying away from areas heavily populated by dolphins, it can probably get more support for its general principles.
- A successful position paper requires more than a forceful statement of personal beliefs. If we can reason logically from principles widely shared by our audience, we are more likely to be successful. If we are going to challenge their beliefs or values, then we need to consider the conciliatory approach as a strategy for getting them to at least listen to our argument.

GUIDELINES for Analyzing a Claim of Value

When reading position papers, what should you look for? Again, the basics of good argument apply here as well as with definition arguments. To analyze claims of values specifically, use these questions as guides:

- **What is the writer's claim?** Is it clear?
- **Is the claim qualified if necessary?** Some claims of value are broad philosophical assertions ("Capital punishment is immoral and bad public policy"). Others are qualified ("Capital punishment is acceptable only in crimes of treason").
- **What facts are presented?** Are they credible? Are they relevant to the claim's support?
- **What reasons are given in support of the claim?** What assumptions are necessary to tie reasons to claim? Make a list of reasons and assumptions and analyze the writer's logic. Do you find any fallacies?
- **What are the implications of the claim?** For example, if you argue for the legalization of all recreational drugs, you eliminate all "drug problems" by definition. But what new problems may be created by this approach? Consider more car accidents and reduced productivity for openers.
- **Is the argument convincing?** Does the evidence provide strong support for the claim? Are you prepared to agree with the writer, in whole or in part?

PREPARING A POSITION PAPER

In addition to the guidelines for writing arguments presented in Chapter 4, you can use the following advice specific to writing position papers or claims of value.

Planning

1. **Think:** What claim, exactly, do you want to support? Should you qualify your first attempt at a claim statement?
2. **Think:** What grounds (evidence) do you have to support your claim? You may want to make a list of the reasons and facts you would consider using to defend your claim.
3. **Think:** Study your list of possible grounds and identify the assumptions (warrants) and backing for your grounds.
4. **Think:** Now make a list of the grounds most often used by those holding views that oppose your claim. This second list will help you prepare counterarguments to possible rebuttals, but first it will help you test your commitment to your position. If you find the opposition's arguments persuasive and cannot think how you would rebut them, you may need to rethink your position. Ideally, your two lists will confirm your views but also increase your respect for opposing views.

5. **Consider:** How can I use a conciliatory approach? With an emotion-laden or highly controversial issue, the conciliatory approach can be an effective strategy. Conciliatory arguments include
   - the use of nonthreatening language,
   - the fair expression of opposing views, and
   - a statement of the common ground shared by opposing sides.

You may want to use a conciliatory approach when (1) you know your views will be unpopular with at least some members of your audience; (2) the issue is highly emotional and has sides that are "entrenched" so that you are seeking some accommodations rather than dramatic changes of position; (3) you need to interact with members of your audience and want to keep a respectful relationship going. The sample student essay on gun control (at the end of this chapter) illustrates a conciliatory approach.

Drafting

1. Begin with an opening paragraph or two that introduces your topic in an interesting way. Possibilities include a statement of the issue's seriousness or reasons why the issue is currently being debated–or why we should go back to reexamine it. Some writers are spurred by a recent event that receives media coverage; recounting such an event can produce an effective opening. You can also briefly summarize points of the opposition that you will challenge in supporting your claim. Many counterarguments are position papers.
2. Decide where to place your claim statement. Your best choices are either early in your essay or at the end of your essay, after you have made your case. The second approach can be an effective alternative to the more common pattern of stating one's claim early.
3. Organize evidence in an effective way. One plan is to move from the least important to the most important reasons, followed by rebuttals to potential counterarguments. Another possibility is to organize by the arguments of the opposition, explaining why each of their reasons fails to hold up. A third approach is to organize logically. That is, if some reasons build on the accepting of other reasons, you want to begin with the necessary underpinnings and then move forward from those.
4. Maintain an appropriate level of seriousness for an argument of principle. Of course, word choice must be appropriate to a serious discussion, but in addition be sure to present reasons that are also appropriately serious. For example, if you are defending the claim that video games should not be subject to content labeling because such censorship is inconsistent with First Amendment rights, do not trivialize your argument by including the point that young people are tired of adults controlling their lives. (This is another issue for another paper.)
5. Provide a logical defense of or specifics in support of each reason. You have not finished your task by simply asserting several reasons for your claim. You also need to present facts or examples for or a logical explanation of each reason.

For example, you have not defended your views on capital punishment by asserting that it is right or just to take the life of a murderer. Why is it right or just? Executing the murderer will not bring the victim back to life. Do two wrongs make a right? These are some of the thoughts your skeptical reader may have unless you explain and justify your reasoning. *Remember:* Quoting another writer's opinion on your topic does not provide proof for your reasons. It merely shows that someone else agrees with you.

A CHECKLIST FOR REVISION

- ☐ Do I have a clear statement of my claim? Is it qualified, if appropriate?
- ☐ Have I organized my argument, building the parts of my support into a clear and logical structure that readers can follow?
- ☐ Have I avoided logical fallacies?
- ☐ Have I found relevant facts and examples to support and develop my reasons?
- ☐ Have I paid attention to appropriate word choice, including using a conciliatory approach if that is a wise strategy?
- ☐ Have I used the basic checklist for revision in Chapter 4 (see p. 106)?

STUDENT ESSAY

EXAMINING THE ISSUE OF GUN CONTROL

Chris Brown

Introduction connects ambivalence in American character to conflict over gun control.

The United States has a long history of compromise. Issues such as representation in government have been resolved because of compromise, forming some of the bases of American life. Americans, however, like to feel that they are uncompromising, never willing to surrender an argument. This attitude has led to a number of issues in modern America that are unresolved, including the issue of gun control. Bickering over the issue has slowed progress toward legislation that will solve the serious problem of gun violence in America, while keeping recreational use of firearms available to responsible people. To resolve the conflict over guns, the arguments of both sides must be examined, with an eye to finding the flaws in both. Then perhaps we can reach some meaningful compromises.

Gun advocates have used many arguments for the continued availability of firearms to the public. The strongest of these defenses points to the many legitimate uses for guns. One use is protection against violence, a concern of some people in today's society. There are many problems with the use of guns for protection, however, and these problems make the continued use of firearms for protection dangerous. One such problem is that gun owners are not always able to use guns responsibly. When placed in a situation in which personal injury or loss is imminent, people often do not think intelligently. Adrenaline surges through the body, and fear takes over much of the thinking process. This causes gun owners to use their weapons, firing at whatever threatens them. Injuries and deaths of innocent people, including family members of the gun owner, result. Removing guns from the house may be the best solution to these sad consequences.

Student organizes by arguments for no gun control.

1. Guns for protection.

Responding to this argument, gun advocates ask how they are to defend themselves without guns. But guns are needed for protection from other guns. If there are no guns, people need only to protect themselves from criminals using knives, baseball bats, and other weapons. Obviously the odds of surviving a knife attack are greater than the odds of surviving a gun attack. One reason is that a gun is an impersonal weapon. Firing at someone from fifty feet away requires much less commitment than charging someone with a knife and stabbing repeatedly. Also, bullet wounds are, generally, more severe than knife wounds. Guns are also more likely to be misused when a dark figure is in one's house. To kill with the gun requires only to point and shoot; no recognition of the figure is needed. To kill with a knife, by contrast, requires getting within arm's reach of the figure, and knowing, for sure, the identity of your presumed opponent.

There are other uses of guns, including recreation. Hunting and target shooting are valid, responsible uses of guns. How do we keep

2. Recreational uses.

guns available for recreation? The answer is in the form of gun clubs and hunting clubs. Many are already established; more can be constructed. These clubs can provide recreational use of guns for responsible people while keeping guns off the streets and out of the house.

3. Second Amendment rights.

The last argument widely used by gun advocates is the constitutional right to bear arms. The fallacies in this argument are that the Constitution was written in a vastly different time. This different time had different uses for guns, and a different type of gun. Firearms were defended in the Constitution because of their many valid uses and fewer problems. Guns were mostly muskets, guns that were not very accurate beyond close range. Also, guns took more than thirty seconds to load in the eighteenth century and could fire only one shot before reloading. These differences with today's guns affect the relative safety of guns then and now. In addition, those who did not live in the city at the time used hunting for food as well as for recreation; hunting was a necessary component of life. That is not true today. Another use of guns in the eighteenth century was as protection from animals. Wild animals such as bears and cougars were much more common. Settlers, explorers, and hunters needed protection from these animals in ways not comparable with modern life.

Finally, Revolutionary America had no standing army. Defense of the nation and of one's home from other nations relied on local militia. The right to bear arms granted in the Constitution was inspired by the need for national protection as well as by the other outdated needs previously discussed. Today America has a standing army with enough weaponry to adequately defend itself from outside aggressors. There is no need for every citizen to carry a musket, or an AR-15, for the protection of the nation. It would seem, then, that the Second Amendment does not fully apply to modern society. While it justifies gun ownership, it is open to restrictions and controls based on the realities of today's world.

To reach a compromise, we also have to examine the other side of the issue. Some gun-control advocates argue that all guns are unnecessary and should be outlawed. The problem with this argument is that guns will still be available to those who do not mind breaking the law. Until an economically sound and feasible way of controlling illegal guns in America is found, guns cannot be totally removed, no matter how much legislation is passed. This means that if guns are to be outlawed for other than recreational uses, a way must be found to combat the illegal gun trade that will evolve. Tough criminal laws and a large security force are all that can be offered to stop illegal uses of guns until better technology is available. This means that, perhaps, a good resolution would involve gradual restrictions on guns, until eventually guns were restricted only to recreational uses in a controlled setting for citizens not in the police or military.

Student establishes a compromise position.

Both sides on this issue have valid points. Any middle ground needs to offer something to each side. It must address the reasons people feel they need guns for protection and allow for valid recreational use, but keep military-style guns off the street, except when in the hands of properly trained police officers. Time and money will be needed to move toward the removal of America's huge gun arsenal. But sooner or later a compromise on the issue of gun control must be made to make America a safer, better place to live.

Conclusion restates student's claim.

Courtesy of Chris Brown.

A PEOPLE'S VACCINE AGAINST A MUTATING VIRUS

NICOLAS J. S. DAVIES

Nicolas J. S. Davies is an independent journalist who has published in a number of outlets including *Huffpost, LA Progressive, Salon, Common Dreams,* and *Truthout.* He is also a researcher with Codepink, a nonprofit organization focused on human rights. His book *Blood on Our Hands: The American Invasion and Destruction of Iraq* was published in 2010. This article was published by *The Progressive* on June 9, 2021.

PREREADING QUESTIONS Since the publication of this article, numerous highly contagious COVID-19 variants emerged to cause even more hospitalizations and deaths worldwide. Can you think of any reasons why wealthier nations should *not* invest heavily in developing and distributing vaccines to nations who cannot afford to develop vaccines themselves?

1 A recent Yahoo News/YouGov poll found that worries about the COVID-19 pandemic in the United States are at their lowest level since it began. Only half of Americans are either "very worried" (15 percent) or "somewhat worried" (35 percent) about the virus, while the other half are "not very worried" (30 percent) or "not worried at all" (20 percent).

2 But the news from around the world makes it clear that this pandemic is far from over, and a story from Vietnam highlights the nature of the danger.

3 Vietnam is a COVID-19 success story, with one of the lowest rates of infection and death in the world. Vietnam's excellent community-based public health system prevented the virus from spreading beyond isolated cases and localized outbreaks, without a nationwide lockdown. With a population of 98 million people, Vietnam has had only 8,883 cases and fifty-three deaths.

4 However, more than half of Vietnam's cases and deaths have come in the last two months, and three-quarters of the new cases have been infected with a new "hybrid" variant that combines the two mutations detected separately in the Alpha (United Kingdom) and Delta (India) variants.

5 Vietnam is a canary in the pandemic coal-mine. The way this new variant has spread so quickly in a country that has fended off every previous form of the virus suggests that this one is much more infectious.

6 This variant must surely also be spreading in other countries, where it will be harder to detect among thousands of daily cases, and will, therefore, likely become widespread before public health officials and governments can respond to it. There may also be other highly infectious new variants spreading undetected among the millions of cases in Latin America and other parts of the world.

7 A new study in *The Lancet* medical journal has found that the Alpha (United Kingdom), Beta (South Africa), and Delta (India) variants are all more resistant to existing vaccines than the original coronavirus, and the Delta variant is still spreading in countries with aggressive vaccination programs, including the United Kingdom.

8 The Delta variant accounts for a two-month high in new cases in the United Kingdom and a new wave of infections in Portugal, just as developed countries are easing restrictions before the summer vacation season, almost certainly opening the door to the next wave. The United Kingdom, which has a slightly higher vaccination rate than the United States, had planned a further relaxation of restrictions on June 21, but that is now in question.

9 China, Vietnam, New Zealand, and other countries defeated the pandemic in its early stages by prioritizing public health over business interests. The United States and Western Europe instead tried to strike a balance between public health and their neoliberal economic systems, breeding a monster that has now killed millions of people. The World Health Organization believes that six to eight million people have died, about twice as many as have been counted in official figures.

Now, the WHO is recommending that wealthier countries who have ample 10
supplies of vaccines postpone vaccinating healthy young people, and instead prioritize sending these vaccines to poorer countries where the virus is running wild.

President Joe Biden has announced that the United States is releasing 11
25 million doses from its stockpiles, most of which will be distributed through the WHO's COVAX program, with another 55 million to follow by the end of June. But this is a tiny fraction of what is needed.

Biden has also agreed to waive patent rights on vaccines under the WTO's 12
TRIPS rules (the Agreement on Trade-Related Aspects of Intellectual Property Rights), but that has so far been held up at the WTO by Canada and rightwing governments in the United Kingdom, Germany, Brazil, Australia, Japan, and Colombia. People have taken to the streets in many countries to insist that a WTO TRIPS Council meeting on June 8 and 9, must agree to waive patent monopolies.

Since all of the countries blocking the TRIPS waiver are U.S. allies, this will 13
be a critical test of the Biden Administration's promised international leadership and diplomacy, which has so far taken a back seat to dangerous saber-rattling against China and Russia, foot-dragging on the JCPOA with Iran, and weapons-peddling to Israel and Saudi Arabia.

Ending international vaccine inequity is not just a matter of altruism, or even jus- 14
tice. It is a question of whether we will end this pandemic before vaccine-resistant, super-spreading and deadlier variants fuel even more toxic new waves. The only way humanity can win this struggle is to act collectively in our common interest.

Public Citizen has researched what it would take to vaccinate the entire 15
world, and concluded that it would cost only $25 billion—3 percent of the annual U.S. budget for weapons and war—to set up manufacturing plants and distribution hubs across the globe and vaccinate all of humanity within a year. Forty-two progressive legislators in Congress have signed a letter to President Biden to urge him to fund such a plan.

If the world can agree to make and distribute a People's Vaccine, it could 16
be the silver lining in this dark cloud, because this ability to act globally and collectively in the public interest is precisely what we need to solve so many of the most serious problems facing humanity today.

For example, the United Nations Environment Program is warning that we 17
are in the midst of a triple crisis of climate change, mass extinction, and pollution. Our neoliberal political and economic system has not just failed to solve these problems. It actively works to undermine efforts to do so, granting people, corporations, and countries who profit from destroying the natural world the freedom to do so without constraint.

That is the very meaning of *laissez-faire*—to let the wealthy and powerful do 18
whatever they want, regardless of the consequences for the rest of us, or even for life on Earth. As the economist John Maynard Keynes reputedly said in the 1930s, "*Laissez-faire* capitalism is the absurd idea that the worst people, for the worst reasons, will do what is best for us all."

Around the world, we are witnessing what can happen when people rise up 19
and act collectively for the common good. That is how we must solve the serious problems we face, from the COVID-19 pandemic to the climate crisis to the terminal danger of nuclear war.

20 Humanity's survival into the twenty-second century and all our hopes for a bright future depend on building new political and economic systems that will simply and genuinely "do what is best for all of us."

Davies, Nicolas J. S. "A People's Vaccine Against a Mutating Virus." *The Progressive*, 9 June 2021. Used with permission.

QUESTIONS FOR READING

1. What information about COVID-19 does Davies provide to help contextualize his article? Do a quick search on the internet to learn about the terms "neoliberalism" and "*laissez-faire* capitalism." What did you find?
2. What examples of robust community-based public health programs does Davies provide?
3. What reasons does Davies offer to develop his subject?
4. What solutions to the problem of a lack of vaccines are offered by the author?

QUESTIONS FOR REASONING AND ANALYSIS

5. Although Davies appears to be writing about the lack of vaccines to address COVID-19 variants, what is his broader subject? What, then, is his main point, his claim?
6. Examine the author's reasons, his value statements; which are most effective in your opinion? Why?
7. Davies argues that people should "act collectively for the common good." What other solutions does he present?

QUESTIONS FOR REFLECTION AND WRITING

8. Davies argues that "humanity's survival into the twenty-second century and all our hopes for a bright future depend on building new political and economic systems that will simply and genuinely 'do what is best for all of us.'" Why do you think he believes this? Do you agree with Davies? Why or why not?
9. How would you refute Davies' argument that we should develop political and economic systems that will do what is best for us all? How would you write an essay that supports Davies' claim and that provided examples of how people in your town could collaborate to bring about positive change for everyone?

IT'S WRONG TO TARGET ASIAN-AMERICAN SCIENTISTS FOR ESPIONAGE PROSECUTION

ALICIA LAI

Alicia Lai graduated from the University of Pennsylvania Carey Law School in 2021 and has a certificate in business management from the Wharton School. She is currently a judicial law clerk for the United States Court of Appeals Federal Circuit. While at the University of Pennsylvania, she worked as the articles editor for the *University of Pennsylvania Law Review* and senior editor for the *Journal of Law & Innovation*. Her research has focused on issues surrounding law and technology. This article was published by *Scientific American* on March 22, 2021.

PREREADING QUESTIONS **What is economic and scientific espionage? What are some examples of racial profiling?**

When trying to catch spies, it is tempting to cast a broad net despite the risk of making false accusations. Recently the U.S. Department of Justice has done just that. In an effort to crack down on what it depicts as an intellectual espionage campaign by China, it has revved up its prosecution of Asian-American citizens for scientific espionage and intellectual-property theft—from the notable case of Wen Ho Lee of Los Alamos National Laboratory in 1999 to Gang Chen of the Massachusetts Institute of Technology this past January. 1

The cycle is familiar yet somehow shocking every time: Immigrant or naturalized scientists are accused of disloyalty. Many are preemptively imprisoned and stripped of professional positions. Accusations of espionage are often found to be erroneous and ungrounded in science and are then dropped. Targeted scientists have raised plausible claims of racial profiling under the Fourth and Fourteenth Amendments, and at least one such case is currently pending in federal court. 2

What is driving this harsh crackdown? One answer is high economic stakes. Intellectual capital sits at the heart of the U.S. economy: an analysis of data from 2014 showed that industries relying on intellectual property directly accounted for 28 million jobs and $6.6 trillion in value. Unsurprisingly, the U.S. reacts aggressively to foreign threats to its source of wealth. And there have been real threats tied to the Chinese government—for instance, inducements offered by the Thousand Talents recruitment program, the Equifax data breach of consumers' personal information and the SolarWinds hack of U.S. government data. Because of long-standing concerns, the Obama administration heightened penalties under the Economic Espionage Act. The Trump administration began the China Initiative to fight what it portrayed as an epidemic of intellectual theft. The Biden administration has already made high-profile arrests. Politicians on both sides of the aisle struggle to avoid appearing "weak on China." It is a persuasively simple narrative: stop foreign spies from stealing America's intellectual property. 3

But there is more to it. Too often prosecutions are mistargeted, and rhetoric ignores clear exculpatory evidence, capitalizing on the perception of Asian-Americans as perpetual foreigners. The sentiment can be traced back to the 1790 Naturalization Act (forbidding Asians and other nonwhite individuals from holding U.S. citizenship) and the 1882 Chinese Exclusion Act (essentially prohibiting all Chinese immigration, initially for 10 years and later indefinitely). And it extends to the current wave of anti-Asian crimes tied to the COVID-19 pandemic. Whereas overall hate crimes in the U.S. decreased by 7 percent during 2020, anti-Asian hate crimes increased by 149 percent. Recent news cycles are studded with violence: a two-year-old toddler stabbed in a Texas wholesale store, a woman doused with acid on her front porch in Brooklyn, a man knifed in Manhattan's Chinatown, a couple beaten with a rock in a sock in Seattle, a mother and her eight-year-old daughter stabbed to death while asleep in their California home, six women gunned down in a mass shooting in Atlanta. 4

5 Although China presents a legitimate national security concern—and genuine instances of espionage should be prosecuted—there is evidence that the U.S. is haphazardly conflating nationality with ethnicity. Representative Ted Lieu of California states that erroneous espionage prosecutions are "the latest example of our government's unfortunate inability to distinguish between American citizens and foreign adversaries." One study found that the proportion of defendants charged under the Economic Espionage Act who were Chinese or Chinese-American rose from 17 to 52 percent between 2009 and 2015. More crucial is the rate of false positives: defendants of Chinese ethnicity have been unjustly accused at twice the rate of non-Chinese defendants. Many of these false positives—cases where the defendant is acquitted at trial, prosecutors drop all charges before trial, or the defendant pleads guilty to minor offenses and receives only probation—could be prevented by carefully examining the evidence before bringing charges, consulting a scientific expert on the merits, and avoiding biased, conclusory rhetoric.

6 The side effects of such a crude policy do more harm than good. Having spent my childhood in an idyllic Pennsylvania university town, I witnessed firsthand the community's reaction when a family friend—a Chinese-American physics professor who was a U.S. citizen—was erroneously accused, arrested and hustled away at gunpoint. Months later the Justice Department realized it had entirely misinterpreted the situation: it had accused him of sending schematics for sophisticated "pocket heater" technology to a colleague in China, but experts later clarified that the confiscated blueprints did not depict a pocket heater at all. The charges were dropped. But the professional, financial and reputational damage was done. The Asian-American community at the university buzzed with apprehension, fearing that no one was safe from unfounded accusations.

7 The current approach sweeps broadly and baselessly. Not only do rash prosecutions subject U.S. citizens to potential civil rights violations, but this climate causes a "brain drain" of intellectual capital. According to the World Intellectual Property Organization, immigrants make up a significant proportion of U.S.-based inventors and have won a third of the Nobel Prizes given to Americans. But now many immigrant scientists and inventors are choosing to leave the U.S. for other countries on the promise of higher pay, prestigious positions, looser regulatory schemes and—most notably—no federal prosecutions for legitimate research activity. Brian Sun, a renowned litigator who successfully represented Lee in his civil lawsuit, explains: "If you're criminally prosecuted and disgraced in this way . . . it's an academic death penalty: What are you left to do but go back to China?"

8 The long-term effect is rather perverse. As Princeton University molecular biologist Yibin Kang notes, "What's happening is doing a great service for the Chinese government. If you turn this into a toxic environment, you're actually helping the Chinese government to then recruit back to China."

9 The U.S. loses in this situation any way you look at it. The country stifles its own innovation ecosystem by discouraging international partnerships, obstructing access to nonclassified federally funded research, renouncing immigrant

intellectual capital and rejecting investments in innovations from certain other countries. On the international stage, it compromises its diplomatic standing by failing to recognize the diverse legal needs of other countries and forcing the harmonization of patent law.

But these harms have gone largely unrecognized. In 2018 the National Institutes of Health—the main source of funding for many academic labs—instructed around 10,000 U.S. research institutions to continue cracking down. Sun calls these "gotcha" cases: they apply disproportionately heavy criminal penalties for mere administrative missteps. Several institutions, such as Emory University in Atlanta and MD Anderson Cancer Center in Houston, subsequently fired a number of their Asian-American researchers. 10

The myopia is astounding. Tensions and violence are escalating every day in courtrooms and on city streets. But at least in the scientific community, prosecutors, legislators, agencies and directors of research institutions have the power to slow down and consider the hard facts of each case. Jumping to conclusory prosecutions and terminations does no good for anyone. 11

By treating Asian-American citizens as perpetual foreigners and prosecuting them without merit or nuance, the U.S. will continue down a self-destructive path, harming its own citizens, innovation and economy 12

Lau, Alicia. "It's Wrong to Target Asian-American Scientists for Espionage Prosecution." *Scientific American*, 22 Mar. 2021. Reproduced with permission. Copyright ©2021 SCIENTIFIC AMERICAN, a Division of Springer Nature America, Inc. All rights reserved. Used with permission.

QUESTIONS FOR READING

1. Why is Lai arguing that it's wrong to target Asian-American scientists for espionage prosecution?
2. What examples are provided of racial profiling? What does the author share about the scientists in these cases?
3. What reasons does Lai offer to build her argument?
4. What solutions to the problem of racial profiling does Lai provide?

QUESTIONS FOR REASONING AND ANALYSIS

5. Although Lai seems like she's writing about racial profiling of Asian-Americans, what is her larger subject? What is her main point–her claim?
6. Examine the author's reasons, her value statements; which are most effective? Why?
7. What solutions does the author provide?

QUESTIONS FOR REFLECTION AND WRITING

8. Lai writes that "By treating Asian-American citizens as perpetual foreigners and prosecuting them without merit or nuance, the U.S. will continue down a self-destructive path, harming its own citizens, innovation and economy." Explain how racial profiling hurts U.S. citizens, U.S. innovation, and the U.S. economy.

9. What does Lai mean when she writes that "the U.S. is haphazardly conflating nationality with ethnicity"? Are there other ways that you notice this happening around you? What can you do to help stop this hurtful conflation?
10. Lai argues that racial profiling hurts innovation. What other policies and practices does Lai cite as also stifling innovation? Do you think these other policies are related to racial profiling? Why or why not?

ON ASSISTED SUICIDE, GOING BEYOND "DO NO HARM"

HAIDER JAVED WARRAICH

Haider Javed Warraich is a graduate of Aga Khan University Medical College in Pakistan and took his residency at Harvard Medical School. He is now a fellow in cardiovascular medicine at the Duke University Medical Center and the author of *Modern Death: How Medicine Changed the End of Life.* This op-ed essay was published in 2016 in the *New York Times.*

PREREADING QUESTIONS How does one go beyond doing no harm? What do you expect the author's focus to be?

1 Durham, N.C.—Out of nowhere, a patient I recently met in my clinic told me, "If my heart stops, doctor, just let me go."

2 "Why?" I asked him.

3 Without hesitating, he replied, "Because there are worse states than death."

4 Advances in medical therapies, in addition to their immense benefits, have changed death to *dying*—from an instantaneous event to a long, drawn-out process. Death is preceded by years of disability, countless procedures and powerful medications. Only one in five patients is able to die at home. These days many patients fear what it takes to live more than death itself.

5 That may explain why this year, behind the noise of the presidential campaign, the right-to-die movement has made several big legislative advances. In June, California became the fifth and largest state to put an assisted suicide law into effect; this week the District of Columbia Council passed a similar law. And on Tuesday voters in Colorado will decide whether to allow physician-assisted suicide in their state as well.

6 Yet even as assisted suicide has generated broader support, the group most vehemently opposed to it hasn't budged: doctors.

7 That resistance is traditionally couched in doctors' adherence to our understanding of the Hippocratic oath. But it's becoming harder for us to know what is meant by "do no harm." With the amount of respirators and other apparatus at our disposal, it is almost impossible for most patients to die unless doctors or patients' families end life support. The withdrawal of treatment, therefore, is now perhaps the most common way critically ill patients die in the hospital.

While "withdrawal" implies a passive act, terminating artificial support feels decidedly active. Unlike assisted suicide, which requires patients to be screened for depression, patients can ask for treatment withdrawal even if they have major depression or are suicidal. Furthermore, withdrawal decisions are usually made for patients who are so sick that they frequently have no voice in the matter. 8

Some doctors skirt the question of assisted suicide through opiate prescriptions, which are almost universally prescribed for patients nearing death. Even though these medications can slow down breathing to the point of stoppage, doctors and nurses are very comfortable giving them, knowing that they might hasten a "natural" death. 9

In extreme cases, when even morphine isn't enough, patients are given anesthesia to ease their deaths. The last time I administered what is called terminal sedation, another accepted strategy, was in the case of a patient with abdominal cancer whose intestines were perforated and for whom surgery was not an option. The patient, who had been writhing uncontrollably in pain, was finally comfortable. Yet terminal sedation, necessary as it was, felt closer to active euthanasia than assisted suicide would have. 10

While the way people die has changed, the arguments made against assisted suicide have not. We are warned of a slippery slope, implying that legalization of assisted suicide would eventually lead to eugenic sterilization reminiscent of Nazi Germany. But no such drift has been observed in any of the countries where it has been legalized. 11

We are cautioned that legalization would put vulnerable populations like the uninsured and the disabled at risk; however, years of data from Oregon demonstrate that the vast majority of patients who opt for it are white, affluent and highly educated. 12

We are also told that assisted suicide laws will allow doctors and nurses to avoid providing high-quality palliative care to patients, but the data suggests the opposite: A strong argument for legalization is that it sensitizes doctors about ensuring the comfort of patients with terminal illnesses; if suicide is an option, they'll do what they can to preclude it. 13

And, again, we are counseled that physicians should do no harm. But medical harm is already one of the leading causes of death—and in any case, isn't preventing patients from dying on their terms its own form of medical harm? 14

With the right safeguards in place, assisted suicide can help give terminally ill patients a semblance of control over their lives as disease, disability and the medical machine tries to wrest it away from them. In Oregon, of the exceedingly few patients who have requested a lethal prescription—1,545 in 18 years—about 35 percent never uses it; for them, it is merely a means to self-affirmation, a reassuring option. 15

Instead of using our energies to obfuscate and obstruct how patients might want to end their lives when faced with life-limiting disease, we physicians need to reassess how we can help patients achieve their goals when the end is near. We need to be able to offer an option for those who desire assisted suicide, so that they can openly take control of their death. 16

17 Instead of seeking guidance from ancient edicts, we need to re-evaluate just what patients face in modern times. Even if it is a course we personally wouldn't recommend, we should consider allowing it for patients suffering from debilitating disease. How we die has changed tremendously over the past few decades—and so must we.

Warraich, Haider. "On Assisted Suicide, Going Beyond 'Do No Harm'" *New York Times*, 4 Nov. 2016. Used by permission of the author.

QUESTIONS FOR READING

1. How has "death" changed today?
2. How do many critically ill patients now die in the hospital?
3. What are the usual arguments against assisted suicide?
4. In Warraich's view, what does assisted suicide give to dying patients?

QUESTIONS FOR REASONING AND ANALYSIS

5. What is Warraich's position on assisted suicide?
6. Who appears to be the author's primary audience for this argument? Why, then, does he publish his argument in a general newspaper? What other audience does he wish to reach and convince?
7. What does the author gain by including the standard arguments against his position?
8. Evaluate Warraich's introduction.

QUESTIONS FOR REFLECTION AND WRITING

9. Which of the arguments against assisted suicide do you think are the most powerful? Why?
10. Which of the author's arguments for assisted suicide are the most effective? Why?
11. Has Warraich changed your thinking on this subject in any way? Why or why not?

WITH AFGHANISTAN'S FALL, THE U.S. CONFRONTS A MORAL NECESSITY IT FACED BEFORE

AMANDA C. DEMMER

Amanda C. Demmer holds a PhD in history from the University of New Hampshire, and she is an assistant professor of history at Virginia Tech, where she teaches courses on the Vietnam War. Her research focuses on human rights, war and society, U.S. history, and migration studies. She has published in peer-reviewed journals, such as *Diplomatic History* and the *Journal of the Early Republic,* and her book, *Moving On: Migrants and the Last Chapter of the Vietnam War,* will be published by Cambridge University Press. This article was published in the *Washington Post* on August 16, 2021.

PREREADING QUESTIONS **What do you know about the Vietnam War and the fall of Saigon? What do you know about the war in Afghanistan (America's longest conflict) and the fall of Kabul? Do a quick search of credible sources on the web to find out more before you read this article.**

After 20 years of fighting, the U.S.-backed regime in Afghanistan has rapidly collapsed. The Taliban has taken over the country for a second time, and its arrival in Kabul triggered panic. As the remaining Americans and thousands of Afghans converged on the airport, desperate scenes unfolded. Multiple people died in the chaos, including some who plunged to their deaths from the air while trying to board departing planes, and the images sparked immediate comparisons to the scenes of South Vietnamese fleeing Saigon. An urgent question resonates between our past and present: What will be the fate of those aligned with the United States? 1

Over 300,000 Afghan civilians have worked with the U.S. in a variety of occupations, including as interpreters and construction workers, according to the International Rescue Committee. At least 18,000 have begun the paperwork to apply for special immigrant visas (SIV) which would allow them to enter the United States but are awaiting final approvals. Taking into account that their immediate families will also need evacuation, the number swells to an estimated 70,000 people in the SIV pipeline. There are so many Afghans who have a reasonable claim to U.S. assistance but who do not qualify for a SIV that the State Department created a Priority 2 designation—intended for activists, journalists and humanitarian aid workers, among others—in early August. Still, the number of Afghans who fear for their lives and want to leave far eclipse the spots available via either designation. 2

The history of the Vietnam War suggests that refugee safety is more than an acute emergency: The question of what we owe those affected by our wars lingers for decades. 3

In early 1975, North Vietnam launched a decisive military offensive. Vast swaths of South Vietnamese territory fell rapidly. When, on March 29, communist troops captured Da Nang, a bustling port metropolis and South Vietnam's second-largest city, officials in Washington and Saigon frantically planned a belated evacuation. The extent and nature of the U.S. obligation to its Vietnamese allies was an immediate and consistent part of these conversations. Efforts to include the South Vietnamese in U.S. evacuation plans faced considerable domestic opposition: War fatigue, economic woes, racism and the tendency to see Vietnamese people as enemies rather than allies all added to the impulse to get the last Americans out and wash the nation's hands of the conflict. 4

Still, in April 1975, 130,000 Vietnamese were evacuated alongside American personnel. The chaos on the ground and the limited number of seats meant that those who resettled in the United States endured a traumatic separation from close family members, who faced incredibly difficult conditions in Vietnam. In the 20 years after the withdrawal, the government directly admitted another half-million individuals with familial and employment ties to the United States through the Orderly Departure Program (ODP). The program allowed this group 5 to leave without the dangers of clandestine flight. After years of negotiations and pressure from NGOs, Vietnam permitted Amerasians (the children of Vietnamese women and American men), those formerly interned in Hanoi's reeducation camps and their close family members to emigrate through subprograms of the ODP.

6 While many American allies remained trapped in Vietnam, others fled—or, in some instances, were expelled—to neighboring countries. The years following the installation of communist governments in Vietnam, Laos and Cambodia saw one of the largest migrations of the 20th century. Between 1975 and 1979, more than 700,000 people reached the shores of first asylum nations. By 1995, the total number of migrants stemming from the conflicts exceeded 1.4 million. At international conferences in 1979 and 1989 aimed at addressing Southeast Asian migrants, Washington accepted the largest number of refugees—around 823,000—and pledged the most money to support the United Nations' refugee programs.

7 Eventually, more than 1 million Vietnamese—universally called "refugees" but occupying a variety of legal categories—resettled in the United States, in addition to hundreds of thousands of Laotians and Cambodians. Facilitating these migrations required negotiating agreements with Hanoi in the absence of formal diplomatic relations and, often, revising U.S. laws. The administrations of Presidents Jimmy Carter, Ronald Reagan, George H.W. Bush and Bill Clinton all supported these resettlements. How do we explain this sustained, bipartisan support, which occurred even as the United States adopted far less generous policies toward migrants from other countries?

8 The highly visible plight of people who fled by sea and revelations of genocide in Cambodia helped prompt action—especially as people around the world confronted the brutal history of the Holocaust. (In a 1979 speech, Vice President Walter Mondale suggested that a failure to respond would be equal to the failure to act to save European Jews on the eve of World War II.) Lawmakers with stark political differences eventually found a common cause in refugee resettlement. Sens. Bob Dole (R-Kan.) and Ted Kennedy (D-Mass.) co-sponsored resolutions that received unanimous support, a level of consensus usually unheard of for a topic related to the Vietnam War. For those who opposed the war, assisting those paying the price for U.S. policy failures seemed an obvious choice and a moral necessity. For those who supported U.S. escalation and remained committed to waging the Cold War, the fact that so many Vietnamese fled their homeland served as a substitute for military victory insofar as it seemed to validate the claim that the war had been a "noble cause" all along.

9 Finally, the tireless work of nongovernmental actors helped keep these questions in front of U.S. officials. The successive waves of migration programs after 1975 were not automatic but instead resulted from hard-fought, intentional lobbying and policymaking.

10 As in 1975, the U.S. government has pledged to include Afghan allies in its evacuation plans. In mid-July, the Pentagon announced Operation Allies Refuge, a program to provide relocation flights for those approved under the SIV program. Those flights began July 30, but their pace has not kept up with

the Taliban's advance. As with the evacuation of Saigon, the military situation in Kabul deteriorated so quickly that belatedly made plans were poorly executed.

Pressures to prolong and expand the evacuation are rising. On Tuesday, a bipartisan group of 40 lawmakers sent President Biden a letter asking the United States to "do everything possible" to secure the airport "until the rescue mission is complete and our citizens, allies, and vulnerable Afghans have had an opportunity to leave." The authors included Republican hawks and Democrats who have been pushing for an end to the war for years. The lawmakers directly challenged the president's timetable, urging that the goal of leaving by Aug. 31 should not apply to the rescue effort and that the United States should stay "as long as is necessary to complete it." President Gerald Ford received a similar letter in 1975. But much has changed since then. 11

So many South Vietnamese were able to evacuate with the United States in 1975 because American officials were willing to postpone most procedural formalities. Throughout that April, many lower-ranking U.S. officials, skeptical about their government's willingness to evacuate allies, snuck out their friends and colleagues on clandestine flights, which often bent if not outright broke immigration laws. (In my research, building on Thurston Clarke's work in "Honorable Exit," I found that most of these actions had the tacit approval of high-ranking officials in Washington and Saigon, who publicly stated that evacuation plans were merely cautionary, even though they privately knew that the country would fall.) The tumultuousness of April 1975 also meant that many South Vietnamese evacuated by chance and did not have formal documents. They were paroled into the United States as a group, with individual processing following thereafter. 12

The laws governing refugee admissions have grown more numerous and more complex since then: Domestic and international refugee norms now favor individual screenings, and the paperwork for a special immigrant visa or other legal paths to the United States is substantial. In his address to the nation Monday, Biden gave no indication that he would override procedural requirements for SIVs or other avenues to the United States, stating that the United States would airlift only "eligible" Afghans. Thus far the White House has been either unable or unwilling to supersede legal formalities as previous administrations did. 13

Policy norms have also shifted notably. While xenophobia has been a potent force throughout U.S. history, the Trump administration set the annual cap for refugees at a historic low last year: 15,000. The Biden administration initially intended to retain this record-low number until pressure from Democratic constituents prompted an increase to 62,500 for this fiscal year. Historically speaking, this figure is also small, especially considering the dramatic increase in the number of displaced peoples around the world. The annual ceiling for refugee admissions during the Reagan years, for instance, ranged from 70,000 to 217,000. Given these trends, it is unclear how many Afghans the United States will ultimately be willing to resettle. 14

As Americans grapple with the loss in Afghanistan, there will be a tendency to ask questions in the past tense: What could have been done differently? Was another outcome possible? For many Afghan allies, however, the war is not 15 over; for them, the most urgent questions remain in the present. What does the United States owe the people with whom it's been aligned for decades? How much effort is it willing to expend, despite public indifference or even opposition, to facilitate their departure and resettlement? The most pressing "lesson of Vietnam" is that these questions should stay with us long after the evacuation of the last Americans from Kabul.

Demmer, Amanda C. "With Afghanistans Fall, the U.S. Confronts a Moral Necessity It Faced Before." *Washington Post*, 16 Aug. 2021. Used with permission.

QUESTIONS FOR READING

1. What are the similarities and differences between the Vietnamese and Afghan refugees noted by the author?
2. Who was eligible for relocation from Vietnam? Who is eligible for relocation from Afghanistan?
3. According to Demmer, why is it more difficult for Afghan refugees to relocate to the United States than it was for refugees from Vietnam?
4. Why is accepting as many refugees as possible from Afghanistan a moral imperative for Demmer?

QUESTIONS FOR REASONING AND ANALYSIS

5. What is Demmer's claim? How does she defend and support it?
6. What strategies does Demmer propose to address the issue of refugees from Afghanistan?
7. Evaluate each section of Demmer's article. What are its strengths and weaknesses? What, if anything, would you do to improve her argument?

QUESTIONS FOR REFLECTION AND WRITING

8. Are you convinced by Demmer's argument? Why or why not?
9. Why do you think some Americans oppose accepting refugees from Afghanistan?
10. In February 2022, Russia invaded Ukraine, displacing millions of people. In the first two months of the war, an estimated 4.2 million refugees fled into neighboring Poland, Romania, Moldova, Hungary, and Slovakia. In March 2022, President Joe Biden stated that the United States would accept up to 100,000 Ukrainian refugees. Why do you think that the U.S. government and Americans in general seemed more willing to accept refugees from Ukraine than from Afghanistan?

SUGGESTIONS FOR DISCUSSION AND WRITING

1. Chris Brown, in the student essay, writes a conciliatory argument seeking common ground on the volatile issue of gun control. Write your own conciliatory argument on this issue, offering a different approach than Brown, but citing Brown for any ideas you borrow from his essay.

2. There are other "hot issues," issues that leave people entrenched on one side or the other, giving expression to the same arguments again and again without budging many, if any, readers. Do not try to write on any one of these about which you get strongly emotional. Select one that you can be calm enough over to write a conciliatory argument, seeking to find common ground.

3. Other issues that call for positions based on values stem from First Amendment rights. Consider a possible topic from this general area.

4. Consider issues related to college life. Should students be automatically expelled for plagiarism or cheating? Should college administrators have any control over what is published in the college newspaper?

CHAPTER 10

Arguments about Cause

LEARNING OUTCOMES

After reading Chapter 10, you will be able to:

- Describe the characteristics of causal arguments.
- Explain how to prepare a causal argument.

Katherine Frey/The Washington Post/Getty Images

READ: What is the setting of this picture, and what subject matter do you think is being covered?

REASON: What argument do you think this picture could be making?

WRITE: If this picture were used to recruit students for this institution, do you think it would be effective? Why or why not?

Because we want to know *why* things happen, arguments about cause are both numerous and important to us. We begin asking why at a young age, pestering adults with questions such as "Why is the sky blue?" and "Why is the grass green?" And, to make sense of our world, we try our hand at explanations as youngsters, deciding that the first-grade bully is "a bad boy." The bully's teacher, however, will seek a more complex explanation because an understanding of the causes is the place to start to guide the bully to more socially acceptable behavior.

As adults we continue the search for answers. We want to understand past events: Why was President Kennedy assassinated? We want to explain current situations: Why do so many college students binge drink? And of course we also want to predict the future: Will the economy improve if there is a tax cut? All three questions seek a causal explanation, including the last one. If you answer the last question with a yes, you are claiming that a tax cut is a cause of economic improvement.

CHARACTERISTICS OF CAUSAL ARGUMENTS

Causal arguments vary not only in subject matter but in structure. Here are the four most typical patterns:

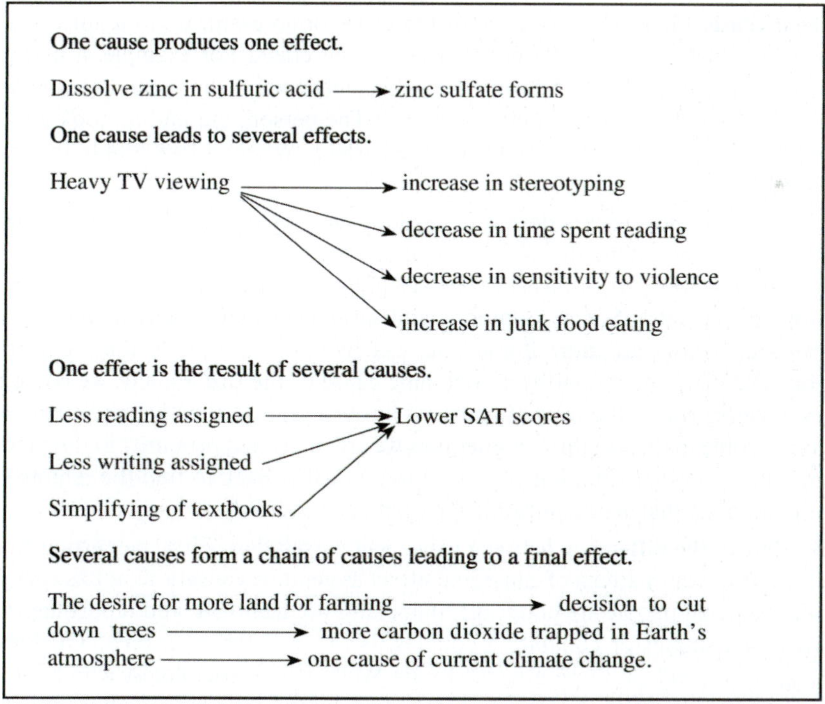

These models lead to several key points about causal arguments:

- **Most causal arguments are highly complex.** Except for some simple chemical reactions, most arguments about cause are difficult, can involve many steps, and are often open to challenge. Think, then, how much more open to debate are arguments about economic fluctuations around the world or arguments about human behavior. Many people think that "it's obvious" that violent TV and video games lead to more aggressive behavior. And yet, psychologists, in study after study, have not demonstrated conclusively that there is a clear causal connection. One way to challenge this causal argument is to point to the majority of people who do not perform violent acts even though they have watched television and played video games while growing up.
- **Because of the multiple and intertwined patterns of causation in many complex situations, the best causal arguments keep focused on their purpose.** For example, you are concerned with global warming. Cows contribute to global warming. Are we going to stop cattle farming? Not likely. Factories contribute to global warming. Are we going to tear down factories? Not likely—but we can demand that smokestacks have filters to reduce harmful emissions. Focus your argument on the causes that readers are most likely to accept because they are most likely to accept the action that the causes imply.
- **Learn and use the specific terms and concepts that provide useful guides to thinking about cause.** First, when looking for the cause of an event, we look for an *agent*—a person, situation, another event that led to the effect. For example, a lit cigarette dropped in a bed caused the house fire—the lit cigarette is the agent. But why, we ask, did someone drop a lit cigarette on a bed? The person, old and ill, took a sleeping pill and dropped the cigarette when he fell asleep. Where do we stop in the chain of causes?

  Second, most events do not occur in a vacuum with a single cause. There are *conditions* surrounding the event. The man's age and health were conditions. Third, we can also look for *influences*. The sleeping pill certainly influenced the man to drop the cigarette. Some conditions and influences may qualify as *remote causes*. *Proximate causes* are more immediate, usually closer in time to the event or situation. The man's dozing off is a proximate cause of the fire. Finally, we come to the *precipitating cause,* the triggering event—in our example, the cigarette's igniting the combustible mattress fabric. Sometimes we are interested primarily in the precipitating cause; in other situations, we need to go further back to find the remote causes or conditions that are responsible for what has occurred.
- **Be alert to the difference between cause and correlation.** First, be certain that you can defend your pattern of cause and effect as genuine causation, not as correlation only. Married people are better off financially, are healthier, and report happier sex lives than singles or cohabiting couples. Is this a correlation only? Or does marriage itself produce these effects? Linda Waite is one sociologist who argues that marriage is the cause. Another example: Girls who participate in after-school activities are much less likely to get pregnant. Are the activities a cause? Probably not. But there are surely conditions and influences that have led to both the decision to participate in activities and the decision not to become pregnant.

An Example of Causal Complexity: Lincoln's Election and the Start of the Civil War

If Stephen Douglas had won the 1860 presidential election instead of Abraham Lincoln, would the Civil War have been avoided? An interesting question posed to various American history professors and others, including Waite Rawls, president of the Museum of the Confederacy. Their responses were part of an article that appeared in the *Washington Post* on November 7, 2010.

Obviously, this is a question that cannot be answered, but it led Rawls to discuss the sequence of causes leading to the breakout of the war. Rawls organizes his brief causal analysis around a great metaphor: the building and filling and then lighting of a keg of powder. Let's look at his analysis.

Existing Conditions

"The wood for the keg was shaped by the inability of the founding fathers to solve the two big problems of state sovereignty and slavery in the shaping of the Constitution."

More Recent Influences

1. "[T]he economics of taxes and the politics of control of the westward expansion were added to those two original issues as the keg was filled with powder."
2. "By the time of the creation of the Republican Party in 1856, the powder keg was almost full and waiting for a fuse. And the election of any candidate from the Republican Party–a purely sectional party–put the fuse in the powder keg, and the Deep South states seceded. But there was still no war."

Proximate Causes

"Two simultaneous mistakes in judgment brought the matches out of the pocket–the Deep South mistakenly thought that Lincoln, now elected, would not enforce the Union, and Lincoln mistakenly thought that the general population of the South would not follow the leadership" of the Deep South states.

Precipitating Causes

1. "Lincoln struck the match when he called the bluff of the South Carolinians and attempted to reinforce Fort Sumter, but that match could have gone out without an explosion."
2. "Lincoln struck a second, more fateful match, when he called for troops to put down the 'insurrection.' That forced the Upper South and Border States into a conflict that they had vainly attempted to avoid." (Blog from the *Washington Post,* November 7, 2010. Reprinted by permission of Waite Rawls.)

Rawls concludes that the election of Lincoln did not start the war; it was only one step in a complex series of causes that led to America's bloodiest war. His analysis helps us see the complexity of cause/effect analysis.

Mill's Methods for Investigating Causes

John Stuart Mill, a nineteenth-century British philosopher, explained in detail some important ways of investigating and demonstrating causal relationships: commonality, difference, and process of elimination. We can benefit in our study of cause by understanding and using his methods.

1. **Commonality.** One way to isolate cause is to demonstrate that one agent is *common* to similar outcomes. For instance, twenty-five employees attend a company luncheon. Late in the day, ten report to area hospitals, and another four complain the next day of having experienced vomiting the night before. Public health officials will soon want to know what these people ate for lunch. Different people during the same twelve-hour period had similar physical symptoms of food poisoning. The common factor may well have been the tuna salad they ate for lunch.
2. **Difference.** Another way to isolate cause is to recognize one key *difference.* If two situations are alike in every way but one, and the situations result in different outcomes, then the one way they differ must have caused the different outcome.

   Studies in the social sciences are often based on the single-difference method. To test for the best teaching methods for math, an educator could set up an experiment with two classrooms similar in every way except that one class devotes fifteen minutes three days a week to instruction by drill. If the class receiving the drill scores much higher on a standard test given to both groups of students, the educator could argue that math drills make a measurable difference in learning math. But the educator should be prepared for skeptics to challenge the assertion of only one difference between the two classes. Could the teacher's attitude toward the drills also make a difference in student learning? If the differences in student scores are significant, the educator probably has a good argument.
3. **Process of elimination.** We can develop a causal argument around a technique we all use for problem solving: *the process of elimination.* When something happens, we examine all possible causes and eliminate them, one by one, until we are satisfied that we have isolated the actual cause (or causes).

   When the Federal Aviation Administration has to investigate a plane crash, it uses this process, exploring possible causes such as mechanical failure, weather, human error, or terrorism. Sometimes the process isolates more than one cause or points to a likely cause without providing absolute proof.

EXERCISE: Understanding Causal Patterns

From the following events or situations, select the one you know best and list as many conditions, influences, and causes—remote, proximate, precipitating—as you can think of. You may want to do this exercise with your class partner or in small groups. Be prepared to explain your causal pattern to the class.

1. Decrease in marriage rates in the United States
2. Arctic ice melt
3. Increase in the numbers of women elected to public office
4. High salaries of professional athletes
5. Increased interest in soccer in the United States
6. Comparatively low scores by U.S. students on international tests in math and science

GUIDELINES for Analyzing Causal Arguments

When analyzing causal arguments, what should you look for? The basics of good argument apply to all arguments: a clear statement of claim, qualified if appropriate; a clear explanation of reasons and evidence; and enough relevant evidence to support the claim. How do we recognize these qualities in a causal argument? Use these points as guides to analyzing:

- **Does the writer carefully distinguish among types of causes?** Word choice is crucial. Is the argument that A and A alone caused B or that A was one of several contributing causes?
- **Does the writer recognize the complexity of causation and not rush to assert only one cause for a complex event or situation?** The credibility of an argument about cause is quickly lost if readers find the argument oversimplified.
- **Is the argument's claim clearly stated, with qualifications as appropriate?** If the writer wants to argue for one cause, not the only cause, of an event or situation, then the claim's wording must make this limited goal clear to readers. For example, one can perhaps build the case for heavy television viewing as one cause of stereotyping, loss of sensitivity to violence, and increased fearfulness. But we know that the home environment and neighborhood and school environments also do much to shape attitudes.
- **What reasons and evidence are given to support the argument?** Can you see the writer's pattern of development? Does the reasoning seem logical? Are the data relevant? This kind of analysis of the argument will help you evaluate it.
- **Does the argument demonstrate causality, not just a time relationship or correlation?** A causal argument needs to prove *agency:* A is the cause of B, not just something that happened before B or something that is present when B is present. March precedes April, but March does not cause April to arrive.
- **Does the writer present believable causal agents, agents consistent with our knowledge of human behavior and scientific laws?** Most educated people do not believe that personalities are shaped by astrological signs or that scientific laws are suspended in the Bermuda Triangle, allowing planes and ships to vanish or enter a fourth dimension.
- **What are the implications for accepting the causal argument?** If A and B clearly are the causes of C, and we don't want C to occur, then we presumably must do something about A and B—or at least we must do something about either A or B and see if reducing or eliminating one of the causes significantly reduces the incidence of C.
- **Is the argument convincing?** After analyzing the argument and answering the questions given in the previous points, you need to decide if, finally, the argument works.

PREPARING A CAUSAL ARGUMENT

In addition to the guidelines for writing arguments presented in Chapter 4, you can use the following advice specific to writing causal arguments.

Planning

1. **Think:** What are the focus and limits of your causal argument? Do you want to argue for one cause of an event or situation? Do you want to argue for several causes leading to an event or situation? Do you want to argue for a cause that others have overlooked? Do you

want to show how one cause is common to several situations or events? Diagramming the relationship of cause to effect may help you see what you want to focus on.

2. **Think:** What reasons and evidence do you have to support your tentative claim? Consider what you already know that has led to your choice of topic. A brainstorming list may be helpful.
3. **Think:** How, then, do you want to word your claim? As we have discussed, wording is crucial in causal arguments. Review the discussion of characteristics of causal arguments if necessary.
4. **Reality check:** Do you have a claim worth defending in a paper? Will readers care?
5. **Think:** What, if any, additional evidence do you need to develop a convincing argument? You may need to do some reading or online searching to obtain data to strengthen your argument. Readers expect relevant, reliable, current statistics in most arguments about cause. Assess what you need and then think about what sources will provide the needed information.
6. **Think:** What assumptions (warrants) are you making in your causal reasoning? Are these assumptions logical? Will readers be likely to agree with your assumptions, or will you need to defend them as part of your argument? For example: One reason to defend the effects of heavy TV watching on viewers is the commonsense argument that what humans devote considerable time to will have a significant effect on their lives. Will your readers be prepared to accept this commonsense reasoning, or will they remain skeptical, looking for stronger evidence of a cause/effect relationship?

Drafting

1. Begin with an opening paragraph or two that introduces your topic in an interesting way. Lester Thurow in "Why Women Are Paid Less Than Men" writes:

   > "In the 40 years from 1939 to 1979 white women who work full time have with monotonous regularity made slightly less than 60 percent as much as white men. Why?"

   This opening establishes the topic and Thurow's purpose in examining causes. The statistics get the reader's attention.
2. Do not begin by announcing your subject. Avoid openers such as: In this essay I will explain the causes of teen vandalism.
3. Decide where to place your claim statement. You can conclude your opening paragraph with it, or you can place it in your conclusion, after you have shown readers how best to understand the causes of the issue you are examining.
4. Present reasons and evidence in an organized way. If you are examining a series of causes, beginning with background conditions and early influences, then your basic plan will be time sequence. Readers need to see the chain of causes unfolding. Use appropriate terms and transitional words to guide readers through each stage in the causal pattern. If you are arguing for an overlooked cause, begin with the causes that have been put forward and show what is flawed in each one. Then present and defend your explanation of cause. This process of elimination structure works well when readers are likely to know what other causes have been offered in the past. You can also use one of Mill's other two approaches, if one of them is relevant to your topic.

5. Address the issue of correlation rather than cause, if appropriate. After presenting the results of a study of marriage that reveals many benefits (emotional, physical, financial) of marriage, Linda Waite examines the question that she knows skeptical readers may have: Does marriage actually *cause* the benefits, or is the relationship one of *correlation* only—that is, the benefits of marriage just happen to come with being married; they are not caused by being married.
6. Conclude by discussing the implications of the causal pattern you have argued for, if appropriate. Lester Thurow ends by asserting that if he is right about the cause of the gender pay gap, then there are two approaches society can take to remove the pay gap. If, in explaining the causes of teen vandalism, you see one cause as "group behavior," a gang looking for something to do, it then follows that you can advise young readers to stay out of gangs. Often with arguments about cause, there are personal or public policy implications in accepting the causal explanation.

A CHECKLIST FOR REVISION

- ☐ Do I have a clear statement of my claim? Is it appropriately qualified and focused? Is it about an issue that matters?
- ☐ Have I organized my argument so that readers can see my pattern for examining cause?
- ☐ Have I used the language for discussing causes correctly, distinguishing among conditions and influences and remote and proximate causes? Have I selected the correct word—either *affect* or *effect*—as needed?
- ☐ Have I avoided the *post hoc* fallacy and the confusing of correlation and cause?
- ☐ Have I carefully examined my assumptions and convinced myself that they are reasonable and can be defended? Have I defended them when necessary to clarify and thus strengthen my argument?
- ☐ Have I found relevant facts and examples to support and develop my argument?
- ☐ Have I used the basic checklist for revision in Chapter 4 (see p. 106)?

FOR ANALYSIS AND DEBATE

"DARING TO DISCUSS WOMEN IN SCIENCE": A RESPONSE TO JOHN TIERNEY

CAROLINE SIMARD

Courtesy of Caroline Simard

Caroline Simard is a board member of the Ada Initiative and research consultant to the Anita Borg Institute for Women and Technology, at the Stanford University School of Medicine. She holds a PhD in communication and social science and works to find ways to increase the number of women and underrepresented racial and ethnic groups in science, technology, engineering, and mathematics (STEM), and business fields.

Simard's essay, a response to an article by John Tierney, was posted to the *Huffington Post* on June 9, 2010.

PREREADING QUESTIONS What type of argument do you anticipate, given the title and headnote information? What other type of argument should you anticipate, given the essay's location in this text?

1 On Monday [June 2010], John Tierney of the *New York Times* published a provocative article, "Daring to Discuss Women in Science," in which he argues that biology may be a factor to explain why women are not reaching high-level positions. He suggests that boys are innately more gifted at math and science and that the dearth of women in science may point to simple biological differences. If this is the case, why would we waste our time trying to get more women in science?

2 Mr. Tierney, let's indeed discuss women in science.

3 First, let me start by saying that I applaud the discussion—all potential explanations for a complex issue and all evidence need to be considered, even the ones that are not popular in the media or not "politically correct." I also believe that Larry Summers's now infamous comments about the possibility that biological differences account for the dearth of women scientists and technologists was, similarly, in the spirit of intellectual debate.

4 The problem with the biology argument that "boys are just more likely to be born good at math and science" isn't that it's not "politically correct"—it's that it assumes that we can take away the power of societal influences, which have much more solid evidence than the biology hypothesis. Tierney makes the point himself in his article—in order to provide evidence for biological differences, he cites a longitudinal Duke [University] study which shows that the highest achievers in SAT math tests (above 750), which counted 13 boys for every girl in the early 80s, became a ratio of 4 boys to 1 girl in 1991, "presumably because of sociocultural factors." Hmm, isn't this actual evidence that biology is not what is at play here? If it is possible to reduce the gender achievement gap in math by 3 thanks to "sociocultural factors," I rest my case. Sociocultural factors are indeed extremely powerful.

5 The Duke study also notes that the 4/1 achievement gap at the highest score hasn't changed in the last 20 years despite ongoing programs to encourage girls in math and science, whereas the highest achievers in writing ability (SAT above 700) shows a ratio of 1.2 girls for every boy, slightly favoring girls. However, if the premise is that boys are inherently "better" at math, and girls are inherently better at writing, why would the achievement gap be so large in math and negligible in writing? The stagnant 4 to 1 ratio is not evidence that there is an innate biological difference in math aptitude, but rather confirmation that persistent sociocultural barriers remain—that is, science and math are still thought of as male domains.

6 Research shows that math and science are indeed thought of as stereotypically male domains. Project Implicit at Harvard University studied half a million

participants in 34 countries and found that 70 percent of respondents worldwide have implicit stereotypes associating science with male more than with female. Years of research by Claude Steele and Joshua Aronson and their colleagues show that implicit stereotypes affect girls' performance in math—a phenomenon called "stereotype threat." When girls receive cues that "boys are better at math," their scores in math suffer. One study in a classroom setting showed that the difference in performance between boys and girls in math SAT scores was eliminated by simply having a mentor telling them that math is learned over time rather than "innate."

The problem is, girls are routinely getting the message that they don't belong in math and science, further undermining their performance (and Mr. Tierney's article isn't exactly helping in changing the stereotype for the general public). The result of this implicit (unconscious) stereotype is that parents, teachers, and school counselors are less likely to encourage girls to pursue math and science than they are boys. These girls are then less likely to seek advanced math classes and would be unlikely, without those opportunities, to make it to the above 700 SAT math score regardless of ability. 7

Anecdotally, I had this experience with my daughter a couple of years ago. At age 10, she had somehow decided that she wasn't good at math (despite being raised in a household with 2 PhDs). With her self-confidence plummeting, math homework became very painful in our household. When I dug deeper, I found that she mistakenly believed that you were either born with math ability or you weren't—that this was an innate biological ability as opposed to something you could learn, and that somehow she hadn't been "born with it." Once I actively dispelled that notion and provided her with additional mentoring, her math performance significantly improved. I never hear her say that she isn't good at math anymore, and her math homework is flawless. 8

The Duke article, and Tierney, raises an important question about preference, however, that research suggests that boys are more interested in "things" and girls are more interested in "people" and thus gravitate towards fields reflecting that interest. In this research too, there is debate about what in this difference is "nature" versus "nurture"—there are powerful socialization forces at play. Regardless, we have to dispel the notion that science is only about "things" and not about people or somehow disconnected from all social relevance. Indeed, some of the most successful interventions to increase girls' interest in math and science have been to reframe the curriculum to provide examples and projects that are grounded in the interests of a diverse population of students. The EPICS program at Purdue University is a great example of grounding engineering disciplines in socially relevant contexts and has been shown to engage a diversity of students. 9

What we need, to put this debate to rest, is to replicate these findings in a country where science and math are not viewed as stereotypically male. The most recent cross-national comparison study, published in 2010 in *Psychological* 10

Bulletin by Nicole Else-Quest and her colleagues and comparing 43 countries, shows that the achievement difference in math between girls and boys varies broadly across countries.

11 Their research shows that country-by-country variation is correlated with gender differences in self-confidence in math, which is compounded by stereotype threat. One of the strongest predictors of the gender gap in math achievement is a given country's level of gender equity in science jobs, consistent with socialization arguments: "if girls' mothers, aunts, and sisters do not have STEM careers, they will perceive that STEM is a male domain and thus feel anxious about math, lack the confidence to take challenging math courses, and underachieve on math tests."

12 Until girls stop getting the signal that math is for boys, the 4 to 1 gender gap in highest achievement categories of math and science will persist. This has nothing to do with innate ability.

13 Mr. Tierney, I look forward to your subsequent articles on this issue. Let's indeed dare to discuss women in science and continue to bring to bear the most relevant research on this issue.

Simard, Caroline. "Daring to Discuss Women in Science:" A Response to John Tierney, *HuffPostTech*, 9 June 2010. http://www.huffingtonpost.com/caroline-simard/daring-to-discuss-women-i_b_605303.html
Used with permission of the author.

QUESTIONS FOR READING

1. What is the occasion for Simard's posting? What is her topic?
2. What is Tierney's position on the issue?
3. What sociocultural factors are the causes of the gender gap in math and science, in Simard's view?

QUESTIONS FOR REASONING AND ANALYSIS

4. What is Simard's claim? (Try to state it with precision.)
5. What *kinds* of grounds does Simard present? What point about Tierney's warrant does the author want to make with the evidence she includes?
6. Examine Simard's style and tone; how do they help her argument?

QUESTIONS FOR REFLECTION AND WRITING

7. In the debate over women in science, there are two related assumptions: (1) Math ability is inborn and (2) Boys are innately better at math than girls. Have you heard either one–or both–of these views? Has Simard convinced you that the evidence challenges these ideas? Why or why not?
8. Why can stereotypes be a "threat"? How can ideas "threaten" us? Explain and illustrate to answer these questions.

WHY FUTURE OFFICERS SHOULD READ SHAKESPEARE, KNOW HISTORY AND UNDERSTAND PSYCHOLOGY

JOSEPH ZENGERLE

Joseph Zengerle is a lawyer and executive director of the Mason Veterans and Servicemembers Legal Clinic, a branch of the George Mason University School of Law. A West Point graduate and retired U.S. Army veteran, he attended the University of Michigan Law School and was a note and comment editor for the *Michigan Law Review*. The following article was published by *Washington Post* on October 3, 2016.

PREREADING QUESTIONS Many college students are pressured to major in "practical" subjects like business or engineering as soon as possible. Yet many of America's most successful people studied a field from the humanities, also known as the liberal arts. How do you think courses in the liberal arts may positively impact your studies and your life?

The U.S. military understood the importance of STEM long before it became the most coveted acronym in education. 1

Recognizing their critical skills in the conduct of war, George Washington appointed the first engineering officers to the Revolutionary Army on June 16, 1775. 2

Military historian Ian Hope describes how "American military thinking emerged in the young republic solidly committed to . . . the discovery of scientific components of war, with complete faith in the power of reason and with an unprecedented belief in the utility of mathematics as key to all scientific endeavors." 3

That philosophy helped guide the development of the country's military academies. In 1802, President Thomas Jefferson signed legislation establishing West Point as the nation's first engineering school. Its first superintendent, Lt. Col. Jonathan Williams, declared that "we must always have it in view that our officers are to be men of science." Superintendent Sylvanus Thayer, often called the "father" of the military academy, later grounded the school's curriculum firmly in mathematics. 4

The academy remained true to that mission when I was at West Point in the 1960s. We had math every morning, beginning with a slide-rule drill, six days a week for our entire first year. Upon graduation, we could select, according to our place in the order of merit, which of the (then five) branches of combat arms we wanted to join. The quota for the Corps of Engineers always ran out first. (I chose Infantry, which never ran out.) Today, the engineering programs at the service academies are among the best in the country. 5

There's an understandable premium on scientific expertise at the Pentagon, too. When I was an assistant secretary of the Air Force in the early 1980s, the defense secretary was a physicist. The current secretary also is a physicist. A technical background makes sense for the leader of an institution responsible for so many complex platforms, including nuclear and satellite systems. The threat of terrorism, the operation of drones and the growing challenge of cyberwarfare further illustrate the demand for uniformed leaders to have a sound grasp of technical fields. 6

7 But even in an age of highly sophisticated warfare, our military leaders should not be too narrowly focused on STEM. If we want leaders who communicate clearly, solve problems creatively and appreciate cultural differences in theaters where they operate, studying the humanities is just as important as science, technology, engineering and math.

8 When I attended Ranger and Airborne schools, a mandatory catchphrase was "move, shoot and communicate." Communication was always a critical component of military tactics, and the more complicated combat has become, the more important it is to ensure clarity of thought and expression that relies upon a grounding in softer disciplines.

9 Those who lead need to be ready for the moments when they must summon their troops—who may be hurt or drained by fatigue—to rise, to respond, to prevail against the odds. That power doesn't come out of the barrel of a gun or the insignia of rank, much less a math formula. It comes from an understanding of human motivation that can be gained by studying psychology, by analyzing history, by reading great literature. Military leaders should know that the familiar notion of troops as a "band of brothers" originates with the stirring speech Shakespeare's Henry V delivers to his outnumbered forces at the Battle of Agincourt.

10 Military leaders also need to be agile thinkers who can assess an unfamiliar situation and strategize a plan. That might require a cost-benefit analysis, but it also requires an understanding that not everything can be quantified. As a special assistant to Gen. William Westmoreland in 1968, I became familiar with the Hamlet Evaluation System, a monthly report that quantified the level of "pacification" by color-coding each village in South Vietnam. When attacks throughout the country erupted during the Tet Offensive, the HES reports were quickly considered an unreliable gauge. By contrast, the success of the 2007 surge in the Iraq War was under the command of Gen. David Petraeus, who, with a PhD in international relations, employed a counterinsurgency strategy based on the Army manual he co-wrote that emphasized leaders' flexibility and adaptability in dealing with indigenous populations.

11 The utility of non-STEM learning is further reflected in the nature of mission assignments. President Lyndon Johnson said victory in Vietnam would depend on our winning the "hearts and minds" of the Vietnamese, an objective necessitating education in relevant history, language and culture for military personnel assigned to advisory roles. That remains true in many conflicts today.

12 The mission of the military has expanded in ways that make a liberal arts background even more important. When Vice President Biden spoke to the graduating class at West Point in May [2016], he told them: "You're gonna need every tool your predecessors possessed . . . but you're gonna need more." He went on to talk about "next-generation technologies, like unmanned systems and autonomous machines" and the need to "dominate the cyber realm." But he also spoke about "building the capacity of emerging countries" and managing "humanitarian crises posed by climate change, mass migration and the spread of infectious disease." To take on these new challenges, rising military leaders benefit from a familiarity with foreign policy, public health and international development issues.

The slide rule my classmates and I struggled to master every day passed out of use a long time ago. But the service academies should be cautious about what they put in its place. If they can expose the minds of officers in training with the right ideas and the right spirit, they will cultivate a cadre of tomorrow's military leaders who will best serve the national interest. 13

Zengerle, Joseph. "Why Future Officers Should Read Shakespeare, Know History and Understand Psychology." *Washington Post*, 9 Oct. 2016. Used with permission of the author.

QUESTIONS FOR READING

1. What are some of the values of a liberal arts education?
2. Why are the liberal arts more important today than they were in the past?
3. How do the humanities, or "softer disciplines," work with fields like engineering and science?
4. What elements of leadership do the liberal arts foster?
5. How do the liberal arts help prepare future generations of people in the armed services in addressing the complex problems facing our nation and the world?

QUESTIONS FOR REASONING AND ANALYSIS

6. What is Zengerle's main argument, and why is he making this claim?
7. How does the author develop his argument? What are his grounds?
8. Zengerle is careful not to dismiss STEM training while making his argument. What is his strategy for including STEM with other disciplines in undergraduate education for military officers?
9. Zengerle focuses on liberal arts at the service academies. Do you think his reasoning applies for curricula at other institutions of higher education, such as community colleges, state and private schools? If so, why? If not, why not?

QUESTIONS FOR REFLECTION AND WRITING

10. When you think of courses to take, do you think about what knowledge or skills you could acquire from those courses? If not, why not? If so, what sorts of knowledge and skills do you anticipate from the courses you are enrolled in now?
11. As you consider the courses you may take during your time in college, do you think about how they might apply to or help you in your future plans for the workplace or graduate school? If so, how? If not, why not?
12. What has been the most valuable course you have taken so far during your time in college? What has been your favorite? If these two courses aren't the same, how might you combine them in some way to work toward a career you love? If they are the same class, how do you plan to apply the knowledge and skills from this course to your pathway to graduate school or the workplace?

SUGGESTIONS FOR DISCUSSION AND WRITING

1. Think about your educational experiences as a basis for generating a topic for a causal argument. For example: What are the causes of writer's block? Why do some apparently good students (based on class work, grades, etc.) do poorly on standardized tests? How does pass/fail grading affect student performance? What are the causes of high tuition and fees? What might be some of the effects of higher college costs? What are the causes of binge drinking among college students? What are the effects of binge drinking?

2. *Elder Scrolls 4: Skyrim* was released over ten years ago, but the game continues to be popular with old and new players. The mod community regularly provides updates, enhanced and improved game play, and new quests–why? What makes it so popular? Why are horror movies so popular? What are the causes for the great success of *The Hunger Games* books? If you are familiar with one of these works, or another work that has been amazingly popular, examine the causes for that popularity.

3. The age-adjusted rates of COVID-19-associated hospitalizations by vaccine status in adults ages 18 and over in 2021 are staggering in their difference. See Figure 5.1 in Chapter 5 for more information on these rates, and then consider the possible causes for these differences. What might be some of the causes for adults not getting vaccinated when by 2021 vaccines were widely available in the United States? Might mis/disinformation have something to do with this situation? Read the articles on mis/disinformation in the text to help you learn more, and then do some research online yourself–using credible sources, of course! Be prepared to discuss some causes of vaccine hesitancy or write an essay on the topic. (Be sure to qualify your claim as appropriate, based on what you know.)

CREDIT

1. Lester Thurow. "Why Women Are Paid Less Than Men." *New York Times,* 8 Mar. 1981.

CHAPTER 11

Presenting Proposals: The Problem/Solution Argument

LEARNING OUTCOMES

After reading Chapter 11, you will be able to:

- Describe the characteristics of problem/solution arguments.
- Explain how to prepare a problem/solution argument.

EyeEm/Alamy Stock Photo

READ: What is the setting of this picture?

REASON: How do you think the climate crisis affects settings like this?

WRITE: What are some strategies you have heard about that might address climate challenges to settings like this one?

You think that your college or university needs a more diverse staff of mental health counselors that better represent the student population. You are concerned that the police in your hometown disproportionately pull over people of color. You believe that LGBTQIA+ people should have the same access to adopting children as anyone else in your state. These are serious local issues; you should be concerned about them. And, perhaps it is time to act on your concerns—how can you do that? You can write a proposal, perhaps a letter to the editor of your college or hometown newspaper.

These three issues invite recommendations for change. And to make a recommendation is to offer a solution to what you perceive to be a problem. Public policy arguments, whether local and specific (college mental health counselors or statewide access to adoption) or more general and far-reaching (e.g., the federal government must stop the flow of illegal drugs into the country), can best be understood as arguments over solutions to problems.

Consider some of these issues stated as policy claims:

- The college needs more mental health counselors who represent the student population.
- We need to spend whatever is necessary to stop the flow of drugs into this country.

Each claim offers a solution to a problem, as we can see:

- More students will be able to get mental health counseling from staff members who have similar life experiences to them if the college hires a more diverse staff.
- The way to address the drug problem in this country is to eliminate the supply of drugs.

The basic idea of policy proposals looks like this:

Somebody	**should (or should not)**	**do X—because:**
(Individual, organization, government)		*(solve this problem)*

Observe that proposal arguments recommend action. They look to the future. And they often advise the spending of someone's time and/or money.

CHARACTERISTICS OF PROBLEM/ SOLUTION ARGUMENTS

- *Proposal arguments may be about local and specific problems or about broader, more general public policy issues.* We need to "think globally" these days, but we still often need to "act locally," to address the problems we see around us in our classrooms, offices, and communities.
- *Proposal arguments usually need to define the problem.* How we define a problem has much to do with what kinds of solutions are appropriate. For example, many people are concerned about our ability to feed a growing world population. Some will argue that the problem is not an agricultural one—how much food we can produce. The problem is a political one—how we distribute the food, at what cost, and how competent or fair some governments are in handling food distribution. If the problem is

agricultural, we need to worry about available farmland, water supply, and farming technology. If the problem is political, then we need to concern ourselves with price supports, distribution strategies, and embargoes for political leverage. To develop a problem/solution argument, you first need to define the problem.

- *How we define the problem also affects what we think are the causes of the problem.* Cause is often a part of the debate, especially with far-reaching policy issues, and may need to be addressed, particularly if solutions are tied to eliminating what we consider to be the causes. Why are illegal drugs coming into the United States? Because people want those drugs. Do you solve the problems related to drug addicts by stopping the supply? Or do you address the demand for drugs in the first place?
- *Proposal arguments need to be developed with an understanding of the processes of government, from college administrations to city governments to the federal bureaucracy.* Are there laws that govern access to adoption state or federal? Are there LGBTQIA+ or civil rights organizations like the ACLU in your area that can be called on to help with the process of presenting proposals to the appropriate people?
- *Proposal arguments need to be based on the understanding that they ask for change–and many people do not like change, period.* Probably all but the wealthiest Americans recognize that our health-care system needs fixing. That doesn't change the fact that many working people struggling to pay premiums are afraid of any changes introduced by the federal government.
- *Successful problem/solution arguments offer solutions that can realistically be accomplished.* Consider Prohibition, for example. This was a solution to problem drinking–except that it did not work, could not be enforced, because the majority of Americans would not abide by the law.

GUIDELINES for Analyzing Problem/Solution Arguments

When analyzing problem/solution arguments, what should you look for? In addition to the basics of good argument, use these points as guides to analyzing:

- **Is the writer's claim not just clear but also appropriately qualified and focused?** For example, if the school board in the writer's community is not doing a good job of communicating its goals as a basis for its funding package, the writer needs to focus just on that particular school board, not on school boards in general.
- **Does the writer show an awareness of the complexity of most public policy issues?** There are many different kinds of problems with American schools and many more causes for those problems. A simple solution—a longer school year, more money spent, vouchers—is not likely to solve the mixed bag of problems. Oversimplified arguments quickly lose credibility.
- **How does the writer define and explain the problem?** Is the way the problem is stated clear? Does it make sense to you? If the problem is being defined differently than most people have defined it, has the writer argued convincingly for looking at the problem in this new way?
- **What reasons and evidence are given to support the writer's solutions?** Can you see how the writer develops the argument? Does the reasoning seem logical? Are the data relevant? This kind of analysis will help you evaluate the proposed solutions.

- **Does the writer address the feasibility of the proposed solutions?** Does the writer make a convincing case for the realistic possibility of achieving the proposed solutions?
- **Is the argument convincing?** Will the solutions solve the problem as it has been defined? Has the problem been defined accurately? Can the solutions be achieved?

Read and study the following annotated argument. Complete your analysis by answering the questions that follow.

Courtesy of Priyamvada Natarajan

WANT MORE SCIENTISTS? TURN GRADE SCHOOLS INTO LABORATORIES

PRIYA NATARAJAN

A professor in both the astronomy and physics departments at Yale University, Priya Natarajan is a theoretical astrophysicist. She was educated first in Delhi and then at MIT. Natarajan's areas of investigation include black hole physics and gravitational lensing. Interested as well in enhancing general science literacy, Natarajan serves on the Advisory Board of NOVA ScienceNow, speaks at conferences, and writes newspaper articles. The following op-ed essay was published on February 5, 2012.

PREREADING QUESTIONS When you were in grade school, did you like to "discover things" in the natural world? How would you encourage early study of science?

1 "What's your major?" Ask a college freshman this question, and the answer may be physics or chemistry. Ask a sophomore or a junior, however, and you're less likely to hear about plans to enter the "STEM" fields—science, technology, engineering and mathematics. America's universities are not graduating nearly enough scientists, engineers and other skilled professionals to keep our country globally competitive in the decades ahead.

Author states problem.

2 And this is despite evidence such as a recent Center on Education and the Workforce report that forecasts skill requirements through 2018 and clearly shows the importance of STEM fields. The opportunities for those with just a high school education are restricted, it says—many high-paying jobs are open only to people with STEM college degrees.

States seriousness of problem.

3 Still, as many as 60 percent of students who enter college with the intention of majoring in science and math change their plans. Because so many students intend to major in a STEM subject but don't follow through, many observers have assumed that universities are where the trouble starts. I beg to differ.

A cause author will refute.

4 I am a professor of astronomy and physics at Yale University, where I teach an introductory class in cosmology. I see the deficiencies that first-year students show up with. My students may have dexterity with the equations they're required to know, but they lack the capacity to apply their knowledge to

real-life problems. This critical shortcoming appears in high school and possibly in elementary grades—long before college. If we want more Americans to pursue careers in STEM professions, we have to intervene much earlier than we imagined.

Author's solution.

Many efforts are underway to get younger students interested in science and math. One example is the Tree of Life's online "treehouse" project, a collection of information about biodiversity compiled by hundreds of experts and amateurs. Students can use this tool to apply what they are learning in the classroom to the world around them. Starting early in children's education, we need to provide these types of engaging, interactive learning environments that link school curricula to the outside world. 5

Specific strategies for solving problem.

My own schooling is an example. Growing up in Delhi, India, I did puzzles, explored numbers and searched for patterns in everyday settings long before I ever saw an equation. One assignment I vividly remember asked us to find examples of hexagons. I eagerly pointed out hexagons everywhere: street tiles, leaves, flowers, signs, buildings. I was taught equations only after I learned what they meant and how to think about them. As a result, I enjoyed math, and I became good at it. 6

Not all American children have this experience, but they can. The Khan Academy, for example, has pioneered the use of technology to encourage unstructured learning outside the classroom and now provides teaching supplements in 36 schools around the country. For instance, recent reports describe a San Jose charter school using Khan's instructional videos in ninth-grade math classes to tailor lessons to each student's pace. 7

Perhaps more than English or history, STEM subjects require an enormous amount of foundational learning before students can become competent. Students usually reach graduate school before they can hope to make an original contribution. They can experiment in high school labs, but the U.S. schools' approach to math and science lacks, in large part, a creative element. We need to help students understand that math and science are cumulative disciplines, and help them enjoy learning even as they gradually build a base of knowledge. 8

One way to do this is to encourage students to engage in self-guided or collaborative research projects—something the Internet has made much more feasible. An example from my own field is Zooniverse, a collection of experimental projects in which students can classify galaxies and search for new planets or supernovae using real data collected by NASA. Taking part in such explorations early will help students understand that science and math aren't just abstract equations, but tools we use to understand our world. By the time they get to college, they will have mastered the rhythm of the scientific method—learn, apply, learn, apply—and enjoy the process. 9

Six years ago, I had a student in an introductory cosmology class for non–science majors who had entered Yale as an economics major, a choice based primarily on pressure from his parents. After one summer researching gamma-ray bursts—the most energetic explosions in the universe—he is currently 10 finishing up a PhD in physics at Berkeley. He was hooked by the opportunity to apply what he learned in the classroom to a challenging scientific problem. He loved the thrill of figuring something out.

11 Without firsthand experience of the scientific method and its eventual payoff, students will continue to flock to other majors when their science and math courses become too demanding. If we want more scientists and engineers later, we need to teach children about the joys of hard work and discovery now.

Author states her claim.

Natarajan, Priya. "Want More Scientists? Turn Grade Schools into Laboratories." *Washington Post*, February 5, 2012. Reprinted by permission of the author.

QUESTIONS FOR READING

1. What are the STEM fields? Why are these fields important?
2. What percentage of college students planning to major in math or science end up changing fields?
3. What do many college students lack that leads them to have trouble in advanced STEM courses?

QUESTIONS FOR REASONING AND ANALYSIS

4. What is the problem Natarajan examines? What has caused this problem, in the author's view? What, then, is her claim?
5. How does the author support her claim?

QUESTIONS FOR REFLECTION AND WRITING

6. Few would question the reality of the problem Natarajan addresses; the issue is how to solve it. Do you agree that at least much of the cause rests with the early teaching of math and science? If yes, why? If no, why not?
7. From your experience, can you suggest other ways to improve early education in math and science?

AIR POLLUTION KILLS. MAKING THAT OFFICIAL CAN HELP US TACKLE IT.

RICHARD MARCANTONIO

Richard "Drew" Marcantonio holds a PhD from the University of Notre Dame in international peace studies and anthropology and is a postdoctoral research associate at the Kroc Institute for International Peace Studies. He teaches and conducts research on environmental violence caused by toxic and nontoxic pollution and has been published in peer-reviewed journals, such as *Science & Policy, Small Wars Journal,* and *Land.* He is currently working on a monograph titled *Environmental Violence in the Earth System and the Human Niche.* This article was published by *The Grist* on February 24, 2021.

PREREADING QUESTIONS What is the air quality like in your hometown or the location of your college? What is the state of other environmental conditions connected to water and land in your hometown or the location of your college? If you don't know, try to find out.

In December, a British coroner ruled that the cause of 9-year-old Ella Adoo-Kissi-Debrah's death in 2013 was "toxic air pollution." On its face this may not seem all that important, given that an estimated 7 million people die annually from air pollution and more than 90 percent of the world's population breathes in hazardous air every day. And yet Ella's certificate of death is the first to formally list toxic air pollution as the cause of death. 1

Ella's case is part of a growing recognition that human-produced toxic pollution is causing a substantial global health crisis, and it has substantial implications for environmental policymaking and for the legal liabilities that pollution producers may face in the future. 2

If the recent cases surrounding glyphosate—the herbicide pioneered by Monsanto in its infamous Roundup weedkiller—are any guide, Ella's case could trigger a potential windfall of cases. After a California court awarded $289 million in damages to Dewayne Johnson, a groundskeeper who used glyphosate for decades, civil cases mounted by the thousands. As a result, Bayer, which acquired Monsanto in 2018, agreed to a $10 billion settlement for all other cases in the U.S. 3

In the U.K., Ella's case has already sparked local action. The British government recently stated that in response to the verdict it would allocate $5.2 billion towards cleaning up vehicle transport emissions in cities and reducing urban nitrogen dioxide levels—the pollutant named as partially responsible for Ella's death in the coroner's report. The mayor of London, Sadiq Khan, said, "Ministers and the previous mayor have acted too slowly in the past, but they must now learn the lessons from the coroner's ruling and do much more to tackle the deadly scourge of air pollution in London and across the country." 4

Living in London, Ella was like many urban-dwelling children who are more likely to develop asthma or other respiratory illnesses due to early and chronic exposure to air pollution from cars, buses, and industry. The coroner concluded that a complex of different noxious gases and particles in the air she breathed daily caused the asthma attack that led to her death. 5

While children's respiratory systems are more vulnerable, adults do not escape the reach of air pollution in cities, where higher rates of dementia and Alzheimer's are linked to exposure to particulate matter of 2.5 microns or less in size. It's also one of the strongest correlates of death or hospitalization due to COVID-19. Spikes in particulate matter, along with other air pollutants like nitrogen oxides, are associated with higher death rates in general in the days following exposure. 6

Here in the United States, there's been relatively little attention paid to Ella's case. Given the pandemic, domestic political struggles, and the transition to a 7 new presidential administration, there is certainly an overload of news competing for attention. But with the renewed focus on climate change and environmental justice signaled by the Biden administration and among U.S. policymakers, Ella's case could be the perfect catalyst for environmental justice, in which poverty, race, and environmental risk exposure intersect. Ella's case sets a legal precedent to do something about it.

8 Death certificates fall under the purview of the Centers for Disease Control and Prevention. Thanks to guidance issued by the Obama administration, environmental exposure may be listed as a contributing factor to a death, but there is currently no code to attribute the immediate cause of death to a toxic pollution exposure. The Biden administration could issue guidance to the CDC to change that, which could shift the way people think about pollution.

9 There are more than 450,000 toxic sites across the U.S. and more than 20,000 active permitted polluters. We need to amend and bolster current domestic environmental legislation to hold polluters accountable and to make the changes permanent, rather than executive orders and programs that can be rolled back by a future administration.

10 Biden's order to build a White House Office of Domestic Climate Policy and an environmental justice interagency council is a formidable start to mitigating and remediating toxic pollution and its unequal distribution. Additionally, the Biden administration needs to put toxic air pollution on the international environmental agenda, for example leading the charge in creating a corollary international agreement to the Paris Climate Agreement.

11 Doing so would signal a shift from treating the outcomes of climate change to treating the causes. For example, in early 2016, the Department of Housing and Urban Development deemed the Isle de Jean Charles along the Louisiana Gulf Coast too risky to live on and granted $48 million to the community to relocate, for the first time codifying the term "climate refugee." But what could have been the start to a long process of redistributive environmental justice to communities threatened by climate change was quickly doused by the incoming Trump team.

12 In that case and in the case of glyphosate, it is the outcomes of pollution that were addressed—either by restitution or relocation—rather than the root cause.

13 Ella's tragic death puts a face to a problem that will be responsible for many more deaths in the future if we don't change our current policies. Let's not let this opportunity for systemic change pass us by.

Marcantonio, Richard. "Air Pollution Kills. Making That Official Can Help Us Tackle It." *Grist*, 24 Feb. 2021. Used with permission.

QUESTIONS FOR READING

1. What are some of the ways that human-produced toxic and nontoxic pollution are affecting people around the world?
2. What has changed recently to increase awareness of the negative effects of human-produced toxic and nontoxic pollutants?

3. Why was the case involving Ella Adoo-Kissi-Debrah so important?
4. Why have environmental and corporate policies changed in an attempt to address human-produced toxic and nontoxic pollution?
5. Why can't the U.S. Centers for Disease Control and Prevention list environmental exposure as a cause of death?

QUESTIONS FOR REASONING AND ANALYSIS

6. What is Marcantonio's claim? How does he defend and support it?
7. The author proposes a few strategies to address human-produced toxic and nontoxic pollution in the United States. First, how do these strategies aid his argument? Second, do his suggestions seem sensible and feasible? Why or why not?

QUESTIONS FOR REFLECTION AND WRITING

8. Marcantonio suggests some pragmatic approaches to addressing human-made toxic and nontoxic pollution. Are you content with these pragmatic approaches? Why or why not?
9. To what extent are we, as consumers of pollution-generating goods and services, to blame for environmental injustice?
10. Why is the environment so important to us, and what are some strategies that you can think of to address human-made pollution beyond the ideas Marcantonio provides?

PREPARING A PROBLEM/SOLUTION ARGUMENT

In addition to the guidelines for writing arguments presented in Chapter 4, you can use the following information to develop a proposal.

The Stases

Answering the *stasis* questions is a helpful way of brainstorming for your problem/solution argument. The stases are organized to take you from fact to proposal in a systematic way.

Fact

- Does the problem exist?
- How did it begin, and what are its causes?
- What has changed to create the problem?

Definition

- What exactly is the problem?
- What is it and what is it not?
- What are the parts of the problem?
- How is it similar to or different than other problems?

Quality (importance of the problem)

- How serious is the problem?
- Does the problem involve laws, rights, common good, or issues of care?

- What are the costs and benefits of addressing the problem?
- What are the alternatives, and are they better or worse than solving the problem?

Policy

- Are we the right people to address the problem?
- Who else might be able to address the problem?
- What should we do about the problem?

Once you've answered some, if not all, of the *stasis* questions, move on to planning.

Planning

1. **Think:** What should be the focus and limits of your argument? There's a big difference between presenting solutions to the problem of physical abuse of women by men and presenting solutions to the problem of sexual assault on your college campus. Select a topic that you know something about, one that you can realistically handle.
2. **Think:** What reasons and evidence do you have to support your tentative claim? Think through what you already know that has led you to select your particular topic. Suppose you want to write on the issues of mental health on college campuses. Where and when were the mental health situations occurring? A brainstorming list may be helpful.
3. **Reality check:** Do you have a claim worth defending? Will readers care? Binge drinking and the polluting of the lake near your hometown are serious problems. Problems with your class schedule may not be–unless your experience reveals a college-wide problem.
4. **Think:** Is there additional evidence that you need to obtain to develop your argument? If so, where can you look for that evidence? Are there past issues of the campus paper in your library? Will the counseling center grant you an interview?
5. **Think:** What about the feasibility of each solution you plan to present? Are you thinking in terms of essentially one solution with several parts to it or several separate solutions, perhaps to be implemented by different people? Will coordination be necessary to achieve success? How will this be accomplished? For the problem of college student mental health, you may want to consider several solutions as a package to be coordinated by the counseling service or an administrative vice president.

Drafting

1. Begin by either reminding readers of the existing problem you will address or arguing that a current situation should be recognized as a problem. In many cases, you can count on an audience who sees the world as you do and recognizes the problem you will address. But in some cases, your first task will be to convince readers that a problem exists that should worry them. If they are not concerned, they won't be interested in your solutions.
2. Early in your essay define the problem–as you see it–for readers. Do not assume that they will necessarily accept your way of seeing the issue. You may need to defend your understanding of the problem before moving on to solutions.

3. If appropriate, explain the cause or causes of the problem. If your proposed solution is tied to removing the cause or causes of the problem, then you need to establish cause and prove it early in your argument. If cause is important, argue for it; if it is irrelevant, move to your solution.
4. Explain your solution. If you have several solutions, think about how best to order them. If several need to be developed in a sequence, then present them in that necessary sequence. If you are presenting a package of diverse actions that together will solve the problem, then consider presenting them from the simplest to the more complex. With the problem of college student mental health, you may want to suggest hiring more diverse counselors plus advocating for an endowment for the counseling center to help make more counseling session visits possible. Just hiring more staff members does not necessarily address the number of times students may visit the counseling center.
5. Explain the process for achieving your solution. If you have not thought through the political or legal steps necessary to implement your solution, then this step cannot be part of your purpose in writing. However, anticipating a skeptical audience that says "How are we going to do that?" you would be wise to have precise steps to offer your reader. You may have obtained the estimated cost of hiring five new counselors. You may have investigated what it would take for your college's advancement office to begin a campaign for endowing the counseling center. Showing readers that you have thought ahead to the next steps in the process can be an effective method of persuasion.
6. Support the feasibility of your solution. Be able to estimate costs. Show that you know who would be responsible for implementation. Specific information strengthens your argument.
7. Show how your solution is better than others. Anticipate challenges by including reasons for adopting your program rather than another program. Explain how your solution will be more easily adopted or more effective when implemented than other possibilities. Of course, a less practical but still viable defense is that your solution is the right thing to do. Values also belong in public policy debates, not just issues of cost and acceptability.

A CHECKLIST FOR REVISION

- ☐ Do I have a clear statement of my policy claim? Is it appropriately qualified and focused?
- ☐ Have I clearly explained how I see the problem to be solved? If necessary, have I argued for seeing the problem my way?
- ☐ Have I presented my solutions—and argued for them—in a clear and logical structure? Have I explained how these solutions can be implemented and why they are better than other solutions that have been suggested?
- ☐ Have I used data that are relevant and current?
- ☐ Have I used the basic checklist for revision in Chapter 4? (See p. 104.)

FOR ANALYSIS AND DEBATE

DOCTORS CAN'T TREAT COVID-19 EFFECTIVELY WITHOUT RECOGNIZING THE SOCIAL JUSTICE ASPECTS OF HEALTH

ZOË JULIAN, RACHEL R. HARDEMAN, AND RYAN HUERTO

Zoë Julian is a health services researcher and clinical instructor at the University of Alabama at Birmingham. She earned her MD and MPH from Emory University and holds a BSE from Washington University in St. Louis. Rachel R. Hardeman is an associate professor and Blue Cross Endowed Professor of Health and Racial Equity in the Division of Health Policy and Management at the University of Minnesota. She holds a PhD and MPH from the University of Minnesota, and a BS in chemistry from Xavier University of Louisiana. Ryan Huerto is a fellow, National Clinician Scholars Program, in the University of Michigan's Department of Family Medicine. He earned his MD from the University of California San Diego and holds an MPH from Harvard University and an MA from Loyola Marymount University.

PREREADING QUESTIONS Why do you think some people might reject the premise that social justice and health care are connected? What do you know about redlining and gentrification in America? Do a quick search of credible sources on the web for the terms redlining and gentrification and find out more before reading this article.

1 Recent data shows that black, Latino, indigenous and immigrant communities are disproportionately affected by COVID-19, due in large part to the persistent legacy of structural racism—practices and policies that systematically benefit white people and harm people of color.

2 From the Bronx and Queens, New York to the Mission District in San Francisco, to the Navajo Nation and black communities of New Orleans, Detroit and Oakland, the message is clear: COVID-19 highlights our societal failures at the intersections of public health, health care and social justice. If health inequities weren't severe and oppressive enough, add on the layer of police brutality that takes black lives on a regular basis. No matter where we look, our system has continually devalued black bodies and lives.

3 As an interdisciplinary team of public health experts, physicians, medical students and critical race scholars, we believe that an important piece of the solution lies in physician training and knowledge of how societal factors affect health. Clinicians in training need to be grounded in the social determinants of health and critical race theory to prepare them for an ethical and effective pandemic response. We'll explain why social justice is so crucial to medical education and the care of marginalized communities.

PUBLIC HEALTH, SOCIAL JUSTICE AND MEDICINE

4 Public health promotes and protects the health of people and the communities where they live, learn, work and play. Traditionally, physicians study purely biological factors that only make up a small proportion of an individual's risk of disease. Public health professionals study the social determinants of

health—factors beyond our bodies that impact health. These include insurance status, access to health care, reliable access to food, safe housing, transportation, education, safety and equal protection under the law.

DO EXPERTS HAVE SOMETHING TO ADD TO PUBLIC DEBATE?

We think so. 5

Social justice is central to public health. This is because research has shown 6 that health disparities are created by social inequities. Public health experts understand that oppressive systems dictate which people have access to key resources that determine health. Racism and classism create conditions where people of color, those living in poverty and other marginalized groups have limited access to resources that impact health—the social determinants.

The social practices that created these gaps in health include redlining, a 7 practice where lenders denied mortgages to eligible buyers solely because of their race. Therefore, black people and other people of color were denied the right of home ownership and upward economic mobility that millions of white people enjoyed. Redlining, now banned, was succeeded by gentrification, whereby middle-class white people come into urban areas and displace black people who have lived in a neighborhood for years.

Both redlining and gentrification perpetuate poverty in communities of 8 color in America's cities. As such, many black and low-income Americans live in communities where clean water for good hand hygiene isn't guaranteed, and social distancing is near impossible in crowded homes. In this way, redlining and gentrification impact the racial inequities seen in COVID-19.

By improving social determinants of health, health care leaders can transform 9 our systems toward adequate COVID-19 prevention, testing and treatment for marginalized communities. But without a critical race lens, experts will still get it wrong. They still might assume that racial and ethnic disparities exist because they believe that race is biological—a longstanding myth. Rather, they must confront how structural racism is a root cause of health inequity.

A strong example of social justice-oriented care is the work of pediatrician 10 Dr. Mona Hanna-Attisha, who helped link toxic lead levels in Flint, Michigan's drinking water with the high lead levels in sick children's blood from Flint. Dr. Hanna-Attisha helped ring the alarm on the Flint Water Crisis, which sparked efforts to clean Flint's drinking water. We believe a similar social justice approach is necessary for beating COVID-19.

COVID MAKES THE CASE CLEAR

Social justice and human rights are at the center of COVID-19. Therefore, they 11 must be centered in clinician training. Courses on inequity and social justice are still optional in many medicals schools. Most of these efforts are student-run, underfunded or assigned to minoritized medical educators.

COVID-19 has revealed how looking at differences in health through biology 12 alone is limited. It is not sufficient in addressing this pandemic. If people perceive inequities as inevitable, they resign marginalized communities to poor health outcomes. When health providers and the health system take accountability for our inequitable health care system, they can better serve patients and communities.

13 As practitioners, scholars and people from communities that are most affected by COVID-19, we see human rights as being at the core of our work. Social justice demands us to see people with their full humanity to ensure equity in and beyond a pandemic. Because so many affected by COVID-19 are navigating poverty, food insecurity, lack of housing, child care and insurance issues, physicians must develop a deep understanding and compassion towards all elements that undergird people's health and well-being.

Hardeman, Rachel R., Ryan Huerto, and Zoe Julian. "Doctors Can't Treat COVID-19 Effectively without Recognizing the Social Justice Aspects of Health." *The Conversation*, 3 June 2020. Used with permission.

QUESTIONS FOR READING

1. According to the authors, why do diseases like COVID-19 affect Black communities and people of color more than white communities?
2. What are some of the social determinants that affect health according to Julian, Hardeman, and Huerto?
3. What happened to the water, and the people who drank it, in Flint, Michigan?
4. What do the authors propose as strategies to address the problem of health inequity in Black communities and among people of color?

QUESTIONS FOR REASONING AND ANALYSIS

5. Write a statement of the authors' claim that reveals their essay as a problem/solution type of argument.
6. What kind of essay do the opening paragraphs suggest? What information do the authors provide in those opening paragraphs?
7. This article is well organized. What do the authors do in each section to make the information they discuss accessible to people outside of the health profession?
8. Julian, Hardeman, and Huerto offer one specific solution: what is it? Evaluate this approach for feasibility and effectiveness.

QUESTIONS FOR REFLECTION AND WRITING

9. Are you convinced by the authors' argument? Why or why not?
10. If you are considering going into a health profession, what might you do to ensure that the authors' solution is a part of your study and experience? If you are not going into a health profession, what might you do to help support equity in health care?

3 INDIGENOUS WOMEN TALK COP26 AND WHAT REAL CLIMATE SOLUTIONS LOOK LIKE

STEPHANIE WOOD

Stephanie Wood holds an MA in journalism from the University of British Columbia and has published in outlets such as *The Tyee, Media Indigena,* Canadian Broadcasting

Corporation, the *National Observer,* and *Yes! Magazine.* She is a Skwxwú7mesh (the name of the Squamish people in the Coast Salish language) writer living in North Vancouver who focuses on Indigenous rights and social justice. This article was published by *Yes! Magazine* on November 8, 2021.

PREREADING QUESTIONS What was COP26, and why was it important for environmentalists and people interested in the climate crisis? If you're not familiar with the First Nations and their languages, do some research on the web. What did you find?

Nuskmata wants to combat myths about mining in Canada. 1

This is one of her goals at the United Nations climate summit in Glasgow. 2

Nuskmata, mining spokesperson for Nuxalk Nation, spoke to *The Narwhal* 3 from her home in British Columbia prior to leaving for the summit, also known as the 26th annual meeting of the Conference of Parties (COP26) to the United Nations Framework Convention on Climate Change. She said she wants to center solutions around Indigenous governance and emphasize how Indigenous Peoples are bearing the burden of climate policies, even well-intentioned ones like switching to electrification and renewable energy—that still requires mining precious metals, she said.

"You can't be sacrificing Indigenous Peoples and clean water in order to get 4 solar panels," she said. "It's not just swapping out oil and gas. It's about changing the system so that it's sustainable for everybody."

Nuskmata is one of many Indigenous delegates at COP26 determined to 5 pursue Indigenous solutions, along with debunking myths and adding context to Canada's global commitments.

She said she also hopes to deliver a message that mining "is not a green 6 solution" to the climate crisis.

At COP26, the more than 100 countries in attendance will update their 2015 7 Paris Agreement commitments to reduce greenhouse gas emissions, intended to meet the urgent need to limit global warming to 1.5°C. This will require profound changes, as the Intergovernmental Panel on Climate Change released a sobering report in August which found Earth could exceed the 1.5°C warming limit by the early 2030s if we don't curb emissions. To stay below 2°C warming, countries have to meet net-zero emissions around 2050, the report found.

Already in Scotland, nearly all countries have signed a deal committing to 8 end deforestation by 2030, including Canada—though logging here is seen as renewable and therefore not affected by the deal. Delegates have pledged $1.7 billion in funding to Indigenous Peoples, recognizing the critical role they play in forest conservation.

On Monday Prime Minister Justin Trudeau pledged to cap and then cut 9 emissions from Canada's oil and gas sector, repeating one of his 2021 campaign promises. But according to a new report from Environmental Defence Canada and Oil Change International, oil and gas producers only have vague commitments that rely on carbon-capture technology. Some critics say COP26 is excluding Indigenous leaders from key parts of the international discussions. Regional Chief of the British Columbia Assembly of First Nations Terry Teegee said in a public statement "there is a noticeable failure to include First Nations while negotiating the collective future of our planet internationally and locally."

10 In further critique, Indigenous people held a memorial at COP26 for 1,005 Indigenous land defenders killed since the Paris Agreement. Indigenous land defender Ita Mendoza, from the state of Oaxaca in Mexico, told *The Guardian* that COP is "a big business, a continuation of colonialism." Despite these concerns, Indigenous leaders are at COP26 pushing for Indigenous Peoples to be at decision-making tables to prevent climate catastrophe.

11 "We have to shift perspectives by sharing who we are, how we live, what our values are, and what our solutions are," Nuskmata said.

12 She is one of three Indigenous women at COP26 who spoke to the Narwhal about what they hope to accomplish at the summit.

13 Here is what they said.

14 "My name, Nuskmata, is ancient. It's older than our forests here," Nuskmata said, explaining her name is an inheritance from her Nuxalk village and bloodline.

15 The ancestor and namesake Nuskmata cleared a path from the coast to the interior of what's now known as British Columbia, Nuskmata said. It makes her think about her responsibility to clear a path in her own way as a spokesperson and advocate.

16 "We may or may not see all the benefits of the work that we're doing, but we have to believe that we are clearing a path for future generations," she said.

17 Nuskmata said she wants to hear about other people's fights to protect their lands at COP26, so she can remember and be inspired by them after she returns home.

18 Taking care of their territory is Nuxalk's "love story with the land," Nuskmata said.

19 "I'm a Nuxalk woman with an ancient name. I still live in the place where my ancestors have been for thousands of years. That's really powerful. That's a beautiful thing. And that's part of my love story."

20 "I want to hear those love stories from all around the world."

21 She will be sharing climate solutions the Nuxalk Nation wants to pursue, including scaling down mining and clearcut logging. In August, the nation issued an eviction notice to Vancouver-based mining company Juggernaut Exploration, which received two permits for exploration from the province without the nation's consent. The nation has not consented to any of the mining on its territory. Many critics have denounced B.C.'s mining laws for being lax on regulation and not requiring Indigenous consent.

22 Juggernaut Exploration missed the eviction deadline.

23 Nuskmata, who is also Secwepemc, has seen first hand the potential dangers of mining, witnessing the 2014 Mount Polley mine disaster on Secwepemc territory, when the tailings pond spilled 24 million cubic metres of contaminated waste into Quesnel Lake. According to critics, B.C.'s mining regulations still fall short on preventing a similar disaster in the future. Nuskmata wants to build more public awareness.

24 "One of the things I learned from Mount Polley is you can never waste a disaster," Nuskmata said. "Within that crisis there are cracks in the system."

Nuskmata also plans to hold B.C. and Canada accountable for their commitments to the United Nations Declaration on the Rights of Indigenous Peoples (UNDRIP). Both levels of government have introduced legislation to adopt UNDRIP. But even though the United Nations Committee on the Elimination of Racial Discrimination called on Canada to halt the Coastal GasLink pipeline, the Trans Mountain pipeline and the Site C dam until obtaining free, prior and informed consent—a central principle of UNDRIP—construction carries on while land defenders continue to fight the projects. 25

"They don't follow their own laws, they adopt stuff and don't implement it," Nuskmata said. "Meanwhile, money keeps flowing out of our territories in the form of trees, minerals, foods and medicines while they keep our communities in stable poverty with their colonial institutions." 26

Her biggest goal for COP26 is to expand her nation's network to share solutions grounded in the principle of reciprocity. 27

"This is a global event, I doubt I will be in any way center stage. But that's not my goal, it's not about me. It's about sharing the work." 28

Kukpi7 Judy Wilson of the Neskonlith Indian Band tried to hail a cab in Vancouver between meetings as we did our interview over the phone, calling her crammed schedule a "typical" day. 29

The prominent Indigenous rights advocate, and secretary-treasurer for the Union of British Columbia Indian Chiefs, celebrated her 60th birthday in October. She has been in politics her whole life, and attended her first United Nations conference sometime in her 40s, though she can't remember what year. For Wilson, advocating for Indigenous Peoples isn't an option. 30

"As an Indigenous person, especially being a woman, we're born into this," she said, standing in the rain with an umbrella as sirens wailed in the background. 31

Indigenous people hold value systems in which "everybody is taken care of," and those values are essential to address global issues of hunger, poverty and climate change, she said. 32

In her experiences attending international events, Wilson noticed Indigenous people have to "carve out their own space" since these events still prioritize state governments. Like Nuskmata, she wants to see more room for Indigenous people to provide solutions. 33

She also wants to bring more international awareness of ongoing Indigenous Rights issues in Canada and their intersections with climate change. 34

"There's a lot happening in our own country with Trans Mountain, Fairy Creek, Site C dam, with Wet'suwet'en," Wilson said. "The real issue is climate change and global warming, but [the government] tries to reduce them to other issues, and our people are criminalized." 35

She wants to spend more time mentoring young people to pick up the fight. 36

"We need to instill climate leadership. I see young people like Autumn Peltier and Greta Thunberg, and I'm so inspired by them," she said. 37

"That's the climate leadership that we need, and I'm not seeing it anywhere else right now. . . It's young people that are going to change the world." 38

Another one of Wilson's priorities at COP26 is to emphasize cumulative effects. Hunting, harvesting, fishing, and collecting medicines is becoming 39 harder in her territory. Less fish are returning in the rivers. This summer, during an extreme heatwave, some Neskonlith families were under an evacuation alert or order due to the White Rock Lake wildfire that burned about 833 square kilometers—an area nearly the size of the City of Calgary. "[Decision-makers] are trying to make it look like there are substantive changes, when it's not enough to reduce emissions to address global warming," she said. "We need to act now."

40 "We have to ensure that these changes are made for the survival of all of our people."

41 In October, Crystal Martin-Lapenskie was in her home near Ottawa Facetiming with her sister in Sanirajak, Nunavut. She asked her how the weather was.

42 To Martin-Lapenskie's shock, her friend stepped outside to show her it was raining.

43 "It shouldn't be raining. It should be snowing," Martin-Lapenskie told The Narwhal on a video call from Glasgow.

44 "As a child, around August there would be snow on the ground. Twenty years later, we're seeing less and less snow. There was no snow in August. You used to be lucky if there's snow in September. Now you're lucky if you see snow in October."

45 "It's really frightening in a short 20-year span that our climate has changed so drastically."

46 Martin-Lapenskie is a former president of the National Inuit Youth Council and a consultant with the Inuit Circumpolar Council. This is her second time at the UN climate summit. She described climate change as a spider web: a series of interwoven issues, and together "it captures all of the necessities in life that you need to survive."

47 Climate change is an urgent issue for Inuit. Their home in the Arctic is warming twice as fast as the rest of the world. Country foods are harder to hunt and harvest. Inuit have even fallen through ice and died when ice typically would have been thick, Martin-Lapenskie said. She also pointed to Nuugaatsiaq, Greenland, which was hit by a tsunami in 2017 caused by a landslide. Residents still aren't able to return home because the area is unstable. Tsunamis are one of the extreme weather events that scientists say will be made more common by climate change.

48 Martin-Lapenskie wants to bring more of these human-centered stories from the Arctic to policy-making at COP26. She wants to amplify Inuit knowledge through the two events the Inuit Circumpolar Council is hosting—one about marine governance and the other about youth and infrastructure.

49 The council is also celebrating International Inuit Day on Nov. 7 in Glasgow with film screenings, Inuit panels, and Inuit drum-dancing and throat-singing.

50 Her primary goal is to get Inuit at decision-making tables.

51 "This week is all about amplifying the need to ensure any policies or decisions that are taking place in the Arctic are being conducted with Inuit," she said.

Wood, Stephanie. "3 Indigenous Women Talk COP26 and What Real Climate Solutions Look Like." *Yes!*, 8 Nov. 2021. Used with permission.

QUESTIONS FOR READING

1. Why did the three Indigenous women Wood interviewed travel to Scotland to attend COP26?
2. According to the article, what are some of the negative effects of climate change they have noticed over the past 20 years?
3. What solutions do the interviewees in the article propose to address the problems they discuss?

QUESTIONS FOR REASONING AND ANALYSIS

4. How does Wood organize her article? Why do you think she structured her piece this way?
5. Wood doesn't really present a clear thesis herself, but rather she allows her interviewees to speak for themselves. Taken together, what are the interviewees asserting?
6. One way to support a claim about climate change is to use traditional research data—rising ocean and temperature levels, extreme weather cycles, increased costs from catastrophic storms caused by the change in climate. What strategy does Wood use? Why do you think Wood and her interviewees use this strategy?
7. Analyze the information Wood provides. Analyze the information the interviewees provide. Which conclusions are inferences and which are judgments?

QUESTIONS FOR REFLECTION AND WRITING

8. Are you convinced by the article's argument? Why or why not?
9. What are the Canadian and U.S. laws governing control of natural resources found on land belonging to an Indigenous nation? Should countries like Canada and the United States be able to utilize natural resources found on these lands without the permission of the Indigenous people? Why or why not?
10. Given that all of the Americas were populated by the First Nations before European colonists arrived, do you think that Indigenous people should play a part in the decision-making process that guides environmental policies of countries like Canada and the United States? Why or why not?

SUGGESTIONS FOR DISCUSSION AND WRITING

1. Think of a problem on your campus or in your community for which you have a workable solution. Organize your argument to include all relevant steps as described in this chapter. Although your primary concern will be to present your solution, depending on your topic you may need to begin by convincing readers of the seriousness of the problem or the causes of the problem—if your solutions involve removing those causes.

2. Think of a problem in education—K-12 or at the college level—that you have a solution for and that you are interested in. You may want to begin by brainstorming to develop a list of possible problems in education about which you could write. Be sure to qualify your claim and limit your focus as necessary to work with a problem that is not so broad and general that your "solutions" become general and vague comments about "getting better teachers." (If one problem is a lack of qualified teachers, then what specific proposals do you have for solving that particular problem?) Include as many steps as are appropriate to develop and support your argument.

3. Think of a situation that you consider serious but that apparently many people do not take seriously enough. Write an argument in which you emphasize, by providing evidence, that the situation is a serious problem. You may conclude by suggesting a solution, but your chief purpose in writing will be to alert readers to a problem.

CHAPTER 12

Locating, Evaluating, and Preparing to Use Sources

LEARNING OUTCOMES

After reading Chapter 12, you will be able to:

- Explain how to select a good paper topic.
- Describe how to write a tentative claim or research proposal.
- Outline how to prepare a working bibliography and manage your paper project.
- Describe how to locate sources for your paper.
- Explain how to conduct field research.
- Outline how to evaluate your paper's sources.
- Describe how to prepare an annotated bibliography.

diego_cervo/123RF

We do research all the time. You would not select a college or buy a car without doing research: gathering relevant information, analyzing that information, and drawing conclusions from your study. You may already have done some research in this course, using sources in this text or finding data online to strengthen an argument. Then you acknowledged your source informally or formally, following the documentation guidelines in this section. So, when you are assigned a more formal research essay, remember that you are not facing a brand-new assignment. You are just doing a longer paper with more sources, and you have this section to guide you to success.

Begin your research process knowing that writing is recursive and often messy, as illustrated in figure 12.1. Though the following steps are presented in a linear order, you will likely find yourself moving back and forth between steps, skipping steps, and even removing and adding steps of your own to complete your research and write your paper. The following steps are basic guidelines. You should meet with your instructor and visit your writing center often during your research to get feedback on how your paper is progressing.

SELECTING A GOOD TOPIC

To get started you need to select and limit a topic. One key to success is finding a workable topic. No matter how interesting or clever the topic, it is not workable if it does not meet the guidelines of your assignment. Included in those guidelines may be a required word count, a required number of assignments, a required number of sources, and a due date. Understand and accept all of these guidelines as part of your writing context.

What Type of Paper Am I Preparing?

Study your assignment to understand the type of project. Is your purpose to write a report essay, an analytical essay, or an argumentative essay? Using these three categories, how would you classify each of the following topics?

1. Explain the chief solutions proposed for increasing the Southwest's water supply.
2. Compare the Freudian and behavioral models of mental illness.
3. Find the best solutions to a current environmental problem.
4. Consider: What twentieth-century invention has most dramatically changed our personal lives?

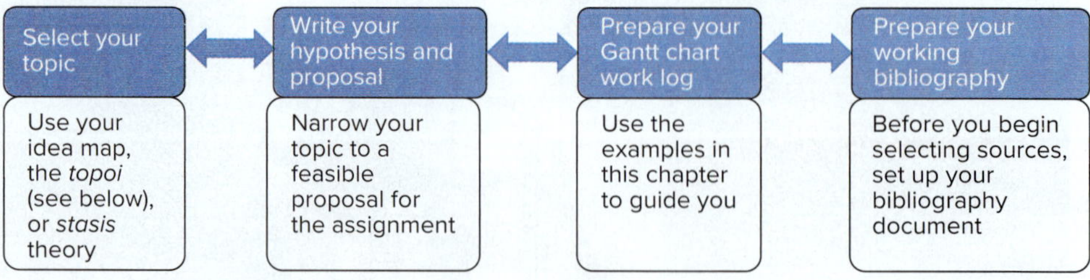

FIGURE 12.1 Recursive Writing Process

Did you recognize that the first topic calls for a report? The second topic requires an analysis of two schools of psychology, so you cannot report on only one, but you also cannot argue that one model is better than the other. Both topics 3 and 4 require an argumentative paper: You must select and defend a claim. If you are not sure about the type of paper you are preparing, meet with your instructor or visit your college writing center and bring the assignment sheet.

Who Is My Audience?

If you are writing in a specific discipline, imagine your instructor as a representative of that field, a reader with knowledge of the subject area. If you are in a composition course, your instructor may advise you to write to a general reader, someone who reads newspapers but may not have the exact information and perspective you have. For a general reader, specialized terms and concepts need definition.

NOTE: Consider the expectations of your readers. A research essay is not a personal essay. It is not about you; it is about a subject. Keep yourself in the background and carefully evaluate any use of the personal pronoun "I."

How Can I Select a Good Topic?

Choosing from assigned topics. At times students are unhappy with topic restriction. Looked at another way, your instructor has eliminated a difficult step in the research process and has helped you avoid the problem of selecting an unworkable topic. If topics are assigned, you will still have to choose from the list and develop your own claim and approach.

Finding a course-related topic. This guideline gives you many options and requires more thought about your choice. Working within the guidelines, try to write about what interests you. Here are examples of assignments turned into topics of interest to the student:

ASSIGNMENT	INTEREST	TOPIC
1. Trace the influence of any twenty-first century event, development, invention.	Music	The influence of hip hop on K-Pop
2. Support an argument on some issue related to the exorbitant amount of money in professional sports.	American baseball, international soccer	Money and cheating in American baseball: the 2017 and 2018 sign stealing scandal of the Houston Astros
3. Demonstrate the popularity of a current myth and then discredit it.	Science fiction	The lack of evidence for the existence of UFOs

Selecting a topic without any guidelines. When you are free to write on any topic, you may need to use some strategies for topic selection.

- Look through your text's table of contents or index for subject areas that can be narrowed or focused.
- Look over your class notes and think about subjects covered that have interested you.
- Consider college-based or local issues.
- Do a subject search in a database to see how a large topic can be narrowed—for example, type in "dinosaur" and observe such subheadings as *dinosaur behavior* and *dinosaur extinction.*
- You may also use one or more of the invention strategies below to narrow and focus a topic:
  - Freewriting
  - Brainstorming
  - Asking questions about a broad subject, using the journalist's questions *who, what, where, when, why* and *how.*
- Use an idea map to freewrite, brainstorm, and/or answer the journalist's questions.

Whichever topic you choose, make sure that it is timely and important, that is, make sure that it is *kairotic.*

What Aristotle Teaches Us About Selecting a Topic

In Chapter 3, you learned about some rhetorical concepts originally developed by Aristotle. In addition to these concepts, Aristotle provided his students with a means for choosing a topic to discuss and different ways to approach a topic once it had been chosen. Aristotle's *topoi,* listed below, may be helpful as you consider the different approaches you can take as you brainstorm about your assignment.

- Definition: defining something or arguing for its inclusion in a group or category
- Compare and contrast: arguing for similar or dissimilar aspects of two or more things, events, etc.
- Cause and effect: arguing the causes and outcomes of something
- Testimony: arguing about something that the author has heard, read, or researched
- Circumstance: arguing whether something is possible or impossible

In the following chapters, you will learn more about some of these *topoi* as they are developed into detailed arguments.

What Kinds of Topics Should I Avoid?

Here are several kinds of topics that are best avoided because they usually produce disasters, no matter how well the student handles the rest of the research process:

1. *Topics that are irrelevant* to your interests or the course. If you are not interested in your topic, you will not produce a lively, informative paper. If you select a topic far

removed from the course content, you may create some hostility in your instructor, who will wonder why you are unwilling to become engaged in the course.

2. *Topics that are broad subject areas.* These result in general surveys that lack appropriate detail and support.
3. *Topics that can be fully researched with only one source.* You will likely produce a summary, not a research paper.
4. *Biographical studies.* Short undergraduate papers on a person's life usually turn out to be summaries of one or two major biographies.
5. *Topics that produce a strong emotional response in you.* If there is only one "right" answer to the abortion issue and you cannot imagine counterarguments, don't choose to write on abortion. Probably most religious topics are best avoided.
6. *Topics that are too technical for you* at this point in your college work. If you do not understand the complexities of the federal tax code, then arguing for a reduction in the capital gains tax may be an unwise topic choice.

Ancient rhetoricians, including Aristotle, also used *stasis* theory to help them discover more about topics for their inquiries. In Chapter 11, you learned how *stasis* theory can help you discover more about an issue you may be addressing in a proposal. Similarly, you can use *stasis* theory in your research project. Again, here are the *stasis* questions with a few questions to help you get started:

Conjecture/Fact

- Is there an act or topic to be considered?
- What do we know about the act or topic?

Definition

- How can we define the act or topic?
- What are the key terms related to the act or topic?

Quality (importance of the topic)

- How important or serious is the act or topic?
- How pressing or urgent is the act or topic?

Policy

- Am I the right person to consider this act or topic?
- What do I think should be done about this act or topic?

WRITING A TENTATIVE CLAIM OR RESEARCH PROPOSAL

Once you have selected and focused on a topic, write a tentative claim or hypothesis, research question, or research proposal. Some instructors will ask to see a statement—from a sentence to a paragraph long—to be approved before you proceed. Others may require a one-page proposal that includes a tentative claim, a basic organizational plan, and a description of types of sources to be used. Even if your instructor does not require anything in writing, you need to write something for your benefit—to direct your reading and thinking. Here are two possibilities:

1. **SUBJECT:** Smartphones

   TOPIC: The impact of smartphones on the twenty-first century

   CLAIM: Smartphones have had the greatest impact of any technological development in the twenty-first century.

   RESEARCH PROPOSAL: I propose to show that smartphones have had the greatest impact of any technological development in the twenty-first century. I will show the influence of smartphones on the economy, on social networking, and on cultural issues to emphasize the breadth of influence. I will argue that other possibilities (such as the laptop computer) did not have the same impact as smartphones. I will check the library's book catalog and databases for sources on technological developments and on smartphones specifically. I will also interview a family friend who works for a company that makes smartphones.

This example illustrates several key ideas. First, the initial subject is both too broad and unfocused (*What* about smartphones?). Second, the claim is more focused than the topic statement because it asserts a position, a claim the student must support. Third, the research proposal is more helpful than the claim only because it includes some thoughts on developing the thesis and finding sources.

2. Less sure of your topic? Then write a research question or a more open-ended research proposal. Take, for example, a history student studying the effects of racism. She is not ready to write a thesis, but she can write a research proposal that suggests some possible approaches to the topic:

   TOPIC: The effects of structural racism in my hometown.

   RESEARCH QUESTION: What are the effects of structural racism in my hometown?

   RESEARCH PROPOSAL: I will examine the effects of structural racism in my hometown (and possibly some long-term effects, depending on the amount of material on the topic). Specifically, I will examine the varying effects of structural racism from redlining, to block busting, to white flight on the current real estate market in my hometown.

PREPARING A WORKING BIBLIOGRAPHY

To begin this next stage of your research, you need to know three things:

- *Your search strategy.* If you are writing on a course-related topic, your starting place may be your textbook for relevant sections and possible sources (if the text contains a bibliography). For this course, you may find some potential sources among the readings in this text. Think about what you already know or have in hand as you plan your search strategy. As part of your research strategy, you may also want to record your tasks and how long your tasks take to complete in a log. Tracking research tasks and time will help you set short- and long-term goals and manage your project.

- *A method for recording bibliographic information.* You have some options: you may use online or downloadable research applications, such as EndNote or EasyBib, you may use a bibliographic application your college provides, you may use a citation generator provided by the publisher or database, or you may track your research in a work log you develop yourself. A work log will help you keep track of your research process, providing a place for recording how you use your time and the sources you find. A work log will also help you reflect on your project management skills so that you can revise how you conduct research and write if you are not happy with the grade you received on your researched paper. If you use a research application, you are still responsible for the accuracy of your listings in your Works Cited page or References page.

Work Log

Keeping a work log helps record the writing process and sources.

DATE	TASKS & SOURCES	TIME SPENT
11/5/2021	Task: Chose concrete topic & answered inquiry questions regarding topic	30 min
11/8/2021	Task: Finding potential articles for topic Sources: www.umsl.edu/socialwork/files/pdfs/Students,%20alums/Engel.%20Jessica%20policy%20brief%20Maternal%20Mortality%20in%20Missouri%20Final.pdf https://storymaps.arcgis.com/stories/40ec06e64b994f2d84ef9ea5e22769c0 https://health.mo.gov/living/families/mch-block-grant/pdf/maternalmortalityandmorbidity_final.pdf www.stltoday.com/opinion/columnists/missouri-needsto-help-its-physicians-prevent-mothers-from-dying/article_053781cc f0b2-5f10-925e-33324128b65d.html	50 min

11/10/2021	Looked for sources www.cdc.gov/healthequity/features/maternal-mortality/index.html Started on presentation	20 min
11/12/21	Finished presentation	1 hr
11/15/2021	Looked for sources www.mhanet.com/mhaimages/SQI/Trajectories/Trajectories_Dec2019_Maternal%20Mortality.pdf www.thinkhealthstl.org/content/sites/stlouisco/MCH/FINAL_2019_MCH_Report.pdf	50 min
11/16/2021	Looked for sources health.mo.gov/data/pamr/pdf/annual-report.pdf www.americanprogress.org/article/eliminating-racial-disparities-maternal-infant- mortality/	30 min
11/17/2021	Created Audience Analysis. Updated and refined primary and secondary question	50 min

Tracking time for each task will help you plan for future writing projects.

Work logs also help you record your sources.

11/18/2021	Started outline and looked for a book source and journalistic sources. Found book source on Saint Louis University database called *Birth Settings in America: Outcomes, Quality, Access, and Choice.* Journalistic source from *New York Times*: www.nytimes.com/2018/04/11/magazine/black-mothers-babies-death-maternal-mortality.html	1 hr
11/20/2021	Completed Project 3 outline and intro paragraph	2 hrs
11/29/2021	Worked on 1st and 2nd body paragraph. Found two additional scholarly sources: *Exploring the Experience of Life Stress Among Black Women with a History of Fetal or Infant Death: a Phenomenological Study. & Exploring Racial Disparity in St. Louis City Fetal-Infant Death.*	2 hrs
12/08/21	Wrote half a third body paragraph.	1 hr
12/11/2021	Worked on annotated bibliography and audience analysis.	2 hrs

12/12/2021	Completed annotated bibliography and audience analysis. Almost completed with the third body paragraph.	2 hrs
12/13/2021	Completed third body paragraph. Last minute editing before turning in the final draft.	5 hrs
	Total Time:	27 hours

Adding up the total amount of time will help you organize you project management in the future.

- *The documentation format you will be using.* You may be assigned the Modern Language Association (MLA) format, or perhaps given a choice between MLA and the American Psychological Association (APA) documentation styles. Once you select the documentation style, skim the appropriate pages in Chapter 14 to get an overview of both content and style.

A list of possible sources is only a *working* bibliography because you do not yet know which sources you will use. (Your final bibliography will include only those sources you cite–actually refer to–in your paper.) A working bibliography will help you see what is available on your topic, note how to locate each source, and contain the information needed to document. Whether you are using research applications or your work log, follow these guidelines:

1. Check all reasonable catalogs, databases, and indexes for possible sources. (Use more than one reference source even if you locate enough sources there; you are looking for the best sources, not the first ones you find.)
2. Complete an entry or listing for every potentially useful source. You won't know what to reject until you start a close reading of sources.
3. Copy (or download from an online catalog) all information needed to complete a citation and to locate the source, including the DOI (digital object identifier), permalink (this is sometimes called a stable URL), or URL if the source is online. (When using an index that does not give all needed information, leave a space to be filled in when you actually read the source.)
4. Put bibliographic information in the correct format for every possible source; you will save time and make fewer errors. Do not mix or blend styles. When searching for sources, have your text handy and use the appropriate models as your guide.

The following brief guide to correct form will get you started. Illustrations are for the work log, but the information and order may be the same in research applications. (Guidelines are for MLA style.)

Basic Form for Articles

The basic MLA form for articles includes the following information in this pattern:

1. The author's full name, last name first
2. The title (and subtitle if there is one) of the article, in italics
3. The facts of the publication: title, volume and issue numbers if they're available, year and pages
4. DOI, permalink, URL, or access number

Include the date, time, and location of your sources so that you can track how much time it's taking you to complete tasks. This will help you manage your time and complete drafts by their deadlines. More information on time management and deadlines is in the following section on Gantt charts.

Gantt Charts

In their most basic form, Gantt charts, named for their designer Henry Gantt, are schedules that help you figure out what you're going to do when. They display tasks, milestones, and deadlines to help you establish a feasible timeline for your research and writing. Learning how to use a Gantt chart in your composition class will help you organize your work so you don't have to cram just before your deadlines. Using a Gantt chart now will also help you prepare for your work after graduation as these types of scheduling models are used in graduate school and in the workplace.

While you can download sophisticated Gantt charts from the web, you can also create a Gantt chart yourself using MS Word, MS PowerPoint, or other similar applications. Use the sample in Figure 12.2 to help you design your own Gantt chart. This Gantt chart is organized into a four-week timeline for a research paper that involves secondary research and one interview.

Task/Date	9/20	9/23	9/25	9/27	9/29	10/1	10/4	10/6	10/8	10/11
Begin work on research paper	Brainstorm paper ideas, start work log, idea map	Finish idea map, meet with instructor, create hypothesis	Start research using Google scholar, revisit hypothesis	Continue research using library database, interview polisci prof						
Begin drafting research paper					Write outline, first paragraph, revisit/affirm hypothesis	Write body paragraphs 1-4, citing as I go				
Workshop, revise research, submit draft							Visit writing center, workshop draft in class, meet with instructor	Write body paragraph 5-9, integrate visuals	Write conclusion, annotated bibliography, finish work log	
Finish research paper and submit final draft										Finish rewriting, submit research paper

FIGURE 12.2 **Research Paper Gantt Chart: A Four-Week Timeline.**

Reading the Gantt chart, you might think that writing is easy and linear–just completion of a list of tasks. It's not. As noted in Chapter 1 and elsewhere in this book, writing is always recursive, often messy, and always challenging. However, organizing your research and writing using a work log and Gantt chart will help you tackle this challenging process.

LOCATING SOURCES

All libraries contain books and periodicals and a system for accessing them. A library's *book collection* includes the general collection, the reference collection, and the reserve book collection. Electronic materials such as CDs, DVDs, and other types of media will also be included in the general "book" collection. The *periodicals collection* consists of popular magazines, scholarly journals, and newspapers. Electronic databases with texts of articles provide alternatives to the print periodicals collection.

Research on the Web and Information Literacy

The web is both disorganized and huge, so you can waste time trying to find information. Moreover, sources on the web vary widely in credibility, so you can also find information that ranges from scholarly data to complete fiction.

The web is good for providing current information, such as news and movie reviews, and it is a great source of government information. However, because anyone can create a website, blog, or social media post and put anything in them, you will have to be especially careful in evaluating web resources. While scholarly articles written by academics have been peer reviewed (vetted by other researchers), and while news sites have been evaluated by editors, personal websites and social media do not require much quality control.

A special word about social media: When conducting research online, you might be tempted to take some shortcuts through social media. While some social media platforms may be useful, you must be especially cautious using Facebook, Twitter, Instagram, TikTok, etc. First, the platforms themselves use algorithms that prioritize or highlight certain types of information above others. For example, a social media platform may use an algorithm that causes an article or post to trend if it causes outrage or negative responses from users. So if someone posts something inflammatory and misleading, it may trend faster because users may be "liking" it and because users may be "disliking" it or raging against the post.

If you find some trusted sources or experts to follow, sources and experts that you have evaluated using the guidelines that follow, then you might consider beginning your research with these resources. But always check multiple reputable sources before using information in your research. In the end, you are responsible for vetting your sources.

Keep in mind these facts about the web:

- The web is both disorganized and huge, so you can waste time trying to find information that is easily obtained in a library reference book or database.
- The web is best at providing current information, such as news and movie reviews. It is also a great source of government information.

- Because anyone can create a website and put anything on it, you will have to be especially careful in evaluating web resources. Remember that articles in magazines and journals have been selected by editors and are often peer reviewed as well, but no editor selects or rejects material on a personal website.

Google

Google, and other search engines like Microsoft Bing, can help you find a lot of information very quickly. However, these search engines prioritize some sources over others so that the engine may display resources higher in the results list than they might normally appear. Search engine algorithms (how website information is found, interpreted, and displayed by the search engines), a website's search engine optimization (SEO), and paid advertising all affect the order in which your research "hits" are presented to you.

For example, Google uses programs called web crawlers (also known as spiders) that move across the web, indexing pages and keywords within those pages. Then when you type in your keywords, Google matches your phrasing with web pages that contain those words. Next, Google ranks these matches to display them in your search list.

Google uses its patented system called PageRank to list and display the results of your search. Technologists believe that PageRank scores search results and displays pages in order according to those scores. It's also believed that PageRank scores and renders search results based on the keyword match, the number of links to the web page, and the age of the web page. Given the number of variables involved in this process, searches can render very different results. Also, results can be manipulated by web designers using SEO. Search engine optimization increases a web page's profile and its chances of being included in a search result. Moreover, SEO increases a web page's chances of being listed at the top of a search.

In its most basic form, SEO works by including keywords in visible content of the page and in the coding of that page that web users cannot see. So a web page's title might be "The Truth About January 6, 2021," which would render good results if someone searched for that title or a keyword combination of words in that title. But to increase SEO effectiveness, a clever designer would also include the page's title in the page description and in the code that makes up the page.

There are other SEO strategies that can improve and skew search engine hits, such as including other related keywords in the web page and in the code. For instance, a savvy designer who wants to mislead users or spread disinformation might also include terms like "free speech," "First Amendment rights," "Second Amendment rights," "Stop the Steal," and "patriotism" in the web page and its code so that when people search for these other terms, a search engine will find, score, and display the page higher in the results list.

A problem with SEO and its impact on your web research is that an excellent source for your paper might not be housed on a website that uses advanced SEO strategies. For-profit companies like TV cable channels and newspapers can pay expert designers to code sophisticated websites that are easily found and highly ranked by search engines like Google. State-sponsored misinformation and disinformation campaigns carried out by hostile intelligence agencies can also rally sophisticated strategies to spread falsehoods or stir up trouble. Moreover, terrorist organizations use misinformation and disinformation tactics online to support their causes.

But public libraries, colleges, nonprofit organizations, and local governments do not usually have the resources to compose websites that can compete with web pages designed using advanced SEO. So, if you search for information on the January 6, 2021, insurrection, some hits may not contain credible information.

Remember, just because someone has included keywords in a web page does not mean that the content of that page is accurate and credible. For instance, many websites include commonly searched terms but also contain misleading or incorrect information created by dubious sources for unethical use. Conspiracy theorists use these types of unethical practices to spread disinformation about the COVID-19 vaccines, and these actions have contributed to the illness, hospitalization, and deaths of thousands of people worldwide.

Lastly, search engines are normally for-profit endeavors. So, companies often purchase ad content that will appear when you use keywords related to their products. These ads generally appear above your search results and might even result in a colorful, animated ad in the margin of your list. While these results usually contain the word "Ad," their placement at the top of the search list often leads confused users to pages posted by companies rather than to pages that contain information related to the user's original search. It's up to you to use critical thinking to judge whether a search and its results are credible.

Google Scholar

Google Scholar will help you find scholarly articles (articles that are peer reviewed by other researchers), which are sources that you can trust. Scholarly articles have been reviewed by experts and editors before publication, and unless an author has purposely misled reviewers or made a grave error in their research, their results are credible.

However, the links in Google Scholar may not take you to a database or journal that permits free downloads. Don't lose hope. Remember that part of your college tuition money supports your library's subscription to databases that do provide free access to research material. So, if Google Scholar doesn't take you to a site that offers free downloads, you can still use the title and author of an article you find to locate that same piece in your library's database. Using that database, you should be able to download articles or order them through Interlibrary Loan (ILL).

REMEMBER: All works, regardless of their source or the format in which you obtain them—and this includes online sources—must be fully documented in your paper.

GUIDELINES for Searching the Web

The web will provide useful sources for many research projects. It will be much less useful than books or online databases for others. One task of the good researcher is to think about the best places to go to get the best material for a specific project. If you think the web will be useful for you, keep these general guidelines in mind to aid your research:

- Bookmark sites you expect to use often so that you do not have to remember a complex URL or do another Google search.
- Make your research terms as precise as possible to avoid getting overwhelmed with hits.

- If you are searching for a specific phrase, put quotation marks around the words. This will reduce the number of hits and lead to more useful sites. Example: "Rainforest depletion." Without the quotation marks, you will get a lot of information about rainforests, but not necessarily about their depletion. You will also get information on the concept of depletion that has nothing to do with rainforests.
- Include your search information in your work log, including the date you accessed your source, for each separate website from which you take material (see Chapter 14 for documentation guidelines).
- Review your online materials carefully to make sure that they are credible sources of information. Some sources are more credible than others. For instance, sites that use .edu (education institutions) and .gov (government organizations) at the end of their URLs may be more appropriate for your project than nonprofits. Lastly, URLs that end with .com are usually for-profit organizations and may or may not be credible sources for your research. (See the Evaluating Sources Guidelines later in this chapter for details.)

The Library Book Catalog

Your chief guide to books and audiovisual materials is the library catalog, usually an electronic database accessed from computer stations in the library or, with an appropriate password, from your PC.

Andrew F. Kazmierski/Shutterstock

One of the famous lions sitting in front of the New York Public Library.

In the catalog there will be at least four ways to access a specific book: the author entry, the title entry, one or more subject entries, and a keyword option. When you pull up the search screen on your library's website, you will probably see that the keyword option is the default. If you know the exact title of the work you want, switch to the title option, type it in, and hit submit. If you want a list of all of the library's books on Ibram X. Kendi, though, click on author and type in "Ibram X. Kendi." Keep these points in mind:

- With a title search, do not type any initial article (a, an, the). To locate *The Beautiful Struggle,* type in Beautiful Struggle.
- Use correct spelling. If you are unsure of spelling, use a keyword instead of an author or title search.
- If you are looking for a list of books on your subject, do a keyword or subject search.
- When screens for specific books are shown, either print screens of potential sources or copy all information needed for documentation–plus the call number for each book.

The Library Reference Collection

The research process often begins with the reference collection. You will find atlases, dictionaries, encyclopedias, general histories, critical studies, and biographies. In addition, various reference tools such as bibliographies and indexes are part of the reference collection.

Many tools in the reference collection that were once found only in print are now also online. Some are now only online. Yet online is not always the way to go. Let's consider some of the advantages of each of the formats:

Advantages of the Print Reference Collection

1. The reference tool may be only in print–use it.
2. The print form covers the period you are studying. (Most online indexes and abstracts cover only from 1980 to the present.)
3. In a book, with a little scanning of pages, you can often find what you need without getting spelling or commands exactly right.
4. If you know the best reference source to use and are looking for only a few items, the print source can be faster than the online source.

Advantages of Online Reference Materials

1. Online databases are likely to provide the most up-to-date information.
2. You can usually search all years covered at one time.
3. Full texts (with graphics) are sometimes available, as well as indexes with detailed summaries of articles. Both can be printed or emailed to your PC.
4. You have access to an amazing amount of material. (Unless you focus your keyword search, however, you may be overwhelmed.)

Before using any reference work, take a few minutes to check its date, purpose, and organization. If you are new to online searching, take a few minutes to learn about each reference tool by working through the online tutorial.

A Word about Wikipedia

Many researchers go first to a general encyclopedia. In the past, these resources were in print and found in a library's reference section. Today, encyclopedias are online. This is not always the best strategy. Often you can learn more about your topic from a current book or a more specialized reference source–which your reference librarian can help you find. Both may give you additional sources for your project. If–or when–you turn to a general encyclopedia, make it a good one that is available online through your library. Some colleges have told their students that *Wikipedia* is not an acceptable source for college research projects.

With this warning in mind, sometimes it is appropriate to begin your research with Wikipedia to learn more about something if the entry seems factual and timely. Double-check the citations at the bottom of Wikipedia pages to review the source of the entry's information. Often, you will find a source in the Wikipedia attributions that you can use for your research.

Library Databases

You will probably access databases by going to your library's home page and then clicking on the appropriate term or icon. (You may have found the book catalog by clicking on "library catalog"; you may find the databases by clicking on "library resources" or some other descriptive label.) You will need to choose a particular database and then type in your keyword for a basic search or select "advanced search" to limit that search by date or periodical or in some other way. Each library will create somewhat different screens, but the basic process of selecting among choices provided and then typing in your search commands remains the same.

GUIDELINES for Using Online Databases

Keep these points in mind as you use online databases:

- **Although some online databases provide full texts of all articles, others provide full texts of only some of the articles indexed.** The articles not in full text will have to be located in a print collection of periodicals.
- **Articles indexed but not available in full text often come with a brief summary or abstract.** This allows you to decide whether the article looks useful for your project. *Do not treat the abstract as the article. Do not use material from it and cite the author. If you want to use the article, find it in your library's print collection or obtain it from another library.*
- **The information you need for documenting material used from an article is not in correct format for any of the standard documentation styles.** You will have to reorder the information and use the correct style for writing titles. If your instructor wants to see a list of possible sources in MLA format, do not hand in a printout of articles from an online database.
- **Because no single database covers all journals, you may want to search several databases that seem relevant to your project.** Ask your reference librarian for suggestions of various databases in the sciences, social sciences, public affairs, and education.

FIELD RESEARCH

Field research, which also includes empirical research, can enrich many projects. For your composition class, it's unlikely you will be completing research that requires the review and approval of an institutional review board (IRB). These boards review research plans to make sure that they are ethical and rigorous and to protect everyone involved.

Nevertheless, if you complete field research, your instructor will expect you to follow strict guidelines for ensuring ethical and rigorous practices. Some of these practices follow.

Regardless of what field you go into after college, you will be expected to conduct thorough research. Work in the sciences, education, engineering, and business will likely require some type of field research. But you might have to conduct field research even if you attend graduate school or work in a field related to the humanities.

Federal, State, and Local Government Documents

In addition to federal documents you may obtain through Public Affairs Information Service or the U.S. Government Publishing Office, department and agency websites, or the Library of Congress's good legislative site *Thomas* (*http://thomas.loc.gov*), consider state and county archives, maps, and other published materials. Instead of selecting a national or global topic, consider examining the debate over a controversial bill introduced in your state legislature. Use online databases to locate articles on the bill and the debate and interview legislators and journalists who participated in or covered the debates or served on committees that worked with the bill.

You can also request specific documents from appropriate state or county agencies and nonprofit organizations. One student, given the assignment of examining solutions to an ecological problem, decided to study the local problem of preserving the Chesapeake Bay. She obtained issues of the Chesapeake Bay Foundation newsletter and brochures prepared by them advising homeowners about hazardous household waste materials that end up in the bay. Added to her sources were bulletins on soil conservation and landscaping tips for improving the area's water quality. Local problems can lead to interesting research topics because they are current and relevant to you and because they involve uncovering different kinds of source materials.

Correspondence

Business and government officials are usually willing to respond to written requests for information. Make sure your correspondence is brief and well written. Either include a self-addressed, stamped envelope for the person's convenience or email your request. If you are not emailing, write as soon as you discover the need for information and be prepared to wait several weeks for a reply. It is appropriate to indicate your deadline and ask for a timely response. Three guidelines for either letters or emails to keep in mind are:

1. Explain precisely what information you need.
2. Do not request information that can be found in your library's reference collection.

3. Explain how you plan to use the information. Businesses especially are understandably concerned with their public image and will be disinclined to provide information that you intend to use as a means of attacking them.

Use reference guides to companies and government agencies or their websites to obtain addresses and the person to whom your letter or email should be sent.

Interviews

Some experts are available for personal interviews. Call, write, or email for an appointment as soon as you know you will conduct an interview. Remember that interviews are more likely to be scheduled with state and local officials than with the president of General Motors. If you are studying a local problem, also consider leaders of the civic association with an interest in the issue. In many communities, the local historian or a librarian will be a storehouse of information about the community. Your former teachers can be interviewed for papers on education. Interviews with doctors or nurses can add a special dimension to papers on medical issues.

If an interview is appropriate for your topic, follow these guidelines:

1. Prepare specific questions in advance.
2. Arrive on time, properly dressed, and behave in a polite, professional manner.
3. If you are interviewing someone via videoconference or phone, make sure you have an alternate way of contacting the person if the video technology fails. Also make sure your audio and video connections are good and that your background is appropriate.
4. Take notes, asking interviewees to repeat key statements so that your notes are accurate.
5. You must also ask permission to record conversations via video and over the phone.
6. If you quote any statements in your paper, quote accurately, eliminating only such minor speech habits as "you know's" and "uhm's." (See Chapter 14 for proper documentation of interviews.)
7. Direct the interview with your prepared questions, but also give interviewees the chance to approach the topic in their own way. You may obtain information or views that had not occurred to you.
8. Do not get into a debate with interviewees. You are there to learn.
9. Afterward, send your interviewees a thank-you email and ask if you may follow up if you have any further questions.
10. If you need to interview someone else, ask if your interviewee knows anyone who might be interested in speaking with you.

Interview Questions

Here are two tips for writing your interview questions:

1. Avoid biased or leading questions: "Some people say that undocumented workers take jobs away from American citizens. Do you believe that jobs should go to American citizens first?" Better to ask this: "What are your thoughts on immigration in America today?"

2. Avoid double-barreled questions: "Shouldn't everyone have the right to defend themselves, and don't you think that it's wrong that if gun control laws pass, only criminals will be able to get guns?" Better to ask this: "What do you think about access to firearms in America? How do you think we can avoid firearms falling into the hands of criminals? How do you think we can avoid firearms falling into the hands of people with mental health issues?

Lectures

Check the appropriate information sources at your school to keep informed of visiting speakers. If you are fortunate enough to attend a lecture relevant to a current project, take careful, detailed notes. Because a lecture is a source, use of information or ideas from it must be presented accurately and then documented. (See Chapter 14 for documentation format.)

Films, DVDs, Television

Your library will have audiovisual materials that provide good sources for some kinds of topics. For example, if you are studying "A Raisin in the Sun," view a videotaped or digital version of the play. Also pay attention to documentaries on public television and to the many news and political talk shows on both public and commercial channels. In many cases, transcripts of shows can be obtained from the TV station or online with permission. Alternatively, record the program while watching it so that you can view it several times. The documentation format for such nonprint sources is illustrated in Chapter 14.

Surveys, Questionnaires, and Original Research

Depending on your paper, you may want to conduct a simple survey or write and administer a questionnaire. Surveys can be used for many campus and local issues, for topics on behavior and attitudes of college students and/or faculty, and for topics on consumer habits. Explore Survey Monkey for help administering an online survey. Simple ones are free! Remember: Surveying fifty of your Facebook friends will not produce a random sample, which is the optimum way of conducting a survey. When writing questions, keep these guidelines in mind:

- Use simple, clear language.
- Devise a series of short questions rather than only a few that have several parts to them. (You want to separate information for better analysis.)
- Phrase questions to avoid wording that seeks to control the answer. For example, do *not* ask "Did you perform your civic duty by voting in the last election?" This is a loaded question.

In addition to surveys and questionnaires, you can incorporate some original research. As you read sources on your topic, be alert to reports of studies that you could redo and update in part or on a smaller scale. Many topics on advertising and television give opportunities for your own analysis. Local-issue topics may offer good opportunities for gathering information on your own, not just from your reading. One student, examining the controversy over a proposed new shopping mall on part of the Manassas Civil War Battlefield in Virginia, made the argument that the mall served no practical need in the community. He supported his position by describing existing malls, including the number and types of stores each contained and the number of miles each was from the proposed new mall. How did he obtain this information? He drove around the area, counting miles and stores. Sometimes a seemingly unglamorous approach to a topic turns out to be an imaginative one.

EVALUATING SOURCES, MAINTAINING CREDIBILITY

As you study your sources, keep rethinking your purpose and approach. Test your research proposal or tentative claim against what you are learning. Remember: You can always change the direction and focus of your paper as new approaches occur to you, and you can even change your position as you reflect on what you are learning.

You will work with sources more effectively if you keep in mind why you are using them. What you are looking for will vary somewhat, depending on your topic and purpose, but there are several basic approaches:

1. *Acquiring information and viewpoints firsthand.* Suppose that you are concerned about the mistreatment of animals kept in zoos. You do not want to just read what others have to say on this issue. If you can, visit a zoo, taking notes on what you see. Then, before you go, plan to interview at least one person on the zoo staff, preferably a veterinarian who can explain the zoo's guidelines for animal care. Primary sources are valuable additions to the secondary sources, such as articles and books, you will use for your research. Many kinds of topics require the use of both primary and secondary sources. If you want to study violence in children's TV shows, for example, you should first spend some time watching specific shows and taking notes.
2. *Acquiring new knowledge.* Suppose you are interested in breast cancer research and treatment, but you do not know much about the choices of treatment and, in general, where we are with this medical problem. You will need to turn to sources first to learn about the topic. Begin with sources that will give you an overview, perhaps a historical perspective. Begin with sources that provide an overview of how knowledge and treatment have progressed in the last thirty years. Similarly, if your topic is the effects of Prohibition in the 1920s, you will need to read first for knowledge but also with an eye to ways to focus the topic and organize your paper.
3. *Understanding the issues.* Suppose you think that you know your views on unauthorized immigration, so you intend to read only to obtain some useful statistical information to support your argument. Should you scan sources quickly, looking for facts you can use? This approach may be too hasty. As explained in Chapter 3, good arguments are built on a knowledge of counterarguments. You are wise to study sources presenting a variety of attitudes on your issue so that you understand–and can refute–the arguments of others. *Remember: With controversial issues often the best argument is a conciliatory one that presents a middle ground and seeks to bring people together.*

When you use facts and opinions from sources, you are saying to readers that the facts are accurate and the ideas credible. If you do not evaluate your sources before using them, you risk losing your credibility as a writer. (Remember Aristotle's idea of *ethos,* how your character is judged.) Just because they are in print, online, or on social media does not mean that a writer's "facts" are reliable or ideas worthwhile. Judging the usefulness and reliability of potential sources is an essential part of the research process.

Lastly, think critically about how the sources you find might be spreading misinformation or disinformation. Check and double-check facts. Use multiple reliable sources. And use your common sense.

For instance, some people don't believe that dinosaurs existed millions of years ago, and you will find multiple sources online that argue strongly for this position. Yet science tells us that dinosaurs did indeed exist millions of years ago. Radiometric dating shows that these curious creatures roamed the earth until at least 65 million years ago. Of course, archaeologists are always finding new fossils, so exact dates change. But testing the properties of isotopes within fossils produces fairly accurate results given that the earth is 4.5 billion years old. The margin of error for radiometric dating is a few thousand years. Conspiracy theorists have spread mis/disinformation online about masks and vaccines not working to slow the spread of COVID-19. Does it make sense that a face mask would help slow the spread of a primarily respiratory disease usually caught by breathing in tiny droplets suspended in the air? Of course it does! Is it common sense that the vast majority of vaccines approved by the Food and Drug Administration are safe—rare side effects notwithstanding—given the millions of doses administered in America? Of course it is!

Moreover, the long history of vaccine success in eliminating dreadful diseases like smallpox and polio prove the effectiveness of vaccine development. Don't let charlatans and conspiracy theorists use their toxic rhetoric to mislead you.

GUIDELINES for Evaluating Sources

Today, with access to so much material online, the need to evaluate is even more crucial. Here are some strategies for evaluating sources, with special attention to online sources:

- **Locate the author's credentials.** Periodicals often list their writers' degrees, current position, and other publications; books, similarly, contain an "about the author" section. If you do not see this information, check various biographical dictionaries (*Biography Index, Contemporary Authors*) or look for the author's website for information. For articles on the web, look for the author's email address or a link to a home page. *Never use an online source that does not identify the author or the organization responsible for the material. Critical question:* Is this author qualified to write on this topic? How do I know?
- **Judge the credibility of the work.** For books, read how reviewers evaluated the book when it was first published. For articles, judge the respectability of the magazine or journal. Study the author's use of documentation as one measure of credibility. Scholarly works cite sources. Well-researched and reliable pieces in quality popular magazines will also make clear the sources of any statistics used or the credentials of any authority who is quoted. One good rule: Never use undocumented statistical information. Another judge of credibility is the quality of writing. Do not use sources filled

with grammatical and mechanical errors. For online sources, find out what institution hosts the site. If you have not heard of the company or organization, find out more about it. *Critical question:* Why should I believe information/ideas from this source? You may also use fact-check websites to investigate claims. Adfontesmedia.com, Snopes.com, and Factcheck.org are good sources to use to double-check information.

- **Select only those sources that are at an appropriate level for your research.** Avoid works that are either too specialized or too elementary for college research. You may not understand the former (and thus could misrepresent them in your paper), and you gain nothing from the latter. *Critical question:* Will this source provide a sophisticated discussion for educated adults?
- **Understand the writer's purpose.** Consider the writer's intended audience. Be cautious using works designed to reinforce biases already shared by the intended audience. Is the work written to persuade rather than to inform and analyze? Examine the writing for emotionally charged language. For online sources, ask yourself why this person or institution decided to have a website or contribute to a newsgroup. *Critical question:* Can I trust the information from this source, given the apparent purpose of the work?
- **In general, choose current sources.** Some studies published years ago remain classics, but many older works are outdated. In scientific and technical fields, the "information revolution" has outdated some works published only five years ago. So look at publication dates (When was the website last updated?) and pass over outdated sources in favor of current studies. *Critical question:* Is this information still accurate?

PREPARING AN ANNOTATED BIBLIOGRAPHY

An annotated bibliography is a list of sources on a topic that includes a summary of each source. As part of your research process, you may be required to prepare either a partial or a complete annotated bibliography. Instructors include this assignment to keep you moving forward in your study of sources; it is a way of checking that you have found and read useful sources in good time to complete your project. Annotating each source also demands careful reading and analysis; it provides a check against skimming a source for some information without taking time to read and understand the context in which the information is presented and the author's position on the topic. You may find that your research paper is more focused and better written if you take the time to write a brief summary statement about each source you plan to use, even if an annotated bibliography is not required.

When preparing an annotated bibliography, list sources alphabetically and in correct MLA (or APA) format (see Chapter 14). Style the source using hanging indentation, just as you would for your list of works cited at the end of your paper. The annotation should appear just below the end of the source entry, indented an inch from the start of the entry to distinguish it from the half-inch hanging indent. *Warning: Do not confuse an annotated bibliography with a Works Cited list.* When you complete your research essay, list all sources used *without* the summaries.

A partial annotated bibliography follows, based on the sample student research essay in Chapter 13. Use this as your model.

SOLUTIONS TO COMBAT HIGH MATERNAL MORTALITY RATES FOR BLACK WOMEN: SELECTED ANNOTATED BIBLIOGRAPHY

Zaryn Kamara

Brown, Kyrah K., Rhonda K. Lewis, Elizabeth Baumgartner, Christy Schunn, J'Vonnah Maryman, and Jamie LoCurto. "Exploring the Experience of Life Stress Among Black Women with a History of Fetal or Infant Death: A Phenomenological Study." *Journal of Racial and Ethnic Health Disparities* vol. 4, no. 3, 2017: 484-496. https://doi/org/10.1007/s40615-016-0250-z.

This article addresses how stress might alter Black women's delivery results. It explains how various stressors from many aspects of life might affect the health of the newborn and the mother. I found the article did an excellent job of emphasizing the need for a life-course perspective in understanding the stress experience of Black women. This article also did a great job of outlining what efforts we could implement to reduce stress and disparities in birth outcomes. I used this source to show how racism-related trauma correlates to increased maternal mortality.

Engel, Jessica, Lindsey Neinstedt, and Leah Kemper. "Maternal Mortality in Missouri: A Review of Challenges and State Policy Options." *Center for Health Economics and Policy,* UMSL, Oct. 2019, www.umsl.edu/~ socialwk/files/pdfs/Students,%20alums/Engel.%20Jessica%20policy%20brief%20Maternal%20Mortality%20in%20Missouri%20Final.pdf.

This source discusses the importance of racial disparity and its effects in Missouri. It also discusses the risk factors, causes, and barriers to care that impact maternal mortality rates, as well as what is being done in different states and especially in Missouri. This source provides excellent background information on maternal mortality. This site also gave figures on Missouri's death rates based on previous studies, proving to be a trustworthy source. I used this source to gain a better understanding of maternal mortality and how it affects women in Missouri, particularly Black women. I also used this source to see what was already being done to address this problem.

Taylor, Jamila, Katie Hamm, Cristina Novoa, and Shilpa Phadke. "Eliminating Racial Disparities in Maternal and Infant Mortality." *Center for American Progress,* Center for American Progress, 2 May 2019, www.americanprogress.org/article/eliminating-racial-disparities-maternal-infant-mortality/.

This article explores a comprehensive policy framework for eradicating racial disparities in maternal and infant mortality. It also looks at whether maternal health care, health literacy, and birthing education can help reduce maternal mortality racial disparities. This source does an excellent job of giving background information on the topic and data. It also offers hypothetical solutions and how those solutions might decrease racial disparities in maternal health care. This source helped me to better outline the solutions that I want to implement. This source also helped me better understand how racial disparities influence all aspects of health care, not just maternal health care.

Courtesy of Zaryn Kamara

CHAPTER 13

Writing the Researched Essay

LEARNING OUTCOMES

After reading Chapter 13, you will be able to:

- Recall steps to avoid plagiarism.
- Explain how to use signal phrases to avoid confusion.
- Describe how to organize a research essay.
- Draft a research essay.
- Revise a research essay.
- Describe what a completed research essay should include.

Tetra Images/Getty Images

You have agonized over your topic choice, searched for good sources, read and thought about your topic, seeking a way to put together a compelling argument—while not forgetting documentation. Whew! Don't rush now. Study this chapter's writing points and apply the guidelines to the writing of a convincing essay.

As noted in Chapter 12, research and writing are recursive processes that do not always follow a linear pattern. Be prepared to move back and forth between steps. Figure 13.1 outlines the next steps you can follow as you begin forming your research into your research paper.

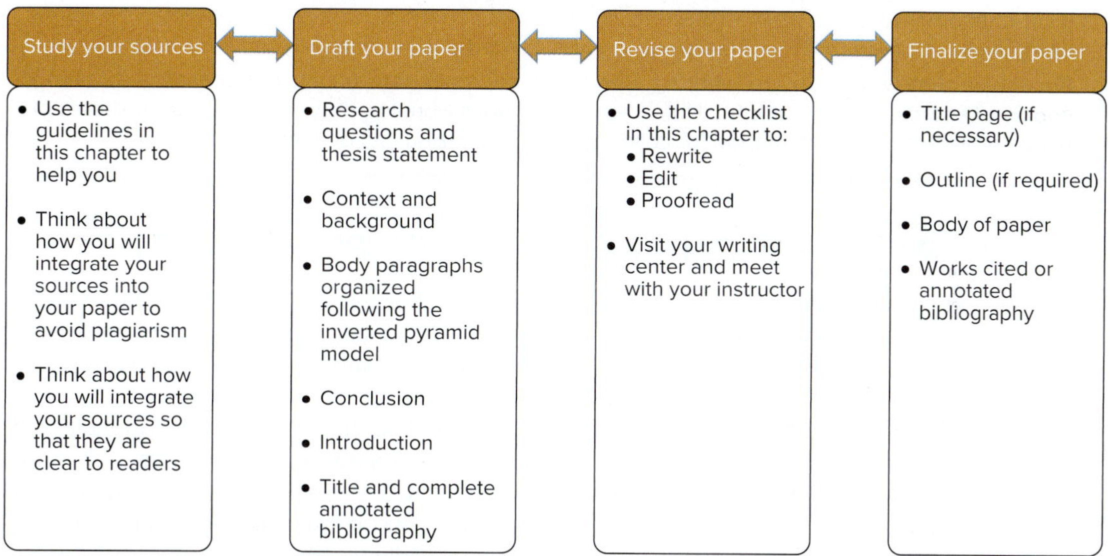

FIGURE 13.1 Research and Writing Process

The following are some general guidelines for studying sources.

GUIDELINES for Studying Sources

1. **Read first; take notes later.** First, do background reading, selecting the most general sources that provide an overview of the topic.
2. **Skim what appear to be your chief sources.** Learn what other writers on the topic consider the important facts, issues, and points of debate.
3. **Annotate photocopies and PDFs**—do not highlight endlessly. Instead, carefully bracket material you want to use. Then write a note in the margin indicating how and where you might use that material.
4. **Either download online sources or take careful notes on the material.** Before preparing a note on content, be sure to copy all necessary information for documenting the material—including the date you accessed the website.
5. **Initially mark key passages in books with Post-its.** Write on the Post-it how and where you might use the material. Alternatively, photocopy book pages and then annotate them. Be sure to record for yourself the source of all copied pages in your work log.

6. **As you study and annotate, create labels for source materials that will help you organize your essay.** For example, if you are writing about the problem of campus sexual assault, you might label passages as: "definitions of the problem," "facts showing there is a problem," "importance of the problem," "causes of the problem," and "possible solutions to the problem." Note how these reminders follow the *stasis* questions. Return to the *stases* to help you learn more about your topic. If you can't answer some of the questions in the *stases,* then you have found a gap in your knowledge. Gaps in knowledge point to the next steps in your research. To fill these gaps, find new sources or pivot to another research method, such as an interview, survey, or observation. For instance, if you can't answer a question through secondary research, perhaps interviewing someone will help.
7. **Recognize that when you are working with many sources, note taking rather than annotating copies of sources is more helpful.** Notes, whether in your work log or typed on separate sheets of paper, provide an efficient method for collecting and organizing lots of information.

ATTRIBUTION AND AVOIDING PLAGIARISM

Documenting sources accurately and fully is required of all researchers. Proper documentation distinguishes between the work of others and your ideas, shows readers the breadth of your research, and strengthens your credibility. In Western culture, copyright laws support the ethic that ideas, new information, and wording belong to their author. To borrow these without acknowledgment is against the law and has led to many celebrated lawsuits. For students who plagiarize, the consequences range from an F on the paper to suspension from college. Be certain, then, that you know what the requirements for correct documentation are; accidental plagiarism is still plagiarism and will be punished. Be certain, then, that you know how to attribute information you gather for your research to the correct source; accidental plagiarism is still plagiarism and will negatively affect your credibility. It may also damage your academic and professional career.

NOTE: MLA documentation requires precise page references for all ideas, opinions, and information taken from sources—except for common knowledge. Author and page references provided in the text are supported by complete bibliographic citations on the Works Cited page.

In sum, you are required to document the following:

- Direct quotations from sources
- Paraphrased ideas and opinions from sources
- Summaries of ideas from sources
- Factual information, except common knowledge, from sources

Understand that putting an author's ideas in your own words in a paraphrase or summary does not eliminate the requirement of documentation. To illustrate, consider the following excerpt from Thomas R. Schueler's report *Controlling Urban Runoff* (Washington Metropolitan Water Resources Planning Board, 1987: pp. 3–4) and a student paragraph based on the report.

SOURCE

The aquatic ecosystems in urban headwater streams are particularly susceptible to the impacts of urbanization. . . . Dietemann (1975), Ragan and Dietemann (1976), Klein (1979) and WMCOG (1982) have all tracked trends in fish diversity and abundance over time in local urbanizing streams. Each of the studies has shown that fish communities become less diverse and are composed of more tolerant species after the surrounding watershed is developed. Sensitive fish species either disappear or occur very rarely. In most cases, the total number of fish in urbanizing streams may also decline.

Similar trends have been noted among aquatic insects which are the major food resource for fish. . . . Higher post-development sediment and trace metals can interfere in their efforts to gather food. Changes in water temperature, oxygen levels, and substrate composition can further reduce the species diversity and abundance of the aquatic insect community.

PLAGIARIZED STUDENT PARAGRAPH

Studies have shown that fish communities become less diverse as the amount of runoff increases. Sensitive fish species either disappear or occur very rarely, and, in most cases, the total number of fish declines. Aquatic insects, a major source of food for fish, also decline because sediment and trace metals interfere with their food-gathering efforts. Increased water temperature and lower oxygen levels can further reduce the species diversity and abundance of the aquatic insect community.

The student's opening words establish a reader's expectation that the student has taken information from a source, as indeed the student has. But where is the documentation? The student's paraphrase is a good example of plagiarism: an unacknowledged paraphrase of borrowed information that even collapses into copying the source's exact wording in two places. For MLA style, the author's name and the precise page numbers are needed throughout the paragraph. Additionally, most of the first sentence and the final phrase must be put into the student's own words or placed within quotation marks. The following revised paragraph shows an appropriate acknowledgment of the source used.

REVISED STUDENT PARAGRAPH TO REMOVE PLAGIARISM

In *Controlling Urban Runoff,* Thomas Schueler explains that studies have shown "that fish communities become less diverse as the amount of runoff increases" (3). Sensitive fish species either disappear or occur very rarely, and, in most cases, the total number of fish declines. Aquatic insects, a major source of food for fish, also decline because sediment and trace metals interfere with their food-gathering efforts. Increased water temperature and lower oxygen levels, Schueler concludes, "can further reduce the species diversity and abundance of the aquatic insect community" (4).

What Is Common Knowledge?

In general, common knowledge includes

- undisputed dates,
- well-known facts, and
- generally known facts, terms, and concepts in a field of study when you are writing in that field.

So, do not cite a source for the dates of the American Revolution. If you are writing a paper for a psychology class, do not cite your text when using terms such as *ego* or *sublimation.* However, you must cite a historian who analyzes the causes of England's loss to the Colonies or a psychologist who disputes Freud's ideas. *Opinions* about well-known facts must be documented. *Discussions* of debatable dates, terms, or concepts must be documented. When in doubt, defend your integrity and document.

USING SIGNAL PHRASES TO AVOID CONFUSION

If you are an honest student, you do not want to submit a paper that is plagiarized, even though that plagiarism was unintentional on your part. What leads to unintentional plagiarism?

- A researcher takes careless notes, neglecting to include precise page numbers on the notes, but uses the information anyway, without documentation.
- A researcher works in material from sources in such a way that, even with page references, readers cannot tell what has been taken from the sources.

Good note-taking strategies will keep you from the first pitfall. Avoiding the second problem means becoming skilled in ways to include source material in your writing while still making your indebtedness to sources absolutely clear to readers. The way to do this: Give the author's name in the essay. You can also include, when appropriate, the author's credentials ("According to Dr. Hays, a geologist with the Department of Interior, . . ."). These *introductory tags* or *signal phrases* give readers a context for the borrowed material, as well as serving as part of the required documentation of sources. *Make sure that each signal phrase clarifies rather than distorts an author's relationship to the ideas presented and your relationship to the source.*

NOTE: Putting a parenthetical page reference at the end of a paragraph is not sufficient if you have used the source throughout the paragraph. Use introductory tags or signal phrases to guide the reader through the material.

GUIDELINES for Appropriately Using and Attributing Sources

Here are three guidelines to follow to avoid misrepresenting borrowed material:

- **Pay attention to verb choice in signal phrases.** When you vary such standard wording as "Cruz says" or "Liu states," be careful that you do not select verbs that misrepresent "Cruz's" or "Liu's" attitude toward the work. Do not write "Liu wonders" when in fact Liu has strongly asserted her views. (See pp. 304–305 for a discussion of varying word choice in signal phrases.)
- **Pay attention to the location of signal phrases.** If you mention Liu after you have presented her views, be sure that your reader can tell precisely which ideas in the passage belong to Liu. If your entire paragraph is a paraphrase of Liu's work, you are plagiarizing to conclude with "This idea is presented by Liu." Which of the several ideas in your paragraph comes from Liu? Your reader will assume that only the last idea comes from Liu.
- **Paraphrase properly.** Be sure that paraphrases are truly *in your own words.* To use Cruz's words and sentence style in your writing is to plagiarize.

EXERCISES: Acknowledging Sources to Avoid Plagiarism

1. The following paragraph (from Franklin E. Zimring's "Firearms, Violence and Public Policy" [*Scientific American*, Nov. 1991]) provides material for the examples that follow of adequate and inadequate acknowledgment of sources. After reading Zimring's paragraph, study the three examples with these questions in mind: (1) Which example represents adequate acknowledgment? (2) Which examples do not represent adequate acknowledgment? (3) In exactly what ways is each plagiarized paragraph flawed?

SOURCE

Although most citizens support such measures as owner screening, public opinion is sharply divided on laws that would restrict the ownership of handguns to persons with special needs. If the U.S. does not reduce handguns and current trends continue, it faces the prospect that the number of handguns in circulation will grow from 35 million to more than 50 million within 50 years. A national program limiting the availability of handguns would cost many billions of dollars and meet much resistance from citizens. These costs would likely be greatest in the early years of the program. The benefits of supply reduction would emerge slowly because efforts to diminish the availability of handguns would probably have a cumulative impact over time. (page 54)

STUDENT PARAGRAPH 1

One approach to the problem of handgun violence in America is to severely limit handgun ownership. If we don't restrict ownership and start the costly task of removing handguns from our society, we may end up with around 50 million handguns in the country by 2040. The benefits will not be apparent right away but will eventually appear. This idea is emphasized by Franklin Zimring (54).

STUDENT PARAGRAPH 2

One approach to the problem of handgun violence in America is to restrict the ownership of handguns except in special circumstances. If we do not begin to reduce the number of handguns in this country, the number will grow from 35 million to more than 50 million within fifty years. We can agree with Franklin Zimring that a program limiting handguns will cost billions and meet resistance from citizens (54).

STUDENT PARAGRAPH 3

According to law professor Franklin Zimring, the United States needs to severely limit handgun ownership or face the possibility of seeing handgun ownership increase "from 35 million to more than 50 million within 50 years" (54). Zimring points out that Americans disagree significantly on restricting handguns and that enforcing such laws would be very expensive. He concludes that the benefits would not be seen immediately but that the restrictions "would probably have a cumulative impact over time" (54). Although Zimring paints a gloomy picture of high costs and little immediate relief from gun violence, he also presents the shocking possibility of 50 million guns by the year 2040. Can our society survive so much firepower?

Clearly, only the third student paragraph demonstrates adequate acknowledgment of the writer's indebtedness to Zimring. Notice that the placement of the last parenthetical page reference acts as a visual closure to the student's borrowing. She then turns to her response to Zimring and her own views on the problem of handguns.

2. Read the following passage and then the three plagiarized uses of it. Explain why each one is plagiarized and how it can be corrected.

   Original Text: Karnow, Stanley. *Vietnam: A History.* Viking Books, 1983, p. 319.

   Lyndon Baines Johnson, a consummate politician, was a kaleidoscopic personality, forever changing as he sought to dominate or persuade or placate or frighten his friends and foes. A gigantic figure whose extravagant moods matched his size, he could be cruel and kind, violent and gentle, petty, generous, cunning, naïve, crude, candid, and frankly dishonest. He commanded the blind loyalty of his aides, some of whom worshipped him, and he sparked bitter derision or fierce hatred that he never quite fathomed.

   a. LBJ's vibrant and changing personality filled some people with adoration and others with bitter derision that he never quite fathomed (Karnow 319).
   b. LBJ, a supreme politician, had a personality like a kaleidoscope, continually changing as he tried to control, sway, appease, or intimidate his enemies and supporters (Karnow 319).
   c. Often, figures who have had great impact on America's history have been dynamic people with powerful personalities and vibrant physical presence. LBJ, for example, was a huge figure who polarized those who worked for and with him. "He commanded the blind loyalty of his aides, some of whom worshipped him, and he sparked bitter derision or fierce hatred" from many others (Karnow 319).

3. Read the following passage and then the four sample uses of it. Judge each of the uses for how well it avoids plagiarism and if it is documented correctly. Make corrections as needed.

Original Text: Karnow, Stanley. *Vietnam: A History.* Viking Books, 1983, p. 327.

On July 27, 1965, in a last-ditch attempt to change Johnson's mind, [Senators] Mansfield and Russell were to press him again to "concentrate on finding a way out" of Vietnam—"a place where we ought not be," and where "the situation is rapidly going out of control." But the next day, Johnson announced his decision to add forty-four American combat battalions to the relatively small U.S. contingents already there. He had not been deaf to Mansfield's pleas, nor had he simply swallowed the Pentagon's plans. He had waffled and agonized during his nineteen months in the White House, but eventually this was his final judgment. As he would later explain: "There are many, many people who can recommend and advise, and a few of them consent. But there is only one who has been chosen by the American people to decide."

a. Karnow writes that senators Mansfield and Russell continued to try to convince President Johnson to avoid further involvement in Vietnam, "a place where we ought not to be," they felt. (327).
b. Though Johnson received advice from many, in particular senators Mansfield and Russell, he believed the weight of the decision to become further engaged in Vietnam was solely his as the one " 'chosen by the American people to decide' " (Karnow 327).
c. On July 28, 1965, Johnson announced his decision to add forty-four battalions to the troops already in Vietnam, ending his waffling and agonizing of the past nineteen months of his presidency. (Karnow 357)
d. Karnow explains that LBJ took his responsibility to make decisions about Vietnam seriously (327). Although Johnson knew that many would offer suggestions, only he had " 'been chosen by the American people to decide' " (Karnow 327).

ORGANIZING THE PAPER

Armed with an understanding of writing strategies to avoid plagiarism, you are now almost ready to draft your essay. Follow these steps to get organized to write:

1. *Arrange notes (or your annotated sources) by the labels you have used and read them through.* You may discover that some notes or marked sections of sources now seem irrelevant. Set them aside, but do not throw them away yet. Some further reading and note taking may also be necessary to fill in gaps that have become apparent.

2. *Reexamine your tentative claim or research proposal.* As a result of reading and reflection, do you need to alter or modify your claim, hypothesis, or research proposal in any way? Or if you began with a research question, what now is your answer to the question? For example, is social media harmful to children?
3. *Decide on the claim that will direct your writing.* To write a unified essay with a "reason for being," you need a claim that meets these criteria:

   - It is a complete sentence, not a topic or statement of purpose.

     TOPIC: Sexual assault on college campuses.

     CLAIM: There are steps that both students and administrators can take to reduce incidents of campus sexual assault.

   - It is limited and focused.

     UNFOCUSED: The Great Recession affected people in many ways.

     FOCUSED: The Great Recession, caused by the subprime mortgage crisis, ruined the lives of many, but it hit minorities especially hard.

   - It establishes a new or interesting approach to the topic that makes your research meaningful.

     NOT INVENTIVE: A regional shopping mall should not be built next to the Manassas Battlefield.

     INVENTIVE: Putting aside an appeal to our national heritage, one can say, simply, that there is no economic justification for the building of a shopping mall next to the Manassas Battlefield.

4. *Write down the organization that emerges from your labels and grouping of sources, and compare this with your preliminary plan.* If there are differences, justify those changes to yourself. Consider: Does the new, fuller plan provide a complete and logical development of your claim? And, will it guide you to an essay that meets your research assignment?

DRAFTING THE ESSAY

Plan Your Time

How much time will you need to draft your essay? Working with sources and taking care with documentation make research paper writing more time consuming than writing an undocumented essay. You also need to allow time between completing the draft and revising. Do not try to draft, revise, and proof an essay all in one day.

Revisit your Gantt chart and work log. Ask yourself some questions: Have I been able to follow my initial schedule? Am I behind? Ahead? How much work have I been able to accomplish? How long is it taking me to complete tasks? How much do I still have to do? If you're honest with yourself and use your Gantt chart and work log, you should be able to plan the next steps of your research and writing to complete your paper on time while producing high-quality work.

Handle In-Text Documentation as You Draft

The Modern Language Association (MLA) recommends that writers prepare their Works Cited page(s) *before* drafting their essay. With this important information prepared correctly and next to you as you draft, you will be less likely to make errors in documentation that will result in a plagiarized essay. Although you may believe that stopping to include parenthetical documentation as you write will cramp your writing, you really cannot try to insert the documentation after completing the writing. The risk of failing to document accurately is too great to chance. Parenthetical documentation is brief; listen to the experts and take the time to include it as you compose.

You saw some models of documentation in Chapter 12. In Chapter 14, you have complete guidelines and models for in-text (parenthetical) documentation and then many models for the complete citations of sources. Study the information in Chapter 14 and then draft your Works Cited page(s) as part of your preparation for writing.

Choose an Appropriate Writing Style

Specific suggestions for composing the parts of your paper follow, but first here are some general guidelines for research essay style.

Use the Proper Person

Research papers are written primarily in the third person (*she, he, it, they*) to create objectivity and to direct attention to the content of the paper. The question is over the appropriateness of the first person (*I, we*). Although you want to avoid writing "as *you* can see," do not try to avoid the use of *I* if you need to distinguish your position from the views of others. It is better to write "I" than "it is the opinion of this writer" or "the researcher learned" or "this project analyzed." On the other hand, avoid qualifiers such as "I think." Just state your ideas. To be safe, though, always ask your instructor what they prefer.

Use the Proper Tense

When you are writing about people, ideas, or events of the past, the appropriate tense is the past tense. When writing about current times, the appropriate tense is the present. Both tenses may occur in the same paragraph, as the following paragraph illustrates:

> In the late 1970s, "personal" computers were all but unheard of. Computers were regarded as unknowable, building-sized mechanized monsters that required a precise 68 degree air-conditioned environment and eggheaded technicians with thick glasses and white lab coats scurrying about to keep the temperamental and fragile egos of the electronic brains mollified. Today's generation of computers is accessible, affordable, commonplace, and much less mysterious.

The astonishing progress made in computer technology in the last few years has made computers practical, attainable, and indispensable. Personal computers are here to stay and are getting more powerful all the time. In fact, today's smartphones are far more powerful than the computers that helped American astronauts walk on the moon in 1969.

In the above example, when the student moves from computers in the past to computers in the present, he shifts tenses accurately.

When writing about sources, the convention is to use the present tense *even* for works or authors from the past. The idea is that the source, or the author, *continues* to make the point or use the technique into the present–that is, every time there is a reader. So, write "Lincoln selects the biblical expression 'Fourscore and seven years ago' " and "King echoes Lincoln when he writes 'five score years ago.' "

Avoid Excessive Quoting

Many students use too many direct quotations. Plan to use your own words most of the time for these good reasons:

- Constantly shifting between your words and the language of your sources (not to mention all those quotation marks) makes reading your essay difficult.
- This is your paper and should sound like you.
- When you take a passage out of its larger context, you face the danger of misrepresenting the writer's views.
- When you quote endlessly, readers may begin to think either that you are lazy or that you don't really understand the issues well enough to put them in your own words. You don't want to present either image to your readers.
- You do not prove any point by quoting another person's opinion. All you indicate is that there is someone else who shares your views. Even if that person is an expert on the topic, your quoted material still represents the view of only one person. You support a claim with reasons and evidence, both of which can usually be presented in your own words.

When you must quote, keep the quotations brief, weave them carefully into your own sentences, and be sure to identify the author in a signal phrase. Study the guidelines for handling quotations on pages 22–25 for models of correct form and style.

Write Effective Introductions

The best introduction is one that presents your subject in an interesting way to gain the reader's attention, states your claim, and gives the reader an indication of the scope and limits of your paper. You might also outline the organization of your paper. In a short research essay, you may be able to combine an attention-getter, a statement of subject, and a claim in one paragraph. More typically, especially in longer papers, the introduction will expand to two or three paragraphs. In the physical and social sciences, the claim may be withheld until the conclusion, but the opening introduces the subject and presents the researcher's hypothesis, often posed as a question. Since students sometimes have trouble with research paper introductions in spite of knowing these general guidelines, several specific approaches are illustrated here:

1. In the opening to her study of car advertisements, a student, relating her topic to what readers know, reminds readers of the culture's concern with image:

   Many Americans are highly image conscious. Because the "right" look is essential to a prosperous life, no detail is too small to overlook. Clichés about first impressions remind us that "you never get a second chance to make a first impression," so we obsessively watch our weight, firm our muscles, sculpt our hair, select our friends, find the perfect houses, and buy our automobiles. Realizing the importance of image, companies compete to make the "right" products, that is, those that will complete the "right" image. Then advertisers direct specific products to targeted groups of consumers. Although targeting may be labeled as stereotyping, it has been an effective strategy in advertising.

2. Terms and concepts central to your project need defining early in your paper, especially if they are challenged or qualified in some way by your study. This opening paragraph demonstrates an effective use of definition:

   William Faulkner braids a universal theme, the theme of initiation, into the fiber of his novel *Intruder in the Dust.* From ancient times to the present, a prominent focus of literature, of life, has been rites of passage, particularly those of childhood to adulthood. Joseph Campbell defines rites of passage as "distinguished by formal, and usually very severe, exercises of severance." A "candidate" for initiation into adult society, Campbell explains, experiences a shearing away of the "attitudes, attachments and life patterns" of childhood (9). This severe, painful stripping away of the child and installation of the adult is presented somewhat differently in several works by American writers.

3. Begin with a thought-provoking question. A student, arguing that the media both reflect and shape reality, started with these questions:

   Do the media just reflect reality, or do they also shape our perceptions of reality? The answer to this seemingly "chicken-and-egg" question is: They do both.

4. Beginning with important, perhaps startling, facts, evidence, or statistics is an effective way to introduce a topic, provided the details are relevant to the topic. Observe the following example:

   Teenagers are working again, but not on their homework. Over 40 percent of teenagers have jobs by the time they are juniors (Samuelson A22). And their jobs do not support academic learning since almost two-thirds of teenagers are employed in sales and service jobs that entail mostly carrying, cleaning, and wrapping (Greenberger and Steinberg 62–67), not reading, writing, and computing. Unfortunately, the negative effect on learning is not offset by improved opportunities for future careers.

Avoid Ineffective Openings

Follow these guidelines for avoiding openings that most readers find ineffective or annoying.

1. *Do not restate the title* or write as if the title were the first sentence in paragraph 1. It is a convention of writing to have the first paragraph stand independent of the title.
2. *Do not begin with "clever" visuals* such as artwork or fancy lettering.
3. *Do not begin with humor* unless it is part of your topic.
4. *Do not begin with a question that is just a gimmick, or one that a reader may answer in a way you do not intend.* Asking "What are the advantages of solar energy?" may lead a reader to answer "None that I can think of." A straightforward research question ("Is *Death of a Salesman* a tragedy?") is appropriate.
5. *Do not open with an unnecessary definition quoted from a dictionary.* "According to Webster, solar energy means . . ." is a tired, overworked beginning that does not engage readers.
6. Reconsider beginning with a purpose statement: "This paper will examine. . ." Although a statement of purpose may be a part of your introduction somewhere, a report still needs an interesting beginning. Set the context first, then explain your purpose.

Compose Solid, Unified Paragraphs

As you compose the body of your paper, keep in mind that you want to (1) maintain unity and coherence, (2) guide readers clearly through source material, and (3) synthesize source material and your own ideas. Do not settle for paragraphs in which facts from notes are just loosely run together. Review the following discussion and study the examples to see how to craft effective body paragraphs.

Provide Unity and Coherence

One way of achieving unity and coherence is by following the inverted pyramid structure, where you begin with general information like your transition, which acts as a guidepost for your readers. Next comes more general information in your topic sentence. Then move from general information like explanation to specific information like examples using paraphrasing and direct quotes. Finish by including your brief wrap-up where you can explain how and why the information you have provided relates to or supports your topic sentence or even your paper's thesis.

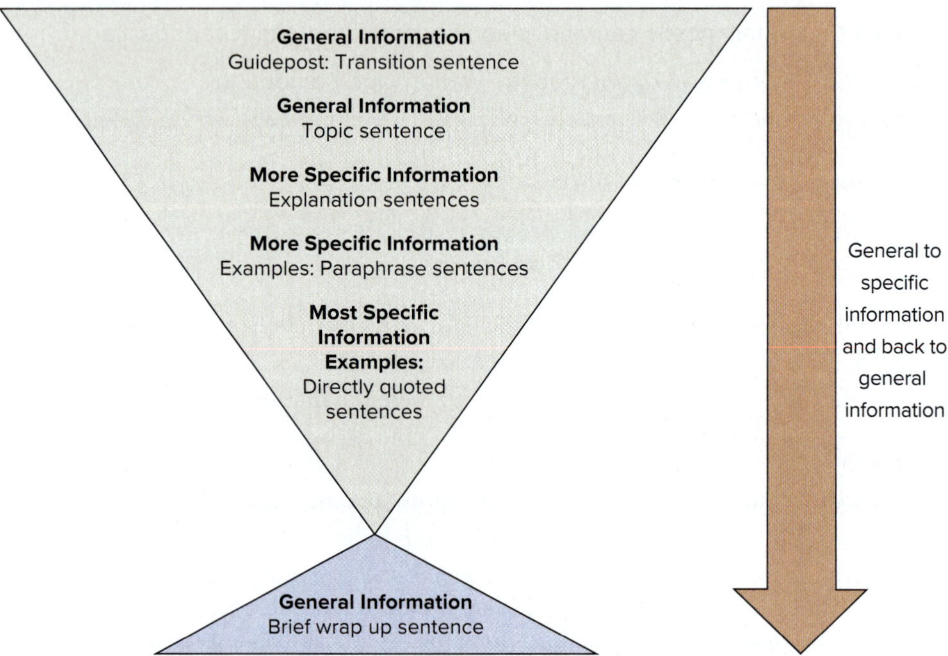

FIGURE 13.2 Inverted Pyramid Paragraph Organization

You achieve paragraph unity when every sentence in a paragraph relates to and develops the paragraph's main idea. Unity, however, does not automatically produce coherence; that takes attention to wording. Coherence is achieved when readers can follow the connection between one sentence and another and between each sentence and the main idea. Strategies for achieving coherence include repetition of key words, the use of pronouns that clearly refer to those key words, moving from general to specific information, repetition of key words, and the use of transition and connecting words. Observe these strategies at work in the following paragraph:

> Perhaps the most important differences between the initiations of Robin and Biff and that experienced by Chick are the facts that Chick's epiphany does not come all at once, and it does not

devastate him. Chick learns about adulthood—and enters adulthood—piecemeal and with support. His first eye-opening experience occurs as he tries to pay Lucas for dinner and is rebuffed (15–16). Chick learns, after trying again to buy a clear conscience, the impropriety and affront of his actions (24). Lucas teaches Chick how he should resolve his dilemma by setting him "free" (26–27). Later, Chick feels outrage at the adults crowding into the town, presumably to see a lynching, then disgrace and shame as they eventually flee (196–97, 210).

Coherence is needed not only within paragraphs but between paragraphs as well. You need to guide readers through your paper, connecting paragraphs and showing relationships by the use of transitions. The following opening sentences of four paragraphs from a paper on solutions to sexual assault on the college campus illustrate smooth transitions:

¶ 3 Specialists have provided a number of reasons why people commit sexual assault.

¶ 4 Some of the causes of sexual assault on the college campus originate with the colleges themselves and with how they handle the problem.

¶ 5 Just as there are a number of causes for campus sexual assaults, there are a number of ways to help solve the problem of these sexual assaults.

¶ 6 If these seem like commonsense solutions, why, then, is it so difficult to significantly reduce the number of sexual assaults on campus?

Without awkwardly writing "Here are some of the causes" and "Here are some of the solutions," the student guides her readers through a discussion of causes for and solutions to the problem of campus sexual assault.

Guide Readers through Source Material

To understand the importance of guiding readers through source material, consider first the following paragraph from a paper on the British coal strike in the 1970s:

The social status of the coal miners was far from good. The country blamed them for the dimmed lights and the three-day workweek. They had been placed in the position of social outcasts and were beginning to "consider themselves another country." Some businesses and shops had even gone so far as to refuse service to coal miners (Jones 32).

Who has learned that the coal miners felt ostracized or that the country blamed them? As readers we cannot begin to judge the validity of these assertions without some context provided by the writer. Most readers are put off by an unattached direct quotation or some startling observation that is documented correctly but given no context within the paper. Using signal phrases that identify the author of the source and, when useful, the author's credentials helps guide readers through the source material. The following revision of the paragraph above provides not only context but also sentence variety:

> The social acceptance of coal miners, according to Peter Jones, British correspondent for *Newsweek,* was far from good. From interviews both in London shops and in pubs near Birmingham, Jones concluded that Britishers blamed the miners for the dimmed lights and three-day workweek. Several striking miners, in a pub on the outskirts of Birmingham, asserted that some of their friends had been denied service by shopkeepers and that they "consider[ed] themselves another country" (32).

Select Appropriate Signal Phrases

When you use signal phrases, try to vary both the words you use and their place in the sentence. Look, for example, at the first sentence in the sample paragraph above. The signal phrase is placed in the middle of the sentence and is set off by commas. The sentence could have been written two other ways:

> The social acceptance of coal miners was far from good, according to Peter Jones, British correspondent for *Newsweek.*
>
> OR
>
> According to Peter Jones, British correspondent for *Newsweek,* the social acceptance of coal miners was far from good.

Whenever you provide a name and perhaps credentials for your source, you have these three sentence patterns to choose from. Make a point to use all three options in your paper. Word choice can be varied as well. Instead of writing "Peter Jones says" throughout your paper, consider some of these verb choices:

Jones *asserts*	Jones *contends*	Jones *attests to*
Jones *states*	Jones *thinks*	Jones *points out*
Jones *concludes*	Jones *stresses*	Jones *believes*
Jones *presents*	Jones *emphasizes*	Jones *agrees with*
Jones *argues*	Jones *confirms*	Jones *speculates*

NOTE: Not all the words in this list are synonyms; you cannot substitute *confirms* for *believes*. First, select the verb that most accurately conveys the writer's relationship to the material. Then, when appropriate, vary word choice as well as sentence structure.

Readers need to be told how to respond to the sources used. They need to know which sources you accept as reliable and which you disagree with, and they need you to distinguish clearly between fact and opinion. Ideas and opinions from sources need signal phrases and then some discussion from you.

Synthesize Source Material and Your Own Ideas

A smooth synthesis of source material is aided by signal phrases and parenthetical documentation because they mark the beginning and ending of material taken from a source. But a complete synthesis requires something more: your ideas about the source and the topic. To illustrate, consider the problems in another paragraph from the British coal strike paper:

> Some critics believed that there was enough coal in Britain to maintain enough power to keep industry at a near-normal level for thirty-five weeks (Jones 30). Prime Minister Heath, on the other hand, had placed the country's usable coal supply at 15.5 million tons (Jones 30). He stated that this would have fallen to a critical 7 million tons within a month had he not declared a three-day workweek (Jones 31).

This paragraph is a good example of random details strung together for no apparent purpose. How much coal did exist? Whose figures were right? And what purpose do these figures serve in the paper's development? Note that the entire paragraph is developed with material from one source. Do sources other than Jones offer a different perspective? This paragraph is weak for several reasons: (1) It lacks a controlling idea (topic sentence) to give it purpose and direction; (2) it relies for development entirely on one source; (3) it lacks any discussion or analysis by the writer.

By contrast, the following paragraph demonstrates a successful synthesis:

> Of course, the iridium could have come from other extraterrestrial sources besides an asteroid. One theory, put forward by Dale Russell, is that the iridium was produced outside the solar system by an exploding star (500). Such an explosion, Russell states, could have blown the iridium either off the surface of the moon or directly from the star itself (500–01), while also producing a deadly blast of heat and gamma rays (Krishtalka 19). This theory seems to explain the traces of iridium

in the mass extinction, but it does not explain why smaller mammals, crocodiles, and birds survived (Wilford 220). So the supernova theory took a backseat to the other extraterrestrial theories: those of asteroids and comets colliding with the Earth. The authors of the book *The Great Extinction,* Michael Allaby and James Lovelock, subtitled their work *The Solution to . . . the Disappearance of the Dinosaurs.* Their theory: an asteroid or comet collided with Earth around sixty-five million years ago, killing billions of organisms, and thus altering the course of evolution (157). The fact that the theory of collision with a cosmic body warrants a book calls for some thought: Is the asteroid or comet theory merely sensationalism, or is it rooted in fact? Paleontologist Leonard Krishtalka declares that few paleontologists have accepted the asteroid theory, himself calling "some catastrophic theories . . . small ideas injected with growth hormone" (22). However, other scientists, such as Allaby and Lovelock, see the cosmic catastrophic theory as a solid one based on more than guesswork (10–11).

This paragraph's synthesis is accomplished by following the inverted pyramid model and by several other strategies: (1) The paragraph has a controlling idea; (2) the paragraph combines information from several sources; (3) the information is presented in a blend of paraphrase and short quotations; (4) information from the different sources is clearly indicated to readers; and (5) the student explains and discusses the information.

You might also observe the different lengths of the two sample paragraphs just presented. Although the second paragraph is long, it is not unwieldy because it achieves unity and coherence. By contrast, body paragraphs of only three sentences are probably in trouble.

Write Effective Conclusions

Sometimes ending a paper seems even more difficult than beginning one. You know you are not supposed to just stop, but every ending that comes to mind sounds more corny than clever. If you have trouble, try one of these types of endings:

1. Do not just repeat your claim exactly as it was stated in paragraph 1, but expand on the original wording and emphasize the claim's significance in your introduction. You might also look to the future and raise some questions that emerged from your research. Here is the conclusion of the solar energy paper:

   The idea of using solar energy is not as far-fetched as it seemed years ago. With the continued support of government plus the enthusiasm of research groups, environmentalists, and private industry, solar energy may become a household word quite soon. With the increasing cost of fossil fuel, the time could not be better for exploring this use of the sun.

2. End with a quotation that effectively summarizes and drives home the point of your paper. Researchers are not always lucky enough to find the ideal quotation for ending a paper. If you find a good one, use it. Better yet, present the quotation and then add your comment in a sentence or two. The conclusion to a paper on the dilemma of defective newborns is a good example:

    Dr. Joseph Fletcher is correct when he says that "every advance in medical capabilities is an increase in our moral responsibility" (48). In a world of many gray areas, one point is clear. From an ethical point of view, medicine is a victim of its own success.

3. If you have researched an issue or problem, emphasize your proposed solutions in the concluding paragraph. The student opposing a mall adjacent to the Manassas Battlefield concluded with several solutions:

    Whether the proposed mall will be built is clearly in doubt at the moment. What are the solutions to this controversy? One approach is, of course, not to build the mall at all. To accomplish this solution, now, with the re-zoning having been approved, probably requires an act of Congress to buy the land and make it part of the national park. Another solution, one that would please the county and the developer and satisfy citizens objecting to traffic problems, is to build the needed roads before the mall is completed. A third approach is to allow the office park of the original plan to be built, but not the mall. The local preservationists had agreed to this original development proposal, but now that the issue has received national attention, they may no longer be willing to compromise. Whatever the future of the William Center, the present plan for a new regional mall is not acceptable.

Avoid Ineffective Conclusions

Follow these rules to avoid conclusions that most readers consider ineffective and annoying.

1. *Do not introduce a new idea.* If the point belongs in your paper, you should have introduced it earlier.
2. *Do not just stop or trail off,* even if you feel as though you have run out of steam. A simple, clear restatement of the claim is better than no conclusion.
3. *Do not offer apologies or expressions of hope.* "Although I wasn't able to find as much on this topic as I wanted, I have tried to explain the advantages of solar energy, and I hope that you will now understand why we need to use it more" is a disastrous ending.

Choose an Effective Title

Give some thought to your paper's title since that is what your reader sees first and what your work will be known by. A good title provides information and creates interest. Make your title informative by making it specific. If you can create interest through clever wording, so much the better. But do not confuse "cutesiness" with clever wording. Review the following examples of acceptable and unacceptable titles:

VAGUE:	A Perennial Issue Unsolved (There are many; which one is this paper about?)
BETTER:	The Perennial Issue of Press Freedom versus Press Responsibility
TOO BROAD:	Earthquakes (What about earthquakes? This title is not informative.)
BETTER:	The Need for Earthquake Prediction
TOO BROAD:	Nikki Giovanni's Poems (Never use just the title of the work under discussion; you can use the work's title as a part of a longer title of your own.)
BETTER:	Joy, Hope, and Food in Nikki Giovanni's Poems
CUTESY:	Babes in Trouble (The slang "Babes" makes this title seem insensitive rather than clever.)
BETTER:	The Effects of Contaminated Drinking Water on African American Newborns in Flint, Michigan

REVISING THE PAPER: A CHECKLIST

After completing a first draft, catch your breath and then gear up for the next step in the writing process: revision. Revision actually involves three separate steps: *rewriting*–adding or deleting text, or moving parts of the draft around; *editing*–a rereading to correct errors from misspellings to incorrect documentation format; and then *proofreading* a new copy that incorporates your edits. If you treat these as separate steps, you will do a more complete job of revision.

Rewriting

Read your draft through and make changes as a result of answering the following questions:

Purpose and Audience

☐ Does my draft meet all of the assignment requirements and my purpose? (Double-check your writing prompt.)

☐ Are terms defined and concepts explained appropriately for my audience?

Content

- ☐ Do I have a clearly stated thesis—the claim of my argument?
- ☐ Have I presented sufficient evidence to support my claim?
- ☐ Are there any irrelevant sections that should be deleted?

Structure

- ☐ Have I ordered my paragraphs to develop my topic logically?
- ☐ Does the content of each paragraph help develop my claim?
- ☐ Is everything in each paragraph on the same subtopic to create paragraph unity?
- ☐ Do body paragraphs have a balance of information and analysis, of source material and my own ideas?
- ☐ Are there any paragraphs that should be combined? Are there any very long paragraphs that should be divided? (Check for unity.)

Editing

Make revisions in response to your application of the rewriting questions. When you are satisfied with your basic content and structure, it is time to edit. This time, pay close attention to sentences, words, and documentation format. Use the following questions to guide editing.

Document Design

- ☐ Have I followed MLA requirements for a 1-inch margin and Times New Roman or similar professional font, set at anywhere between 11 and 13 points?
- ☐ Have I double-spaced throughout, including the Works Cited pages?

Coherence

- ☐ Have I used connecting words, and have I repeated key terms to produce paragraph coherence?
- ☐ Have I used transitions to show connections between paragraphs?

Sources

- ☐ Have I paraphrased instead of quoted whenever possible?
- ☐ Have I used signal phrases to create a context for source material?
- ☐ Have I documented all borrowed material, whether quoted or paraphrased?
- ☐ Are parenthetical references properly placed after borrowed material?

Style

- ☐ Have I varied sentence length and structure?
- ☐ Have I avoided long quotations?
- ☐ Do I have correct form for quotations? For titles?

- ☐ Is my language specific and descriptive?
- ☐ Have I avoided inappropriate shifts in tense or person?
- ☐ Have I removed any wordiness, deadwood, trite expressions, or clichés?
- ☐ Have I used specialized terms correctly?
- ☐ Have I avoided contractions as too informal for most research papers?
- ☐ Have I maintained an appropriate style and tone for academic work?

Proofreading

When your edits are complete, check that your paper format matches the guidelines described and illustrated in the research paper below. Print a copy of your paper for final proofreading and make corrections as needed. Correct all errors and keep a file of your paper before submitting a copy to your instructor.

THE COMPLETED PAPER

Your research paper should be double-spaced throughout (including the Works Cited page) with 1-inch margins on all sides. Your project will contain the following parts, in this order:

1. *A title page* (if needed) with your title, your name, your instructor's name, the course name or number, and the date, neatly centered, if an outline follows. If there is no outline, place this information at the top left of the first page.
2. *An outline,* or statement of purpose, if required.
3. *The body or text of your paper.* Number all pages consecutively, including pages of works cited, using arabic numerals. Place numbers in the upper right-hand corner of each page. Include your last name before each page number.
4. *A list of works cited,* beginning on a separate page, follows the text. Title the first page "Works Cited." (Do not use the title "Bibliography.")

SAMPLE STUDENT ESSAY IN MLA STYLE

The following paper illustrates an argumentative essay using sources documented in MLA style.

Zaryn Kamara is a third-year biology major with a minor in public health at Saint Louis University (SLU). She is passionate about health care and how it impacts racial minorities and individuals with socioeconomic challenges. Currently, she is exploring the regulation of glucose transport in skeletal muscle cells in an undergraduate research lab with Dr. Jonathan Fisher, Professor of Biology at SLU.

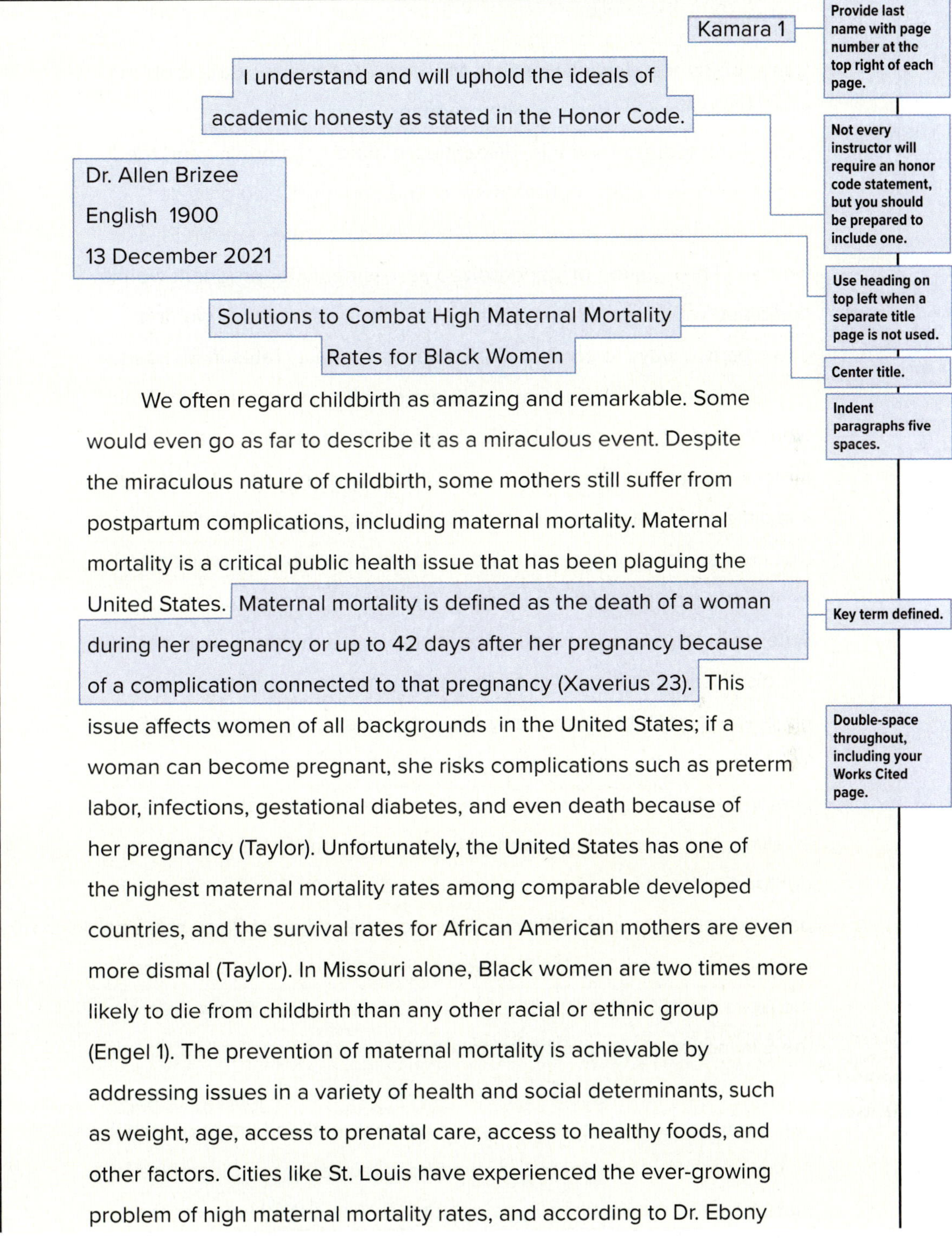
Kamara 1
Provide last name with page number at the top right of each page.
I understand and will uphold the ideals of academic honesty as stated in the Honor Code.
Not every instructor will require an honor code statement, but you should be prepared to include one.
Dr. Allen Brizee
English 1900
13 December 2021
Use heading on top left when a separate title page is not used.
Solutions to Combat High Maternal Mortality Rates for Black Women
Center title.
Indent paragraphs five spaces.
We often regard childbirth as amazing and remarkable. Some would even go as far to describe it as a miraculous event. Despite the miraculous nature of childbirth, some mothers still suffer from postpartum complications, including maternal mortality. Maternal mortality is a critical public health issue that has been plaguing the United States. Maternal mortality is defined as the death of a woman during her pregnancy or up to 42 days after her pregnancy because of a complication connected to that pregnancy (Xaverius 23). This issue affects women of all backgrounds in the United States; if a woman can become pregnant, she risks complications such as preterm labor, infections, gestational diabetes, and even death because of her pregnancy (Taylor). Unfortunately, the United States has one of the highest maternal mortality rates among comparable developed countries, and the survival rates for African American mothers are even more dismal (Taylor). In Missouri alone, Black women are two times more likely to die from childbirth than any other racial or ethnic group (Engel 1). The prevention of maternal mortality is achievable by addressing issues in a variety of health and social determinants, such as weight, age, access to prenatal care, access to healthy foods, and other factors. Cities like St. Louis have experienced the ever-growing problem of high maternal mortality rates, and according to Dr. Ebony
Key term defined.
Double-space throughout, including your Works Cited page.

Carter of Barnes–Jewish Hospital, Missouri OB/GYNs lack the tools to track risk factors associated with pregnancy (Prabu). The aim of this paper is to address the racial disparities in maternal mortality and the consequences it has on prenatal care. The paper will also provide ways to address the continuance of high mortality rates among Black women. The creation of standardized assessments for pregnant women combined with the provision of prenatal resources for Black women could be two ways to combat high maternal mortality rates in St. Louis.

Clear opening leads to student's thesis, which in this case is a proposal to address a local and national problem.

Maternal death and near-death are problems that persist for Black women of all socio-economic backgrounds. No matter what resources a Black woman has access to, these will not lower her risk of mortality. It is difficult for Black women in America to escape the systemic racism that creates psychological stress that affects their health, particularly the health of expectant mothers (Brown). The societal racism that pervades America creates a longstanding racial bias in health care, which leads to the dismissal of legitimate concerns and symptoms that these women have, which contributes to poor birth outcomes. According to the *New York Times* article "Why America's Black Mothers and Babies Are in a Life-or-Death Crisis," Simone Landrum experienced symptoms of fatigue, swelling, and nausea and reported these symptoms to her doctor. Her doctor dismissed her concerns, and a few days later, Landrum lost her baby and almost her life (Villarosa). As more tragedies of Black maternal mortality increased, Monica Simpson believed it was time to address the issue. In 2014, she stood before the United Nations Committee on the Elimination of Racial Discrimination and called on the United States to "eliminate racial disparities in sexual and reproductive health and standardize the data-collection system on maternal and infant deaths in all states to effectively identify and address the causes of disparities in maternal—and infant-mortality rates" (qtd. in Villarosa). However, there

Paragraph developed using paraphrase and direct quotations from several sources.

Kamara 3

has been no effort to standardize the data collection system. Racism and bias in the health care system must be addresses as we consider maternal mortality.

The United States spends proportionally more money on its maternity system than any other country, yet has significantly poorer outcomes based on measures of mortality and morbidity. Further, these poorer outcomes disproportionately affect Black women, their newborns, and their families (Scrimshaw 15). The racial disparity in maternal mortality attributes to the structural racism in healthcare and social service delivery that causes African American women to receive a poorer quality of care (Taylor). It is important to note that the United States has a unique maternity system that causes women to pay for care through different mechanisms. For example, the United States uses a rationalized system of maternity care that involves potential transfers to many levels. Because there are transfers, it requires pregnant women to build strong relationships between each facility level to receive the care (Scrimshaw 45). This can be exceptionally difficult for women who cannot travel to multiple locations and afford the multiple levels of care.

Student explains the problem.

While racism drives racial disparities in maternal mortality, health care programs like Medicaid, Temporary Assistance for Needy Families (TANF), and nutrition assistance contribute to the negative trends in maternal mortality. In recent years, these programs have been experiencing a steady erosion of funds or budget cuts (Taylor). These cuts have a harmful effect on families of color as they rely on these programs the most because of the barriers to economic opportunity. It is important to note that while there are programs set in place to aid pregnant women in the substantial costs of prenatal care, many low-income childbearing women do not qualify for them. In Missouri, Medicaid coverage has not expanded to include low-income women of childbearing

Student explains why the problem needs to be addressed now.

age as eligible. This is especially concerning because Missouri's maternal mortality rate is 22.1. However, St. Louis City, where there is a high African American population, had a maternal mortality rate of 51.1 (Prabu). With such rates, it is important that strategies are put in place to address it.

Student transitions from explaining problem to presenting proposals to address problem.

Given the pressing nature of this issue, I am proposing the following strategies to reduce maternal mortality, focusing on the group most in need—African American women. The current system places an emphasis on medical research on white people. However, every race has their own specific set of risk factors that physicians must consider. For instance, Black women are more likely to suffer from high blood pressure and hypertension, which could lead to the pregnancy complications of preeclampsia and eclampsia (Taylor). Because the risk factors are different for each racial group, I propose that standardized risk assessment tests should be created for each group to assess their current risk. The creation of these standardized tests will allow physicians to better care for all pregnant women of all different backgrounds. This allows physicians to catch health complications before they get worse. To be combined with the standardized risk assessment test, a family history of female pregnancies should also be considered. If someone's mother suffered from postpartum complications, the offspring will likely suffer from those same complications. This approach allows the physicians and all those caring for the pregnant women to prepare for specific situations.

In addition to standardized risk assessment tests, a standardized evaluation equivalent to the Apgar test should also be created. For this to be feasible, a committee of OB/GYNs will be selected to create the Apgar score to improve the quality and trigger necessary medical interventions for mothers (Taylor). An Apgar score was created by Dr. Virginia Apgar and is used as a method of assessing the clinical status of newborns in the minutes immediately after delivery (Taylor). The Apgar score will focus

Kamara 5

on identifiable characteristics that are crucial to monitor after birth, such as heart rate, respiratory breathing, muscle tone and other factors.

Adapting the Apgar score for moms might help medical staff prevent severe maternal morbidity and mortality and reduce possible subjectivity and biases. Risk assessments are necessary, but it is also crucial to facilitate access to comprehensive, inexpensive, high-quality healthcare to eliminate racial disparities in maternal mortality.

Therefore, I propose providing prenatal resources tailored to African American women to ensure that they receive the best possible care. The Center for American Progress states "Lack of access to both quality, affordable health care and insurance coverage fuel poor health outcomes and racial and ethnic health disparities" (qtd. in Taylor). While we cannot change Missouri's non-expansive Medicaid, we can provide resources that aid low-income mothers to still receive proper prenatal care. To ensure that low-income pregnant women are receiving the proper prenatal care, I propose partnering with Planned Parenthood, an essential health care service organization that provides STD testing and treatment, birth control, prenatal care and so much more at a free or low cost. To implement my proposed strategies, pop-up clinics should also be created in partnership with Planned Parent hood for women who cannot travel to prenatal appointments and obstetric services.

While the pop-up clinics will increase the number of women receiving prenatal care, there needs to be services in place for delivery. Most insurance companies do not cover the cost for women to hire midwives or doulas, and so moms are left with the option of having a hospital birth (Scrimshaw 46). For pregnant women looking for alternative birth settings, volunteer doulas and midwives should be present to provide information on their jobs and to assist women with their deliveries. By implementing all of these strategies, maternal mortality may decrease.

Student explains strategies here and above for addressing problem. Student also explains how strategies would be implemented.

Kamara 6

Racism and institutional racism are pervasive in our culture and impact the health outcomes of Black women. This reality is seen in the higher number of maternal death rates for African American women; their symptoms are dismissed, their access to critical health care treatments is difficult, and their medical practitioners continue to be prejudiced. We can address the high maternal mortality rate in St. Louis and the United States by increasing access to maternity services and increasing awareness of risk factors for all racial and ethnic groups. While it will take time for genuine change to be enacted, the desire for progress will maintain the momentum of the strategies outlines in this paper. Maternal mortality is at an all-time high, and it is time we did something to minimize it.

Student concludes by overviewing problem and proposed solutions and ends with a call to action.

Kamara 7

Start a new page for the Works Cited.

Works Cited

Brown, Kyrah K., Rhonda K. Lewis, Elizabeth Baumgartner, Christy Schunn, J'Vonnah Maryman, and Jamie LoCurto. "Exploring the Experience of Life Stress Among Black Women with a History of Fetal or Infant Death: A Phenomenological Study." *Journal of Racial and Ethnic Health Disparities* vol. 4, no. 3, 2017: 484–496. https://doi.org/10.1007/s40615-016-0250-z.

Danawi, Hadi, and Marie Peoples. "Exploring Racial Disparity in St. Louis City Fetal-Infant Death." *Walden University ScholarWorks,* School of Health Sciences Publications, Apr. 2015, pp. 39–43. scholarworks.waldenu.edu/cgi/viewcontent.cgi?article=1073&context=shs_pubs.

Engel, Jessica, Lindsey Neinstedt, and Leah Kemper. "Maternal Mortality in Missouri: A Review of Challenges and State Policy Options." *Center for Health Economics and Policy,* UMSL, Oct. 2019, www.umsl.edu/~socialwk/files/pdfs/Students,%20alums/Engel.%20Jessica%20policy%20brief%20Maternal%20Mortality%20in%20Missouri%20Final.pdf.

Prabu, Anirudh, and Ishaan Shah. "Missouri Needs to Help Its Physicians Prevent Mothers from Dying." *St. Louis Post-Dispatch,* Ian Caso, 7

For online sources, include a URL or a DOI.

Double-space Works Cited.

List sources alphabetically by last name.

Feb. 2018, www.stltoday.com/opinion/columnists/missouri-needs-to-help-its-physicians-prevent-mothers-from-dying/article_053781ce-f0b2-5f10-925e-33324128b65d.html.

Scrimshaw, Susan C., and Emily P. Backes. *Birth Settings in America: Outcomes, Quality, Access, and Choice*. National Academies Press, 2020.

Taylor, Jamila, Katie Hamm, Cristina Novoa, and Shilpa Phadke. "Eliminating Racial Disparities in Maternal and Infant Mortality." *Center for American Progress,* Center for American Progress, 2 May 2019, www.americanprogress.org/article/eliminating-racial-disparities-maternal-infant-mortality/.

Villarosa, Linda. "Why America's Black Mothers and Babies Are in a Life-or-Death Crisis." *The New York Times,* The New York Times, 11 Apr. 2018, www.nytimes.com/2018/04/11/magazine/black-mothers-babies-death-maternal-mortality.html.

Xaverius, Pamela K. "Maternal and Child Health Profile." *Think Health St. Louis,* Conduent Healthy Communities Institute, Oct. 2019, https://www.thinkhealthstl.org/content/sites/stlouisco/MCH/FINAL_2019_MCH_Report.pdf.

Use hanging indention.

Courtesy of Zaryn Kamara

For this proposal assignment, students created PowerPoint slides and discussed them in five-minute presentations. Zaryn developed the slides below to accompany her proposal.

When designing your slides, follow the CARP model: Contrast, Alignment, Repetition, Proximity.

These bullet items are aligned with the slide title.

Why is Maternal Mortality an Issue?

- In 2019, Missouri ranked in the top 10 in U.S. for maternal mortality
- In Missouri, Black women are two times more likely to die from pregnancy-related causes
- St. Louis lacks a system that allows OB-GYNs to track relevant pregnancy-related statistics, standard protocols for pregnancy-related emergencies
- Due to Missouri's lack of Medicaid expansion, low-income women are not eligible for Medicaid coverage before, after pregnancy (Engel 2019)

The slide titles are all in the same location, providing the repetition you want in a presentation.

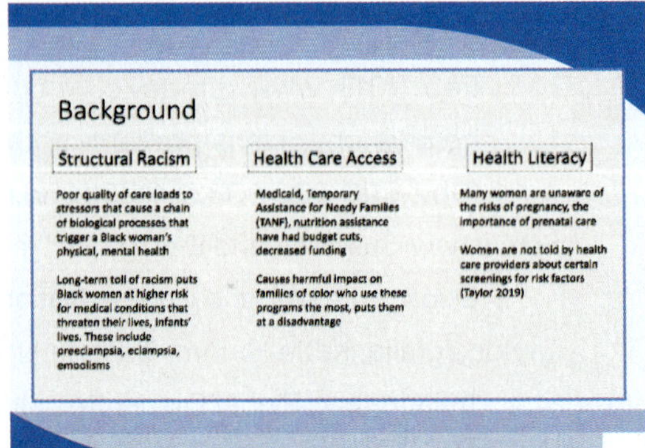

Each column is close to its header, providing proximity of information.

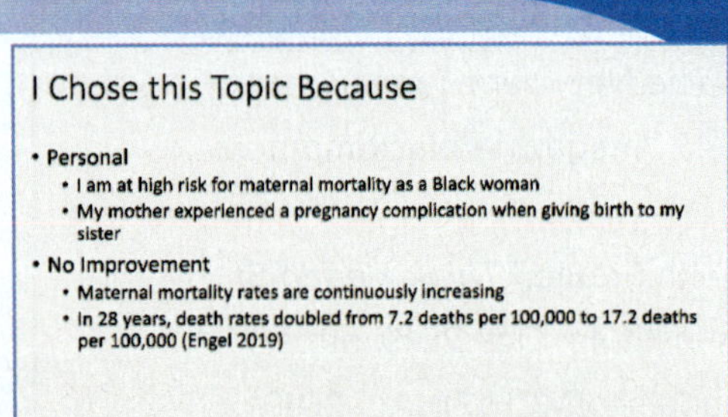

While these slides are not fancy, they are clear and readable, which is what you want. Beginning with a basic design like this allows you to augment your information with images.

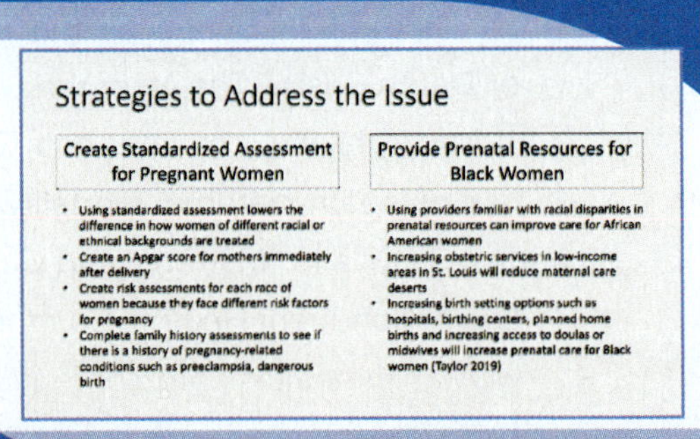

Be aware, however, that when you use images, you need to cite their sources and use alt-text to describe them for blind and low vision users.

Conclusion

- Maternal mortality among Black women is a serious problem in U.S. and St. Louis that we must address now
- Creating standardized assessments, providing prenatal and postnatal resources will increase maternal health care and decrease maternal mortality among Black women

The student wraps up the presentation by restating the issue, noting its timeliness, and summarizing the proposed strategies for addressing the problem.

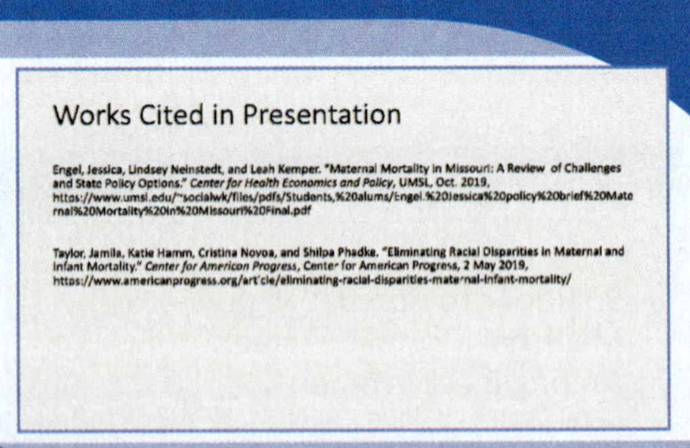

Check with your instructor to see if the works cited in your presentation needs to adhere to citation guidelines precisely. Here, for example, the student has used MLA but has opted – with permission from the instructor – to list sources single-spaced without hanging indents.

CHAPTER 14

Formal Documentation: MLA Style, APA Style

LEARNING OUTCOMES

After reading Chapter 14, you will be able to:

- Recall how to use the simplest patterns of parenthetical documentation.
- Place parenthetical documentation.
- Describe how to use parenthetical citations of complex sources.
- Prepare MLA citations for a Works Cited list.
- Use APA style to prepare a list of references.

fizkes/Shutterstock

In Chapter 12 you were shown, in a sample work log, what information about a source you need to prepare the documentation for a researched essay. In Chapter 13 you were shown in-text documentation patterns as part of the discussion of avoiding plagiarism and writing effective paragraphs. The format shown is for MLA (Modern Language Association) style, the documentation style used in most of the humanities disciplines. APA (American Psychological Association) style is used in the social sciences. The sciences and other disciplines also have style sheets, but the most common documentation patterns used by undergraduates are MLA and APA, the two patterns explained in this chapter.

Remember that MLA recommends that writers prepare their Works Cited list–a list of all sources they have used–before drafting the essay. This list can then be used as an accurate guide to the in-text/parenthetical documentation that MLA requires along with the Works Cited list at the end of the essay. Heed this good advice. This chapter begins with guidelines for in-text documentation and then provides many models of full documentation for a Works Cited list.

As you now know, MLA documentation style has two parts: in-text references to author and page number and then complete information about each source in a Works Cited list. Because parenthetical references to author and page are incomplete–readers could not find the source with such limited information–all sources referred to by author and (usually) page number in the essay require the full details of publication in a Works Cited list that concludes the essay. General guidelines for in-text citations are given below.

NOTE: You need a 100 percent correspondence between the sources listed in your Works Cited and the sources you actually cite (refer to) in your essay. Do not omit from your Works Cited any sources you refer to in your essay. Do not include in your Works Cited any sources not referred to in your paper.

GUIDELINES for Using Parenthetical Documentation

- The purpose of documentation is to make clear exactly what material in a passage has been borrowed and from what source the borrowed material has come.
- Parenthetical in-text documentation requires specific page references for borrowed material—unless the source is not a print one.
- Parenthetical documentation is required for both quoted and paraphrased material and for both print and nonprint sources.
- Parenthetical documentation provides as brief a citation as possible consistent with accuracy and clarity.

THE SIMPLEST PATTERNS OF PARENTHETICAL DOCUMENTATION

The simplest in-text citation can be prepared in one of three ways. The highlighted text below illustrates examples of these three approaches.

1. Give the author's last name (full name in your first reference to the writer) in the text of your essay and put the appropriate page number(s) in parentheses following the borrowed material.

   Frederick Lewis Allen observes that, during the 1920s, urban tastes spread to the country (146).

2. Place the author's last name and the appropriate page number(s) in parentheses immediately following the borrowed material.

   During the 1920s, "not only the drinks were mixed, but the company as well" (Allen 82).

3. On the rare occasion that you cite an entire work rather than borrowing from a specific passage, give the author's name in the text and omit any page numbers.

   Leonard Sax explains, to both parents and teachers, the specific ways in which gender matters.

Each one of these in-text references is complete *only* when the full citation is placed in the Works Cited section of your paper:

Allen, Frederick Lewis. *Only Yesterday: An Informal History of the Nineteen-Twenties.* Harper and Row, 1931.

Sax, Leonard. *Why Gender Matters.* Random House, 2005.

The three patterns just illustrated should be used in each of the following situations:

1. The source referred to is not anonymous–the author is known.
2. The source referred to is by one author.
3. The source cited is the only work used by that author.
4. No other author in your list of sources has the same last name.
5. The source has page numbers.

PLACEMENT OF PARENTHETICAL DOCUMENTATION

The simplest placing of an in-text reference is at the end of the sentence *before* the period. When you are quoting, place the parentheses *after* the final quotation mark but still before the period that ends the sentence.

During the 1920s, "not only the drinks were mixed, but the company as well" (Allen 82).

NOTE: Do not put any punctuation between the author's name and the page number.

If the borrowed material forms only a part of your sentence, place the parenthetical reference *after* the borrowed material and *before* any subsequent punctuation. This placement more accurately shows readers what is borrowed and what are your own words.

Sport, Allen observes about the 1920s, had developed into an obsession (66), another similarity between the 1920s and the 1980s.

If a quoted passage is long enough to require setting off in display form (block quotation), then place the parenthetical reference at the end of the passage, *after* the final period. Remember: Long quotations in display form *do not* have quotation marks.

It is hard to believe that when he writes about the influence of science Allen is describing the 1920s, not the 1980s:

> The prestige of science was colossal. The man in the street and the woman in the kitchen, confronted on every hand with new machines and devices which they owed to the laboratory, were ready to believe that science could accomplish almost anything. (164)

And to complete the documentation for all three examples:

Works Cited

Allen, Frederick Lewis. *Only Yesterday: An Informal History of the Nineteen-Twenties.* Harper and Row, 1931.

PARENTHETICAL CITATIONS OF COMPLEX SOURCES

Not all sources can be cited in one of the three patterns illustrated above, for not all meet the five criteria listed on page 321. Works by two or more authors, for example, will need somewhat fuller references. Each sample form of in-text documentation given below must be completed with a full Works Cited reference, as shown above.

Two Authors, Mentioned in the Text

Richard Herrnstein and Charles Murray contend that it is "consistently . . . advantageous to be smart" (25).

Two Authors, Not Mentioned in the Text

The advantaged smart group forms a "cognitive elite" in our society (Herrnstein and Murray 26-27).

A Book in Two or More Volumes

Sewall analyzes the role of Judge Lord in Dickinson's life (2: 642-47).

OR

Judge Lord was also one of Dickinson's preceptors (Sewall 2: 642-47).

NOTE: The number before the colon always signifies the volume number. The number(s) after the colon represents the page number(s).

A Book Listed by Title—Author Unknown

According to *The Concise Dictionary of American Biography,* William Jennings Bryan's 1896 campaign stressed social and sectional conflicts (117).

***The New York Times*' editors were not pleased with some of the changes in welfare programs ("Where" 4: 16).**

Always cite the title of the article, not the title of the journal, if the author is unknown. With no opening noun or noun phrase, abbreviate the title with the first word. This is sufficient to guide readers to the correct Works Cited item.

William Jennings Bryan's 1986 campaign stressed social and sectional conflicts (*Concise Dictionary* 117).

If the title begins with a noun or noun phrase (noun plus adjective), shorten the title as shown.

A Work by a Corporate Author

> A report by the Institute of Ecology's Global Ecological Problems Workshop argues that the civilization of the city can lull us into forgetting our relationship to the total ecological system on which we depend (13).

Although corporate authors may be cited with the page number within the parentheses, your writing will be more graceful if corporate authors are introduced in the sentence. Then only page numbers go in parentheses.

Two or More Works by the Same Author

> During the 1920s, "not only the drinks were mixed, but the company as well" (Allen, *Only Yesterday* 82).
>
> Frederick Lewis Allen contends that the early 1900s were a period of complacency in America (*Big Change* 4-5).
>
> In *The Big Change,* Allen asserts that the early 1900s were a period of complacency (4-5).

If your list of sources contains two or more works by the same author, the fullest parenthetical citation includes the author's last name, followed by a comma; the work's title, shortened if possible; and the page number. If the author's name appears in the text—or the author and title both appear as in the third example above—omit these items from the parenthetical citation. When you have to include the title to distinguish among sources, it is best to put the author's name in the text.

Two or More Works in One Parenthetical Reference

> Several writers about the future agree that big changes will take place in work patterns (Toffler 384-87; Naisbitt 35-36).

Separate each author with a semicolon. But if the parenthetical reference becomes disruptively long, cite the works in a "See also" note rather than in the text.

A Source without Page Numbers

It is usually a good idea to name the nonprint source within your sentence so that readers will not expect to see page numbers.

> Although some still disagree, the *Oxford English Dictionary Online* defines global warming as "The gradual increase in the overall temperature of the earth's atmosphere due to the

greenhouse effect caused by increased levels of carbon dioxide, CFCs, and other pollutants."

Complete Publication Information in Parenthetical Reference

At times you may want to give complete information about a source within parentheses in the text of your essay. Then a Works Cited list is not used. Use square brackets for parenthetical information within parentheses. This approach may be a good choice when you use only one source that you refer to several times. Literary analyses are one type of essay for which this approach to citation may be a good choice. For example:

> Edith Wharton establishes the bleakness of her setting, Starkfield, not just through description of place but also through her main character, Ethan, who is described as "bleak and unapproachable" (*Ethan Frome* [Charles Scribner's Sons, 1911, Print] 3. All subsequent references are to this edition). Later Wharton describes winter as "shut[ting] down on Starkfield" and negating life there (7).

Additional-Information Footnotes or Endnotes

At times you may need to provide additional information that is not central to your argument. These additions belong in a content note. However, use these sparingly and never as a way of advancing your thesis. Many instructors object to content notes and prefer only parenthetical citations.

"See Also" Footnotes or Endnotes

More acceptable is the note that refers to other sources of evidence for or against the point to be established. These notes are usually introduced with "See also" or "Compare," followed by the citation. For example:

> Chekhov's debt to Ibsen should be recognized, as should his debt to other playwrights of the 1890s who were concerned with the inner life of their characters.[1]

[1] See also Eric Bentley, *In Search of Theater* (Vintage, 1959) 330; Walter Bruford, *Anton Chekhov* (Yale UP, 1957) 45.

PREPARING MLA CITATIONS FOR A WORKS CITED LIST

The partial in-text citations described and illustrated above must be completed by a full reference in a list given at the end of the essay. To prepare your Works Cited list, alphabetize, by author last name, the sources you have actually referred to in your paper and complete each citation according to the forms explained and illustrated below. (Guidelines for formatting a finished Works Cited page are found on p. 310.)

You can search the examples that follow to find the appropriate model for each of your sources, but you are less likely to make errors when you also understand the basic pieces of information—and the order of their presentation—essential to every citation.

Remember the purpose of your list: to provide the information that will let your readers locate each source you used. For example, if you used a book in a revised edition, readers must know that. Or if you used articles initially published in a magazine that you found in this textbook, then you must provide that additional information. The additional information is essential to identifying the actual source you used. MLA invites researchers to think in terms of a "container"—or a series of containers—for each source. A book has as its container the name of its publisher and the date of publication.

However, an article in this textbook would have two containers. First, the initial facts of publication for the magazine article followed by all of the details that identify *Read, Reason, Write,* namely author, title, publisher and date (this book's container) plus the page numbers on which the article appears here. Articles you find and use from an online database would also have two containers. The articles you actually used were originally published elsewhere and then reproduced in the database.

Books require the following information, in the order given, with periods after each of the four major elements:

- Author, last name first.
- Title—and subtitle if there is one—all in italics.
- The publisher's name, followed by a comma, and the date of publication, followed by a period.

Author	Title	Facts of Publication
Bellow, Saul.	*A Theft.*	Viking Books, 1989.

Forms for Books: Citing the Complete Book

A Book by a Single Author

Seyler, Dorothy U. *The Obelisk and the Englishman: The Pioneering Discoveries of Egyptologist William Bankes.* Prometheus Books, 2015.

The subtitle is included, preceded by a colon, even if there is no colon on the book's title page.

A Book by Two or Three Authors

Brizee, Allen, and Jaclyn M. Wells. *Partners in Literacy: A Writing Center Model for Civic Engagement.* Rowman & Littlefield Publishers, 2016.

Second (and third) authors' names appear in normal signature order.

A Book with Three or More Authors

Baker, Susan P., et al. *The Injury Fact Book.* Oxford UP, 1992.

Use the name of the first person listed on the title page followed by a comma and "et al." Shorten "University Press" to "UP."

Two or More Works by the Same Author

Goodall, Jane. *In the Shadow of Man.* Houghton Mifflin, 1971.

---. *Through a Window: My Thirty Years with the Chimpanzees of Gombe*. Houghton Mifflin, 1990.

Give the author's full name with the first entry. For the second (and additional works), begin the citation with three hyphens followed by a period. Alphabetize the entries by the books' titles.

A Book Written Under a Pseudonym with Name Supplied

Wrighter, Carl P. [Paul Stevens]. *I Can Sell You Anything.* Ballantine Books, 1972.

An Anonymous Book

Beowulf: A New Verse Translation. Translated by Seamus Heaney. Farrar, Straus, and Giroux, 2000.

An Edited Book

Hamilton, Alexander, et al. *The Federalist Papers.* Edited by Isaac Kramnick. Viking Books, 1987.

Lynn, Kenneth S., editor. *Huckleberry Finn: Text, Sources, and Critics.* Harcourt Brace, 1961.

If you cite the author's work, put the author's name first and the editor's name after the title. If you cite the editor's work (an introduction or notes), then place the editor's name first, followed by a comma and "editor."

A Translation

Schulze, Hagen. *Germany: A New History.* Translated by Deborah Lucas Schneider. Harvard UP, 1998.

Cornford, Francis MacDonald, translator. *The Republic of Plato.* Oxford UP, 1945.

If you cite the author's work, place the author's name first and the translator's name after the title. If the translator's work is the important element, place the translator's name first. If the author's name does not appear in the title, give it after the title. For example: By Plato.

A Book in Two or More Volumes

Spielvogel, Jackson J. *Western Civilization.* West Publishers, 1991. 2 vols.

A Book in Its Second or Subsequent Edition

O'Brien, David M. *Storm Center: The Supreme Court and American Politics.* 2nd ed. W. W. Norton, 1990.

A Book in a Series

Parkinson, Richard. *The Rosetta Stone.* British Museum, 2005. British Museum Objects in Focus.

Provide the series title–and number if there is one–after publication information. Capitalize but do not italicize the series name.

A Reprint of an Earlier Work

Twain, Mark. *Adventures of Huckleberry Finn.* 1885. Centennial Facsimile Edition. Introduction by Hamlin Hill. Harper & Row, 1962.

Faulkner, William. *As I Lay Dying.* 1930. Vintage Books/Random House, 1964.

Provide the original publication date as well as the facts of publication for the reprinted version. Indicate any new material, as in the first example. The second example illustrates the paperback reprint by the original publisher.

A Book with Two or More Publishers

Green, Mark, et al. *Who Runs Congress?* Bantam Books/Grossman Publishers, 1972. Ralph Nader Congress Project.

Separate the publishers with a forward slash.

A Corporate or Governmental Author

U.S. Environmental Protection Agency. *Chesapeake Bay: Introduction to an Ecosystem.* Government Printing Office, 2012.

American Indian Education Handbook. California Department of Education Unit, 1991.

When the author and the publisher are the same, begin with the title; do not repeat author and publisher.

Religious Texts

The Holy Bible

The Reader's Bible: A Narrative. Edited with introduction by Roland Mushat Frye. Princeton UP, 1965.

Provide facts of publication for versions not well known. In the text, capitalize religious texts such as the Bible or the Koran, but do not use italics except in the Works Cited.

Forms for Books: Citing Part of a Book

A Preface, Introduction, Foreword, or Afterword

Sagan, Carl. Introduction. *A Brief History of Time: From the Big Bang to Black Holes.* By Stephen Hawking. Bantam Books, 1988, pp. ix-x.

Use this form if you are citing the author of the introduction, preface, etc. Provide an identifying word after the author's name and give inclusive page numbers for the part of the book you are citing.

An Encyclopedia Article

Ostrom, John H. "Dinosaurs." *McGraw-Hill Encyclopedia of Science and Technology.* 1957 edition.

"Benjamin Franklin." *Concise Dictionary of American Biography.* Edited by Joseph E. G. Hopkins. Charles Scribner's Sons, 1964.

One or More Volumes in a Multivolume Work

James, Henry. *The Portrait of a Lady.* Vols. 3 and 4 of *The Novels and Tales of Henry James.* Charles Scribner's Sons, 1908.

A Work in an Anthology or Collection

Hurston, Zora Neale. *The First One. Black Female Playwrights: An Anthology of Plays Before 1950.* Edited by Kathy A. Perkins. Indiana UP, 1989, pp. 80-88.

Comstock, George. "The Medium and the Society: The Role of Television in American Life." *Children and Television: Images in a Changing Sociocultural World.* Edited by Gordon L. Berry and Joy Keiko Asamen. Sage Publications, 1993, pp. 117-31.

Give inclusive page numbers for the particular work you have used.

An Article in a Collection, Casebook, or Sourcebook

Yancy, George. "I Am a Dangerous Professor." *The New York Times.* November 2016. Reprinted in *Read, Reason, Write: An Argument Text and Reader,* 13th ed. By Dorothy U. Seyler and Allen Brizee. McGraw Hill, 2024, pp. 380–83.

Many articles in collections have been previously published, so you must provide the original facts of publication (excluding page numbers if they are not readily available), and then the facts of publication for the collection. End with inclusive page numbers for that part of the book that you used.

Cross-References

If you are citing several articles from one collection, you can provide a citation for the entire book and then provide just the author, title, and page numbers for each specific article used. Include a cross-reference to the editor(s) of the collection with each specific article you cite.

Head, Suzanne, and Robert Heinzman, editors. *Lessons of the Rainforest.* Sierra Club, 1990.

Bandyopadhyay, J., and Vandana Shiva. "Asia's Forest, Asia's Cultures." Head and Heinzman, pp. 66-77.

Forms for Digital Sources

Remember that the purpose of a citation is to lead readers to the exact source you have used. This means that if you access an article in a digital database that was initially published in a print source, you must include this additional container, the information about the database. Researchers also use other kinds of online sources, and citations for these usually require more information than for printed sources. Include as many of the items listed below, in the order given here, as are relevant–and available–for each source. Take the time to search a website's home page to locate as much of the information as possible.

- Author (or editor, compiler, translator), last name first, ending in a period.
- Title of the work, in quotation marks if it is part of a site, in italics if it is a complete and separate work, such as an online novel, ending in a period.

- Facts of publication of the print version if the item was originally published in print, ending in a period.
- Title of the website, in italics–unless it is the same as the title of the work.
- Publisher of the site–organization or person who owns or sponsors the site.
- Date of publication.
- Digital object identifier (DOI), if any–the most preferred choice–permalink, or URL, preferably a stable URL, followed by a period.
- Your date of access only if the source is undated, likely to change, or likely to be removed.

NOTE: MLA recommends including DOIs, permalinks, and/or URLs, but you should omit them if your instructor prefers that you do so. Also, some articles in library databases with DOIs may not be accessible online.

Study this annotated citation of an article in an online news publication as a general model:

author · title of work · sponsor of website

Yancy, George. "I Am a Dangerous Professor." *The New York Times*, 30 Nov. 2016, www.nytimes.com/2016/11/30/opinion/i-am-a-dangerous-professor.html?ref=opinion&_r=0.

date of publication · website URL

A Published Article in an Online Database

Shin, Michael S. "Redressing Wounds: Finding a Legal Framework to Remedy Racial Disparities in Medical Care." *California Law Review*, vol. 90, no. 6, 2002, pp. 2047–2100. *JSTOR*, www.jstor.org/stable3481439.

Kumar, Sanjay. "Scientists Accuse Animal Rights Activists of Stifling Research." *British Medical Journal*, vol. 325, no. 7374, 23 Nov. 2002, p. 1192. *EBSCOhost*, https://doi.org/10.1136/bmj.325.7374.1192/d.

No access date is used with databases of printed articles.

An Article in a Reference Source

"Prohibition." *Encyclopaedia Britannica Online*, 11 June 2014, www.britannica.com/topic/prohibition-alcohol-interdict.

An Online News Source

Associated Press. "Russia Voted Off UN Human Rights Council." *WTOP,* 28 Oct. 2016, wtop.com/europe/2016/10/russia-voted-off-unhuman-rights-council/. Accessed 30 Oct. 2016.

An Article in an Online Magazine

Kinsley, Michael. "Politicians Lie. Numbers Don't." *Slate,* 16 Sept. 2008, www.slate.com/articles/news_and_politics/readme/2008/09/politicians_lie_numbers_dont.html.

A Poem in a Scholarly Project

Keats, John. "Ode to a Nightingale." *Poetical Works of John Keats.* 1884. *Bartleby.com,* www.bartleby.com/126/40.html.

Information from a Government Site

"The 2008 HHS Poverty Guidelines." *ASPE,* U.S. Department of Health and Human Services, 23 Jan. 2008, aspe.hhs.gov/2008-hhs-poverty-guidelines.

Information from a Professional Site

"Every Student Succeeds Act: Resources for Orchestras." League of American Orchestras, 9 Nov. 2020, americanorchestras.org/every-student-succeeds-act-resources-for-orchestras.

Information from a Professional Blog

Leta, Vicky, et al. "Women Inventors Whose Contributions Still Bless Us Today." *Mashable,* 24 Mar. 2016. mashable.com/2016/03/24/women-inventors/?utm_cid=hp-hh-sec#yLcwQAqKgkqT.

Home Page for a Course or Academic Department

Saint Louis University English Department. www.slu.edu/arts-and-sciences/english/index.php. Accessed 4 Oct. 2021.

Twitter

@ProfAllenBrizee. "I'd rather be playing Skyrim." *Twitter,* 21 Aug., 2021, 4:11 p.m., twitter.com/ProfAllenBrizee/status/1429189553559113733.

YouTube

DJ Luter One. "90s House Music Mix vol. 3." *YouTube,* uploaded by DJ Luter One, 28 May 2021, www.youtube.com/watch?v=LpcLrcJWiH8.

Forms for Other Print and Nonprint Sources

The materials in this section, although often important to research projects, do not always lend themselves to documentation by the forms illustrated above. Follow the basic order of author, title, and facts of publication as much as possible. Add more information as needed to make the citation clear and useful to a reader. Citations for such sources as films, television and podcast episodes, and other media will likely need to include additional container information (e.g., the physical media, website, app, or streaming service you used to acccess the material).

Audio (or Video) from a Website

Vachss, Andrew. "Dead and Gone." Interview by Bill Thompson. *Eye on Books,* 24 Oct. 2000. *The Zero.* www.vachss.com/av_interviews/eye_books.html. Accessed 25 Sept. 2008.

A Recording (Physical format or from a Website, app, or streaming service)

Stein, Joseph. *Fiddler on the Roof.* Jerry Bock, composer. Original-Cast Recording with Zero Mostel. Original cast recording. RCA, 1964. Vinyl.

Rose, Frankie. "Dancing Down the Hall." *Interstellar,* Slumberland Records, 2017. *Spotify* app.

The conductor and/or performers help identify a specific recording.

Plays, Concerts, or Other Performances

Beckett, Samuel. *Waiting for Godot.* Performers Ian McKellen and Patrick Stewart. Directed by Sean Mathias, 26 Nov. 2013, Cort Theatre, New York City.

Principal actors, singers, musicians, and/or the director can be added as appropriate.

A Television Episode

"Meetings Have Biscuits." *Killing Eve.* Created by Phoebe Waller-Bridge, season 3, episode 3, BBC America, 25 Apr. 2020. *Amazon Prime Video* app.

An Interview

Plum, Kenneth. Personal Interview, 5 Mar. 2012.

A Lecture

Brizee, Allen. "Writing Ethical and Effective Proposals." Saint Louis University, 30 Sep. 2021. Lecture.

A Personal Letter or E-mail

Usick, Patricia. "Bankes' Chapel." E-mail to the author. 3 Aug. 2015.

Maps and Charts

Hampshire and Dorset. Map. Geographers' A–Z.

Cartoons and Advertisements

Halleyscope. "Halleyscopes Are for Night Owls." Advertisement. *Natural History,* Dec. 1985, p. 15.

United Airlines Advertisement. ESPN. 8 Aug. 2008. Television.

A Published Dissertation

Brotton, Joyce D. *Illuminating the Present through Literary Dialogism: From the Reformation through Postmodernism.* 2002. George Mason U, PhD dissertation. UMI, 2002.

Government Documents

United States, Environmental Protection Agency. *The Challenge of the Environment: A Primer on EPA's Statutory Authority.* Government Printing Office, 1972.

If the author is not given, cite the name of the government first followed by the name of the department or agency. If the author is known, give the author's name first, followed by the title, and then appropriate facts for accessing the material.

Geller, William. *Deadly Force. U.S. Department of Justice National Institute of Justice Crime File Study Guide.* U.S. Department of Justice, www.ncjrs.gov/pdffiles1/Digitization/ 100734NCJRS.pdf. Accessed 24 Mar. 2016.

Constitutions

The Constitution of the United States: A Transcription. National Archives, Article 1, section 3, U.S. National Archives and Records Administration, 15 April 2021, www.archives.gov/founding-docs/constitution-transcript.

The Constitution is referred to by article and section. When citing a court case, give the name of the case, the volume, page of the report, and the date.

Court Cases

Turner v. Arkansas. 407 U.S. 366. 1972.

skynesher/Getty Images

Forms for Periodicals: Articles in Magazines, Journals, and Newspapers

Articles from the various forms of periodicals, when read in their print format, require the following information, in the order given:

- Author, last name first, followed by a period.
- Title of the article, in quotation marks, followed by a period inside the final quotation mark.
- Facts of publication, which usually include the title of the periodical in italics followed by a comma, the volume number or volume and issue number followed by a comma, the date of publication followed by a comma, inclusive page numbers for the article preceded by p. or pp., and then a period.

For articles accessed in their print format, think of the facts of publication–the details about the specific periodical–as the article's container. Articles, unlike books, are not published separately; they are "contained" within a periodical or in a book collection of articles. Articles of various kinds can also be found on a website, in which cases the website becomes the container. Identifying facts of the website must be supplied for your readers to find the work you are citing.

Article in a Journal Paged by Year

Brown, Jane D., and Carol J. Pardun. "Little in Common: Racial and Gender Differences in Adolescents' Television Diets." *Journal of Broadcasting and Electronic Media,* vol. 48, no. 2, 2004, pp. 266-78.

Article in a Journal Paged by Issue

Lewis, Kevin. "Superstardom and Transcendence." *Arete: The Journal of Sport Literature,* vol. 2, no. 2, 1985, pp. 47-s54.

If the journal uses both volume and issue numbers, provide both regardless of the journal's choice of paging.

Article in a Monthly Magazine

Wegner, Mary-Ann Pouls. "Gateway to the Netherworld." *Archaeology* Jan./Feb. 2013, pp. 50-53.

Do not use volume or issue numbers with popular magazines. Cite the month(s) and year of publication and inclusive page numbers. Abbreviate all months except May, June, and July.

Article in a Weekly Magazine

Stein, Joel. "Eat This, Low Carbers." *Time,* 15 Aug. 2005, p. 78.

Provide the complete date, using the order of day, month, year.

An Anonymous Article

"Death of Perestroika." *The Economist,* 2 Feb. 1991, pp. 12-13.

The missing name indicates that the article is anonymous. Alphabetize under D.

A Published Interview

Angier, Natalie. "Ernst Mayr at 93." Interview. *Natural History Magazine,* May 1997, pp. 8-11.

Follow the pattern for a published article, but add the descriptive label "Interview" (followed by a period) after the article's title.

A Review

Whitehead, Barbara D. "The New Segregation." Review of *Coming Apart: The State of White America,* 1960-2010, by Charles Murray. *Commonweal,* 4 May 2012.

If the review is signed, begin with the author's name and then the title of the review article. Also provide the title of the work being reviewed and its author, preceded by "Review of." For reviews of art shows, videos, or computer software, provide place and date or descriptive label to make the citation clear.

Forms for Periodicals: Articles in Newspapers Accessed in Print

Article in a Newspaper

Arguila, John. "What Deep Blue Taught Kasparov—and Us." *Christian Science Monitor,* 16 May 1997, p. 18.

A newspaper's title should be cited as it appears on the masthead.

Article in a Newspaper with Lettered Sections

Taub, Amanda. "Why Some Wars Get More Attention Than Others." *New York Times,* 2 Oct. 2016, p. A8.

Place the section letter immediately before the page number without any spacing. If the paging of the article is not consecutive, give the first page and the plus (+) sign.

An Article in a Newspaper with a Designated Edition

Pereria, Joseph. "Women Allege Sexist Atmosphere in Offices Constitutes Harassment." *The Wall Street Journal,* eastern ed. 10 Feb. 1988, p. 23.

Cite the edition used after the title of the newspaper.

An Editorial

"Japan's Two Nationalisms." Editorial. *The Washington Post,* 4 June 2000: B6.

Add the descriptive label "Editorial" after the article title.

A Letter to the Editor

Wiles, Yoko A. "Thoughts of a New Citizen." Letter. *The Washington Post,* 27 Dec. 1995: A22.

A Review

Doerr, Anthony. "Running through Time." Review of *Time Travel: A History* by James Gleick. *The New York Times Book Review,* 2 Oct. 2016, pp. 1+.

If the review is signed, begin with the author's name and then the title of the review article. Then provide the title of the work being reviewed and its author, preceded by "Review of." For reviews of art shows, videos, or computer software, provide place and date or descriptive label to make the citation clear.

APA STYLE

The *APA system* identifies a source by placing the author's last name and the publication year of the source within parentheses at the point in the text where the source is cited. The in-text citations are supported by complete citations in a list of sources at the end of the paper. Most disciplines in the social sciences use APA style. The guidelines given here follow the style of the *Publication Manual of the American Psychological Association* (7th ed., 2020).

APA Style: In-Text Citations

The simplest parenthetical reference can be presented in one of three ways. The highlighted text below illustrates examples of these three approaches.

1. Place the year of publication within parentheses immediately following the author's name in the text.

    In a typical study of preference for motherese, Fernald (1985) used an operant auditory preference procedure.

Within the same paragraph, additional references to the source do not need to repeat the year, if the researcher clearly establishes that the same source is being cited.

> Because the speakers were unfamiliar subjects, Fernald's work eliminates the possibility that it is the mother's voice per se that accounts for the preference.

2. If the author is not mentioned in the text, place the author's last name followed by a comma and the year of publication within parentheses after the borrowed information.

    The majority of working women are employed in jobs that are at least 75 percent female (Lawrence & Matsuda, 1997).

3. Cite a specific passage by providing the page, chapter, or figure number following the borrowed material. *Always* give specific page references for quoted material.
    - A brief quotation:

      Deuzen-Smith (1988) believes that counselors must be involved with clients and "deeply interested in piecing the puzzle of life together" (p. 29).

    - A quotation in display form:

      Bartlett (1932) explains the cyclic process of perception:

        Suppose I am making a stroke in a quick game, such as tennis or cricket. How I make the stroke depends on the relating of certain new experiences, most of them visual, to other

> immediately preceding visual experiences, and to my posture, or balance of posture, at the moment. (p. 201)

Use this style with a quotation of forty words or more. Indent a block quotation five spaces from the left margin, do not use quotation marks, and double-space throughout. To show a new paragraph within the block quotation, indent the first line of the new paragraph an additional five spaces. Note the placing of the year after the author's name, and the page number at the end of the direct quotation.

More complicated in-text citations should be handled as follows:

Two Authors, Mentioned in the Text

> Kuhl and Meltzoff (1984) tested 4- to 5-month-olds in an experiment . . .

Two Authors, Not Mentioned in the Text

> . . . but are unable to show preference in the presence of two mismatched modalities (e.g., a face and a voice; see Kuhl & Meltzoff, 1984).

Give both authors' last names each time you refer to the source. Connect their names with "and" in the text. Use an ampersand (&) in the parenthetical citation.

More Than Three Authors

For works coauthored by three or more people, provide the name of the first author only, followed by "et al." Use this format in every citation, including the first, unless doing so would cause ambiguity.

> As Price-Williams et al. have shown (1969), . . .
>
> **OR**
>
> Studies of these children have shown (Price-Williams et al., 1969) . . .

Corporate Authors

In general, spell out the name of a corporate author each time it is used. If a corporate author has well-known initials, the name can be abbreviated after the first citation.

FIRST IN-TEXT CITATION:	(National Institutes of Health [NIH], 1989)
SUBSEQUENT CITATIONS:	(NIH, 1989)

Two or More Works within the Same Parentheses

When citing more than one work by the same author in a parenthetical reference, use the author's name only once and arrange the years mentioned in order; thus:

> Several studies of ego identity formation (Marcia, 1966, 1983) . . .

When an author, or the same group of coauthors, has more than one work published in the same year, distinguish the works by adding the letters *a, b, c,* and so on, as needed, to the year. Give the last name only once, but repeat the year, each one with its identifying letter; thus:

> Several studies (Smith, 1990a, 1990b, 1990c) . . .

When citing several works by different authors within the same parentheses, list the authors alphabetically; alphabetize by the first author when citing coauthored works. Separate authors or groups of coauthors with semicolons; thus:

> **Although many researchers (Archer & Waterman, 1983; Grotevant, 1983; Grotevant & Cooper, 1986; Sabatelli & Mazor, 1985) study identity formation . . .**

Personal Communication

Cite information obtained via interview, phone, letter, text message, and e-mail communication.

> **According to Sandra Haun (personal interview, September 7, 2018) . . .**

Because readers cannot retrieve information from these personal sources, do *not* include a citation in your list of references.

Secondary Sources

Make every effort to find, read, and cite original works. When this is not possible—the work is now out of print or the writer is quoting someone from a speech or personal communication—cite the secondary source this way:

> **Jennings disputes Smith's claims by recounting what she said in a recent radio interview: "I will not be running for re-election in the House" (as cited in Kim, 2017).**

APA STYLE: PREPARING A LIST OF REFERENCES

All sources cited parenthetically in your paper—except for all types of personal communication—need a complete citation. These complete citations are placed on a separate page (or pages) after the text of the paper and before any appendices included in the paper. Sources are arranged alphabetically, and the first page is titled "References." Begin each source flush with the left margin and indent second and subsequent lines five spaces. Double-space throughout the list of references. Follow these rules for alphabetizing:

1. Organize two or more works by the same author, or the same group of coauthors, chronologically.

   Beck, A. T. (1991).

   Beck, A. T. (1993).

2. Place single-author entries before multiple-author entries when the first of the multiple authors is the same as the single author.

   Grotevant, H. D. (1983).

   Grotevant, H. D., & Cooper, C. R. (1986).

3. Organize multiple-author entries that have the same first author but different second or third authors alphabetically by the name of the second author or third and so on.

Gerbner, G., & Gross, L.

Gerbner, G., Gross, L., Jackson-Beeck, M., Jeffries-Fox, S., & Signorielli, N.

Gerbner, G., Gross, L., Morgan, M., & Signorielli, N.

4. Organize two or more works by the same author(s) published in the same year alphabetically by title.

Form for Books

A book citation contains these elements in this form:

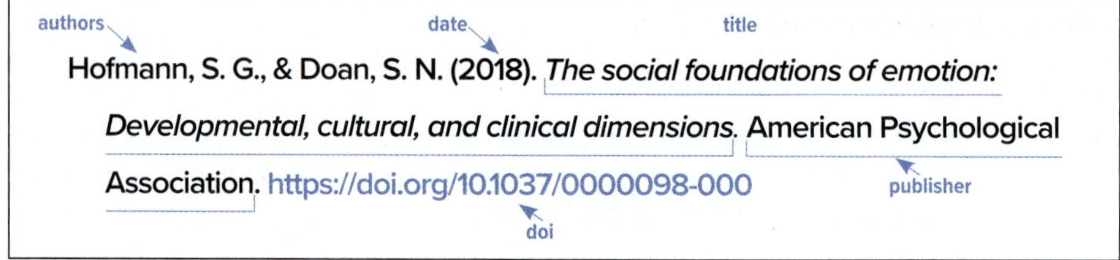

Authors

Give all authors' names, last name first, and initials. Separate authors with commas, use the ampersand (&) before the last author's name, and end with a period. For edited books, place the abbreviation "Ed." or "Eds." in parentheses following the last editor's name.

Date of Publication

Place the year of publication in parentheses followed by a period.

Title

Capitalize only the first word of the title and of the subtitle, if there is one, and any proper nouns. Italicize the title and end with a period. Place additional information such as number of volumes or an edition in parentheses after the title, before the period.

Burleigh, N. (2007). *Mirage: Napoleon's scientists and the unveiling of Egypt.*

Publication Information

Give the publisher's name, eliminating unnecessary terms such as *Publisher, Co.,* and *Inc.* End the citation with a period.

Mitchell, J. V. (Ed.). (1985). *The ninth mental measurements yearbook.* University of Nebraska Press.

National Institute of Drug Abuse. (1993, April 13). *Annual national high school senior survey.* Author.

Newton, D. E. (1996). *Violence and the media.* ABC-Clio.

Give a corporate author's name in full. When the organization is both author and publisher, place the word *Author* after the place of publication.

Retrieval Information

Whether a source is retrieved in print or digital form, include a live-linked DOI, or digital object identifier, whenever one is available. DOIs are a series of numbers and letters that provide a link to a specific item, and this link does not change with time. Although DOIs are often on the first page of a document, they can, at times, be hard to locate. For digital sources, APA prefers that you always choose a source's DOI over its URL, if you can find it. Place the DOI at the end of the citation, as a live link to the source, and introduce the number thus: https://doi.org/[follwed by the DOI number]. Do not end the citation with a period.

Form for Electronic Sources

As a minimum, an APA reference for any type of online source should include the following information: a document title or description, the date of publication, a way to access the document online, and, when possible, an author name.

When the online address (URL) is likely to be stable, you can cite that address. For example: https://www.nytimes.com. However, a good source that you find during your research may not be found later by your readers with the URL that you used. APA recommends, therefore, that such sources be documented with the item's DOI (digital object identifier) instead of its URL.

Do not place URLs within angle brackets (< >). Do not place a period at the end of the URL, even though it concludes the citation.

Here are a few examples of citations for online sources:

Journal Article Retrieved Online

Habermas, Jürgen. (2006). Political communication in media society. *Communication Theory, 16*(4), 411–426. https://doi.org/10.1111/j.1468-2885.2006.00280.x

Gardiner, K., Herault, Y., Lott, I., Antonarakis, S., Reeves, R., & Dierssen, M. (2010). Down syndrome: From understanding the neurobiology to therapy. *Journal of Neuroscience, 30*(45), 14943–14945. https://doi.org/10.1523/JNEUROSCI.3728-10.2010

Electronic Daily Newspaper Article Available by Search

Olalde, M., & Menenez, R. (2020, February 6). Toxic legacy of old oil wells. *Los Angeles Times.* https://www.latimes.com/projects/california-oil-well-drilling-idle-cleanup/#nt=liK0promoLarge-7030col1-7030col1nt=liH1promoXSmall-7030col2

Journal Article Available from a Periodical Database

If you retrieved the article from an online database that is not easily accessed by readers, include the URL that links to the home page for the database, or to the login page (for example, "Retrieved from PsycARTICLES, http://psycnet.apa.org)."

Dixon, B. (2001, December). Animal emotions. *Ethics & the Environment, 6*(2), 22. Retrieved from JSTOR, https://www.jstor.org

U.S. Government Report on a Government Website

U.S. General Accounting Office. (2002, March). *Identity theft: Prevalence and cost appear to be growing.* https://www.gao.gov/new.items/d02363.pdf

Cite a message posted to a newsgroup or electronic mailing list in the reference list. Cite an e-mail from one person to another *only* in the essay, not in the list of references.

Form for Articles

An article citation contains these elements in this form:

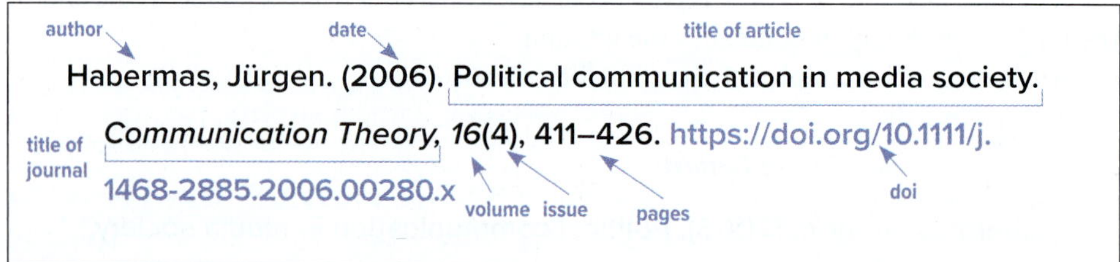

Date of Publication

Place the year of publication for articles in scholarly journals in parentheses, followed by a period. For articles in newspapers and popular magazines, give the year followed by month and day (if appropriate).

(1997, March).

Title of Article

Capitalize only the title's first word, the first word of any subtitle, and any proper nouns. Place any necessary descriptive information in square brackets immediately after the title.

Krenkler, R. (2020, February 25). Ban polystyrene [Letter to the Editor]. *Los Angeles Times,* p. B10.

Publication Information

Cite the title of the journal in full, capitalizing according to conventions for titles. Italicize the title and follow it with a comma. Give the volume number, italicized, followed by a comma, and then inclusive page numbers followed by a period. *If* a journal begins each issue with a new page 1, then also cite the issue number in parentheses immediately following the volume number. Do not use "p." or "pp." before page numbers when citing articles from scholarly journals; do use "p." or "pp." in citations to newspaper and magazine articles. Note that the citation should end with a DOI, if available.

Martin, C. L., Wood, C. H., & Little, J. K. (1990). The development of gender stereotype components. *Child Development, 61,* 1891–1904. https://doi.org/10.2307/1130845

Leakey, R. (2000, April/May). Extinctions past and present. *Time,* p. 35.

An Article or Chapter in an Edited Book

Goodall, J. (1993). Chimpanzees—bridging the gap. In P. Cavalieri & P. Singer (Eds.), *The great ape project: Equality beyond humanity* (pp. 10–18). St. Martin's.

Cite the author(s), date, and title of the article or chapter. Then cite the name(s) of the editor(s) in signature order after "In," followed by "Ed." or "Eds." in parentheses; the title of the book; the inclusive page numbers of the article or chapter, in parentheses, followed by a period. End with the publisher of the book.

A Report

U.S. Merit Systems Protection Board. (1988). *Sexual harassment in the federal workplace: An update.* U.S. Government Printing Office.

SAMPLE STUDENT ESSAY IN APA STYLE

The following student essay illustrates APA style. Use 1-inch margins and double-space throughout, including any block quotations. Block quotations should be indented *five* spaces from the left margin (in contrast to the half an inch required by MLA style). Observe the following elements: title page, running head, abstract, author/year in-text citations, subheadings within the text, and a list of references. This student sample is an analysis of President Barack Obama's speech included in this text in Chapter 17, Race in America.

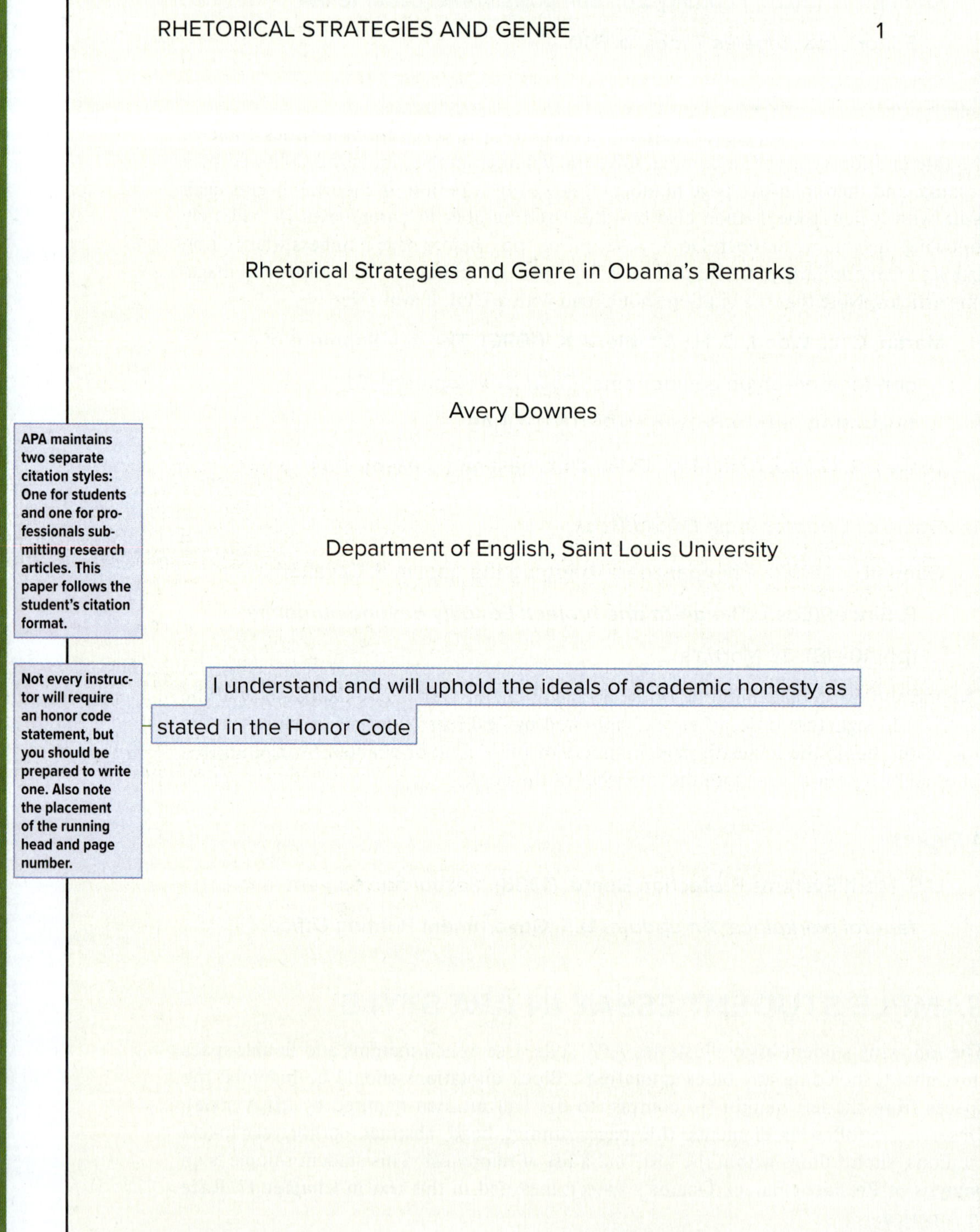

RHETORICAL STRATEGIES AND GENRE 1

Rhetorical Strategies and Genre in Obama's Remarks

Avery Downes

Department of English, Saint Louis University

I understand and will uphold the ideals of academic honesty as stated in the Honor Code

APA maintains two separate citation styles: One for students and one for professionals submitting research articles. This paper follows the student's citation format.

Not every instructor will require an honor code statement, but you should be prepared to write one. Also note the placement of the running head and page number.

Abstract

This paper examines the effectiveness of rhetorical strategies and genre of former President Barack Obama's speech commemorating the 50th anniversary of the march on Selma. Obama uses pathos, ethos, and logos throughout his speech. Within his use of logos, he utilizes inductive reasoning to argue the idea that America is a just, fair, inclusive, and generous country and that it will triumph. He uses deductive reasoning to argue that Americans need to register and vote. The use of rhetorical strategies like these allows Obama to argue his points effectively. However, due to faulty or hasty generalizations, Obama's argument is not completely flawless. Overall, however, Obama does an effective job using the problem-solution genre and his rhetorical strategies while delivering his speech.

Papers in APA style usually begin with an abstract.

Keywords: pathos, ethos, logos, induction, deduction, faulty generalizations

Place keywords below the abstract.

Student sets the context in the opening section of the intro-duction before presenting the paper's thesis.

As the 50th anniversary of the march from Selma to Montgomery arrived, former 44th President, Barack Obama, took time to reflect on this historic event. Obama served from 2008 until 2016 as the first Black president after his time spent working at the Illinois State Senate and the United States Senate. Through his reflection on the march from Selma to Montgomery led by Martin Luther King, Jr., Obama reminds Americans of the racial injustices the country faced while offering them hope and realistic solutions to continue fighting for equality as the past several generations did. By using rhetorical strategies and the problem-solution argumentative genre, Obama delivers a fairly effective speech, while only committing a few errors in logic.

Since the argu-mentative genre is not common knowledge, the student cites the source that provided that information – this book!

Here and below, the student sets the context of the rhetorical analysis by providing infor-mation about the speech, its place in history, and its author, as well as the genre the author uses.

Obama uses the problem-solution argumentative genre to communicate his views (Seyler & Brizee, 2019). Authors or speakers using the argumentative genre define the problem and may explain how the problem affects the audience. The problem, according to Obama, is that. Americans' rights to vote is threatened by people lacking interest. His solution is that Americans need to register and vote so they maintain their power. The way an author frames a problem may cause the audience to view the causes and solutions to the problem differently. Using this genre requires realistic solutions and ability to ask the audience to change despite their potential hesitations. Using this genre helps Obama as he describes the issues he sees in the country and allows him to inspire his audience to accept the change he believes is necessary.

The purpose of this speech is to remind the audience of racial injustices that Americans have faced throughout multiple generations and to attempt to give logical solutions that lead to a more equal future. Obama speaks to the American public—both present and future generations—and to other countries around the world as America navigates their democratic experiment. Obama gave this speech in 2015, making the timing especially important. Many Americans did not like Obama because he was Black. This dislike is a direct continuation of what Martin Luther King, Jr., fought against 50 years ago. Obama asks Americans to take action steps to help end inequality; then he tells his audience why they should do this. He also describes how prominent American leaders should model their behavior because those individuals fought for the rights to do the action steps Obama describes.

The rhetorical proofs Obama uses include ethos, pathos, and logos. For this paper, I am analyzing logos through induction and deduction. Ethos, which shows the speaker's credibility, exists through Obama's jobs and education rather than what he says. First, Obama served as President of the United States, which shows he deserves respect from his audience. Besides his title of President, Obama also proves his credibility through his high level of education. He attended Columbia University in New York City and graduated with a political science degree. To further continue his education, Obama attended Harvard Law School. With his educational background, Obama ran for political office. He started as an Illinois State Senator and then ran for United States Senate (Nelson, 2021). Due to Obama's jobs in government roles, he proves himself qualified to give a speech on how his audience can fight inequality through their government given rights.

Student explains key terms and overviews structure of this section.

Besides ethos, Obama uses pathos to evoke his audience's emotions. During his Presidency, Obama was determined to create unity in the United States. In his speech, Obama uses the desire Americans have for unity as a way to evoke empathy in his audience. By doing this, his audience is more likely to receive his solutions positively. While describing what happened when Black Americans and allies marched from Selma, Obama tells his audience,

> Because of what they did, the doors of opportunity swung open not just for black folks, but for every American. Women marched through those doors. Latinos marched through those doors. Asian Americans, gay Americans, Americans with disabilities—they all came through those doors. (as cited in Seyler & Brizee, 2019)

In APA, direct quotes of 40 or more words must be indented.

Obama's audience can see themselves as members in the various groups described. While seeing themselves in these groups, they feel more attached to the message and have the capacity to empathize with the injustices faced by Black Americans.

Obama then continues to describe who Americans are by stating, "We are Lewis and Clark and Sacajawea, pioneers who braved the unfamiliar, followed by a stampede of farmers and miners, and entrepreneurs and hucksters. That's our spirit. That's who we are" (as cited in Seyler & Brizee, 2019). If an individual could not identify with the previous statements, Obama goes on to describe groups that anyone could identify with. He allows his audience time and options to find where they identify with his message, generating empathy.

Student provides direct quotes to provide examples and support claims.

Obama uses logos through both induction and deduction. Inductive reasoning uses facts to reach inferences (Seyler & Brizee, 2019). Obama infers through a series of historical events that "the idea of a just America and a fair America, an inclusive America, and a generous America—that idea ultimately triumphed" (as cited in Seyler & Brizee, 2019). He believes that no matter what injustices threaten the country, America will turn out just, fair, inclusive, and generous. To make this inference difficult to rebut, Obama uses a significant number of historical events beginning with the march on Selma as "part of a broader campaign that spanned generations; the leaders that day part of a long line of heroes" (as cited in Seyler & Brizee, 2019). Selma is described as one event in the long history of fighting inequality instead of as an isolated event. Obama also brings in others, including

RHETORICAL STRATEGIES AND GENRE 6

"founders like Franklin and Jefferson" and "leaders like Lincoln and FDR," as they used their positions of power to work toward equality (as cited in Seyler & Brizee, 2019). Each of these individuals believed the idea that America is just, fair, inclusive, and generous. Lastly, Obama mentions specific sites that "are places and moments in America where this nation's destiny has been decided. Many are sites of war—Concord and Lexington, Appomattox, Gettysburg" (as cited in Seyler & Brizee, 2019). These places show the lengths Americans are willing to go to create a more just, fair, inclusive, and generous nation and support Obama's inference about the country.

Due to this inference, Obama moves to offer solutions that today's Americans can use. These solutions will continue supporting citizens as they push for America to be a just, fair, inclusive, and generous place. He describes how laws across the country are preventing people from using their right to vote. To keep America just and fair, each citizen must have the capability to use their right to vote. Without this capability, the idea that America will ultimately be a fair, just, inclusive, and generous nation will fail instead of triumph. To prevent these laws from continuing, Obama believes the people need to register and vote. If citizens want to have power in their country, they need to use their rights. Obama also claims that even without these laws, America would have a very low voter turnout (as cited in Seyler & Brizee, 2019). If Americans want to have a fair and just country, they need to register and vote. The reason why registering and voting is a logical conclusion is argued through Obama's deductive reasoning found later in his speech.

Each citation style requires different formatting. APA requires ampersands for in-text citation.

Deductive reasoning uses a major premise and minor premise to reach a conclusion. The relationship between the major premise and minor premise allows a logical conclusion to be reached (Seyler & Brizee, 2019). The major premise in Obama's speech is that democracy and voting are vital to equality. His minor premise states that voting is jeopardized by the American public lacking interest. Obama states, "if every new voter-suppression law was struck down today, we would still have, here in America, one of the lowest voting rates among free peoples" while describing how important voting was and is in the United States. He wonders how our voting rate is so low, and asks, "how do we so casually discard the right for which so many fought?" (as cited in Seyler & Brizee, 2019). This approach to low voting turnout helps Obama reach the conclusion that Americans need to register and vote. Obama believes the American public gives away their power when they refuse to vote and low voter turnout is an example of Americans giving away their power.

Student transitions from analysis of rhetorical strategies to analysis and evaluation of logical fallacies.

This argument appears logically sound, as Obama is a skilled speaker and has impressive writers assisting him while crafting his speeches. However, when looking at his claims, there is a logical fallacy. Logical fallacies exist when the logic has errors due to overgeneralizing, not having enough information, or being desperate for an answer (Seyler & Brizee, 2019). Obama uses hasty or faulty generalizations when arguing his points. At certain points while giving his speech, Obama aims to inspire more than present logical arguments. Through his deductive reasoning, he says all Americans need to vote, which is an overgeneralization. Some Americans are not awarded the luxury to freely use their voting rights.

According to the American Civil Liberties Union (ACLU), 48 states introduced more than 400 voter suppression bills (2021). Voter suppression includes strict ID laws, limiting early voting, and purges to voter rolls. This impacts people of color, people with disabilities, and the elderly disproportionately and limits their ability to use their right to vote. As an example of voter suppression found in Georgia, specifically communities of color, legislators "made it a crime to provide food and water to voters standing in line at the polls" (ACLU, 2021). The lines at these polls are extremely long, and this pushes people to leave without voting because they need food and water.

Voter purges also exist, which invalidate people's voter registration due to felony convictions. However, some of these individuals are eligible to vote despite the felony conviction (Hardy, 2016). According to the Prison Policy Initiative (2020), people of color are pulled over, arrested, jailed, and given longer sentences at significantly higher rates than white Americans. So, as voting purges occur, they more likely impact people of color (The Sentencing Project, 2017). If these individuals cannot use their right to vote, they cannot express what would benefit that identity group. Due to these unfair obstacles certain Americans face, telling people to register and vote as a solution to inequality is only a viable solution to people who are not affected by voter suppression.

Student provides ample support for the claim that the author has used the overgeneralization fallacy.

Obama limits his speech's effectiveness due to this logical fallacy. Only certain Americans can take his solution and make it work, but not all Americans. Minimizing low voter turnout to lacking interest does not acknowledge those who have to go through obstacles to vote. Besides his solutions to register and vote, not many other solutions are offered. And the other solutions are vague and only noted to inspire rather than calling Americans to act. The problem-solution argumentative genre requires realistic solutions, and Obama only provides a real solution if the individual can vote.

Overall, Obama's speech aims to inspire and call Americans toward the problems rather than pushing them away. He gives his audience a reason to care by allowing them to see themselves as benefitting from the work done to make America a more equal place. He attempts to offer solutions fit to work in modern times, although his argument is limited due to some overgeneralizations. Nevertheless, Obama's use of rhetorical strategies and the problem-solution argumentative genre is mostly effective; the speech still makes readers reflect on the past and look toward the future with a desire to create change.

Student concludes by restating major points, noting the strengths and weaknesses of the author's argument and providing a final evaluation.

APA Style

RHETORICAL STRATEGIES AND GENRE 9

Title the page "References."

Double-space throughout. In each citation, use a hanging indent. Note APA style in placing dates.

References

Block the vote: How politicians are trying to block voters from the ballot box. (2021). American Civil Liberties Union (ACLU). https://www.aclu.org/news/civil-liberties/block-the-vote-voter-suppression-in-2020/

Hardy, B. (2016). Data mix-up from Ark. Secretary of state purges unknown number of eligible voters. *Arkansas Times*. https://arktimes.com/arkansas-blog/2016/07/25/data-mix-up-from-ark-secretary-of-state-purges-unknown-number-of-eligible-voters

Nelson, M. (2021). *Barack Obama: Life before the presidency.* UVA Miller Center. https://millercenter.org/president/obama/life-before-the-presidency

Race & justice news: One-third of black men have felony convictions. (2017). The Sentencing Project. https://www.sentencingproject.org/news/5593/

Seyler, D.U. & Brizee, A. (2019). *Read, reason, write: An argument text and reader.* McGraw Hill Education.

Courtesy of Avery Downes

SECTION 5

A Collection of Readings

Rise Images/Alamy Stock Photo

This section is divided into seven chapters, each one on a current topic or set of interrelated issues open to debate. The chapters contain four to six articles to remind us that complex issues cannot be divided into simple "for" or "against" positions. This point remains true even for chapters on a specific topic. It is not sound critical thinking to be simply for or against any complicated public policy initiative. No one is "for" or "against" protecting our environment, for example. The debate begins with restrictions on the use of fossil fuels or energy use or elephant poaching. It is only when we get into policy decisions—and ways of funding those decisions or strategies for enforcing those decisions—that citizens have opposing views.

Questions follow each article to aid reading, analysis, and critical responses. In addition, each chapter opens with a visual both to enjoy and to consider seriously as a contribution to the issues discussed in the chapter. Following each opening image is a brief introduction to the chapter and several general questions to focus your thinking as you read.

CHAPTER 15

The Media: Image and Reality

REUTERS/Anthony Bolante/Alamy Stock Photo

READ: What is the situation? Who is speaking? Who is listening and watching?

REASON: What role do you think ratings play in the 24-hour cable news cycle?

WRITE: Where do you get your news? How do you know you can trust that source? What are the merits of obtaining news from multiple sources?

Although we may not agree with Marshall McLuhan that the medium itself *is* the message, we still recognize that the various media influence us. They stir emotions, shape our vision of the world, and dramatically present a message designed to alter our lives. The essays in this chapter explore the effects of different types of media on the way we perceive the world and construct our lives from those impressions. Note that the chapter opens with a picture of someone watching CNN, a popular cable news network. The 24-hour cable news cycle, the internet, and social media have fundamentally changed how we obtain our information and thus perceive the world around us. Be sure to take time to study and reflect on the implications of this phenomenon throughout this text.

Surely we are influenced by media messages, by the "reality" they present to us. How extensive is this influence? Most of us make purchases that have been determined at least to some extent by advertising. And we know that news sites online created for the purpose of spreading misinformation have led people to act on fake news. Is this a problem—or an inescapable part of life? Is there anything that can—or should—be done in response to the media's desire to shape our thoughts and engage our emotions?

PREREADING QUESTIONS

1. If cable news is driven by ratings, how might this increase news channels' coverage of events and commentary?
2. How do films reflect our world and also shape our ideas of that world?
3. What do the various forms of music (jazz, rock, rap, K-pop) tell us about ourselves and our world? What does your music preference tell us about you?
4. How does advertising shape our images of the world? How realistic are these images? Do we want ads to be "realistic"? Have ads become too invasive in our lives?
5. How accurate is our press coverage? Media outlets around the world do not portray the same worldview; is this a problem? What about media conglomerates owned by one person or only a few corporate entities? Should a small number of people control such large swaths of media influence?
6. What standards of reliability, objectivity, and fairness should be set for the media? Should these differ from one medium to another?

"I'M PREJUDICED," HE SAID. AND THEN WE KEPT TALKING.

HEATHER C. MCGHEE

Heather McGhee is president of Demos, a public-policy organization working for equal opportunity. She is a member of the World Economic Forum's Global Agenda Council on Civic Participation and also sits on several boards. Holding a law degree from the University of California at Berkeley, McGhee writes for newspapers and magazines and also appears frequently on television talk shows such as *Meet the Press*. The essay here was first published in the *New York Times*.

PREREADING QUESTIONS What is your reaction to the author's title? Did she get your attention?

One morning in August, when I was a guest on C-Span, I got a phone call that took my breath away. 1

"I'm a white male," said the caller, who identified himself as Garry from North Carolina. "And I'm prejudiced." 2

As a black leader often in the media, I have withstood my share of racist rants, so I braced myself. But what I heard was fear—of black people and the crime he sees on the news—not anger. 3

"What can I do to change?" he asked. "To be a better American?" 4

I thanked him for admitting his prejudice, and gave him some ideas—get to know black families, recognize the bias in news coverage of crime, join an interracial church, read black history. In a professional capacity, I typically speak about race in terms of law and policy. But with this man on the phone it felt right to speak to the basic human need I heard in his voice: to connect. 5

The video of us went viral, surpassing eight million views. After a racially charged summer, a lot of people saw something they hungered for in our exchange. To white viewers, here was a black woman who was morally clear but not angry. To people of color, here was a white man admitting his racism—finally. 6

Garry found me on Twitter after our televised call, and shortly before the [2016] election, I visited him near his hometown in the Appalachian foothills of North Carolina. We met on a patio amid the changing fall colors as his dog kept a watchful eye nearby. There we were: two products of this country who couldn't be more different, having the oft-invoked but seldom practiced "conversation about race." 7

I was surprised when he said that he had followed my suggestions and was dedicated to "getting right about this before I die." He talked about the fear he carried toward people of color, and how it had become a physical weight. "It's killing me on the inside," he said. "If I don't change things, I could have a stroke." 8

Although Garry didn't vote for Donald J. Trump, he is the media's image of a Trump voter: a rural, middle-aged white male from a working-class background. "We're a troubled group right now," he said to me when we met. "We're not a growing part of the population, we're diminishing. I think our culture is mixing real fast. Instead of the usual 20 years it takes to change society, it's happening in five years. It feels like an overwhelming wave is rushing over us." 9

Research shows that when white people become attuned to demographic change, they become more conservative. The right-wing narrative is that such change is the unmaking of America. I told Garry I believed it was the fulfillment of our country. 10

We talked about what it would mean to be the "better American" he invoked on our call. I said that person would be able to find common cause with people of all backgrounds. Garry's eyes brightened, but he said that it would take time. 11

"I speak for a lot of unspoken people," he told me. "Maybe millions of white people who are afraid to admit" their racial fears and prejudices. "They're not bad people. They just don't know how to behave and how to interact" with people of different races. 12

Garry had some advice for me, too. "Talk to white people," he said. "We need a little bit of guidance. We're not really getting it from our politicians. They want to play one side against the other for votes." 13

14 We steered clear of politics in our first few conversations, but after the election, he was eager to talk. Garry saw Mr. Trump as the peddler of all the toxic ideas about people of color that he now avoids on television. (He said "watching too much TV" is something he has in common with both Mr. Trump and his voters; we did meet, after all, through a C-Span call.) He thinks many Trump voters could benefit from the journey he's taken.

15 With Mr. Trump headed to the White House, my now-friendship with the "racist caller" on C-Span seems like a glimpse of a path not taken. Garry makes me believe that even though a man endorsed by the Ku Klux Klan won the majority of white support, people can change. He told me he now notices his own stereotypes and is eager to replace them with something more generous and true about his fellow Americans.

16 We need conversations like mine and Garry's to happen across the country, outside of politics. Societies that have been through traumas have embarked on racial reconciliation processes; South Africa's is the most famous, but there are dozens more. There's no reason we can't do that here.

17 Demos, the think tank I run, is working with a variety of other groups on such an effort in 10 communities next year. I spent the past week meeting with hundreds of people—librarians and teachers, community organizers and police officers—who are preparing for conversations in their communities.

18 "What can I do to change?" Garry asked when he called in this summer.

19 I was able to answer him because he had first acknowledged what so many people deny: the persistence of prejudice. That's the first step for all of us to become better Americans.

McGhee, Heather C. "'I'm Prejudiced,' He Said. Then We Kept Talking." *New York Times*, December 10, 2016. Used with permission of the author.

QUESTIONS FOR READING

1. What is the situation McGhee introduces as her subject?
2. What was McGhee's response to her caller? What did Garry and McGhee do later?
3. What did Garry observe about watching TV?
4. Why does the author think that Americans can change?

QUESTIONS FOR REASONING AND ANALYSIS

5. Analyze McGhee's essay. What are its marks of a personal essay?
6. What makes this essay also an argument? What is the author's claim?
7. McGhee supports her claim with, essentially, an extended example. What does Garry reveal about the causes of prejudice? What solution does the author recommend?

QUESTIONS FOR REFLECTION AND WRITING

8. Psychologists tell us that it is difficult to change until we acknowledge a problem. Does this make sense to you? Is Garry on the right track, then?

9. If prejudice stems from a lack of knowledge, then the suggestion that Garry find ways to interact with African Americans seems good advice. But what about Garry's fears? Is fear also caused by a lack of knowledge, or are there other causes that should be considered? What does Garry suggest as possible causes of his anxiety? Reflect on these questions.
10. Is the medium of television part of the problem? Wouldn't the answer depend on what TV is watched? For example, if one watched reliable news and then a lot of sports–especially football and basketball–would this TV experience lead to prejudice against Black people? Are there other viewing habits that might reinforce prejudice? Be prepared to discuss the role of TV in encouraging vs. debunking racial and/or ethnic stereotypes.

MOTHER NATURE IS BROUGHT TO YOU BY. . .

TIM WU

Tim Wu, a native Washingtonian, is a professor at Columbia Law School. A graduate of Harvard Law School, Wu clerked for Justice Stephen Breyer. He has published widely in newspapers and magazines, including *The New Republic, Slate,* and *The New Yorker.* Wu is the author of *The Master Switch* and is best known for creating the term "net neutrality." His most recent book is *The Attention Merchants: The Epic Scramble to Get inside Our Heads* (2016), a study of the many ways that businesses seek to reach us with ads.

PREREADING QUESTIONS Based on Wu's essay title, what do you expect his subject to be? Based on what you have learned from the biographical headnote, what else might you expect the essay to explore?

This year, parks in several states including Idaho and Washington, and the National Park Service, will be blazing a new trail, figuratively at least, as they begin offering opportunities to advertisers within their borders. 1

King County in Washington, which manages 28,000 acres of parkland surrounding Seattle, offers a full branding menu: Naming rights or sponsorships may be had for park trails, benches and even trees. "Make our five million visitors your next customers," the county urges potential advertisers. 2

King County already partnered with Chipotle to hide 30 giant replica burritos on parkland bearing the logo of the agency and the restaurant chain. People who found the burritos won prizes from Chipotle. 3

In May, the National Park Service proposed allowing corporate branding as a matter of "donor recognition." As the *Washington Post* reported, under new rules set to go into effect at the end of the year, "an auditorium at Yosemite National Park named after Coke will now be permitted" and "visitors could tour Bryce Canyon in a bus wrapped in the Michelin Man." 4

The logic behind these efforts is, in its own way, unimpeachable. Many millions of people—that is, "green consumers"—visit parks every day, representing an unrealized marketing opportunity of great value. Yes, parks are meant to be 5 natural, not commercial, but times are tough, or so say the backers of the new schemes.

6 The spread of advertising to natural settings is just a taste of what's coming. Over the next decade, prepare for a new wave of efforts to reach some of the last remaining bastions of peace, quiet and individual focus—like schools, libraries, churches and even our homes.

7 Some of this reflects technological change, but the real reason is the business model of what I call the "attention merchants." Unlike ordinary businesses, which sell a product, attention merchants sell people to advertisers. They do so either by finding captive audiences (like at a park or school) or by giving stuff away to gather up consumer data for resale.

8 Once upon a time, this was a business model largely restricted to television and newspapers, where it remained within certain limits. Over the last decade, though, it has spread to nearly every new technology, and started penetrating spaces long thought inviolate.

9 In school districts in Minnesota and California, student lockers are sometimes covered by large, banner-style advertisements, so that the school hallways are what marketers call a fully immersive experience. Other schools have allowed advertising inside gymnasiums and on report cards and permission slips. The Associated Press reported this year that a high school near South Bend, Ind., "sold the naming rights to its football field to a bank for $400,000, its baseball field to an auto dealership, its softball field to a law firm, its tennis court to a philanthropic couple and its concession stands to a tire and auto-care company and a restaurant."

10 Even megachurches, with their large and loyal congregations, have come to see the upside of "relevant" marketing, yielding the bizarre spectacle of product placements in sermons. In one of the first such efforts, pastors in 2005 were offered a chance to win $1,000 and a trip to London if they mentioned *The Chronicles of Narnia* during services. For the 2013 release of *Superman: Man of Steel,* pastors were supplied with notes for a sermon titled *Jesus: The Original Superhero.*

11 Nor are our workplaces and social spheres immune. The time and energy we spend socializing with friends and family has, almost incredibly, been harnessed for marketing, through the business models of Facebook, Instagram and other social media. At the office, the most successful of the productivity-killing distraction engines, BuzzFeed, brags of luring a "bored at work" network hundreds of millions strong.

12 Unfortunately, there is worse yet to come: The nation's most talented engineers now apply themselves to making marketing platforms out of innovations—A.I. assistants like the Amazon Echo or self-driving cars. Here the intrusions will be subtle, even disguised, so as not to trip our defenses, but they will be even more powerful, going after our very decision-making processes. Consider how much we already depend on Siri or Google Maps: What happens when our most trusted tools have mixed motives?

13 Advertising revenue often seems like "free money," but there are enormous risks for the character of any institution once it begins to rely heavily on advertising income. History and logic suggest that, once advertisers become a major

funding source, they create their own priorities, and unless carefully controlled they will warp the underlying space to serve their interests.

This development raises questions beyond the mere issue of how annoying ads can be. The model of individual liberty and a self-reliant citizenry was proposed by the founders and influenced by philosophers like John Stuart Mill, who envisioned sufficient time and space for self-development of character and room for making decisions that are truly ours. 14

Similar ideas about the prerequisite of free will are to be found in the great spiritual traditions, which sanctify certain times and spaces for the sake of our spiritual development. 15

These ideals are threatened by a way of doing business that by its nature seeks to invade the most sanctified of spaces. 16

If you don't like the sound of this future, resistance is not futile—it is necessary. A commercial dystopia can be averted only by private resistance and principled decisions by the leaders of institutions. 17

The first simply requires redrawing the lines that have been eroded. Where once upon a time, tradition or religion drew those lines for us, blocking out times for family and faith, nowadays personal or family initiative are required to define parts of our lives as off limits. The default setting will always be intrusion and distraction. We need to flip the switch. 18

The second should be to reduce the attention economy by patronizing businesses or institutions with subscription models or those that keep advertising within reasonable limits. 19

Third, the leaders of schools, libraries and even the more principled technology firms should understand that there is always a hidden cost to the proposition offered by advertising. Once an institution is dependent on ad revenue, it's impossible to put the Crest 3D White Radiant Mint toothpaste back in the tube. 20

Above all, we should not simply resign ourselves to a world saturated by commercial appeals at the cost of our private and sacred spaces. As the great legal scholar Charles Black Jr. once put it, "I tremble for the sanity of a society that talks, on the level of abstract principle, of the precious integrity of the individual mind, and all the while, on the level of concrete fact, forces the individual mind to spend a good part of every day under bombardment with whatever some crowd of promoters want to throw at it." 21

Wu, Tim. "Mother Nature Is Brought to You By. . ." *New York Times*, 2 Dec. 2016. Used with permission of the author.

QUESTIONS FOR READING

1. What can we expect to find in parks when we visit? Why is this happening?
2. In what other new venues can we expect to find advertising?
3. Who is creating these new venues for ads?
4. What might we be losing with the increasing number of venues for ads?
5. What steps should we be taking, in the writer's view, to stop the increasing spread of advertising into so many new venues?

QUESTIONS FOR REASONING AND ANALYSIS

6. What is Wu's subject? (Restating the essay's title is not sufficient.) What is the claim of his argument?
7. Examine the essay's organization. What *type* of essay is this?
8. Wu reminds readers that originally advertising could be found mostly in newspapers and on television. Where else do we regularly find ads today? Given the spread we already live with, are you surprised to read that you may see ads in parks, schools, libraries, churches, and homes? If so, why? If not, why not?
9. Wu provides some examples of the newest ad venues, but he doesn't have to go on for pages because he knows you can add to his examples. Why is he now objecting to advertising's newest venues? What are his reasons? Is his argument convincing? Why or why not?

QUESTIONS FOR REFLECTION AND WRITING

10. Examine the author's suggestions for addressing the problem. Do these seem reasonable steps we can and should take? If so, why? If not, why not?
11. Does the branding of sports facilities (stadiums) and events (tournaments) bother you? What about at the high school level? What about billboards in state and national parks? What about all of the ads that attach themselves to websites you visit? Do you "draw the line" against ads in all of these places? Some? None? Be prepared to defend your position on venues appropriate–or inappropriate–for advertising.

MISINFORMATION, DISINFORMATION, AND HOAXES: WHAT'S THE DIFFERENCE?

MICHAEL J. O'BRIEN AND IZZAT ALSMADI

Mike O'Brien, PhD, is provost and vice president for academic affairs at Texas A&M University San Antonio, where he is also a professor of history. His research focuses on evolutionary archaeology and biology. Author of twenty-six books, his latest monograph, *The Importance of Small Decisions: How People Make Decisions in an Era of Too Much Information and Fake News,* was published by MIT Press in 2019. Izzat Alsmadi, PhD, is an assistant professor at Texas A&M University San Antonio, and he teaches in the Department of Computing and Cyber Security. His most recent book, *The NICE Cyber Security Framework: Cyber Security Intelligence and Analytics* was published in 2019. This article was published in *The Conversation* on April 21, 2021.

PREREADING QUESTIONS What are your definitions of misinformation, disinformation, and hoaxes?

1 Sorting through the vast amount of information created and shared online is challenging, even for the experts.

2 Just talking about this ever-shifting landscape is confusing, with terms like "misinformation," "disinformation" and "hoax" getting mixed up with buzzwords like "fake news."

Misinformation is perhaps the most innocent of the terms—it's misleading 3
information created or shared without the intent to manipulate people. An example would be sharing a rumor that a celebrity died, before finding out it's false.

Disinformation, by contrast, refers to deliberate attempts to confuse or manip- 4
ulate people with dishonest information. These campaigns, at times orchestrated by groups outside the U.S., such as the Internet Research Agency, a well-known Russian troll factory, can be coordinated across multiple social media accounts and may also use automated systems, called bots, to post and share information online. Disinformation can turn into misinformation when spread by unwitting readers who believe the material.

10 TYPES OF MIS- AND DISINFORMATION

False Connection: The content is not supported by headlines, visuals or captions

False Context: False contextual information surrounds accurate content

Manipulated Content: Content or images are changed in an attempt to deceive

Satire or Parody: Content is not intended to deceive, but potentially can

Misleading Content: Incorrect, incomplete or misleading content frames an individual or issue

Imposter Content: Genuine sources are impersonated

Fabricated Content: False content is used with the purpose to deceive or harm

Propaganda: Content designed to influence attitudes, values, beliefs, and knowledge

Sponsored Content: Content is created by advertisers or PR firms to look like editorial content

Error: Genuine and established organizations make mistakes

5 Hoaxes, similar to disinformation, are created to persuade people that things that are unsupported by facts are true. For example, the person responsible for the celebrity-death story has created a hoax.

6 Though many people are just paying attention to these problems now, they are not new—and they even date back to ancient Rome. Around 31 B.C., Octavian, a Roman military official, launched a smear campaign against his political enemy, Mark Antony. This effort used, as one writer put it, "short, sharp slogans written on coins in the style of archaic Tweets." His campaign was built around the point that Antony was a soldier gone awry: a philanderer, a womanizer and a drunk not fit to hold office. It worked. Octavian, not Antony, became the first Roman emperor, taking the name Augustus Caesar.

THE UNIVERSITY OF MISSOURI EXAMPLE

7 In the 21st century, new technology makes manipulation and fabrication of information simple. Social networks make it easy for uncritical readers to dramatically amplify falsehoods peddled by governments, populist politicians and dishonest businesses.

8 Our research focuses specifically on how certain types of disinformation can turn what might otherwise be normal developments in society into major disruptions.

9 One sobering example we've reviewed in detail is a situation you might remember: racial tensions at the University of Missouri in 2015, in the wake of Michael Brown's death in Ferguson, Missouri. One of us, Michael O'Brien, was dean of the university's College of Arts and Science at the time and saw first-hand the protests and their aftermath.

10 Black students at the university, just over 100 miles to the west of Ferguson, raised concerns about their safety, civil rights and racial equity in society and on campus. Unhappy with the university's responses, they began to protest.

11 The incident that got the most national attention involved a white professor in the communication department pushing student journalists away from an area where Black students had congregated in the center of campus, yelling, "I need some muscle over here!" in an effort to keep reporters at bay.

12 Other events didn't get as much national coverage, including a hunger strike by a Black student and the resignations of university leaders. But there was enough publicity about racial tensions for Russian information warriors to take notice.

13 Soon, the hashtag #PrayforMizzou, created by Russian hackers using the university's nickname, began trending on Twitter, warning residents that the Ku Klux Klan was in town and had joined the local police to hunt down Black students. A photo surfaced on Facebook purporting to show a large white cross burning on the lawn of the university's library.

14 A Twitter user claimed the police were marching with the KKK, tweeting: "They beat up my little brother! Watch out!" and a picture of a black child with a severely bruised face. This user was later found to be a Russian troll who went on to spread rumors about Syrian refugees.

15 These were a rich mix of different types of false information. The photos of the burning cross and the bruised child were hoaxes—the photos were legitimate, but

their context was fabricated. A Google search for "bruised black child," for example, revealed that it was a year-old picture from a disturbance in Ohio.

The rumor about the KKK on campus started as disinformation by Russian hackers and then spread as misinformation, even ensnaring the student-body president, a young Black man who posted a warning on Facebook. When it became clear the information was false, he deleted the post. 16

THE FALLOUT

Undoubtedly, not all of the fallout from the Mizzou protests was the direct result of disinformation and hoaxes. But the disruptions were factors in big changes in student numbers. In the two years following the protests, the university saw a 35% drop in freshman enrollment and an overall enrollment drop of 14%. That caused campus university officials to cut about 12%—or US$55 million—from the university's budget, including significant layoffs of faculty and staff. Even today, the campus is not yet back to what it was before the protests, financially, socially or politically. 17

The take-home message is clear: the world is a dangerous place, made all the more so by malevolent intent, especially in the online age. Learning to recognize misinformation, disinformation and hoaxes helps people stay better informed about what's really happening. 18

O'Brien, Michael J., and Izzat Alsmadi. "Misinformation, Disinformation and Hoaxes: What's the Difference?" *The Conversation*, 21 Apr. 2021. Used with permission.

QUESTIONS FOR READING

1. What are the authors' definitions of disinformation, misinformation, and hoaxes?
2. According to O'Brien and Alsmadi, what is one of the first examples of disinformation?
3. What happened at the University of Missouri that caused Russian trolls to launch a disinformation campaign?
4. What were the results of the disinformation campaign?

QUESTIONS FOR REASONING AND ANALYSIS

5. What are O'Brien and Alsmadi arguing?
6. How do the authors organize their article to support their claims?
7. What do the authors do in the final paragraph to convey a clear message?

QUESTIONS FOR REFLECTION AND WRITING

8. Are you convinced by O'Brien and Alsmadi? Why or why not?
9. What makes these authors credible?
10. Some politicians and pundits (political commentators) have stoked an anti-intellectual movement against academics like O'Brien and Alsmadi. Why do you think the anti-intellectual movement in America has taken off, and what, if anything, do you think this has to do with the spread of dis/misinformation?

7 WAYS TO AVOID BECOMING A MISINFORMATION SUPERSPREADER

H. COLLEEN SINCLAIR

H. Colleen Sinclair is an associate professor of social psychology at Mississippi State University, where she teaches courses on interpersonal relationships, experimental and social psychology, and psychology and the law. She has published in scholarly journals like *Personal Relationships, The Journal of Social Psychology,* and *Sex Roles.* This article was published in *The Conversation* on March 18, 2021.

PREREADING QUESTIONS Have you accidentally spread misinformation? What happened afterward, and did you do anything to address it?

1 Internet platforms like Facebook and Twitter have taken some steps to curb its spread and say they are working on doing more. But no method yet introduced has been completely successful at removing all misleading content from social media. The best defense, then, is self-defense.

2 **Misleading or outright false information—broadly called "misinformation"—can come from websites pretending to be news outlets, political propaganda or "pseudo-profound" reports that seem meaningful but are not.** Disinformation is a type of misinformation that is deliberately generated to maliciously mislead people. Disinformation is intentionally shared, knowing it is false, but misinformation can be shared by people who don't know it's not true, especially because people often share links online without thinking.

3 Emerging psychology research has revealed some tactics that can help protect our society from misinformation. Here are seven strategies you can use to avoid being misled, and to prevent yourself—and others—from spreading inaccuracies.

1. EDUCATE YOURSELF

4 The best inoculation against what the World Health Organization is calling the "infodemic" is to understand the tricks that agents of disinformation are using to try to manipulate you. One strategy is called "prebunking"—a type of debunking that happens before you hear myths and lies. Research has shown that familiarizing yourself with the tricks of the disinformation trade can help you recognize false stories when you encounter them, making you less susceptible to those tricks.

5 Researchers at the University of Cambridge have developed an online game called "Bad News," which their studies have shown can improve players' identification of falsehoods.

6 In addition to the game, you can also learn more about how internet and social media platforms work, so you better understand the tools available to people seeking to manipulate you. You can also learn more about scientific research and standards of evidence, which can help you be less susceptible to lies and misleading statements about health-related and scientific topics. Badges identify ways misinformation exploits people's minds

2. RECOGNIZE YOUR VULNERABILITIES

7 The prebunking approach works for people across the political spectrum, but it turns out that people who underestimate their biases are actually more vulnerable to being misled than people who acknowledge their biases.

8 **Research has found people are more susceptible to misinformation that aligns with their preexisting views.** This is called "confirmation bias," because a person is biased toward believing information that confirms what they already believe.

9 The lesson is to be particularly critical of information from groups or people with whom you agree or find yourself aligned—whether politically, religiously, or by ethnicity or nationality. Remind yourself to look for other points of view, and other sources with information on the same topic.

10 **It is especially important to be honest with yourself about what your biases are.** Many people assume others are biased but believe they themselves are not—and imagine that others are more likely to share misinformation than they themselves are.

3. CONSIDER THE SOURCE

11 Media outlets have a range of biases. The Media Bias Chart describes which outlets are most and least partisan as well as how reliable they are at reporting facts.

12 You can play an online game called "Fakey" to see how susceptible you are to different ways news is presented online.

13 When consuming news, make sure you know how trustworthy the source is—or whether it's not trustworthy at all. Double-check stories from other sources with low biases and high fact ratings to find out who—and what—you can actually trust, rather than just what your gut tells you.

14 **Also, be aware that some disinformation agents make fake sites that look like real news sources—so make sure you're conscious of which site you are actually visiting.** Engaging in this level of thinking about your own thinking has been shown to improve your ability to tell fact from fiction.

4. TAKE A PAUSE

15 When most people go online, especially on social media, they're there for entertainment, connection or even distraction. Accuracy isn't always high on the priority list. Yet few want to be a liar, and the costs of sharing misinformation can be high—to individuals, their relationships and society as a whole. Before you decide to share something, take a moment to remind yourself of the value you place on truth and accuracy.

16 Thinking "is what I am sharing true?" can help you stop the spread of misinformation and will encourage you to look beyond the headline and potentially fact-check before sharing.

17 **Even if you don't think specifically about accuracy, just taking a pause before sharing can give you a chance for your mind to catch up with your emotions.** Ask yourself whether you really want to share it, and if so, why. Think about what the potential consequences of sharing it might be.

18 Research shows that most misinformation is shared quickly and without much thought. The impulse to share without thinking can even be more powerful than partisan sharing tendencies. Take your time. There is no hurry. You are not a breaking-news organization upon whom thousands depend for immediate information.

5. BE AWARE OF YOUR EMOTIONS

19 **People often share things because of their gut reactions, rather than the conclusions of critical thinking.** In a recent study, researchers found that people who viewed their social media feed while in an emotional mindset were significantly more likely to share misinformation than those who went in with a more rational state of mind.

20 Anger and anxiety, in particular, make people more vulnerable to falling for misinformation.

6. IF YOU SEE SOMETHING, SAY SOMETHING

21 Stand up to misinformation publicly. It may feel uncomfortable to challenge your friends online, especially if you fear conflict. The person to whom you respond with a link to a Snopes post or other fact-checking site may not appreciate being called out.

22 But evidence shows that explicitly critiquing the specific reasoning in the post and providing counterevidence like a link about how it is fake is an effective technique.

23 Even short-format refutations—like "this isn't true"—are more effective than saying nothing. Humor—though not ridicule of the person—can work, too. When actual people correct misinformation online, it can be as effective, if not more so, as when a social media company labels something as questionable.

24 People trust other humans more than algorithms and bots, especially those in our own social circles. That's particularly true if you have expertise in the subject or are a close connection with the person who shared it.

25 An additional benefit is that public debunking notifies other viewers that they may want to look more closely before choosing to share it themselves. So even if you don't discourage the original poster, you are discouraging others.

7. IF YOU SEE SOMEONE ELSE STAND UP, STAND WITH THEM

26 If you see someone else has posted that a story is false, don't say "well, they beat me to it so I don't need to." When more people chime in on a post as being false, it signals that sharing misinformation is frowned upon by the group more generally.

27 Stand with those who stand up. If you don't and something gets shared over and over, that reinforces people's beliefs that it is OK to share misinformation—because everyone else is doing it, and only a few, if any, are objecting.

28 Allowing misinformation to spread also makes it more likely that even more people will start to believe it—because people come to believe things they hear repeatedly, even if they know at first they're not true.

There is no perfect solution. Some misinformation is harder to counter than others, and some countering tactics are more effective at different times or for different people. But you can go a long way toward protecting yourself and those in your social networks from confusion, deception and falsehood. 29

Sinclair, H. Colleen. "7 Ways to Avoid Becoming a Misinformation Superspreader," *The Conversation*, 18 Mar. 2021. Used with permission.

QUESTIONS FOR READING

1. What are the authors' definitions of disinformation and misinformation?
2. What is the "infodemic" and who coined this term?
3. What are the seven steps you can use to avoid becoming a misinformation superspreader?
4. According to Sinclair, what online games can you play to help educate yourself about misinformation and prevent spreading it? Did you play them? What happened? What did you think of them?
5. What are the outcomes of spreading misinformation according to Sinclair?

QUESTIONS FOR REASONING AND ANALYSIS

6. What is Sinclair claiming in this article? What does she want you to believe? What does she want you to do?
7. How does Sinclair present information that supports her claims?
8. How does Sinclair end her article to compel readers to take action?

QUESTIONS FOR REFLECTION AND WRITING

9. Do you think you will follow all or some of Sinclair's suggestions? Why or why not?
10. What do you think about Sinclair's list? Are there steps you can think of that you would add to the list? Are there any you would remove?
11. Have you been the victim of misinformation? How did it make you feel?

CHAPTER 16

Misinformation, Disinformation, and the Role of Social Media

BigTunaOnline/Shutterstock

READ: What, if any, social media platforms do you use? Why do you (or do you not) use social media?

REASON: What role do you think social media plays in the spread of misinformation and disinformation?

WRITE: What are some ways we might address the spread of misinformation and disinformation on social media?

The influence of misinformation and disinformation today–especially as a source of knowledge on important topics like politics and public health–is so impactful and so complex that it warrants its own chapter. Virtually no one under fifty today has an online presence without some sort of social media account. Meanwhile, people of all ages are barraged with mis/disinformation of one kind or another, leading to a troubling disconnect between fact and fiction and the rise of fake news and truth decay. We must consider that the point of mis/disinformation is not always to convince, it is also to confuse. And the audience of mis/disinformation is not always reasonable media consumers. Conspiracy theorists devour and then disgorge mis/disinformation to support dangerous ideas like the claim that microchips have been implanted in vaccines and that crisis actors played the shooting victims at Sandy Hook Elementary School. If we are to overcome mis/disinformation and use social media positively, we must first understand the challenges we are facing, which is the goal of the readings that follow. Consider the questions below as you read and study the essays in this chapter.

PREREADING QUESTIONS

1. Has social media made us more knowledgeable or less?
2. Are Twitter, Instagram, Facebook, TikTok, etc., useful forms of communication or a waste of time? What about Snapchat?
3. What is the difference between having knowledge and having access to knowledge? Can the difference affect critical thinking?
4. What do we do about the digital divide that prevents people from accessing online knowledge?
5. What role did mis/disinformation play in the pandemic? The January 6, 2021, attack on the Capitol? The war in Ukraine?
6. How can we use social media to bridge gaps that divide us rather than enlarging those gaps?

WE ARE ALL PROPAGANDISTS NOW

JENNIFER MERCIECA

Jennifer Mercieca is a professor of communication at Texas A&M, where she teaches courses on propaganda, political communication, social movements, and rhetoric. At Texas A&M, Mercieca conducts research on the public sphere, communication, and democracy. She has published in scholarly journals as well as *USA Today* and the *Washington Post*. This article was published in *The Conversation* on July 20, 2021.

PREREADING QUESTIONS Given Mercieca's title, what do you think her article will be about? Can you anticipate her position—or will you have to read to discover it?

The U.S. is in an information war with itself. The public sphere, where Americans discuss public issues, is broken. There's little discussion—and lots of fighting. 1

2 One reason why: Persuasion is difficult, slow and time-consuming—it doesn't make good television or social media content—and so there aren't a lot of good examples of it in our public discourse.

3 What's worse, a new form of propaganda has emerged—and it's enlisted us all as propagandists.

PERSUASION VERSUS PROPAGANDA

4 I teach classes on political communication and propaganda in America. Here's the difference between the two:

5 Political communication is persuasion used in politics. It helps to facilitate the democratic process.

6 Propaganda is communication as force; it's designed for warfare. Propaganda is anti-democratic because it influences while using strategies like fear appeals, disinformation, conspiracy theory and more.

7 Since there are few examples of persuasion in our public sphere these days, it is difficult to know the difference between persuasion and propaganda. That's worrisome because politics is not war, so political communication isn't—and shouldn't be—the same as propaganda.

THE MANUFACTURE OF CONSENT

8 Mass propaganda techniques emerged with mass communication technologies like posters, pictures and movies during the first World War.

9 That old propaganda model was designed by political elites to "manufacture consent" at home so that citizens would support the war, and to demoralize the enemy abroad.

10 According to linguist and social critic Noam Chomsky, the manufacture of consent was believed by elites to be necessary because they thought "the mass of the public are just too stupid to be able to understand things. . . We have to tame the bewildered herd, not allow the bewildered herd to rage and trample and destroy things."

11 During World War I, George Creel's Committee on Public Information, a federal agency, oversaw the production of pro-war films like the 1918 silent film "America's Answer." When Americans went to see the film in theaters, they would often encounter a speech from one of the "Four Minute Men"—the local citizens whom Creel enlisted to give patriotic speeches during the four minutes it took to change the movie reels.

12 After World War I, according to Herman and Chomsky, all sorts of elites turned to propaganda to "tame the bewildered herd." The old propaganda was good at taming citizens. But there was a nasty side effect that played out over almost a century of its use: disengagement. Political communication scholars in the 1990s and early 2000s worried about what they saw as the crisis in democracy, which was civic disengagement characterized by low voter turnout, low political party affiliation and rising distrust, cynicism and disinterest in politics.

THE MANUFACTURE OF DISSENT

The elite-controlled old vertical propaganda model couldn't withstand the changes in communication brought on by the new participatory media—first talk radio, then cable, email, blogs, chats, texts, video and social media. 13

According to recent Pew research, 93% of Americans are connected to the internet and 82% of Americans are connected to social media. We now all have direct access to communicate in the public sphere—and, if we choose, to create, circulate and amplify propaganda. 14

A lot of people use their social media connections and platforms to knowingly and unknowingly spread misinformation, disinformation, conspiracy and partisan talking points—all forms of propaganda. We're all propagandists now. 15

Rather than the elite manufacturing consent, a new propaganda model has emerged in the 21st century: what I call the "manufacture of dissent." 16

NEW CRISIS IN DEMOCRACY

The "manufacture of dissent" model takes advantage of our individual abilities to produce, circulate and amplify propaganda. It sets us in motion to, in Chomsky's words, "rage and trample and destroy things." 17

The new propaganda can emerge from anyone, anywhere—and it is designed to create chaos so no one knows whom to trust or what is true. 18

Now we have a new crisis in democracy. 19

Citizens are called upon and trained by political parties, media, advocacy organizations, platforms, corporations—and more—to become propagandists, even without realizing it. Though both sides of the political spectrum can and have used the new propaganda, it has been embraced more on the right, largely to counter the old manufacture of consent model embraced by the mainstream. 20

For example, the slogan topping daily emails sent by ConservativeHQ, a longstanding and influential conservative news blog, says, "The home for grassroots conservatives leading the battle to educate and mobilize family, friends, neighbors, and others to defeat the anti-God, anti-America, Marxist New Democrats." 21

From this perspective, politics is a "battle," it's warfare and ConservativeHQ's readers can fight by educating and mobilizing—by spreading ConservativeHQ's propaganda. 22

Likewise, the conspiracy website InfoWars tells its audience, "There's a war on for your mind." 23

Social media platforms train users to communicate as propagandists: Recent research shows that platform users learn to express polarizing emotions like outrage through "social learning." Social media users are taught through app feedback—positive reinforcement through notifications—and peer-learning—what they see others do—to post outrage even if they don't feel outraged and they don't want to spread outrage. 24

The more outrage we see, the more outrage we post. 25

DISSENT AND DISTRUST

26 Today's new model of propaganda has dangerous consequences.

27 The Jan. 6, 2021, insurrection was a direct result of the manufacture of dissent. Right-wing politicians, citizens and media used disinformation, misinformation, conspiracy, fear appeals and outrage circulated via the old and new propaganda to cast doubt on the nation's electoral process.

28 President Trump primed his followers to believe that the election would be "rigged," which led people to look for and circulate so-called "evidence" of fraud.

29 Courts and election officials certified the integrity of the election. Conspiracists saw that as further evidence of the "plot" and supported Trump's Big Lie that the election had been stolen.

30 Trump's supporters amplified the conspiracy via posts on social media, videos, text messages, emails and secret groups—spreading doubt about the election to their friends, neighbors and audiences.

31 When Trump told people to march on the Capitol to defend their freedom, they did.

POLITICS IS WAR

32 But the Big Lie that led to the Jan. 6, 2021, insurrection was merely part of an even bigger lie. Since the 1990s and the emergence of the manufacture of dissent, right-wing propaganda's major premise has been that "politics is war and the enemy cheats." Every news story from that perspective is an elaboration on that theme, including those about the 2020 election.

33 When politics is seen as war and the enemy can't be trusted, then every election is seen as dire and the electoral process that denies your side victory is seen as unfair. According to a recent Monmouth University poll, 30% of Americans still believe Trump's Big Lie.

34 The legitimacy of the American political system requires the actual consent of the governed, and its vitality and health requires we allow actual dissent. But our broken public sphere has neither. Both come from persuasion, not propaganda.

35 This isn't about nostalgia for traditional propaganda. Both the old propaganda and the new propaganda are anti-democratic. The old propaganda manufactured Americans' consent, using communication as force to keep people disengaged and compliant.

36 The new propaganda manufactures dissent. It uses communication as force to keep people engaged and outraged—and it sets us in motion to trample and destroy things.

Mercieca, Jennifer. "We Are All Propagandists Now." *The Conversation*, 20 July 2021. Used with permission.

QUESTIONS FOR READING

1. What is Mercieca's subject? (Be precise.)
2. According to Mercieca, what has happened to the public sphere?
3. How did we arrive at our current state of civic discourse according to Mercieca?

4. In Mercieca's view, what is the difference between persuasion and propaganda?
5. Mercieca argues that persuasion helps democracy and propaganda damages democracy. How does she explain these assertions?

QUESTIONS FOR REASONING AND ANALYSIS

6. What is Mercieca's primary claim?
7. How does she support her claim? How does she use reasoning and evidence? Are you persuaded? If so, why? If not, why not?
8. Mercieca's tone is somber, and she ends her article with a discouraging image of our potential future. But she also states that we can resist spreading misinformation and propaganda. Now that you've read Mercieca's article, how might you approach your news sources differently and act differently when you're using social media?

DISINFORMATION IS EVOLVING TO MOVE UNDER THE RADAR

ALEXANDRE ALAPHILIPPE

With a background in communication and digital information, Alexandre Alaphilippe is an internationally recognized expert on disinformation. He is the co-founder and executive director of the EU DisinfoLab and contributes regularly to conferences where he discusses the connections between digital information, civil society, and democracy. This article was published by The Brookings Institute on February 4, 2021.

PREREADING QUESTIONS What are some connections you notice between digital information, civil society, and democracy? What is the current state of these connections today?

For disinformation, 2020 was a pivotal year. The novel coronavirus spread around the world accompanied by viral medical falsehoods. Political leaders became bolder in their use of disinformation to maintain power and sow discord. Online conspiracy movements grew rapidly, gaining untold adherents. And online platforms made unprecedented, though inconsistent, moves to moderate content on their services. 1

These developments have required groups that peddle disinformation to evolve. Malicious and sophisticated actors, confronted by this unprecedented response from platforms, have tried to find alternative strategies to spread disinformation, increasingly moving under the radar to evade detection from researchers, journalists, and fact checkers. Meanwhile, online infrastructure continues to enable both widespread disinformation campaigns and the proliferation of misinformation. 2

GOING UNDER THE RADAR

With platforms investing more resources in detecting information operations, sophisticated purveyors of disinformation are going to greater lengths to 3 obscure their identities and the origin of their propaganda. In June 2020, the EU DisinfoLab exposed the link between Observateur Continental, a French-language website producing disinformation, and InfoRos, a Moscow-based company tied to Russian Military intelligence (GRU). Observateur Continental relied on content laundering—the use of proxies to endorse disinformation. Through partnerships with conspiracy-oriented websites on the right-wing fringe, Observateur Continental disseminated its material to specific audiences and attempted to obscure the Russian origin of the content. The Peace Data operation, exposed in September of last year and linked to Russia's infamous Internet Research Agency, followed a similar pattern, hiring independent journalists in the United States to write stories around the U.S. election while obscuring the identity of those behind the operation.

4 These obfuscating strategies have proven successful and growing in popularity. A 15-year-long disinformation operation exposed by EU DisinfoLab in December relied on the fake media website EU Chronicle to discredit Indian adversaries in South Asia and succeeded in rallying international policymakers to its campaign. These campaigns reveal the vulnerabilities in democratic systems that increasingly embrace transparency as a tonic to disinformation but are reluctant to take the tough decisions necessary to hold actors accountable by, for example introducing sanctions. Both operations (Observateur Continental and Indian Chronicles) remain active today even after their exposure.

5 Indeed, the Indian Chronicles and Observateur Continental operations share several similarities in design and outcome:

6 • Both efforts lacked a sophisticated online presence;

7 • Neither turned to "active" methods, such as online advertisement or amplification through the use of troll farms;

8 • Both had an active offline partnership strategy contingent on finding allies in the real world: namely, partnering with established websites and soliciting content from external contributors, such as freelancers or policymakers, who could publish on their own;

9 • Both used content laundering to broadcast their messages to targeted communities;

10 • Both stayed under the radar and were only exposed after long investigations.

UNCOVER THE BROADER DISINFORMATION ECOSYSTEM

11 Online platforms have stepped up their efforts to limit the spread of disinformation, providing context to misinformation and developing new content moderation policies, including bans on prominent figures. But this whack-a-mole strategy has been insufficient to the challenge of widespread misinformation. Confronted with resilient malicious actors and recurring narratives, journalists, fact-checkers, and investigators have repeatedly debunked false content, only for the same actors to return again and again. Those fighting disinformation have felt like Sisyphus, pushing the same rock every day up the mountain.

Assessing who is accountable for the distribution of disinformation must be expanded. The year 2020 showed that the distribution of disinformation stems not only from a list of online assets readily available on large platforms, such as Facebook pages, Twitter accounts, and YouTube channels, but also relies on a combination of active measures and a passive ecosystem. Active measures include the production and dissemination of disinformation through content production, publication, paid and/or coordinated amplification, while the passive ecosystem includes the mechanisms that allow this content to be hosted and spread, and sometimes to hide ownership, such as DNS infrastructure, adtech, and algorithmic recommendation. This passive ecosystem allows for the use of cross-platform strategies—the hosting of content on a less moderated platform, amplifying it on another, and monetizing it through crowdfunding—to be used to spread disinformation. 12

It is the passive ecosystem that enables under the radar campaigns to flourish. If we want to tackle disinformation in the long term, we need to better address the passive ecosystem contributing to the distribution of disinformation in our analysis. This research would allow researchers to better describe the impact of malicious actors in our societies. It would also help us to better identify how to hold bad actors accountable and improve regulation efforts. 13

The increasing sophistication of disinformation actors requires those investigating disinformation to see beyond the usual scapegoats—most commonly Russia, troll farms, and Twitter bots. We also need to stop basing disinformation reporting on arbitrary and unverifiable performance indicators, such as the number of fake accounts in a campaign or the number of countries effected. Applying greater rigor to disinformation studies will only grow in importance as actors in the field evolve. In response to de-platforming and improved content moderation, disinformation actors are joining less moderated online spaces, such as Gab, Telegram, or Parler. Where they once had monetized their work on YouTube, these actors are now leaving the streaming platform for crowdfunding services (Tipeee, Patreon, GoFundMe, etc.). As a direct consequence, these new infrastructures cannot be left out of the broader conversation of the online distribution. 14

After years of a hands-off approach in moderating online content, profit-oriented platforms need to be held accountable for their role in actively supporting the spread of disinformation and harmful content. This is also why it is time to open the black box of online distribution of information, the business models of algorithms, domain name registration, syndicated content, and programmatic advertising systems. In order to do so, civil society groups investigating disinformation need better access to data—access that social media companies have so far denied. 15

There is no accountability without transparency. Stemming the spread of online disinformation requires defining sanctions for malicious actors and the online architecture that allows disinformation to spread. Otherwise, the systemic causes of this issue will remain with us, and disinformation will continue to spread under the radar and work against democratic societies. 16

Alaphilippe, Alexandre. "Disinformation Is Evolving to Move under the Radar." *Brookings*, 4 Feb. 2021. Used with permission.

QUESTIONS FOR READING

1. According to Alaphilippe, what has happened recently that has made investigating and exposing purveyors of disinformation more difficult and time consuming?
2. What have been the results of the increase in and sophistication of disinformation?
3. According to Alaphilippe, how does the increase of disinformation jeopardize public health and democracy?
4. What is content laundering, and why is it so dangerous?

QUESTIONS FOR REASONING AND ANALYSIS

5. What is Alaphilippe's claim? How does he defend and support it?
6. What does Alaphilippe insist we must do to avoid and defeat disinformation? How does he present this information?
7. Evaluate each section of Alaphilippe's article. What are its strengths and weaknesses? What, if anything, would you do to improve his argument?

QUESTIONS FOR REFLECTION AND WRITING

8. Are you convinced by Alaphilippe's argument? Why or why not?
9. Why do you think some Americans fall victim to disinformation (check out other articles in this book to read about possible reasons)?
10. A vast web of disinformation has duped millions into believing that the 2020 presidential election was stolen by President Biden through massive voter fraud. Though there exists plenty of evidence pointing to bad actors, such as Russia and right-wing conspiracy theorists propping up this big lie, large numbers of people still fall victim to this disinformation. What might we do to help people think more critically about their sources of information so that they can resist disinformation?

I AM A DANGEROUS PROFESSOR

GEORGE YANCY

Courtesy of Dr. George Yancy

George Yancy is a philosophy professor at Emory University with research interests in the philosophy of race. He is the author, coauthor, or editor of many books and articles. He is author of *Black Bodies, White Gazes: The Continuing Significance of Race in America* (2016) and editor of the Philosophy of Race book series for Lexington Books. The following essay appeared in the *New York Times* in November 2016.

PREREADING QUESTIONS What is your reaction to Yancy's title? To a reference to *1984* in the opening sentence?

1 Those familiar with George Orwell's *1984* will recall that "Newspeak was designed not to extend but to *diminish* the range of thought." I recently felt the

weight of this Orwellian ethos when many of my students sent emails to inform me, and perhaps warn me, that my name appears on the Professor Watchlist, a new website created by a conservative youth group known as Turning Point USA.

I could sense the gravity in those email messages, a sense of relaying what 2
is to come. The Professor Watchlist's mission, among other things, is to sound an alarm about those of us within academia who "advance leftist propaganda in the classroom." It names and includes photographs of some 200 professors.

The Watchlist appears to be consistent with a nostalgic desire "to make 3
America great again" and to expose and oppose those voices in academia that are anti-Republican or express anti-Republican values. For many black people, making America "great again" is especially threatening, as it signals a return to a more explicit and unapologetic racial dystopia. For us, dreaming of yesterday is not a privilege, not a desire, but a nightmare.

The new "watchlist" is essentially a new species of McCarthyism, especially 4
in terms of its overtones of "disloyalty" to the American republic. And it is reminiscent of Cointelpro, the secret F.B.I. program that spied on, infiltrated and discredited American political organizations in the '50s and '60s. Its goal of "outing" professors for their views helps to create the appearance of something secretly subversive. It is a form of exposure designed to mark, shame and silence.

So when I first confirmed my students' concerns, I was engulfed by a feeling 5
of righteous indignation, even anger. The list maker would rather that we run in shame after having been called out. Yet I was reminded of the novel *The Bluest Eye* in which Toni Morrison wrote that anger was better than shame: "There is a sense of being in anger. A reality and presence. An awareness of worth." The anger I experienced was also—in the words the poet and theorist Audre Lorde used to describe the erotic—"a reminder of my capacity for feeling." It is that feeling that is disruptive of the Orwellian gestures embedded in the Professor Watchlist. Its devotees would rather I become numb, afraid and silent. However, it is the anger that I feel that functions as a saving grace, a place of being.

If we are not careful, a watchlist like this can have the impact of the philosopher 6
Jeremy Bentham's Panopticon—a theoretical prison designed to create a form of self-censorship among those imprisoned. The list is not simply designed to get others to spy on us, to out us, but to install forms of psychological self-policing to eliminate thoughts, pedagogical approaches and theoretical orientations that it defines as subversive.

Honestly, being a black man, I had thought that I had been marked enough— 7
as bestial, as criminal, as inferior. I have always known of the existence of that racialized scarlet letter. It marks me as I enter stores; the white security guard never fails to see it. It follows me around at predominantly white philosophy conferences; I am marked as "different" within that space not because I *am* different, but because the conference space is filled with whiteness. It follows me as white police officers pull me over for no other reason than because I'm black. As Frantz Fanon writes, "I am overdetermined from without."

But now I feel the multiple markings; I am now "un-American" because of my 8
ideas, my desires and passion to undo injustice where I see it, my engagement

in a form of pedagogy that can cause my students to become angry or resistant in their newfound awareness of the magnitude of suffering that exists in the world. Yet I reject this marking. I refuse to be philosophically and pedagogically adjusted.

9 To be "philosophically adjusted" is to belie what I see as one major aim of philosophy—to speak to the multiple ways in which we suffer, to be a voice through which suffering might speak and be heard, and to offer a gift to my students that will leave them maladjusted and profoundly unhappy with the world as it is. Bringing them to that state is what I call doing "high stakes philosophy." It is a form of practicing philosophy that refuses to ignore the horrible realities of people who suffer and that rejects ideal theory, which functions to obfuscate such realities. It is a form of philosophizing that refuses to be seduced by what Friedrich Nietzsche called "conceptual mummies." Nietzsche notes that for many philosophers, "nothing actual has escaped from their hands alive."

10 In my courses, which the watchlist would like to flag as "un-American" and as "leftist propaganda," I refuse to entertain my students with mummified ideas and abstract forms of philosophical self-stimulation. What leaves their hands is always philosophically alive, vibrant and filled with urgency. I want them to engage in the process of freeing ideas, freeing their philosophical imaginations. I want them to lose sleep over the pain and suffering of so many lives that many of us deem disposable. I want them to become conceptually unhinged, to leave my classes discontented and maladjusted.

11 Bear in mind that it was in 1963 that the Rev. Dr. Martin Luther King, Jr., raised his voice and said: "I say very honestly that I never intend to become adjusted to segregation and discrimination. I never intend to become adjusted to religious bigotry. I never intend to adjust myself to economic conditions that will take necessities from the many to give luxuries to the few. I never intend to adjust myself to the madness of militarism, to self-defeating effects of physical violence."

12 I also recall the words Plato attributed to Socrates during his trial: "As long as I draw breath and am able, I shall not cease to practice philosophy." By that Socrates meant that he would not cease to exhort Athenians to care more for justice than they did for wealth or reputation.

13 So, in my classrooms, I refuse to remain silent in the face of racism, its subtle and systemic structure. I refuse to remain silent in the face of patriarchal and sexist hegemony and the denigration of women's bodies, or about the ways in which women have internalized male assumptions of how they should look and what they should feel and desire.

14 I refuse to be silent about forms of militarism in which innocent civilians are murdered in the name of "democracy." I refuse to remain silent when it comes to acknowledging the existential and psychic dread and chaos experienced by those who are targets of xenophobia and homophobia.

15 I refuse to remain silent when it comes to transgender women and men who are beaten to death by those who refuse to create conditions of hospitality.

16 I refuse to remain silent in a world where children become targets of sexual violence, and where unarmed black bodies are shot dead by the state and its

proxies, where those with disabilities are mocked and still rendered "monstrous," and where the earth suffers because some of us refuse to hear its suffering, where my ideas are marked as "un-American," and apparently "dangerous."

Well, if it is dangerous to teach my students to love their neighbors, to think and rethink constructively and ethically about who their neighbors are, and how they have been taught to see themselves as disconnected and neoliberal subjects, then, yes, I am dangerous, and what I teach is dangerous. 17

Yancy, George. "I Am a Dangerous Professor." *New York Times*, 30 Nov. 2016. Used with permission of the author.

QUESTIONS FOR READING

1. What is the Professor Watchlist? What seems to be its purpose?
2. What is the reaction of many Black people to the nostalgic "make America great again" idea?
3. Why is the reaction of anger better than a reaction of shame?
4. How does Yancy want to influence his students?

QUESTIONS FOR REASONING AND ANALYSIS

5. You know the occasion for Yancy's essay; what is his claim?
6. How does Yancy develop and support his position? Is his support effective for his subject and claim?
7. Examine the author's use of a rhetorical strategy in the latter part of his essay. What makes this strategy effective?
8. What are the essay's earmarks of a personal essay? Explain why the essay is still an argument.

QUESTIONS FOR REFLECTION AND WRITING

9. Yancy uses a number of quotations. Which one(s) would you choose as most effective? Why?
10. Would you choose to take a class from a professor on the watchlist? If so, why? If not, why not?

HOW TO COMBAT DISINFORMATION TARGETING BLACK COMMUNITIES

AMY YEE

PREREADING QUESTIONS **What is a bot? What is a troll? Why do you think people ("bad actors") and countries like Russia use bots and trolls?**

1 Earlier this year, Jessica Ann Mitchell Aiwunyor saw a friend arguing on Twitter about Black identity. Aiwuyor noticed that the Twitter account her friend was fighting with was a new one, with zero followers and also wasn't following anyone else. She told her friend he was probably arguing with a bot or troll. The revelation stopped the online debate in its tracks: her friend stopped engaging with the suspicious account.

2 When Aiwuyor tells others that infuriating online debates could be with bots or trolls, those incendiary exchanges begin to come into focus, and lose some of their power. "They are happy to hear they haven't lost their minds," said Aiwuyor, a communications specialist based near Washington, D.C.

3 Indeed, her friend may have been a victim of a broad disinformation campaign aimed at the Black community in the U.S. by Russian-backed Internet Research Agency or other bad actors.

4 During the 2016 presidential campaign, "no single group of Americans was targeted by IRA information operatives more than African-Americans," according to a Senate Intelligence Committee report released in October 2019.

5 Ahead of the general election, U.S. intelligence agencies such as the FBI have been sounding the alarm about disinformation and malicious attempts to "manipulate public opinion, discredit the electoral process, and undermine confidence in U.S. democratic institutions."

6 Aiwuyor was alarmed about the ongoing problem, and this October launched the National Black Cultural Information Trust to challenge disinformation.

7 Disinformation—falsehoods and rumors, purposefully meant to cause harm—is "a perpetual attempt to tarnish and erode our democracy," said the NAACP in October.

8 Along with the National Black Cultural Information Trust, the NAACP and other groups are countering disinformation aimed at the Black community by spreading accurate information, becoming reliable resources in communities, and tapping local influencers to be trusted messengers.

9 Researchers found that Twitter accounts operated by Russian trolls posing as Black activists "received more engagement than other types of inauthentic accounts," said Deen Freelon of the University of North Carolina at Chapel Hill and lead author of a study published this year in *Social Science Computer Review.*

10 Ahead of 2016 elections, Blacktivist, a Russian-created campaign with social media accounts, spewed intentionally divisive posts and racked up 11.2 million engagements on Facebook alone, such as likes and shares.

11 This year, an unprecedented pandemic, race-related protests, and polemical U.S. elections, provide ample fodder for disinformation campaigns. Bad information can discourage people from voting, exacerbate COVID-19 health risks, and sow distrust in government and institutions.

12 Twitter in October suspended fake Black accounts after shutting down nearly 1,600 accounts, including some based in Iran that inflamed conversations about Black Lives Matter and other racially charged issues. Facebook also recently suspended hundreds of fake accounts.

13 Recent disinformation has spread falsehoods about voting station locations, or that voting by mail doesn't work. In Michigan, people are receiving robocalls claiming that voting will put people on government watchlists, said Rai Lanier, a director at nonprofit Michigan Liberation.

Other falsehoods claimed that Black people couldn't contract COVID-19 or that the virus is caused by 5G cellphone technology. Getting reliable information "is a life or death situation. It's not intellectual conversations," said Nse Ufot, executive director of New Georgia Project, a civic engagement nonprofit. 14

Black people are particularly vulnerable to false health information because they are more likely to have existing and untreated health conditions. Distrust exists in Black communities "due to a long-documented history of medical experimentation, neglect, and the limited diversity of the medical profession," according to a report from the Shorenstein Center at Harvard Kennedy School. 15

But various organizations are combating disinformation in innovative ways. New Georgia Project, based in Atlanta, forges connections with young people, especially Black and other people of color, through hackathons and video game launches to get them interested in elections. In November 2019, some 150 coders, designers and esports players attended a "game jam" to come up with apps and games to demystify elections. 16

Those connections with communities help defuse falsehoods and rumors. "The more they see us as a trusted messenger, the better we get at combating disinformation," Ufot said. 17

New Georgia Project also sends out shareable messages with accurate information through social media platforms such as Twitter, Instagram, and TikTok. 18

It even made a cheeky video featuring pole dancers. "There's nowhere we won't go to meet our folks," Ufot said. She estimated the New Georgia Project has reached 3 million Georgians of color via social media in 2020. 19

There are signs that outreach has resonated with people. In 2014, New Georgia Project registered roughly 69,000 new voters. It has registered 455,000 Georgians in total since its founding. 20

The National Black Cultural Information Trust released a short guide about disinformation that warns about "digital Black face," in which fake social media accounts and bots masquerade as Black people to discourage voting and create conflict within Black communities. 21

The guide advises checking social media accounts for suspicious signs by asking whether they were just recently created, or had very few or zero followers. "Beware of abnormal social media handles, accounts with no profile photos, or strange images and vernacular," the group advises. 22

In 2019, Andre Banks, CEO of communications firm A/B Partners, started Win Black/Pa'lante, a digital strategy coalition to counter disinformation targeting Blacks and Latinos, who are also prime targets. 23

During the 2016 election, disinformation was "actually targeted to make sure Black voters were not fully able to express our political power," he said. 24

Banks was aware of academics and analysts gathering data on disinformation campaigns. He started Win Black/Pa'lante to "listen and learn from that research quickly and create content that groups across the country could use." 25

Voter suppression, intimidation, and propaganda are not new, but the internet makes it easier to spread. "These are old-school tactics but weaponized with digital media," observed Ashley Bryant, co-lead of Win Black/Pa'lante. 26

27 Win Black analyzes disinformation trends on social media and then arms about 100 progressive organizations and advocacy partners in 21 states with accurate, catchy content to share on social media. It has reached millions of people through posts and videos.

28 However, organizations sometimes need training and tools to accurately spread awareness. "Without education, a lot of groups are inadvertently amplifying these narratives," said Bryant.

29 Education may need to be tailored to reach the grassroots level. Nonprofit First Draft administers a two-week disinformation training course by SMS text messages in English and Spanish. It sends daily lessons via text because people might lack robust internet connections, especially during the pandemic lockdown. The SMS lessons have reached dozens of community organizations like youth groups and women's clubs and hundreds of individuals.

30 Messages in mainstream media and newspaper op-eds also may not reach people on the ground or resonate with marginalized groups, so trusted messengers within communities are key.

31 Influential conversations are happening in "nail salons, barbershops, on the stoop in front of houses, in parks, churches," said Amalia Deloney, co-executive director of Media Democracy Fund.

32 The National Black Cultural Information Trust also raises awareness through events such as a virtual town hall on reparations with Black academics and other experts. An upcoming webinar will feature *The Christian Recorder,* the newspaper of the influential African Methodist Episcopal Church.

33 "You're more likely to trust people you can see and engage with," said founder Jessica Aiwuyor.

34 In addition to church leaders, NBCIT reaches out to other important Black influencers, including Black media like podcasts, radio stations in Philadelphia, Washington, D.C., and Louisiana, and newspapers such as *The Afro,* and public television outlets and cable, such as Black News Channel.

35 Aiwuyor also spreads the word through Black Bloggers Connect, an online community and newsletter with 10,000 members that she started as a graduate student in 2009.

36 Disinformation is in the spotlight because of elections, but it also widens fissures within the Black community that can have long-lasting impact. Bad actors "are using our cultural conversations to sway the way we think about each other and ourselves," Aiwuyor said.

37 Disinformation can, for example, stoke "animus for a Jamaican or an African immigrant and blame them for our social woes or vice versa. Then that sways how we think about immigration," she explained.

38 "It's kind of attacking us from within. It's using our cultural conversations against us," said Aiwuyor. "It harms our ability to unite around issues. What we need to do is band together."

Yee, Amy. "How to Combat Disinformation Targeting Black Communities." *Yes!* 3 Nov. 2020. Used with permission.

QUESTIONS FOR READING AND ANALYSIS

1. How did Russia and other "bad actors" influence the 2016 elections in America?
2. According to Yee, why were Black users more likely to be influenced by political and health disinformation?
3. What social media platforms do bots and trolls use to spread disinformation?
4. What other venues are spreading disinformation to Black people?
5. What have people done to counter disinformation in Black communities? How might these venues be used to counter disinformation?

QUESTIONS FOR REASONING AND ANALYSIS

6. Why does Yee believe that disinformation targeted to Black communities is a serious problem? What is her claim?
7. How does she support her claim? How does she use reasoning and examples?

QUESTIONS FOR REFLECTION AND WRITING

8. Were you persuaded by Yee's argument? If so, why? If not, why not?
9. Do you think that you've ever been targeted by a bot or troll? What happened?
10. Now that you've read Yee's article, how will you approach social media differently?

CHAPTER 17

Race in America

Maskot/Getty Images

READ: What do you know about the history and current events of race in America?

REASON: Why do you think it's important to have honest, ongoing discussions about race in America? Why do you think some people don't even want to talk about race in America?

WRITE: Read some of the articles in this chapter and other articles on race in this book. Then write a short essay on some ideas that you have to improve the dialogue in America about race.

Over two decades into the twenty-first century, we might be forgiven for harboring some uncertainties about the country's future. Although some have written of America's decline, we seem to have survived the COVID-19 pandemic and its economic fallout, and we are still a country of entrepreneurs that drive technological innovation. Access to a good education and the possibility of owning a home mean that some Americans can still enjoy a large measure of success. All too often, however, BIPOC (Black, Indigenous, and people of color) communities struggle to access good education and home ownership due to systemic racism embedded in institutions like schools and housing.

School districts that serve BIPOC communities are perennially underfunded, leading to a disparity in educational resources that negatively affects students in those areas. Andre Perry, a research fellow at the Brookings Institute, explains that school systems attended by students of color "receive an annual $23 billion less than majority-white institutions."[1] Perry also states that "massive racial disparities in funding disempower students of color, who make up the majority of those who attend public schools." Since these inequities are caused by the downgrading of "residential properties in Black communities" by "federal and local actors," there is little people of color can do to increase the tax base that funds their schools.

Due to the dramatic decrease in affordable housing in America, BIPOC communities are forced to rent rather than own their homes. And when renting a home requires spending 30% or more of a family's income, the "cost-burden" makes it difficult for people to afford "food, clothing, transportation, and medical care."[2] If BIPOC families struggle to afford these types of necessities, their ability to obtain a mortgage and make a down payment to purchase a home is unlikely. According to a Pew Institute study published in 2017, white families are far more likely to obtain a mortgage than Black and Hispanic families. Forty-one percent of Black families own their own home, and 47% of Hispanic families own their own home, whereas 71.9% of white families own their own home (Desilver and Bialik).[3] Clearly, we must do something about inequities built into systems that are supposed to provide Americans with opportunity to succeed.

There is some good news here. Younger Americans are more concerned about racism and its effects and are far more accepting of diversity than older Americans. If the country's youth will commit to becoming and staying informed and to participating in elections (older Americans vote in far greater numbers than younger Americans) based on knowledgeable consideration of the candidates and the country's needs, there is hope that we can make ourselves anew and journey forward together, as so eloquently put by both Abraham Lincoln and Barack Obama.

You can begin by seeking out the authors in this text who have impressed you with their knowledge, wisdom, and perhaps calm approach to examining problems and offering solutions. Learn and reflect on what you learn. Think about the kind of world you want to have for yourself and for generations to come. You might also ask yourself: What can I do to make a difference?

A NEVER ENDING WAR

KAYE WISE WHITEHEAD

Amy Davis/ Baltimore Sun/ Tribune News Service/Getty Images

Karsonya (Kaye) Wise Whitehead is an associate professor of communication and African and African American Studies in the Department of Communication at Loyola University Maryland. A former Baltimore City middle school teacher, she is the founding executive director of the Black Feminist Writer's Project. She is also the author of four books, the most recent of which is *RaceBrave: New and Selected Works*. Her commentary below was published in *the Baltimore Sun* in 2014.

PREREADING QUESTIONS Knowing that the author is an associate professor of communication who studies race, class, and gender, what do you expect Whitehead's subject to be? What makes Whitehead's title catchy and compelling?

1 In the days leading up to the end of the Michael Dunn "loud music" case—in which a white Florida man shot and killed a 17-year-old black teen after getting into an argument over the boy's so-called "thug" music—I was overwhelmed with feelings of restlessness, worry, frustration and fear.

2 They were the same feelings I had at the end of the George Zimmerman trial. The same ones I have when I think about the day when my sons will be old enough to drive or walk to the store by themselves. I worry so much about what could happen to them simply because they are black and male. I feel like my husband and I are in the midst of this never-ending war, the same war that my parents and my grandparents fought. It is the same war that black people have been fighting in this country since American slavery was first legalized. This war is simply to keep our boys safe in a society that devalues them, suspects them, fears them and often dismisses them. It is a war that I now fear I am losing.

3 When my sons were first born, we held them in our arms and promised them that we would love and protect them. When they learned how to crawl, we ran around the house moving things out of their way. When they learned how to toddle, we walked behind them, always ready to catch them right before they fell. When they started school, we used to check in with their teachers every day to make sure that they were comfortable and safe and happy. We taught them how to say please and thank you, how to raise their hands in school before they spoke and how to wait their turn. We taught them to be respectful and polite. We spent hours reading to and with them, taking them to the library, to the museums and to see Shakespeare in the Park. We saved our money, moved into a safe neighborhood and sacrificed so that they could attend the best schools, take piano and play sports. We took them to church and made sure that they learned their scriptures and prayed before they ate their food. We really believed that we were doing everything that we could do to keep them safe, to beat the odds and to win this war. There was a moment when Barack Obama was first elected president that I thought that the war had finally ended and that we had won. We celebrated because we believed that the work that had been done to create a fair and just society. We believed that America was finally colorblind and post racial. We have come to realize that we were wrong.

We are still living in a country where our sons will be judged by the color of their skin and not the content of their character. I believe that it does not matter how much education they have or how polite they are or how much money we make or that they can play the piano and fence and swim. In this country, no matter where they are or what they are doing, they will still be seen as threats and thugs and criminals. They will be seen as disposable. 4

Whitehead, Karsonya Wise. "A Never Ending War." *Baltimore Sun*, 18 Feb. 2014. Used with permission of the author.

QUESTIONS FOR READING

1. What caused the author to feel restless, worried, frustrated, and fearful?
2. What steps has the author taken to try to keep her sons safe?
3. What war is the author referring to?

QUESTIONS FOR REASONING AND ANALYSIS

4. What leads the author to think that America was "finally colorblind"?
5. What is the ethical issue the author is trying to understand and deal with in her op-ed?
6. What position does she reach on the issue? Does she offer a specific claim statement or imply one?

QUESTIONS FOR REFLECTION AND WRITING

7. What kind of evidence does Whitehead use to support her claims? Do you think her evidence is legitimate? Do you think her claims are effective? Why or why not? Explain.
8. Do you think that people of color, especially males, are at greater risk when they wear a hoodie or listen to loud music in their cars? Be prepared to defend your view.
9. Many states have "stand-your-ground" laws that allow people to use deadly force in self-defense if they feel their lives are threatened. Are stand-your-ground laws necessary and moral? Are they effective in reducing crime? How might these laws be manipulated in cases where self-defense is not clear? Be prepared to discuss or write about this issue.

REMARKS BY THE PRESIDENT AT THE 50TH ANNIVERSARY OF THE SELMA TO MONTGOMERY MARCHES

BARACK H. OBAMA

Scott Olson/ Getty Images

The forty-fourth president of the United States was born in Hawaii on August 4, 1961, to a white American mother and a Black Kenyan father while both were in college. After Obama attended Columbia College and Harvard Law School—where he became the first African American editor of the *Harvard Law Review*—Obama returned to Chicago to teach at the University of Chicago Law School and to practice civil rights law. Elected first to the Illinois State Senate, he was then, in 2004, elected to the U.S. Senate. In 2008, Obama became the first African American president of the United States. He was reelected in 2012 to a second term as president. Obama delivered the following address to commemorate the 50th anniversary of the Selma to Montgomery civil rights marches led by Dr. Martin Luther King Jr.

PREREADING QUESTIONS You may already know about the Selma to Montgomery civil rights marches, but perhaps you do not. How does Obama help people who do not know about the original marches understand the history and significance of the commemoration so that he reaches the broadest possible audience?

Edmund Pettus Bridge
Selma, Alabama
2:17 P.M. CST

1 AUDIENCE MEMBER: We love you, President Obama!

2 THE PRESIDENT: Well, you know I love you back. (Applause.)

3 It is a rare honor in this life to follow one of your heroes. And John Lewis is one of my heroes.

4 Now, I have to imagine that when a younger John Lewis woke up that morning 50 years ago and made his way to Brown Chapel, heroics were not on his mind. A day like this was not on his mind. Young folks with bedrolls and backpacks were milling about. Veterans of the movement trained newcomers in the tactics of non-violence; the right way to protect yourself when attacked. A doctor described what tear gas does to the body, while marchers scribbled down instructions for contacting their loved ones. The air was thick with doubt, anticipation and fear. And they comforted themselves with the final verse of the final hymn they sung:

5 "No matter what may be the test, God will take care of you; Lean, weary one, upon His breast, God will take care of you."

6 And then, his knapsack stocked with an apple, a toothbrush, and a book on government—all you need for a night behind bars—John Lewis led them out of the church on a mission to change America.

7 President and Mrs. Bush, Governor Bentley, Mayor Evans, Sewell, Reverend Strong, members of Congress, elected officials, foot soldiers, friends, fellow Americans:

8 As John noted, there are places and moments in America where this nation's destiny has been decided. Many are sites of war—Concord and Lexington, Appomattox, Gettysburg. Others are sites that symbolize the daring of America's character—Independence Hall and Seneca Falls, Kitty Hawk and Cape Canaveral.

9 Selma is such a place. In one afternoon 50 years ago, so much of our turbulent history—the stain of slavery and anguish of civil war; the yoke of segregation and tyranny of Jim Crow; the death of four little girls in Birmingham; and the dream of a Baptist preacher—all that history met on this bridge.

10 It was not a clash of armies, but a clash of wills; a contest to determine the true meaning of America. And because of men and women like John Lewis, Joseph Lowery, Hosea Williams, Amelia Boynton, Diane Nash, Ralph Abernathy, C.T. Vivian, Andrew Young, Fred Shuttlesworth, Dr. Martin Luther King, Jr., and so

many others, the idea of a just America and a fair America, an inclusive America, and a generous America—that idea ultimately triumphed.

As is true across the landscape of American history, we cannot examine this moment in isolation. The march on Selma was part of a broader campaign that spanned generations; the leaders that day part of a long line of heroes. 11

We gather here to celebrate them. We gather here to honor the courage of ordinary Americans willing to endure billy clubs and the chastening rod; tear gas and the trampling hoof; men and women who despite the gush of blood and splintered bone would stay true to their North Star and keep marching towards justice. 12

They did as Scripture instructed: "Rejoice in hope, be patient in tribulation, be constant in prayer." And in the days to come, they went back again and again. When the trumpet call sounded for more to join, the people came—black and white, young and old, Christian and Jew, waving the American flag and singing the same anthems full of faith and hope. A white newsman, Bill Plante, who covered the marches then and who is with us here today, quipped that the growing number of white people lowered the quality of the singing. (Laughter.) To those who marched, though, those old gospel songs must have never sounded so sweet. 13

In time, their chorus would well up and reach President Johnson. And he would send them protection, and speak to the nation, echoing their call for America and the world to hear: "We shall overcome." (Applause.) What enormous faith these men and women had. Faith in God, but also faith in America. 14

The Americans who crossed this bridge, they were not physically imposing. But they gave courage to millions. They held no elected office. But they led a nation. They marched as Americans who had endured hundreds of years of brutal violence, countless daily indignities—but they didn't seek special treatment, just the equal treatment promised to them almost a century before. (Applause.) 15

What they did here will reverberate through the ages. Not because the change they won was preordained; not because their victory was complete; but because they proved that nonviolent change is possible, that love and hope can conquer hate. 16

As we commemorate their achievement, we are well-served to remember that at the time of the marches, many in power condemned rather than praised them. Back then, they were called Communists, or half-breeds, or outside agitators, sexual and moral degenerates, and worse—they were called everything but the name their parents gave them. Their faith was questioned. Their lives were threatened. Their patriotism challenged. 17

And yet, what could be more American than what happened in this place? (Applause.) What could more profoundly vindicate the idea of America than plain and humble people—unsung, the downtrodden, the dreamers not of high station, not born to wealth or privilege, not of one religious tradition but many, coming together to shape their country's course? 18

What greater expression of faith in the American experiment than this, what greater form of patriotism is there than the belief that America is not yet finished, that we are strong enough to be self-critical, that each successive generation 19 can look upon our imperfections and decide that it is in our power to remake this nation to more closely align with our highest ideals? (Applause.)

20 That's why Selma is not some outlier in the American experience. That's why it's not a museum or a static monument to behold from a distance. It is instead the manifestation of a creed written into our founding documents: "We the People . . . in order to form a more perfect union." "We hold these truths to be self-evident, that all men are created equal." (Applause.)

21 These are not just words. They're a living thing, a call to action, a roadmap for citizenship and an insistence in the capacity of free men and women to shape our own destiny. For founders like Franklin and Jefferson, for leaders like Lincoln and FDR, the success of our experiment in self-government rested on engaging all of our citizens in this work. And that's what we celebrate here in Selma. That's what this movement was all about, one leg in our long journey toward freedom. (Applause.)

22 The American instinct that led these young men and women to pick up the torch and cross this bridge, that's the same instinct that moved patriots to choose revolution over tyranny. It's the same instinct that drew immigrants from across oceans and the Rio Grande; the same instinct that led women to reach for the ballot, workers to organize against an unjust status quo; the same instinct that led us to plant a flag at Iwo Jima and on the surface of the Moon. (Applause.)

23 It's the idea held by generations of citizens who believed that America is a constant work in progress; who believed that loving this country requires more than singing its praises or avoiding uncomfortable truths. It requires the occasional disruption, the willingness to speak out for what is right, to shake up the status quo. That's America. (Applause.)

24 That's what makes us unique. That's what cements our reputation as a beacon of opportunity. Young people behind the Iron Curtain would see Selma and eventually tear down that wall. Young people in Soweto would hear Bobby Kennedy talk about ripples of hope and eventually banish the scourge of apartheid. Young people in Burma went to prison rather than submit to military rule. They saw what John Lewis had done. From the streets of Tunis to the Maidan in Ukraine, this generation of young people can draw strength from this place, where the powerless could change the world's greatest power and push their leaders to expand the boundaries of freedom.

25 They saw that idea made real right here in Selma, Alabama. They saw that idea manifest itself here in America.

26 Because of campaigns like this, a Voting Rights Act was passed. Political and economic and social barriers came down. And the change these men and women wrought is visible here today in the presence of African Americans who run boardrooms, who sit on the bench, who serve in elected office from small towns to big cities; from the Congressional Black Caucus all the way to the Oval Office. (Applause.)

27 Because of what they did, the doors of opportunity swung open not just for black folks, but for every American. Women marched through those doors. Latinos marched through those doors. Asian Americans, gay Americans, Americans with disabilities—they all came through those doors. (Applause.)

Their endeavors gave the entire South the chance to rise again, not by reasserting the past, but by transcending the past.

What a glorious thing, Dr. King might say. And what a solemn debt we owe. 28
Which leads us to ask, just how might we repay that debt?

First and foremost, we have to recognize that one day's commemoration, no 29
matter how special, is not enough. If Selma taught us anything, it's that our work is never done. (Applause.) The American experiment in self-government gives work and purpose to each generation.

Selma teaches us, as well, that action requires that we shed our cynicism. 30
For when it comes to the pursuit of justice, we can afford neither complacency nor despair.

Just this week, I was asked whether I thought the Department of Justice's 31
Ferguson report shows that, with respect to race, little has changed in this country. And I understood the question; the report's narrative was sadly familiar. It evoked the kind of abuse and disregard for citizens that spawned the Civil Rights Movement. But I rejected the notion that nothing's changed. What happened in Ferguson may not be unique, but it's no longer endemic. It's no longer sanctioned by law or by custom. And before the Civil Rights Movement, it most surely was. (Applause.)

We do a disservice to the cause of justice by intimating that bias and dis- 32
crimination are immutable, that racial division is inherent to America. If you think nothing's changed in the past 50 years, ask somebody who lived through the Selma or Chicago or Los Angeles of the 1950s. Ask the female CEO who once might have been assigned to the secretarial pool if nothing's changed. Ask your gay friend if it's easier to be out and proud in America now than it was thirty years ago. To deny this progress, this hard-won progress—our progress—would be to rob us of our own agency, our own capacity, our responsibility to do what we can to make America better.

Of course, a more common mistake is to suggest that Ferguson is an iso- 33
lated incident; that racism is banished; that the work that drew men and women to Selma is now complete, and that whatever racial tensions remain are a consequence of those seeking to play the "race card" for their own purposes. We don't need the Ferguson report to know that's not true. We just need to open our eyes, and our ears, and our hearts to know that this nation's racial history still casts its long shadow upon us.

We know the march is not yet over. We know the race is not yet won. We 34
know that reaching that blessed destination where we are judged, all of us, by the content of our character requires admitting as much, facing up to the truth. "We are capable of bearing a great burden," James Baldwin once wrote, "once we discover that the burden is reality and arrive where reality is."

There's nothing America can't handle if we actually look squarely at the 35
problem. And this is work for all Americans, not just some. Not just whites. Not just blacks. If we want to honor the courage of those who marched that day, then all of us are called to possess their moral imagination. All of us will need to feel as they did the fierce urgency of now. All of us need to recognize as they did that change depends on our actions, on our attitudes, the things we teach our

children. And if we make such an effort, no matter how hard it may sometimes seem, laws can be passed, and consciences can be stirred, and consensus can be built. (Applause.)

36 With such an effort, we can make sure our criminal justice system serves all and not just some. Together, we can raise the level of mutual trust that policing is built on—the idea that police officers are members of the community they risk their lives to protect, and citizens in Ferguson and New York and Cleveland, they just want the same thing young people here marched for 50 years ago—the protection of the law. (Applause.) Together, we can address unfair sentencing and overcrowded prisons, and the stunted circumstances that rob too many boys of the chance to become men, and rob the nation of too many men who could be good dads, and good workers, and good neighbors. (Applause.)

37 With effort, we can roll back poverty and the roadblocks to opportunity. Americans don't accept a free ride for anybody, nor do we believe in equality of outcomes. But we do expect equal opportunity. And if we really mean it, if we're not just giving lip service to it, but if we really mean it and are willing to sacrifice for it, then, yes, we can make sure every child gets an education suitable to this new century, one that expands imaginations and lifts sights and gives those children the skills they need. We can make sure every person willing to work has the dignity of a job, and a fair wage, and a real voice, and sturdier rungs on that ladder into the middle class.

38 And with effort, we can protect the foundation stone of our democracy for which so many marched across this bridge—and that is the right to vote. (Applause.) Right now, in 2015, 50 years after Selma, there are laws across this country designed to make it harder for people to vote. As we speak, more of such laws are being proposed. Meanwhile, the Voting Rights Act, the culmination of so much blood, so much sweat and tears, the product of so much sacrifice in the face of wanton violence, the Voting Rights Act stands weakened, its future subject to political rancor.

39 How can that be? The Voting Rights Act was one of the crowning achievements of our democracy, the result of Republican and Democratic efforts. (Applause.) President Reagan signed its renewal when he was in office. President George W. Bush signed its renewal when he was in office. (Applause.) One hundred members of Congress have come here today to honor people who were willing to die for the right to protect it. If we want to honor this day, let that hundred go back to Washington and gather four hundred more, and together, pledge to make it their mission to restore that law this year. That's how we honor those on this bridge. (Applause.)

40 Of course, our democracy is not the task of Congress alone, or the courts alone, or even the President alone. If every new voter-suppression law was struck down today, we would still have, here in America, one of the lowest voting rates among free peoples. Fifty years ago, registering to vote here in Selma and much of the South meant guessing the number of jellybeans in a jar, the number of bubbles on a bar of soap. It meant risking your dignity, and sometimes, your life.

41 What's our excuse today for not voting? How do we so casually discard the right for which so many fought? (Applause.) How do we so fully give away our

power, our voice, in shaping America's future? Why are we pointing to somebody else when we could take the time just to go to the polling places? (Applause.) We give away our power.

Fellow marchers, so much has changed in 50 years. We have endured war and we've fashioned peace. We've seen technological wonders that touch every aspect of our lives. We take for granted conveniences that our parents could have scarcely imagined. But what has not changed is the imperative of citizenship; that willingness of a 26-year-old deacon, or a Unitarian minister, or a young mother of five to decide they loved this country so much that they'd risk everything to realize its promise. 42

That's what it means to love America. That's what it means to believe in America. That's what it means when we say America is exceptional. 43

For we were born of change. We broke the old aristocracies, declaring ourselves entitled not by bloodline, but endowed by our Creator with certain inalienable rights. We secure our rights and responsibilities through a system of self-government, of and by and for the people. That's why we argue and fight with so much passion and conviction—because we know our efforts matter. We know America is what we make of it. 44

Look at our history. We are Lewis and Clark and Sacajawea, pioneers who braved the unfamiliar, followed by a stampede of farmers and miners, and entrepreneurs and hucksters. That's our spirit. That's who we are. 45

We are Sojourner Truth and Fannie Lou Hamer, women who could do as much as any man and then some. And we're Susan B. Anthony, who shook the system until the law reflected that truth. That is our character. 46

We're the immigrants who stowed away on ships to reach these shores, the huddled masses yearning to breathe free—Holocaust survivors, Soviet defectors, the Lost Boys of Sudan. We're the hopeful strivers who cross the Rio Grande because we want our kids to know a better life. That's how we came to be. (Applause.) 47

We're the slaves who built the White House and the economy of the South. (Applause.) We're the ranch hands and cowboys who opened up the West, and countless laborers who laid rail, and raised skyscrapers, and organized for workers' rights. 48

We're the fresh-faced GIs who fought to liberate a continent. And we're the Tuskeegee Airmen, and the Navajo code-talkers, and the Japanese Americans who fought for this country even as their own liberty had been denied. 49

We're the firefighters who rushed into those buildings on 9/11, the volunteers who signed up to fight in Afghanistan and Iraq. We're the gay Americans whose blood ran in the streets of San Francisco and New York, just as blood ran down this bridge. (Applause.) 50

We are storytellers, writers, poets, artists who abhor unfairness, and despise hypocrisy, and give voice to the voiceless, and tell truths that need to be told. 51

We're the inventors of gospel and jazz and blues, bluegrass and country, and hip-hop and rock and roll, and our very own sound with all the sweet sorrow and reckless joy of freedom. 52

53 We are Jackie Robinson, enduring scorn and spiked cleats and pitches coming straight to his head, and stealing home in the World Series anyway. (Applause.)

54 We are the people Langston Hughes wrote of who "build our temples for tomorrow, strong as we know how." We are the people Emerson wrote of, "who for truth and honor's sake stand fast and suffer long;" who are "never tired, so long as we can see far enough."

55 That's what America is. Not stock photos or airbrushed history, or feeble attempts to define some of us as more American than others. (Applause.) We respect the past, but we don't pine for the past. We don't fear the future; we grab for it. America is not some fragile thing. We are large, in the words of Whitman, containing multitudes. We are boisterous and diverse and full of energy, perpetually young in spirit. That's why someone like John Lewis at the ripe old age of 25 could lead a mighty march.

56 And that's what the young people here today and listening all across the country must take away from this day. You are America. Unconstrained by habit and convention. Unencumbered by what is, because you're ready to seize what ought to be.

57 For everywhere in this country, there are first steps to be taken, there's new ground to cover, there are more bridges to be crossed. And it is you, the young and fearless at heart, the most diverse and educated generation in our history, who the nation is waiting to follow.

58 Because Selma shows us that America is not the project of any one person. Because the single-most powerful word in our democracy is the word "We." "We the People." "We Shall Overcome." "Yes We Can." (Applause.) That word is owned by no one. It belongs to everyone. Oh, what a glorious task we are given, to continually try to improve this great nation of ours.

59 Fifty years from Bloody Sunday, our march is not yet finished, but we're getting closer. Two hundred and thirty-nine years after this nation's founding our union is not yet perfect, but we are getting closer. Our job's easier because somebody already got us through that first mile. Somebody already got us over that bridge. When it feels the road is too hard, when the torch we've been passed feels too heavy, we will remember these early travelers, and draw strength from their example, and hold firmly the words of the prophet Isaiah: "Those who hope in the Lord will renew their strength. They will soar on [the] wings like eagles. They will run and not grow weary. They will walk and not be faint." (Applause.)

60 We honor those who walked so we could run. We must run so our children soar. And we will not grow weary. For we believe in the power of an awesome God, and we believe in this country's sacred promise.

61 May He bless those warriors of justice no longer with us, and bless the United States of America. Thank you, everybody. (Applause.)

END
2:50 P.M. CST

Remarks by President Obama at the 50th Anniversary of the Selma to Montgomery Marches (2015).

QUESTIONS FOR READING

1. Why is it especially poignant that Obama delivered this address?
2. Why were the original protestors marching in Selma, Alabama? Be more specific than "they were marching for civil or equal rights."
3. What idea from the Declaration of Independence does Obama use in his speech?
4. What events does Obama reference as reminders that racism still exists in America? How does he tie these events to the continuing struggle for equal rights for all Americans?
5. What does Obama want attendees of this event and readers of this speech to do to honor those who protested and died during the Selma to Montgomery marches?

QUESTIONS FOR REASONING AND ANALYSIS

6. Normally, U.S. presidents begin speeches by acknowledging other elected officials. How does Obama do this? Why do you think he begins his speech in this way?
7. What is Obama's primary claim, and how does he support it?
8. Obama's speech is meant to be part history lesson, part tribute, and part call to action. How does he interweave these elements throughout his address?
9. Political scientists and experts in speech communication have noted that Obama is one of the most gifted public orators of our time. Do you agree? If so, why? If not, why not?

QUESTIONS FOR REFLECTION AND WRITING

10. The civil rights movement in America did not begin in the 1960s; rather, it has been a part of our history from the beginning—original signers of the Declaration of Independence wrangled over slavery, an issue that eventually led to the Civil War. What are your thoughts and concerns about race relations and civil rights in America today?
11. Are you registered to vote? If so, do you participate in local and national elections? If not, why not? Are you involved in political civil activities and why? If so, what do you do? If not, what would it take for you to be more civically engaged?

IMMIGRATE, ASSIMILATE

AMY CHUA

LEE Seung-Hwan/ Getty Images

A professor at Yale Law School since 2001, Amy Chua specializes in international business transactions, ethnic conflict, and globalization and the law. She is the author of *Battle Hymn of the Tiger Mother* (2011). She cowrote *The Triple Package: How Three Unlikely Traits Explain the Rise and Fall of Cultural Groups* with her husband, Jed Rubenfeld, in 2014. Her essay on immigration, published February 3, 2008, was a special to the *Washington Post.*

PREREADING QUESTIONS Given the title, where do you expect to find Chua on the immigration debate? Given her education and expertise, how do you expect her to support her argument?

1 If you don't speak Spanish, Miami really can feel like a foreign country. In any restaurant, the conversation at the next table is more likely to be in Spanish than English. And Miami's population is only 65 percent Hispanic. El Paso is 76 percent Latino. Flushing, N.Y., is 60 percent immigrant, mainly Chinese.

2 Chinatowns and Little Italys have long been part of America's urban landscape, but would it be all right to have entire U.S. cities where most people spoke and did business in Chinese, Spanish or even Arabic? Are too many Third World, non-English-speaking immigrants destroying our national identity?

3 For some Americans, even asking such questions is racist. At the other end of the spectrum, conservative talk-show host Bill O'Reilly* fulminates against floods of immigrants who threaten to change America's "complexion" and replace what he calls the "white Christian male power structure."

4 But for the large majority in between, Democrats and Republicans alike, these questions are painful, and there are no easy answers. At some level, most of us cherish our legacy as a nation of immigrants. But are all immigrants really equally likely to make good Americans? Are we, as Samuel Huntington warns, in danger of losing our core values and devolving "into a loose confederation of ethnic, racial, cultural and political groups, with little or nothing in common apart from their location in the territory of what had been the United States of America"?

5 My parents arrived in the United States in 1961, so poor that they couldn't afford heat their first winter. I grew up speaking only Chinese at home (for every English word accidentally uttered, my sister and I got one whack of the chopsticks). Today, my father is a professor at Berkeley, and I'm a professor at Yale Law School. As the daughter of immigrants, a grateful beneficiary of America's tolerance and opportunity, I could not be more pro-immigrant.

6 Nevertheless, I think Huntington has a point.

7 Around the world today, nations face violence and instability as a result of their increasing pluralism and diversity. Across Europe, immigration has resulted in unassimilated, largely Muslim enclaves that are hotbeds of unrest and even terrorism. The riots in France late last year were just the latest manifestation. With Muslims poised to become a majority in Amsterdam and elsewhere within a decade, major West European cities could undergo a profound transformation. Not surprisingly, virulent anti-immigration parties are on the rise.

8 Not long ago, Czechoslovakia, Yugoslavia and the Soviet Union disintegrated when their national identities proved too weak to bind together diverse peoples. Iraq is the latest example of how crucial national identity is. So far, it has found no overarching identity strong enough to unite its Kurds, Shiites and Sunnis.

9 The United States is in no danger of imminent disintegration. But this is because it has been so successful, at least since the Civil War, in forging a national identity strong enough to hold together its widely divergent communities. We should not take this unifying identity for granted.

---

* O'Reilly was fired by Fox News in 2017.–Ed.

The greatest empire in history, ancient Rome, collapsed when its cultural 10
and political glue dissolved, and peoples who had long thought of themselves as Romans turned against the empire. In part, this fragmentation occurred because of a massive influx of immigrants from a very different culture. The "barbarians" who sacked Rome were Germanic immigrants who never fully assimilated.

Does this mean that it's time for the United States to shut its borders and 11
reassert its "white, Christian" identity and what Huntington calls its Anglo-Saxon, Protestant "core values"?

ANTI-IMMIGRANT MISTAKES

No. The anti-immigration camp makes at least two critical mistakes. 12

First, it neglects the indispensable role that immigrants have played in build- 13
ing American wealth and power. In the 19th century, the United States would never have become an industrial and agricultural powerhouse without the millions of poor Irish, Polish, Italian and other newcomers who mined coal, laid rail and milled steel. European immigrants led to the United States' winning the race for the atomic bomb.

Today, American leadership in the Digital Revolution—so central to our mili- 14
tary and economic preeminence—owes an enormous debt to immigrant contributions. Andrew Grove (co-founder of Intel), Vinod Khosla (Sun Microsystems) and Sergey Brin (Google) are immigrants. Between 1995 and 2005, 52.4 percent of Silicon Valley startups had one key immigrant founder. And Vikram S. Pundit's recent appointment to the helm of Citigroup means that 14 CEOs of Fortune 100 companies are foreign-born.

The United States is in a fierce global competition to attract the world's best 15
high-tech scientists and engineers—most of whom are not white Christians. Just this past summer, Microsoft opened a large new software-development center in Canada, in part because of the difficulty of obtaining U.S. visas for foreign engineers.

Second, anti-immigration talking heads forget that their own scapegoating 16
vitriol will, if anything, drive immigrants further from the U.S. mainstream. One reason we don't have Europe's enclaves is our unique success in forging an ethnically and religiously neutral national identity, uniting individuals of all backgrounds. This is America's glue, and people like Huntington and O'Reilly unwittingly imperil it.

Nevertheless, immigration naysayers also have a point. 17

America's glue can be subverted by too much tolerance. Immigration 18
advocates are too often guilty of an uncritical political correctness that avoids hard questions about national identity and imposes no obligations on immigrants. For these well-meaning idealists, there is no such thing as too much diversity.

MAINTAINING OUR HERITAGE

The right thing for the United States to do—and the best way to keep Americans 19
in favor of immigration—is to take national identity seriously while maintaining

our heritage as a land of opportunity. U.S. immigration policy should be tolerant but also tough. Here are five suggestions:

Overhaul Admission Priorities.

20 Since 1965, the chief admission criterion has been family reunification. This was a welcome replacement for the ethnically discriminatory quota system that preceded it. But once the brothers and sisters of a current U.S. resident get in, they can sponsor their own extended families. In 2006, more than 800,000 immigrants were admitted on this basis. By contrast, only about 70,000 immigrants were admitted on the basis of employment skills, with an additional 65,000 temporary visas granted to highly skilled workers.

21 This is backward. Apart from nuclear families (spouse, minor children, possibly parents), the special preference for family members should be drastically reduced. As soon as my father got citizenship, his relatives in the Philippines asked him to sponsor them. Soon, his mother, brother, sister and sister-in-law were also U.S. citizens or permanent residents. This was nice for my family, but frankly there is nothing especially fair about it.

22 Instead, the immigration system should reward ability and be keyed to the country's labor needs, skilled or unskilled, technological or agricultural. In particular, we should significantly increase the number of visas for highly skilled workers, putting them on a fast track for citizenship.

Make English the Official National Language.

23 A common language is critical to cohesion and national identity in an ethnically diverse society. Americans of all backgrounds should be encouraged to speak more languages—I've forced my own daughters to learn Mandarin (minus the threat of chopsticks)—but offering Spanish-language public education to Spanish-speaking children is the wrong kind of indulgence. Native-language education should be overhauled, and more stringent English proficiency requirements for citizenship should be set up.

Immigrants Must Embrace the Nation's Civic Virtues.

24 It took my parents years to see the importance of participating in the larger community. When I was in third grade, my mother signed me up for Girl Scouts. I think she liked the uniforms and merit badges, but when I told her that I was picking up trash and visiting soup kitchens, she was horrified.

25 For many immigrants, only family matters. Even when immigrants get involved in politics, they often focus on protecting their own and protesting discrimination. That they can do so is one of the great virtues of U.S. democracy. But a mind-set based solely on taking care of your own factionalizes our society.

26 Like all Americans, immigrants have a responsibility to contribute to the social fabric. It's up to each immigrant community to fight off an "enclave" mentality and give back to their new country. It's not healthy for Chinese to hire only Chinese, or Koreans only Koreans. By contrast, the free health clinic set up by Muslim Americans in Los Angeles—serving the entire poor community—is a model to emulate. Immigrants are integrated at the moment they realize that their success is intertwined with everyone else's.

Enforce the Law.

Illegal immigration, along with terrorism, is the chief cause of today's anti-immigration backlash. It is also inconsistent with the rule of law, which, as any immigrant from a developing country will tell you, is a critical aspect of U.S. identity. But if we're serious about this problem, we need to enforce the law against not only illegal aliens, but also against those who hire them. 27

It's the worst of all worlds to allow U.S. employers who hire illegal aliens—thus keeping the flow of illegal workers coming—to break the law while demonizing the aliens as lawbreakers. An Arizona law that took effect Jan. 1 tightens the screws on employers who hire undocumented workers, but this issue can't be left up to a single state. 28

Make the United States an Equal-Opportunity Immigration Magnet.

That the 11 million to 20 million illegal Immigrants are 80 percent Mexican and Central American is itself a problem. This is emphatically not for the reason Huntington gives—that Hispanics supposedly don't share America's core values. But if the U.S. immigration system is to reflect and further our ethnically neutral identity, it must itself be ethnically neutral, offering equal opportunity to Sudanese, Estonians, Burmese and so on. The starkly disproportionate ratio of Latinos—reflecting geographical fortuity and a large measure of lawbreaking—is inconsistent with this principle. 29

Immigrants who turn their backs on American values don't deserve to be here. But those of us who turn our backs on immigrants misunderstand the secret of America's success and what it means to be American. 30

Chua, Amy. "Immigrate, Assimilate." *Washington Post*, 3 Feb. 2008. Reprinted by permission of the author.

QUESTIONS FOR READING

1. What is Huntington's concern for America?
2. What has happened in some European cities? To several European countries? What causes internal conflict in Iraq?
3. What are the two mistakes of those who oppose immigration, in the author's view?
4. What are the author's suggestions for a tough immigration policy? State her five proposals in your own words.

QUESTIONS FOR REASONING AND ANALYSIS

5. Why does Chua provide her immigrant experience and family success story? As a part of her argument, what purpose does it serve?
6. What is clever about her concluding paragraph? How does it mirror the approach of her argument?
7. What is Chua's claim? Express her position as a problem/solution argument.
8. Look at Chua's five proposals. What kinds of grounds does she provide in support?
9. Is the author convincing? If so, what makes her argument effective? If not, why not?

QUESTIONS FOR REFLECTION AND WRITING

10. Chua asserts that the chief cause of anti-immigration attitudes is a combination of terrorism and illegal aliens. Do you agree with this assessment? If not, why not?
11. Where do you stand on immigration? In opposition? Embracing diversity? Or somewhere in the middle? Has Chua established a good argument for the middle ground? Why or why not?
12. Is there any specific proposal with which you disagree? If so, why? How would you refute Chua's defense of that proposal?

DEB HAALAND IS TAKING ON RACIST NAMES ON FEDERAL LANDS

ADAM MAHONEY

Adam Mahoney is an environmental justice journalist at *Grist* and a Reporting Fellow at *ProPublica*. He also writes about crime and justice, as well as U.S. and world politics. Mahoney's work has appeared in *The Guardian, U.S. News and World Report, Rolling Stone, Salon,* and the *Chicago Sun-Times*. In 2019, he won the Society of Professional Journalists Award for Opinion Writing. Mahoney earned his BS in journalism and sociology from Northwestern University in 2020. This article was published in *Grist* on November 23, 2021.

PREREADING QUESTIONS **How do you think names of places can be racist?**

1 At the urging of Interior Secretary Deb Haaland, a member of the Pueblo of Laguna who is the first Indigenous person to hold a cabinet-level position in a U.S. presidential administration, the federal government is beginning a formal process to remove racist and derogatory names from lands under its jurisdiction.

2 Last week, Haaland ordered the Interior Department's Board on Geographic Names to institute procedures to remove terms such as "squaw," which is found in the names of more than 650 federal sites. For the first time in U.S. history, a federal order now explicitly designates "squaw," a racist and misogynist term used as a slur against Indigenous women by settlers, as a derogatory term.

3 In a statement, Haaland said that the move marks a "significant step in honoring the ancestors who have stewarded our lands since time immemorial."

4 "Racist terms have no place in our vernacular or on our federal lands," she added. "Our nation's lands and waters should be places to celebrate the outdoors and our shared cultural heritage —not to perpetuate the legacies of oppression."

5 The new task force charged with implementing the process will be made up of representatives from federal land management agencies, while history experts, members of the general public, and representatives of Indigenous communities will be tapped to create an advisory board to review and recommend the name changes, according to the order. This move accompanies pending Congressional legislation to rename more than 1,000 names on federal land that currently include derogatory terms.

The Native American Rights Fund, which has long called for the removal of derogatory place names, applauded the move. 6

"Names that still use derogatory terms are an embarrassing legacy of this country's colonialist and racist past," said John Echohawk, the group's executive director. "It is well-past time for us, as a nation, to move forward, beyond these derogatory terms, and show Native people—and all people—equal respect." 7

The order could empower activists across the country, including those living in the area currently named Squaw Valley, located in Fresno County, California. For two years, residents have claimed that local officials have been unwilling to meet with them to discuss renaming the valley. 8

Following Haaland's announcement, Fresno County Supervisor Nathan Magsig indicated that the federal order would not necessarily alter the stance of county officials. "When I saw the Secretary make that decision that they made, I was a little bit taken aback because they are one individual," he told the *Fresno Bee*. "But there are other voices that are out there that need to be heard, too, that are just as valuable as her opinion." 9

While changing federal names has historically been an arduous process that can take many years in some cases, several name changes have established a precedent that Haaland is building upon. For example, following the internment of Japanese Americans during World War II and the peak of the Civil Rights Movement in the 1960s, the Board on Geographic Names took actions to eliminate the use of derogatory terms for Black and Japanese Americans. And in recent years, states like Oregon, Maine, Montana, and Minnesota have passed legislation prohibiting the use of the word "squaw" in place names. 10

Mahoney, Adam. "Deb Haaland Is Taking on Racist Names on Federal Lands." *Grist*, 23 Nov. 2021. Used with permission.

QUESTIONS FOR READING

1. What recent event has led to Mahoney's article?
2. Mahoney notes that Deb Haaland is "the first Indigenous person to hold a cabinet-level position in a U.S. presidential administration." Why is this important to know?
3. What names and terms is Secretary Haaland attempting to change?
4. What does Secretary Haaland mean by "legacies of oppression" when justifying the name changes?

QUESTIONS FOR READING AND ANALYSIS

5. Mahoney's article could be described as a "hard news" piece as he doesn't overtly take a position. Nonetheless, raising awareness of the topic matter might also be described as a rhetorical move to advocate for antiracist language. In these types of articles, the author still has the responsibility of ensuring trustworthiness. What sort of information does Mahoney cite to support his credibility as a journalist?
6. How does Mahoney organize his article to make it inviting to people who might not be experts in the topic?
7. What sort of language does Mahoney use to explain complex information to non-experts?

QUESTIONS FOR REFLECTION AND WRITING

8. How do you feel about changing racist names of parks and other geographic locations?
9. Do a quick search for state and federal parks in your area. Do any of them use racist language in their names or descriptions? If so, how might you try to advocate for changing this language? What would be your first steps?
10. Some people are critical of changing historic—yet racist—names to more accurately and inclusively describe geographic locations. They claim that such action is revisionist history and that it erases the achievements of (mostly) white European colonists. How might you respond to someone who disagrees with what Secretary Haaland is doing?

WHAT *SHANG-CHI AND THE LEGEND OF TEN RINGS* GETS RIGHT ABOUT CHINESE FOOD

XINROU SHU

Xinrou Shu writes about diverse subjects like social justice, race, food, fashion, and culture. As a journalist, she has published in *V Magazine, Shangrao Daily, SupChina,* and *Salon.* She holds a BA in psychology and social behavior, with a minor in journalism, from the University of California, Irvine, and an MFA in literary reportage from New York University's Arthur L. Carter Journalism Institute. She works in both Chinese and English. This article was published in *Salon* on October 25, 2021.

PREREADING QUESTIONS With an article title that includes the name of a Marvel Comics movie and Chinese food, how do you think the author might integrate a discussion of race?

1 I have a confession to make: I was never a huge Marvel fan. To be honest, I was indifferent to Thanos' death, as well as the superheroes' victory. While audiences were applauding for the supervillain's death, I felt a bit of emptiness as I didn't feel a huge connection between my background as a Chinese woman and the depictions of the heroes on screen.

2 My feelings have changed since the release of "Shang-Chi and the Legend of the Ten Rings"—specifically after watching a particular scene involving food.

On a Sunday night, sitting in a theater, oddly enough, I empathized with the characters. All the ingredients were there: the predominantly Asian cast (I grew up watching Tony Leung's movies), the perfect Mandarin pronunciation, the traditional Chinese elements running through the film. These all pulled me closer to my memories; my heritage and language; and to my Chinese background.

3 During the movie, I was especially struck by a small detail: the rice porridge in the breakfast scene. When Shaun/Shang-Chi (Simu Liu) was at Katy's (Awkwafina) door, her mom said to him: "She's not ready. Come have some zhōu while you wait."

4 Inside, the family was having a nice breakfast of congee together. A large bowl of rice porridge was placed on the dining table, waiting to be distributed.

Oh, my dear zhōu! It was at that moment I knew the movie was going to make a difference.

5 After all, it's not orange chicken.

6 Despite the fact that I do like the taste of orange chicken, being born and raised in China, I can tell you that orange chicken, much like Americanized Mandarin, is Americanized from Chinese roots.

7 In the U.S., Americanized Chinese food isn't uncommon. David R. Chan, a Chinese food expert who has eaten at more than 7,400 Chinese restaurants in America, explained the invention of this variety was out of "historical accidents."

8 It's a product of two separate eras, first adapted for ingredients found in the U.S. and later adapted to American tastes by Taishanese migrants in the 19th century. Then culinary traditions that were brought from Sichuan, Hunan and other mainland areas to Taiwan were eventually transported again to New York by Taiwanese chefs, who were cooking for a non-Chinese customer base.

9 "Because both classes of Americanized Chinese food really are historical accidents, I kind of dismiss it as 'faux Chinese food,'" Chan said. "Not that I mind Americanized Chinese food, since I find some of it good for what it is. And given that these Americanized Chinese dishes have been around for so long, who's to say they're not their own cuisine now?"

10 I'm with Chan on that. You can't expect to completely learn Mandarin from the Americanized standards. For the same reason, you can't fully understand Chinese culture by a variation of Chinese food that only has shallow Chinese roots.

11 That's why I was so frustrated by the misrepresentation of Chinese culture on TV—especially the Chinese food culture. According to a study from USC Annenberg Inclusion Initiative, in 1,100 popular films from 2007 to 2017, the prevalence of Asians on screen only increased from 3.4% to 4.8%.

12 Even if Asians, especially Chinese, are on screen, they always speak accented English and Americanized Mandarin Chinese. What's worse, orange chicken, depicted as a popular Chinese dish, is often under the spotlight.

13 But the congee at the breakfast table in "Shan-Chi" is a game changer. It's definitely a "Chinese-approved" dish. Though the origin of congee is still a mystery, it likely originated in China. The earliest reference can be traced back to the Chinese Zhou dynasty, circa 1,000 BCE.

14 This fits within a larger trend of seeing more accurate representations of diverse food cultures on TV. Actually, according to Krishnendu Ray, the associate professor of food studies at New York University, the representations of the East are shifting from "etic" to "emic"—that is, from looking at a culture from an outsider's point of view to an insider's point of view.

15 He explained that, due to the rise of East Asia in both hard power and soft power, the relationship between Asian and American populations is changing. Also, with the democratization of social media like Instagram and TikTok, information spreads. People have a place to learn about food cultures, and people in the dominant culture—especially young people—are more omnivorous when it comes to authenticity.

16 "The representation is changing dramatically. [The congee] in 'Shang-Chi and the Legend of Ten Rings' is a terrific example," Ray said. "And I think that's the future very clearly, with the rise of Asian cultures."

17 In Chinese culture, breakfast is the most important meal of the day. The old saying, "Have a good breakfast, a full lunch and a small dinner," runs through generation to generation. It basically means, "Breakfast like a king, lunch like a prince, dine like a pauper." Breakfast, according to Chan, "does have an important role in Chinese food culture, in some ways more important than other meals since it is the most likely meal to be eaten at home."

18 Not only is breakfast eaten at home, but also eaten with family—the Chinese value family and harmony. As the most common breakfast pick on the dining table, isn't congee a bond that ties the family closer?

19 Simmer either long-grain or short-grain rice in extra water until it's fully softened, then you get a pot of thick congee. A staple food across Asia, congee has various regional versions. *Kayu* in Japan, *juk* in Korea, *babor* in Cambodia, *lugaw* in Philippines, *chok* or *jok* in Thailand—the list can go on and on. The preparation differs slightly depending on the culture. For instance, some cultures substitute water with chicken stock, while others cook the rice along with other ingredients like seafood.

20 Regardless of the names and regional varieties, congee is a get-better food across cultures. If you feel sick, softened rice and rice soup will warm you up, gently comforting you from the stomach to the whole body. Going back to when I was in kindergarten and was too sick to eat, my dad always cooked plain congee and carefully fed me with a spoon.

21 "Have some báizhōu (plain congee), then you'll get better soon," he said.

22 His words have been a curse. Even after two decades, I can still remember him sitting at my bedside and blowing the congee to cool. Those memories were so vivid that plain congee has become my instinct when dealing with sickness. I guess congee, above a traditional cultural food, is a universal language for reticent Asian parents to say, "I love you," and a way of demonstrating care for early morning visitors who show up on your doorstep, much like Shang-Chi.

Shu, Xinrou. "What 'Shang-Chi and the Legend of Ten Rings' Gets Right about Chinese Food." Salon.com, 25 Oct. 2021. Used with permission.

QUESTIONS FOR READING

1. What event from the movie *Shang-Chi and the Legend of Ten Rings* sparks Shu's interest in the plot and characters?
2. According to Shu, what do most Americans consider to be Chinese food? Why do they think this? Why is this negative, according to Shu?
3. What information does Shu cite to highlight "the misrepresentation of Chinese culture on TV"?
4. What do we need to do, according to Shu, to develop a more accurate view of Chinese culture?

QUESTIONS FOR REASONING AND ANALYSIS

5. What is Shu's claim? Where does she state it?
6. How does she support her claim?
7. How does Shu try to relate to her readers?
8. According to the author, what role does social media play in the future of intercultural understanding?

QUESTIONS FOR REFLECTION AND WRITING

9. Do you have a "get better" food? If so, how did it evolve into your get better dish, and how does it improve your well-being?
10. Our perceptions of people and cultures different from us often develop from the movies, TV shows, and online content we ingest. As such, we can sometimes form inaccurate ideas about people and cultures if we have limited exposure to a wide variety of media. What sources of information do you use? Where do you go online to find out more about people and cultures you don't know? What other ways might you learn more about people and cultures different from you?

TEXAS REPUBLICANS TO INVESTIGATE SCHOOL DISTRICTS' BOOKS THAT MENTION RACE AND SEXUALITY

BRIAN LOPEZ

Courtesy of the Texas Tribune

Brian Lopez is the public education reporter for the *Texas Tribune.* Before working at the *Texas Tribune,* Lopez wrote for the *Fort Worth Star-Telegram,* where he focused on issues involving local government. Lopez worked for *The Shorthorn,* the student-run newspaper, before graduating in 2020 from the University of Texas at Arlington. This article was published by *Salon* on October 27, 2021.

PREREADING QUESTIONS From the title of this article, can you tell what the writer's position will be? Does it seem like an argument article? Or does it seem like an analysis article? Might it be both?

A Republican state lawmaker has launched an investigation into Texas school districts over the type of books they have, particularly if they pertain to race or sexuality or "make students feel discomfort." 1

State Rep. Matt Krause, in his role as chair of the House Committee on General Investigating, notified the Texas Education Agency that he is "initiating an inquiry into Texas school district content," according to an Oct. 25 letter obtained by the *Texas Tribune.* 2

Krause's letter provides a 16-page list of about 850 book titles and asks the districts if they have these books, how many copies they have and how much money they spent on the books. 3

His list of titles includes bestsellers and award winners alike, from the 1967 Pulitzer Prize-winning novel *The Confessions of Nat Turner* by William Styron and *Between the World and Me* by Ta-Nehisi Coates to last year's book club favorites: *Hood Feminism: Notes from the Women that a Movement Forgot* by Mikki Kendall and Isabel Wilkerson's *Caste: The Origins of Our Discontents.* 4

But race is not the only thing on the committee chair's list. Other listed books Krause wants school districts to account for are about teen pregnancy, abortion 5 and homosexuality, including *LGBT Families* by Leanne K. Currie-McGhee, *The Letter Q: Queer Writers' Notes to their Younger Selves* edited by Sarah Moon, and Michael J. Basso's *The Underground Guide to Teenage Sexuality: An Essential Handbook for Today's Teens and Parents.*

6 Krause, a Fort Worth lawmaker and founding member of the House Freedom Caucus, is running for state attorney general against Ken Paxton. Krause declined to comment and no explanation was given as to how these books were chosen.

7 Krause sent notice of the investigation to Lily Laux, the Texas Education Agency deputy commissioner of school programs, as well as some Texas school superintendents. His letter did not specify which school districts Krause was investigating.

8 Krause informs districts they must provide the committee with the number of copies they have of each book, on what part of campus those books are located and how much money schools spent on the books, as well as information on any other book that violates House Bill 3979, the so-called "critical race theory law" designed to limit how race-related subjects are taught in public schools. Critical race theory, the idea that racism is embedded in legal systems and not limited to individuals is an academic discipline taught at the university level. But it has become a common phrase used by conservatives to include anything about race taught or discussed in public secondary schools.

9 The law states a teacher cannot "require or make part of a course" a series of race-related concepts, including the ideas that "one race or sex is inherently superior to another race or sex" or that someone is "inherently racist, sexist, or oppressive" based on their race or sex.

10 School officials have until Nov. 12 to respond. It is unclear what will happen to the districts that have such books.

11 The letter did not give a specific reason that Krause was launching the investigation, only that "the committee may initiate inquiries concerning any 'matter the committee considers necessary for the information of the legislature or for the welfare and protection of state citizens.'"

12 Lake Travis Independent School District officials received the letter and are trying to figure out what the next steps are, a spokesperson said. Officials in that Austin-area school district are speaking with other school districts to figure out what this means for them. In nearby Round Rock Independent School District, the district spokesperson, Jenny Caputo, texted that it will "take significant staff time to gather the information to reply to this request." The district's legal team is still reviewing the request.

13 State Rep. Victoria Neave, D-Dallas, who is vice chair of the committee, said she had no idea Krause was launching the investigation but believes it's a campaign tactic. She found out about the letter after a school in her district notified her.

14 "His letter is reflective of the Republican Party's attempt to dilute the voice of people of color," she said.

15 Neave said she doesn't know what Krause is trying to do but will investigate the motive and next steps.

The TEA and the rest of the Committee on General Investigating members 16
did not immediately respond to requests for comment.

Brandon Rottinghaus, a political science professor at the University of 17
Houston, said it doesn't surprise him that Krause has taken initiative on a conservative item, especially since there is a crowded field in the Texas attorney general race.

"He's not well known statewide, and so he needs to put down a pretty tall 18
conservative flag to get notice," Rottinghaus said. "As a political statement, it certainly conveys the clear message that the Republicans are watching."

Rottinghaus said he doesn't recall a time in recent memory when legisla- 19
tures have taken the role of investigating school districts.

"The monitoring of this definitely is a political statement and so the fact that 20
the legislature is attentive to it definitely implies that they're not going to drop the issue," he said.

Jim Walsh, an attorney who often represents school districts, pointed out there 21
is nothing in the law that says books must be removed and Krause's investigation also doesn't call for books to be removed. For now, it's up to school districts to decide how they will respond, but what's certain is that it will add more workload to Texas schools that are already struggling from the effects of the pandemic.

Texas State Teachers Association President Ovidia Molina said in a state- 22
ment that the investigation is a "witch hunt" and that nothing in state law gives lawmakers the right to go after educators.

"This is an obvious attack on diversity and an attempt to score political points 23
at the expense of our children's education," she said.

Krause's investigation comes after several school districts across the state 24
removed books from libraries because of parental outcry.

Earlier this month, the Carroll Independent School District board in Southlake 25
reprimanded a fourth grade teacher who had an anti-racist book in her classroom after a parent complained about it last year.

Then, in a separate incident this month, a Carroll ISD administrator asked 26
teachers to provide materials that presented an "opposing" perspective of the Holocaust in an effort to comply with HB 3979. The law, which comes with little to no guidance, has caused confusion and fear among teachers and administrators, who have seemingly misinterpreted the law.

In the Katy Independent School District, a school removed a book after par- 27
ents claimed it promoted "critical race theory," which the district later found to be untrue and reinstated the book.

Lopez, Brian. "Texas House Committee to Investigate School Districts' Books on Race and Sexuality." *Texas Tribune*, 26 Oct. 2021. Used with permission.

QUESTIONS FOR READING

1. What is Lopez's subject? (Be precise.)
2. According to Lopez, what has happened recently to warrant an investigation into books held by public schools?

3. How does the House Committee on General Investigating member State Representative Matt Krause justify his request for his list of books?
4. What are some of the books on the list?
5. What is critical race theory? Is it taught in elementary, middle, or high schools? Does it claim that one race is better than any of the others or that people are inherently racist?

QUESTIONS FOR REASONING AND ANALYSIS

6. At first blush, Lopez's article might seem like an analysis. But looking closely at the organization of the article, one can see a subtle argument. What is that argument? Note the sources of his interviews and where their information is placed within the article.
7. What subtle argument might Lopez be making in this article?
8. Does Lopez do an effective job of presenting information in a fair and balanced way? What is your position on this topic after reading Lopez's article?

QUESTIONS FOR REFLECTION AND WRITING

9. Who should have final say in determining the content of public libraries? The librarians? The teachers? The principal? The students? The board of education? The state legislature?
10. Lopez quotes University of Houston political science professor Brandon Rottinghaus, who says that Krause likely has political aspirations for higher office and that this is really the reason he began the inquiry. What do you think about this? Is this an ethical or unethical way of spending taxpayers' money?
11. Based on what you read in Lopez's article, and given recent legislation around reproductive rights, what do you think may happen to books on reproductive health in schools? What segments of the population do you think will be most adversely affected by the removal of books on race, sexuality, and reproductive health? If you don't know, do some research on this question to find out more.
12. Should schools ban books? Do some quick research to find out the history of book banning and the reasons behind it. Write a 250-word response about what you find.

CREDITS

1. https://www.edweek.org/policy-politics/opinion-black-families-dont-need-fixing-they-need-better-school-financing/2020/08
2. https://www.huduser.gov/portal/pdredge/pdr_edge_featd_article_092214.html
3. https://www.pewresearch.org/fact-tank/2017/01/10/blacks-and-hispanics-face-extra-challenges-in-getting-home-loans/

CHAPTER 18

Gender and Gender Identity

New Africa/Shutterstock

READ: What do you know about the reasons why gender roles and gender identities are changing in America? Where did you get your information?

REASON: What impact do you think the overturning of *Roe v. Wade* might have on gender roles and gender identities in America?

WRITE: What are the mental health outcomes for people dealing with gender roles and gender identity when they are positively supported? What are the outcomes when they are not?

The six articles in this chapter on gender and gender identity provide much for readers to reflect upon and debate. The writers examine the incredible–and in some cases controversial–changes to the concepts of gender, sexuality, and gender identity that the world has experienced in the past two decades. In many cases, this change represents great strides in freedom, empowerment, and personal safety for people challenging traditional and sometimes oppressive ideas of gender and gender identity. Women now serve in combat roles in the U.S. military; same-sex marriage is legal–for now–in the United States; and more attention is being paid to the violence that often accompanies hypermasculine cultures, such as sports and caustic online communities.

In some cases, however, these changes have been achieved at the high cost of discrimination and lives lost. Yet according to a Gallup poll from 2021, 66% of Americans surveyed support openly transgender men and women serving in the military.[1] Not surprising, then, that Gallup also found that 53% of Americans surveyed in 2019 supported new laws to reduce discrimination against lesbian, gay, bisexual, and transgender people.[2]

Some of the writers in this chapter approach the changes in gender and gender identity–and their effects on our politics, our culture, and our personal lives–from a social science perspective; others take a more empirical approach; others develop arguments from emotions or from an academic perspective. Some express strongly held views; others seek common ground. But whatever the writer's topic, or the basis for the argument, or the values expressed, all would agree that the changes of the past two decades have had a profound effect on our lives. All would likely also agree that while some issues–transgender and nonbinary rights specifically–will continue to benefit from both research and reflection, the reality is that the majority of Americans have accepted an inclusive approach to gender roles and LGBTQIA+ relationships.

PREREADING QUESTIONS

1. Do you expect to have a career? To have a partner or spouse and children? Should society support all genders having these choices? If so, how?
2. What role, if any, should government and the courts have in defining marriage and the rights of transgender, nonbinary, and LGBTQIA+ people?
3. What has been meant by "traditional genders" in the past? In what ways have these traditional roles and identities changed in the twenty-first century?
4. Do you have a position on transgender, nonbinary, and LGBTQIA+ rights? On partnership recognition? If you have a position, what is it, and what is its source?
5. Do you expect to develop a romantic relationship with someone while in college? If so, how do you want your peers, family, college, church (if you are a person of faith), employer, etc., to handle that choice? If you don't plan to develop a romantic relationship while in college, or ever for that matter, how do you want your peers, family, college, church (if you are a person of faith), etc., to handle that choice?
6. What are the most important issues we need to address regarding gender, sexuality, and gender identities? Why do you feel strongly about these? What should we do to address them?

WOMEN WILL MAKE UNITS STRONGER

LISA JASTER

Courtesy of Lisa Jaster

One of only three women to complete the U.S. Army Ranger School, Major Lisa Jaster, now in the Army Reserve, is an engineer with Shell Oil. Jaster completed the elite training program as a wife and mother aged thirty-seven, an amazing feat. Her article below was initially published in 2015.

PREREADING QUESTIONS From Jaster's biography, what "units" do you think she will be writing about? If women are the "weaker sex," how might women make units stronger?

Last week, Defense Secretary Ashton B. Carter directed that all jobs in the U.S. military be opened to women. The announcement provoked strong reactions, but all sides concurred that we cannot let our standards fall or force quotas on our combat units. As an Army officer, a combat veteran and one of the first three women to graduate from U.S. Army Ranger School, I strongly agree. 1

The critics worry about strength and stamina, often comparing infantry units to professional sports teams. But just as a successful football team needs a smart quarterback, fast receivers, strong linemen and talented special teams, our war fighters must dominate all aspects of the battle space. At Ranger School, individuals are referred to as either Strong Rangers or Smart Rangers. Some exceptional soldiers are both, but most fit predominantly into one category or the other. I wasn't the strongest Ranger, but I spent almost every morning in the center of the patrol base helping plan the day's mission. Did my intellect make me an asset to the team? I know a few guys who would say it did. As with every team, some members need to be smarter while others need to be stronger. But no one can be a physical liability. 2

I keep hearing that the change means politicians will force military training schools to graduate women. Some think that if allowances are not made, no women will successfully graduate from some schools or be able to join certain units. But that's okay—no one wants those allowances. Secretary Carter said there would be no quotas, and there shouldn't be. Elite training courses such as Basic Underwater Demolition ensure that only individuals with extremely high levels of mental and physical prowess can serve in these niche capacities. That should not change. 3

Just as the military gets tested on tactical tasks, everyone in the ranks should get tested on job-specific physical requirements. For example, if you want to be in an armor or field artillery unit, you must prove that you are capable of lifting and moving the heaviest round in the arsenal. Consideration should be given to the addition of job-specific physical testing, which could solve a problem in many of our combat units and may quell concerns around the integration of women. 4

Many comments I have seen about this topic allude to "female issues." Look, women have been running around the woods for hundreds of years without anyone having to tell them how to deal with bodily functions. Trust me, we got this. 5

6 Countless people also question how units will maintain the mystical alchemy of the bro-bond once women join the ranks, but unit cohesion doesn't develop because men act like teenagers in a locker room. Overcoming adversity builds that bond. Ask a cop after a shootout or a firefighter who ran into a burning building. The man or woman to his left or right becomes his "brother" regardless of gender, religion or politics.

7 None of these arguments is new. And all of them ignore the fundamental fact that brute strength is not the only, or even the most important, factor in a successful combat mission. Courage, ingenuity, strategic thinking, levelheadedness, marksmanship and an ability to read people all factor into whether a unit succeeds or a mission goes south. Yes, we will maintain physical standards, and some women will fail, but the ones who succeed will bring new strengths as well, making their units stronger and more agile.

8 Finally, a word to those women interested in joining combat arms: Carry your load. Meet or exceed the same standard as a man your size, and be prepared for the possibility of failure. Above all, strive to be an asset to our forces daily. Understand that your behavior will affect generations to come. Women don't have to prove we are worthy of this opportunity, but we have to make sure that we don't prove the naysayers right.

Jaster, Lisa. "Women Will Make Units Stronger." *Washington Post*, 12 Dec. 2015. Used with permission of the author.

QUESTIONS FOR READING

1. What announcement has led to Jaster's essay?
2. What responses to the announcement does Jaster agree with? How do these agreements reinforce Jaster's argument?
3. How should physical requirements and standards be maintained?
4. How do military units form a "brotherhood"?
5. What qualities are important to a successful mission?

QUESTIONS FOR READING AND ANALYSIS

6. Around what points does Jaster organize her essay? Then, what *type* of argument is this? State her claim to reveal her approach.
7. If Jaster argues to maintain standards and opposes any use of quotas, how does she support her position that women will make units "stronger"?
8. Find a metaphor and explain how the author uses it to support her position.

QUESTIONS FOR REFLECTION AND WRITING

9. Has Jaster convinced you that women can strengthen army units? If so, why? If not, why not?
10. Is it time to stop defining–and limiting–individuals by their gender and instead evaluate each person on his or her particular skills and abilities? This is a key question for our times, worthy of serious reflection.

SUPREMACY CRIMES

GLORIA STEINEM

Gabriel Olsen/FilmMagic/Getty Images

Editor, writer, and lecturer, Gloria Steinem has been cited in *World Almanac* as one of the twenty-five most influential women in America. She is the cofounder of *Ms.* magazine and of the National Women's Political Caucus and is the author of a number of books and many articles. The following article appeared in *Ms.* in the August/September 1999 issue.

PREREADING QUESTIONS **Who are the teens who commit most of the mass shootings at schools? Who are the adults who commit most of the hate crimes and sadistic killings? What generalizations can you make about these groups based on your knowledge from media coverage?**

You've seen the ocean of television coverage, you've read the headlines: "How to Spot a Troubled Kid," "Twisted Teens," "When Teens Fall Apart." 1

After the slaughter in Colorado that inspired those phrases, dozens of copycat threats were reported in the same generalized way: "Junior high students charged with conspiracy to kill students and teachers" (in Texas); "Five honor students overheard planning a June graduation bombing" (in New York); "More than 100 minor threats reported statewide" (in Pennsylvania). In response, the White House held an emergency strategy session titled "Children, Violence, and Responsibility." Nonetheless, another attack was soon reported: "Youth With 2 Guns Shoots 6 at Georgia School." 2

I don't know about you, but I've been talking back to the television set, waiting for someone to tell us the obvious: it's not "youth," "our children," or "our teens." It's our sons—and "our" can usually be read as "white," "middle class," and "heterosexual." 3

We know that hate crimes, violent and otherwise, are overwhelmingly committed by white men who are apparently straight. The same is true for an even higher percentage of impersonal, resentment-driven, mass killings like those in Colorado; the sort committed for no economic or rational gain except the need to say, "I'm superior because I can kill." Think of Charles Starkweather, who reported feeling powerful and serene after murdering ten women and men in the 1950s; or the shooter who climbed the University of Texas Tower in 1966, raining down death to gain celebrity. Think of the engineering student at the University of Montreal who resented females' ability to study that subject, and so shot to death 14 women students in 1989, while saying, "I'm against feminism." Think of nearly all those who have killed impersonally in the workplace, the post office, McDonald's. 4

White males—usually intelligent, middle class, and heterosexual, or trying desperately to appear so—also account for virtually all the serial, sexually motivated, sadistic killings, those characterized by stalking, imprisoning, torturing, and "owning" victims in death. Think of Edmund Kemper, who began by killing animals, then murdered his grandparents, yet was released to sexually torture and dismember college students and other young women until he himself 5 decided he "didn't want to kill all the coeds in the world." Or David Berkowitz, the Son of Sam, who murdered some women in order to feel in control of all women. Or consider Ted Bundy, the charming, snobbish young would-be lawyer who tortured and murdered as many as 40 women, usually beautiful students who were symbols of the economic class he longed to join. As for John Wayne Gacy, he was obsessed with maintaining the public mask of masculinity, and so hid his homosexuality by killing and burying men and boys with whom he had had sex.

6 These "senseless" killings begin to seem less mysterious when you consider that they were committed disproportionately by white, non-poor males, the group most likely to become hooked on the drug of superiority. It's a drug pushed by a male-dominant culture that presents dominance as a natural right; a racist hierarchy that falsely elevates whiteness; a materialist society that equates superiority with possessions; and a homophobic one that empowers only one form of sexuality.

7 As Elliott Leyton reports in *Hunting Humans: The Rise of the Modern Multiple Murderer,* these killers see their behavior as "an appropriate—even 'manly'—response to the frustrations and disappointments that are a normal part of life." In other words, it's not their life experiences that are the problem, it's the impossible expectation of dominance to which they've become addicted.

8 This is not about blame. This is about causation. If anything, ending the massive cultural cover-up of supremacy crimes should make heroes out of boys and men who reject violence, especially those who reject the notion of superiority altogether. Even if one believes in a biogenetic component of male aggression, the very existence of gentle men proves that socialization can override it.

9 Nor is this about attributing such crimes to a single cause. Addiction to the drug of supremacy is not their only root, just the deepest and most ignored one. Additional reasons why this country has such a high rate of violence include the plentiful guns that make killing seem as unreal as a video game; male violence in the media that desensitized viewers in much the same way that combat killers are desensitized in training; affluence that allows maximum access to violence-as-entertainment; a national history of genocide and slavery; the romanticizing of frontier violence and organized crime; not to mention extremes of wealth and poverty and the illusion that both are deserved.

10 But it is truly remarkable, given the relative reasons for anger at injustice in this country, that white, non-poor men have a near-monopoly on multiple killings of strangers, whether serial and sadistic or mass and random. How can we ignore this obvious fact? Others may kill to improve their own condition, in self-defense, or for money or drugs; to eliminate enemies; to declare turf in drive-by shootings; even for a jacket or a pair of sneakers—but white males addicted to supremacy kill even when it worsens their condition or ends in suicide.

11 Men of color and females are capable of serial and mass killing, and commit just enough to prove it. Think of Colin Ferguson, the crazed black man on the Long Island Railroad, or Wayne Williams, the young black man in Atlanta who kidnapped and killed black boys, apparently to conceal his homosexuality. Think of Aileen Carol Wuornos, the white prostitute in Florida who killed abusive johns "in self-defense," or Waneta Hoyt, the upstate New York woman who strangled

her five infant children between 1965 and 1971, disguising their cause of death as sudden infant death syndrome. Such crimes are rare enough to leave a haunting refrain of disbelief as evoked in Pat Parker's poem "jonestown": "Black folks do not/Black folks do not/Black folks do not commit suicide." And yet they did.

Nonetheless, the proportion of serial killings that are not committed by white 12 males is about the same as the proportion of anorexics who are not female. Yet we discuss the gender, race, and class components of anorexia, but not the role of the same factors in producing epidemics among the powerful.

The reasons are buried deep in the culture, so invisible that only by revers- 13 ing our assumptions can we reveal them.

Suppose, for instance, that young black males—or any other men of 14 color—had carried out the slaughter in Colorado. Would the media reports be so willing to describe the murderers as "our children"? Would there be so little discussion about the boys' race? Would experts be calling the motive a mystery, or condemning the high school cliques for making those young men feel like "outsiders"? Would there be the same empathy for parents who gave the murderers luxurious homes, expensive cars, even rescued them from brushes with the law? Would there be as much attention to generalized causes, such as the dangers of violent video games and recipes for bombs on the Internet?

As for the victims, if racial identities had been reversed, would racism remain 15 so little discussed? In fact, the killers themselves said they were targeting blacks and athletes. They used a racial epithet, shot a black male student in the head, and then laughed over the fact that they could see his brain. What if that had been reversed?

What if these two young murderers, who were called "fags" by some of the 16 jocks at Columbine High School, actually had been gay? Would they have got the same sympathy for being gay-baited? What if they had been lovers? Would we hear as little about their sexuality as we now do, even though only their own homophobia could have given the word "fag" such power to humiliate them?

Take one more leap of the imagination: suppose these killings had been 17 planned and executed by young women—of any race, sexuality, or class. Would the media still be so disinterested in the role played by gender-conditioning? Would journalists assume that female murderers had suffered from being shut out of access to power in high school, so much so that they were pushed beyond their limits? What if dozens, even hundreds of young women around the country had made imitative threats—as young men have done—expressing admiration for a well-planned massacre and promising to do the same? Would we be discussing their youth more than their gender, as is the case so far with these male killers?

I think we begin to see that our national self-examination is ignoring some- 18 thing fundamental, precisely because it's like the air we breathe: the white male factor, the middle-class and heterosexual one, and the promise of superiority it carries. Yet this denial is self-defeating—to say the least. We will never reduce the number of violent Americans, from bullies to killers, without challenging the assumptions on which masculinity is based: that males are superior to females, that they must find a place in a male hierarchy, and that the ability to dominate someone is so important that even a mere insult can justify lethal revenge. There are plenty of studies to support this view. As Dr. James Gilligan concluded in *Violence: Reflections on a National Epidemic,* "If humanity is to evolve beyond the propensity toward violence . . . then it can only do so by recognizing the extent to which the patriarchal code of honor and shame generates and obligates male violence."

19 I think the way out can only be found through a deeper reversal: just as we as a society have begun to raise our daughters more like our sons—more like whole people—we must begin to raise our sons more like our daughters—that is, to value empathy as well as hierarchy; to measure success by other people's welfare as well as their own.

20 But first, we have to admit and name the truth about supremacy crimes.

Steinem, Gloria. "Supremacy Crimes." *Ms.* August/September 1999. Reprinted by permission of the author.

QUESTIONS FOR READING

1. What kinds of crimes is Steinem examining? What kinds of crimes is she excluding from her discussion?
2. What messages, according to Steinem, is our culture sending to white, non-poor males?
3. How does Elliott Leyton explain these killers' behavior?
4. What is the primary reason we have not examined serial and random killings correctly, in the author's view? What is keeping us from seeing what we need to see?
5. What do we need to do to reduce "the number of violent Americans, from bullies to killers"?

QUESTIONS FOR REASONING AND ANALYSIS

6. What is Steinem's claim? Where does she state it?
7. What is her primary type of evidence?
8. How does Steinem qualify her claim and thereby anticipate and answer counterarguments? In what paragraphs does she present qualifiers and counterarguments to possible rebuttals?
9. How does the author seek to get her readers to understand that we are not thinking soundly about the mass killings at Columbine High School? Is her strategy an effective one? Why or why not?

QUESTIONS FOR REFLECTION AND WRITING

10. Steinem concludes by writing that we must first "name the truth" about supremacy violence before we can begin to address the problem. Does this make sense to you? How can this be good advice for coping with most problems? Think of other kinds of problems that this approach might help solve.
11. Do you agree with Steinem's analysis of the causes of serial and random killings? If yes, how would you add to her argument? If no, how would you refute her argument?

FEMINISM'S LEGACY SEES COLLEGE WOMEN EMBRACING MORE DIVERSE SEXUALITY

SEAN G. MASSEY, MEI-HSIU CHEN, AND SARAH YOUNG

Sean G. Massey is an associate professor of women, gender, and sexuality studies at Binghamton University. At Binghamton, he conducts research on anti-LGBTQIA+ prejudice and racial bias in education and law enforcement. Mei-Hsiu Chen is Director of Statistical Consulting Services and lecturer in the Department of Mathematical Sciences at Binghamton. Sarah Young is the BSW program director and assistant professor of social work at Binghamton, where she conducts research on LGBTQIA+ youth and safe school policies. This article was published by *Conversation* magazine on April 28, 2021.

PREREADING QUESTIONS Why do you think it's important for all students to feel safe at their schools?

Most adults identify themselves as heterosexual, meaning they report being attracted to, and engaging in sex with, only members of the other sex. However, women ages 18 to 29 are increasingly rejecting exclusive heterosexuality and describing their sexual orientation in other ways. These changes in women's sexuality are not mirrored by their male peers. 1

Percentage of men's and women's attraction to each sex over time.

Year	2011	2012	2013*	2014	2015	2016	2017	2018	2019
Other Sex Only									
Men	84.60	83.70		86.80	88.60	840	85.30	81.40	85.70
Women	76.90	81.40		68.20	68.70	71.20	67.30	62.10	64.90
Other Sex Mostly									
Men	8.70	7.90		6.40	5.40	8.80	6.50	7.40	7.20
Women	15.60	10.80		22.40	22.60	16.40	22.30	20.50	17.00
Other Sex Somewhat More									
Men	0.00	1.40		1.30	0.30	0.80	1.20	0.00	2.5
Women	2.00	2.10		2.66	2.10	3.60	2.50	5.50	5.10
Both Sexes									
Men	1.00	1.00		1.90	0.80	2.10	2.40	4.10	2.10
Women	3.40	3.90		3.90	5.10	5.80	4.70	9.90	9.80
Same Sex Somewhat More									
Men	0.0	1.0		0.6	0.5	0.0	0.0	1.2	0.0
Women	0.7	0.7		0.6	0.2	0.7	1.4	0.3	0.8
Same Sex Mostly									
Men	2.90	1.20		1.30	2.10	1.30	0.6	2.50	1.70
Women	0.00	0.20		1.30	1.10	1.50	0.70	0.70	1.10
Same Sex Only									
Men	2.90	3.80		1.60	2.30	2.90	4.10	3.30	0.80
Women	1.40	1.00		0.90	0.20	0.70	1.10	1.00	1.30

*No data provided for 2013

Source: https://theconversation.com/feminisms-legacy-sees-college-women-embracing-more-diverse-sexuality-159023

2 That's the primary finding in our most recent report on nine years of surveys at the Binghamton Human Sexualities Research Lab, just published in "Sexuality in Emerging Adulthood." Together with our Binghamton University colleagues Richard E. Mattson, Melissa Hardesty, Ann Merriwether and Maggie M. Parker, we conclude that changes in young adults' sexual orientation are not just as a result of increased social acceptance of LGBT people—but also are related to feminism and the women's movement.

LGBT PROGRESS

3 These findings align with recent polling by the Gallup Organization, which found that American adults are increasingly identifying as lesbian, gay, bisexual, transgender or more than one of those. The Gallup report attributed these changes to increasing public awareness and acceptance of people who identify as LGBT, as well as the influence of a 2015 U.S. Supreme Court case legalizing same-sex marriage nationwide. Another potential factor was proposed federal legislation banning discrimination on the basis of gender identity or sexual orientation.

Year	2011	2012	2013*	2014	2015	2016	2017	2018	2019
Other Sex Only									
Men	0.885	0.901		0.920	0.925	0.903	0.871	0.880	0.911
Women	0.912	0.923		0.850	0.862	0.858	0.856	0.833	0.824
Other Sex Mostly									
Men	0.038	0.019		0.019	0.018	0.034	0.047	0.017	0.038
Women	0.054	0.041		0.090	0.098	0.080	0.090	0.096	0.085
Other Sex Somewhat More									
Men	0.010	0.010		0.003	0.003	0.008	0.018	0.008	0.004
Women	0.000	0.007		0.019	0.013	0.022	0.011	0.014	0.013
Both Sexes									
Men	0.000	0.014		0.013	0.005	0.013	0.018	0.025	0.017
Women	0.020	0.009		0.017	0.017	0.022	0.014	0.034	0.051
Same Sex Somewhat More									
Men	0.010	0.002		0.006	0.000	0.000	0.000	0.008	0.004
Women	0.000	0.002		0.004	0.002	0.000	0.011	0.007	0.005
Same Sex Mostly									
Men	0.010	0.005		0.013	0.018	0.017	0.000	0.017	0.008
Women	0.000	0.003		0.007	0.002	0.007	0.004	0.007	0.003
Same Sex Only									
Men	0.048	0.048		0.026	0.031	0.025	0.047	0.045	0.017
Women	0.014	0.015		0.013	0.006	0.011	0.014	0.010	0.019

*No data provided for 2013

Source: https://theconversation.com/feminisms-legacy-sees-college-women-embracing-more-diverse-sexuality-159023

But our study goes beyond those poll results, showing that young American adults are shifting away from heterosexuality not just in how they identify themselves when asked about their identities, but also how they describe whom they are attracted to and with whom they have sex. That indicates something more is happening than an increasing willingness to "come out" and identify as LGBT. 4

The fact that these differences are larger among women than men indicates, we believe, that feminism and the women's movement have, in fact, begun to change female sex and gender roles. 5

COMPULSORY HETEROSEXUALITY

In the early 1980s, lesbian feminist Adrienne Rich argued that what she called "compulsory heterosexuality" was the primary cause of gender inequality. She said that because social pressures and threats of violence—as well as actual violence—force heterosexuality on women, that made women dependent on and subservient to men in all areas of life, including gender roles and sexual expression. 6

Our research indicates that one outcome of more than a century of feminist activism and progress may be women's increasing resistance to compulsory heterosexuality and its consequences. As a result, more women under 30 are moving away from exclusive heterosexuality than men in the same age group. 7

Year	2011	2012	2013*	2014	2015	2016	2017	2018	2019
Neither Agree Nor Disagree									
Men	0.167	0.155		0.192	0.157	0.176	0.146	0.172	0.166
Women	0.19	0.19		0.169	0.188	0.183	0.152	0.209	0.182
Somewhat Agree									
Men	0.059	0.076		0.077	0.074	0.129	0.128	0.076	0.094
Women	0.156	0.184		0.188	0.184	0.144	0.215	0.133	0.11
Somewhat Disagree									
Men	0.324	0.261		0.296	0.314	0.313	0.305	0.277	0.328
Women	0.259	0.205		0.276	0.228	0.247	0.263	0.252	0.227
Totally Agree									
Men	0.088	0.116		0.071	0.082	0.073	0.122	0.109	0.072
Women	0.238	0.216		0.198	0.255	0.266	0.17	0.122	0.184
Totally Disagree									
Men	0.363	0.392		0.364	0.372	0.309	0.299	0.366	0.34
Women	0.156	0.205		0.169	0.144	0.16	0.2	0.284	0.297

*No data provided for 2013

Source: https://theconversation.com/feminisms-legacy-sees-college-women-embracing-more-diverse-sexuality-159023

In a related development, we found that women in this age group are also reporting more open attitudes toward sex than previous generations of women. They are separating sex from traditional love relationships, describing themselves 8 as enjoying casual sex with different partners and more likely to have sex with a person before being sure the relationship would become serious or long term. These attitudes are more akin to those of their male peers.

9 The shift is more pronounced among women who are moving away from exclusive heterosexuality, and less obvious among women who report they are exclusively heterosexual.

THERE'S MUCH MORE TO LEARN

10 We still have a lot of questions about these trends. We wonder how they affect the ways that these young adults engage in sex and relationships. We also don't know how women who identify themselves as not exclusively heterosexual negotiate and navigate sexual relationships with men—or whether these trends will continue as they age.

Year	2011	2012	2013*	2014	2015	2016	2017	2018	2019
Neither Agree Nor Disagree									
Men	0.218	0.176		0.198	0.210	0.177	0.177	0.143	0.226
Women	0.095	0.154		0.200	0.150	0.133	0.197a	0.219	0.188
Somewhat Agree									
Men	0.208	0.223		0.218	0.242	0.220	0.274	0.235	0.226
Women	0.116	0.117		0.143	0.139	0.129	0.160	0.133	0.148
Somewhat Disagree									
Men	0.129	0.144		0.164	0.122	0.194	0.159	0.168	0.153
Women	0.272	0.260		0.245	0.256	0.262	0.208	0.198	0.218
Totally Agree									
Men	0.287	0.347		0.302	0.301	0.297	0.207	0.319	0.289
Women	0.088	0.084		0.129	0.099	0.141	0.141	0.241	0.210
Totally Disagree									
Men	0.158	0.111		0.117	0.125	0.112	0.183	0.134	0.106
Women	0.429	0.385		0.283	0.355	0.335	0.294	0.209	0.237

*No data provided for 2013

Source: https://theconversation.com/feminisms-legacy-sees-college-women-embracing-more-diverse-sexuality-159023

11 We are also interested in why men in this age group are less likely than women to reject exclusive heterosexuality—but are more likely to report exclusive homosexuality. And we'd like to know whether, or at what point, those who are not exclusively heterosexual might come out to family and friends—and if they deal with things like anti-LGBT prejudice.

12 As human sexuality becomes increasingly diverse, it remains unclear whether the political and social landscape will affirm these changes or threaten those who are expressing that diversity. We are hopeful that the continued success of the LGBT and feminist movements will push society toward an affirming future.

Massey, Sean G., Mei-Hsiu Chen, and Sarah Young. "Feminism's Legacy Sees College Women Embracing More Diverse Sexuality." *Conversation*, 28 Apr. 2021. Used with permission.

QUESTIONS FOR READING

1. According to the authors, what has happened in the past nine years at Binghamton University that is notable and the reason they wrote this article?
2. Massey, Chen, and Young note that their research findings align with results of polling conducted by the Gallup Organization. What were those results?
3. According to the authors, what are the reasons college-age people who identify as women are changing how they respond to questions about sex, sexuality, and gender identification?
4. The authors mention a concept known as "compulsory heterosexuality." What is that, and why do they mention it in the article?

QUESTIONS FOR REASONING AND ANALYSIS

5. This article seems like a report on research the authors conducted at their institution. Yet if analyzed closely enough, one might tease out an argument. What is that argument?
6. How do Massey, Chen, and Young develop their argument?
7. Evaluate each section of this article. What are its strengths and weaknesses? What, if anything, would you do to improve the argument?

QUESTIONS FOR REFLECTION AND WRITING

8. Are you convinced by the authors' argument? Why or why not?
9. Why do you think some Americans act violently toward people who identify as nonbinary, trans, or LGBTQIA+?
10. Why do you think the data reported by people who identify as male did not change as much as the data reported by people who identify as female?

THE TRANS HISTORY YOU WEREN'T TAUGHT IN SCHOOLS

CATHERINE ARMSTRONG

Catherine Armstrong is the Director of People and Culture and a lecturer in Modern History at Loughborough University in the UK. At Loughborough, she teaches courses in American history and conducts research on the histories of transgender people in the East Midlands in England. She completed her PhD at the University of Warwick and has held positions at Oxford Brookes University and Manchester Metropolitan University. She became a fellow of the Royal Historical Society in 2013 and has published in scholarly journals like *Counseling Psychology Review, Atlantic Studies,* and *Slavery and Abolition.* In 2020, she published her book *American Slavery, American Imperialism US Perceptions of Global Servitude, 1870–1914* with Cambridge University Press. This article was published by *Yes!* magazine on June 7, 2021.

PREREADING QUESTIONS **Were you taught anything about transgender people in your K-12 experience? What did you learn? What do you wish you had learned?**

1 Nonbinary and trans people have always been here, not least in every recorded society from the ancient world onwards. Why is it then that they're often absent from the tales and lists of historical figures we hear about? The answer lies, in part, with how history is recorded and who records it.

2 People who belong to groups that fear being ostracized and persecuted often only reveal their true selves to a few people. As a result, the visibility of LGBT+ people, even during moments in history when they have faced hostility, is often limited. Coupled with that is a dearth of historical records because authors of these historical accounts were often prejudiced and did not want to record the experiences of those considered shameful under the values of their time.

3 Historians working on the queer past need to understand why LGBT+ people, along with members of other marginalized groups, don't appear as often in recorded history compared with those outside of these communities. Fortunately, historians are now beginning to look around more carefully to find these important stories.

GENDER PRESENTATION IN THE 18TH AND 19TH CENTURIES

4 Our understanding of being transgender has evolved considerably in the past few decades. Transgender experiences aren't necessarily limited to people who undergo medical procedures to alter their body; they also include people who present themselves as different from the gender they were assigned at birth.

5 Much of society now appreciates that the gender to which a person is assigned at birth might be entirely different from their gender identity, which is different again to their gender expression. On one level, a person's gender is defined by how they identify, that is, how they feel internally: as a woman, or a man, as neither, or as anything in between on the gender spectrum. But what is also important is your gender expression, that is, the deliberate and accidental signals you give to others about your gender through aspects such as what you wear and how you cut your hair.

6 Although the terminology we use to describe gender would have been alien in the 18th and early 19th centuries, in those eras, many people would have understood these concepts. Some women who were sexually and romantically attracted to other women, then as now, presented as more masculine, both for personal gratification and sometimes to be accepted by society.

7 Anne Lister (or "Gentleman Jack"—the subject of a recent TV series starring Suranne Jones) is a good example. Under 19th century ideas of gender, she would have been perceived by others as masculine, and not until 1988 did the biographer Helena Whitbread decode her diaries and discover the true extent of her lesbian relationships and life.

8 Other women presented themselves as men for reasons of career ambition, because they wished to make life choices denied to the half of the population assigned female at birth. In the American Civil War, Franklin Thompson and Harry

Buford were widely praised soldiers who fought for and spied for the Confederate states. Both were women passing as men, or in the phrase of historian Matthew Teorey who has worked on their cases, women who "unsexed" themselves.

An earlier example of gender fluidity is the 18th century case of the Chevalier 9
D'Eon, who worked for French King Louis XV as a spy in London before later claiming political exile in England. The Chevalier became a minor society celebrity and presented as a man and a woman at various points in their life, until aged about 50 they began to live permanently as a woman.

BEING TRANSGENDER IN A GLOBAL CONTEXT

It is important to understand that the lives of LGBT+ people in the past were 10
experienced differently in cultures outside Europe. The notion of a third gender or "Mahu" is part of Polynesian culture. It can mean a gender between male and female, or gender fluid. In Hawai'i and Tahiti, Mahu people were highly respected in native culture as keepers of oral traditions and historical knowledge. They often taught the hula dance, famous to the region, which has a leisure function but also an important spiritual meaning. Mahu people exist not only in the past but are an important part of queer culture in Hawaii today.

Other native cultures also display a deep respect for gender diversity. 11
The Navajo tribe from the southwest United States have a gender category called Nadleeh, which can refer to transgender people who have transitioned in one direction along the gender binary (having been assigned male at birth, and now identifying as female, or assigned female at birth and now identifying as male), gender-fluid people and those whose gender presentation is more masculine or feminine than their gender identity suggests. Nadleehi in Navajo culture have a spiritual function as well as being respected tribal members in their own right.

Compared to Western society, this difference in perception was noted by 12
anthropologists as early as the 1920s. Author William Willard Hill was surprised that Navajo society considered a transgender person "very fortunate," unlike in his own culture in the U.S., for which gender fluidity caused anxiety in mainstream society. A timely reminder that it's always important to look outside one's own culture to learn about inclusion and diversity. You might be surprised by what you discover.

Armstrong, Catherine. "The Trans History You Weren't Taught in Schools." *Yes!*, 7 Jun. 2021. Used with permission.

QUESTIONS FOR READING

1. According to Armstrong, what has determined whether trans and nonbinary people have been recorded in history?
2. What are some examples of historical figures who were trans or nonbinary?
3. What are the terms that other cultures use to describe trans or nonbinary people?
4. How have other cultures treated trans or nonbinary people?

QUESTIONS FOR REASONING AND ANALYSIS

5. What is Armstrong's argument?
6. How does the author organize this article to support her argument? How does she structure her reasoning? How does she use and explain her examples?
7. Evaluate each section of Armstrong's article. What are its strengths and weaknesses? What, if anything, would you do to improve her argument?

QUESTIONS FOR REFLECTION AND WRITING

8. Are you convinced by Armstrong's argument? Why or why not?
9. Why do you think other cultures, such as the Polynesian culture, have been more accepting of trans and nonbinary people than European and American cultures?
10. Why do you think it's important for history to be presented in an honest and factual manner? What happens when people or events are omitted from historical accounts?

Courtesy of Braden Hill

Courtesy of Stevie Lane

NO, YOU CAN'T IDENTIFY AS "TRANSRACIAL." BUT YOU CAN AFFIRM YOUR GENDER

BRADEN HILL AND STEVIE LANE

Professor Braden Hill conducts research on Aboriginal, Indigenous, and LGBTQIA+ issues at Edith Cowan University in Australia. He is a Nyungar (Wardandi) man and serves as Edith Cowan University's Pro-Vice-Chancellor and Head of Kurongkurl Katitjin, the institution's Centre for Indigenous Australian Education and Research. Stevie Lane serves as Edith Cowan University's Equity Projects Officer, and they are an activist in the LGBTQIA+ community. They have published in written and multimodal formats including *Out in Perth* and *The Queer AV.* This article was published by *Conversation* magazine on July 1, 2021.

PREREADING QUESTIONS How do you think trans or nonbinary people or members of the LGBTQIA+ community have been affected by the discrimination and violence committed against them?

1 Earlier this week, online influencer Oli London responded to criticism after saying they identify as Korean. Having undergone surgeries to change their appearance, they equated being "transracial" with the experiences of transgender people who affirm their gender.

2 The same reasoning behind London's Korean identity (they have asked to be called Jimin after a K-Pop star) can be compared to that of Rachel Dolezal, a white woman who identifies as Black and made headlines in 2015. Debates about "transracialism" followed. Unfortunately, it seems we haven't learned much in this space.

3 At their core, London's words and actions are a prime example of racism, cultural appropriation, and transphobia, enacted from a perspective of considerable privilege. Trans and gender diverse experiences don't equate with someone

deciding to change their appearance to be part of a group whose experiences, community and struggles they can't fully understand.

RACE AND GENDER ARE NOT BUILT THE SAME

Gender is our internal sense of self, whether that be man, woman, neither or both. Most people have an idea about their gender at two to three years old—this may not align with the sex assigned to them at birth. 4

Unlike gender, race presents as categorized (often physical) traits that are socially constructed and understood. You can't inherit your gender, this is internal and something individual to you—but you do inherit the social construct of race. There is also much more to one's racial identity than physical appearance—it's also about culture, community, connection and even trauma. 5

While multicultural communities and LGBTQ+ experiences of discrimination are sometimes compared, it is important to understand these experiences are different and complex. This is particularly the case, for example, in considering trans people of color and their experiences of both racism and transphobia. 6

People who face discrimination based on their race or cultural background can usually go home to members of their family who understand them. This is often not the case for trans and gender diverse people. 7

Race and gender have very different histories, understandings, experiences, and implications in the face of discrimination. The very idea of being able to transition to a difference race discredits trans and gender diverse people's experiences of gender affirmation. It also undermines the importance of cultural connections for many communities. 8

PICKING AND CHOOSING

London, who is non-binary and uses they/them pronouns, has actively chosen a "transracial" identity. But trans and gender diverse people's decision to transition (whether that be social, medical and/or legal) is almost always involuntary and out of necessity to live their lives authentically. 9

Almost 50% of trans young people in Australia have attempted suicide at least once in their lives. Trans and gender diverse young people experience higher levels of psychological distress than their cisgender peers. 10

This is not because there is anything inherently wrong with trans people, but because of how trans people are treated by others. Conflating racial identity with gender identity implies that being trans is a choice, and therefore so is race. The reality is that transitioning as a trans person is a difficult and taxing process, one that can be dangerous but also lifesaving and celebrated. 11

It is racist to think someone can pick and choose parts of a race or culture they like, then distance themselves from that culture when it suits them. They avoid the burden of discrimination while reaping the rewards of white privilege, taking the necessary resources and voices from the communities who need it. 12

There is a difference between affirming your gender as a trans person, which doesn't harm anyone else, and choosing to live and appropriate another culture. 13

What's more, the word "transracial" is already in use, usually referring to adoption practices in which white parents adopt children of color. So it's misleading when used to talk about someone changing their appearance. 14

15 Gender understandings can also be different based on their cultural context.

16 The gender binary we've come to think of as usual—male and female—has previously been enforced upon people, cultures and countries through colonization. Rigid understandings of gender are imposed upon cultures where gender fluidity was previously more accepted.

17 Trans and gender diverse experiences have existed in many Indigenous cultures around the world for thousands of years, including in Australia.

AMPLIFYING DIVERSITY

18 It's important for us to acknowledge that talking about "transracial" identities as something you can be for or against only further marginalizes and harms people of color and trans and gender diverse people. This marginalization is compounded for trans people of color.

19 Instead of the pursuit of fame and followers, we need to prioritize amplifying the experiences of diverse peoples in ways that not only focus on discrimination and abuse, but also celebrate people being their authentic selves.

Hill, Braden, and Stevie Lane. "No, You Can't Identify as 'Transracial'. But You Can Affirm Your Gender." *Conversation*, 1 Jul. 2021. Used with permission.

QUESTIONS FOR READING

1. According to Hill and Lane, why shouldn't Oli London identify as "transracial"?
2. How do the authors define gender? How do they define race?
3. What alarming statistic do the authors use to argue that Australian trans and gender diverse young people experience more psychological distress?
4. Hill and Lane use the term "colonization" in their article. What do they mean by colonization, and why do they use this term?

QUESTIONS FOR REASONING AND ANALYSIS

5. What is Hill and Lane's primary argument?
6. What are some secondary arguments the authors present in their article?
7. How do Hill and Lane mix inferences and judgments to support their arguments?

QUESTIONS FOR REFLECTION AND WRITING

8. Are you persuaded by Hill and Lane's article? Why or why not?
9. Why do you think Oli London wanted to identify as transracial?
10. Research shows that the LGBTQIA+ community struggles more with mental health issues, suicidal ideation, and suicide than members of the CisHet community (people who identify with the gender they were assigned at birth and who choose opposite sex romantic partnerships). Do some research on the efforts your college has taken to address this issue. What has your college done? What is it working on, and what does it plan to accomplish? What else might your institution do to address student well-being?

THE SECRET TO EFFICIENT TEAMWORK IS RIDICULOUSLY SIMPLE

ERIN BRODWIN

Erin Brodwin is the science editor for *Business Insider* and has published in other magazines, such as *Scientific American, Popular Science, Newsweek,* and *Psychology Today.* She received a bachelor's from the University of California, San Diego, and a master's degree from the City University of New York's Graduate School of Journalism. This article was published in *Business Insider* on January 23, 2015.

PREREADING QUESTIONS Why do you think women are paid less than men? Why do you think women do not advance as far as men in the workplace?

Want to avoid another boring, unproductive meeting? 1

Invite more Women. 2

Two new studies from scientists at MIT, Carnegie Mellon, and Union College 3
suggest the most efficient groups—the ones who are the best at collaborating, analyzing problems, and solving them the fastest and most effectively—weren't comprised simply of the smartest people.

Instead, they had just three things in common, one of which was simply that 4
they had more women.

You might be thinking to yourself, well of course the more *diverse* teams did 5
better; the greater the range of opinions and ideas, the better, right?

Not quite. The groups in the study didn't get smarter when they simply 6
included an even number of women and men. It was even more specific than that: **The more women a team had, the better they performed.**

This result makes a little more sense in light of another part of the study 7
which looked at how well the members of a team could read the emotions of their fellow teammates. Women did consistently better on this test, which involved looking at images of people's faces in which only their eye regions were showing and identifying what complex emotion they were feeling, from shame to curiosity.

Here's a female example from the emotion-reading test: The word choices 8
were reflective, aghast, irritated, and impatient. Which emotion do you think she's feeling?

Reflective was the correct choice. 9

In this test and others designed to measure how well a person can read and 10
interpret others' feelings, women consistently score higher than men—a concept known as "emotional intelligence" and first coined by psychologist Daniel Goleman in 1995.

In another large study from this year of more than 4,600 people, for exam- 11
ple, women scored higher in almost all aspects of emotional intelligence (labeled EIQ in this chart for shorthand), including understanding, facilitating, and managing emotions, than their male counterparts.

	MALES	FEMALES
Perception	7.40 (1.8)	8.03 (1.7)
Understanding	6.78 (1.6)	7.43 (1.6)
Facilitation	6.55 (1.6)	7.02 (1.5)
Management	5.88 (1.4)	6.57 (1.4)
TIE Total	26.62 (5.2)	29.06 (5.0)

Women outperformed men in every subscale of the TIE, and consequently in the total score.
"TIE: An Ability Test of Emotional Intelligence," PLOS One.

12 These results held steady even when teams weren't physically together but instead worked exclusively online. Even without being able to see their fellow team-members' faces, women performed consistently better than men at gauging other people's emotions.

13 How do they do this? It's called *reading between the lines.*

14 Oh yeah. Recent research has suggested that when it comes to picking out the emotional undercurrents of emails and texts, the vast majority of us are usually way off base (Does an extra exclamation mark mean she's being sarcastic, or extra enthusiastic?!).

15 But those of us who can accurately detect the hidden emotions in the written word are also, perhaps, the ones who are better at working together in groups. And more often than not, those people tend to be female.

16 This finding squares with other research on women in professional leadership roles. One recent report found, for example, that companies with women on their boards had far higher average returns on equity than those without women on their boards; another concluded that companies led by female CEOs outperform companies led by male CEOs by nearly 50%.

Brodwin, Erin. "The Secret to Efficient Teamwork Is Ridiculously Simple." *Business Insider*, 23 Jan. 2015. Copyright ©2015 Business Insider. Used with permission.

QUESTIONS FOR READING

1. What is Brodwin's subject? (Women in the workplace is not sufficiently precise as an answer.)
2. What does new research show about women and their impact on teams and efficiency in the workplace?
3. According to psychologists, what are the reasons behind the differences between women and men who work in teams?

QUESTIONS FOR REASONING AND ANALYSIS

4. What is Brodwin's claim?
5. What is her primary support? (Add a "because" clause to her claim to find her grounds.)
6. Review the author's comments about women in the workplace. What, in Brodwin's view, is their reason for performing differently than men? Does the author provide evidence for this warrant? Is support needed?

QUESTIONS FOR REFLECTION AND WRITING

7. Reflect on the author's position regarding women in the workplace. Do you believe Brodwin's claim? Do you agree with her conclusion?
8. Brodwin asserts that women simply *read between the lines* more effectively than do men. If this is the case, how might businesses and non-profit organizations apply this skill to increase efficiency? And how might these organizations "train up" men who may be lagging in emotional IQ, or EIQ?
9. How can professional organizations increase their number of female employees?

CREDITS

1. https://news.gallup.com/poll/1651/gay-lesbian-rights.aspx
2. https://news.gallup.com/poll/1651/gay-lesbian-rights.aspx

CHAPTER 19

Laws and Rights: Issues of Gun Safety and Policing

John Moore/Getty Images

READ: What do you notice about the children and adults who were shot and killed at Sandy Hook Elementary School in 2012?

REASON: Why do you think it took ten years for the federal government to pass consequential legislation that addresses mass shootings like the one that occurred at Sandy Hook?

WRITE: After the mass shooting in Uvalde, Texas, where nineteen students and three adults were killed, President Biden signed the bipartisan "Protecting Our Kids" Act. Do some quick research on this law to find out more, and then write a short response to these questions: Does the law go far enough? Why or why not? What would you change, and why would you change it?

Gun safety and policing issues in the United States are two of the most challenging laws and rights problems facing the country. Since 2012, there have been over 125 mass shootings in the United States. Most data tracking organizations and publications define mass shootings as having four or more people shot in one incident. Do some quick math, and you will discover the appalling numbers behind these terrible tragedies. Some of these shootings have even occurred in schools. During one of the most horrendous mass school shootings in U.S. history, twenty-eight people, including children between ages six and seven, were shot and killed at Sandy Hook Elementary School in Newtown, Connecticut, in 2012.

The lack of gun safety doesn't just affect shooting victims. According to a 2021 Pew Research Center article, "In 2020, 54% of all gun-related deaths in the U.S. were suicides (24,292)."[1] Yet state and federal legislators usually seem reluctant to increase gun safety. Regardless of how you feel about Second Amendment rights, it's reasonable to conclude that we all want America to be as safe as possible. The challenge lies in how we get there. Two of the articles in this chapter will help you think about and reflect on this issue, while the other three discuss policing issues.

Two recent events involving police brutality were flash points that sparked unified public outrage. The 2014 fatal shooting of Michael Brown in Ferguson, Missouri, and the death of Freddie Gray in Baltimore, Maryland, in 2015 drew attention to the disproportionate fatalities suffered by Black people at the hands of police. In the summer of 2020, two fatalities caused by law enforcement sparked more protests, which began as local responses and grew into nationwide demonstrations against police brutality. Protestors rallied to draw attention to Breonna Taylor's fatal shooting by police officers in Louisville, Kentucky, and George Floyd's murder by officer Derek Chauvin in Minneapolis, Minnesota. The two common threads to the deaths from 2014, 2015, and 2020 are that the victims were Black, and they were all killed by police. How did we get here, and how do we address police brutality, especially when it seems focused on people of color? In 2020, the Black Lives Matter movement cohered to raise awareness of and address these issues. But today, the country still struggles with finding common ground and moving forward in positive ways.

As of April 18, 2022, the *Washington Post*'s "Fatal Force" database had recorded 1,019 cases of fatal shootings in the United States by police in the past twelve months. Most of the people shot and killed by police were young Black men.[2] Why is this? And what can we do to address police brutality when police unions make it difficult to hold bad cops accountable? This chapter raises these and other tough questions. Reflect on the following as a guide to your study of the current debates on gun safety and policing issues.

PREREADING QUESTIONS

1. What kinds of restrictions–if any–on firearms should be enacted to protect public safety while protecting Second Amendment rights?
2. Why do you think so many people own so many guns in America? Should there be a limit on the number of firearms one can buy and sell in a year? Should there be a limit on the types of firearms one can buy and sell?
3. Should local municipalities and states determine police conduct and how police are trained, or should police unions control how police act and prepare for their jobs?

4. Should police who disregard their training and department regulations be held responsible for their actions? If so, how long should violations be kept in officers' personnel records?
5. What are some ways police departments can build trust among communities who have been traumatized by the long history of police brutality?
6. If data show that a hands-off approach to policing decreases crime, why do you think more police departments haven't adopted this model?

THREE MILLION MORE GUNS: THE SPRING 2020 SPIKE IN FIREARM SALES

PHILLIP LEVINE AND ROBIN MCKNIGHT

Phillip Levine is a nonresident fellow at the Brookings Institute and the A. Barton Hepburn and Katherine Coman Professor of Economics at Wellesley College. At Wellesley, Levine teaches courses in statistical and econometric methods. Levine is widely published in scholarly and mass media outlets, and his book *Mismatch: The New Economics of Financial Aid and College Access* was published in 2021.

Robin McKnight is a professor of economics at Wellesley College and teaches courses in probability and statistics and intermediate microeconomics as well as courses in health economics. This article was published by the Brookings Institute on Monday, July 13, 2020.

PREREADING QUESTIONS Does the idea of three million more guns in America make you feel more or less safe?

1 When Americans are concerned about their personal security, they buy firearms. Such concerns have been rampant since March, initially due to the onset of the COVID-19 pandemic and then the social unrest in June that followed George Floyd's killing. Our estimates indicate that almost three million more firearms have been sold since March than would have ordinarily been sold during these months. Half of that increase occurred in June alone. This pattern highlights an important potential consequence that may result from this tumultuous period: more firearms in the hands of private citizens.

SPIKES IN GUN SALES OVER A DECADE

2 Past spikes in firearms sales have occurred when individuals worried about possible restrictions (see figure below). Following President Obama's calls to impose modest restrictions on firearm sales in response to the Sandy Hook elementary school shooting and the San Bernardino terrorist attack, sales jumped by 3 million and 1.6 million, respectively, beyond the expected level over the few months of elevated sales. Protests demanding gun control legislation led by students in Parkland, Florida, the site of the most recent high-profile school shooting, led to another spike in sales of 700,000.

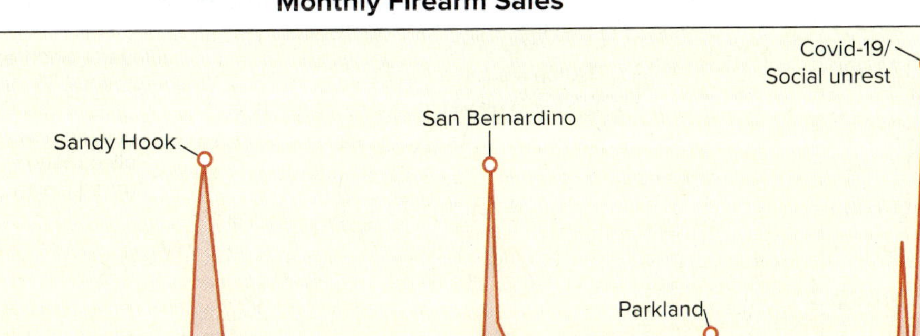

The data presented here are from background checks conducted by the FBI before a firearm is sold by a licensed dealer. These data do not perfectly measure firearm sales, but they are highly correlated with sales and are commonly used by researchers. In past work, we have used these data to show that the spike in firearm sales following the Sandy Hook school shooting led to a spike in accidental firearm deaths, particularly among children. 3

The 2020 spike, however, is less about concerns regarding access to firearms, than personal safety. In March, concerns about personal safety arose from both a deadly new virus and an economy in free fall. By June, concerns about the virus and the economy remained, and were compounded by new evidence of racial injustice in policing, widespread protests, and discussions of defunding the police. 4

EMERGENCY = GUN SALES

Daily data allows us to better identify the sources of fears about personal safety. As the following figure shows, the average daily level of firearm sales in January and February was 92,000. Within that period, daily sales varied within the range of 80,000 to 100,000 per day. 5

On March 13, President Trump issued a proclamation declaring a national emergency concerning the COVID-19 outbreak. Over the next 12 days (including that day), firearm sales surged, jumping to over 120,000 per day, and peaking at 176,000 on March 16. Over 700,000 additional firearms were sold in March. 6

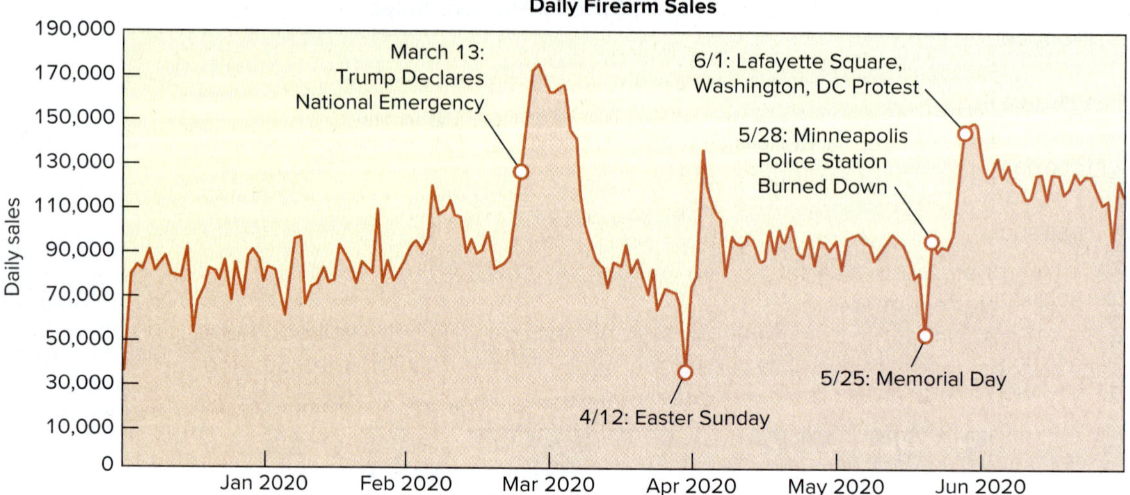

7 The geographic pattern in the additional sales is not correlated with COVID-19 death rates nor with increases in unemployment rates. This suggests that the spike in firearm sales resulted from a general sense of national apprehension, rather than a response to differential deterioration in local conditions. Over the next two months, as the country settled into its new environment and even moved into a period of scheduled re-openings, firearm sales stabilized, if perhaps at a slightly higher level than earlier in the year (seasonal variation is modest during this period of the year).

PROTESTS = GUN SALES

8 Then George Floyd was killed on May 25, which started a chain of events leading to a Minneapolis police station being burned down on May 28. Protests then spread nationwide, including to Lafayette Square in Washington, DC, where the federal government forcibly removed protesters, reportedly using chemical agents and rubber bullets, on June 1. Additional protests, including clashes with police, continued for several days.

9 The onset of these protests started another surge in firearm sales, reaching 150,000 per day on June 2 and June 3. The protests faded but, as public discussions about Black Lives Matter and defunding the police persisted, firearm sales remained elevated throughout the month of June.

10 As a result of these events, firearm sales in June were the highest on record (since data collection began in 1998), with 3.9 million firearms sold. This includes an additional 1.4 million firearms beyond the number that we would normally expect to be sold in June.

THE ROLE OF RACISM

11 Along with the general concern for personal security that these protests may have unleashed, additional data suggests that inherent racial tensions in our society also contributed to the June spike in firearm sales.

To examine this issue, we augment our analysis with data from Google Trends, which indicates the relative frequency with which individuals search for certain terms. Following an approach used in prior research, we track searches for a common racial epithet as a measure of racial animus. 12

The figure below presents daily Google Trends index values for that search term in the United States. Google does not release actual counts of searches, but creates an index, where the day with the highest search totals is recorded as a 100. Other values represent the ratio between that highest day and the search counts on other days (i.e., a day with a value of 50 has half the searches for that term as the highest day). 13

In March, when the pandemic hit and firearm sales initially spiked, there were no substantive changes in search frequency for the racial epithet. Starting in late May and early June, though, those searches jumped, hitting their peak on June 19 (Juneteenth). 14

The increase in firearm sales in June may have had nothing to do with racial animus, though. The protests could have engendered concerns regarding personal security, and therefore greater firearm sales, with no relationship to the simultaneous increase in racial animus. The correlation in the timing of these changes need not imply a causal relationship. 15

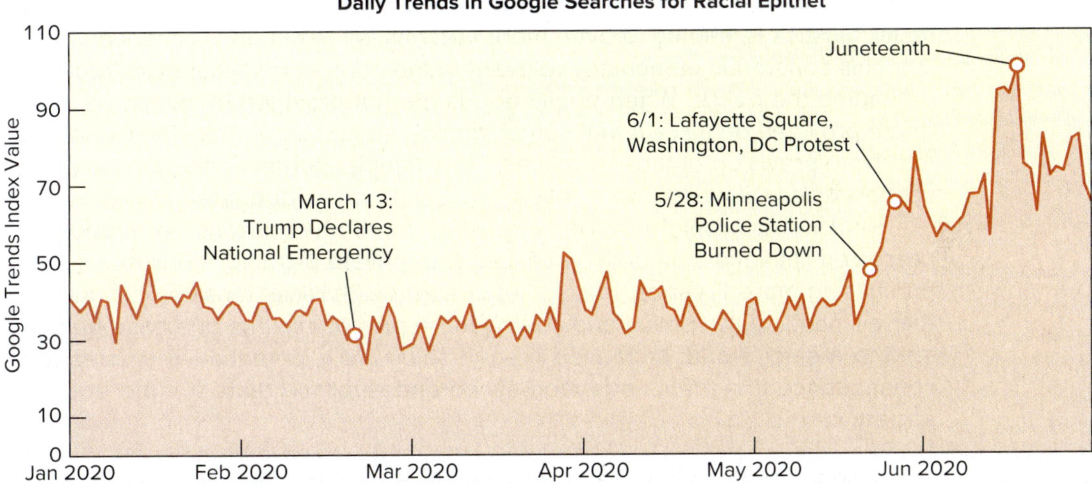

To shed further light on the relationship between gun sales and racial animus, we examined geographic variation in these measures. Specifically, we explored whether the June spike in firearm sales (measured relative to sales in June 2019) was larger in states where racial animus is greater. We measured state-level racial animus using Google Trends data on the relative prevalence of the same search term across the 50 states in 2019. We use the state-specific firearm sales spikes in March (relative to March of 2019) to capture state-level differences in the way that personal security concerns translate into firearm purchases. 16

17 We find that states where individuals are more likely to search for racial epithets experienced larger increases in June firearm sales, even after adjusting for the personal security concerns that likely generated the March spikes in gun sales. This pattern suggests that part of the concern regarding personal security that led to firearm sales increases in June was related to the racial tensions. We do not observe the same relationship between increases in firearm sales and racial animus at the state level in any of the previous spikes in sales.

18 It is unclear who was buying those firearms. Concerns regarding personal security related to racial tensions could lead individuals of any race, including Blacks or whites, to buy firearms. In general, however, whites are far more likely to own firearms than Blacks (49 percent versus 32 percent).

GUN SALES AND UNINTENDED CONSEQUENCES

19 There are more guns than people in the United States (400 million are in circulation for a population of 330 million). In just the first six months of 2020, approximately 19 million firearms have been sold, representing more than one firearm for every 20 Americans.

20 The presence of so many guns complicates discussions of public policy. Injustices committed by the police, and systemic racism in society more broadly need to end. It is concerning that the necessary national discussion regarding racial injustice is leading to even more firearms in the hands of Americans.

21 This concern is particularly relevant in the context of discussions regarding defunding the police. When public goods are not provided by the government, or are provided on a scale that some consider to be inadequate, individuals turn to private provision of these services. For example, parents often turn to private schools when they perceive public education to be inadequate.

22 Similarly, it would not be surprising for some citizens to respond to perceived limitations on police services with private provision. This may include purchasing more firearms. In a society fraught with racial tension, it is not clear that dismantling the police and seeing more private citizens purchase guns will lead to a safer world. Increased firearm sales are a potential—if unintended—consequence that merits attention as we endeavor to create a more equitable society.

Levine, Phillip, and Robin McKnight. "Three Million More Guns: The Spring 2020 Spike in Firearm Sales." Brookings, 13 Jul. 2020. Used with permission.

QUESTIONS FOR READING

1. What events lead to higher gun sales according to Levine and McKnight?
2. Findings from Levine and McKnight's research show that there may be a connection between racism and increased firearm sales. However, they point out that the connection may be correlation rather than causal. What do they mean by this?
3. What is the difference between correlation and causation? Why is this difference important to this article?

4. Despite the qualification for correlation versus causation, what do the authors argue about the connection between racism and the spike in gun sales?
5. Who buys more guns in America?
6. What are some of the unintended consequences of gun purchases?

QUESTIONS FOR REASONING AND ANALYSIS

7. Though the article seems like a presentation of research findings with analysis, the authors do make a primary claim along with several secondary claims. What are they arguing? Are you persuaded? If so, why? If not, why not?
8. How do the authors structure their article to support their argument?
9. What research methods did Levine and McKnight use to gather their data?
10. How do Levine and McKnight use visuals to help explain the complex information they are conveying in their article?

QUESTIONS FOR REFLECTION AND WRITING

11. A 2019 study published in the *American Journal of Preventive Medicine* reveals that gun ownership increases the chances of domestic homicides and suicide (DOI: https://doi.org/10.1016/j.amepre.2019.04.009). Given the increased risk associated with gun ownership, why do you think many people purchase firearms when they feel less safe? Based on this article, and the other articles included in this section, do you think you will purchase a firearm in the future? If so, why? If not, why not? If you already own a firearm, what are you doing to prevent the use of your weapon in domestic homicide or suicide?

THE SENTENCING OF DEREK CHAUVIN IS PUNISHMENT—NOT JUSTICE

KASSIDY TARALA

Kassidy Tarala is the Web Editor and Audience Engagement Coordinator at *The Progressive*. Her work has also appeared in the *Minnesota Daily*, the *Minnesota Monthly*, and *Lavender Magazine*. She writes about LGBTQIA+ issues and issues related to social justice. She holds a BA in journalism with minors in social justice and gender, women, and sexuality studies. This article was published in *The Progressive* on June 25, 2021.

PREREADING QUESTIONS What is the difference between punishment and justice?

Gianna Floyd just wants to play with her dad. 1

That's what she said in her victim impact statement via video during the sentencing of Derek Chauvin for the murder of Gianna's father, George Floyd. Chauvin was sentenced by Judge Peter Cahill to twenty-two-and-one-half years in prison. He also can never own firearms again, and he must register as a predatory offender upon release. 2

3 After seven-year-old Gianna Floyd made her statement, George Floyd's nephew, Brandon Williams, and two brothers, Terrence and Philonise Floyd, shared their own statements and asked that Chauvin be given the maximum sentence of forty years without parole.

4 "My family and I have been given a life sentence," Philonise Floyd said. "We will never be able to get George back."

5 On behalf of the prosecution team, Assistant Minnesota Attorney General Matthew Frank addressed the impact that Chauvin's murder of George Floyd has had on the community, specifically the Floyd family. During his statement, he referred to Chauvin's treatment of George Floyd as "torture," recalling the nine-and-a-half minutes that Chauvin held his knee on Floyd's neck, and asked that Cahill sentence Chauvin to thirty years.

6 For the first time since the trial began, Derek Chauvin spoke. "At this time, due to some additional legal matters at hand, I'm not able to give a full statement, but very briefly I want to send my condolences to the Floyd family," he said.

7 Chauvin, however, did not apologize to the Floyd family for murdering their loved one. Instead, he said, "There's going to be some other information in the future that would be of interest, and I hope things will give you some peace of mind."

8 Chauvin's mother, Carolyn Pawlenty, also made a statement in which she described Chauvin as "honorable" and insisted that she will maintain his innocence regardless of his sentence.

9 There have been ongoing protests and actions in the Twin Cities since George Floyd was murdered last summer. In response to Chauvin's sentencing, there is a "Justice 4 All Stolen Lives" march this evening in downtown Minneapolis, followed by a "One Down, Three to Go" protest at 9 tonight, calling for the other officers involved in the murder of George Floyd to be charged as well.

11 While the sentencing of Derek Chauvin offers a bit of relief for the community, many are still hesitant to call it "justice." As people fight for abolition there are mixed feelings regarding the use of the criminal justice system and prison to punish Chauvin.

12 Chauvin's sentence is not justice—it is punishment. It is not accountability, as he has yet to accept responsibility for the murder he committed and make reparations to the Floyd family and the community at large.

13 True justice would be abolishing the system that allowed George Floyd to be murdered in the first place. It would look like no more Black lives being taken by state-sanctioned violence, law enforcement, or incarceration. It would look like an end to the surveillance of communities of color.

14 It would look like reparations, restitution, and recognition that Black lives do, in fact, matter.

Tarala, Kassidy. "The Sentencing of Derek Chauvin Is Punishment—Not Justice." *The Progressive*, 25 Jun. 2021. Used with permission.

QUESTIONS FOR READING

1. What event precipitated Tarala's short but powerful article?
2. Derek Chauvin was serving as a Minneapolis police officer when he killed George Floyd during his arrest. Why was Chauvin convicted of murdering Floyd?
3. During the sentencing phase of the trial, Chauvin was allowed to make a statement. What did he say?
4. Floyd's family and friends, as well as Chauvin's mother, were also allowed to speak. What did they say?
5. What occurred in Minneapolis and across the United States in response to Floyd's murder?

QUESTIONS FOR REASONING AND ANALYSIS

6. What is Tarala's claim? (Be precise.)
7. Tarala's article is not very long, but it is powerful. What approach does she take to relate to and connect with her readers?
8. What facts does she use to support her claim?

QUESTIONS FOR REFLECTION AND WRITING

9. Tarala calls for some sweeping overhauls of law enforcement. What do you think about these ideas?
10. Do some research on police violence and strategies to address this problem. If we are to reform law enforcement in the United States, what do you think needs to happen? What would a reformed police system consist of?

END POLICE VIOLENCE AGAINST BLACK AMERICANS

AMANDA CALHOUN

Amanda Calhoun received her MD and master of public health degrees from Saint Louis University's School of Medicine in 2019. Currently, she is completing her adult/child psychiatry residency at the Yale Child Study Center in the Yale School of Medicine. As a health care practitioner and activist, she raises awareness of racism in America's medical system by developing antiracist teaching material, running antiracist workshops, and writing about social justice. Her award-winning work has appeared in mass media publications and scholarly journals like the *Journal of Racial and Ethnic Disparities* and *Academic Psychiatry.* This article was published on May 2, 2022, by *The Progressive* magazine.

PREREADING QUESTIONS What does disproportionate mean? If you don't know, look it up. Then try to answer this question: Why do you think Black Americans suffer violence disproportionately when they interact with police?

1 On April 4, an unarmed Black man named Patrick Lyoya was killed by police in Grand Rapids, Michigan, after being pulled over for having mismatched license plates; a white officer shot him in the back of his head. On April 17, Syracuse police aggressively detained a Black boy, just eight years old, after he allegedly stole a bag of chips. The next day, police in upstate New York tackled a young Black boy with autism (ironically during Autism Acceptance Month) for no clear reason as he stood in line at Target.

2 As I scroll through social media, I keep wondering: where are all of the staunch opposers of violence? Where are the people who claimed to be allies, who swore their allegiance to support Black Americans after the police murder of George Floyd? We still need that level of outrage directed toward the disproportionate violence Black people experience in the United States on a regular basis.

3 It is now well documented that Black people are punished more harshly than white people under the law, and that they undergo disproportionate violence at the hands of the police. Black individuals with disabilities, like the 14-year-old thrown to the ground in Target, are more likely to be harmed by the police than their white counterparts.

4 The media certainly plays a role in this racism. White mass shooters, it's been found, are more likely to have sympathetic descriptors than Black ones. Black boys as young as preschoolers are more likely to be watched by their teachers for bad behavior than white boys. Black children are more likely to be suspended in schools for the same behaviors as white children and six times more likely to be shot by the police.

5 None of this is surprising if you know the history of policing in the United States. Police forces in this country were originally created as slave patrols—a joint force between slaveowners and white supremacy groups. Their purpose was to nab runaway slaves. Police have remained a symbol of violence and death to Black Americans, from slavery to Jim Crow to present day.

6 A recent survey showed that individuals' views of the police differ significantly based on race. White Americans were more likely to trust the police than Black Americans. Is it any wonder?

7 Some might argue that, since Lyoya was struggling with a police officer, the use of force was warranted. Even still, did the police officer have to shoot him in the head? Were there no other options to de-escalate the situation?

8 And it's unclear whether Lyoya was struggling in the first place because he was attempting to harm the police officer or because he feared for his life. Given the rampant police brutality directed toward Black Americans, it is plausible that Lyoya might have felt the need to physically defend himself.

9 And what about Black children who are aggressively detained by police? There is no justification for throwing a child with autism to the ground or holding an eight-year-old to the point of tears for allegedly stealing chips. These scenarios are what racism and white supremacy look like.

10 Black Americans need continued anti-violence support from the wider community. We still need your op-eds, your protests and your public outrage in the face of excessive, unwarranted violence. We need the collective public to demand accountability when it comes to police brutality.

We need you to keep the same energy you had when you first declared yourself an ally, and we need it now. Black Americans are still fighting. Stand with us. 11

Calhoun, Amanda. "End Police Violence Against Black Americans." *The Progressive*, 2 May 2022. Used with permission.

QUESTIONS FOR READING

1. How does the title of Calhoun's article serve as a lead-in to her subject?
2. What events motivated the author to write her article?
3. What new facts did you learn while reading this article?

QUESTIONS FOR REASONING AND ANALYSIS

4. What is Calhoun's main idea or thesis?
5. What examples illustrate the problem Calhoun discusses in her article? What evidence does she present to support her main idea or thesis?
6. What solution does Calhoun suggest?

QUESTIONS FOR REFLECTION AND WRITING

7. What are your thoughts on this topic? Were you convinced by Calhoun's argument? Why or why not?
8. What do you think you can do to help address the problem Calhoun discusses?
9. Do some quick research on your own using credible sources to discover the facts about police violence toward Black people in your hometown or the area in which your college is located. What did you find? What are people doing to help address this issue locally?
10. Write a 500-word essay on your findings and discuss what you think about the strategies local residents are using to address this issue. Will they work? Why or why not? What are your ideas for addressing the problem?

GUN VIOLENCE RESEARCH MATTERS. HERE'S WHY.

LORNET TURNBULL

Lornet Turnbull is an award-winning freelance writer based in Seattle. With two decades of media experience, she has published her work in numerous outlets including the *Washington Post,* the *Boston Globe,* the *Denver Post,* and the *Toronto Star.* Her investigative journalism has covered a wide variety of topics, such as labor unions, politics, homelessness, and refugees in the West Bank. This article was published on October 1, 2019, in *Yes!* magazine.

PREREADING QUESTION Why do you think some people and gun rights organizations do not want data collected on gun violence?

1 The California Department of Justice took a call about a 21-year-old man threatening to shoot his co-workers after being fired from his job. A search of his home uncovered 400 rounds of ammunition.

2 And a 24-year-old California man with a history of alcohol and drug abuse told his mother he was going to kill employees and relatives in the family business, and then himself by shooting or bombing. His uncle closed the business the next day and three days later called police, who confiscated 26 firearms, including 18 semiautomatic pistols.

3 In both instances, which occurred between 2016 and 2018, court-issued extreme risk protection orders allowed law enforcement to step in and temporarily remove the men's weapons.

4 These so-called red-flag orders, which family members or police can ask a judge to issue to help prevent mass shootings or suicides, are examples of the kinds of gun policies coming out of the work research scientists are doing across the country.

5 Almost unseen and against the backdrop of a raging gun control debate, their work is being funded, not by the federal government, but increasingly by private and individual donors and—most recently—a handful of states.

It's all rooted in a basic premise: To address the nation's gun violence problem, we must first understand it.

6 "For the first time in our history, everybody sees firearm violence as a problem that could personally affect them," says Garen Wintemute, a recognized national authority on the epidemiology of firearm violence and professor of emergency medicine at University of California, Davis. "It's no longer just people who live in places I don't live or who don't look like me," he says. "It's people like me."

7 Wintemute directs the Firearm Violence Research Center and the Violence Prevention Research Program at UC Davis and helped draft California's protective order statute, the first in the nation. Buttressed by the fact that nearly 80 percent of the perpetuators of mass public shootings make explicit threats, the policy has been adopted in 17 states and is the subject of bipartisan legislation in Congress.

8 The fact that his home state of California, with some of the nation's lowest gun ownership rates, also has one of its lowest gun-death rates and most aggressive gun laws, is in no small part because of the scientist's three decades of research work.

9 Mass shootings, he says, have focused public attention on a public health crisis that kills more than 100 people a day.

10 "What we've done with that attention is broaden it so that people understand research to prevent firearm violence can't just focus on mass shootings," he says. "We could zero out deaths from mass shootings, and public mass shootings, and still have 99% of the problem with us. And nobody's happy with that."

11 This summer, after shootings in Dayton, Ohio, and El Paso, Texas, one-third of adults in an American Psychological Association survey said the fear of mass shootings stops them from going to certain places and events. At the same time, Amnesty International issued a travel advisory warning visitors to be "extra

vigilant," "wary of the ubiquity of firearms among the population," and to avoid places where large numbers of people gather. The organization calls gun violence in the U.S. a human rights crisis.

ATTENTION BRINGS FUNDS

The deadly roll call of the mass killings, culminating with the slaughter of 27 chil- 12
dren and adults at Sandy Hook Elementary School, made 2012 a watershed year.

Firearm violence went from being a law enforcement problem of the "inner- 13
city" to a public health crisis that could affect anyone, anywhere.

"We can say that 2012 did set us off in a new direction," Wintemute says. 14
"And since then, the conversation, the level of concern kind of intensified, it's become possible to get more research funding."

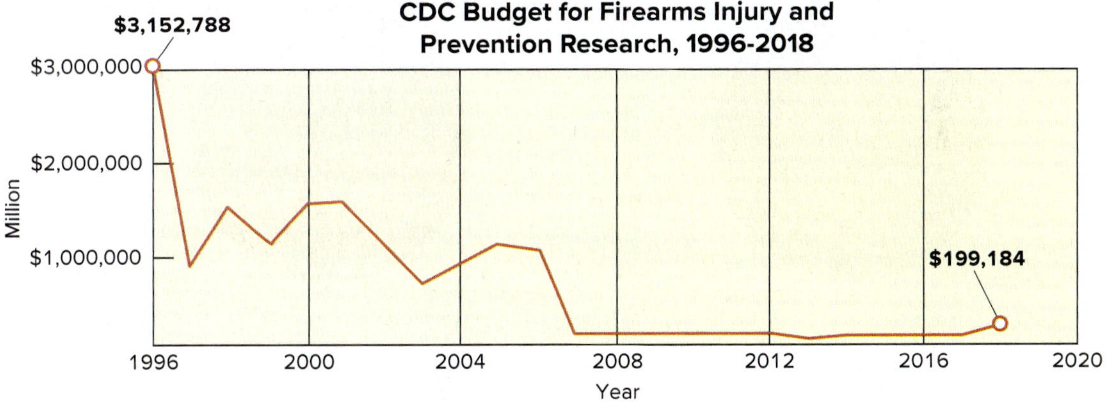

But the problem remains much bigger than the response. "There's still 15
almost no federal funding for research, which is one of the reasons that states and private foundations have stepped up," he says.

The federal government was essentially barred from funding firearm vio- 16
lence research in 1996 after Congress passed the Dickey Amendment, prohibiting federal funds from being used to "advocate or promote gun control."

Between 1996 and 2018, Centers for Disease Control and Prevention fund- 17
ing for gun injury prevention fell by 94 percent. Among the 30 leading causes of death, firearm violence ranks 29th for the amount of federal funding dedicated to research—only ahead of accidental falls.

Last year, after the Parkland school shooting, Congress clarified that the ban 18
did not apply to all gun violence research, but it earmarked no extra money for research.

So with limited financial help from a few donors and federal agencies, such as 19
the National Institutes of Health and National Institute for Justice, scientists such as Wintemute and others at places like Northeastern, Duke and Johns Hopkins universities and elsewhere, largely agnostic to the politics of guns, were left to operate mostly on shoestring budgets.

That began to change after the mass shootings of 2012. 20

21 In 2018, the Laura and John Arnold Foundation, a subsidiary of Arnold Ventures, created the National Collaborative on Gun Violence Research backed by $20 million, an amount "of the scope that we'd ordinarily expect to see from the federal government," Wintemute points out.

22 The National Collaborative is funding 17 research projects to explore the impact of gun violence—from suicides and officer-involved shootings to firearm safety.

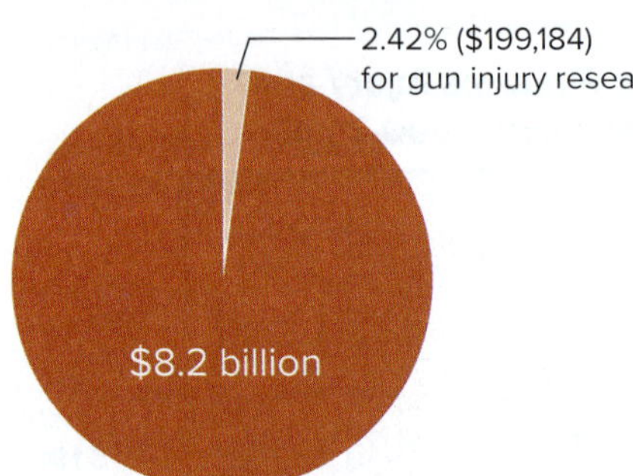

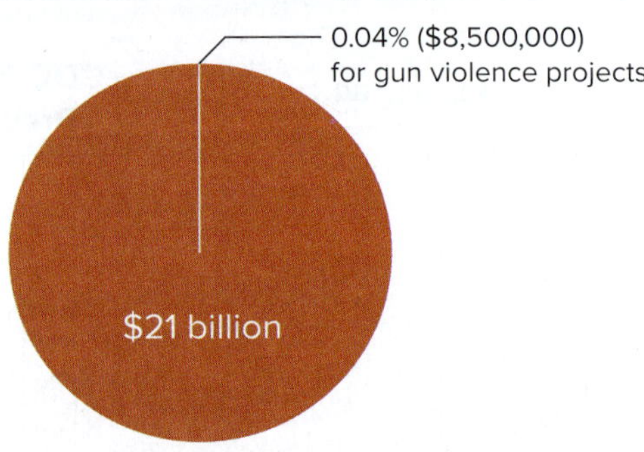

23 "We have lost an entire generation of research on gun violence to a two-decade long political stalemate," says Asheley Van Ness, who as director of criminal justice leads gun violence research work at Arnold Ventures.

24 "We need scientific research to point the way toward effective interventions that save lives and protect Second Amendment rights, because solutions to the gun violence epidemic can do both," she says. "And we need this research now, at a scale commensurate to the problem."

STATES OFFER UP FUNDS FOR RESEARCH

25 Left to confront the damage of mass shootings, states are also investing in the search for answers.

26 In 2018, New Jersey added $2 million in its state budget to establish the New Jersey Center of Gun Violence Research at Rutgers University.

27 And earlier this year, the state of Washington approved $1 million over two years for researchers at the Harborview Injury Prevention Research Center to study risk factors associated with gun deaths and injuries, evaluate gun laws, and develop strategies to reduce the firearm death toll.

28 Ali Rowhani-Rahbar, co-director of the Firearm Injury & Policy Research Program and director of the Research Core at Harborview, says firearm laws and policies have tremendous nuance that can affect their overall effectiveness.

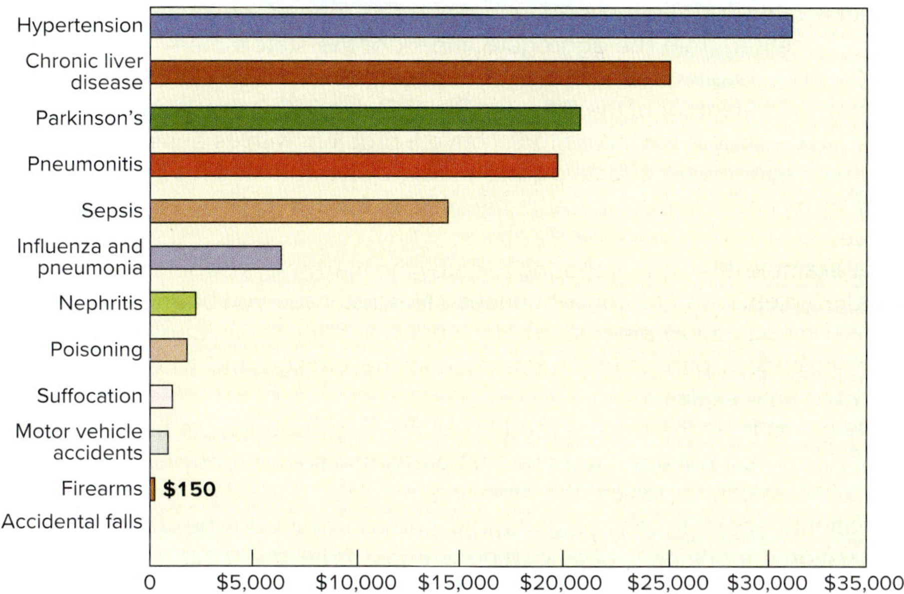

"How many times have you heard of a mass shooting that occurred because 29
of a failed background check or some loophole?" he asks.

"We need research not only to inform the creation of new policies, but also to 30
inform what is going on right now in terms of the policies already in place. There are many unanswered questions as it relates to the policy arena in this area of work."

Back in 2017, for example, Wintemute, studied Washington's and Colorado's 31
comprehensive background check policies and found they'd had little measurable effect—likely explained by lack of both compliance and enforcement.

Rowhani-Rahbar says Harborview is grateful for the state funding, which will 32
allow researchers to "scratch the surface to get some urgent answers." But in the long term, he says, broader federal government support is vital.

"Think of the other leading causes of death in this country: cancer, cardio- 25
vascular disease, not to mention motor vehicle collisions . . . that have been decreasing in terms of trends over time," he says.

"That was not possible until we had a major commitment to support broad 26
and sustained research over a period of time. A very large program of research with a much broader scope and over a longer period of time is needed for us to reduce the toll of the crisis of gun violence."

CALIFORNIA TAKES THE LEAD

California became the first state to fund gun violence research when it 25
established the Firearm Violence Research Center in 2016. By then, Wintemute had been doing the work for more than three decades, at times using his own money to finance it.

26 The $5 million in state funds over five years allow the new research center to build on work already being done at the Violence Prevention Research Program next door. California's 8% gun death rate, one of the lowest rates in the country, benefited from the aggregate impact of the state's many gun policies, many of which resulted from the doctor's research.

27 A one-time member of the Rifle and Pistol Club at UC Davis, Wintemute says, "I don't have a problem with the tool; I have a problem with its abuses."

28 With an eye toward affecting state policy, Wintemute and his team are continuing to examine some of the many unanswered questions around firearm violence.

29 For example, they are preparing to study the many ways people are exposed to firearm violence and its consequences. "Not just 'have you been shot, but has someone in your family been shot? Has your neighbor committed suicide? Was firearm violence a part of the soundtrack in the background where you grew up?'" Wintemute explains.

30 "My guess is by the time we add up all the ways people can be exposed to firearm violence, it will turn out to be that pretty much everybody is."

31 A 2017 article, in which the doctor advocated for other doctors to ask their patients about access to guns and counsel them on the dangers, grew into a national movement after getting a boost from the most unlikely place. The National Rifle Association, a regular Wintemute critic, had tweeted that the doctors should "Stay in their lane," to which the doctors tweeted back, "#ThisIsOurLane."

32 Now, California is prepared to fund the nation's first statewide program to train doctors and other health professionals on how to incorporate firearm violence prevention into their clinical practice.

33 Wintemute believes that properly designed comprehensive background check policies, solid enforcement, and compliance, together with extreme risk protection orders, which in California are known as gun violence restraining orders, have the potential to save lives.

34 He and his team are now evaluating the effectiveness of California's gun violence restraining orders' statute by examining court records for orders issued between 2016 and 2018.

35 In an article in the Annals of Internal Medicine, Wintemute highlighted 21 cases his team examined, (including the two referenced above), noting that in none of the cases, which covered schools, workplaces, domestic and other situations, were the threatened shootings carried out.

36 No one knows whether violence would have occurred had the extreme risk protection orders not been issued, Wintemute says in reference to the 21 cases in his team's report. "But there's at least the possibility that mass shootings are something we can take emergency action on and prevent."

Turnbull, Lornet. "Gun Violence Research Matters. Here's Why." *Yes!* 1 Oct. 2019. Used with permission.

QUESTIONS FOR READING

1. What is the topic of Turnbull's article, and why is it important to explore now?
2. What events motivated the author to write her article?
3. What new facts did you learn while reading this article?
4. What information does Turnbull provide to help her readers trust the facts she includes in the article?

QUESTIONS FOR REASONING AND ANALYSIS

5. What is Turnbull's thesis?
6. What examples illustrate the problem Turnbull discusses in her article? What evidence does she present to support her thesis?
7. What solutions are included in the article?

QUESTIONS FOR REFLECTION AND WRITING

8. What are your thoughts on this topic? Were you convinced by Turnbull's argument? Why or why not?
9. Why do you think it's important to collect data and use systematic methods to analyze this data when addressing problems facing our society?
10. Do some quick research on your own using credible sources to discover the facts about gun violence research taking place in your hometown/state or the location of your university. What did you find? What are people doing to help address this issue locally?
11. Write a 500-word essay on your findings, and discuss what you think about the strategies local residents are using to address gun violence research. Will they work? Why or why not? What are your ideas for addressing the problem?

CREDITS

1. https://www.pewresearch.org/fact-tank/2022/02/03/what-the-data-says-about-gun-deaths-in-the-u-s/
2. https://www.washingtonpost.com/graphics/investigations/police-shootings-database/

CHAPTER 20

The Environment: How Do We Address the Climate Crisis?

Maja Hitij/Getty Images

READ: What do you know about the climate crisis, and how do you feel about it?

REASON: There have been other well-known climate activists—Sir David Attenborough, Jacques Cousteau, David Bloomberg, Pope Francis. Why do you think Greta Thunberg is so popular and successful in raising awareness about the climate crisis?

WRITE: There are many aspects to the climate crisis: air, water, and ground pollution; renewable energy; environmental racism, etc. Write a short essay on which one is most important to you, and present some general strategies you think may work in addressing these areas of environmental justice.

In 2005, psychology professor Glenn Shean published a book titled *Psychology and the Environment.* Dr. Shean argues that we are behaving as if we have no environmental problems to face, and that therefore the biggest first step to solving problems related to environmental degradation is to make people aware of and concerned about the interconnected issues of climate change, the heavy use of fossil fuels, and species extinction. Because we are programmed to make quick decisions based on immediate dangers, we find it difficult to become engaged with dangers that stretch out into an indeterminate future. There is always tomorrow to worry about the polar bears or the increasing levels of CO^2 in the atmosphere, or the rapidly melting ice caps. And besides, who wants to give up a comfortable lifestyle because it might affect future life on this planet?

By 2008, the Bush administration began to give voice to the concerns of environmentalists such as Dr. Shean. During the Obama administration, concerns with the rising sea levels and water pollution and widespread destruction of coral reefs led to the 2016 international Paris Agreement that set goals and guidelines for nations to use to hold temperature increases around the globe. In 2017, the Trump administration announced that the United States would withdraw from the Paris Agreement, which took effect on November 4, 2020. Under the Biden administration, however, the United States rejoined the Paris Agreement on February 19, 2021. Quite a wild ride. And yet climate change deniers persist, perhaps couching their objections in the context that mandating restrictions and controls is not the business of government.

Why do we resist accepting responsibility for adding to the problem? Because to admit to being a cause means that we have to accept being part of the solution–we have to agree to change some of the things we are doing that are heating up the atmosphere. And here is where sacrifice and cost enter the picture. Do we expect factories to shut down? No, but regulations governing pollutants from their smokestacks will help the atmosphere–at a cost to doing business. Do we expect people to stop enjoying the beach? No, but we could have restrictions on building that destroys the barrier islands and marshlands protecting shorelines from erosion and destruction from storms. Do we expect people to stop driving cars? No, but the government could require manufacturers to build more fuel-efficient cars–at a cost to doing business.

And so, even though the conversation has changed somewhat since 2005, the debate continues over the extent to which human actions make a difference and then what should be done, at what cost, and at whose expense. In six articles, a variety of voices are heard on this debate.

Professor Alan Townsend of the University of Colorado has expressed an even larger worry–a concern that even though science "sustains us, transports, protects us," our trust in science seems to be eroding. When "science is chewed up in the ugly machinations of partisan politics," Townsend writes, it "threatens society as a whole." Do we want vaccines that save lives to be called into question? Do we want to stop funding the work of protecting endangered species? There is much to consider as you explore the issues raised by the writers in this chapter.

PREREADING QUESTIONS

1. To whom do you listen primarily when you explore scientific questions? Scientists? Politicians? Religious leaders? What is the reasoning behind your choice?
2. How green is your lifestyle? Do you think it matters? Why or why not?

3. Does Dr. Shean describe you when he writes of those who are complacent about environmental problems because there does not seem to be an immediate danger? If so, do you think you should reconsider your position? Why or why not?
4. If you accept that we have a problem, what solutions would you support? Reject? Why?
5. How much regulation should we allow government to have over actions that affect the environment? Should companies who pollute the environment and/or jeopardize people's safety have to pay fines and reparations for their actions? Why or why not?

HOW TO SABOTAGE CLIMATE LEGISLATION? AN EXXON LOBBYIST EXPLAINS

KATE YODER

Kate Yoder writes about the environment, climate, culture, language, and history, and she has been published by outlets like *National Magazine, The Guardian, WIRED, Business Insider, HuffPost, Salon,* and *Mother Jones.* Currently, she is the news editor at *Grist.* She attended Goshen College, where she studied English writing and art, graduating summa cum laude. This article was published by *Grist* on July 2, 2021.

PREREADING QUESTIONS Should members of the U.S. Congress be able to own stocks in companies or receive income from organizations that might benefit from their legislative work? Why or why not? Should fossil fuel companies or their trade organizations be allowed to contribute to legislators when the corporations have deliberately misled and/or endangered the American public? Why or why not?

1 All the billions ExxonMobil spent on PR went up in flames this week after a sting operation by Greenpeace recorded one of the oil giant's lobbyists talking about what goes on behind the scenes—sabotaging climate legislation, secretly manufacturing cancer-causing chemicals, and using trade groups as "whipping boys" to evade public scrutiny.

2 "It's pretty damning stuff," said Geoffrey Supran, a Harvard researcher who investigates fossil fuel propaganda.

3 The lobbyist, Keith McCoy, has been representing Exxon on Capitol Hill for eight years, chatting with senators as a senior director of the company's federal affairs team. Earlier this year, an undercover reporter with Unearthed, an investigative site run by Greenpeace, posed as a recruiter and got in touch with McCoy.

4 In the resulting Zoom job interview in May—segments of which first aired on the British network Channel 4 on Wednesday—McCoy outlines the ways that Exxon is actively sabotaging climate legislation and trying to avoid public scrutiny. A second installment of the interview that aired on Thursday revealed that Exxon manufactures and uses so-called "forever chemicals" linked to cancer, hormone disruption, and more—and used the American Petroleum Institute, a trade organization, to lobby against legislation that would regulate the chemicals.

5 The oil giant has a well-established history of sowing public doubt about the science of climate change despite knowing its catastrophic potential. But in

recent years, Exxon has taken some climate-friendly stances, backing a carbon tax, supporting the Paris Agreement, and committing to help the Biden administration and Congress pass new laws to take on climate change. McCoy's comments, however, suggest that was all for show.

In the video recording, McCoy admits that Exxon fought to undermine climate 6
science and legislation. "Did we aggressively fight against some of the science? Yes," he tells the undercover reporter. "Did we hide our science? Absolutely not. Did we join some of these 'shadow groups' to work against some of the early efforts? Yes, that's true. But there's nothing illegal about that. You know, we were looking out for our investments, we were looking out for our shareholders."

McCoy talks about his cozy relationships with members of Congress. He 7
apparently has weekly chats with Joe Manchin, a moderate Democrat from West Virginia who has received tens of thousands of dollars from Exxon and its trade associations, and names 10 other senators he calls "crucial" to Exxon's business. McCoy explains how Exxon's lobbying helped remove the "negative stuff"—in other words, the landmark climate change measures—from President Joe Biden's infrastructure bill currently in Congress.

During an interview on Channel 4 Thursday, Representative Alexandria 8
Ocasio-Cortez, a Democrat from New York, remarked how rare it was to hear about Exxon's intervention in climate policy as it was happening, as opposed to finding out about it from investigations years later. "There is an understanding that there's a dark underbelly of Washington that works this way," she said. "Rarely do we see it exposed in real-time of real legislation right before us in Congress."

McCoy also says in the recording that the company's support for a carbon 9
tax is simply a "talking point" to avoid public pressure. Given the lack of appetite for this kind of tax, he says, it'll never happen: "The bottom line is it's going to take political courage, political will in order to get something done. And that just doesn't exist in politics. It just doesn't."

The secret tapes "prove straight from the horse's mouth, straight from an 10
Exxon insider, what our and others' research has indicated for so long," Supran said. "Although Exxon and the fossil fuel industry's tactics have evolved, the end goal remains the same, and that is to stop action on climate change."

In a response to the debacle, Exxon's CEO condemned and apologized 11
for McCoy's comments. Darren Woods said that the statements "in no way represent the company's position on a variety of issues, including climate policy, and our firm commitment that carbon pricing is important to addressing climate change," adding that McCoy's remarks were "entirely inconsistent with the way we expect our people to conduct themselves." On LinkedIn, McCoy wrote that he was "deeply embarrassed" by what he had said on camera.

Supran suggested that Exxon's apology was more of a "sorry we got caught" 12
sentiment. "This guy's paid to further the position of the company on Capitol Hill, and the idea that he's so out of the loop that he's misrepresenting the company seems quite far-fetched," he said.

Yoder, Kate. "How to Sabotage Climate Legislation? An Exxon Lobbyist Explains." *Grist*, 2 Jul. 2021.
Used with permission.

QUESTIONS FOR READING

1. What event is Yoder reporting on in this article?
2. According to Yoder, what have ExxonMobil and the American Petroleum Institute been doing to ensure that their interests are protected even when climate legislation does pass?
3. How have ExxonMobil and the American Petroleum Institute influenced legislators according to Yoder?
4. What impact have ExxonMobil and the American Petroleum Institute's actions had on public opinion regarding the climate crisis according to Yoder?

QUESTIONS FOR REASONING AND ANALYSIS

5. Some arguments are more obvious than others. While Yoder's piece may not contain an overt claim, what might readers feel after finishing this article?
6. Raising awareness can be activism. How does this news article raise awareness of the climate crisis?
7. How does the author organize this article, and what sort of information does she use to convey important points in a clear, concise manner?

QUESTIONS FOR REFLECTION AND WRITING

8. How do you feel after reading this article?
9. Publicly traded companies like ExxonMobil have a fiduciary responsibility to make decisions that benefit their shareholders. What responsibility do these companies have to protect the health of the general public? The environment? Do they have an obligation to communicate clearly and truthfully about the adverse and negative effects of their products? Why or why not?
10. Exxon has a long history of apathy toward the environment. In 1989, the *Exxon Valdez,* a supertanker, struck Bligh Reef in Prince William Sound, Alaska. Within a week, the *Valdez* spilled over ten million gallons of crude oil, which caused the deaths of hundreds of thousands of animals and ruined the local fishing industry. One cause of the accident was Exxon's failure to repair the *Valdez*'s collision avoidance system, which had been broken for over a year. Given this background and what you read in Yoder's article, how do you feel about ExxonMobil as a company, and what can we do to more effectively regulate companies that continue to jeopardize the environment and human life?

THE KEY TO BEATING FOSSIL FUEL CORPS? GLOBAL COLLABORATION

PABLO FAJARDO MENDOZA AND SRIRAM MADHUSOODANAN

An Ecuadorian activist and lawyer, Pablo Fejardo Mendoza has been involved with environmental justice since 1993 when he began representing the seventy-five (later 30,000) Indigenous people negatively impacted by the Texaco (obtained by Chevron Corporation in 2001) Lago Agrio oil field disaster. Sriram Madhusoodanan is International Strategy Lead with the Gulf Coast Center for Law and Policy, where he works on climate reparations. He has published in outlets like *Entrepreneur* magazine, *Salon,* and *AlterNet.* This article was published by *Grist* on February 22, 2021.

PREREADING QUESTIONS Should fossil fuel companies pay legal settlements or reparations when they have harmed people or the environment through their actions or inactions? Why or why not?

Last summer, Delaware, Connecticut, and other states joined cities like Hoboken, New Jersey, and Charleston, South Carolina, in suing fossil fuel corporations including Exxon Mobil, BP, Chevron, and Shell for misleading the public about the climate impacts of burning fossil fuels. That now makes 16 U.S. cities, counties, states, and the District of Columbia with active litigation. 1

For justice to be truly served in U.S. courts, however, policymakers and communities trying to hold the fossil fuel industry accountable must do everything in their power to secure justice and restitution for those most impacted around the globe. A critical first step is teaming up and aligning strategies to end the legal loopholes corporations use to escape liability. 2

To achieve this, a global coalition of liability experts, social justice activists, and NGOs—including one of ours, Corporate Accountability—teamed up to create a tool for governments and civil society movements. Called the Liability Roadmap, it pulls together the expertise of Indigenous and frontline communities that are fighting the worst polluters and setting global legal precedents. A key element for success is collaboration. 3

While U.S.-based fossil fuel corporations have run roughshod over human rights, democracy, and the environment around the world in pursuit of profit, frontline communities have been waging legal battles for decades. They've won many favorable rulings. For example, in 2019, a Dutch court ruled in favor of four Nigerian women in a decades-long suit against Royal Dutch Shell for its complicity in the 1995 deaths of their husbands, allowing the suit to proceed. In Chad in 2016, a court fined Exxon $74 billion in back taxes and royalties. And in Ecuador, Indigenous communities won a judgment ordering Chevron to pay $9.5 billion for the corporation's extraction, damages, and pollution in the Amazon. 4

Yet in many of these cases, the defendants have yet to pay a dime. In Ecuador, for example, Chevron countersued the country, leveraging a bilateral investment treaty to avoid paying. In isolation, these cases face long odds against the financial, legal, and political might of Big Polluters, which threaten endless counter-litigation and legal intimidation to escape accountability. Land and environmental defenders are also at high risk of violence. According to Global Witness, 2019 was the deadliest year on record. In Colombia and elsewhere, fossil fuel, mining, and agribusiness corporations have been accused of complicity. 5

To succeed against these odds, litigants and civil society must join together to share resources and strategy, just as the world did against another deadly 6 industry, tobacco. One of the inspirations for the Liability Roadmap is found in a little-known public health treaty of the World Health Organization called the Framework Convention on Tobacco Control. Among other critical measures, it details how governments could recoup immense tobacco-related health care costs. Included in the framework is a civil liability toolkit to help countries use their laws and international agreements to the greatest effect, along with suggestions for changing laws and pursuing precedents that prevent corporations from exploiting trade agreements to avoid liability.

7 Collaboration can take a multitude of forms. In many cases, it's as simple as sharing intelligence on industry operations and legal strategy. But it can also mean international collaboration between countries. Legal cases seek justice in the form of criminal and civil liability for abuses, but their purpose is often broader: ending the fossil fuel industry's long record of political manipulation. The first step for those taking on Big Polluters in the U.S. is to reach out to those around the globe who have been doing the same.

8 The success of U.S.-based fossil fuel corporations like Chevron has depended upon the exploitation and abuse of resources and people in the Global South. So it is also imperative legal victories benefit those communities that have endured the greatest impacts of corporate abuse. Justice in the U.S. must be restorative beyond its borders.

9 There's a growing call for such equity at negotiating meetings of the UN Framework Convention on Climate Change, the global climate treaty that the Paris Agreement is part of. Climate-justice and environmental groups are calling for governments negotiating the implementation of the treaty to establish a fund that would support nations hit hard by climate impacts. As part of that process, governments could require that wealthy nations allocate a percentage of fossil fuel litigation proceeds to such a fund. This would be groundbreaking and provide a path toward repairing the deliberate harm caused by polluting corporations.

10 We know going it alone doesn't work. It's time to work together to catalyze a just and equitable transition from fossil fuels. It's time to make Big Polluters pay.

Mendoza, Pablo Fajardo, and Sriram Madhusoodanan. "The Key to Beating Fossil Fuel Corps? Global Collaboration." *Grist*, 22 Feb. 2021. Used with permission.

QUESTIONS FOR READING

1. Mendoza and Madhusoodanan are responding to an injustice they perceive in legal settlements against fossil fuel companies. What is this injustice?
2. According to the authors, what tool might "governments and civil society movements" use to address this injustice?
3. Who has been negatively impacted by fossil fuel pollution according to Mendoza and Madhusoodanan?
4. What strategies do the authors recommend to help victims of fossil fuel pollution?

QUESTIONS FOR REASONING AND ANALYSIS

5. Mendoza and Madhusoodanan lay out a clear and concise argument in their article. What is this argument?
6. What information do the authors provide to support their argument and show that their strategy will work?
7. What key terms do the authors use to create a compelling article? What tone do they strike, and how do you think readers will react?

QUESTIONS FOR REFLECTION AND WRITING

8. Are you convinced by the article? Why or why not?
9. Do some research on the Lago Agrio oil field disaster. What happened? Why is this considered a disaster? Should Chevron be forced to pay fines and reparations to help repair the ecological and human suffering the disaster has caused? Why or why not?
10. On February 24, 2022, one of the world's largest oil and gas producing countries, Russia, invaded its neighbor Ukraine. In response to this brutal and unprovoked attack, Western nations leveed sanctions and embargoes against Russia and its oligarchs. But many countries, such as Germany and the U.S., continued to import Russian fuel, paying Russia billions of dollars. Ukrainian President Volodymyr Zelensky asserted that the West was subsidizing Russia's war with his country and, in effect, paying blood money for fuel. Given this, and what you read in the article by Mendoza and Madhusoodanan, can you think of reasons why the world shouldn't do more to wean itself off of fossil fuels? What are some ways ordinary citizens can help reduce dependence on fossil fuels?

TRASH TALK: REFLECTIONS ON OUR THROWAWAY SOCIETY

GREGORY M. KENNEDY, S.J.

A Canadian, Fr. Kennedy, S.J., holds a PhD in philosophy from the University of Ottawa. He entered the Society of Jesus (known as the Jesuits) in 2006 and earned a master of divinity in 2014, then continued advanced studies at the University of Bogotá. He has spent summers working on organic farms and expects to return from Colombia to the Jesuits' organic farm in Canada.

Courtesy of Greg Kennedy

PREREADING QUESTIONS Knowing that the author is a Jesuit, would you necessarily expect his position on trash to be different from that of any other writer on this topic? How might his education and training influence his approach or writing style?

Every morning my colleague's desk captured my passing eye. Nestled beneath the computer screen, between her cup of pens and a stapler, she kept her mid-morning snack. Sometimes it was two chocolates in gold foil, or a pair of sugar biscuits bound together in cellophane, sometimes rose-colored paper 1 enveloping a candy from the Philippines. And always fruit. One day it was an apple, another an orange, a third day a banana. Regardless of the variety, the fruit was invariably as meticulously wrapped as its companion foodstuffs.

2 Now plastic wrap around an apple struck me as redundant. Plastic wrap around a banana or orange still snug in its peel struck me as downright ridiculous. I could not help staring incredulously each morning at these doubly embedded specimens, but never gathered the gumption to query my colleague about her logic.

3 Why, I wondered, would a person spend time, energy, and money to shroud a banana in plastic, which would later require more time, energy and money to get rid of? After all, the good Creator already outfitted the banana with an effective, protective cover. What purpose does that extra layer of petrochemical veneer serve?

4 By no means would my colleague stand alone in the dock before such questions. Nearly every retailer and almost as many customers in this country suspect that no licit commercial transaction has occurred if, in the end, there isn't a bag, or a box, a bottle, or a blister pack to pitch into the garbage pail.

5 In *Gone Tomorrow: The Hidden Life of Garbage,* Heather Rogers estimates that 80% of U.S. products, like plastic wrap, are discarded after a single use. Of course, it takes a special kind of person to use a banana more than once. Food, the quintessential consumer good, has become a Grade-A disposable in the overstocked market. A supersized portion of comestibles in this country does not receive even the fleeting honor of a single use. The average American household wastes a quarter of all the food it presumably worked hard to bring home. Add to that the other waste occurring along the entire length of the production and distribution line—from the farm to the supermarket deli—and the total percentage of food wasted before tasted approaches a shocking and shaming forty percent.

6 Except in rare instances, for example, pie-throwing contests, food is not intentionally produced in order to be tossed. The same does not hold for food's innumerable, protective accessorizing. Of all municipal solid waste, the single largest share goes to containers and packaging at 30%. Juice boxes, polystyrene clamshells, tin cans, plastic this, that and the other thing—nary a bite comes to our lips that has not recently emerged from an artificial peel.

7 At first glance, it may seem that the plastic cling wrap and the organic banana peel differ only chemically, since they share the same function: packaging. Ever since Aristotle, philosophers have looked to an object's putative purpose in seeking to define its particular essence. This technique often succeeds with manufactured objects, but always stumbles over natural things. Only the consumer conveniently regards the banana peel as packaging. From the standpoint of the banana tree, the peel plays a vital part in procreation. To the soil the peel means future nutrients and increased fertility.

8 Irreducible to a single purpose, natural things exist as waste only temporarily and conditionally. When out one evening picking saskatoon berries, a friend expressed his anxiety to me about the coming nightfall. "If we don't pick these bushes clean, all their berries will go to waste." I conceded a limited truth to this

statement. As far as our stomachs were concerned, the berries would not fulfill their function if they never reached our mouths.

Had we consulted the bush and berries, however, we might have slowed our hurried harvest. With respect to reproduction, the berries existed as ingeniously designed aerial seed-distribution units. In boyishly biological terms: birds eat the berries, fly a while and poop out the seeds across all the various kinds of soils one hears about in parables. However, we, the civilized consumers, would, by eating the seeds, destine them to destruction in the sewage treatment plant. So where exactly was the waste, on the bush or in our plumbing? 9

Plastic wrap does not enjoy this multiplicity of purpose, nor the redemptive ambiguity of "waste." Its design is much less intelligent. Once the wrap fulfills its single function, it is good for nothing. In fact, it is about as good *as* nothing, because it has no more to achieve. If function and essence do go together in manufactured objects, then a consumer item deprived of function will also be devoid of essence. It becomes waste unconditionally and forever, since it no longer serves any possible end. 10

Since it was originally conceived and produced to lose its function after a single use, the object was in a sense already wasted even before it performed its purpose. So here we have an object that already existed as waste. Planned obsolescence, you could say, renders objects presently obsolete. Such absolute waste, waste considered from all possible angles, waste built right into the conception of an object, I philosophically classify as "trash." 11

The word "trash" has a modern ring. The reality began littering history only after the Industrial Revolution, when the mass production of goods took off, leaving the ground piled up with discarded, worn out bags. Albert Borgmann, philosopher of technology at the University of Montana, locates the key to modern industry in its division of labor. This is standard history. What moves Borgmann's interpretation well beyond mediocrity is where he draws the most basic lines of division: not between human workers, but within technology itself. 12

The genius of modern technology, he demonstrates, lies in its unprecedented ability to split the product from its production. Consumers desire commodities, such as tasty food, amusing entertainment, easy transportation. Devices deliver these desirables. Their delivery advances toward perfection the closer they come to providing products in demand without demanding anything in return. Thus the perfect device remains completely hidden behind the convenience of the consumable commodity. 13

Convenience, the rock on which we have built the consumer world, relies absolutely on the division between commodity and device. Digging your own potatoes is not terribly convenient, especially when compared to dashing into 7-11 for a sealed-fresh bag of salt-and-vinegar chips. A complex, technological and all but invisible industrial food system is the globalized device feeding our hunger for fast-food convenience items. Packaging, of course, is an essential ingredient for making food convenient. 14

As part of the device, packaging has a sole function: to deliver the commodity of food as safely and conveniently as possible. Its single function necessitates its single use. If the consumer had to fold the plastic wrap and bring it home for 15 tomorrow's snack, or had to wash and dry the take-away cup in preparation for the next injection of java, or had to return the aluminum can to the cola company for refills, then these devices would be delivering their goods inconveniently. But by definition, the device can't make such demands; its whole point is to disappear. As soon as it has accomplished its mission of delivery, the packaging device exhausts the conditions of its existence. It is trash, pure and simple. Into the void of the trash or recycling bin it vanishes.

16 So the banana peel and the plastic wrap differ much more than just chemically. The peel, not limited to a single purpose, exists and functions within an integrated web of relationships. Each relationship lets it be in a unique way. The peel exists as waste only within a limited subset of its total interconnections.

17 The plastic wrap, on the other hand, was expressly designed to deliver just one value: the protection of goods from air, dirt and germs. Once the food is gone then so goes the plastic's *raison d'etre*. The wrap has nothing left to live for; it is curled up and buried. Materially, the object has the same qualities as it had when it first spooled off the roll. But as far as the consumer is concerned, it has instantly become irredeemable waste. How many of us would entrust another sandwich to it? No, it simply must be trashed. It belongs nowhere in our consumer world.

18 We all know that, despite our worst intentions, the disposables we discard do not really disappear. Yet we like to pretend that they do. As consumers we have precious little business with the trash we generate. Our elaborate system of garbage collection, incineration, disposal and recycling is a sophisticated device that delivers to most urban consumers the commodities of sanitation and cleanliness. Undoubtedly, swept streets and clean homes count as real blessings. But hiding our trash within the technological division of commodity and device allows us to consume without concerning ourselves about consequences.

19 And the consequences keep piling up. In spite of all our roused environmental consciousness and the de-materialization of the digital age, our quantity of trash compounds. According to the EPA, Americans generated 2.68 lbs of municipal solid waste per person per day in 1960. By 2010 that total had bloated to 4.43 lbs. The fatter the wedge we drive between the commodity and its device, the more trash we inevitably stuff into the gap.

20 We can and must do otherwise. Some years after WWII, French philosopher Jean-Paul Sartre said: "We were never more free than during German occupation." Sartre had a flair for paradox. Under occupation, every act took on significance; every act, no matter how prosaic, held out the chance for bravery and non-conformity. In a throw-away society, analogous opportunities prevail. Every shopping bag you refuse, every coffee cup you reuse, every piece of plastic you eschew is an act of freedom and conscience against our thoughtless slavery to trash.

Kennedy, Gregory M. "Trash Talk." *America: The National Catholic Weekly*, 7 May 2012. Reprinted by permission of the author.

QUESTIONS FOR READING

1. What percentage of food is wasted?
2. What percentage of solid waste is composed of packaging? How does packaging's purpose differ from food's purpose?
3. How does plastic covering differ from organic covering–such as the banana peel?
4. What do modern consumers want? How does plastic packaging help to deliver this?

QUESTIONS FOR REASONING AND ANALYSIS

5. Explain why plastic packaging is "trash" whereas organic "waste" is not.
6. Our digital age has presumably resulted in less paper, and yet our volume of solid waste continues to increase. What–implies Kennedy–is contributing to the increased tonnage of trash?
7. Review elements of style in Chapter 2 and then analyze Kennedy's writing, focusing on three characteristics that you select to study. How does his style contribute to his argument?

QUESTIONS FOR REFLECTION AND WRITING

8. What specific suggestions for wasting less food and tossing less trash do you have to add to Kennedy's discussion? Explain and defend your suggestions. If you don't think that wasting food along the way or filling solid waste dumps are really that big a problem, prepare your rebuttal of Kennedy's argument.
9. Kennedy concludes his essay by quoting Sartre. Explain Sartre's point and how Kennedy uses it to support his concluding point. Contemplate other ways in which we could use these ideas as guides to living.

A COSMIC PERSPECTIVE

NEIL DEGRASSE TYSON

Rick Kern/WireImage/Getty Images

An astrophysicist whose research interests include star formation and the structure of the Milky Way, Neil deGrasse Tyson is director of the Hayden Planetarium in New York City and the author of ten books. He is also one of today's most important figures in bringing science to the nonspecialist. He was host of the PBS show *NOVA ScienceNOW* for its five seasons and was on-camera host and narrator of *Cosmos: A Space Odyssey* for thirteen episodes. He wrote 100 monthly essays for *Natural History* magazine, concluding with the following essay in April 2007.

PREREADING QUESTIONS What does the phrase "cosmic perspective" mean to you? What do you expect Tyson to explore in this essay?

Of all the sciences cultivated by mankind, Astronomy is acknowledged to be, and undoubtedly is, the most sublime, the most interesting, and the most 1 *useful. For, by knowledge derived from this science, not only the bulk of the Earth is discovered . . . ; but our very faculties are enlarged with the grandeur of the ideas it conveys, our minds exalted above [their] low contracted prejudices.*

—James Ferguson, *Astronomy Explained upon Sir Isaac Newton's Principles, and Made Easy to Those Who Have Not Studied Mathematics* (1757)

2 Long before anyone knew that the universe had a beginning, before we knew that the nearest large galaxy lies two and a half million light-years from Earth, before we knew how stars work or whether atoms exist, James Ferguson's enthusiastic introduction to his favorite science rang true. Yet his words, apart from their eighteenth-century flourish, could have been written yesterday.

3 But who gets to think that way? Who gets to celebrate this cosmic view of life? Not the migrant farmworker. Not the sweatshop worker. Certainly not the homeless person rummaging through the trash for food. You need the luxury of time not spent on mere survival. You need to live in a nation whose government values the search to understand humanity's place in the universe. You need a society in which intellectual pursuit can take you to the frontiers of discovery, and in which news of your discoveries can be routinely disseminated. By those measures, most citizens of industrialized nations do quite well.

4 Yet the cosmic view comes with a hidden cost. When I travel thousands of miles to spend a few moments in the fast-moving shadow of the Moon during a total solar eclipse, sometimes I lose sight of Earth.

5 When I pause and reflect on our expanding universe, with its galaxies hurtling away from one another, embedded within the ever-stretching, four-dimensional fabric of space and time, sometimes I forget that uncounted people walk this Earth without food or shelter, and that children are disproportionately represented among them.

6 When I pore over the data that establish the mysterious presence of dark matter and dark energy throughout the universe, sometimes I forget that every day—every twenty-four-hour rotation of Earth—people kill and get killed in the name of someone else's conception of God, and that some people who do not kill in the name of God kill in the name of their nation's needs or wants.

7 When I track the orbits of asteroids, comets, and planets, each one a pirouetting dancer in a cosmic ballet choreographed by the forces of gravity, sometimes I forget that too many people act in wanton disregard for the delicate interplay of Earth's atmosphere, oceans, and land, with consequences that our children and our children's children will witness and pay for with their health and well-being.

8 And sometimes I forget that powerful people rarely do all they can to help those who cannot help themselves.

9 I occasionally forget those things because, however big the world is—in our hearts, our minds, and our outsize atlases—the universe is even bigger. A depressing thought to some, but a liberating thought to me.

10 Consider an adult who tends to the traumas of a child: a broken toy, a scraped knee, a schoolyard bully. Adults know that kids have no clue what constitutes a genuine problem, because inexperience greatly limits their childhood perspective.

As grown-ups, dare we admit to ourselves that we, too, have a collective immaturity of view? Dare we admit that our thoughts and behaviors spring from a belief that the world revolves around us? Apparently not. And the evidence abounds. Part the curtains of society's racial, ethnic, religious, national, and cultural conflicts, and you find the human ego turning the knobs and pulling the levers. 11

Now imagine a world in which everyone, but especially people with power and influence, holds an expanded view of our place in the cosmos. With that perspective, our problems would shrink—or never arise at all—and we could celebrate our earthly differences while shunning the behavior of our predecessors who slaughtered each other because of them. 12

Back in February 2000, the newly rebuilt Hayden Planetarium featured a space show called "Passport to the Universe," which took visitors on a virtual zoom from New York City to the edge of the cosmos. En route the audience saw Earth, then the solar system, then the 100 billion stars of the Milky Way galaxy shrink to barely visible dots on the planetarium dome. 13

Within a month of opening day, I received a letter from an Ivy League professor of psychology whose expertise was things that make people feel insignificant. I never knew one could specialize in such a field. The guy wanted to administer a before-and-after questionnaire to visitors, assessing the depth of their depression after viewing the show. "Passport to the Universe," he wrote, elicited the most dramatic feelings of smallness he had ever experienced. 14

How could that be? Every time I see the space show (and others we've produced), I feel alive and spirited and connected. I also feel large, knowing that the goings-on within the three-pound human brain are what enabled us to figure out our place in the universe. 15

Allow me to suggest that it's the professor, not I, who has misread nature. His ego was too big to begin with, inflated by delusions of significance and fed by cultural assumptions that human beings are more important than everything else in the universe. 16

In all fairness to the fellow, powerful forces in society leave most of us susceptible. As was I . . . until the day I learned in biology class that more bacteria live and work in one centimeter of my colon than the number of people who have ever existed in the world. That kind of information makes you think twice about who—or what—is actually in charge. 17

From that day on, I began to think of people not as the masters of space and time but as participants in a great cosmic chain of being, with a direct genetic link across species both living and extinct, extending back nearly 4 billion years to the earliest single-celled organisms on Earth. 18

I know what you're thinking: we're smarter than bacteria. 19

No doubt about it, we're smarter than every other living creature that ever walked, crawled, or slithered on Earth. But how smart is that? We cook our food. We compose poetry and music. We do art and science. We're good at math. Even if you're bad at math, you're probably much better at it than the smartest chimpanzee, whose genetic identity varies in only trifling ways from ours. Try as they might, primatologists will never get a chimpanzee to learn the multiplication table or do long division. 20

21 If small genetic differences between us and our fellow apes account for our vast difference in intelligence, maybe that difference in intelligence is not so vast after all.

22 Imagine a life-form whose brainpower is to ours as ours is to a chimpanzee's. To such a species our highest mental achievements would be trivial. Their toddlers, instead of learning their ABCs on Sesame Street, would learn multivariable calculus on Boolean Boulevard. Our most complex theorems, our deepest philosophies, the cherished works of our most creative artists, would be projects their schoolkids bring home for Mom and Dad to display on the refrigerator door. These creatures would study Stephen Hawking (who occupies the same endowed professorship once held by Newton at the University of Cambridge) because he's slightly more clever than other humans, owing to his ability to do theoretical astrophysics and other rudimentary calculations in his head.

23 If a huge genetic gap separated us from our closest relative in the animal kingdom, we could justifiably celebrate our brilliance. We might be entitled to walk around thinking we're distant and distinct from our fellow creatures. But no such gap exists. Instead, we are one with the rest of nature, fitting neither above nor below, but within.

24 Need more ego softeners? Simple comparisons of quantity, size, and scale do the job well.

25 Take water. It's simple, common, and vital. There are more molecules of water in an eight-ounce cup of the stuff than there are cups of water in all the world's oceans. Every cup that passes through a single person and eventually rejoins the world's water supply holds enough molecules to mix 1,500 of them into every other cup of water in the world. No way around it: some of the water you just drank passed through the kidneys of Socrates, Genghis Khan, and Joan of Arc.

26 How about air? Also vital. A single breathful draws in more air molecules than there are breathfuls of air in Earth's entire atmosphere. That means some of the air you just breathed passed through the lungs of Napoleon, Beethoven, Lincoln, and Billy the Kid.

27 Time to get cosmic. There are more stars in the universe than grains of sand on any beach, more stars than seconds have passed since Earth formed, more stars than words and sounds ever uttered by all the humans who ever lived.

28 Want a sweeping view of the past? Our unfolding cosmic perspective takes you there. Light takes time to reach Earth's observatories from the depths of space, and so you see objects and phenomena not as they are but as they once were. That means the universe acts like a giant time machine: the farther away you look, the further back in time you see—back almost to the beginning of time itself. Within that horizon of reckoning, cosmic evolution unfolds continuously, in full view.

29 Want to know what we're made of? Again, the cosmic perspective offers a bigger answer than you might expect. The chemical elements of the universe are forged in the fires of high-mass stars that end their lives in stupendous explosions, enriching their host galaxies with the chemical arsenal of life as we know it. The result? The four most common chemically active elements in the

universe—hydrogen, oxygen, carbon, and nitrogen—are the four most common elements of life on Earth. We are not simply in the universe. The universe is in us.

Yes, we are stardust. But we may not be of this Earth. Several separate lines of research, when considered together, have forced investigators to reassess who we think we are and where we think we came from. 30

First, computer simulations show that when a large asteroid strikes a planet, the surrounding areas can recoil from the impact energy, catapulting rocks into space. From there, they can travel to—and land on—other planetary surfaces. Second, microorganisms can be hardy. Some survive the extremes of temperature, pressure, and radiation inherent in space travel. If the rocky flotsam from an impact hails from a planet with life, microscopic fauna could have stowed away in the rocks' nooks and crannies. Third, recent evidence suggests that shortly after the formation of our solar system, Mars was wet, and perhaps fertile, even before Earth was. 31

Those findings mean it's conceivable that life began on Mars and later seeded life on Earth, a process known as panspermia. So all earthlings might—just might—be descendants of Martians. 32

Again and again across the centuries, cosmic discoveries have demoted our self-image. Earth was once assumed to be astronomically unique, until astronomers learned that Earth is just another planet orbiting the Sun. Then we presumed the Sun was unique, until we learned that the countless stars of the night sky are suns themselves. Then we presumed our galaxy, the Milky Way, was the entire known universe, until we established that the countless fuzzy things in the sky are other galaxies, dotting the landscape of our known universe. 33

Today, how easy it is to presume that one universe is all there is. Yet emerging theories of modern cosmology, as well as the continually reaffirmed improbability that anything is unique, require that we remain open to the latest assault on our plea for distinctiveness: multiple universes, otherwise known as the "multiverse," in which ours is just one of countless bubbles bursting forth from the fabric of the cosmos. 34

The cosmic perspective flows from fundamental knowledge. But it's more than just what you know. It's also about having the wisdom and insight to apply that knowledge to assessing our place in the universe. And its attributes are clear: 35

The cosmic perspective comes from the frontiers of science, yet it's not solely the province of the scientist. The cosmic perspective belongs to everyone. 36

The cosmic perspective is humble. 37

The cosmic perspective is spiritual—even redemptive—but not religious. 38

The cosmic perspective enables us to grasp, in the same thought, the large and the small. 39

The cosmic perspective opens our minds to extraordinary ideas but does not leave them so open that our brains spill out, making us susceptible to believing anything we're told. 40

The cosmic perspective opens our eyes to the universe, not as a benevolent cradle designed to nurture life but as a cold, lonely, hazardous place. 41

The cosmic perspective shows Earth to be a mote, but a precious mote and, for the moment, the only home we have. 42

43 The cosmic perspective finds beauty in the images of planets, moons, stars, and nebulae but also celebrates the laws of physics that shape them.

44 The cosmic perspective enables us to see beyond our circumstances, allowing us to transcend the primal search for food, shelter, and sex.

45 The cosmic perspective reminds us that in space, where there is no air, a flag will not wave—an indication that perhaps flag waving and space exploration do not mix.

46 The cosmic perspective not only embraces our genetic kinship with all life on Earth but also values our chemical kinship with any yet-to-be discovered life in the universe, as well as our atomic kinship with the universe itself.

47 At least once a week, if not once a day, we might each ponder what cosmic truths lie undiscovered before us, perhaps awaiting the arrival of a clever thinker, an ingenious experiment, or an innovative space mission to reveal them. We might further ponder how those discoveries may one day transform life on Earth.

48 Absent such curiosity, we are no different from the provincial farmer who expresses no need to venture beyond the county line, because his forty acres meet all his needs. Yet if all our predecessors had felt that way, the farmer would instead be a cave dweller, chasing down his dinner with a stick and a rock.

49 During our brief stay on planet Earth, we owe ourselves and our descendants the opportunity to explore—in part because it's fun to do. But there's a far nobler reason. The day our knowledge of the cosmos ceases to expand, we risk regressing to the childish view that the universe figuratively and literally revolves around us. In that bleak world, arms-bearing, resource-hungry people and nations would be prone to act on their "low contracted prejudices." And that would be the last gasp of human enlightenment—until the rise of a visionary new culture that could once again embrace the cosmic perspective.

Tyson, Neil deGrasse. "Cosmic Perspective." *Natural History*, April 2007. Used with permission of Natural History Magazine, Inc.

QUESTIONS FOR READING

1. Who gets to celebrate a cosmic view of life? Who does not usually have that chance?
2. What might astrophysicists forget about when they are busy studying the universe far away from what humans are experiencing here and now?
3. How can a cosmic perspective alter the way we perceive daily problems?
4. Although a cosmic perspective can make us feel small, it can also make us feel "alive" and "connected." Why?
5. How is the universe "in us"?
6. How is it possible that we could be descendants of Martians?
7. Why is continued exploration so important?

QUESTIONS FOR REASONING AND ANALYSIS

8. In general, what does Tyson mean by a cosmic perspective? Why does he think it is so important? What, then, is his claim?
9. What does the author accomplish with his opening quotation?

10. How does Tyson use his example of the psychology professor to develop and support his claim? How do his examples of quantity, size, and scale advance his argument?
11. Study Tyson's twelve advantages of the cosmic perspective both as a rhetorical strategy and as support for his claim. What makes his list an effective strategy?

QUESTIONS FOR REFLECTION AND WRITING

12. Which of the twelve items in the cosmic perspective list do you find most moving? Most surprising? Most worthy of sharing with others? Select at least one for each of the three questions and support your choice. If none strike you as memorable, explain why.
13. Tyson asserts at the end that exploration is essential to human enlightenment. Do you agree? If so, why? If not, why not?
14. Are you fascinated and in awe of the universe, or does it bother or depress you? Explain your reaction and reflect on it.

MISSING FROM COP26: LIFESTYLE CHOICES OF MIDDLE-CLASS AND RICH CONSUMERS

HOMI KHARAS

Homi Kharas is a senior fellow and deputy director of the Global Economy and Development Program at the Brookings Institute. He holds a PhD in economics from Harvard University and an MA and BA from King's College, University of Cambridge. Kharas has worked at the World Bank and has advised the United Nations on sustainable economic development. He has written four books, including his latest, *The Last Mile in Ending Extreme Poverty,* which was published in 2015. He has also published widely in journals and edited collections. This article was published by the Brookings Institute on November 22, 2021.

PREREADING QUESTION What changes to your lifestyle and consumer habits are you willing to make to help address the climate crisis?

Negotiations at COP26 focused on green technology and finance. 1
Governments pledged money, businesses committed to net-zero production, and ordinary citizens . . . did nothing! Individual activists made a lot of noise, but there was no systematic effort to organize the change in consumption patterns needed to reach our shared goal of keeping climate warming to less than 1.5 degrees Celsius. The Chichester Festival Theater organized a crowd of eco-activists to spell out "commit," and to pledge to reduce food waste and the like, but the lifestyle and behavior changes of individuals, especially middle-class and rich consumers, received far less attention than warranted. The richest 10 percent of consumers account for 44 percent of consumption-related carbon emissions.

A few facts can provide context. About two-thirds of global greenhouse 2
gas (GHG) emissions are linked to household consumption. This is why the U.N. Environment Program's (UNEP) 2020 Emissions Gap Report concluded

that major lifestyle changes will be required. Consumers will need to reduce their carbon footprint from a global average of around 6 tons of CO_2 equivalent (CO_2eq) per person to 2–2.5 tons by 2030 and to 0.7 tons by 2050. Some of this is done automatically when businesses produce in more sustainable ways. For example, when utility companies substitute renewable sources for fossil fuels, the indirect emissions of consumers in heating and cooling their homes using electricity automatically decline. The consumer is not being asked to do anything except, perhaps, to switch to electric appliances. They can retain their consumption pattern. But this will not suffice. Changes in lifestyles are needed. That's why Sustainable Development Goal 12 is responsible consumption and production.

3 Every little bit counts given the scale and urgency of reducing emissions, but where consumers are concerned there is a flood of suggestions and recommendations that generate more confusion than actionable information. Research on how consumer lifestyle choices are affecting aggregate carbon emissions has lagged.

4 We know something about the differences between countries. The average consumer in the United States, for example, emits about 17.6 tons of CO_2eq per capita, more than double that of the European Union and the U.K. (7.9 tons), and 10 times as much as India (1.7 tons). What we don't know with any degree of robustness is how much this is simply due to higher income and spending levels in the U.S. (rich people emit more than poor people), how much is due to temperature and other natural conditions, and how much is due to policy choices.

5 A just transition would take into account all these issues (and unsurprisingly, available research identifies North America as a positive outlier in emissions). It would also help to pinpoint policy actions that can encourage consumers to reduce emissions.

AVOID-SHIFT-IMPROVE

6 An easy framework for thinking about lifestyle changes, developed by Felix Creutzig and others, is Avoid-Shift-Improve. Avoidance is best understood as reducing the overall level of consumption. For example, a key "ask" of consumers is to avoid long-haul and medium-haul flights, as these have considerable carbon emissions associated with them. Smaller houses, reductions in food waste, and living car-free (thanks to the availability of carsharing through businesses like Uber) can be added to this list. On shifting, use of public transport, shifting diets to reduce beef and lamb consumption, and buying local produce are part of the answer. On improving energy efficiency, transitioning to electric cars and purchasing sustainably produced products are the main drivers.

7 In each of these cases, there is a public policy reason to encourage the shifts in consumer behavior, and this is most readily achieved through differentiated taxes. There is plenty of talk about taxing carbon, but a uniform tax on carbon is not an efficient nor a fair solution. Application of the Ramsey optimal tax rule would suggest that the appropriate tax rate on a good be proportional to the unit contribution of that good to carbon emissions, and inversely proportional to the elasticity of demand of the good in question. This is the set of taxes that would minimize the deadweight welfare loss stemming from taxation.

With this in mind, there are three priorities for lifestyle changes: 8

1. Impose a tax on the main areas where "avoidance" is the priority—air flights, 9
beef, and lamb are huge sources of carbon. In today's world, they should be considered a luxury and taxed accordingly. As these industries reduce emissions (for example, the addition of kelp to animal feed appears promising in reducing methane emissions), the optimal tax rate should decline.
2. Use the revenues to subsidize the choices to which consumers should 10
shift—public transport and local food producers of vegan products.
3. Set standards and encourage business research to develop efficient appli- 11
ances, most importantly electric cars, trucks, and buses.

The Ramsey rule tells economists how to set *relative* tax rates across goods. The 12
absolute level of taxes depends on how much revenues need to be raised. Similarly, the level of the Ramsey carbon taxes described above depends on the global carbon budget that must be respected. In practical terms, much of this depends on global population. I have written before on how the best investment in reducing carbon emissions is investing in girls' secondary education in high-fertility countries. This remains true—by a large margin. It is disappointing that at COP26, even in the special session on climate change and health, there was no mention of education.

COP26 missed an important opportunity to highlight the role that lifestyle changes 13
can bring about, and to prepare the ground for policies that will surely need to be implemented to make these lifestyle choices acceptable to the population. People accepted taxes on cigarettes as a tool to reduce smoking and increase life expectancy. They need similar efforts to understand why flying and eating meat deserve similar treatment. What's more, they need to understand that the demographic impact on each of us of lower population growth in poor countries is large. That's why combining climate finance and development finance makes so much sense.

So let's not forget about what each of us can do to consume in more respon- 14
sible ways. Let's also understand the big picture. Reducing food waste is good, but small compared to avoiding a single flight. Reducing meat consumption is as important as giving up your car. At the time of COP27, when more ambitious targets and actions are expected, we should look for proposals to encourage low-carbon lifestyle choices. And we should redouble efforts to accelerate girls' education.

Kharas, Homi. "Missing from COP26: Lifestyle Choices of Middle-Class and Rich Consumers." Brookings, 23 Nov. 2021. Used with permission.

QUESTIONS FOR READING

1. What issue is Kharas responding to with this article?
2. According to Kharas, which consumers produce the most carbon emissions?
3. What three-step action plan does the author cite as being a helpful strategy for addressing the climate crisis?
4. In addition to altering consumer habits, what other area does Kharas suggest we address to make a difference in carbon emissions?

QUESTIONS FOR REASONING AND ANALYSIS

5. Kharas is able to break down a very complex issue into clear, concise explanations and strategies. What is his argument?
6. What sort of qualitative and quantitative information does Kharas use, and where does he place this information in his article? You may have to look up the definitions of qualitative and quantitative.
7. How does Kharas mix inferences and judgments to support his argument? You may have to review the sections in this book that explain inferences and judgments.

QUESTIONS FOR REFLECTION AND WRITING

8. Are you convinced by the article? Why or why not?
9. Do some research on COP26. What happened? Who was there? What did they do? What have been the outcomes and impacts of COP26, if any?
10. After reading this article, what are some things you can do to help address carbon emissions? Are you willing to do these? Why or why not?

AN AMBITIOUS STRATEGY TO PRESERVE BIODIVERSITY

DAVID SHIFFMAN

David Shiffman holds a PhD in interdisciplinary ecosystem science and policy from the University of Miami, an MS in marine biology from the College of Charleston, and a BS in biology with a concentration in marine science from Duke University. Currently, he is a conservation biologist at Arizona State University, where he conducts research with the Marine Stewardship Council. He has published in scholarly journals like *Aquatic Ecology* and *Arctic Science* and in popular outlines, such as the *Washington Post, Nature,* and the *St. Louis Post-Dispatch.* He has been interviewed over 200 times, mostly about sharks. His book *Why Sharks Matter: A Deep Dive with the World's Most Misunderstood Predator* was published in 2022. This article was published by *Scientific American* on October 4, 2020.

PREREADING QUESTIONS Why do you think the debate over conservation is split so dramatically between the two largest political parties in America? What can we do to bridge that gap?

1 The recently released 2020 Democratic Party platform contains a lot of policies that will excite scientists and environmentalists, including an aggressive agenda to fight climate change, the return of science-based decision making to the EPA, and environmental justice. There's one game-changing passage, however, that's received shockingly little notice outside of a small circle of experts—who are no less than ecstatic to see it mentioned at this level. Indeed, the inclusion of a statement like this in a national party platform and a presidential campaign promise represents the largest shift in United States science-based biodiversity conservation policy since the Endangered Species Act.

I'm speaking about "30 by 30," the goal of using science-based decision-making to protect 30 percent of U.S. lands and waters by the year 2030. "Vice President Biden is committed to making the country more resilient to climate change and securing environmental justice, so I suggested that including the goal of conserving 30 percent of America's lands and oceans by 2030 would be a perfect fit for his platform," Representative Deb Haaland (D–N.M.), a member of the Platform Drafting Committee and author of a 30 by 30 resolution in Congress, told me in a statement. (The platform reads "Democrats will protect wildlife habitats and biodiversity, slow extinction rates, and grow America's natural carbon sinks by conserving 30 percent of our lands and waters by 2030." Or, as it's phrased in Joe Biden's climate change plan, a commitment to "Protecting biodiversity, slowing extinction rates and helping leverage natural climate solutions by conserving 30 percent of America's lands and waters by 2030.") 2

The 30 by 30 goal isn't new, and it isn't radical eco-extremism run amok. This goal been discussed for years by the science-based conservation community and has been examined in peer-reviewed scientific journal articles and detailed reports from well-respected nonprofits like Defenders of Wildlife and the Center for American Progress. A resolution in support of this goal has been introduced in Congress and in several state legislatures including that of South Carolina—hardly a hotbed of far-left activism. 3

It's based on a huge and growing body of scientific evidence that says that the world's wildlife and wild places face existential threats, and a commitment to help save these places not only for the abstract goal of "protecting the environment," but because it matters for people, too. As Kate Kelly, the public lands director at the Center for American Progress, told me, "30 by 30 is a recognition that we have a nature crisis on our hands, and it's a commitment to pursue ambitious and inclusive conservation policies—because we have a problem, all is not well on planet Earth." 4

According to Lindsay Rosa, a senior conservation GIS scientist at Defenders of Wildlife's Center for Conservation Innovation, the most commonly used figures suggest that currently about 12 percent of U.S. land and 26 percent of U.S. waters are protected—but troublingly, there's a lot of land that's important for biodiversity conservation that isn't yet protected, but could be. "About 80 percent of our highest-biodiversity hotspots are currently not protected," Rosa told me. "We have a long way to go, but there's still plenty of opportunity left." 5

It's also important to note here that experts I spoke to stressed that it matters *which* 30 percent we protect. Conserving a giant, undeveloped stretch of land where little lives and that no one wanted to develop anyway is not especially helpful to biodiversity conservation or climate resilience. We need to protect at least some of every major ecosystem, an ecological concept called "representativity." We need to protect habitats that species of concern actually live in, which you'd think would be obvious but is often ignored when protected areas don't involve scientific input from the start. 6

When we're dealing with migratory species, it's important to protect their migratory routes and not just their destination, a concept known as corridor conservation. Not all habitats are equally helpful in terms of climate resilience. 7

And, obviously, human needs are vital when determining which habitats should be off-limits to large-scale resource extraction and development; while some top-down coordination is necessary, local voices have to have a say, especially concerning natural resource management on Indigenous lands. And since unequal access to wild spaces and the mental and physical health benefits they provide is a major environmental justice issue, Kelly told me that 30 by 30 isn't just about biodiversity conservation, but "is an opportunity to hit the reset button on who conservation is for, and who nature can benefit."

8 A national program to enact 30 by 30 won't just be a series of new national parks declared by the President, but will include things like national wildlife refuges, national monuments, state-level protected areas, conservation easements on private land, and co-management with tribal leadership. Local consultation and support will have to be part of it from the beginning, but it won't be successful without support and leadership from the federal government. This level of preservation is necessary but isn't guaranteed to happen. "We need continued U.S. leadership to reach the goal of 30 by 30," Justin Kenney, the director of the 30x30 Ocean Alliance, told me. "And it's gaining more and more momentum each day!"

9 Does such a bold, ambitious, science-based environmental plan have a chance of happening in our hyperpolarized government? It really does, because conserving wildlife and wild places often has huge bipartisan support; in fact, 86 percent of voters somewhat or strongly support the specific goal of 30 by 30, including 76 percent of Republican voters, according to a poll conducted by the Center for American Progress.

10 Kenney pointed out that President George W. Bush created what was at the time the largest marine protected area in the world. "Americans are proud of their land, water and wildlife and want to protect them," Kelly told me. Jacob Malcom, the director of Defender of Wildlife's Center for Conservation Innovation, is optimistic that this plan will attract broad support, telling me that "we have to do this to protect nature and protect ourselves, and our political leaders will realize that."

11 30 by 30 represents the last best hope for saving many of the United States' iconic species and wild places, and is a key step in fighting climate and restoring justice. It's widely supported by experts and can be achieved in a way that helps everyone. It won't, however, happen if Donald Trump is reelected to the presidency; not only is there no pledge like 30 by 30 in President Trump's campaign materials, but he has focused on removing such protections; the Center for American Progress has described him as "the only president in U.S. history to have removed more public lands than he protected."

12 *Scientific American*'s historic endorsement of Joe Biden noted that Biden "has a record of following the data and being guided by science." With his campaign's incorporation of 30 by 30 goals, that's also true when it comes to biodiversity conservation. We have to do this. We can do this. And if Joe Biden becomes the next President of the United States, we will.

Shiffman, David. "An Ambitious Strategy to Preserve Biodiversity." *Scientific American*, 4 Oct. 2020.
Reproduced with permission. Copyright ©2020 SCIENTIFIC AMERICAN, a Division of Springer Nature America, Inc. All rights reserved.

QUESTIONS FOR READING

1. What announcement is Shiffman responding to with this article?
2. What is the 30 by 30 plan?
3. What nonprofit organizations support the 30 by 30 plan? What legislative bodies support the plan?
4. What is "representativity," and why is it important to biodiversity and conservation?

QUESTIONS FOR REASONING AND ANALYSIS

5. What is Shiffman's argument in this article, and how does he support it?
6. Reread the article. Note the sentence structure and word choice Shiffman uses. What sort of tone does he achieve with his style, and what effect do you think these rhetorical choices have on his readers? How does he strike a balance on a divisive topic?
7. Toward the end of his article, Shiffman makes it clear who he supported in the 2020 election. Why do you think he saved this information for his conclusion?

QUESTIONS FOR REFLECTION AND WRITING

8. Are you persuaded by Shiffman's argument? Why or why not?
9. How can ordinary citizens support the 30 by 30 plan and the vision set forth by the "America the Beautiful" report?
10. While we now know the results of the 2020 presidential election–Joe Biden won–the fate of the 30 by 30 plan is less certain. After the election, President Biden committed to bold environmental goals through the America the Beautiful report. But critics have noted the lack of details in the report explaining how the country will follow through on these goals. Do some research on the America the Beautiful report and actions taken to enact its vision. What did you find?

Understanding Literature

The same process of reading nonfiction can be used to understand literature–fiction, poetry, and drama. You still need to read what is on the page, looking up unfamiliar words and tracking down references you don't understand. You will still need to examine the context, to think about who is writing to whom, under what circumstances, and in what literary format. And, to respond fully to the words, sounds, or images, you need to analyze the writer's techniques for developing ideas and expressing attitudes.

Although it seems logical that the reading process should be much the same regardless of the work, not all readers of literature are willing to accept that logic. Some readers want a work of literature to mean whatever they think it means. But what happened to the writer's desire to communicate? If you decide that a Robert Frost poem, for example, should mean whatever you are feeling when you read it, you might as well skip the reading of Frost and just commune with your feelings. Presumably you read Frost to gain some new insight from him, to get beyond just your vision and see something of human experience and emotion from a new vantage point.

Other readers of literature hesitate over the concept of *literary analysis,* or at least over the word *analysis.* These readers complain that analysis will "tear the work apart" and "ruin it." If you are inclined to share this attitude, stop for a minute and think about the last sports event you watched. Perhaps a friend explained: "Bayern München is so good at set pieces that Borussia Dortmund will have to stay on the offensive to keep the ball out of their end of the pitch to have a chance to win the game." The soccer game is being analyzed! And that analysis makes the event more fully experienced by those who understand at least some of the elements of soccer.

The analogy is clear. You, too, can be a fan of literature and use literary analysis to better understand the author's intents. You can enjoy reading and discussing your reading once you learn to use your active reading and analytic skills to open up a poem or story, and once you sharpen your knowledge of literary terms and concepts so that you can "speak the language" of literary criticism with the same confidence with which you discuss the merits of a 4-2-3-1 soccer formation.

The works of literature in this Appendix represent a wide variety of genres from a wide span of time periods and authors. While this is only an overview, this section will give you a chance to learn and practice some of the basics of literary analysis.

GETTING THE FACTS: ACTIVE READING, SUMMARY, AND PARAPHRASE

Let's begin with the following poem by Paul Dunbar. As you read, make marginal notes, circling a phrase you fancy, putting a question mark next to a difficult line, underscoring words you need to look up. Note, too, your emotional reactions as you read.

PROMISE

PAUL LAWRENCE DUNBAR

Smith Collection/Gado/Getty Images

Born of former slave parents, Dunbar (1872–1906) was educated in Dayton, Ohio. After a first booklet of poems, *Oak and Ivy,* was printed in 1893, several friends helped Dunbar get a second collection, *Majors and Minors,* published in 1895. A copy was given to author and editor William Dean Howells, who reviewed the book favorably, increasing sales and Dunbar's reputation. This led to a national publisher issuing *Lyrics of Lowly Life* in 1896, the collection that secured Dunbar's fame.

I grew a rose within a garden fair,
And, tending it with more than loving care,
I thought how, with the glory of its bloom,
I should the darkness of my life illume;
And, watching, ever smiled to see the lusty bud
Drink freely in the summer sun to tinct its blood.

My rose began to open, and its hue
Was sweet to me as to it sun and dew;
I watched it taking on its ruddy flame
Until the day of perfect blooming came,
Then hasted I with smiles to find it blushing red—
Too late! Some thoughtless child had plucked my rose and fled!

Dunbar, Paul Laurence. *Lyrics of Lowly Life*. New York: Dodd, Mead and Company, 1896.

"Promise" should not have been especially difficult to read, although you may have paused a moment over "illume" before connecting it to "illuminate," and you may have to check the dictionary for a definition of "tinct." Test your knowledge of content by listing all the facts of the poem. Pay attention to the poem's basic situation. Who is speaking? What is happening, or what thoughts is the speaker sharing? In this poem, the "I" is not further identified, so you will have to refer to him or her as the "speaker." You should not call the speaker "Dunbar," however, because you do not know if Dunbar ever grew a rose.

In "Promise" the speaker is describing an event that has taken place. The speaker grew a rose, tended to it with care, and watched it begin to bloom. Then, when the rose was in full bloom, some child picked the rose and took it away. The situation is fairly simple, isn't it? Too simple, unfortunately, for some readers who decide that the speaker never grew a rose at all. But when anyone writes, "I grew a rose within a garden fair," it is wise to assume that the writer means just that. People do grow roses, most often in gardens, and then the gardens are made "fair" or beautiful by the flowers growing there. Read first for the facts; try not to jump too quickly to broad generalizations.

As with nonfiction, one of the best ways to make certain you have understood a literary work is to write a summary or paraphrase. Since a summary condenses, you are most likely to write a summary of a story, novel, or play, whereas a paraphrase is usually reserved for poems or complex short passages. When you paraphrase a difficult poem, you are likely to end up with more words than in the original because your purpose is to turn cryptic lines into more ordinary sentences. For example, Dunbar's "Then hasted I with smiles" can be paraphrased to read: "Then, full of smiles, I hurried."

When summarizing a literary work, remember to use your own words, draw no conclusions, giving only the facts, but focus your summary on the key events in the story. (Of course, the selecting you do to write a summary represents preliminary analysis; you are making some choices about what is important in the work.) Read the following short story by Kate Chopin and then write your own summary. Finally, compare yours to the summary that follows the story.

THE STORY OF AN HOUR

KATE CHOPIN

The Picture Art Collection/Alamy Stock Photo

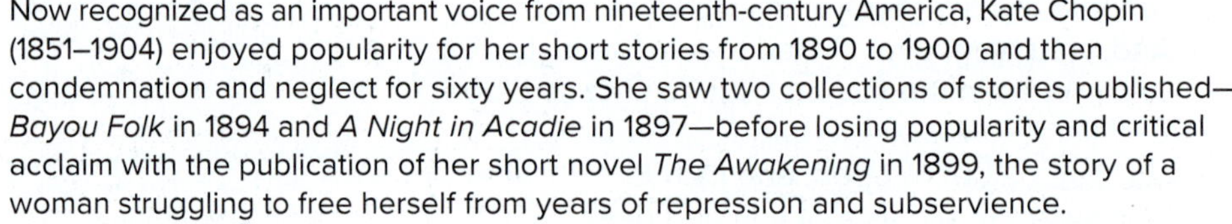

Now recognized as an important voice from nineteenth-century America, Kate Chopin (1851–1904) enjoyed popularity for her short stories from 1890 to 1900 and then condemnation and neglect for sixty years. She saw two collections of stories published—*Bayou Folk* in 1894 and *A Night in Acadie* in 1897—before losing popularity and critical acclaim with the publication of her short novel *The Awakening* in 1899, the story of a woman struggling to free herself from years of repression and subservience.

1 Knowing that Mrs. Mallard was afflicted with a heart trouble, great care was taken to break to her as gently as possible the news of her husband's death.

2 It was her sister Josephine who told her, in broken sentences; veiled hints that revealed in half concealing. Her husband's friend Richards was there, too, near her. It was he who had been in the newspaper office when intelligence of the railroad disaster was received, with Brently Mallard's name leading the list of "killed." He had only taken the time to assure himself of its truth by a second telegram, and had hastened to forestall any less careful, less tender friend in bearing the sad message.

3 She did not hear the story as many women have heard the same, with a paralyzed inability to accept its significance. She wept at once, with sudden, wild abandonment, in her sister's arms. When the storm of grief had spent itself she went away to her room alone. She would have no one follow her.

4 There stood, facing the open window, a comfortable, roomy armchair. Into this she sank, pressed down by a physical exhaustion that haunted her body and seemed to reach into her soul.

5 She could see in the open square before her house the tops of trees that were all aquiver with the new spring life. The delicious breath of rain was in the air. In the street below a peddler was crying his wares. The notes of a distant song which some one was singing reached her faintly, and countless sparrows were twittering in the eaves.

There were patches of blue sky showing here and there through the clouds 1
that had met and piled one above the other in the west facing her window.

She sat with her head thrown back upon the cushion of the chair, quite 7
motionless, except when a sob came up into her throat and shook her, as a child who has cried itself to sleep continues to sob in its dreams.

She was young, with a fair, calm face, whose lines bespoke repression and 8
even a certain strength. But now there was a dull stare in her eyes, whose gaze was fixed away off yonder on one of those patches of blue sky. It was not a glance of reflection, but rather indicated a suspension of intelligent thought.

There was something coming to her and she was waiting for it, fearfully. 9
What was it? She did not know; it was too subtle and elusive to name. But she felt it, creeping out of the sky, reaching toward her through the sounds, the scents, the color that filled the air.

Now her bosom rose and fell tumultuously. She was beginning to recognize 10
this thing that was approaching to possess her, and she was striving to beat it back with her will—as powerless as her two white slender hands would have been.

When she abandoned herself a little whispered word escaped her slightly 11
parted lips. She said it over and over under her breath: "free, free, free!" The vacant stare and the look of terror that had followed it went from her eyes. They stayed keen and bright. Her pulses beat fast, and the coursing blood warmed and relaxed every inch of her body.

She did not stop to ask if it were or were not a monstrous joy that held her. 12
A clear and exalted perception enabled her to dismiss the suggestion as trivial.

She knew that she would weep again when she saw the kind, tender hands 13
folded in death; the face that had never looked save with love upon her, fixed and gray and dead. But she saw beyond that bitter moment a long procession of years to come that would belong to her absolutely. And she opened and spread her arms out to them in welcome.

There would be no one to live for her during those coming years; she would 14
live for herself. There would be no powerful will bending hers in that blind persistence with which men and women believe they have a right to impose a private will upon a fellow-creature. A kind intention or a cruel intention made the act seem no less a crime as she looked upon it in that brief moment of illumination.

And yet she had loved him—sometimes. Often she had not. What did it matter! 15
What could love, the unsolved mystery, count for in face of this possession of self-assertion which she suddenly recognized as the strongest impulse of her being!

"Free! Body and soul free!" she kept whispering. 16

Josephine was kneeling before the closed door with her lips to the keyhole, 17
imploring for admission. "Louise, open the door! I beg; open the door—you will make yourself ill. What are you doing, Louise? For heaven's sake open the door."

"Go away. I am not making myself ill." No; she was drinking in a very elixir of 18
life through that open window.

Her fancy was running riot along those days ahead of her. Spring days, and 19
summer days, and all sorts of days that would be her own. She breathed a quick prayer that life might be long. It was only yesterday she had thought with a shudder that life might be long.

20 She arose at length and opened the door to her sister's importunities. There was a feverish triumph in her eyes, and she carried herself unwittingly like a goddess of Victory. She clasped her sister's waist, and together they descended the stairs. Richards stood waiting for them at the bottom.

21 Someone was opening the front door with a latchkey. It was Brently Mallard who entered, a little travel-stained, composedly carrying his grip-sack and umbrella. He had been far from the scene of accident, and did not even know there had been one. He stood amazed at Josephine's piercing cry; at Richards' quick motion to screen him from the view of his wife.

22 But Richards was too late.

23 When the doctors came they said she had died of heart disease—of joy that kills.

Chopin, Kate. "The Story of an Hour." *Vogue*, 6 Dec. 1894.

Summary of "The Story of an Hour"

> Mrs. Mallard's sister Josephine and her husband's friend Richards come to tell her that her husband has been listed as killed in a train accident. They try to be gentle because Mrs. Mallard has a heart condition. She cries and then goes to her bedroom alone. She sits in an armchair and gazes out the open window. Her dull stare gives way to some new thought that she cannot push away. She whispers the word "free" and thinks about a future directed by herself. Responding to Josephine's pleas, she leaves the bedroom and sees Richards below–and then Mr. Mallard letting himself in the front door. Mrs. Mallard dies, and the doctors who attend her say she died of heart disease–of "joy that kills."

Note that the summary is written in the present tense. Brevity is achieved by leaving out dialogue and the details of what Mrs. Mallard sees outside her window and the future life she imagines. Observe that the summary is not the same as the original story. The drama and emotion are missing, details that help us to understand the story's ending.

Now for a paraphrase. Read the following sonnet by Shakespeare, looking up unfamiliar words and making notes. Remember to read to the end of a unit of thought, not just to the end of a line. Some sentences continue through several lines; if you pause before you reach punctuation, you will be confused. Write your own paraphrase, not looking ahead in the text, and then compare yours with the one that follows the poem.

SONNET 116

WILLIAM SHAKESPEARE

Digital Image: Yale Center for British Art

Surely the best-known name in literature, William Shakespeare (1564–1616) is famous as both a dramatist and a poet. Rural Warwickshire and the market town of Stratford upon-Avon, where he grew up, showed him many of the character types who were to enliven his plays, as did the bustling life of a young actor in London. Apparently his sonnets were intended to be circulated only among his friends, but they were published nonetheless in 1609. His thirty-seven plays were first published together in 1623. Shakespeare's 154 sonnets vary, some focusing on separation and world-weariness, others on the endurance of love.

Let me not to the marriage of true minds
Admit impediments. Love is not love
Which alters when it alteration finds,
Or bends with the remover to remove.
O, no! it is an ever-fixed mark
That looks on tempests and is never shaken;
It is the star to every wand'ring bark,
Whose worth's unknown, although his height be taken.
Love's not Time's fool, though rosy lips and cheeks
Within his bending sickle's compass come;
Love alters not with his brief hours and weeks,
But bears it out even to the edge of doom.
If this be error and upon me proved,
I never writ, nor no man ever loved.

Shakespeare, William. "Sonnet 116," 1609.

Paraphrase of "Sonnet 116"

> I cannot accept barriers to the union of steadfast spirits. We cannot call love love if it changes because it discovers change or if it disappears during absence. On the contrary, love is a steady guide that, in spite of difficulties, remains unwavering.
>
> Love can define the inherent value in all who lack self-knowledge, though superficially they know who they are. Love does not lessen with time, though signs of physical beauty may fade. Love endures, changeless, eternally. If anyone can show me to be wrong in this position, I am no writer and no man can be said to have loved.

We have examined the facts of a literary work, what we can call the internal situation. But, as we noted in Chapter 2, there is also the external situation or context of any piece of writing. For many literary works, the context is not as essential to understanding as it is with nonfiction. You can read "The Story of an Hour," for instance, without knowing much about Kate Chopin, or the circumstances in which she wrote the story, although such information would enrich your reading experience. There is a body of information, however, that is important: the external literary situation. Readers should take note of these details before they begin to read:

- First, don't make the mistake of calling every work a "story." Make clear distinctions among stories, novels, plays, and poems.
- Poems can be further divided into narrative, dramatic, and lyric poems.
- A *narrative poem,* such as Homer's *The Iliad,* tells a story in verse. A *dramatic poem* records the speech of at least one character.

- A poem in which only one figure speaks–but clearly addresses words to someone who is present in a particular situation–is called a *dramatic monologue.*
- *Lyric poems,* Dunbar's "Promise" for example, may place the speaker in a situation or may express a thought or feeling with few, if any, situational details, but lyric poems have in common the convention that we as readers are listening in on someone's thoughts, not listening to words directed to a second, created figure. These distinctions make us aware of how the words of the poem are coming to us. Are we hearing a storyteller or someone speaking? Or are we overhearing someone's thoughts?

REMEMBER: Active reading includes looking over a work first and predicting what will come next. Do not just start reading words without first understanding what kind of work you are about to read.

Lyric poems can be further divided into many subcategories or types. Most instructors will expect you to be able to recognize some of these types. You should be able to distinguish between a poem in *free verse* (no prevailing metrical pattern) and one in *blank verse* (continuous unrhymed lines of iambic pentameter). (*Note:* A metrical line will contain a particular number–pentameter is five–of one kind of metrical "foot." The iambic foot consists of one unstressed syllable followed by one stressed syllable.) You should also be able to tell if a poem is written in some type of *stanza* form (repeated units with the same number of lines, same metrical pattern, and same rhyme scheme), or if it is a *sonnet* (always fourteen lines of iambic pentameter with one of two complex rhyme schemes labeled either "English" or "Italian"). You want to make it a habit to observe these external elements before you read. To sharpen your observation, complete the following exercise.

EXERCISE: Observing Literary Types and Using Literary Terms

1. After surveying this appendix, make a list of all the works of literature by primary type: short story, poem, play.
2. For each work on your list, add two more pieces of information: whether the author is American or British, and in what century the work was written. Why should you be aware of the writer's dates and nationality as you read?
3. Further divide the poems into narrative, dramatic, or lyric.
4. List as many of the details of type or form as you can for each poem. For example, if the poem is written in stanzas, describe the stanza form used: the number of lines, the meter, the rhyme scheme. If the poem is a sonnet, determine the rhyme scheme. (*Note:* Rhyme scheme is indicated by using letters, assigning *a* to the first sound and using a new letter for each new sound. Thus, if two consecutive lines rhyme, the scheme is *aa, bb, cc, dd,* and so on.)

SEEING CONNECTIONS: ANALYSIS

Although we read first for the facts and an initial emotional response, we do not stop there, because as humans we seek meaning. Surely there is more to "The Story of an Hour" than the summary suggests; emotionally we know this to be true. As with nonfiction, one of the best places to start analysis is with a work's organization or structure. Lyric poems will be shaped by many of the same structures found in essays: chronological, spatial, general to particular, particular to general, a list of particulars with an unstated general point, and so forth. In "Promise," Dunbar gives one illustration, recounted chronologically, to make a point that is left unstated. "Sonnet 116" contains a list of characteristics of love underscored in the conclusion by the speaker's conviction that he is right.

Analysis of Narrative Structure

In stories (and plays and narrative poems) we are given a series of events, in time sequence, involving one or more characters. In some stories, episodes are only loosely connected but are unified around a central character (Mark Twain's *Adventures of Huckleberry Finn,* for example). Most stories present events that are at least to some extent related causally; that is, action A by the main character leads to event B, which requires action C by the main character. This kind of plot structure can be diagrammed, as in Figure 1.

Figure 1 introduces some terms and concepts useful in analyzing and discussing narratives. The story's *exposition* refers to the background details needed to get the story started, including the time and place of the story and relationships of the characters. In "The Story of an Hour," a key detail of exposition is the fact that Mrs. Mallard has a heart condition. The *complication* refers to an event: Something happens to produce tension or *conflict.* In Chopin's story, the announcement of Mr. Mallard's death seems to be an immediate complication. But, after her initial tears, we do not see Mrs. Mallard dealing with this complication in the "typical" way. Instead, when she sits in her bedroom, she experiences a *conflict.* She struggles within herself. Why does she struggle? Why not just embrace the new idea that comes to her?

Although some stories present one major complication leading to a *climax* of decision or insight for the main character, many actually repeat the pattern, presenting several complications—each with an attempted resolution that causes yet another complication—until we reach the high point of tension, the *climax.* The action—or inaction—of the climactic moment leads to the story's *resolution* and ending.

These terms are helpful in analysis, even though some stories end abruptly, with little apparent resolution. A stark "resolution" is part of the modern writer's view of

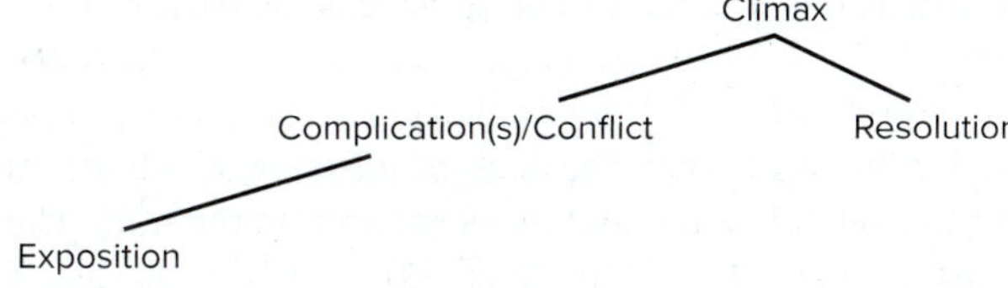

FIGURE 1 Plot Structure

reality, that life goes on, with problems often remaining unresolved. A character in an unpleasant marriage continues in that marriage, perhaps ruefully, perhaps a bit wiser but no happier and unable to act to change the situation. What is the climactic moment in "The Story of an Hour"? How is the story resolved? What is significant about the doctors' explanation at the end? Are they correct?

Analysis of Character

An analysis of plot structure suggests to us that Mrs. Mallard is not in conflict over her husband's death. She is in conflict, initially, over her reaction to that death, but she resolves her conflict, only to have Mr. Mallard open the front door. Note the close connection between complication (event) and conflict (what the characters are feeling). Fiction requires both plot and character, events and players in those events. In serious literature the greater emphasis is usually on character, on what we learn about human life through the interplay of character and incident.

As we shift from plot to character, we can enhance our analysis by considering how writers present character. Writers will usually employ several techniques from the following list:

- Descriptive details. (Mrs. Mallard's heart condition. Josephine and Richards worry about her health.)
- Dramatic scenes. (Instead of telling, they show us. Much of "The Story of an Hour" is dialogue. When Mrs. Mallard is in her bedroom alone, we overhear her internal dialogue.)
- Contrast among characters. (Josephine assumes that Mrs. Mallard continues to be the distraught, bereft widow, whereas she is actually embracing a future on her own. Note the contrast between the gentle, kind control of Mr. Mallard in their marriage and the way the control actually feels in his wife's experience of it.)
- Other elements in the work. (Names can be significant, or characters can become associated with significant objects, or details of setting can become symbolic. Note all of the specific details of events outside Mrs. Mallard's window. What, altogether, do they represent?)

Understanding character can be a challenge because we must infer from a few words, gestures, and actions. Looking at all of a writer's options for presenting character will keep us from overlooking important details.

Analysis of Elements of Style and Tone

All the elements, discussed in Chapter 2, that shape a writer's style and create tone can be found in literary works as well and need to be considered as part of your analysis. We can begin with Chopin's title. How much can happen in one hour? Well, the person we thought was dead is alive, and the "widow" ends up dead, quite a reversal of fortunes in such a short time. This situation is filled with irony. The doctors' misunderstanding of the cause of Mrs. Mallard's shock at the sight of her husband also adds irony to the story. The doctors express society's conventional thinking: Dear Mrs. Mallard is so happy that her husband is really alive that her heart cannot stand it. But is that really what shocks her into an early death?

Shakespeare's "Sonnet 116" develops the speaker's ideas about love through a series of metaphors. The rose in Dunbar's "Promise" is not a metaphor, though, because it is not part of a comparison. Yet, as we read the poem we sense that it is about something more serious than the nurturing and then stealing of one flower, no matter how beautiful. The poem's title gives us a clue that the rose stands for something more than itself; it is a symbol. Traditionally the red rose is a symbol of love. To tie the poem together, we will have to see how the title, the usual symbolic value of the rose, and specifics of the poem connect.

DRAWING CONCLUSIONS: INTERPRETATION

We have studied the facts of several works and analyzed their structures and other key elements. To reach some conclusions and shape our thinking into a coherent whole is to offer an interpretation of the work. At this point, readers can be expected to disagree somewhat, but if we have all read carefully and applied our knowledge of literature, differences should, most of the time, be ones of focus and emphasis. Presumably no one is prepared to argue that "Promise" is about pink elephants or "The Story of an Hour" about the Queen of England. Neither work contains any facts to support those conclusions.

What conclusions can we reach about "Promise"? A beautiful flower has been nurtured into bloom by a speaker who expects it to brighten life. The title lets us know that the rose represents great promise. Has a rival stolen the speaker's loved one, represented symbolically by the rose? A thoughtless child would not be an appropriate rival for an adult speaker. In the context of this poem, the rose represents, more generally, something that the speaker cherishes in anticipation of the pleasure it will bring, only to lose that something.

What conclusions have you reached about "The Story of an Hour"? What is the real irony of the story? When Mr. Mallard, very much alive, opens the door to his home, what door does he shut for Mrs. Mallard?

WRITING ABOUT LITERATURE

When you are assigned a literary essay, you will usually be asked to write either an explication or an analysis. An *explication* presents a reading of a complex poem. It will combine paraphrase and explanation to clarify the poem's meaning. A *literary analysis* can take many forms. You may be asked to analyze one element in a work: character conflict, the use of setting, the tone of a poem. Or you could be asked to contrast two works. Usually an analytic assignment requires you to connect analysis to interpretation, for we analyze the parts to better understand the whole. If you are asked to examine the metaphors in a Shakespeare sonnet, for example, you will want to show how understanding the metaphors contributes to an understanding of the entire poem. In short, literary analysis is much the same as a style analysis of an essay. Thus the guidelines for writing about style discussed in Chapter 2 apply here as well. Successful analyses are based on accurate reading, reflection on the work's emotional impact, and the use of details from the work to support conclusions.

Literary analyses can also incorporate material beyond the particular work. We can analyze a work in the light of biographical information or from a particular political ideology. Or we can study the social-cultural context of the work, or relate it to a literary tradition. These are only a few of the many approaches to the study of literature, and they depend on the application of knowledge outside the work itself. For undergraduates, topics based on these approaches usually require research. The student research essay at the end of the appendix is a literary analysis. Alan examines Faulkner's *Intruder in the Dust* as an initiation novel. He connects his analysis to works by Hawthorne and Arthur Miller. What is taken from his research is documented and helps develop and support his own conclusions about the story.

To practice close reading, analysis, and interpretation of literature, read the following works. Use the questions after each work to aid your response.

TO HIS COY MISTRESS

ANDREW MARVELL

One of the last poets of the English Renaissance, Andrew Marvell (1621–1678) graduated from Cambridge University, spent much of his young life as a tutor, and was elected to Parliament in 1659. He continued in public service until his death. Most of his best-loved lyric poems come from his years as a tutor. "To His Coy Mistress" was published in 1681.

Had we but world enough, and time,
This coyness, lady, were no crime.
We would sit down, and think which way
To walk, and pass our long love's day.
Thou by the Indian Ganges' side
Shouldst rubies find; I by the tide
Of Humber would complain. I would
Love you ten years before the Flood,
And you should, if you please, refuse
Till the conversion of the Jews.
My vegetable° love should grow *slowly vegetative*
Vaster than empires, and more slow;
An hundred years should go to praise
Thine eyes, and on thy forehead gaze;
Two hundred to adore each breast,
But thirty thousand to the rest;
An age at least to every part,
And the last age should show your heart.
For, lady, you deserve this state,
Nor would I love at lower rate.
   But at my back I always hear
Time's wingèd chariot hurrying near;
And yonder all before us lie
Deserts of vast eternity.
Thy beauty shall no more be found,
Nor in thy marble vault shall sound
My echoing song; then worms shall try
That long preserved virginity,

And your quaint honor turn to dust,
And into ashes all my lust.
The grave's a fine and private place,
But none, I think, do there embrace.
  Now therefore, while the youthful hue
Sits on thy skin like morning dew,
And while thy willing soul transpires
At every pore with instant fires,
Now let us sport us while we may,
And now, like amorous birds of prey,
Rather at once our time devour
Than languish in his slow-chapped power.
Let us roll all our strength and all
Our sweetness up into one ball,
And tear our pleasures with rough strife
Thorough° the iron gates of life. *through*
Thus, though we cannot make our sun
Stand still, yet we will make him run.

Marvell, Andrew. "To His Coy Mistress," 1681.

QUESTIONS FOR READING, REASONING, AND REFLECTION

1. Describe the poem's external form.
2. How are the words coming to us? That is, is this a narrative, dramatic, or lyric poem?
3. Summarize the speaker's argument, using the structures *if, but,* and *therefore.*
4. What figure of speech do we find throughout the first verse paragraph? What is its effect on the speaker's tone?
5. Find examples of irony and understatement in the second verse paragraph.
6. How does the tone shift in the second section?
7. Explain the personification in line 22.
8. Explain the metaphors in lines 30 and 45.
9. What is the paradox of the last two lines? How can it be explained?
10. What is the idea of this poem? What does the writer want us to reflect on?

THE PASSIONATE SHEPHERD TO HIS LOVE

CHRISTOPHER MARLOWE

Cambridge graduate, Renaissance dramatist second only to Shakespeare, Christopher Marlowe (1564–1593) may be best known for this lyric poem. Not only is it widely anthologized, it has also spawned a number of responses by such significant writers as the seventeenth-century poet John Donne and the twentieth-century humorous poet Ogden Nash. For the Renaissance period, the shepherd was a standard figure of the lover.

Come live with me and be my love,
And we will all the pleasures prove
That valleys, groves, hills, and fields,
Woods, or steepy mountain yields.

And we will sit upon the rocks,
Seeing the shepherds feed their flocks,
By shallow rivers to whose falls
Melodious birds sing madrigals.

And I will make thee beds of roses
And a thousand fragrant posies,
A cap of flowers, and a kirtle
Embroidered all with leaves of myrtle;

A gown made of the finest wool
Which from our pretty lambs we pull;
Fair lined slippers for the cold,
With buckles of the purest gold;

A belt of straw and ivy buds,
With coral clasps and amber studs:
And if these pleasures may thee move,
Come live with me, and be my love.

The shepherds' swains shall dance and sing
For thy delight each May morning:
If these delights thy mind may move,
Then live with me and be my love.

Marlowe, Christopher. "The Passionate Shepherd to His Love," 1599.

QUESTIONS FOR READING, REASONING, AND REFLECTION

1. Describe the poem's external structure.
2. What is the speaker's subject? What does he want to accomplish?
3. Summarize his "argument." How does he seek to convince his love?
4. What do the details of his argument have in common—that is, what kind of world or life does the speaker describe? Is there anything missing from the shepherd's world?
5. Would you like to be courted in this way? Would you say yes to the shepherd? If not, why?

THE NYMPH'S REPLY TO THE SHEPHERD

SIR WALTER RALEIGH

The Print Collector/ Alamy Stock Photo

The renowned Elizabethan courtier Sir Walter Raleigh (1552–1618) led a varied life as both a favorite of Queen Elizabeth and out of favor at court, as a colonizer and writer, and as one of many to be imprisoned in the Tower of London. In the following poem, Raleigh offers a response to Marlowe, using the nymph as the voice of the female lover.

If all the world and love were young,
And truth in every shepherd's tongue,
These pretty pleasures might me move
To live with thee and be thy love.

Time drives the flocks from field to fold
When rivers rage and rocks grow cold,
And Philomel becometh dumb;
The rest complains of cares to come.

The flowers do fade, and wanton fields
To wayward winter reckoning yields;
A honey tongue, a heart of gall,
Is fancy's spring, but sorrow's fall.

Thy gowns, thy shoes, thy beds of roses,
Thy cap, thy kirtle, and thy posies
Soon break, soon wither, soon forgotten,—
In folly ripe, in reason rotten.

Thy belt of straw and ivy buds,
Thy coral clasps and amber studs,
All these in me no means can move
To come to thee and be thy love.

But could youth last and love still breed,
Had joys no date nor age no need,
Then these delights my mind might move
To live with thee and be thy love.

Raleigh, Sir Walter. "The Nymph's Reply to the Shepherd," 1600.

QUESTIONS FOR READING, REASONING, AND REFLECTION

1. Describe the poem's external structure.
2. What is the context of the poem, the reason the speaker offers her words?
3. Analyze the speaker's argument, using *if* and *but* as your basic structure–and then the concluding, qualifying *but.*
4. What evidence does the speaker provide to support her argument?
5. Who has the more convincing argument: Marlowe's shepherd or Raleigh's nymph? Why?

IS MY TEAM PLOUGHING

A. E. HOUSMAN

British poet A. E. Housman (1859–1936) was a classicist, first a professor of Latin at University College, London, and then at the University of Cambridge. He spent the rest of his life at Trinity College, Cambridge. He is best known for his first volume of poetry, *A Shropshire Lad* (1896), a collection of crystal-clear and deceptively simple verses that give expression to a world that has been lost—perhaps the innocence of youth.

"Is my team ploughing,
  That I was used to drive
And hear the harness jingle
  When I was man alive?"

Ay, the horses trample,
  The harness jingles now:
No change though you lie under
  The land you used to plough.

"Is football playing
  Along the river shore,
With lads to chase the leather,
  Now I stand up no more?"

Ay, the ball is flying,
  The lads play heart and soul;
The goal stands up, the keeper
  Stands up to keep the goal.

"Is my girl happy,
  That I thought hard to leave,
And has she tired of weeping
  As she lies down at eve?"

Ay, she lies down lightly,
  She lies not down to weep:
Your girl is well contented.
  Be still, my lad, and sleep.

"Is my friend hearty,
  Now I am thin and pine,
And has he found to sleep in
  A better bed than mine?"

Yes, lad, I lie easy,
  I lie as lads would choose;
I cheer a dead man's sweetheart,
  Never ask me whose.

Houseman, A. E. *A Shropshire Lad*. London: Grant Richards, 1898.

QUESTIONS FOR READING, REASONING, AND REFLECTION

1. Classify the poem according to its external structure.
2. Is this a narrative, dramatic, or lyric poem? How are we to read the words coming to us?
3. What is the relationship between the two speakers? What has happened to the first speaker? What has changed in the life of the second speaker?
4. What ideas are suggested by the poem? What does Housman want us to take from his poem?

TAXI

AMY LOWELL

Bettmann/Getty Images

Educated at private schools and widely traveled, American Amy Lowell (1874–1925) was both a poet and a critic. Lowell frequently read her poetry and lectured on poetic techniques, defending her verse and that of other modern poets.

When I go away from you
The world beats dead
Like a slackened drum.
I call out for you against the jutted stars
And shout into the ridges of the wind.
Streets coming fast,
One after the other,
Wedge you away from me,
And the lamps of the city prick my eyes
So that I can no longer see your face.
Why should I leave you,
To wound myself upon the sharp edges of the night?

Lowell, Amy. *Sword Blades and Poppy Seed*. New York: The Macmillan Company, 1914.

QUESTIONS FOR READING, REASONING, AND REFLECTION

1. Classify the poem according to its external structure.
2. Is this a narrative, dramatic, or lyric poem?
3. Explain the simile in the opening three lines and the metaphor in the last line of the poem.
4. What is the poem's subject? What seems to be the situation in which we find the speaker?
5. How would you describe the tone of the poem? How do the details and the emotional impact of the metaphors help to create tone?
6. What is the poem's meaning or theme? In other words, what does the poet want us to understand from reading her poem?

JOSEPHINE

Courtesy of J Mase III

J MASE III

J Mase III is the author of two books: *And Then I Got Fired: One Transqueer's Reflection on Grief, Unemployment, & Inappropriate Jokes About Death* and *White Folks Be Trippin': An Ethnography Through Poetry & Prose*. His award-winning work has appeared on MSNBC, and in the *New York Times*, the *Huffington Post*, and the *Root*. As an educator active in Seattle, Washington, J Mase III has led workshops on LGBTQIA+ and racial justice in the United States and Canada, as well as the United Kingdom. He is also a slam poet who has appeared with Chuck D and the Indigo Girls. What follows is a poem by J Mase III, a trans BIPOC (Black, Indigenous, and people of color) poet, in honor of Transgender Day of Remembrance, November 20, 2020.

She asks if she can talk to me about Jesus at 3 A.M. on the C train
because something about my queer face means
clearly, I'm on a path straight to Hell
I've come to expect this type of reaction
from strangers
at least once a week
since the first time I was exorcised at 16
But today
I've grown tired
and I've decided it is my turn to proselytize
So, before you do any of that
I want to know from you
Have you heard the good word about
Joseph of Genesis?
See
Joseph
Josephine
Jo of Genesis
favorite child of Jacob
aka Israel
when asked
what you wanted
you desired one thing:
a kethoneth passim (כְּתֹנֶת פַּסִּים)
Pastor called this a royal coat
And
Jo
I had never read the Bible before
found you and kept reading
Josephine
I got to 2nd Samuel
and realized your coat of many colors
was a princess dress

Joseph
your father must have really loved you
Because he got it for you
and you wore it with pride
Jo
when your brothers saw you
in your flowing dress
in your glory
they became enraged
I am sorry for the beating your received
Sorry they destroyed your dress
and smeared it with the red paint of your swollen veins
Josephine
Did you know they told your father you were dead
so he'd never come looking for you
Never knew your brothers sold you as a slave into Egypt
and once you were stolen from your home fields
the earth dried up
Jo
the very ground on which you walked
mourned the loss of its genderqueer child
and all the plants died
and the animals no longer had the will to live
Josephine
your family nearly starved
Saw the formation of ribs
where once grew flesh
and belly fat
And they
hungry and desperate
traveled into Egypt
And what must they have seen, Jo?
See, in Egypt people discovered you
not as a f**
not as tr****
They saw you in totality
You went from slave
to leader over lands
There you were, Josephine
You looked magnificent
As you
Your family couldn't even recognize you through the glare of divinity
But you saw them shivering in fear
Waiting to hear what this regal leader might say
Wondering if your spirit might see fit
to grant them the grain needed to survive

and Joseph
love broke through
the darkness of resentment
And for the first time
your family saw you
as you
as Magnificent
for it was your word
that saved them from starvation
Dear Joseph of Genesis
aka Josephine
aka Jo
I am claiming your story
for every queer kid told
they are unholy
for every queer told
in order to love
we must let our faith die
I am going to put it in a pocket
over my heart
next to Ruth & Naomi
next to David & Jonathan
next to Hegai & Deborah
and seat them at the last Passover
with Jesus and Lazarus
Yes
I am taking Jesus with me too
Dear pastor
To you who claim your words are from God
but whose book is pledged to King James
know what allegiances you keep
You've been lying about my people for too long

Mase, J III. "Josephine," 2020. Used with permission of the author.

QUESTIONS FOR READING, REASONING, AND REFLECTION

1. Slam poetry is a relatively new genre, though you can still analyze it using the traditional terms included in this chapter. So, do you think this is a narrative, dramatic, or lyric poem? What other ideas from literary analysis might help you understand this poem?
2. In the beginning of the poem, J Mase III uses the Old Testament term "kethoneth passime." What does that mean, and why do you think he would use this term in this way?
3. The lack of stanzas, traditional punctuation, and set patterns of rhyme are a hallmark of slam poetry. As such, slam poetry usually follows a hip-hop style of rhythm and free-verse stream of consciousness. How does J Mase III harness these literary elements to convey his ideas?

4. What is the subject of the poem? What seems to be the situation in which we find the speaker?
5. How would you describe the tone of the poem? How do the details and the emotional impact of the metaphors help create tone?
6. What is the poem's meaning or theme? What does the poet want us to understand from the reading of this poem?
7. Many of the poems in this chapter deal with love and the complexities of love, romantic and otherwise. The poems of the eighteenth, nineteenth, and twentieth centuries explored love in more opaque ways, whereas J Mase III considers love–of God and of one another–in a style that is clear and abrupt. Why do you think the treatment of love differs so much from one century to the next?

12. CARRIZO

CRISOSTO APACHE

Courtesy of Crisosto Apache

Crisosto Apache holds an MFA and an AFA from the Institute of American Indian Arts in Santa Fe, New Mexico, and a BA in English and creative writing from Metropolitan State University of Denver. He has published his work in a variety of journals, such as *Common Place: The Journal of Early American Life, Yellow Medicine Review, Denver Quarterly,* and *Hawaii Review.* In 2014, he was nominated for the Pushcart Prize. He is a Mescalero Apache, Chiricahua Apache, and Diné (Navajo) Native American, and his poems focus on cultural identity and LGBTQIA+ and "two spirit" issues. Currently, he teaches writing in the Denver, Colorado, area.

For Edgar

The submarine's inside was dim.
— *Ryūnosuke Akutagawa, tr. by Will Petersen*

in my youth, I hitched a ride to San Diego, across
chirping desert and distant night, I gazed upon a slow-moving
dark, encasing a convex cerulean cavity

each night, I stood beneath the sky for hours mesmerized
at the perplex reformatory, twinkling lights of broken
glass fragments spreading against a glistening sunset

a faceless man behind a lost reflection of glass
at a drive-up window informs me,
too bad, you know nothing of your own past
how far will I walk against the night?
conforming to a captivity I had never realized

some years later, under the kitchen table, they all huddle,
as the rampage continues toward the back of the house,
a clash of debris from the other room recoils
and broken sounds escape the barricade of doors

I remember I returned in 1970,
all they remember is me sitting at the edge of my bed,
with the war still in my hands

Apache, Crisosto. "12. Carrizo." Poem. In *Ghostword*, 2021. Used with permission.

QUESTIONS FOR READING, REASONING, AND REFLECTION

1. Apache begins his poem by dedicating it to someone named Edgar. Why do you think poets and authors sometimes dedicate their work to other people?
2. Apache follows his dedication with a short quote from Ryūnosuke Akutagawa, a Japanese poet and short story writer who committed suicide when he was 35. Why do you think Apache included this quote from this particular writer? Do some quick research on the web to find out more about Akutagawa.
3. Classify Apache's poem according to its external structure.
4. Is this a narrative, dramatic, or lyric poem?
5. Explain the metaphor in the second line.
6. What is the poem's subject? What seems to be the situation in which we find the speaker?
7. How would you describe the tone of the poem? How do the details and the emotional impact of the metaphors help to create tone?
8. Why do you think Apache italicized the line "*too bad, you know nothing of your own past*"?
9. What do you think Apache means by the line "with the war still in my hands"?
10. What is the poem's meaning? What does Apache want us to understand from reading his poem?

THE VIEW FROM MOUNT FUJI

ALEX RUBI

Courtesy of Reje Tenchavez

Alessandra "Alex" Rubi is a second-year undergraduate student at Saint Louis University (SLU), where she is majoring in English with a minor in psychology. She is concentrating in creative writing with a focus on literary fiction and fantasy. As an author of Filipino descent, Alex writes about Asian cultures and issues related to LGBTQIA+ communities. Her work has been published in *Kiln* and *Via,* SLU's undergraduate journals, and she received the 2022 Albert J. Montesi Award for Creative Achievement for "The View from Mount Fuji." "The View from Mount Fuji" was based on a research project Alex completed on LGBTQIA+ communities in Japan.

CHARACTERS

AIKO. Twenty-nine year old writer. Calm natured and quiet. Loves Yuri.

YURI. Twenty-nine year old secretary. Hardworking and passionate. Loves Aiko.

SCENE 1

Outskirts of Kyoto, Japan. 2012.

Lights up on a Japanese dining table. Aiko, a young woman with short dark hair, sits at the table hunched over her writing. Only Aiko and the table are lit up. She is all focus and determination.

YURI (*offstage*): I'm home!

(*Aiko shoots up, startled. She looks around as if just realizing how late in the day it is. Lights up on a simple living room as Yuri walks through the door. Yuri, a young woman with untamed hair — a stark contrast to her pressed white shirt and black pants, enters the room and leans against the door frame. She looks weary from a long day at work, but her face brightens as she looks at Aiko.)*

YURI: Have you been cooped up in here all day?

AIKO: I'm working.

(*Yuri huffs, but the sound is fond. She walks towards Aiko, dumping her bag on the table - numerous papers spilling out, and plops on a cushion opposite her.)*

YURI: What are you writing about this time? I wanna see— (*she reaches for the papers on the desk. Aiko slaps her hand lightly to stop her.*)

AIKO: It's not done yet.

YURI (*whining*): But I want to read it. . .

AIKO: There's hardly anything there anyways.

YURI: Still. . .

(*Yuri and Aiko stare at each other. Yuri pouts, trying to convince her to let her read her work. Aiko stares back with a straight face, not yielding to Yuri. This goes on for a long moment. Yuri gives up with a sigh, but she is smiling. She reaches over and steals Aiko's pencil, using it for her own work.)*

YURI (*nonchalantly*): Well, then you'll have to tell me all about it on our way up.

AIKO: Our way up? Are we going somewhere?

YURI: Let's just say, you might need to pack a jacket.

AIKO: Why? Where are we going, Mt. Fuji?

YURI: (*pause*) Well, it was supposed to be a surprise. Although I guess maybe it was obvi—(*Aiko springs up from her chair, walks around the table, and throws her arms around Yuri's neck. Yuri drops the pencil, her work abandoned.)*

YURI: Oh Aiko. (*she wraps her arms around Aiko's small frame, burying her face in her hair*).

I'm sorry it took so long—

AIKO: Thank you, Yuri.

(*They are both silent. Yuri kisses Aiko's forehead and closes her eyes. Lights down.)*

SCENE 2

Fujiyoshida, Japan. Halfway up Mount Fuji. September, 2012.

Aiko and Yuri are walking through the trail with bulky hiking backpacks and jackets. It is nighttime. They are hoping to make it to the summit before the sun comes up.

AIKO: You know, these trails are just like the ones in my story.

YURI: Yeah?

AIKO: Yeah. The journey to Hoshi must be made through Heaven's Steps. That's how the firefly gets their miracle.

YURI: Tell me the story.

AIKO: There once was a firefly and the firefly was happy. The little firefly had a loving family and friends and never wanted anything more than that.

But one day, the little firefly's light began to go out. And no one knew why. This scared the little firefly since they loved their small light. The little firefly began to seek help, but none of the others knew what to do. So they began to feel helpless. Then one day, the little firefly heard a rumour. That on the mountain top in Hoshi, there is a little shrine, and there miracles become reality.

The little firefly knew they had to go. But the journey was dangerous. They would have to climb up hundreds and thousands of stairs called Heaven's Stairs, and the journey would have to be made through the frigid cold season. Most never made it. But the firefly wanted their light badly. So the firefly made the journey.

YURI: Was it hard?

AIKO: It was excruciating. The mountains were cold and miserable and the stairs seemed endless. And most of all, the firefly was lonely. They had no friends or family with them, just their flickering light. It was getting dark and the mountaintop still seemed so far away. Throughout the journey, the firefly's light got dimmer and dimmer. Eventually, the little firefly couldn't go on any longer.

They collapsed there, halfway up Heaven's Stairs, shivering and crying in the snow. It was dim and quiet, and for a while, there was nothing.

YURI: And then?

AIKO: And then, a light came through the darkness.

YURI: Who was it? What was it?

AIKO: (*a moment*) I don't know.

YURI: What do you mean you don't know?? You can't leave me hanging!

AIKO: I haven't gotten that far yet. I'm thinking something about dragons. . . (*she trails off, thinking about her story*)

YURI: But does the little firefly get their miracle? How does the story end?

AIKO (*shrugs*): I'll let you know once I find out how their story ends. But as of now, their future is uncertain.

(Aiko looks distant for a moment. Suddenly, she begins to cough. Yuri ushers her to sit down and take a drink.)

YURI: Let's take a break.

AIKO: I'm okay, I'm okay. . . Just give me a moment.

(*There's a moment of silence while Aiko catches her breath. Yuri fidgets with a worried expression.*)

YURI: You know what I'm going to pray for? When we get to the top of Mt. Fuji?

AIKO: What?

YURI: I'm gonna pray for a better government.

AIKO (*laughing*): Huh?

YURI: I'm serious! It's because of them that we're not married already.

AIKO: They're making progress.

YURI: Not fast enough. That's what I'll pray for. That one day I'll have enough money to move to Australia, somewhere that would let us get married right now. I'd wish for enough money to live happily, somewhere with the best doctors and the prettiest house — you could spend your entire day writing by the desert and I'd spend all my time right here with you instead of doing silly paperwork all day.

AIKO (*laughs*):	But I like watching you do paperwork.
YURI (*smiles*):	So? That doesn't mean I like doing it. And why are you laughing? What are you having second thoughts about me, is that it?
AIKO:	I've been with you for thirteen years, and I've known you for even longer. In my eyes, we already *are* married.
YURI:	Well then, what are you going to pray for? Once we make it to the top. (*Aiko looks at Yuri smiling, but the sight is somehow sad.*)
AIKO:	I'll pray for a miracle. *(Yuri is silent. Then she pulls Aiko up.)*
YURI:	Then what are you waiting for! Let's go already! (*Aiko laughs as Yuri drags her along. Together they walk offstage. Lights off.*)

SCENE 3

The summit of Mount Fuji. Just before sunrise.

Aiko stands alone looking out to the audience. The sky is still dark. Aiko is bundled in her jacket. Her eyes are wide. Yuri walks up with a cup of coffee. Her nose is red from the cold. She hands the cup to Aiko which she accepts gratefully. They stand quietly for several moments, shoulders touching. They look at the horizon where the night is slowly turning to day, streaks of blue appearing through the dark night.

AIKO (*breathless*):	We made it. (*Yuri looks at her.*)
AIKO:	I made it. I didn't think-
YURI:	Since when have you ever doubted yourself? You were always going to make it, Aiko. (*she takes a deep breath, the sound uneasy*) You are going to be fine, okay? You're here! Look at you! You just climbed Fujiyama in less than ten hours and you are standing right here with me. You're okay, you're okay— (*Yuri breaks off and looks down, blinking furiously. She brings a hand to her mouth to muffle a cry. Aiko reaches out. Her soft hand on Yuri's cheek.*)
AIKO (*softly*):	Don't cry.
YURI (*sniffing*):	I'm not crying, you're crying. (*Aiko laughs, the sound soft as snow.*)
AIKO:	Sorry, you're right. I'm the one crying. (*Yuri wipes her eyes and places her hand over the one on her cheek.*)

YURI: Don't be sorry. Just— don't, okay? Don't.

AIKO: Okay. I won't.

YURI: Good, good.

(They turn back towards the horizon. Yuri leans her head on top of Aiko's, holding her hand tightly. The sun is rising, bathing the sky is splashes of pink, yellow, and blues.)

AIKO: Sun's coming up.

YURI: It's a miracle.

AIKO: It is.

(The sky is bright. Together, hand-in-hand, they watch the sun rise. Lights down.)

SCENE 4

Lights up on a hospital room.

Aiko lays in bed. She is sleeping. In the background, the steady beating of a heart monitor is heard. Yuri sits next to her, holding Aiko's hand. She holds a book in her other hand — Aiko's book. The title, in gold lettering, reads The Little Firefly. Yuri opens the book to the first page and starts to read the dedication aloud.

YURI: To Yuri, you are my miracle. Watching you lift a pencil was worth a wedding day with anyone else.

(Yuri puts the book down and kisses Aiko's cheek. A moment.) Lights off.

Courtesy of Alex Rubi

QUESTIONS FOR READING, REASONING, AND REFLECTION

1. Explain the situation as the play begins.
2. Examine the dialogue of the two characters. What is revealed about Aiko and Yuri's relationship through their dialogue?
3. Examine the stage direction; it is italicized and placed within parentheses. What does the stage direction–that is, what the actors are supposed to be *doing*–reveal about Aiko and Yuri's relationship?
4. What do we learn about the characters themselves through their dialogue and action?
5. What is the significance of Aiko and Yuri's hiking trip to Mount Fuji? Why does it seem to mean so much to them?
6. What do the fireflies symbolize in Aiko's story? What is the significance of the unfinished story of the fireflies?
7. Why does Aiko say that she will pray for a miracle when they reach the top of Mount Fuji?
8. What is the play about primarily? Is it a political story? A love story? Both? Neither? Or is it about cultural norms and expectations? In a few sentences, state what you consider to be the play's dominant theme. Then list the evidence you would use to support your conclusion.

SAMPLE STUDENT LITERARY ANALYSIS

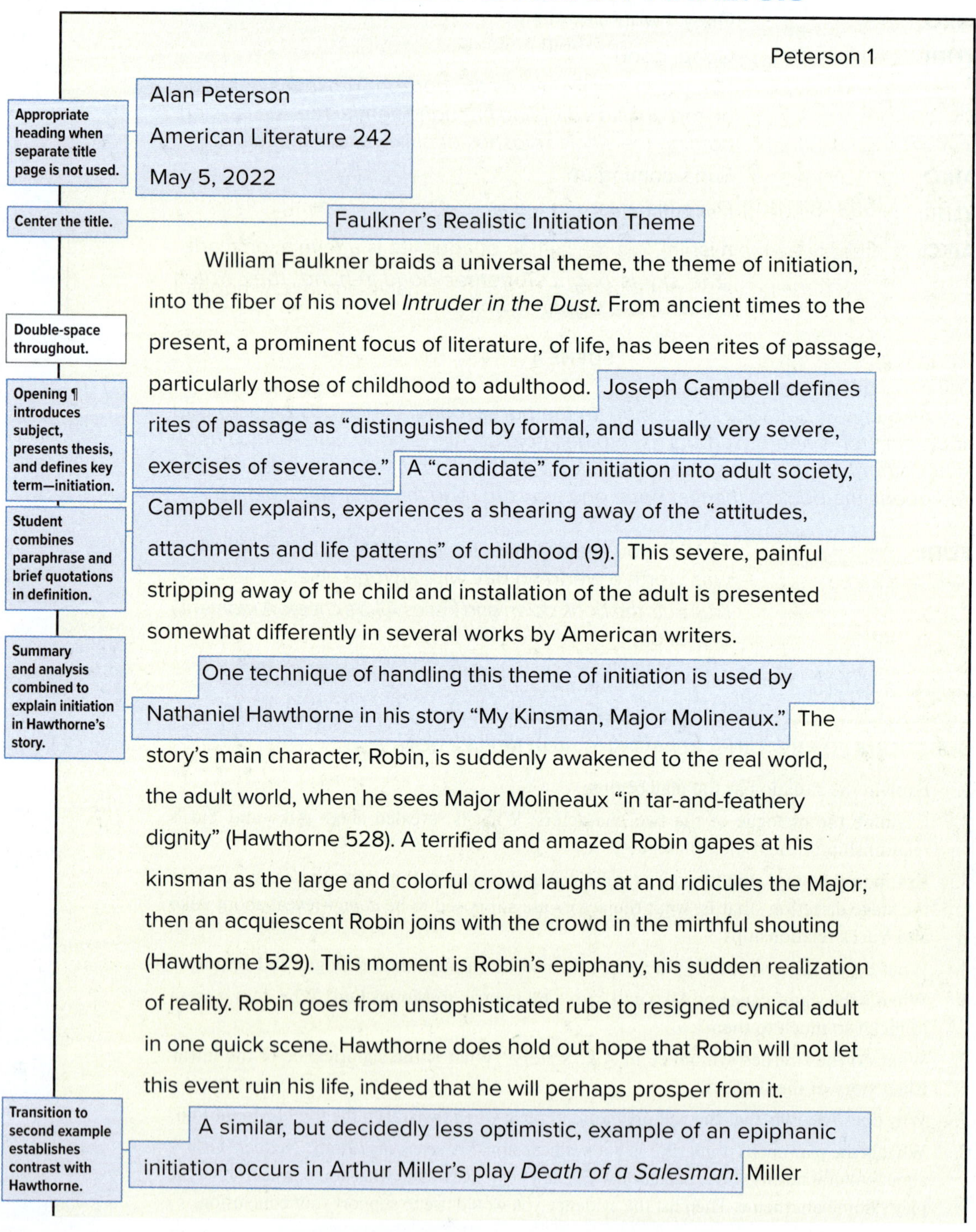

Peterson 1

Alan Peterson

American Literature 242

May 5, 2022

Faulkner's Realistic Initiation Theme

William Faulkner braids a universal theme, the theme of initiation, into the fiber of his novel *Intruder in the Dust*. From ancient times to the present, a prominent focus of literature, of life, has been rites of passage, particularly those of childhood to adulthood. Joseph Campbell defines rites of passage as "distinguished by formal, and usually very severe, exercises of severance." A "candidate" for initiation into adult society, Campbell explains, experiences a shearing away of the "attitudes, attachments and life patterns" of childhood (9). This severe, painful stripping away of the child and installation of the adult is presented somewhat differently in several works by American writers.

One technique of handling this theme of initiation is used by Nathaniel Hawthorne in his story "My Kinsman, Major Molineaux." The story's main character, Robin, is suddenly awakened to the real world, the adult world, when he sees Major Molineaux "in tar-and-feathery dignity" (Hawthorne 528). A terrified and amazed Robin gapes at his kinsman as the large and colorful crowd laughs at and ridicules the Major; then an acquiescent Robin joins with the crowd in the mirthful shouting (Hawthorne 529). This moment is Robin's epiphany, his sudden realization of reality. Robin goes from unsophisticated rube to resigned cynical adult in one quick scene. Hawthorne does hold out hope that Robin will not let this event ruin his life, indeed that he will perhaps prosper from it.

A similar, but decidedly less optimistic, example of an epiphanic initiation occurs in Arthur Miller's play *Death of a Salesman*. Miller

Peterson 2

develops an initiation theme within a flashback. A teenaged Biff, shockingly confronted with Willy's infidelity and weakness, has his boyhood dreams, ambitions—his vision—shattered, leaving his life in ruins, a truth borne out in scenes in which Biff is an adult during the play (1083–84, 1101). Biff's discovery of the vices and shortcomings of his father overwhelms him. His realization of adult life is a revelation made more piercing when put into the context of his naive and overly hopeful upbringing. A ravaged and defeated Biff has adulthood wantonly thrust upon him. Unlike Hawthorne's Robin, Biff never recovers.

¶ concludes with emphasis on contrast.

William Faulkner does not follow these examples when dealing with the initiation of his character Chick in *Intruder in the Dust*. In Robin's and Biff's cases, each character's passage into adulthood was brought about by realization of and disillusionment with the failings and weaknesses of a male adult playing an important role in his life. By contrast, Chick's male role models are vital, moral men with integrity. Chick's awakening develops as he begins to comprehend the mechanisms of the adult society in which he would be a member.

Transition to Faulkner's story by contrast with Hawthorne and Miller.

Faulkner uses several techniques for illustrating Chick's growth into a man. Early in the novel, at the end of the scene in which Chick tries to pay for his dinner, Lucas warns Chick to "stay out of that creek" (Faulkner 16).[1] The creek is an effective symbol: it is both a physical creek and a metaphor for the boy's tendency to slide into gaffes that perhaps a man could avoid. The creek's symbolic meaning is more evident when, after receiving the molasses, Chick encounters Lucas in town. Lucas again reminds Chick not to "fall in no more creeks this winter" (24). At the end of the novel, Lucas meets Chick in Gavin's office and states: "you ain't fell in no more creeks lately, have you?" (241). Although Lucas phrases

Footnote first parenthetical reference to inform readers that subsequent citations will exclude the author's name and give only the page number.

[1] Subsequent references to Faulkner's novel cite page numbers only

Peterson 3

this as a question, the answer is obvious to Lucas, as well as to the reader, that indeed Chick has not blundered into his naive boyhood quagmire lately. When Lucas asks his question, Chick's actual falling into a creek does not occur to the reader.

Note transition.

Another image Faulkner employs to show Chick growing into a man is the single-file line. After Chick gets out of the creek, he follows Lucas into the house, the group walking in single file. In the face of Lucas's much stronger adult will, Chick is powerless to get out of the line, to go to Edmonds's house (7). Later in the novel, when Miss Habersham, Aleck Sander, and Chick are walking back from digging up the grave, Chick again finds himself in a single-file line with a strong-willed adult in front. Again he protests, then relents, but clearly he feels slighted and wonders to himself "what good that [walking single file] would do" (130). The contrast between these two scenes illustrates Chick's growth, although he is not yet a man.

Note interpolation in square brackets.

Faulkner gives the reader other hints of Chick's passage into manhood. As the novel progresses, Chick is referred to (and refers to himself) as a "boy" (24), a "child" (25), a "young man" (46), "almost a man" (190), a "man" (194), and one of two "gentlemen" (241). Other clues crop up from time to time. Chick wrestles with himself about getting on his horse and riding away, far away, until Lucas's lynching is "all over finished done" (41). But his growing sense of responsibility and outrage quell his boyish desire to escape, to bury his head in the sand. Chick looks in the mirror at himself with amazement at his deeds (125). Chick's mother serves him coffee for the first time, despite the agreement she has with his father to withhold coffee until his eighteenth birthday (127). Chick's father looks at him with pride and envy (128–29).

Good use of brief quotations combined with analysis.

Peterson 4

Perhaps the most important differences between the epiphanic initiations of Robin and Biff and that experienced by Chick are the facts that Chick's epiphany does not come all at once and it does not devastate him. Chick learns about adulthood—and enters adulthood—piecemeal and with support. His first eye-opening experience occurs as he tries to pay Lucas for dinner and is rebuffed (15–16). Chick learns, after trying again to buy a clear conscience, the impropriety and affront of his actions (24). Lucas teaches Chick how he should resolve *his* dilemma by setting him "free" (26–27). Later, Chick feels outrage at the adults crowding into the town, presumably to see a lynching, then disgrace and shame as they eventually flee (196–97, 210). As in most lives, Chick's passage into adulthood is a gradual process; he learns a little bit at a time and has support in his growing. Gavin is there for him, to act as a sounding board, to lay a strong intellectual foundation, to confirm his beliefs. Chick's initiation is consistent with Joseph Campbell's explanation: "all rites of passage are intended to touch not only the candidate, but also every member of his circle" (9). Perhaps Gavin is affected the most, but Chick's mother and father, and Lucas as well, are influenced by the change in Chick.

Characteristics of Chick's gradual and positive initiation explained. Observe coherence techniques.

In *Intruder in the Dust,* William Faulkner has much to say about the role of and the actions of adults in society. He depicts racism, ignorance, resignation, violence, fratricide, citizenship, hope, righteousness, lemming-like aggregation, fear, and a host of other emotions and actions. Chick learns not only right and wrong, but that in order to be a part of society, of his community, he cannot completely forsake those with whom he disagrees or whose ideas he challenges. There is much compromise in growing up; Chick learns to compromise on some issues, but not all. Gavin's appeal to Chick to "just don't stop" (210) directs him to conform enough to be a part of the adult world, but not to lose sight of, indeed instead to embrace, his own values and ideals.

Student concludes by explaining the values Chick develops in growing up.

Paging is continuous.

Place Works Cited on separate page.

Double-space throughout.

Use hanging indentation.

Peterson 5

Works Cited

Campbell, Joseph. *The Hero with a Thousand Faces.* Princeton UP, 1949.

Faulkner, William. *Intruder in the Dust.* Random House, 1948.

Hawthorne, Nathaniel. "My Kinsman, Major Molineaux." *The Complete Short Stories of Nathaniel Hawthorne.* Doubleday, 1959, pp. 517–30.

Miller, Arthur. *Death of a Salesman.* 1949. *An Introduction to Literature.* 9th edition. Edited by Sylvan Barnet, et al. Little Brown, 1985, pp. 1025–111.

Courtesy of Alan Peterson

SUGGESTIONS FOR DISCUSSION AND WRITING

1. Prepare an explication of either Amy Lowell's "Taxi" or Sir Walter Raleigh's "The Nymph's Reply to the Shepherd." You will need to explain both what the poem says and what it means–or what it accomplishes.

2. Analyze A. E. Housman's attitudes toward life and human relationships in "Is My Team Ploughing."

3. Analyze Mrs. Mallard's conflict, and decision about that conflict, as the basis for your understanding of the dominant theme in "The Story of an Hour."

4. Slam poetry is often political and confrontational; it's meant to be heard live. See if you can find an online clip of J Mase III reading his poetry, and write a paragraph about the similarities and differences you notice between the live delivery and the written word.

5. John Donne in "The Bait" and Ogden Nash in "Love Under the Republicans (or Democrats)" also have responses to Marlowe's "The Passionate Shepherd to His Love." Select one of these poems, find a copy, read and analyze it, and then evaluate its argument as a response to Marlowe's shepherd.

Index